No.1
BEST SELLER

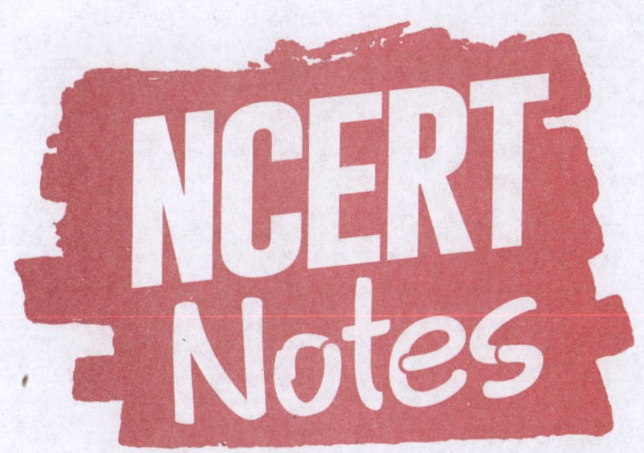

Indian History

Class 6-12 (Old+New)

No.1
BEST SELLER

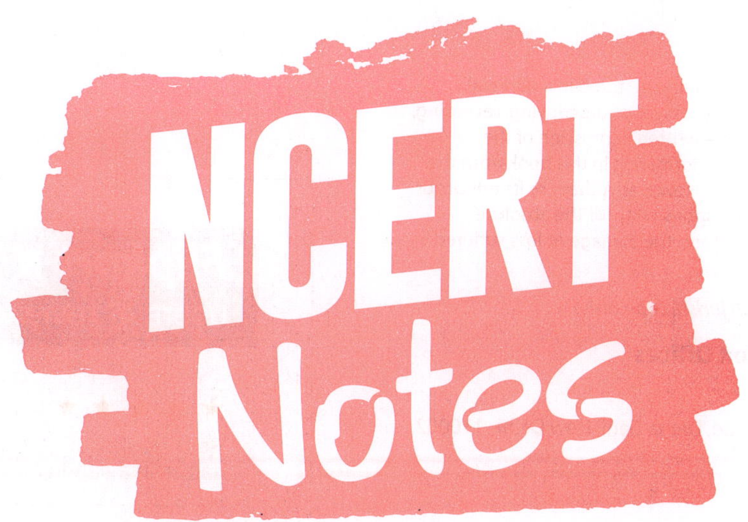

Indian History

Class 6-12 (Old + New)

Authors
Mudit Sharma
Aashutosh Jaishwal
Series Editor
Santosh Dutt Pandey

ARIHANT PUBLICATIONS (INDIA) LIMITED

Administrative & Production Offices

Regd. Office

'Ramchhaya' 4577/15, Agarwal Road, Darya Ganj, New Delhi -110002
Tele: 011- 47630600, 43518550

Head Office

Kalindi, TP Nagar, Meerut (UP) - 250002
Tel: 0121-7156203, 7156204

Sales & Support Offices

Agra, Ahmedabad, Bengaluru, Bareilly, Chennai, Delhi, Guwahati, Hyderabad, Jaipur, Jhansi, Kolkata, Lucknow, Nagpur & Pune.

PRICE ₹285.00

PO No : TXT-29-T070627-4-26

Published by Arihant Publications (India) Ltd.

For further information about the books published by Arihant, log on to www.arihantbooks.com or e-mail at info@arihantbooks.com

Follow us on   

Two Words

NCERT are the Foundation in the Journey of IAS...

Civil Services Examinations are the most prestigious and coveted examinations in India. Being the toughest exam, it automatically consists of a vast and a detailed syllabus. Aspirants often find it difficult to cover the entire syllabus and lack a right direction for a proper and a systematic study for the exam.

The most important aspect of this preparation journey are the **NCERT books**. Every year approximately **35-40 questions** directly come from NCERT books.

NCERT books also play a key role in understanding the **Basic Concepts**; so that aspirants can easily form the basic foundation of the entire syllabus. But due to the demand for many NCERT books which are required for study, it becomes exhausting to cover each and every NCERT book.

NCERT NOTES SERIES presented by Arihant Publications covers complete text from Class 6th to 12th NCERT books in a comprehensive manner.

Features of Revised Edition

- Extra and relevant facts from exam point of view are covered from Tamil Nadu Board Books.
- Most important facts from NIOS books also compiled to enrich the content.
- Theory in each chapter is facilited with charts, tables, etc. to make the preparation easy and convenient.
- Exam focused last minute revision topics are also covered in the appendix.

The book is adorned with questions prepared by a team of experts along with a vital role played by the Project Management team with members: Mona Yadav (Project Manager), Prachi Parshuram (Project Coordinator), Seema Saini (Proof Reading TL), Pradeep Chaudhary, (DTP TL), Bilal Hashmi, Rakesh Rawat and Ankit Tyagi (Cover and Inner designer).

We hope this book will help the aspirants to achieve their goals of clearing UPSC as well as State PCS exams. Your valuable suggestions have always inspired us to strive for useful, authentic and more trustworthy publications. So your inputs and suggestions are welcomed for subsequent editions.

We wish you all the very best for your preparation and journey!!

Authors

CONTENTS

ANCIENT HISTORY

MEDIEVAL HISTORY

MODERN HISTORY

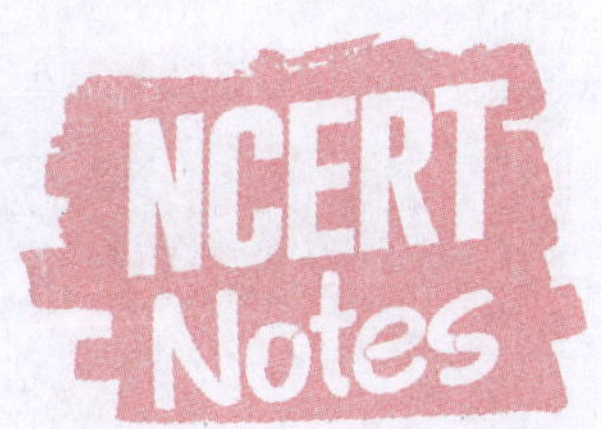
NCERT
Notes

ART AND CULTURE

Ancient History

Sources of Ancient Indian History

[SOURCES]

Class VI New NCERT Chap 4 (What Books and Burials Tell Us), Class-XI Old NCERT (I) Chap 2 (The Importance of Ancient Indian History), Class-XI Old NCERT (II) Chap 2 (Modern Historians of Ancient India), Class-XI Old NCERT Chap 3 (Types of Sources and Historical Construction), Class-XII New NCERT Chap 1 (Bricks, Beads and Bones), Chap 2 (Kings, Farmers and Towns) Tamil Nadu Board (Class XI), NIOS

- **The study of Ancient Indian history is important as it tells us how, when and where people developed the earliest cultures in our country.**
- **It indicates how they started their agriculture which made life secure and settled. It shows how the Ancient Indians discovered and utilised natural resources and how they created the means for their livelihood.**
- **Sources that are responsible for providing information about history are known as Historical Sources.**

Sources of Ancient Indian History

The sources responsible for the information about ancient history can be broadly categorised as archaeological and literary sources.

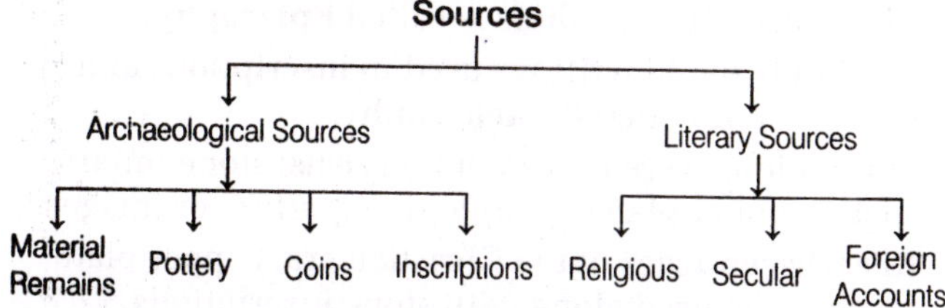

Archaeological Sources

These sources include material remains, pottery, inscriptions and coins. The one who studies archaeological sources is known as archaeologist.

Material Remains

- Archaeological excavations show the layout plan of the settlements in which people lived, the type of pottery they used, the form of houses in which they dwelt, the kind of cereals they used as food and the type of tools and implements they handled.
- Vertical digging of sites provides us a good chronological sequence of material culture. It also tells us about the material culture of the ancient period.
- Buildings made of stone and bricks tell us of great building activities in the past.
- Ring wells are rows of pots or ceramics rings arranged one on top of other. They have been found in many cities and seem to have been used as toilets as drains and garbage dumps. These were usually found in individual houses.
- In South India, megaliths provide us information about the life of people of post iron age. Some of the largest collection of iron tools and weapons were found in the megalithic burials.
- The use of iron began in the Indian sub-continent around 3000 years ago. Around 2500 years ago, there are evidences of ample use of iron tools, which include iron axes for clearing forests and the iron ploughshare.

Major Archaeological Sites and their Findings

Sites	Findings
Narmada Valley	Early hunting and gathering communities
North of Vindhyas	Rice was first grown here (in India)
Rajgrih	The first kingdom of India (Magadha) established here
Sulaiman and Kirthar hills to the North-West	The first crops such as wheat and barley about 8000 years ago began to grow here
Garo hills	Early agriculture in India
Indus and its tributaries	The first cities in Indian sub-continent (Harappa civilisation)
The Ganga valley	Cities developed about 2500 years ago (2nd urbanisation)

Dating in Archaeology

- The dates of material remains are fixed according to the radio-carbon method (Carbon-14 dating). The history of climate and vegetation is known through an examination of plant residue and especially through pollen-analysis.
- Carbon dating has suggested that agriculture was practiced in Rajasthan and Kashmir as far back as 6000 BC.
- An examination of the animal bones enables us to find out whether the animals were domesticated and for finding out their use.

Various Types of Datings

Bio-stratigraphy	Focuses on using fossil population found within rock layers
Stratigraphy	Layers of soil
Flourine dating	Life of fossils/bones/skeletons
Radio-carbon	Gauges the radio-active carbon-14 isotope's degradation
ESR dating	Dating technique for time between 60,000 to 2,00,000 years
Argon/potassium dating	Life span of Rock

Pottery

- Various kinds of pottery have been discovered during excavations.
- Red and Black pottery was used by the people of Indus Valley Civilisation. While the **Painted Grey Ware** (PGW) pottery was used during the Vedic Age.

Coins

- The study of coins is called **Numismatics**.
- Ancient coins were made of various metals like copper, silver, gold or lead.
- **Coin moulds**, made of burnt clay have been discovered in large numbers belong to **Kushana period**. Such moulds disappeared in the Post-Gupta period.
- The earliest coins, called the **Punch-Marked Coins**, were largely made up of silver. They contain a few symbols but the later coins mention the names of kings, gods or dates of issuance. They were generally rectangular or sometimes square or round in shape.
- The coins were not inscribed, but were stamped with symbols using dies or punches. Hence, they are called **Punch-Marked Coins**. These coins are found over most parts of the sub-continent and remained in circulation till the early centuries AD.

Punch-Marked Coins

- The largest numbers of coins were found in post-Mauryan times. These were made of lead, potin, copper, bronze, silver and gold.

Importance of Coins

The importance of coins are follows as :

- The areas of their findings indicate the region of coinage circulation. This enables to reconstruct the history of several ruling dynasties, especially of the Indo-Greeks.
- Coins also throw significant light on the economic history. The coins issued by the guilds of merchants and goldsmiths show that craft and commerce had become important.
- The **Guptas** issued the largest number of gold coins. It indicates that trade and commerce flourished, especially in the post-Mauryan and Gupta times.
- Only a few coins belonging to post-Gupta period have been found. It indicates the decline of trade and commerce at that time.
- Coins also contain religious symbols and legends, which throw light on the art and religion of the time.
- They also give information about natural resources available in various regions. **Satavahanas**, who ruled in Andhra Pradesh and Maharashtra in the first two centuries AD, issued a large number of lead coins since, the Andhra region possessed rich sources of lead.

Inscriptions

- The study of inscriptions is called **Epigraphy**.
- The study of old writings used in inscriptions and old record is called **Palaeography**.
- Inscriptions were carved out on seals, stone pillars, rocks, copper plates, temple walls, bricks or images.
- In early centuries of the Christian era, copper plate began to be used along with stone inscriptions.
- The earliest inscriptions are found on the seals of Harappa belonging to about 2500 BC, but they have not been deciphered so far.
- The oldest inscription deciphered so far is **Brahmi script** that was issued by **Ashoka** in the third century BC.

- The Ashokan epigraphs were first deciphered in 1837 by **James Princep**, a civil servant in the employment of the East India Company.
- Two Ashokan pillars were found by **Firoz Shah Tughlaq** and re-established by him at Firoz Shah Kotla Fort and in ridge area in Delhi near university of Delhi.

Language Used in Inscriptions

- The earliest inscriptions were written in the **Prakrit language** in the third century BC. Sanskrit was adopted as an epigraphic medium in the second century AD. In the ninth and tenth centuries AD, the inscriptions began to be composed in regional languages.
- Ashokan inscriptions were engraved in the **Brahmi script**, which was written from left to right. Some inscriptions were written in **Kharosthi script** which was written from right to left.
- **Brahmi script** was prevailed in the whole country, except for the North-Western part. It continued to be the main script till the end of **Gupta era**.
- Greek and Aramaic scripts were used in writing Ashokan inscriptions in Afghanistan.
- The **Boghaz-Koi inscription** found in Asia Minor mentions Vedic Gods *Mitra, Varuna, Indra* and *Nasatya*.

Ancient Inscription

Types of Inscriptions

The following four types of inscriptions help us in understanding history of Ancient India :

(i) Some inscriptions convey royal orders and decisions regarding social, religious and administrative matters to officials and public in general. Ashokan inscriptions are of this category.

(ii) Other inscriptions are votive records of the followers of Buddhism, Jainism, Vaishnavism, etc, who put up pillars, tablets, temples or images as marks of devotion.

(iii) The third types of inscriptions throw light on attributes and achievements of kings and conquerors. Allahabad pillar inscription of Samudragupta belongs to this category.

(iv) Finally, there are donation records which refer specially to gifts of money, cattle, land, etc, mainly for religious purposes, made not only by kings and princes but also by artisans and merchants.

- Inscriptions recording land grants, made mainly by chiefs and princes, are very important for the study of the land system and administration in Ancient India. These were mostly engraved on copper plates. They contain the grants of lands revenues and villages made to monks, priests, temples, monasteries, vassals and officials.

Important Ancient Inscriptions

Inscriptions	Location	Significance
Uttaramerur Inscription	Chengalpattu (now Kanchipuram) district South of Chennai	• It is noted for its temple inscriptions that describe a self-governance system existing around seventh to ninth centuries AD.
Eran Inscription	Sagar district, Madhya Pradesh on the Bank of Bina river	• It is an earliest evidence of *Sati* found in India here.
Besnagar/ Vidisha Inscription	Vidisha in present Madhya Pradesh	• This pillar inscription was constructed by Heliodorus, a Greek ambassador and belongs to Shunga period (second century BC). • It is written in Prakrit language (with a few Sanskritic spellings) and Brahmi script. • This pillar inscription is devoted to Lord Vasudeva.
Junagarh Inscription	Junagarh district, Gujarat	• It is first pure Sanskrit inscription, by King Rudradaman of Saka dynasty in around 150 AD. • It says that Pushyagupta, the Governor of Chandragupta Maurya, built a dam on Sudarshan lake.
Mehrauli Inscription/ Garuda pillar	Originally at Vishnupada (Udayagiri), Madhya Pradesh but was transported to Delhi later	• It is probably erected by Chandragupta Vikramaditya. • It mentions Chandragupta II conquest over Vanga countries and Vatakas. The pillar bears a Sanskrit inscription in Brahmi script.
Aihole Inscription	Bagalkot, Karnataka	• It is a eulogy of Chalukya King Pulakeshin II and mentions his victory over Harshavardhana. • It is written in Sanskrit, composed by Ravikirti, the court poet of Pulakeshin II.

Inscriptions	Location	Significance
Allahabad Pillar Inscription (Prayag Prasasti)	Prayagraj, Uttar Pradesh	• It is issued by Samudragupta and composed by Harisena. • It is written in refined Sanskrit language in Champu Kavya style. • It mentions the conquest of Samudragupta both in North and South and described the boundaries of Gupta Empire and his diplomatic relations.
Hathigumpha Inscription	Udayagiri, near Bhubaneshwar , (Odisha)	• It was erected by Kharavela, the ruler of Kalinga during second century BC. • It mentions the military expeditions carried by Kharavela.
Lumbini Pillar Inscription	Located in Nepal	• It is a royal commemorative inscription recording Ashoka's visit to Buddha's birth place.
Mandasaur Inscription of Yashodharman	Mandsaur district, Madhya Pradesh	• It mentions the rule of Yashodharman, a local king. • It is composed by Veersena.

Literary Sources

- Literary sources are the most authentic sources for the reconstruction of history.
- The most ancient manuscripts, hand written material, in India are not older than the fourth century AD and have been found in **Central Asia**.
- In India, they were written on **birch bark** and **palm leaves**, but in Central Asia manuscripts were written on **sheep leather** and **wooden tablets**.
- The literature can be classified into religious and secular literature.

Religious Literature

- The Vedic, Buddhist, Jain and other contemporary literature are the religious literary sources of Ancient Indian History.
- They throw light on the social and cultural conditions of ancient times but it is difficult to make use of them in the context of time and place.

Vedic Literature

- The Vedic literature gives us a clear picture of the political, social and economic life of the Aryans and of the conflict between the Aryans and the non-Aryans.

Puranas

- The Puranas contain mythological information.
- There exists total **18 Puranas.** They give the genealogical records (*Vanshavali*) of the ancient rulers of Kali Yuga.
- They are very much useful for studying history. Important Puranas are **Vayu Purana**, **Skanda Purana**, **Matsya Purana**, **Vishnu Purana**, etc.

Mahabharata and Ramayana

- The two epics *Mahabharata* and *Ramayana* seem to have been finally compiled by 400 AD. Of this, the *Mahabharata* is older and possibly reflects the state of affairs from the 10th century BC, to the fourth century AD.
- Originally, it consisted of 8800 verses and was called *Jaya Samhita* or the collection dealing with victory. These were raised to 24000 and came to be known as **Bharata**.
- The final compilation brought the verses to 100,000 which came to be known as the **Mahabharata** or the **Satasahasri Samhita**. It contains narrative, descriptive and didactic material.
- *Ramayana* originally consisted of 12000 verses, which were later raised to 24000. It seems to have been composed later than the *Mahabharata*.

Jaina and Buddhist Literature

- The religious books of Jainas and Buddhists refer to historical personalities and incidents.
- The earliest Buddhist texts were written in **Pali language**, which was common man's language in Magadha or South Bihar.
- They were finally compiled in the second century BC in Sri Lanka, but the canonical portions reflect the state of affairs in the age of Buddha in India.
- They tell us not only about the life of Buddha but some of the Buddhist kings who ruled over Magadha, Northern Bihar and Eastern Uttar Pradesh.
- **Jatakas** are the birth stories of Buddha's previous years. These were probably composed by ordinary people and then written down and preserved by Buddhist monks. They throw light on social and economic conditions between fifth to second century BC. They also make incidental references to political events in the age of Buddha.
- The Jaina texts were written in **Prakrit** and were finally compiled in sixth century AD at **Vallabhi** in **Gujarat**. They contain many passages which help us to reconstruct political history of Eastern Uttar Pradesh and Bihar in the age of Mahavira. The Jaina texts refer repeatedly about trade and traders.

Secular Literature

- Secular class of literature refers to the law-books called the *Dharamsutras, Smritis,* biographies, plays, dramas and the literature of South India called Sangam literature.
- The *Dharamsutras* were compiled in 500-200 BC, and the principal *Smritis* were codified in the first six centuries of Christian era. They laid down the

duties or different Varnas as well about the kings and their officials.

- They prescribed the rules according to which property is to be held, sold and inherited. They also prescribe punishments for person guilty of theft, assault, murder, adultery, etc.
- An important law book is the *Arthashastra* of **Kautilya**. It is divided into 15 Adhikarans, of which Adhikaran II and III may be regarded of an earliest date.
- The book was put in its final form in the beginning of Christian era. Its earliest portions reflect the state of society and economy in the age of Mauryas. It provides rich material for the study of Ancient Indian polity and economy.
- The secular literature also includes the work of **Bhasa**, **Kalidasa** and **Banabhatta**. They throw light on the conditions of the time to which these writings belonged. They also throw light on the social and cultural life of Northern and Central India in the age of Guptas.
- The works of Kalidasa comprise kavyas and dramas, the most famous of which is *Abhijyana Shakuntalam*.
- *Harshacharita* by **Banabhatta** in the seventh century AD, is a semi-biographical work written in Sanskrit language and in fancy style.
- It describes the early career of Harshavardhana. It gives excellent idea of the court life under Harsha and the social and religious life in his age.
- **Sandhyakar Nandi's** *Ramcharitam* narrates the story of conflict between the Kaivarta peasants and the Pala prince Rampala.
- **Bilhana's** *Vikramankadevacharita* recounts the achievements of his patron, Vikramaditya VI (1076-1127), the Chalukyan King of Kalyan.
- The *Rajatarangini* or *The Stream of Kings* written by **Kalhana** in 12th century AD. It is an oldest fullest record of history of Kashmir.

Sangam Literature

- It comprises the earliest Tamil texts, composed around 2300 years ago in assemblies (known as Sangama) of poets that were held in city of Madurai.
- It is a major source of information regarding social, economic and political life of the people living in the delta.

Foreign Accounts

- The Greek, Roman, Chinese and Arab visitors came to India, either as sailors, travellers or religious missionaries. They left behind accounts of details that they saw in India.

Greek and Roman Sources

- The accounts of Greek and Roman authors, such as **Megasthenes**, **Arian**, **Curtius**, **Plutarch**, **Diodorus**, **Dionysics**, etc, gave valuable information of India's contemporary situation.

  The Greek writer, **Herodotus**, had never been to India and yet his book has reference to the conquests of North-Western India by the Persian emperors. It constituted the twentieth province of the empire of Darius, the Persian emperor.
- The Greek visitors mention **Sandrokottas**, who is identified with Chandragupta Maurya, whose date of accession is fixed at 322 BC.
- The *Indica* of **Megasthenes**, who came to the court of Chandragupta Maurya, has been lost and preserved only in fragments quoted by subsequent classical writers. *Indica* furnishes valuable information not only about Mauryan administration but also about social classes and economic activities in that period.
- Greek and Roman accounts of the first and second centuries AD mentioned many Indian ports and various items of trade between India and Roman empire.
- The *'Periplus of The Erythraean Sea'* by unknown author and **Ptolemy's** *Geography* (150 AD), both written in Greek, provide valuable data for the study of ancient geography and commerce.
- An account of a Greek sailor provides detailed account of port of Barygaza (the Greek name of Bharuch).

Chinese Sources

- Fa-Hien (fifth century AD) and **Hiuen Tsang** (seventh century AD), were Buddhist travellers from China, who came to visit the Buddhist shrines and to study Buddhism.
- Fa-Hien describes the social, religious and economic conditions of India in the age of Guptas and Hiuen Tsang presents a similar account of India in the age of Harsha.
- **I-Tsing** visited India in seventh century after the death of Harsha.
- Hiuen Tsang, also known as Xuan Zang, visited Nalanda and spent time in studying with other pilgrims. He came during the reign of Harshavardhana.

Arab Sources

- Some earlier Arab writers were **Sulaiman** (*Silsilat-ut-Tawarikh*) and **Al Masudi** (*Muruj-ul-Zahab*).
- **Al-Biruni** gave important information about India in his books *'Tahqiq-i-Hind'* and *Kitab-ul-Hind*. He was Arab scholar and contemporary of Mahmud of Ghazni.
- Al-Biruni studied Sanskrit and acquired knowledge of Indian literature. He did not give any political information of his times but gave details insights of contemporary society and culture.

Modern Historians of Ancient India

- The first book, which was translated by the East India Company in India was *Manusmriti*, that was published as 'A Code of Gentoo Laws' in English by **Nathaniel Brassey Halhed** in 1776 AD.
- The Asiatic Society of Bengal was established in 1784 AD by Sir William Jones in Calcutta. He later translated *Abhijyana Shakuntalam* into English in 1789 AD.
- **William Jones** was the first scholar to propogate the deep relationship between the Indo-European languages with Sanskrit as well as Persian.
- In the year 1785, **Sir Charles Wilkins** translated the Bhagavad Gita into English as *Bhagavad Gita-Dialogues of Krishna*.
- German scholar, **Max Muller** contributed immensely on Indology. He translated Vedas, Upanishads, Hitopadesha, etc and published as *Sacred Books of the East* in total 50 part series.
- *The Early History of India* Book written by **Vincent Arthur Smith** (1843-1920) in 1904, is considered as the first systematic work in Ancient Indian History.
- An eminent scholar **RG Bhandarkar**, reconstructed Satavahana dynasty in Deccan as well Vaishnavism and other religious sects.
- Social Activist **Pandurang Vaman Kane** (1880-1972) wrote the History of *Dharmashastras*, which is considered as Encyclopedia of social code and Ethics.
- **Raja Rajendralal Mitra** was among the first Indian cultural researcher and historian who published various manuscripts of Vedic literature. He also wrote *the Sanskrit Buddhist Literature of Nepal* in 1882.
- Eminent historian **RC Majumdar** (1888-1980) had presented *History and Culture of Indian people*, where he propounded Indian Renaissance in descriptive manner.
- Another scholar **Nilakantha Shastri** has vividly described about the history of South India in his work *History of South India*.
- Historian **KP Jayaswal** in his work 'Hindu Polity' in 1924 had proved the existence of Mahajanapadas and other republic states in Ancient period.
- The book, early Indus civilisation, 1948 has been written by **Ernest Mackay**. It gives elaborates description of Harappan cities.
- British historian and noted Indologist **AL Basham** had written the book *The Wonder that Was India in 1951*, where he attempted to correct the negative stereotypes of India.
- **DD Koshambi** in his book 'An Introduction to the Study of Indian History' published in 1956 revolutionised Indian Historiography with his realistic and scientific approach.

Important Books and Their Authors

Books	Authors
Mudrarakshasa	Vishakadatta
Rajatarangini	Kalhana
Kathasaritsagar	Somdeva
Kamasutra	Vatsayana
Prashnottarmalika	Amoghavarsha
Swapanvasdattam	Bhasa
Buddha Charita	Asvaghosa
Natyashastra	Bharata
Abhigyan Shakuntalam, Vikramorvasiyam Raghuvansam	Kalidasa
Amarkosha	Amarsimha
Panchasidhantika, Brihat Samhita	Varahamihira
Surya Sidhanta	Aryabhatta
Panchatantra	Vishnu Sharma
Nitisara	Kamandaka
Aihole Prasasti	Ravi Kriti
Indica	Megasthenes
Arthasastra	Kautilya
Charaka Samhita	Charaka
Lilawati	Bhaskaracharya
Harshacharita, Kadambari	Banbhatta
Naganand a and Ratnavali	Harshavardhana
Gathasaptashati	Hala
Ashtadhyayi	Panini
Mahabhasyam	Patanjali
Naishadhacharitra	Sri Harsha
Mrichhakatikam	Shudraka
Gitagovinda	Jayadev

Extra Facts From Tamil Nadu Board and NIOS

- **The Zend Avesta** is a Persian/Iranian text of Zoroastrianism. This book speaks about the lands and Gods of the people speaking the Indo-Persian languages. It has references to the regions of North-Western part of India. It has a linguistic similarity with Veda.
- **Gatha Saptasati**, a prakrit text composed by the Satavahana king Hala. It talks about evolution of society in South Indian states.
- The classical sangam corpus consists of **Tholkappiyam**, the eight anthologies **(Ettuthokai)**, Ten Idylls **(Paththuppattu)**. These texts elaborate about society of Sangam period.

02

Pre-Historic Cultures

[SOURCES]

Class-VI New NCERT Chap 2 (From Hunting-Gathering to Growing Food), Class-VI Old NCERT Chap 1 (Early Man), Class-IX Old NCERT Chap 1 (Life in Pre-historic Times), Class-XI Old NCERT Chap 1 (The Stone Age : The Early Man), Class-XI Old NCERT Chap 6 (Chalcolithic Farming Cultures) Tamil Nadu Board (Class XI), NIOS

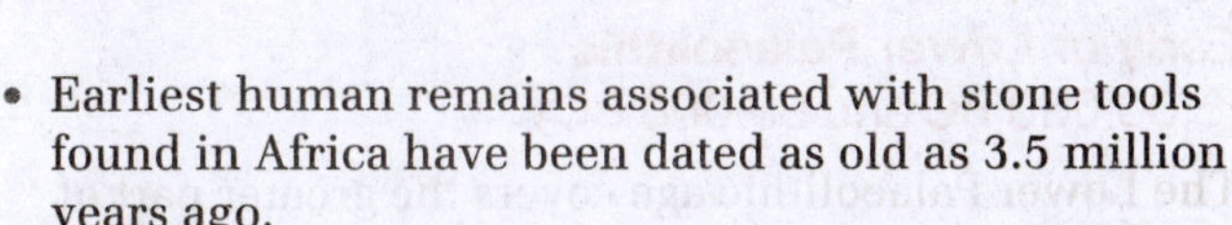

- Earliest human remains associated with stone tools found in Africa have been dated as old as 3.5 million years ago.
- In India, the evidence of first occupation are not earlier than the **Middle Pleistocene**, which began about 5,00,000 years ago. Initially, men were **nomads**. They wandered in groups from place-to place in search of food and shelter. There was no cultivation. So, they consumed all they could find in a certain place and had to move place-to-place in search of food. They also hunted animals and they had to go elsewhere in their search.
- People either lived in caves or built small shelters on the leafy branches of large trees.
- In the later part of **stone age** (Neolithic), man stopped being a nomad and began to settle down in one place as an agriculturist.
- It took almost 3,00,000 years for men to change from a '**food-gatherer**' to a '**food producer**'.

Division of Ancient Indian History

History of Ancient India has been divided by the historian into three heads as follows:

1. **Pre-Historic Period** It is the period of human culture for which no written records are available. The humans of this period were not civilised. The history of this period is studied by archaeological evidences only. This period is divided into three parts *viz.* Palaeolithic Age, Mesolithic Age and Neolithic Age.
2. **Proto-history Period** It is the period between pre-history and history during which a culture or civilisation has not yet developed writing, but other cultures have already noted its existence in their own writings. Duration of this period is 2500 BC to 600 BC.
3. **Historical Period** It is the period whose information is available in written records. Humans of this period were civilised and historical activities after 600 BC included in this period.

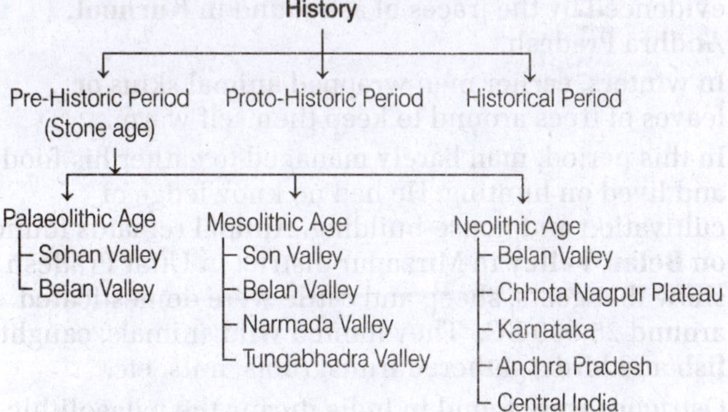

Palaeolithic Age: Hunters and Food Gatherers

- The earliest period is called the Palaeolithic. The term is derived from two Greek words, 'palaeo', meaning old and 'lithos', meaning stone. This period developed in the **Pleistocene period** or the Ice Age.

- The Palaeolithic period extends from 2 million years ago to about 12,000 years ago. This long span of time covers 99% of human history.
- As per the evidences found in form of tools in **South India** and in the **Sohan Valley** in Pakistan, humans have been living in India roughly from 5,00,000 BC. Such sites have also been discovered in **Kashmir**.
- The early man used stone tools for hunting, cutting and other purposes. The tools were made of stone, wood and bone.
- Some of these stone tools, were used to cut meat and bone, scrape bark (from trees) and hides (animal skins), chop fruit and roots.
- Some may have been attached to handles of bone or wood, to make spears and arrows for hunting. Other tools were used to chop wood, which was used as firewood.

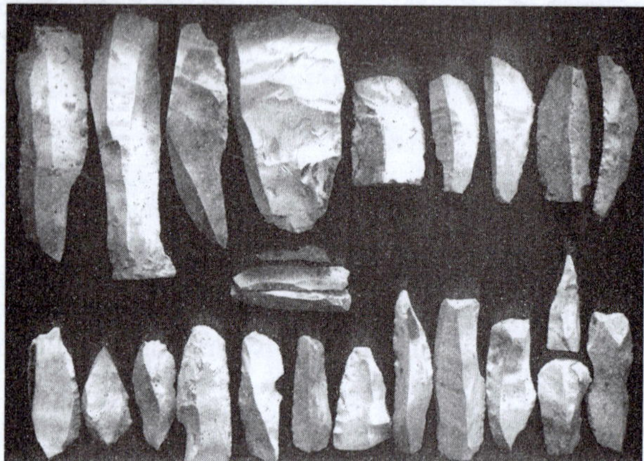

Tools of Palaeolithic Age

- The Palaeolithic men discovered fire, which is evidenced by the traces of ash found in **Kurnool**, Andhra Pradesh.
- In winters, earlier men wrapped animal skins or leaves of trees around to keep themself warm.
- In this period, man barely managed to gather his food and lived on hunting. He had no knowledge of cultivation and house-building. Animal remains found on **Belan Valley** in Mirzapur district in Uttar Pradesh show that goats, sheep and cattle were domesticated around 25,000 BC. They hunted wild animals, caught fish and birds, gathered fruits, roots, nuts, etc.
- Ostriches were found in India during the palaeolithic age. In Patne, Maharashtra some ostrich eggshells were found with engraved designs.
- The life was not settled yet, the hunter-gatherers of this age moved from place-to-place :
  - in search of food
  - to follow the movements of animals they hunted
  - in search of different kind of plants
  - to meet their friends and relatives
- Around 12,000 years ago, there were major changes in the climate of the world, with a shift to relatively warm conditions. In many areas, this led to the development of grasslands. This in turn led to an increase in the number of deer, antelope, goat, sheep and cattle, i.e., animals that survived on grass.
- This helped people to start thinking about herding and rearing these animals. Fishing also became an important occupation.
- This was also the period when several grain bearing grasses, including wheat, barley and rice grew naturally in different parts of the sub-continent.
- Men, women and children probably collected these grains as food, learnt where they grew and when they ripened. This may have led them to think about growing plants on their own.

Phases in the Palaeolithic Age

- The Palaeolithic Age in India is divided into three phases. According to the nature of the stone tools used by the people and also to the nature of change in the climate.

1. Early or Lower Palaeolithic (5,00,000 BC and 50,000 BC)

- The Lower Palaeolithic age covers the greater part of the Ice Age. Its characteristic feature is the use of **hand-axes, cleavers** and **choppers**.
- Its sites are found in the Valley of River Soan or Sohan in Punjab, (now in Pakistan). Other sites were found at **Hunsgi**, Karnataka.
- The Early Palaeolithic tools have found in the **Belan Valley**. The Belan sites contain caves and rock shelters, which could have served as seasonal camps for human beings.
- The sites found in the desert area of **Didwana** in Rajasthan, in the Valleys of the Belan and the Narmada (Madhya Pradesh) and in the caves and rock shelters of **Bhimbetka** near Bhopal in Madhya Pradesh roughly belong to 1,00,000 BC.
- At some sites, a large number of tools, were found that were used for all sorts of activities. These were probably **habitation-cum factory sites**.

Habitation and Factory Sites

- **Habitation sites** These were the places where people lived. These include caves and rock shelters. They provided shelter from the rain, heat and wind.
- **Factory sites** These were the places where stone was found and where people made tools.
- **Habitation-cum-factory sites** These were the sites where people lived for longer time. Here large number of tools are found.

2. Middle Palaeolithic (50,000 BC and 40,000 BC)

- The Middle Palaeolithic industries are mainly based upon **flakes**, which are found in different parts of India and show regional variations.
- The principal tools are varieties of **blades**, **points**, **borers** and **scrapers** made of flakes.
- Middle Palaeolithic sites are found in **Soan Valley**, **Narmada river valley** and at places South of Tungabhadra river.

3. Upper Palaeolithic (40,000 BC and 10,000 BC)

- The Upper Palaeolithic phase was less humid. It coincided with the last phase of the **Ice Age**, when climate became comparatively warm.
- In the world context, it marks the appearance of new flint industries and modern men (*Homo sapiens*).
- Caves and rock shelters used by human beings in the Upper Palaeolithic phase have been discovered at **Bhimbetka**, 45 km South of Bhopal. This phase was characterised by massive flakes, blades, burins and scrappers, which have been found in upper level of Gujarat dunes.

The Mesolithic Age: Hunters and Herders

- The Upper Palaeolithic Age came to an end with the end of Ice Age around 9000 BC and the climate became warm and dry.
- From 9000 BC, an intermediate stage emerged in Stone Age culture, which is called the Mesolithic Age.
- It intervened as a transitional phase between the Palaeolithic Age and the Neolithic or new Stone Age. It is also called the **Later Stone Age**.
- In case of India, it started about 8000 BC and continued upto 4000 BC.
- The characteristic tools of the Mesolithic Age are **microliths**.
- The Mesolithic people lived on hunting, fishing and food gathering. At a later stage, they also domesticated animals.
- **Adamgarh** in Madhya Pradesh and **Bagor** in Rajasthan provide the earliest evidence for the domestication of animals. The dog was the first animal to be domesticated.
- Mesolithic sites are found in Chhota Nagpur plateau, Central India and South of River Krishna.
- The Mesolithic Site **Bagor** in Rajasthan is very well preserved. It had a distinctive microlithic industry, and its inhabitants depended on hunting and pastoralism.

Pre-Historic Art

- The people of Palaeolithic and Mesolithic ages practiced painting.
- Pre-historic art appears at several places, but **Bhimbetka** is a striking site which has more than 500 painted rock shelters, distributed in an area of 10 sq km.
- The rock paintings extend from the Palaeolithic to the Mesolithic period, but a majority of rock shelters are associated with the Mesolithic occupation.
- Many birds, animals and human beings are painted. Most probably, most of the birds and animals that appear in paintings were hunted for the sake of livelihood. Perching birds, which live upon grain, are absent in the earliest group of painting.

Tools of Mesolithic Age

The Neolithic Age: Food Producers

- In the context of the world, the **New Stone Age** began in 9000 BC. However, the Neolithic settlements in the Indian sub-continent are not older than 7000 BC. Whereas Neolithic settlements found in South India are not older than 2500 BC. The people of this age used tools and implements of polished stone. They particularly used stone axes.
- The Neolithic settlers were the earliest farming communities. They also started to tame animals. Animals like sheep, goat, cattle and pig were domesticated by them and they became herders.
- With various discoveries and developments, the Neolithic man settled in one place, forming a village. These were the earliest village. They were to be found all over India but more often in river valleys and on the flat plains, where the soil was more fertile and it was easier to grow crops.
- The Neolithic villages were small and the houses were made of mud and reed and situated close to each other. The area of huts was probably surrounded by a **mud wall** or **fence**. The field lay outside the fence.
- The village itself was usually built on slightly higher ground than the fields. The huts were thatched and

ordinarily consisted of just one room. A fire was lit in the hut, on which the cooking was done. They cultivated crops like rice, wheat, barley, ragi and horsegram (*Kulathi*).

- Since, in the Neolithic phase several settlements came to be acquainted with the cultivation of cereals and the domestication of animals, they needed pots in which they could store their food grains. Hence, pottery first appears in this phase. In many areas, they began making large clay pots or wove baskets or dug pits into the ground. Hand-made potter is found in the early stage. Later, they used **wheel made pottery**.
- A very important discovery was that of the **wheel**. Its discovery led to a big advance in the pattern of living. It helped men to travel easily from one place to another. The use of wheel also improved the making of pottery.

Neolithic Society

- When men became settled, it became necessary to make rules of conduct. The first thing was to decide what each person's job was to be. There used to be division of labour and men and women had to perform different functions/ tasks. Generally, the oldest man in the village had to be leader who could give commands. But sometimes, it was the strongest and the bravest man.

Religion in Neolithic Age

Sky-God and **Earth-Goddess** were worshipped. The dead were buried in a grave. Several burial sites have been found at **Mehrgarh**. In one instance, the dead person was buried with goats.

Neolithic Areas

- The sites are found all over the sub-continent. Some of the most important ones are in the North-West, in present-day **Kashmir** and in East and South India.
- **Mehrgarh** was the earliest Neolithic settlement found in Indian sub-continent, which is located in a fertile plain near the **Bolan Pass**, at **Baluchistan** (Pakistan). It was probably one of the places where people learnt to grow barley and wheat, and rear sheep and goats for the first time in this area.
- It is one of the earliest villages, that we know about and dates back to 7000 BC. Archaeologists have found evidence of many kinds of animal bones from the earliest levels. These included bones of wild animals such as the deer and pig.
- The Neolithic people of **Mehrgarh** were more advanced. They produced wheat, cotton and lived in mud-brick houses. Other finds at Mehrgarh include remains of square or rectangular houses. Each house had four or more compartments, some of which may have been used for storage.

First Area

- **Burzahom**, situated near **Srinagar** (Jammu and Kashmir), dated back to 2400 BC. The Neolithic people of Burzahom lived there on a lake-side in pits and probably had hunting and fishing economy. They were not acquainted with agriculture or domestication of animals. They used tools and weapons made of polished stone and bone. They used coarse grey pottery. Domestic dogs were found to be buried with their masters in their graves.
- Gufkral (literally the 'cave of the potter') is another Neolithic site located 41 km South-West of Srinagar. The people of Gufkral practiced both agriculture and domestication of animals.
- Chirand, near Patna, dates back to 1600 BC. It is the only site in India where bone implements have been found in large number.
- In addition, sites in **Mirzapur** and **Allahabad** have been found. The site in Allahabad district is noted for the cultivation of the rice in the 6th millennium BC.

Second Area

- The second group of Neolithic people lived in **South India** to the South of river **Godavari**. The Neolithic phase in South India seems to have covered the period from 2500 BC to 1000 BC. Here, the people settled on the tops of granite hills or on the plateau near the river banks. They possessed cattle, sheep and goats.
- They used stone **axes** and **stone blades**. The rubbing stone shows that, they were acquainted with art of producing grains.

Neolithic ground stone axe

- The important sites in South are **Maski**, **Brahmagiri**, **Hallur**, Kodekal, Sangankallu, Tirumakudal Narsipur, Takkalakota in Karnataka, Paiyampalli in Tamil Nadu and Utnur and Piklihal in Andhra Pradesh.
- The Neolithic settlers in **Piklihal** were cattle herders. They domesticated cattle, sheep and goats, etc. It is evidenced by the ash mounds and habitation sites discovered in Piklihal.

Third Area

- The third area from which Neolithic tools have been recovered in the hills of Assam. Neolithic tools have been found in the **Garo Hills** in the Meghalaya as well.
- **Daojali-hading** is a site on the hills near the Brahmaputra Valley, close to routes leading into China and Myanmar. Here stone tools, including mortars and pestles, have been found. These indicate that people were probably growing grain and preparing food from it.

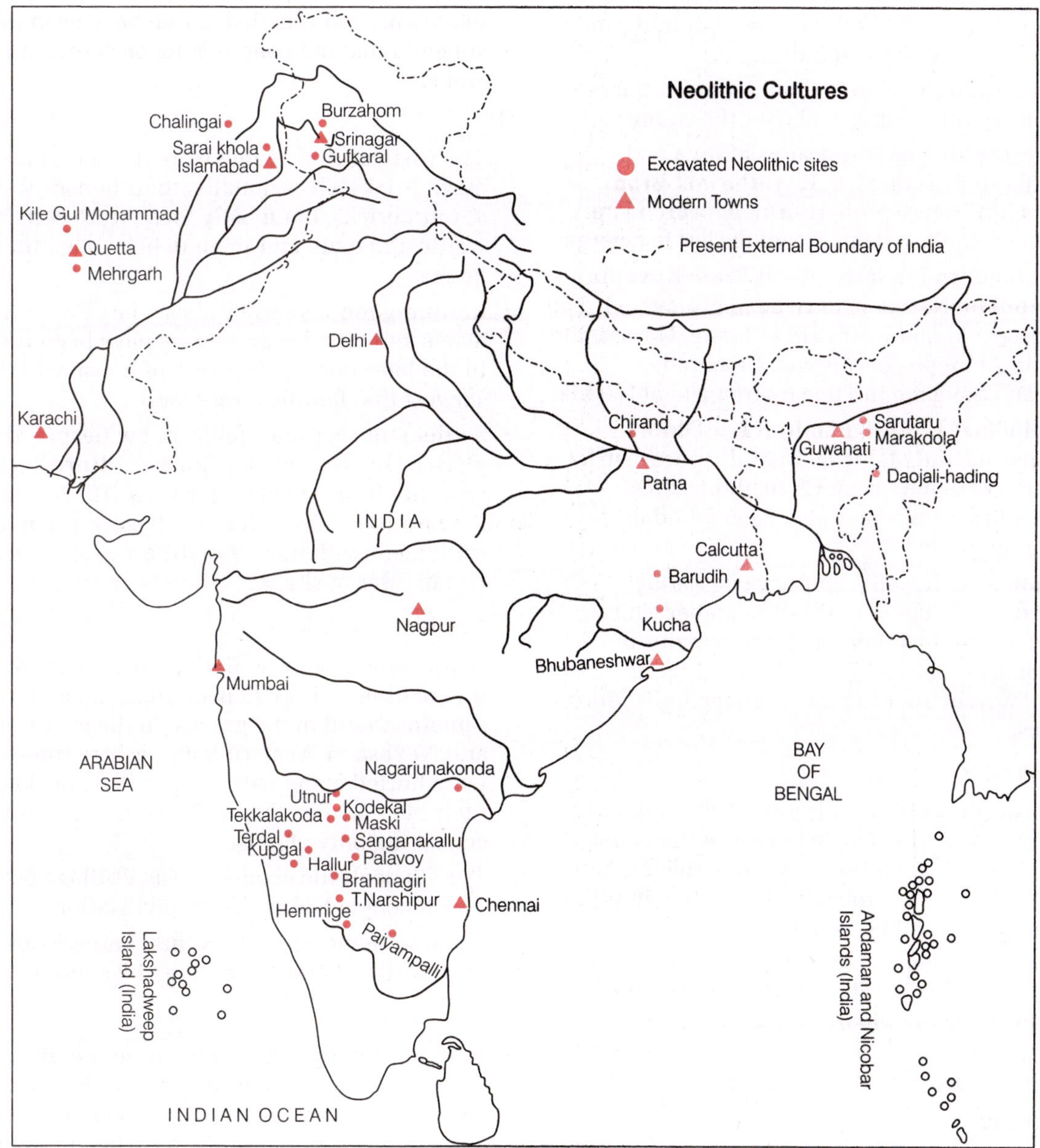

*From Tamil Nadu Board

Chalcolithic Age

- The use of metal began towards the end of the Neolithic age and thus the Chalcolithic age. The first metal to be used was copper. Later, it was mixed with metals such as tin, zinc and lead to make new metal of alloy called **bronze**.
- The Chalcolithic man was fond of **ornaments** and **decoration**. The women wore ornaments of shell and bone. Man had invented the technique of spinning and weaving cloth.
- There were several cultures that were using stone implements along with the copper implements. Such cultures are called **Chalcolithic cultures**.

- As per scientific analysis, Chalcolithic cultures were not older than 1800 BC. They seem to have continued in some areas till 1000 BC and in other areas till 800 BC.

The Early Settlers

- The Chalcolithic communities founded the first villages in India (not in Indian sub-continent) and cultivated barley, wheat, lentil in Western India and rice in Southern and Eastern India.
- Except for the alluvial plains, Chalcolithic cultures have been discovered almost all over the country.
- Their earliest settlements appear in **Malwa** and Central India such as those in **Kayatha** and **Eran**. Settlements in Western Maharashtra appeared later and settlements in West Bengal were the last to emerge.
- In Western Madhya Pradesh sites at **Eran**, **Kayatha** and **Navdatoli** on Narmada have been discovered. The sites in Western Maharashtra are at Jorwe, Nevasa and Daimabad in Ahmednagar district; Chandoli, Inamgaon and Songaon in Pune district and at Nashik.
- In Eastern India, **Chirand**, **Pandu Rajar Dhibi** in Burdwan district and Mahisdal in Midnapore district in West Bengal are important Chalcolithic sites. Some Chalcolithic sites have also been found in Allahabad region.
- The settlements at Kayatha and Eran in Madhya Pradesh and at Inamgaon in Western Maharashtra were fortified. On the other hand, the remains of structures in Chirand and Pandu Rajar Dhibi in Eastern India were poor in nature, giving indications of sinkholes.

Tools and Weapons

- The people of Chalcolithic cultures used small tools and weapons made of stone. In certain settlements, copper implements are found in good numbers. At **Ahar**, stone tools are completely absent. In **Gilund**, copper blade industry has been found.
- The Chalcolithic people used different types of pottery, one of which is called Black and Red. It was wheel made and occasionally painted with white linear designs. However, people of different cultures used different types of pottery and implements.

Known Animals

- The people living in South-Eastern Rajasthan, Western Madhya Pradesh and Western Maharashtra domesticated animals and cultivated foodgrains. They domesticated cow, sheep, goat, pig, buffalo and hunted deer.
- Remains of camel have also been found. It is not clear whether, they were acquainted with the horse. Some animal remains are identified either to the horse or donkey or wild ass.

Food

- They used to cultivate wheat, rice, bajra, lentil, green gram, black gram and grass pea. All these foodgrains have been found at **Navadatoli** in Maharashtra. In addition, ber, linseed, ragi and cotton were also grown.
- They also ate non-vegetarian food. In Eastern India, fish hooks and remains of rice have been found, which suggests that the people in Eastern region lived on fish and rice.

Houses

- The Chalcolithic people were not acquainted with burnt bricks. Occasionally, their houses were made up of mud bricks, but mostly these were constructed with wattle and daub and seem to have been thatched houses.
- In **Inamgaon**, in earlier phase, large mud houses with ovens and circular pit houses have been discovered. In the later phase, discovery of house with five rooms suggest that families were large.
- Settlements became stable and widespread in this phase. This is termed as **Jorwe culture** because of its type-site is provided by Jorwe, a village situated near Pravara river. Every Jorwe village was a nucleated settlement with houses of different size, circular or rectangular in shape.

Social Inequalities

- In this phase, we also find the beginning of social inequalities. It is evidenced from the material/ remains found in the graves. In the graves at **Chandoli** and **Nevasa** in Western Maharashtra some children were buried along with copper-bead necklaces around their neck while other children had grave goods consisting only of pots.
- The Chalcolithic economy was a village economy. These people had no urban civilisation.
- Some settlements such as **Inamgaon**, **Eran**, **Kayatha** were fortified and surrounded by a **moat**.

Art and Crafts

- A little is known about their art and crafts. They knew the art of copper smelting. They were expert coppersmiths and also good workers in stone as a large number of microliths have been found. They knew the art of **spinning** and **weaving**. **Spindle whorls** have been discovered in **Malwa** and cotton and silk have been found in Maharashtra.

Burial Practices

- Unlike Harappans, they did not use separate cemeteries. They had different burial practices. In Maharashtra, people used to bury their dead in urns under the floor of their house in the North-to-South position in the South India in the East-West position.

- Almost complete or extended burial obtained in Maharashtra, but post-extraction or fractional burial prevailed in West Bengal.

Religion

- **Terracotta** figures of women found in Inamgaon suggest that the Chalcolithic people prayed the Mother Goddess. In Malwa and Rajasthan stylised bull terracotta show that, the bull served as a religious cult.

Important Chalcolithic Cultures in India

Chalcolithic Culture	Sites of Chalcolithic Culture	Feature Shade
Ahara Culture (3000-1500 BC)	Ahara (Rajasthan), Balathal, Gilund, etc.	• The distinctive feature is black and red ware, decorated with the white designs.
Kayatha Culture (2000-1800 BC)	Near river in Chambal and its tributaries.	• The sturdy red slipped ware with chocolate colour designs is main feature.
Malwa Culture (1700-1200 BC)	Narmada and its tributaries in Gujarat.	• One of the largest Chalcolithic settlements. • The Malwa ware is slightly coarse in fabric, but has a thick buff surface over which designs were made either in red or black.
Svalda Culture (2300-2000 BC)	Dhulia district of Maharashtra.	• Known for its non-Harappan culture.
Prabhas and Rangpur Culture (1700-1400 BC)	Prabhas Patan and Rangpur, Gujarat	• Both of them are derived from the Harappa Civilisation. The polished red ware is the hall mark of this culture.

Importance of Chalcolithic Cultures

- Except for alluvial plains and the thickly forested areas, traces of Chalcolithic cultures have been found almost all over the country.
- They used microliths and other stone tools supplemented by a little use of copper tools. It seems that most of them knew, the art of copper smelting.
- Almost all Chalcolithic communities used black and red wheel-turned pots. They were, the first to use painted pottery. Their pots were meant for cooking, eating and storing. They used the *lota*, but there is no trace of the *thali*.
- In South India, the Neolithic phase imperceptibly faded into the stone-copper phase and so, these cultures are called **Neolithic-Chalcolithic**.
- In other parts, especially in Western Maharashtra and Rajasthan, the Chalcolithic people seems to have been colonisers.
- The Chalcolithic communities founded the first villages in India and cultivated far more cereals than is known in case of the Neolithic communities.
- The burial practices were different in Maharashtra the dead body was placed in the North-South position, but in South India, towards East-West position. Almost complete or extended burial obtained in Maharashtra, but post-extraction or fractional burial prevailed in West Bengal.

Limitations in Chalcolithic Cultures

- In spite of a food-producing economy, the rate of Infant Mortality was very high. It is evident from the large number of children graves in Western Maharashtra.
- Though the copper metal was known but the Chalcolithic culture was a rural culture since, as a metal copper has its limitations and its supply was also limited.
- Further, people did not know the art of mixing copper with tin and thus, forging much stronger and useful metal called **Bronze**. It was the bronze tools, which facilitated the rise of earliest civilisations. They also did not know the art of writing nor did they live in cities.
- Although, the Chalcolithic cultures came much later than the Indus Valley Civilisation, they did not derive any substantial benefit from the advance technological knowledge of the Indus people.

Copper Age in India

- Hoards of copper objects have been found in a wide area ranging from the Chhota Nagpur plateau to the Upper Gangetic basin but, they are concentrated in **Ganga-Yamuna doab**.
- The artefacts found indicate good technological skill and knowledge on the part of the copper smiths and cannot be the handwork of nomadic people or hunters.
- At several places artefacts have been discovered in association with ochre-coloured pots and some mud structures, which shows that the people who used the copper hoards led a settled life and were one of the earliest primitive agriculturists and artisans to settle in doab.

  - The period covered by the **ochre-coloured pottery culture** is roughly placed between 2000 BC and 1800 BC.
  - The end of these settlements is not clear, but the sanctity and religious purity attached to copper vessels, utensils, etc, in Hindu religion may have started in the copper age.
  - The people of Copper Hoard Culture were contemporaries of Harappans and the ochre-coloured pottery area in which they lived was not far removed from that of Harappans. Therefore, some kind of barter system between these copper-using people and the bronze using Harappans can be expected.

Megalithic Culture or Iron Age

- Till second century BC, the phenomenon of large scale agricultural communities using iron implements, rise of social classes, use of writing are not found in peninsula.
- The Southern tip of Peninsular India was inhabited by the people called **Megalith builders**. Megaliths usually refer to graves, which are encircled by big pieces of stone.
- The beginning of megaliths can be traced to 1000 BC, but in many cases Megalithic phase lasted from about the fifth century to first century BC and in a few places this phase persisted even upto the **early Christian era**.
- The Megalithic people did not practice advance type of agriculture. It is evidenced from the fact that compared to the number of agricultural tools those meant for fighting and hunting have been found in the megaliths.
- The Megaliths are found in all upland areas of Peninsular India, but their concentration seems to be in Eastern Andhra Pradesh and in Tamil Nadu.
- The **Chera**, **Chola** and **Pandyas** mentioned in the **Ashokan Inscriptions** were probably in the Megalithic phase of material culture.
- The Megalithic people in the Southern districts of Tamil Nadu had certain peculiar characteristics. They buried the skeleton of the dead in urns made of red pottery in pits.
- The practice of urn-burial was different from that of pit-burial surrounded by stone circles, which practice prevailed in **Krishna-Godavari Valley**.
- The Megalith is contain not only skeletons of people but also pottery and iron objects. It indicates their belief in the next world. These goods also give good idea about source of their livelihood.
- The Megalithic people produced ragi and paddy but their area of cultivable land used by them was very limited and generally, they did not settle on the plains or the low lands.
- By the beginning of the **Christian era**, Megalithic people moved from uplands into fertile river basins and reclaimed marshy deltaic areas.
- Under the stimulus of contact with the elements of material culture brought from the North to the South by traders, conquerors and Jain and Buddhist missionaries, they came to practice wet paddy cultivation. They also founded numerous villages and towns and came to have social classes. All these created conditions for the rise of imperial States in the Southern India.

Extra Facts From Tamil Nadu Board and NIOS

- The first Palaeolithic tools were identified at the site of Pallavaram near Chennai by Robert Bruce Foote in 1863.
- Acheulean and Sohanian were cultural tradition of Palaeolithic period. Acheulean were known for the use of hand axe and Sohanian were known for the use of pebble-flake.
- The only well-known hominin fossil of India was found at Hathnora near Hoshangabad in Madhya Pradesh. Animal fossils of **Elephas Namadicus, Stegodon Ganesa** and **Bos Namadicus** have been discovered in Narmada Valley. These site are related to Palaeolithic age.
- In India, the Middle Palaeolithic phase was first identified by **HD Sankalia** on the Pravara river at Nevasa.
- People, in Upper Palaeolithic, lived in caves. The important sites of this period were Meralbhavi in Karnataka, **Kurnool caves** in Andhra Pradesh, **Godavarikhani** in Telangana, **Baghor** I and **Baghor III** of Son Valley in Madhya Pradesh.
- An Upper Palaeolithic shrine was found at Baghor in Uttar Pradesh, it is the earliest known shrine in India.
- Mesolithic sites in India are found in Paisra (Bihar), Langhnaj (Gujarat), Baghor II, Chopani, Mando, Sarai Nahar Rai Mahadaha and Damdama (all in Uttar Pradesh), Sankanakallu (Andhra Pradesh), Kibbanahalli (Karnataka) and Bagor and Tilwara in Rajasthan.
- Mesolithic people were made circular huts for temporary use. They buried the dead, which suggest their belief and humane relationship. At **Mahadaha**, a man and a woman were buried together.
- The Neolithic people of Burzahom traded with the people of the Harappan civilisation. The important tools of Neolithic period were stone axes, chisels, adzes, pounders, maceheads, points and picks. Awls were used for stitching skins into clothes to beat the weather.
- Nagarjunakonda, Rampuram in Andhra Pradesh, Watkal, Hallur and Piklihal in Karnataka and Paiyyampalli in Tamil Nadu are important Neolithic sites in South India. Daojali Hading and Sarutaru are the Neolithic sites in the Assam region.
- The important Palaeolithic site in Maharashtra were Nevasa on tributary of Godavari and Patne in the Tapti river system. The important site of Palaeolithic in Tamil Nadu was Attirampakkam.
- Neolithic people produced pottery for the purpose of storing grains. This period is famously known as 'the Neolithic Revolution'. The houses of Neolithic period were build by dried bricks.

Indus Valley Civilisation

[SOURCES]

Class-VI Old NCERT Chap 3 (Man Takes to City Life),
Class-XI Old NCERT Chap 7 (Harappa Civilisation : Bronze Age Civilisation),
Class-XII New NCERT Chap 1 (Bricks, Beads and Bones : The Harappan Civilisation)
Tamil Nadu Board (Class XI), NIOS

Origin and Geographical Extent

- The Indus Valley Civilisation or Harappan culture, was discovered in 1921 at the modern site of Harappa in West Punjab in Pakistan. It covered parts of Punjab, Haryana, Sind, Baluchistan, Gujarat, Rajasthan and some areas of Uttar Pradesh.
- The area formed a triangle and accounted for about 12,99,000 km^2, which was larger than ancient Egypt and Mesopotamia.
- **Cunningham**, the first Director-General of the Archaeological Survey of India (ASI) is often called the father of Indian Archaeology. He began archaeological excavations of Harappan culture in the mid-19th century.
- Seals were discovered at Harappa by archaeologists such as **Daya Ram Sahni** and **RD Banerjee** in the early decades of the 20th century.
- On the basis of these findings, **John Marshall**, Director-General of the ASI, announced the discovery of a new civilisation in the Indus Valley to the world in 1924.
- **Radiocarbon dating** has determined the most acceptable time period of Indus Valley Civilisation between 2350-1750 BC.
- At that time, the Northern and Western parts of India (now in Pakistan) were covered with forests. The climate was moist and humid. The areas of Sind and Rajasthan were not deserts.
- The origin of Harappan culture is not clear. However, it is said to be evolved out of indigenous settlements.
- There are no evidences which prove that the influence of Mesopotamia or Egypt helped the rise of Harappan culture.

Major Developments in Harappan Archaeology

Year	Development
1875	Report of Alexander Cunningham on Harappan seal.
1921	Daya Ram Sahni began excavations at Harappa.
1925	Excavations began at Mohenjodaro.
1946	REM Wheeler started excavations at Harappa.
1955	SR Rao began excavations at Lothal.
1960	BB Lal and BK Thapar began excavations at Kalibangan.
1974	MR Mughal began explorations in Bahawalpur, Pakistan.
1980	A team of German and Italian archaeologists began surface explorations at Mohenjodaro.
1986	American team began excavations at Harappa .
1990	RS Bisht began excavations at Dholavira.

Phases of Indus Valley Civilisation

The period of Harappan culture is divided into three phases which are as follows :

Early Harappan Phase (3300 to 2600 BC)

- The Early Harappan Phase is related to the **Hakra Phase**, identified in the **Ghaggar-Hakra River Valley**.
- This phase stands characterised by centralised authority and an increasingly urban quality of life.

- Trade networks had been established and there are also evidences of the cultivation of crops. Peas, sesame seeds, dates, cotton, etc., were grown during this time.
- The site **Kot-Diji** represents the phase leading upto Mature Harappan Phase.

Mature Harappan Phase (2600 to 1900 BC)

- By 2600 BC, the Indus Valley Civilisation had entered into a mature stage.
- The early Harappan communities were turning into large urban centers, like **Harappa** and **Mohenjodaro** in Pakistan and **Lothal** in India.
- Sites of this phase were Harappa, Mohenjodaro, **Chanhudaro**, Lothal, **Kalibangan**, **Banawali**, **Sutkagendor and Surkotada**.

Extent of Indus Valley Civilisation

- **Easternmost site** Alamgirpur (Meerut, Uttar Pradesh)
- **Westernmost site** Sutkagendor (Baluchistan)
- **Northernmost site** Manda (Jammu)
- **Southernmost site** Daimabad (Maharashtra)

Late Harappan Phase (1900 to 1300 BC)

- The signs of a gradual decline of the Harappan Civilisation are believed to have started around 1800 BC and by 1700 BC, most of the cities were abandoned.
- However, various elements of the ancient Harappan Civilisation can be seen in later cultures.
- Archaeological data indicates the continuation of the Late Harappan culture till 1000-900 BC.
- The evidences of late Harappan phase is found in **Rangpur** and **Rojdi** in Kathiawar peninsula (Gujarat).

Contemporary Civilisations of Indus Valley Civilisation

Civilisation	Banks of River	Description
Egypt	Nile river	This was the civilisation of the Pharaohs who built the pyramids at this time.
Mesopotamia (Modern Iraq)	Euphrates and Tigris rivers	This was the Sumerian civilisation and Harappans had trading contacts with it.
Hwang Ho (China)	Hwang Ho river	—

Cities of Indus Valley Civilisation

Some of the prominent cities of Indus Valley Civilisation are discussed below :

Harappa

- It is located on the banks of the River Ravi and was the first Indus site to be discovered and excavated in 1921 by **Daya Ram Sahani. Charles Masson** first visited Harappa near Sahiwal in Punjab, (now in Pakistan) in 1826-1827 and gave its earliest reference.
- In 1912, **J Fleet** discovered the Harappan seals and promoted the excavations under **Sir John Marshall.** It was visited by **Cunningham** in 1853 and 1873.
- The Indus Valley Civilisation was originally called **Harappa Civilisation** after the discovery of this site.

Mohenjodaro

- It is the **largest site** of the Harappan Civilisation, discovered by **RD Banerjee** in 1922. In Sindhi language, the word 'Mohenjodaro' means **Mound of the Dead.**
- **The Great Bath of Mohenjodaro** is the most important public place, measuring 39 feet in length, 23 feet wide and 8 feet deep.

  It is located at the centre of the citadel and is remarkable for its beautiful brickwork. Its floor is made of burnt bricks set in gypsum and mortars.
- **The Great Granary** is the largest building of this civilisation measuring 150 feet in length and 50 feet in width. It is located within the citadel.
- Other buildings include an angular multi-pillared assembly hall and a big rectangular building which served administrative purpose.

Great Bath of Mohenjodaro

Chanhudaro

- It is known as the **Lancashire of India** and is the only Indus city without a citadel. Chanhudaro was perhaps a great centre of bead manufacturing.

Kalibanga

- The literal meaning of Kalibanga is **black bangle.** Kalibangan has the largest concentration of Harappan settlements and yields evidence of early Harappan period.
- Many houses of this city had their own wells. Three different cultural layers, (i.e.,) **Indus, Jhukar** and **Jhangar** can be seen here.

Ropar

- It was the first site to be excavated after independence. Buildings found here were made of stone and soil. It is located in Punjab and has yielded a sequence of six cultural periods or phases with some break from Harappa i.e., **Painted Grey Ware** (PGW) **Culture, Northern Black Polished** (NBP) **Ware Culture**, Kushana, Gupta, Medieval to the present day.

Lothal

- The most unique feature of Lothal was its dockyard, the world's first tidal port. It served as a main seaport for the Indus people. **Baked bricks** with lime plaster were used in the dockyards of Lothal.
- It is situated in Gujarat and served long distance trade and also supplied the cities along the banks of the Indus with raw materials such as cotton from Gujarat and copper from Rajasthan.
- Lothal has been perceived by the historians to be an outpost for sea-trade with contemporary West Asian Societies, particularly Oman.
- It is known as the **Manchester of Harappan Civilisation** for its cotton trade.

Banawali

- It is the only Harappan city with oval-shaped settlements, radial streets and lack of systematic drainage pattern. Both **Pre-Harappan** and **Harappan phases** are found here.
- Artefacts recovered from here include, **8-shaped jars**, cooking vessels, ovens and painted earthen pots. Interestingly a **wash basin type structure** is also found in house at Banawali.

Dholavira

- The city of Dholavira was located on Khadir Beyt (also spelled as Bet) in the Rann of Kutch.
- It is one of the two largest Harappan settlements in India, the other being Rakhigarhi in Haryana.

Dholavira

- The most unique feature of the site is its **division into three sections**. Two of these parts were protected by strong rectangular fortifications, with entrances through gateways.
- It is the **warehousing settlement** of Harappan Civilisation. Dholavira also consists of a large open area in the settlement where public ceremonies could be held.
- A public inscription with **10 large sized signs** of the Harappan scripts are also discovered here besides water reservoirs.

Town Planning

The Harappan culture is distinguished by its system of town planning. The city was divided into two parts i.e., the **citadel** on West and the **Lower town** on the East.

Citadel

- The citadel was built on a mud brick platform. It was smaller in size and was walled. It was occupied by the members of the ruling class.
- Evidences of such structure are found on the citadel that were probably used for special public purposes. These include the warehouse (Granary) and the Great Bath.
- **Granary** is largest building in Mohenjodaro measuring 45.7×115.23 m. Granaries are also found in Kalibangan.
- The **Great Bath** in Mohenjodaro, which served ritual bathing, is situated in the citadel mound. It was a large rectangular tank in a courtyard surrounded by a corridor on all four sides.
- There were two flights of steps on the North and South leading into the tank, which was made watertight by setting bricks on edge and using a mortar of gypsum.
- There were rooms on three sides, in one of which was a large well. Its floor was made of burnt bricks. Water in the Great Bath was drawn from a large well in an adjacent room and an outlet from the corner of the Bath led to a drain.

Drainage System

- One of the most distinctive features of Harappan cities was the carefully **planned drainage system.** Water flowed from the house to streets which had drains. These drains were covered with bricks or stone slabs. The street drains were equipped with manholes. It seems that streets with drains were laid out first and then houses built along them.
- Total number of wells found in Mohenjodaro was about 700.
- Drainage systems were not unique to the larger cities, but also found in smaller settlements as well. For instance, at Lothal, houses were built of mud bricks, while drains were made of burnt bricks.

Variations in Plan of Cities

- While most Harappan settlements have uniform plan, there are variations.
- At sites such as **Dholavira** and **Lothal** (Gujarat), the entire settlement was fortified and sections within the town were also separated by walls.
- The citadel within Lothal was not walled off, but was built at a height. Dholavira was divided into three parts.

Important Sites of Indus Valley Civilisation

Site	Location	Excavated by	Year of excavation	Major Findings
Harappa	Montgomery, Pakistan on the bank of Ravi river	Daya Ram Sahni	1921	Granary, workmen's quarter, vanity case, furnaces, piece of pottery with Indus script, cubical limestone weight, copper bullock cart, coffin burials, cemetery, terracotta figurines, evidence of horse at superficial level, etc.
Mohenjodaro	Larkana District of Sind on the bank of Indus river	RD Banerjee	1925	Great Bath, Granary, unicorn seals, Bronze Dancing Girl statue, Pashupati seal, steatite statue of Beard Priest, piece of woven cloth, etc.
Sutkagendor	Baluchistan on Dasht river	Auriel Stein	1929	Trade point between, Harappa and Babylon, flint blades, stone vessels, stone arrowheads, shell beads, pottery, horse remains, etc.
Chanhudaro	Mullan Sandha, Sindh on the Indus river	NG Majumdar	1931	Bangle factory, inkpot, bead-makers shop, the footprint of a dog chasing a cat, cart with a seated driver, it is the only city without a citadel, etc.
Rangpur	Kathiawad (Gujarat), on the Madar river	MS Vats, SR Rao	1931, 1957	Post-Harappan site, rice husk, six types of pottery, etc.
Amri	Close to Baluchistan, on the bank of Indus river	NG Majumdar	1935	Antelope evidence, rhinoceros' evidence, etc.
Kot-Diji	Khairpur (Sindh, Pakistan), on the Indus river	Fazal Ahmad, Ghurrey	1935, 1955	Figurine of ox, steatite seal, terracotta beads, etc.
Kalibanga	Hanumangarh district, Rajasthan on the bank of Ghaggar river	Amlanand Ghose	1953	Granary, ploughed field, wooden drainage, evidence of earthquake, wooden plough, camel's bone, fire alters, earthen bricks instead of baked one, etc.
Ropar	Punjab, on the river Sutlej	YD Sharma	1953	Five-fold sequence of culture, stone and mud house, evidence of dog burial, alongwith human burial, etc.
Lothal	Ahmedabad, Gujarat on Bhogva river near the Gulf of Cambay	R Rao	1955	Divided into six sections, bead making factory, rice husk, ivory weight balance, dockyard, fire alters, terracotta figure of horse, etc.
Alamgirpur	Meerut (UP), on the Hindon river	YD Sharma	1958	Pottery, animal bones, plant fossils, copper tools, etc.
Desalpur or Gunthli	Nakhtrana Taluka, Gujarat	SR Rao, A Ghosh	1963	Copper and teracotta seals, brown pottery.
Surkotada	Gujarat	JP Joshi	1964	Bones of horses, beads, stone covered beads, etc.
Rakhigarhi	Hisar (Haryana), on the Drishdavati river	Surajbhan	1969	Largest Harappan site, fire alters, cylindrical seal, terracotta wheel, etc.
Balakot	Arabian Sea (Baluchistan, Pakistan)	George F Dales	1973-1979	Early Harappan findings, bricks, bead workshop.
Banawali	Fatehabad district of Haryana	RS Bisht	1974	Remains of street and drains, beads, barley, oval shaped settlement, the only city with radial streets, toy plough, the largest number of barley grains, etc.
Dholavira	Gujarat in Rann of Kutch	RS Bisht	1990	Only site to be divided into three parts, giant water reservoir, unique water harnessing system, dams, embankments, signboard with Indus script, etc.

Lower Town

- The lower town which was below the citadel was larger in size and was inhabited by the common people.
- The houses in the lower cities of all Indus settlements followed the **grid system** (roads cut across one another at right angles) and the city was divided into blocks.
- Streets were wide; the main street being about ten metre wide.

Lower Town

Residential Buildings

- Generally, houses were either one or two storeys high, with rooms built around a courtyard.
- Houses were built of bricks and had thick, strong walls, which were plastered and coloured.
- The roofs of the houses were flats. There were few windows but had numbers of doors, which were probably made of wood.
- The kitchen had a **fire-place** and **large jars of pottery** for storing grain or oil. Adjacent to it was the drain. Bathrooms were built on one side of the house and had drains which were connected with street drain.
- The courtyard had an oven for baking bread. It was probably the centre of activities such as cooking and weaving, particularly during hot and dry weather.
- There are no windows in the walls along the main road which shows the Harappans had concern for privacy. Besides, the main entrance does not give a direct view of the interior or the courtyard.
- Some houses had their own wells, which meant water was always available inside the house. Some houses also have remains of staircases to reach a second storey or the roof.
- The people of Harappa civilisation were used **burnt bricks** while in **Egypt** dried bricks were used and in **Mesopotamia** use of baked bricks was found.

Economic Conditions in Indus Valley Civilisation

The Economic condition of Harappa Civilisation (Indus Valley Civilisation) was largely based on Agriculture. The people of this civilisation were also engaged in trade and various other occupations.

Agriculture

The Harappan villages, mostly situated near the flood plains, helped in producing sufficient foodgrains not only to feed themselves but also the town people.

Activities of Harappa people associated with agriculture are discussed as follows :

Sowing

- The Indus people sowed seeds in the flood plains in the month of November, when the flood water receded and reaped their harvests of wheat and barley in April before the advent of the next flood.

Plough

- The Harappans probably used **wooden ploughshare** and **stone sickles** for harvesting the crops.
- Representations on seals and terracotta sculpture indicate that the bull was known to them and used for ploughing.
- Archaeologists have also found evidence of a ploughed field at **Kalibangan** (Rajasthan), associated with **Early Harappan Period**.
- The field had two sets of furrows at right angles to each other, suggesting that two different crops were grown together.

Crops

- The Indus people were the earliest ones to produce cotton. Findings of rice cultivation are relatively rare. However, remains show that the people of Lothal used rice.
- Main crops grown here are wheat, barley, mustard, peas, sesame, lentil, millets, rice, etc.
- Barley has been discovered at **Banawali**. Millets are found from sites in **Gujarat**.

Irrigation

- Most Harappan sites were located in semi-arid lands, where irrigation was required for agriculture.
- *Gabarbands* or *nalas* enclosed by dams were used for storing water in Baluchistan but channel or canals seem to be absent.
- Traces of canals have been found at the Harappan site of **Shortughai** in Afghanistan, but not in **Punjab** or **Sindh**. It is possible that ancient canals dried up long ago.

- It is also likely that water drawn from wells was used for irrigation. Besides, water reservoirs found in **Dholavira** (Gujarat) may have been used to store water for agriculture.

Storage

- Foodgrains were stored in granaries, the remains of which have been found in **Mohenjodaro**, **Harappa** and **Kalibanga**.

Domestication of Animals

- In Harappan times, animals were domesticated on a large scale. Oxen, buffalo, goat, sheep, dog, cat and pig were domesticated.
- Camels and asses were used for carriage purposes. The humped bulls were favoured by the Harappan.
- Evidence of the horse comes from a doubtful **terracotta figurine** from **Lothal**. The remains of the horse are reported from **Surkotada** (Gujarat). But horse was not in regular use in Harappan times.
- **Elephants** and **rhinoceros** were also known to Harappans and people in Gujarat domesticated elephants. Other animals known to the Harappan people are bull, camel, donkey, etc.

Occupations

- Harappans were engaged in a number of occupations. They were weavers, mason, potters, bead-makers, boat-maker, seal-maker.
- Bead-making factories have been found at **Chanhudaro** and **Lothal**.

Trade and Commerce

- The importance of trade in the life of the Indus people is known by the presence of numerous seals, uniform scripts and regulated weights and measures.
- They carried on trade in stone, metal, shell, etc. They did not use metal money. All exchanges were carried on through **barter**.
- The Harappans were engaged in internal as well as external trade. For the internal trade, carts with solid wheel were used while the external trade was carried out through ships. They practiced navigation on the coast of the Arabian Sea.
- The Harappan had commercial links with **Rajasthan**, **Afghanistan** and **Iran**. Many seals of Harappan civilisation have been discovered in Mesopotamia.
- The **Mesopotamian records** from about 2350 BC refer to trade relations with **Meluha,** which was ancient name given to Indus region.
- The Mesopotamian texts speak of two intermediate trading stations called **Dilmun** and **Magan**, which lay between Mesopotamia and Meluha. Dilmun can be identified with Bahrain on the Persian Gulf. The merchandise was shipped from Lothal and incoming good were received here.
- Items of exports includes pottery, grains, cotton goods, spices, stone beads, pearls and eye paint.
- The Harappans also carried on long distance trade for *lapis lazuli* (Blue rock); lapis may have contributed to the social prestige of the ruling class. Harappans had set up a trading colony in Northern Afghanistan which evidently facilitated trade with Central Asia.
- They imported gold from Karnataka and other precious stone from Gujarat, Iran and Afghanistan.

Lists of Imports during Indus Valley Civilisation

Items of Import	Place
Gold	Afghanistan, Karnataka
Silver	Afghanistan
Copper	Khetri (Rajasthan), Oman
Tin	Afghanistan, Iran
Carnelian	Saurashtra
Jade	Central Asia
Amethyst	Maharashtra
Turquoise	Central Asia, Iran

Social Conditions in Indus Valley Civilisation

- The Harappan society was egalitarian i.e., all people were treated equal socially, politically and economically. The caste system does not found to be existed. However, the varying size of the houses indicates the prevalence of a kind of class system.

Food

- Archaeologists have been able to reconstruct dietary practices from finds of charred grains and seeds. These are studied by archaeo-botanists, who are specialists in ancient plant remains.
- The people of Harappan Civilisation ate a wide range of plant and animal products including fish and meat, wheat, barley, maize, millet, pulses, rice, fruits and other eatables. For this, cattle, sheep, goat, buffalo and pig were domesticated by the Harappans.

Clothes

- They knew how to weave cotton. It is known by the finding of clay spindles. Mostly clothes were of cotton, but some wool clothes were also used.
- The women wore a short skirt. The men wrapped a long piece of cloth around themselves.
- Cotton was probably grown at Mehrgarh from about 7000 years ago. Actual pieces of cloth were found

attached to the lid of a silver vase and some copper objects at Mohenjodaro.

- Both men and women were fond of wearing ornaments. The men wore amulets and the women wore **bracelets** and **necklaces**. These were made of **beads of shell** for common people and of **gold** and **silver** for the rich people.

Amusements and Toys

- For children, there were small clay carts resembling the modern *ekkas*, figures of animals, whistles made in the form of birds and rattles of all kinds.
- Marbles were also popular among children. For girls, there were dolls too. The older people spent their time in **gambling**, **dancing** and **hunting**.

Burials

- Harappans used to bury their dead in **pits**. Some graves contain pottery and ornaments, perhaps indicating a belief that these could be used in the after life.
- Jewellery has been found in burials of both men and women. In some instances, the dead were buried with copper mirrors.

Harappan Burials

Art and Crafts of Indus Valley Civilisation

The Harappan culture belongs to the **Bronze Age**. The Harappan people were well aware of various crafts like weaving, spinning and bead-making.

In order to identify centres of craft production, archaeologists usually look for raw material such as stone nodules, whole shells, copper ore, tools, unfinished objects; rejects and waste material.

Metallurgy and Bronze Craft

- The Harappans used many tools made of stone, but they were very well-acquainted with the manufacture and use of Bronze. Bronze was made by mixing tin with copper.
- The discovery of bronze goods suggests that the **metal-workers** (bronzesmiths) constituted an important group of artisans in Harappan society.
- They produced not only images and utensils but also various tools and weapons such as axes, saws, knives and spears.
- A bronze statue of **dancing girl** found in Mohenjodaro, is the best specimen of that time.

Terracotta Figurines

- A number of figurines made of fire-baked **earthen clay** (Terracotta) have been found from Harappan sites. These were either used as toys or objects of worship.
- Terracotta models of the plough have been found at sites in Cholistan and at Banawali (Haryana).
- They represent birds, dogs, sheep, cattle, monkeys, men and women. But the terracotta pieces represent unsophisticated artistic works.
- The Terracotta figurines, the paintings on the pottery and the bronze images from the Harappan sites.

Weights and Measures

- The Harappan used weights and measures for trade and other transactions.
- Numerous articles used for weights have been found. They show that in weighing mostly 16 or its multiples were used; e.g., 16, 64, 160, 320 and 640.
- The lower denomination of the weights were binary (1, 2, 4, 8, 16, 32 etc. upto 12800) while the higher denominations followed the decimal system.
- Weights were usually made up of chert stone, generally cubical with no markings.
- The Harappans also knew the **art of measurement**. Sticks inscribed with measure marks have been found.

Pottery

- The Harappans were expert in the use of the potter's wheel. The Harappans produced their own characteristic pottery, which was glossy and shiny.
- The Harappans used **Red and Black Ware** (RBW) pottery. Most of them were made on reddish clay and – lines, dots, geometrical designs, tree and leaf designs and animal figures were painted in black on them.

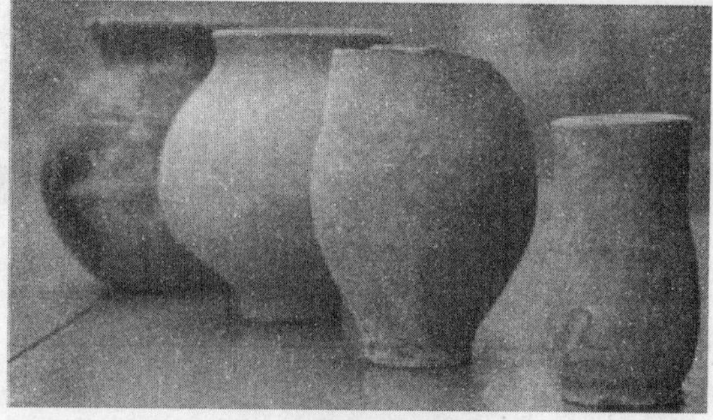

Harappan Pottery

Harappan Script

- The Harappans invented the art of writing. Although, the earliest specimen of Harappan script was noticed in 1853, but it has not been deciphered so far.
- Most inscriptions are short, the longest containing about 26 signs.
- Unlike the **Egyptians** and **Mesopotamians**, the Harappans did not write long inscriptions. Most inscriptions were recorded on seals and contain only a few words.
- The Harappan script is not alphabetical but mainly **pictographic** written in alternate lines of writing, are reverse with reversed letters (**Boustrophedon**).
- Around 250 to 400 pictographs are found and in the form of a picture, each letter stands for some sound, idea or object.
- These pictographs are the indigenous work of the Indus region and does not show any influence of the scripts of **Western Asia**.

Seals

- The greatest artistic creation of the Harappan culture are the seals. They are made of **steatite stone** (soft stone) and often carry short inscriptions with pictures of the one-horned animal (called **Unicorn**), the buffalo, the tiger, the rhinoceros, the goat and the elephant.
- Seals and sealing (impression of the seal) were used to facilitate long distance communication. The seals were perhaps used by the merchants and traders to stamp their goods. The sealing also conveyed the identity of the sender.
- The most famous seal is the **Pashupati Seal** of Harappa Civilisation from Mohenjodaro. It is a seal with a figure seated cross-legged in the centre with animals around; an elephant and a tiger to the right of the figure and rhino and a buffalo to its left. At his feet appear two deer.

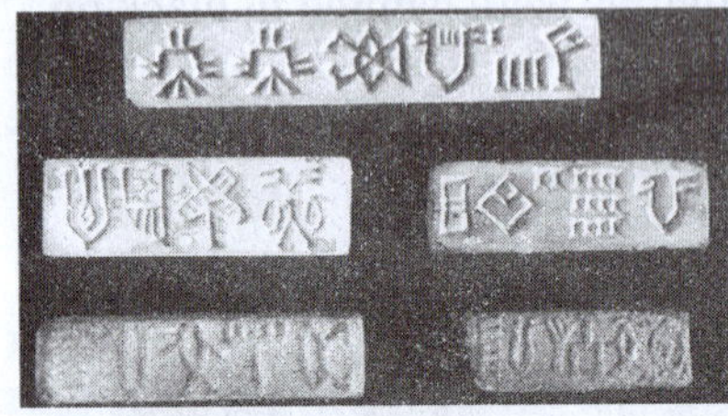

Harappan Seals

Pashupati Seal

Bead-making

- The Harappans were also experts in bead-making.
- The variety of materials used to make beads i.e., **stones** like carnelian, jasper, crystal, quartz and steatite; **metals** like copper, bronze and gold and **shell**, **faience** and **terracotta** or **burnt clay**.
- Some beads were made of two or more stones, cemented together, some of stone with gold caps. The shapes were numerous – disc-shaped, cylindrical, spherical, barrel-shaped, segmented, etc.
- Some were decorated by incising or painting and some had designs etched onto them.

Craft Production Centres

- **Chanhudaro** was almost exclusively devoted to craft production, including bead-making, shell-cutting, metal-working, seal-making and weight-making.
- Specialised drills have been found at Chanhudaro, **Lothal** and **Dholavira. Nageshwar** and **Balakot** were specialised centres for making shell objects, including bangles, ladles and inlay.

Religious Practices of Indus Valley Civilisation

- The people of this civilisation worshipped Gods in the form of nature such as trees, animals and human beings. But the Gods were not placed in temples.
- In Harappa, numerous terracotta figurines of women have been found. So, it is evident that they probably worshipped **mother goddess.**
- In one figurine, a plant is shown growing out of the embryo of a woman. Probably, it represents the **goddess of Earth** and it was intimately connected with the origin and growth of plants.
- Therefore, it is perceived that the Harappans, looked upon the Earth as a fertility goddess and worshipped her in the same manner as the Egyptians worshipped the **Nile Goddess Isis.**
- The **male deity** is represented on a seal. This god has three-horned heads. The depicted god is identified as **Pashupati**. But the identification is doubtful, because horned gods also appear in other ancient civilisations.
- The picture of a deity is represented on a seal in the midst of the branches of a sacred tree pipal.
- In addition, there was the prevalence of **phallus worship,** which became connected with *Shiva* in later time. Numerous symbols of the phallus have been found in Harappa which were possibly meant for worship.
- **Animals** were also worshipped in Harappan times. The most important of them is the **humped bull.**
- Findings of **amulets** in large numbers indicate that the Harappans believed in ghosts and evil forces. The Atharva Veda, contains many charms and spells and recommends amulets are must for warding off diseases and evil forces.

Political Organisation in Indus Valley Civilisation

- There is no clear idea about the political organisation of the Harappans.
- In contrast to Egypt and Mesopotamia, no temple or religious structure has been found at any Harappan site. Therefore, the priests cannot said to be the rulers of Harappa.
- Perhaps, the Harappan rulers were more concerned about commerce than the conquests. Harappans were possibly ruled by a class of merchants.
- The Harappans were peace loving people since the findings from Harappan sites lack any type of weapons.

Palaces and Kings

- Archaeological records provide no immediate answers for a centre of power or for depictions of people in power.
- A large building found at **Mohenjodaro** was labelled as a palace by archaeologists. A stone statue was labelled and continues to be known as the **priest-king**.

The **priest-king**

- Some archaeologists had an opinion that Harappan society had no rulers and everybody enjoyed equal status. Others believe that there was no single ruler but several rulers.
- The third opinion is that there was a single state due to, similarity in artefacts, the evidence for planned settlements and the standardised ratio of brick size.

Decline of Indus Valley Civilisation

- By 1800 BC, most of the mature Harappan sites were abandoned. Simultaneously, there was an expansion of population into new settlements in Gujarat, Haryana and Western Uttar Pradesh.
- In the few Harappan sites that continued to be occupied after 1900 BC, there was a transformation of material culture, marked by the disappearance of the distinctive artefacts i.e., weight, seals, special beads. Writing, long-distance trade and craft specialisation also disappeared.
- Different theories states that causes of decline may be Aryan invasion, climate change, deforestation, excessive floods, epidemic, shifting or drying up of rivers, ecological imbalance, etc.
- However, some of these causes do not explain the decline of the entire civilisation.
- **Aryan invasion theory** was propounded by **Mortimer Wheeler**. This theory was supported by the fact that some exotic tools and pottery indicate the entry of new people. A few signs of violence appear in the last phase of Mohenjodaro.
- Traces of new people appear in a cemetery belonging to late phase of Harappa. However, there is no evidence of any mass-scale confrontation between the Harappan and the Aryans.
- Thus, the causes of the decline of this civilisation have not been firmly established. Archaeologists now believe that the civilisation did not come to an abrupt end but gradually declined.
- The ecological imbalance theory of **Walter Fairservis** best explains this belief.

Different Opinions about the Decline of Indus Valley Civilisation

Thinkers	Opinion
Stuart Piggott and Gordon-Childe	External Aggression *(Aryan Invasion)*
MR Sahni	Inundation
KAR Kennedy	Epidemic
Marshall and Raikes	Tectonic Disturbances (e.g. *Dholavira)*
Aurel Stein and AN Ghosh	Climatic Change
Walter Fairservis	Deforestation, scarcity of resources, ecological imbalances
Marshal, SR Rao, Maickey	Flood (e.g. *Mohenjodaro)*
GF Hales	Drought due to change in the course of river Ghaggar

Post-Urban Phase of the Harappan Culture

- The post-urban phase of the Harappan culture is also known as the **Sub-Indus culture**.
- This culture was earlier considered **Post-Harappan**, but now it is more popularly known as the **Late Harappan Culture**. The Late Harappan Culture was primarily Chalcolithic in which tools of stone and copper are used.
- A number of sites of these cultures have been found in **Rajasthan**, **Madhya Pradesh**, **Maharashtra** and **Eastern India**.

- Though most of these cultures belong to a period after that of the Harappan culture, they were much less advanced than the Harappan culture. They neither had any cities nor any system of writing.
- The **chalcolithic people** in the later Harappan phase lived in villages and practiced agriculture, stock raising, hunting and fishing.
- During the later phase of the Harappan culture, some exotic tools and pottery indicate the slow percolation of new people in the Indus basin.

Contribution of Indus Valley Civilisation

- The Harappan culture has contributed a lot to the Indian culture, society, polity and economy. The Harappan culture did not end; rather its traits were adopted by the subsequent cultures over the period of time. Even today, a number of factors can be analysed which traces their origin to the culture of Indus Valley Civilisation.
- The Harappan civilisation developed the first accurate system of standardised **weights and measures**.
- Harappans created **sculpture**, **seals**, **pottery** and **jewellery** from materials, such as terracotta, metal and stone. Evidence shows Harappans participated in a vast **maritime trade network** extending from Central Asia to modern-day Iraq, Iran, Kuwait and Syria.
- The planning of cities on **Grid Pattern** was practiced by the Harappan people. The underground covered drainage system was also a unique feature which was not available in the contemporary civilisation.

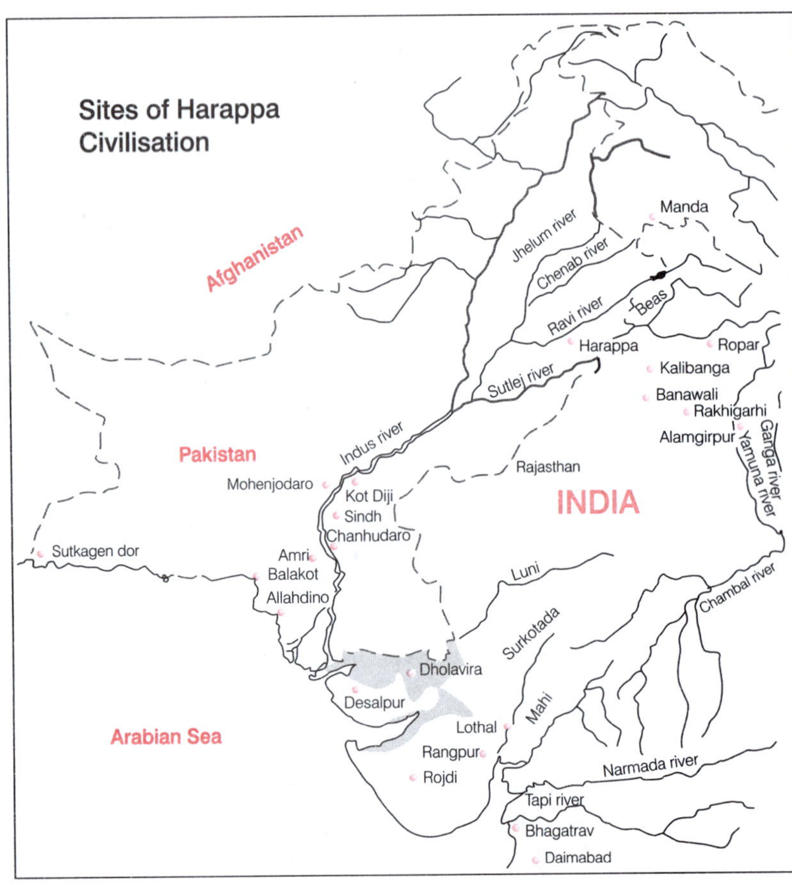

- The Harappans started the practice of **multi-cropping system**. They had efficient methods of irrigation. Their contribution in culture cannot be ignored.
- The people of Harappan culture used to bury their dead.
- At present time, people have adopted the **practice of worshiping** *Shiva, phallus, peepal*, Mother Goddess and bull from Harappan culture. The worship of *Shiva* and the Mother Goddess and the practice of religious bathing are examples of continuing traditions of the Harappan culture.

Extra Facts From Tamil Nadu Board and NIOS

- Agriculture was an important source of subsistence for the Harappans. They adopted a double cropping system.
- The Zebu bulls were probably domesticated by Harappans for agriculture. It is a large breed, often representative in their seals.

Major Centre of Craft Production

Material	Site or Source
Shell	Nageshwar and Balakot
Lapis Lazuli	Shortughai
Steatite	South Rajasthan

- **Rohri Chert** a fine grained sedimentary rock, was found in the region of Rohri in Pakistan. It was used by the Harappans for making stone blades and tools.
- Rajasthan region is rich in copper deposits and the Harappans acquired copper mainly from the Khetri mines located here.
- The painted motifs, generally noticed on the pottery are peepal leaves, fish scale design, zig-zag lines, horizontal bands and geometrical motifs with floral and faunal patterns.
- Kolar goldfields of Karnataka and the river-beds of Himalayan rivers, might have supplied gold.
- The source of silver is believed to be Jwar mines of Rajasthan.
- The evidence of fire worship has been found at some sites such as **Kalibanga** and **Lothal**.

The Vedic Age

(SOURCES)

Class-VI New NCERT Chap 4 (What Books and Burials Tell us),
Class-VI Old NCERT Chap 3 (Life in the Vedic Age),
Class-IX Old NCERT Chap 3 (Early Iron-Age Civilisation),
Class-XI Old NCERT Chap 8 (The Advent of Aryans and Age of Rig Veda),
Class-XI Old NCERT Chap 9 (Transition to State and Social Formation)
Tamil Nadu Board (Class XI), NIOS

- The Vedic Age refers to the period when the Vedic Sanskrit texts were composed in India.
- It is the age of the **Aryans** who are supposed to have migrated from **Central Asia** into the Indian sub-continent in several stages during 2000 to 1500 BC.

Advent of the Aryans in India

- The term **'Aryan'** literally means the **'best'** or **'eminent'**. It is not evident that all the earliest Aryans belonged to one race, but their culture was of the same type. They were distinguished by their common language. They spoke the Indo-European languages.
- Originally, the Aryans seem to have lived areas of Southern Russia to Central Asia. They used horses and their swiftness enabled them and some allied people to make successful advent in West-Asia from about 2000 BC onwards.
- The **Rig Veda** gives information about the Aryans in India. The term 'Arya' appeared 36 times in this text and generally indicates a cultural community.
- The Rig Veda is the earliest text of the Indo-European languages and has many things in common with the **Avesta,** which is the oldest text in the Iranian language. The two texts use the same names for several gods and even for social classes.
- Also, the earliest specimen of the Indo-European language is found in an inscription of about 2200 BC from Iraq.
- Later such specimens occur in **Hittite** inscriptions in Anatolia (Turkiye) from the 19th to the 17th centuries BC.
- Aryan names appear in **Kassite** inscription of about 1600 BC from Iraq and in **Mitanni** inscription of the 14th century BC from Syria. But so far no such inscriptions have been found in India.
- The Aryans migrated to India in several stages. The earliest stage is represented by the Rig Vedic people, who appeared in the sub-continent in about 1500 BC.

Vedic Literature

- The Vedic literature gives us a clear idea of the political, social and economic life of the Aryans and their conflict with the non-Aryans.

Four Vedas

- The Vedic literature can be classified into the four Vedas i.e., the **Rig**, **Sama**, **Yajur** and **Atharva** and their Vedangas, the Brahamansa, the Aranyaksa and the Upanishads.
- The Vedas are the large bodies of religious text that are composed of Vedic Sanskrit and originated in Ancient India.
- They form the oldest scriptures of Hinduism and the oldest layer of Sanskrit literature. The Vedas are said to have passed on through verbal transmission from one generation to the next. Therefore, they are also known as **Shruti**.

Rig Veda

- It is the **oldest Veda** and depicts the life of early Vedic people in India. It was compiled between 1500 BC to 1000 BC.
- Its text consists of **1028 hymns** (Sukta) which are divided into **10 Mandalas** or books.
  - **Mandala I** is primarily dedicated to Indra and Agni. Varuna, Surya, Mitra, Rudra and Vishnu have also been mentioned.
  - **Mandalas II – VII** form the oldest part of the Rig Veda Samhita and are called 'family books' as they are ascribed to particular families of *rishis*.
  - In **Mandala VIII**, the hymns are dedicated to various gods and have been mostly composed by the Kanva clan.
  - In **Mandala IX**, all the hymns are dedicated entirely to Soma.
  - **Mandala X** contains Nadi Stuti Sukta praising the rivers. It also contains Nasadiya Sukta and Purush Sukta. It contains hymns that are traditionally chanted during marriage and death rituals.
- The Upaveda of Rig Veda is the **Ayurveda**.

Sama Veda

- The Sama Veda or the **Veda of Chants** is the collection of verses drawn from the Rig Veda.
- These verses are provided with musical notations and are intended as an aid to the performance of sacred songs.
- It was compiled between 1000 BC to 600 BC.
- Recensions or Branches (Shakhas) of the Sama Veda are **Kauthuma, Ranayaniya** and **Jaiminiya** (Talavakara).
- The Upaveda of Sama Veda is the **Gandharva Veda.**

Yajur Veda

- Yajur Veda (Worship or ritual knowledge) was compiled between 1000 BC to 600 BC.
- It deals with the procedure for the performance of sacrifices. It is further divided into :
  - **Shukla Yajur Veda/ Vajasaneya / White Yajur Veda** It contains only the mantras. It contains the Madhyandina and Kanva recensions.
  - **Krishna Yajur Veda / Black Yajur Veda** It includes mantras as well as prose explanations/ commentary. It contains Kathaka, Maitrayani, Taittiriya and Kapishthala recensions.
- The Upaveda of the Yajur Veda is the **Dhanur Veda.**

Atharva Veda

- Atharva Veda was also compiled between 1000 BC to 600 BC. It concerns with magic spells to ward off evil spirits or dangers.
- It is classified into 20 *khandas* or books, with 711 hymns.
- It contains **Shaunaka** and **Paippalada** recensions.
- The Upaveda of Atharva Veda is **Shilpa Veda.**

Brahamanas

- The Brahamanas are the prose texts that explain the hymns in the Vedas.
- In addition to explaining the symbolism and meaning of the **Samhitas**, Brahmana literature also provide scientific knowledge of the Vedic period, including observational astronomy altar construction and geometry.
- Each Veda has one or more of its own Brahmanas.
  - **Aitareya** and **Kaushitaki** Brahamanas were allotted to the Rig Veda,
  - **Tandya** and **Jaiminiya** Brahamanas to Sama Veda
  - **Taittiriya** and **Shatpatha** Brahamanas to Yajur Veda
  - **Gopath Brahamanas** to the Atharva Veda for detailing.

Aranyakas

- The Aranyakas are the philosophies written mainly for the forest-dwelling hermits and their disciples. They are appendices to Brahamanas.
- They can be considered as the bridge between the Brahamanas that talk about ritual sacrifices and the Upanishads that talk about knowledge and spirituality.

Upanishads

- The Upanishads contain philosophical ideas about the sacrifice, body and universe. There are **108 Upanishads.**
- The concepts of **'Atman'** and **'Brahman'** are majorly explained by Upanishads.
- The Brihadaranyaka Upanishad, one of the earliest Upanishads, contain a list of successive generation of teachers and students, many of whom were designated by metronymics.

Vedangas

Vedangas are limbs of Vedas and are written for how to chant Vedas properly. There are six Vedangas, as follows :

- *Siksha*, which covers Phonetics (sounds)
- *Nirukta*, which covers Etymology (origin of words)
- *Chandas*, which covers Metrics
- *Vyakarana*, which covers Grammar
- *Jyotisha*, which covers Astrology
- *Kalpa*, which covers Rituals

Upavedas

- There are four Upavedas which are **Ayurveda** (Veda about life), **Gandharva Veda** (Veda about music), **Shilpa Veda** (Veda about architecture) and **Dhanur Veda** (Veda about archery and warfare).
- Some school of thoughts consider **Arthashastra** as fifth Upaveda.

Sutra Sahitya

- The period of 600 BC to 300 BC is known as **period of Sutra**, when various literatures of Sutras were written. Sutras first appear in the Vedic literature known as **Brahamana** and **Aranyaka**.
- It was a period of general upheaval of social, political and religious thought occurred in India.

Six Sutras

Sutra	Description
Kalpa Sutra	It contains the sacrificial practice and systematic sutras.
Srautasutras	It contains teaching of the performance of the great sacrifices.
Sulvasutras	It is related to geometry and mathematics.
Gruhasutras	It contains rules of domestic life.
Dharmasutras	It has various customs and social duties.

Vedic Age (1500-1000 BC)

The age of the Vedic Period or Rig Vedic Period corresponds with the date of the composition of the Rig Vedic hymns. This date has been fixed between 1500 BC and 1000 BC.

Geographical Knowledge of Vedic Age

- The earliest Aryans lived in the geographical area covered by Eastern Afghanistan, North-West Frontier Province, Punjab and parts of Western Uttar Pradesh.
- Some rivers of Afghanistan such as the river **Kubha** (Kabul) and the river **Indus** (Sindhu) and its five branches, are mentioned in the Rig Veda.
- The Sindhu is the river par excellence of the Aryans and it is repeatedly mentioned in Rig Veda.
- Some of the hymns in the Rig Veda are in the form of dialogues. This is part of one such hymn, a dialogue between a sage named Vishvamitra, and two river (Beas and Sutlej) that were worshipped as goddesses.
- Another river, the **Saraswati**, is called *Naditama* or the best of the rivers in the Rig Veda. It is identified with the **Ghaggar-Hakra channel** in Haryana and Rajasthan. Rig Vedic description shows it to be the **Avestan river Harakhwati** or the **Helmand river** in South Afghanistan from where the name Saraswati was transferred to India.
- The whole region in which the Aryans first settled in Indian sub-continent called the **Land of the Seven Rivers**. The word **Samudra** is mentioned in the Rig Veda but it mainly denotes a collection of water.

Rivers and Their Ancient Names

Ancient Name	Modern Name
Vitasta	Jhelum
Askini	Chenab
Parushni	Ravi
Vipasa	Beas
Sutudri	Sutlej
Gomati	Gomal
Kubha	Kabul
Sadanira	Gandak
Saraswati	Ghaggar

Vedic Polity

- It was a nomadic system of government in which the military element was strong.
- The administrative machinery of the Aryans in the Early Vedic period worked with the tribal chief in the centre, because of his successful leadership in war. He was called *Rajan*. The king's post had become hereditary.
- The *Rajan* was a kind of chief and he did not exercise unlimited power, as he had to reckon with the tribal organisation.
- The king was called the protector of his tribe. He protected its cattle, fought wars and offered prayers to gods on its behalf.
- Several tribal or the clan-based assemblies such as the *sabha, samiti, vidatha, gana,* etc, are mentioned in the Rig Veda. They exercised deliberative, military and religious functions.
- The two most important assemblies were the *Sabha* and the *Samiti*. The most important functionary seems to have been the *Purohita*.
- The two priests who played a major part in the time of Rig Veda are **Vasishtha** and **Vishvamitra**. Vishvamitra composed the *Gayatri Mantra* to widen the Aryan world.
- The next important functionary seems to be the *senani*. The Rig Veda does not mention any officer for administering justice. But it was not an ideal society. There were cases of theft and burglary and especially the theft of cows.

- Spies were employed to keep an eye on such antisocial activities. The officer who enjoyed authority over a large pasture ground was called *Vrajapati*. He led heads of the families called *Kulapas*, or the heads of the fighting hordes called *Gramanis*, to battle. In the beginning, the *gramani* was just the head of a small tribal fighting unit.
- Sanskrit text use the term Kula to designate families and jnati for the larger network of kinfolk. The term 'Vamsha' is used for lineage.
- The king did not maintain any regular or standing army, but in times of war he bring together a militia whose military functions were performed by different tribal groups called *vrata, gana, grama, sardha*.
- Probably, the chiefs received voluntary offerings from the people called *Bali*.

Vedic Society

- Kinship was the basis of social structure in the **Early Vedic society**. A man was identified by the clan to which he belonged, as can be seen in the names of several Rig Vedic Kings.
- People gave their primary loyalty to the tribe, which was called *Jana*. The term *'Jana'* occurs at about 275 places in the Rig Veda and the term *'anapada'* or territory is not used even once.
- The people were attached to the tribe, since the kingdom was not yet established.
- Another important term which stands for the tribe in the Rig Veda was *Vis*; it is mentioned 170 times in the text. It is evident that family in Early Vedic phase was indicated by the term *griha*.
- The Rig Veda shows some consciousness of the physical appearance of people. *Varna* was the term used for colour, which provided the identity mark for the social order. Rig Veda mentions *arya* and *dasa varna*.
- People who composed the hymns described themselves as Aryas and called their opponents Dasas or Dasyus.
- Rig Vedic society was a **patriarchal society**. In the Rig Veda, no desire is expressed for daughters, though the desire for children and cattle is a repeated theme in the hymns. The birth of a son was desired and people prayed to the gods especially for the brave sons to fight the wars.

Position of Women

- Women were given opportunities for spiritual and intellectual development. They could attend assemblies and also used to offer sacrifices.
- The institution of marriage was established, although symbols of primitive practices survived. There are some instances of **polygamy**.
- The practice of **levirate** (Practice of marrying brother's widow) and **widow remarriage** is in the Rig Veda.
- There are **no instances of child-marriage**. The marriageable age in the Rig Veda seems to have been 16 to 17; although it is not mentioned specifically.

Social Divisions

- The conquest of the indigenous inhabitants by the Aryans contributed most to the creation of social divisions is Early Vedic age.
- The *Dasas* and the *Dasyus* conquered by the Aryans, were treated as **slaves and shudras.**
- Varna was the term used for colour. It seems that the Aryans were fair and the indigenous inhabitants were dark in complexion.
- The tribal chiefs and the priests acquired a larger share of the booty and they naturally grew at the cost of their kinsmen, which created social inequalities in the tribe.
- Gradually, the tribal society was divided into three groups i.e., **warriors, priests** and the **people.**
- The fourth division, the shudras appeared towards the end of the Rig Vedic period. Slaves were given as gifts to the priests. They were mainly women slaves.
- Those who performed tasks such as handling corpses and dead animals are known as chandalas (untouchable).
- In the age of the Rig Veda, differentiation based on occupations had started, but this division was not very sharp.
- Unequal distribution of the spoils of war created social inequalities and this helped the rise of princes and priests at the cost of the common tribal people. But since economy was mainly pastoral and not food-producing, the scope for collecting regular tributes from the people was very limited.
- Tribal elements in society were stronger and social divisions based on collection of taxes or accumulation of landed property was absent. The society was still tribal and largely **egalitarian.**

Findings of Bhagwanpura

- A site called Bhagwanpura has been excavated in Haryana and in all these cases **Painted Grey Ware** have been found.
- Findings of Bhagwanpura ranges from 1600 BC to 1000 BC which was also roughly the period of the Rig Veda.
- A thirteen-roomed mud house have been discovered at Bhagwanpura. Cattle bones have been found in good quantity in all these sites and in Bhagwanpura horse bones have also been found.

Vedic Economy

- There are so many references to the cow and the bull in the Rig Veda. The Rig Vedic Aryans can be called predominantly a **pastoral people**.
- Most of their wars were fought for the sake of cows. The terms for war in the Rig Veda is *gavishthi* or search or cows.
- The cow seems to have been the most important form of wealth. Gifts made to priests usually consist of cows and women slaves.
- The Rig Vedic people possessed better knowledge of agriculture. They knew sowing, harvesting and threshing and also had knowledge about the different seasons.
- The Rig Veda mentions artisans such as the **carpenter**, the **chariot-maker**, the **weaver**, the **leather worker**, the potter, etc. Early Vedic age was rural in nature. Aryans did not live in cities.

Vedic Religious Life

- The Aryans personified natural forces and looked upon them as living beings for which they gave human or animal forms.
- The dominant mode of worshipping the Gods was through the recitation of prayers and offering of sacrifices.
- **Offerings of vegetables, barley**, etc were made to Gods, but in Rig Vedic times, the process was not accompanied by any ritual.
- They did not worship gods for their spiritual uplift or for ending the miseries of existence. They asked mainly for *praja* (children), *pashu* (cattle), food, wealth, health, etc.

Important Vedic Gods

- The most important divinity in the Rig Veda is **Indra**. Indra was called **Purandara** or breaker of forts. Indra played the role of a warlord, leading the Aryan soldiers to victory against the demons. There are 250 hymns devoted to him in the Rig Veda. He is considered to be the rain god and thought to be responsible for causing rainfall.
- The second position is held by **Agni** (fire god) to whom 200 hymns are devoted. In Vedic times, Agni acted as a kind of intermediary between the Gods and the people.
- The third important position is occupied by **Varuna** who personified water. Varuna was supposed to uphold the natural order and whatever happened in the world was thought to be the reflection of his desires.
- **Soma** was considered to be the God of plants and an intoxicating drink.
- **Maruts** was considered as the God of the storm.
- Some female divinities such as **Aditi** and **Usha** are also mentioned in Rig Veda who represented the appearance of the dawn.
- But they were not prominent in the time of the Rig Veda. In the patriarchal set-up, the male Gods were far more important than the female Goddesses.

Aryan-Dasyu Conflicts

- The **Dasyus** in the Rig Veda represent the original inhabitants of the country and an Aryan chief who overpowered them were called Trasadasyu.
- The **Aryans** came into conflict with the indigenous inhabitants called the Dasas, Dasyus, etc. The Rig Veda mentions the defeat of Sambara by a chief called Divodasa, who belonged to the Bharata clan.
- The Aryan chief was soft towards the Dasas, but strongly hostile to the Dasyus. The term **'Dasyuharta'**, (slaughter of the Dasyus), is repeatedly mentioned in the Rig Veda.
- According to tradition, the Aryans were divided into five tribes called Panchajana but there might have been other tribes also. The Aryans fought amongst themselves also.
- The famous **Battle of Ten Kings** or the **Dasrajan Yudha** was fought between the tribe **Bharatas**, led by King **Sudas** and the Confederacy of the other ten tribes – Puru, Yadu, Turvasa, Anu, Druhyu, Alina, Paktha, Bhalanas, Shiva and Vishanin.
- The former five are said to be Aryan tribes while the later five are said to be Non-Aryan tribes.
- The Bharatas emerged victorious in the battle, which was fought on the banks of river **Parushni** (present Ravi).

Important Ratnis and Other Important Officials

Official	Description
Purohita	Chief priest, also sometimes referred to as the *Rastragopa*
Senani	Supreme Commander of the Army
Vrajapati	Officer Incharge of the Pasture Land
Jivagribha	Police Officer
Spasas/Dutas	Spies, who also sometimes worked as messengers
Gramani	Head of the Village
Kulapati	Head of the Family
Madhyamasi	Mediator of Disputes
Bhagadugha	Revenue Collector
Sangrihitri	Treasurer
Mahishi	The Chief Queen
Suta	Charioteer
Govikartana	Keeper of Games and Forests

Official	Description
Palagala	Messenger
Kshatta	Chamberlain
Akshavapa	Accountant
Sthapati	Chief Judge
Takshan	Carpenter

Later Vedic Age (1000-600 BC)

- Around 1000 BC, the use of iron appeared in Eastern Punjab, Western Uttar Pradesh, Madhya Pradesh and Rajasthan. **Iron** is referred to as *Shyama* or *Krishna* ayas in the later Vedic texts.
- Excavations show that iron weapons such as **arrow-heads** and **spear-heads** came to be commonly used in Western Uttar Pradesh from about 800 BC onwards.
- With iron weapons, the Vedic people may have defeated the few adversaries that may have faced them in the upper portion of the doab.
- Agriculture and various crafts enabled the later Vedic people to lead a settled life.
- Although the term **'Nagara'** is used in later Vedic texts, beginnings of towns can be traced towards the end of the later Vedic period.
- The later Vedic period saw certain important changes such as the beginning of territorial kingdoms. Wars were fought not only for the possession of cattle but also for the territory.
- The predominantly pastoral society of early Vedic times had become agricultural. The tribal pastoralists came to be transformed into peasants who could maintain their chief with frequent tributes. The shudras were still a small serving order.
- The tribal society broke up into a **varna-divided society**.

Geographical Expansion During Later Vedic Age

- The Aryans expanded from Punjab over the whole of Western Uttar Pradesh covered by the Ganga-Yamuna doab. In the beginning, they lived between the **Saraswati** and the **Drishadvati** rivers.
- The **Kurus** occupied Delhi and the upper portion of the doab, the area called **Kurukshetra** or the **land of the Kurus**.
- Gradually, they amalgamated with a people called the **Panchalas** who occupied the middle portion of the doab. They set up their capital at **Hastinapur** situated in the district of Meerut (Uttar Pradesh).
- The **Mahabharata war** of this age is supposed to have been fought around 950 BC.
- The Later Vedic people succeeded in the second phase of their expansion because they used iron weapons and horse drawn chariots.

Later Vedic Polity

- In Later Vedic times, Rig Vedic popular assemblies lost importance and royal power increased.
- The *vidatha* completely disappeared. The *sabha* and *samiti* continued to hold the position, but their character changed. They came to be dominated by chiefs and rich nobles.
- In this phase, women were no longer permitted to attend the *sabha* and it was now dominated by nobles and brahmanas.
- The formation of bigger kingdoms made the chief or the king more powerful.
- In the beginning each area was named after the tribe which settled there first. At first, **Panchala** was the name of a people and then it became the name of a region.
- The term *Rashtra*, which indicates territory, first appears in the period. Traces of the election of the chief or the king also appear in **Later Vedic texts**.
- The king's influence was strengthened by rituals. He performed the *Rajasuya* sacrifice, which was supposed to confer supreme power. He performed the *ashvamedha yajna*, which meant unquestioned control over an area in which the royal horse ran uninterrupted.
- He also performed the *Vajapeya* or the chariot race, in which the royal chariot was made to win the race against his kinsmen. All these rituals impressed the people with the increasing power and prestige of the king.
- During this period collection of taxes and tributes seems to have become common. They were probably deposited with an officer called *Sangrihitri.*
- However, even in Later Vedic times the king did not possess a standing army. Tribal units were assembled in times of war.

Later Vedic Economy

- **Agriculture** was the chief means of livelihood of the Later Vedic people. Later Vedic texts mention about use of oxen to the plough.
- The *Shatapatha Brahmana* speaks at length about the ploughing rituals. *Janaka*, the king of Videha and father of Sita, lent his hand of the plough. *Balarama*, the brother of Krishna, is called **Haladhar** or '**wielder of the plough**'.

- The Vedic people continued to produce barley, but during this period rice and wheat became their chief crops.
- In this age, the Vedic people came to be acquainted with rice in the doab for the first time. It is called **Vrihi** in the Vedic texts.
- The Vedic texts also refer to the **seas** and **sea voyages.**
- This suggests some kind of commerce which may have been stimulated by the rise of new arts and crafts in Later Vedic age.
- Copper was one of the first metals to be used by the Vedic people. Copper objects have been found in Painted Grey Ware sites. They were used mainly for war, hunting and ornaments.
- The Later Vedic people were acquainted with four types of pottery - **black and red ware, black-slipped ware, Painted Grey Ware** and **red ware.**
- The last type of pottery was most popular and its use has been found almost all over Western Uttar Pradesh.

Later Vedic Society

- The Later Vedic society came to be divided into four Varnas called the **Brahmanas, Kshatriyas, Vaishyas** and **Shudras.**
- The growing cult of sacrifices enormously added to the power of the Brahmanas, Kshatriya constituted **Warrior class.**
- The Vaishyas constituted the common people and they were assigned to do the production functions such as agriculture, cattle-rearing, etc.
- Towards the end of the Vedic period, they began to engage in trade. The Vaishyas appear to be the only **tribute-payers** in Later Vedic times.
- All the three higher Varnas shared one common feature i.e., they were entitled to **Upanayana** or investiture with the sacred thread according to the Vedic mantras.
- The fourth Varna was deprived of the sacred thread ceremony and the recitation of the *Gayatri Mantra*. With this, discrimination began with shudras.
- **Aitareya Brahmana**, is a text of the Later Vedic period. In this text, Shudra is called the servant of higher caste, to be made to work at will by another and to be beaten at will.
- Generally, the Later Vedic texts draw a line of demarcation between the three higher orders on the one hand and the Shudras on the other.
- Certain sections of artisans such as *Rathakara* or chariot-maker enjoyed a high status and were entitled to the sacred thread ceremony.

Position of Women

- Women were generally given a lower position in the Later Vedic societies.
- Some women theologians took part in philosophic discussions and some queens participated in coronation rituals, but ordinarily women were thought to be inferior and subordinate to men.

Different Types of Marriages

There were eight types of marriages in existance

Asura Marriage by purchase.

Gandharva Marriage by the consent of two parties ; a special form of it was *syamvara* or self-choice.

Brahma Marriage of a duly dowered girl to a man of the same Varna with Vedic rites and rituals.

Daiva Father gives the daughter to the sacrificial priests as part of fee or Dakshna.

Arsa A token bride-price of a cow and a bull is given.

Prajapati Marriage without dowry and bride-price.

Paisacha It is seduction of a girl while asleep, mentally deranged or drunk, hence it can hardly be called a marriage.

Rakshasa Marriage by capture.

Rise of New Social Order

- The institution of *gotra* appeared in later Vedic times. Literally, *gotra* means the cow-pen or the place where cattle belonging to the whole clan are kept. But in course of time, it signified descent from a common ancestor.
- People began to practice *gotra exogamy* (Marriage outside *gotra*).
- Ashramas or four stages of life were not well established in Later Vedic times. In the post-Vedic texts, four ashramas were of **Brahmachari** (student), **Grihastha** (householder), **Vanaprastha** (retired) and **Sanyasa** or ascetic who completely renounced the worldly life.
- Only the first three are mentioned in the Later Vedic texts; the last or the fourth stage had not been well established in Later Vedic times though ascetic life was not unknown.
- Even in post-Vedic times only the stage of the householder was commonly practiced by all the Varnas.

The Sixteen Sanskaras

1. Garbhadhana – Ceremony for conception.
2. Pumsavana – To secure the birth of male child.
3. Simantonayana – Parting the hair.
4. Jatakarma – Natal rites (Ceremony for a newborn child).
5. Namakarana – Ceremony for naming the child.
6. Nishkramana – First outing (Exposure to Sun).
7. Annaprasana – First feeding with boiled rice in the 6 months.
8. Chudakarana – Arrangement of the hair tuft.
9. Karnavedha – Piercing the earlobes.
10. Vidyarambha – Learning the alphabet.
11. Upanayana – Holy thread ceremony.
12. Vedarambha – First study of the Vedas.
13. Keshanta and Ritusuddhi – Cutting the hair.
14. Samavartana – Graduation ceremony (on returning home after completing studentship).
15. Vivaha – Marriage.
16. Antyeshti – Funeral.

Religious Life of Later Vedic Age

- In the Later Vedic period, Aryan culture developed under Brahmanical influence.
- The cult of sacrifice central of this culture was accompanied by rituals and formulae.
- The two prominent Rig Vedic Gods, *Indra* and *Agni*, lost their importance in Later phase.
- **Prajapati** the creator, come to occupy the supreme position in the Later Vedic age.
- Some of the other minor Gods of the Rig Vedic period also came to the forefront. **Rudra**, the God of animals, became important in Later Vedic times.
- **Vishnu** came to be conceived as the preserver and protector of the people who now led a settled life instead of a semi-nomadic life as they did in Rig Vedic times.
- In addition, some objects began to be worshipped as symbols of divinity; signs of idolatry appear in later Vedic times.
- As society became divided into social classes, some of the social orders came to have their own deities.
- **Pushan**, who was supposed to look after cattle, regarded as the God of the Shudras.
- People worshipped Gods for the same material reasons in this period as they did in earlier times.
- However, the mode of worship changed considerably. Prayers continued to be recited, but they ceased to be the dominant mode of pleasing the Gods as in earlier times.
- Sacrifices became far more important and they assumed both public and domestic character. Public sacrifices involved the king and the whole of the community.
- Sacrifices involved the killing of animals on a large scale. They were accompanied by formulae which had to be carefully pronounced by the sacrificer. The sacrificer was known as the *Yajamana*, the performer of Yajna.
- These formulae and sacrifices were invented, adopted and elaborated by the priests.
- The Brahmanas claimed a monopoly of priestly knowledge and expertise. They invented a number of rituals, some of which were adopted from the Non-Aryans.
- Cows, gold, cloth and horses were given as sacrificial gifts.
- Sometimes, the priests claimed portions of territory as *Dakshina*, but the grant of land as sacrificial fee was not well established in the Later Vedic period.
- The *Shatapatha Brahmana* states that in the *Ashvamedha,* North, South, East and West all should be given to the priest.

Kingdoms of the Later Vedic Period

Kingdoms	Locations
Panchal	Badayun and Farrukhabad in Uttar Pradesh
Kushinagar	Northern region of Uttar Pradesh
Kashi	Modern Varanasi
Koshal	Ayodhya in Uttar Pradesh
Uttara Madra	Near Amritsar
Southern Madra	Kashmir
Eastern Madra	Near Kangra
Kekaya	On the bank of Beas river East of Gandhara kingdom
Gandhara	Rawalpindi and Peshawar and parts of North-East Afghanistan

Extra Facts From Tamil Nadu Board and NIOS

- Though the Rig Veda is in Sanskrit, about 300 words of the Munda and Dravidian languages have been identified in it, suggesting cultural mix with earlier inhabitation.
- Bali as a kind of tax were received by the *Rajanya* or *Kshatriya*, they were the warriors.
- Important crop during Vedic age were **barley** (Yavam) and **wheat** (Godhuma).

Religious Movements

(SOURCES)

Class-VI New NCERT Chap 6 (New Questions and Ideas),
Class-VI Old NCERT Chap 9 (Traders, Kings and Pilgrims),
Class-XI Old NCERT Chap 10 (Jainism and Buddhism),
Chap 13 (State and Varna at the Age of Buddha),
Class-XII New NCERT Chap 4 (Thinkers, Beliefs and Buildings)
Tamil Nadu Board (Class XI), NIOS

Rise of New Religious Sects

- In Sixth century BC witnessed rise of numerous heterogeneous religions in India. They mainly originated in middle Gangetic plain.
- As 62 **religious sects** were present at that time among which Jainism and Buddhism gained prominence and became torchbearer of religious reforms in Ancient India.

Causes of Origin

- In Post-Vedic period, Varna system became rigid and it was determined on the basis of birth rather than profession. The society was divided in four Varnas i.e., Brahmin, Kshatriya, Vaishya and Shudra.
  - **Brahmanas** were at highest position in the hierarchy and given many privileges, including gifts, no taxation and no punishment as evident in post-Vedic times.
  - **Kshatriyas** occupied second highest position in the hierarchy. They governed the people and collected taxes from them.
  - **Vaishyas** were mainly agriculturalists, traders, merchants, etc and were the principal taxpayers. Along with Brahmanas and Kshatriyas, they enjoyed the status of Dvij (Twice born), allowed to study Vedas and their sacred thread ceremony was conducted.
  - **Shudras** occupied the last position in the hierarchy and meant to serve the other three Varnas as domestic slaves, hired labourers, craftsmen. They were not allowed to study Vedas. They were cruel, greedy and thieves in habit and some of them were also considered as untouchables.
- Persons with higher Varna were considered as purer and accordingly their punishments were lenient. In other words, higher the *Varna*, lower the punishment and vice-versa.
- **Varna based society** caused tensions among Varnas and Kshatriya who were the governing class opposed to the ritualistic domination of Brahmanas. This led to protest over the Varna system based on birth.
- Another significant reason was the development of new agricultural economy in Eastern India including Eastern Uttar Pradesh and Bihar. The area received rainfall more than 100 cm and previously thickly forested, the area was cleared with the use of iron axes.
- The **new agrarian economy** used iron ploughs which require to be pulled by bullocks. However, Vedic practices of killing cattle in sacrifices slowly diminished the livestock population. This also made agriculture more difficult. In order to make new economy stable, practice of animal sacrifice was needed to be stopped.
- Vaishya gained prominence economically and wanted upliftment in the social hierarchy. For this, Vaishyas looked for a new religion which would improve their position.

- The Vaishyas and trader class made generous support to **Vardhaman Mahavira** and **Gautama Buddha**. There are multiple reasons behind it, such as :
  - Buddhism and Jainism didn't laid importance on existing Varna system.
  - Both the religions preached non-violence, which was very essential for the stability and promotion of agrarian economy. Further, non-violence would have increased greater trade and commerce.
  - The Brahmana class criticised the system of money lending and that's why Vaishyas, were held in low esteem.
  - Both Buddhism and Jainism suggested to live a puritan and ascetic life. They were supporter to live the life only with the basic necessities and not for luxury. This simple living system attracted many people who became followers of Jainism and Buddhism.

Jainism

- Jaina word comes from the term Jina, meaning conqueror.
- Origin of Jainism goes back to the ancient time. **Rishabhanatha** (born in Ayodhya) is believed to be the first **Tirthankara**.
- Most of the early Tirthankaras believed to be born in Ganga basin except Parshvanatha (23rd Tirthankara) who was born in **Varanasi** and attained Nirvana in **Bihar**.

Vardhaman Mahavira

- Vardhaman Mahavira was 24th and the **last Tirthankara** of Jainism.
- He was born in 540 BC in **Kundagrama**, a village near **Vaishali**. His father **Siddhartha** was head of Jnatrika clan and his mother **Trishala** was sister of King **Chetaka** who was a Lichchavi Prince of Vajji Ganasangha.
- He left his house at the age of 30 and attained enlightenment 12 years later at the age of 42 years. He preached for next 30 years in Kosala, Magadha, Mithila, Champa, etc. He died at the age of 72 at Pavapuri near modern **Rajgir**.
- Through *Kaivalya*, Mahavira conquered misery and happiness, and called as *Jina* (great conqueror). Later his followers were known as **Jainas**. Mahavira taught simple doctrine of '*Ahimsa*' (Non-violence), in Prakrit language which was a common man's language at that time.

Doctrines of Jainism

- Jainism taught about five great vows/doctrines :
  1. Do not commit violence
  2. Do not speak a lie
  3. Do not steal
  4. Do not possess any property
  5. Observe Brahamacharya (celibacy) [Added by Mahavira]
- **Parsvanatha** talked about covering upper and lower portion of the body, but **Mahavira** asked followers to discard clothes altogether. Jainism recognised existence of God but placed them below Jina. Jainism also not condemned the Varna system.
- Jainism made serious attempts to counter the evils existed in the Varna system and ritualistic order. Jaina teachings talk about the cycle of *Karma*, which results in birth and rebirth.
- According to Jainism, ascetism and penance are required to free oneself from the cycle of Karma. Therefore, salvation (Liberation) can be achieved only when one renounce the world and accept monastic way of life. Liberation can also be attained by pure and meritorious conduct even by a person of lower origin.
- Three jewels of Jainism which believed to lead the path towards liberation are :
  - **Right Knowledge** (*Samyak Gyana*)
  - **Right Faith** (*Samyak Darshana*)
  - **Right Conduct** (*Samyak Charitra*)

Tirthankaras with their Symbols

Tirthankaras	Symbols	Tirthankaras	Symbols
Rishabhanatha (*Adinath*)	Bull or Ox	Vimalanatha	Bear
Ajitnatha	Elephant	Anantnatha	Falcon
Sambhavanath	Horse	Dharmanatha	Vajra
Abhinandananatha	Monkey	Shantinatha	Deer
Sumatinatha	Red Goose	Kunthunatha	He-Goat
Padmaprabha	Lotus	Arahnatha	Fish
Suparshvanatha	Swastika	Mallinatha	Kalash
Chandra Prabhu	Crescent (*new moon*)	Munisuvrata	Tortoise
Pushpadanta	Crocodile	Naminatha	Blue Water Lily
Shitalanatha	Kalpa-Vriksha	Neminatha	Shankh
Shreyansnatha	Rhinoceros	Parshvanatha	Snake
Vasupujya	Buffalo	Mahavira	Lion

Philosophy of Jainism

- Jainism believed in the **theory of Syadvada** (Theory of Conditional Judgement), i.e., Theory of Relativity of Knowledge. It is believed that there is no absolute answer to a question. Every object exists in relation with other objects. In one way, it is not only an extension of *Anekanta* ontology but a separate system of logic.
- The main features of Jaina philosophy remain in its dualistic metaphysics, which states that there are two categories of living :
  1. Conscious being (*Jiva*)
  2. Non-living being (*Ajiva*)

Sallekhana/Santhara

- It is a form of penance where an individual perform in order to get rid the cycle of birth and rebirth. It is a form of starvation in which a person consumes less food and water; gradually, fasting into death.

Spread of Jainism

- **Mahavira** organised Jainism in a *Sangha* in which both men and women were allowed. He preached his teachings in Prakrit and gave his first sermon near Rajgir.
- Jainism spread to different parts in India, such as Gujarat, Tamil Nadu and Karnataka. It is believed that Jainism was spreaded to Karnataka by **Chandragupta Maurya**, who became a Jain monk himself.
- Second cause of the spread of Jainism was that North India was famine struck and Jain monks went to South under the leadership of **Bhadrabahu**. When they came back, there were certain visible changes in the two groups of Jainism.
- It spreaded to Kalinga during fourth century BC and given patronage by its ruler **Kharavela**. It is believed that from here, it spreaded to Tamil Nadu.

Jain Councils

Council	Year	Place	Leader	Main Point
First	300 BC	Pataliputra	Sthulabhadra	12 Angas were compiled
Second	512 AD	Vallabhi	Devardhi Kshemashramana	12 lost Angas were compiled and 12 Upangas were created

Sects of Jainism

- Mahavira had eleven ardent disciples, ten of whom died before Mahavira. **Sudharma** was the only disciple remained alive after his death who became the first **Theda** (pontiff).
- The two factions of Jainism, one who left for South India and the other remained in Magadha called as **Digambara** and **Shwetambara** respectively.
- Digambara or sky clads remained the ardent followers of the doctrines/principles given by Mahavira, whereas Shwetambara adopted various changes in order to face famine in Magadha.

Contributions of Jainism

- Jaina followers discarded Sanskrit initially and preached in **Prakrit** (language of masses). Their adoption of Prakrit, developed the popularity of the religion and also developed various regional languages.
- Jain literature has been written in Prakrit, **Ardhamagadhi**, which were finally compiled in second Jain Council. This resulted in development of various regional languages such as **Sauraseni**, which led to the development of **Marathi** language.
- Jaina literature consists of epics, puranas, novels and dramas. There are many old manuscripts even today confined in the Jain shrines of Rajasthan and Gujarat.
- Initially, Jaina followers were not idol worshippers. Later on, they began to worship Mahavira and other 23 Tirthankaras.
- They started sculpting images of them on stone and this led to the development of art and architecture in the region especially in South, Western and Central India.

Jaina Literature

Jaina Literature can be divided in two categories :

1. Agama Literature

It include sacred literature, written in Ardhamagadhi such as :

Angas	–	12
Upangas	–	12
Prakirnas	–	10
Chhedasutra	–	6
Mulasutra	–	4

2. Non-Agama Literature

These are commentaries, explanation of Agama literature, independent work of scholars and ascetics. Major examples of it are :

Kalpa Sutra	–	Bhadrabahu
Theravali	–	Merutunga
Padma-Charita	–	Vimala Suri
Antara Katha	–	Rajshekhara
Parisishtha Parwan	–	Hemachandra

Jaina Architecture

- Earliest evidence of Jaina architecture was found in caves (*viharas*) of Odisha, such as in **Khandagiri**, **Udayagiri** (first century BC), **Hanthigumpha** (first century BC) and **Ellora** (11th and 12th centuries AD) in Maharashtra.
- **Jaina temples at Dilwara** in Rajasthan were built by Solanki rulers. They were dedicated to Jain Tirthankara. These temples were completely built of white marble and are also famous for their unique and distinct style.
- **Ranakpura Jaina temple** was attributed to first **Tirthankara Adinath**. It was built in *Chaumukh* design of architecture. The temple was built in 15th century AD.
- **Statue of Gomateshwara** (Bahubali) at Shravanabelagola in Karnataka and temples at Gwalior, Khajuraho, Deogarh, Chanderi, etc are the examples of rich heritage of Jaina architecture.
- 84 feet high statue of **Rishabhdeva** has been built at Bawangaja (Badwani district of Madhya Pradesh). It was created in 13th century AD.

Decline of Jainism

The reasons for the decline of Jainism are :

- **Lack of Royal Patronage** Later kings like Harsha and Kanishka promoted Buddhism, which resulted in decline of royal patronage of Jaina religion.
- **Easy Living by Monks** Monks did not put efforts to spread and popularise Jainism. Traders and merchants remained loyal but do not promoted Jainism.
- **Jaina Philosophy** The philosophy of austerity and penance were harsh as compared to Buddha's middle path, which attracted common people more into Buddhism than in Jainism.
- **Division of Jainism** In later phase, Jainism was divided in two factions namely Shwetambara and Digambara. This led to division of the followers resulting in overall loss of relevance.

Buddhism

Buddhism was another prominent religious movement, which arose in India during sixth century BC and had an impact on the existing social and religious order. It was started by **Gautama Buddha** after attaining enlightenment.

Gautama Buddha

- Siddhartha (Gautama Buddha) was born in 563 BC in the Shakya Kshatriya clan at **Lumbini** near **Kapilvastu** (Piprahwa district of Nepal).
- His father **Shuddodhana** was the elected ruler of Kapilvastu (the head of republic clan of Shakya). His mother **Maya** died 7 days after the birth of Siddhartha. After, the death of his mother, Siddhartha was brought up by foster mother **Mahapajapati Gautami**.
- From early childhood, Buddha showed a meditative state of mind. He gave up his married life and left his home, at the age of 29 years.
- He was moved by looking the misery of the people. Particularly, he saw an old man sick person, a dead body and an ascetic.
- He kept wandering for 6-7 years and at the age of 35, he got enlightenment under the pipal tree at **Bodh Gaya** where he was called Buddha (the Enlightened one).
- After giving his **first sermon at Sarnath**, Buddha wandered from one place to another giving sermons for next 40 years; resting only during the rainy season.
- Gautama Buddha passed away at the age of 80 years in 483 BC at a place called **Kushinagar** (Uttar Pradesh).
- Viharas were the place where Buddhist monk (Bhikkus and Bhikkhunis) stay or live and chaitya were the place monk worships or pray.

Doctrines of Buddhism

- Buddha gave four noble truths (*Arya Satya*) :
  1. **Dukkha** The world is full of sorrows.
  2. **Samudaya** Desire is the root cause of all the sorrows.
  3. **Nirodha** Nirvana can be attained by conquering desires.
  4. **Magga/Marga** There is a path for cessation of sorrows.
- **Nirvana** is the path for the cessation of the sorrows. According to Buddha, this can be done by following of Ashtangik Marga (Eight-Fold path).

These Eight-fold path are :

1. Right Observation
2. Right Determination
3. Right Speech
4. Right Action
5. Right Livelihood
6. Right Exercise
7. Right Memory
8. Right Meditation

- According to Buddha, following these **Madhyam Marga**, an individual will lead to attainment of Nirvana.

- According to Buddha, if a person follows eight-fold path, he doesn't require priest to attain Nirvana.
- *Pratitya Samudpada* is the continuous cycle of birth and rebirth. Its root cause is ignorance.
- Buddha, *Dhamma* and *Sangha* are the Triratnas (three Jewels) of Buddhism.
- If we get what we want, we are not satisfied and want even more. The Buddha described this as thirst or tanha. He taught that this constant craving could be removed by following moderation in everything.

Dasa Shilas (10 Percepts)

1.	Don't Tell Lie
2.	Don't Steal
3.	Observe Celibacy (Brahmacharya)
4.	Do not Acquire Gold or Silver
5.	Observe Non-Violence
6.	Do not Consume Intoxicants
7.	Don't Indulge in Corrupt Practices
8.	Don't use Flower, Scents and Perfumes
9.	Don't take Food after Midday
10.	Avoid Comfortable Bed

- According to the Buddhist philosophy, the world is transient (Anicca) and constantly changing. It is also soulless (Anatta) as there is nothing permanent.

Spread of Buddhism

- Buddhism doesn't recognise the existence of God but was silent about soul. It considered every human as equal irrespective of his caste and Varna. This attracted common people. Women were also included in Sangha; this brought them at par with man.
- Buddhism made special appeal to the people outside **Aryavarta** (a land belongs to Aryans). People in Magadha readily embraced Buddhism.
- Personality of Buddha and his methodologies attracted many as he countered hatred with love and evil by good.
- The Buddha's foster mother, Mahapajapati Gautami was the first woman to be ordained as a Bhikkhuni.
- Use of **Pali** as a language to propagate also helped Buddhism to flourish among common man as it was the language of the masses. Further the rules for entry into Sangha were very simple and it was open to all. The only condition was to follow the rules of the monastic order.
- Adoption of Buddhism by **Ashoka** was the most important event for the popularity of Buddhism as Ashoka sent religious mission to various kingdoms of South-East Asia, West Asia, China and Sri Lanka to propagate Buddhism. This led to flourishment of Buddhism outside India.
- Even today, Buddhism flourish in Sri Lanka, China, South-East Asia despite its decline in the land of its origin.
- Buddha's speeches were written and compiled by his disciple. These compilation is known as **Tipitaka.** Three basket to hold different types of texts. First, *Vinaya Pitaka* included rules and regulation for those who joined the Sangha or monastic order. Second, *Sutta Pitaka* and third *Abhidhamma Pitaka* dealt with philosophical matter of Buddha's life.
- **Dipavamsa** and **Mahavamsa** were the chronicle of Buddha's life.
- Hagiography is biography of a saint or religious leader. Hagiographies often praise the saint's achievements and may not always be literally accurate. They tell us about the beliefs of the followers of that particular tradition.

Buddhist Councils

Buddhist Councils	Places	Years	Presidents	Rulers/ Kings
1st Buddhist Council	Satapani Cave (Rajgriha)	483 BC	Mahakassapa	Ajatashatru
2nd Buddhist Council	Vaishali	383 BC	Sabakami	Kalashoka
3rd Buddhist Council	Pataliputra	250 BC	Mogaliputta Tissa	Ashoka
4th Buddhist Council	Kashmir	First century AD	Vasumitra	Kanishka

Sects of Buddhism

Bhuddhist texts mention that about 64 sects or schools of Buddhism were in existance. Some of these are–

- **Sthaviravada/Theravada** They depicted Buddhism in the most simple way and considered Buddha as God of Gods (Devatideva). They also preached the teachings of Buddha in simple way and language.
- **Sarvastivadina** They believed in Sabbamatthi (all things exists). This doctrine is given in Samyutta Nikaya. Vasubandhu was the greatest exponent.
- This unique Buddhist text, part of the Sutta Pitaka, is a collection of verses composed by Bhikkhunis and also known as Therigatha.
- **Mahasanghika** They bestowed Buddha with superpowers and consider him as super human. Importance of *Bodhisattva* is more than *Arhats.* They were influential in regions around Amravati, Nagarjunakonda.

- **Hinayana** They are also called as 'Lesser Wheels'. They believed in original teachings of Buddha. Salvation can be achieved through self-discipline and meditation. The worshipped Buddha using symbols rather than idol worship.
- **Mahayana** They are called as the 'Greater Wheel'. They represented Buddha as a great human. Started idol worship and recognised Buddha as incarnation of God. The ideal of *Bodhisattva* who are concerned with the salvation of others was also central to this.
- **Vajrayana** This is the tantric form of Buddhism. Emerged in seventh century AD. This school believed in salvation by attaining magical powers and spells. It became popular in Bengal, Bihar and Tibet.

Differences between Hinayana and Mahayana

Basis	Theravada/ Hinayana	Mahayana
Locations	Southern *(Sri Lanka, Thailand, Burma, Laos, Cambodia parts of South-East Asia)*	Northern *(Tibet, China, Taiwan, Japan, Korea, Mongolia parts of South-East Asia)*
Schools and Sects	One school survived *(as many as 18 existed at one time)*	8 major schools: four practice based *(Zen, Pure land, Vajrayana, Vinaya)*; four philosophy based *(Tendai, Avamtasaka, Yogacara and Madhyamika)*
Buddhist Scriptures	Pali Canon/Tripitaka only	Books of the *Theravada Tripitaka* , in addition to many other Sutras (e.g. *Lotus Sutra*)
Buddhas	Historical Buddha *(Gautama)* and previous Buddhas only	Gautama Buddha plus Amitabha, Medicine Buddhas and others
Bodhisattvas	*Maitreya only*	Maitreya plus Avalokitesvara, Manjusri, Ksitigarbha and Samanthabadra
Goal of Training	*Arhat*	Buddhahood *via* Bodhisattva path
3 Buddha Bodies (*Trikaya*)	Very limited emphasis; mainly on *Nirmana kaya* and *Dharma kaya*	Emphasised, including the *Samboga kaya* or reward/enjoyment body

Causes of Decline of Buddhism

By 11th and 12th century, Buddhism almost vanished from India, due to various reasons :

- It became victim of the same **ritualistic tendencies**, which it opposed in the initial stage.
- Buddhist monks cut off from common people. They gave up Pali and adopted **Sanskrit as a language**. Further they started receiving **gifts and donations** from the kings and aristocrats. Almost 200 village's revenue were attached to **Nalanda University**.
- By seventh century AD, Buddhist monastery became a place of ease living and centre of corrupt practice. Enormous wealth received by the monasteries further corrupted them and women are now considered as an object of lust.
- Various later rulers persecuted Buddhist monks. Shunga ruler **Pushyamitra Shunga** and Huna ruler **Mihikula** were prominent among them.
- Shaivite king **Shashanka** of Goud cut off the Bodhi tree at Gaya. According to **Hiuen Tsang**, 1600 Buddhist stupas and monasteries were destroyed and thousands of worshippers and monks were killed.
- The riches monasteries also drew Turkish invaders towards them and they became easy target for loot. Numerous monks fled to Nepal and Tibet.

Significance and Impact of Buddhism

- Buddhism showed a keen awareness on the existing social and economic problems and emphasised that all people need to be treated equally. People should not gather wealth.
- Buddha talked about elimination of poverty by providing farmers with grain, labours with wages and traders with money. This will eliminate the cruelty, hatred and violence arouse out of poverty.
- The code of conduct prescribed for monks were the guidelines against the materialistic world, sexual desires, wealth and desires. It was a revolt against the use of money by Buddha. It presented a simple way of life in sixth century BC.
- The rules of *Sangha* took full account of existing and emerging material conditions as debtors and slaves were not allowed in the Sangha unless freed by the master. Further, women and shudras were provided equal status to that of others.
- Both Buddhism and Buddhist monks were not against the existing social and political order, they respected political order and recognised social order on the basis of occupation.
- Buddhism talked about attainment of **Nirvana** however, it was for the monks and not for worshippers. Lay followers were supposed to live in the existing social order.
- Buddhist text, *Sutta Nipata* considered cattle as the giver of *Annada, Vannada* and *Sampada*. Hence, they need to be protected and Buddhist doctrine of non-violence also restricted killing of animals.

- Buddhist monasteries developed great learning centres of the time. **Nalanda**, **Vallabhi** and **Vikramshila** were prominent ones among them.
- Buddhism laid the foundation of idol worship in India; the first image worship belonged to Buddha. It has depictions of various life events of Buddha at **Bodh Gaya**, **Sarnath** and **Bharhut**.
- From first century onwards, the panel images of Buddha were made. Greek and Indian sculptors worked together and created, what is later called as **Gandhara School to Art** in North-West Frontier Region of India.

Similarities and Difference Between the Two Religions

Feature	Jainism	Buddhism
Existence of soul	Believed in soul	Didn't believed in soul
Practices	Extreme austerity and penance	Majjim-marg or moderate Path
Non-violence	Extreme	Moderate/Practical
Faith and karma	Believed	Believed
Founder	Kshatriya	Kshatriya

Other Heterodox Religious Movements

Ajivika and **Unchedvadi** were the prominent heterodox religious movements in India.

Ajivika

- **Makkhali Gosala** was the proponent of this sect. He was the first disciple of Vardhaman Mahavira. According to him, every object of the universe is coordinated with fate and destiny.
- He believed in Karma, fatalism and extreme inactions. It was very popular during the time of Bindusara of Mauryan dynasty.

Unchedvadi

- The leader of this school of sect was **Ajita Kesakambali**, who was an ancient Indian philosopher in the sixth century BC.
- He is considered as the first known proponent of Indian materialism. According to him, all is annihilated with death and there is no after life.

Bhagwatism

- Bhagwatism sect originated in **post-mauryan period**.
- Bhagwat means **'One Devoted to God'**. Bhagwat sect was highly devotional system, which revolved around a personal God known as **Vishnu**, Vasudev Krishna, Hari or Narayan. The worshippers of Narayan/Bhagwat were called **Bhagwatas**.
- By the sixth century BC, Vishnu became a member of the trinity of God along with **Shiva** and **Brahma**. It was believed that Narayan bestowed good fortune to his worshippers and in return of that the worshippers offered their loving devotion or *bhakti* to him.
- It presented the doctrine of incarnation or *avatar* of Vishnu. It believed that whenever, the social order faced crisis, Vishnu incarnated in human form to save it.

Ten Avatars of Vishnu

- Matsya (fish), Kurma (tortoise), Varaha (boar), Narasimha (man-lion), Vaman (dwarf), Parashurama, Rama, Krishna, Buddha and Kalki were ten avatars of Vishnu.

- The sect originated from **Mathura** region and then spread to North-West, Northern Deccan and then South India.
- After sixth century BC, several texts were written to popularise the virtues of worshipping him and the most important was the **Bhagwat Purana**.
- Patrons of Bhagwatism/Vaishnavism were **Heliodorus**, **Huvishka**, Gupta rulers, Chalukyas of Badami, **Lakshmana Sen** of Bengal and Eastern Gangas of Odisha.

Popularity of Bhagwat Sect

- The sect was sufficiently liberal to attract foreigners. As the sect propagated *bhakti* and *ahimsa* (non-killing of animals), it attracted agricultural society and appealed to artisans, merchants, women, Vaishya and Shudras.
- The main emphasis of this sect is to adopt **Bhakti**, **Karma** and **Jnana** marg to attain *moksha*.

Idol Worship

- The earliest images are found from Mathura region. From Gupta periods onwards, idol worship in temples became common feature of Hinduism.
- The Bhagwat sect was remained prominent until at least the 11th century AD, when Bhakti was reactivated by the great theologian **Ramanuja**.
- The devotees of Vishnu in South India, were popularly known as **Alvars**. They were 12 in numbers. They composed songs devoted to Lord Vishnu. Among these Alvar saints, **Sri Andal** was the only female saint.
- **Goudiya Vaishnav** branch contributed in gaining popularity of Vaishnavism internationally.

Cults of Bhagwat Vaishnavism

Vishishtadvaita, Dvaita, Shuddhadvaita and Achintya Bheda Abheda were cults of Bhagwat Vaishnavism.

Vishishtadvaita

- Vishishtadvaita (Advait with uniqueness; Qualification) is a non-dualism of the qualified whole, in which brahman alone exists, but is characterised by multiplicity. The school believes in all diversity subsuming to an underlying unity.
- **Ramanuja** was the main proponent of the philosophy of Vishishtadvaita. According to him, the *Prasthan Trayi* (*Upanishads*, *Bhagwat Gita* and *Braham* Sutra) should be interpreted in such a way that shows a unity in diversity.
- Ramanuja teachings said that whatever exists, is brahman; but brahman is not of a homogenous nature, but contains within itself elements of plurality owing to which it truly manifests itself in a diversified world.
- Three key principles of Vishishtadvaita :
  - **Tattva** The knowledge of three real entities namely Jiva, Ajiva and Ishvara.
  - **Hita** The means of realisation, as through devotion and self-surrender.
  - **Purushartha** The goal is to attain *moksha* or liberation from bondages.

Dvaita

- It is Dualism (a strict distinction between the parmatman the God and jivatman the individual soul). Philosophy was given by **Madhavacharya** (1238-1317).
- Madhav Acharya said that individual souls of beings are not created by God, but dependent on him for their existence.

Shuddhadvaita

- It is pure non-dualism philosophy given by **Vallabhacharya**. He is founding philosopher of Pushtimarg (The Path of Grace) focused on the worship of Krishna.
- Vallabhacharya propagated that God is pure and non-dualistic.

Achintya Bheda Abheda

- Inconceivable duality and non-duality (Achintya means inconceivable, *Bheda* means difference and *Abheda* means as non-difference) Philosophy was given by Chaitanya.
- **Chaitanya Mahaprabhu** founded *Gaudiya* tradition of Vaishnavism. The Achintya Bheda Abheda propound that the supreme lord and his energies are one as well as different from each other.
- As the individual is a part of the Supreme lord which is infinite, the individual souls are infinitesimal and dependent upon the Supreme lord eternally.
- The Supreme energy cannot be ascertained through logics and speculation.

New Dynamic Force : Islam

- From the seventh century onwards, Asia and North Africa were slowly made aware of a new and dynamic force which arose in Arabia. This was Islam and India too experienced the rise and spread of it.
- Arabia at that time was a centre of trade. The two important cities were **Mecca** and **Medina**, where the wealthy merchants who owned big camel caravans lived.
- **Muhammad** was the prophet of this new religion. Muhammad believed that there was only one God. He began to think more and more about these ideas.
- Those who accepted his idea, were called **Muslims** and their religion were called **Islam**.
- Islam spread very rapidly after the death of Muhammad in 632 AD. The caliphate was established over the area stretched from Western Asia right across Northern Africa and upto Spain.
- **'Caliph'** or **successor of the Prophet** was the title given to the ruler of this territory.
- In 712 AD, the Arabs conquered Sindh and threatened Western India, but were hold back by the local rulers. They kept their political control over Sindh. It was in this part of India that Islam first became an important religion.

Important Terms Related to Jainism and Buddhism

- **Avasarpini** The descending order of the six periods of the Jain cosmic cycle.
- **Ajnanavada** The Jain doctrine of agnosticism or scepticism. The Jain texts mentioned 67 kinds of Ajnanavada.
- **Anuvratas** These are five principles, which are less rigorous in nature and are to be followed by a follower of Jainism.
- **Dohakosa** The last Buddhist text produced in India.
- **Dukham-Dhukam Kal** The sixth and the last period of the Jain cosmic cycle, a very wretched period.
- **Mahavratas** Five principles observed by the Jain monks.

- **Posadha** Fasting by the Jain members on the full Moon and the new Moon day.
- **Pavarna** Also known as *Uposatha* or *Upavastha*, it was the ceremony when Buddhist monks met to confess their offences.
- **Prajnaparamita** Collection of *Sutras*, which deal with the Doctrine of *Sunya* or Nothingness.
- **Samachari** Part of the Kalpasutra, which deals with the Jain monks.
- **Sukham-Sukham Kal** The first cosmic cycle of Jainism.
- **Sanghathera** Also known as *Samgha Parinayaka*, *Sanghathera* was the elected President of the fortnightly assembly of Buddhist monks.
- **Trisastisalaka Purushacharita** The longest poem composed by Jain scholar Hemachandra, dealing with the deeds of 63 enlightened men, including the 24 Tirthankaras.
- **Shramana** Monk or ascetics.
- **Theravali** The second section of the Jain Kalpasutra containing a list of schools (aonas) and their heads.
- **Tathagata** One who has attained the truth.
- **Utsarpini** The ascending order of Jain cosmic cycle.
- **Upasikas** The followers of Buddhism.

Extra Facts From Tamil Nadu Board and NIOS

- Bhagavatisutra is an Jain text, provides a poor account of Makkhali Ghoshe.
- Buddhist text, Samannaphala Sutta, mentioned about Ajatashatru of Magadha meeting with Gautama Buddha.
- The invasion of Huns gave a death blow to Buddhism. Toramana and Mihirakula, the two Hun chiefs had a deep-seated hatred for Buddhism.
- **Manimekalai** by Sattanar one of the twin epics of the post-Sangam age is a Buddhist literature.
- **Ajivikas** in Tamil Land-*Manimekalai*, *Nilakesi* and *Sivagnana Siddhiyar* have reference to Ajivika doctrine. Nilakesi's quest for truth takes her to Buddha and Puranan. Puranan was the leader of the Ajivika sect.

06

Mahajanapadas

[SOURCES]

Class-VI New NCERT Chap 5 (Kingdoms, Kings and Early Republic), Class-VI Old NCERT Chap 4 (India from 600 BC to 400 BC), Class-XI Old NCERT Chap 11 (Territorial States and First Magadhan Empire), Chap 12 (Iranian and Macedonian Invasion), Class-XII New NCERT Chap 2 (Kings, Farmers and Towns), Chap 3 (Kinship Caste and Class) Tamil Nadu Board (Class XI), NIOS

Emergence of Mahajanapadas

- The word **Janapada** literally means the land where the Jana set its foot and settled down.
- In sixth century BC, widespread use of iron started. This led to the clearing of forest area over Gangetic plain and ultimately large settlements came into existence in the region.
- New iron tools and weapons increased production of food grains as well as developed the art of warfare.
- Emergence of new agrarian economy, development of large settlements (cities), surplus production, army led to creation of large area under one command known as **Janapadas**.
- The important excavation settlements in the Janapadas were Purana Qila in Delhi, Hastinapura near Meerut and Atranjikhera near Etah (Uttar Pradesh).
- **Panchala**, **Kosala**, **Kashi**, **Surasena**, **Videha** were among these Janapadas and named after the rulers who ruled them. These Janapadas were either kingdoms or republics (*Gana Sangha*). Republic is an area governed by a group of people under one elected head.
- In ancient republics, it was Kshatriya clan which owned and ruled the land. Some historians also called them oligarchy as they didn't allow non-Kshatriya to govern the republic.
- Over the period of time, some Janapadas emerged as **Mahajanapadas** after gaining great territorial control and increasing their power. They were constantly fighting with one another in order to extend their area of dominance or control.

Sixteen Mahajanapadas

- In the age of Buddha, 16 Mahajanapadas are mentioned, out of which Magadha, Avanti, Kosala, Vatsa were the most powerful.
- Majority of these Mahajanapadas were located North of Vindhyan region and extended from North-West Frontier region to Bihar.
- These Mahajanapadas fought with each other constantly and over the period of time Magadha became most powerful Mahajanapada. Ultimately, it became first powerful kingdom of India.
- Most Mahajanapadas were ruled by Kings, some known as Ganas or Sanghas, were oligarchies, where power was shared by a number of men, often collectively called Rajas. Both Mahavira and the Buddha belonged to such Ganas.

Description of Sixteen Mahajanapadas

- **Kashi** It was the most powerful Mahajanapada. It was famous for its cotton textiles and market for horses.
- **Kosala** Its most popular king was Prasenjit. He was the contemporary of Buddha.

- **Anga** It was a great centre of trade and commerce. In middle of sixth century BC, it was annexed by Magadha under Bimbisara.
- **Vajji** It represented a confederacy of eight clans of whom Videhas were the most well-known. The Videhas has also had their capital at Mithila.
- **Malla** Buddha died in this Mahajanapada at Kushinagar. Magadha annexed it after Buddha's death.
- **Chedi** The territory of Chedi corresponded to the Eastern parts of modern Bundelkhand. A branch of Chedis founded a royal dynasty in the kingdom of Kalinga.
- **Vatsa** It was situated around the region of Allahabad (now prayagraj). Its most powerful king was Udayin.
- **Kuru** (Situated in Meerut, Delhi and Thaneshwar) At the Buddha's time, Kuru country was ruled by a chieftain named Kauravya.
- **Panchala** It was located in Rohilkhand and parts of Central Doab.
- **Matsya** It was located in the region of Rajasthan. Sujata ruled over both the Chedis and the Matsyas.
- **Surasena** It had a republican form of government. Avantiputra, the King of Surasena, was amongst the first chief disciples of the Buddha.
- **Asmaka** It was located on the bank of the river Godavari. It was the Southernmost Mahajanapada ruled by the Ikshvaku Kshatriyas.
- **Avanti** It was located around the region of Ujjain district in Madhya Pradesh. Chanda Pradyota was the most powerful King of Avanti.

- **Gandhara** It was famous for education and learning traditions in Ancient India. *Panini* and *Kautilya* were the world renowned alumnus of the Taxila University situated in Gandhara.
- **Kamboja** Kautilya's Arthashastra and Ashoka's Edict. XIII attested that the Kambojas followed a Republican Constitution.
- **Magadha** This Mahajanapada started the policy of Imperialism. The founders of the kingdom were perceived to be Jarasandha and Brihadratha. However, its real imperial foundation was laid by Bimbisara and Ajatashatru.
- Most of these Mahajanapadas had capital. The important features of their capital was that highly protected through huge walls of wood, brick or stone. These capitals were protected from attacks from other kings.

List of Sixteen Mahajanapadas

S. No.	Mahajanapada	Capital	Present Day
1.	Anga	Champa	Bhagalpur and Mungher (Bihar)
2.	Asmaka	Pratisthan/ Paithan	Banks of Godavari (Telangana)
3.	Avanti	Mahismati and Ujjaini	Malwa region of Madhya Pradesh
4.	Chedi	Suktamati	Bundelkhand region of Uttar Pradesh and Madhya Pradesh
5.	Gandhara	Taxila	North-Western frontier region (Pakistan)
6.	Kashi	Kashi	Banaras in Uttar Pradesh
7.	Kamboja	Rajapura	Poonch and Hazra district of Jammu and Kashmir
8.	Kosala	Shravasti	Eastern Uttar Pradesh
9.	Kuru	Indraprastha and Hastinapur	Delhi and Meerut region
10.	Magadha	Rajgriha and Patliputra	Patna region of Bihar
11.	Malla	Kushinara and Pava	Deoria region in Uttar Pradesh
12.	Matsya	Viratnagar	Jaipur region of Rajasthan
13.	Panchala	Ahichchatra and Kampilya	Bareily and Farrukhabad region of Uttar Pradesh
14.	Surasena	Mathura	Mathura region of Uttar Pradesh
15.	Vajji	Vaishali	Northern Uttar Pradesh and Nepal
16.	Vatsa	Kaushambi	Banks of Yamuna in Uttar Pradesh

Republics in the Sixth Century AD

Among 16 Mahajanapadas were many republics states and other smaller Janapadas existed in the sixth century AD. Prominent among these were :

- Mallas of Pava
- Mallas of Kushinara
- Bhaggas (Mirzapur, Uttar Pradesh)
- Kaliya (Ramagama, Nepal)
- Moriya (Pippalivana in the foothills of Himalayas)
- Shakya of Kapilvastu (Kapilvastu, Indo-Nepal border)
- Lichchavis of Vaishali (Muzzaffarpur, North Bihar)
- Kalama (Kesaputta, East Champaran, Bihar)
- Butis (Allakappa, Bihar)

Dynasties of Magadha (Rise of Magadha)

Important dynasties of Magadha Mahajanapada age are as follows :

Haryanka Dynasty

The Haryanka dynasty was the first to rule in the Magadha Mahajanapada. It was founded by Bimbisara.

Bimbisara (544-492 BC)

- He was the first ruler of the Mahajanapada and contemporary of **Gautama Buddha**. Bimbisara adopted various mechanisms to increase the geographical area and dominance of Magadha.
- He defeated **Anga** capital and established matrimonial relations with **Kosala** (Mahakoshaladevi), **Lichchavi** (Chellana) and **Madra** clan. This made the position of Bimbisara strong. The Gandhara Ruler of Taxila Pukkusati sent an embassy to Bimbisara.

Ajatashatru (492-460 BC)

- He killed his father Bimbisara and became the ruler of Magadha Kingdom. He did not believe in matrimonial alliance-based relationships.
- He attacked and defeated **Prasenjit** (King of Kosala). He also defeated **Lichchavi** king after 16 years of war.
- During his reign, first Buddhist Council was convened at **Rajgriha** after the death of Gautam Buddha.

Udayin (460-444 BC)

- He was son and successor of Ajatashatru. He was a weak ruler as compared to his predecessors.
- He built the fort at **Pataliputra** and shifted capital from Rajgriha to Pataliputra.

Shishunag Dynasty

- **Shishunag** (412-394 BC) was the officer of **Udayin,** who replaced Udayin and started a new dynasty rule under his name.
- During his reign, the supremacy of Magadha established over **Avanti** (in other words, Magadha became the sole super Mahajanapada). He was succeeded by Kalashoka (Kak varna).
- **Kalashoka** (394-366 BC) shifted capital from Vaishali to Pataliputra and also convened **Second Buddhist Council** in Vaishali.

Nanda Dynasty

- Shishunags were replaced by **Nandas**, who are considered as first empire builders of India.
- They defeated the kingdom of **Kalinga** for the first time and brought image of **Jina** as a victory trophy.
- Prominent Nanda ruler was **Mahapadmananda** who has a mighty army consisted of large number of soldiers, elephants, chariots. It was believed that Mahapadmananda's army stopped Alexander to proceed further Eastwards.
- **Dhanananda** was the last ruler of Nanda dynasty and was replaced by Chandragupta Maurya, who established Mauryan dynasty.

Causes of the Rise of Magadha

Various factors were responsible for Magadha's rise into prominence. Some of these were :

- **Ambitious Rulers** Magadha was ruled by numerous ambitious rulers like, Bimbisara, Ajatashatru, Ashoka, etc.
- **Location** Both Rajgriha and Pataliputra were located strategically. As a result, Magadha can control Uttar Patha as near as Central and Eastern parts.
- **Fertile Soil** Alluvial soil of Gangetic plain helped in producing surplus in Magadha Province.
- **Natural Resource** Abundance of natural resources like iron enabled Magadha to equip with better weapons and tools to develop new agrarian economy.
- **Rise of Towns** Use of metallic money led to growth of trade and commerce which resulted in increase of prosperity of Magadha and developed many towns.
- **Use of Elephants** Using elephants in war which were found in Magadha region also helped in Magadha's rise.

Foreign Invasion

In fourth century BC, **Greeks** and **Iranians** fought for the supremacy in the Indian sub-continent region. Greek rulers not only conquered Asia minor region but also marched towards India beyond Indus plains.

Iranian or Persian Invasion

- The **Achaemenian rulers** of Iran, who expanded their empire at the same time as done by Magadhan kings, took advantages of the political disunity of the North-Western frontier.
- **Herodotus,** the Greek historian, also known as the Father of History states that in 516 BC, **Darius** (552-486 BC), the grandson of Cyrus, sent a naval expedition to explore the valley of the Sindhu river and annexed a part of Punjab and Sindh.
- The Indian soldiers formed a part of the Achaemenian army that conquered Greece in the time of the Persian ruler **Xerxes** (465-456 BC).
- The successor of **Darius I**, **Darius III** also enlisted Indian soldiers and sent them to fight with **Alexander**.

Effects of the Persian Invasion

- It led to the introduction of the **Aramaic** form of writing, which later developed into the **Kharosthi** alphabets.
- It led to the promotion of **Indo-Iranian trade**.
- Geographical exploration of the Indus and Arabian Sea, lead to the opening up of a new water route.
- Fusion of the **Persian art** forms became, quite visible in the Mauryan art and architecture.

Greek Invasion

- In the fourth century BC, the Greeks and the Iranians fought for the supremacy of the world. The Greek ruler **Alexander** conquered not only Asia Minor and Iraq, but also Iran. From Iran, he marched towards India as he was attracted by its wealth.
- Alexander who came through the **Khyber pass**, conquered the major principalities one by one. Among the rulers of these territories, two well-known were, **Ambhi,** the prince of Taxila and **Porus**, whose kingdom lay between the Jhelum and the Chenab.
- Ambhi, readily submitted to the invader, augmented his army and replenished his treasure. On the other hand, another Indian ruler, Porus fought bravely, but was defeated.

Battle of Hydaspes

- The Battle of Hydaspes was fought between **Alexander the Great** and **King Porus** in 326 BC. The Battle took place on the banks of the Jhelum river, which was known as Hydaspes to ancient Greeks.
- In the battle, Porus surrendered and the Alexander emerged victorious.
- After the battle, the Alexander was deeply impressed by the bravery and resistance by Porus and made Porus his *satraps* (Viceroy to the king).

Effects of the Greek Invasion

- It opened up the trade route between the North-West India and Western Asia and Europe.
- Opening up of **four distinct routes** between India and Greece by land and sea paved the way for increased trade and cultural contacts between the two regions.
- Not only did the Greek invasion led to the coming up of guilds (*Shreni*), but also facilitated trade due to the fact that money also got introduced post the invasion.
- The **Greek Art** influenced the architecture of the period, for instance, the **Ashokan pillars** have been influenced by the same.
- Many **Greek scholars** came to India and wrote on Indian history, now of immense relevance in the reconstruction of the then contemporary socio-religious aspects.
- The Greek invasion also further helped in the **expansion of Mauryan empire** in North-West India, since, the local powers were already subsumed by Alexander.

Extra Facts From Tamil Nadu Board and NIOS

- The source of revenue during Mahajanapadas period were Kara and Shulka. The King raised revenue through taxes to maintain and elaborate administrative structure and an army.
- The richer landowner were called Grihapatis. These landowners employed labourers called Dasas or Karmakaras. The smaller landowners were known as Kassakas or Krishakas.

07

Mauryan Empire

[SOURCES]

Class-VI Old NCERT Chap 5 (The Mauryan Empire), Class-VI New NCERT Chap 7 (From a Kingdom to an Empire), Class-VI Old NCERT Chap 7 (Ashoka, the Emperor Who Gave up War), Chap 10 (Buildings, Paintings and Books), Class-XI Old NCERT Chap 14 (The Age of Mauryas), Chap 15 (Significance of the Mauryan Rule), Class-XII New NCERT Chap 4 (Thinkers, Beliefs and Buildings)
Tamil Nadu Board (Class XI), NIOS

- After Nandas, a powerful **Mauryan dynasty** established itself on the throne of Magadha. Later on, it became one of the most important dynasties in Ancient Indian History.
- The Mauryan Empire was established in 322 BC with its capital in patliputra, which is known as **Patna** know.

Sources of Mauryan Dynasty

- Both Indian and classical sources suggest that **Alexander's** retreat from India facilitated Chandragupta to carve out a kingdom for himself.
- **Kautilya's** *Arthashastra* is one of the greatest treatises on economical, socio-political condition of the contemporary period. It gives fair idea about foreign affairs, administration, military arts, war and religion of Mauryan empire.
- *Mudrarakshasa* a historical play in Sanskrit by **Vishakhadatta** of fourth century AD narrated the ascent of the King Chandragupta Maurya to power in Northern India with the aid of Chanakya. It gives an account of socio-economic conditions of that era.
- *Parisisthaparvana,* a Jain work, written by **Hemachandra** is a biography of Chanakya.
- It also provides crucial information about Chandragupta Maurya, such as his early life, his conquest of Magadha, the famine in Magadha and his conversion to Jainism.
- Other sources, namely, *Rajatarangini* of **Kalhana**, *Kathasaritsagar* of **Somadev** and *Brihatkathamanjari* of **Kshemendra** also provide vital information about the Mauryan period.
- **Buddhist Jatakas** describe the stories of previous births of Gautama Buddha. They tell us about the prevalent social order, existence of guilds, popular customs which flourished till the Mauryan age.
- **Manjusrimulkalpa** is a non-canonical Buddhist work that covers wide historical period from the seventh century BC to the eighth century AD. It also contains important information about the Nandas and Mauryas.
- Greek Governor **Strabo** (64 BC-19 AD) wrote important geographical works named *'Geographica'*. He also refers to the matrimonial alliance between Seleucus Nicator and Chandragupta Maurya and the women bodyguards of Chandragupta.
- The work of **Diodorus** (First century BC) is the earliest available Greek account of India named *Bibliotheca Historica*. His accounts on India are derived from **Megasthenes Indica**.
- **Pliny** (First century AD) is the author of *Natural History* (75 AD) and gives the account of India based on Greek sources and reports by Western merchants.

Rulers of Mauryan Dynasty

Prominent rulers of Mauryan dynasty are discussed as follows :

Chandragupta Maurya

- Mauryan dynasty was established by Chandragupta Maurya. He belonged to an ordinary family.
- According to Brahmin traditions/sources, Chandragupta Maurya belonged to a humble origin and lived in **Nanda king's palace** (*Ranawas*).
- Chandragupta, with the help of **Kautilya** (Chanakya) overthrew the Nanda ruler **Dhanananda** and established Mauryan dynasty.
- According to a Greek historian **Justin,** in order to establish his dominance, Chandragupta started a military campaign with six lakh soldiers in whole India.
- Chandragupta Maurya also fought war with Indo-Greek ruler **Seleucus Nicator** in which the Chandragupta emerged victorious. Seleucus married his daughter **Helena** to Chandragupta Maurya.
- Seleucus Nicator also sent his ambassador **Megasthenes** to the Mauryan court. **Megasthenes** book *Indica* is a very important source of Mauryan empire.
- During the time of Chandragupta, the Mauryan rule was spread in the whole of Indian sub-continent except Tamil Nadu and North-East parts of India.
- In the last phase of his life, Chandragupta Maurya left the throne, embrassed Jainism from Jain Sage **Bhadrabahu** and died performing Sallekhana (Fasting into death) at Shravanabelagola (Mysore).

Kautilya's Arthashastra

- *Arthashastra* is considered as the greatest piece of work in the history of the Mauryas. Kautilya composed the book in Sanskrit. It is the most significant text to know about contemporary Mauryan administrative system.
- In general, *Arthashastra* is an authoritative book on polity and public administration. It is divided into 15 parts, 180 chapters and 6000 shlokas.
- It is in both prose and verse style, which is commonly called **Mahabharata style.**

Bindusara

- After Chandragupta, his son Bindusara became the ruler of the Mauryan empire.
- During the reign of Bindusara, the Maurya empire spread to the South as far as Mysore and thus included almost the entire country (except Kalinga and Southern kingdoms).
- The Greeks called Bindusara *Amitrochatas* (Amitraghat in Sanskrit).
- During the reign of Bindusara, **Antiochus,** the ruler of Syria, sent dry figs, wine to Bindusara but refused to send a Sophist (philosopher).
- **Deimachus,** an ambassador of Antiochus I was at the court of Bindusara.
- **Ptolemy II Philadelphus,** the ruler of Egypt, sent an ambassador named **Dynosis** to the court of Bindusara.
- Buddhist text *Mahavamsa* suggests that Bindusara was the follower of Brahamanism, but various other Buddhist books mentioned that he embrassed Ajivika sect under the guidance of **Pingalavatsa**.

Ashoka

- Ashoka was the **Governor** of **Avanti**, before ascending the throne.
- During his fathers' reign, he also went **Taxila** to supress the rebellion.
- According to the Buddhist traditions, Ashoka was extremely cruel in his early life and sat on the throne after killing his 99 brothers, however there is no historical authenticity of this. **Dipavamsa** states that in the year 273 BC, he captured the Magadha empire but crowned in 269 BC with the help of his abled minister **Radhagupta**.
- Ashoka was the first Indian king, who gave Royal public orders through his Edicts.
- Information about Ashoka's reign can be obtained from his inscriptions, which can be categorised in five types:
  1. Major rock inscriptions
  2. Minor rock inscriptions
  3. Separate inscriptions
  4. Major pillar inscriptions
  5. Minor pillar inscriptions
- Ashoka addressed his subjects as 'son' and called himself as *'Devanam Piyadassi'*. His name Ashoka was found only at three places in Karnataka and one in Madhya Pradesh.
- Ashoka's inscriptions have been found in present-day **India**, **Nepal** and **Afghanistan**. So far, these inscriptions have been found in 45 places in a total of 182 recitations.
- Ashoka's inscriptions composed in **Prakrit** and are written in **Brahmi script** in most parts of the empire however, inscriptions from North-Western part are written in **Kharosthi** and **Aramaic script**.

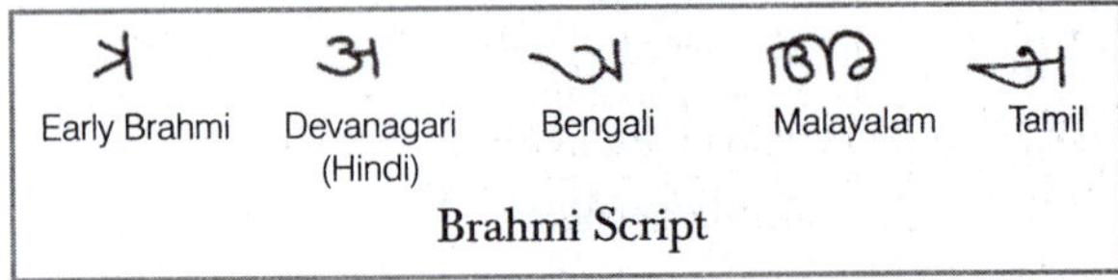

Brahmi Script

Major Rock Edicts

- They were found at distant locations of Mauryan empire i.e.,

Kalsi	Uttarakhand
Sopara	Maharashtra
Girnar	Gujarat
Yerragudi	Andhra Pradesh
Dhauli and Jaugada	Odisha
Manshera and Shahbazgarhi	Pakistan
Kandahar	Afghanistan

Fourteen Major Rock Edicts

S. No.	Major Rock Edicts	Discription
1.	MRE I	It prohibits animal slaughter particularly during festive season. Only two peacocks and one deer were allowed to be killed in his royal kitchen.
2.	MRE II	It provides medical treatment for man and animal. The edict also talks about four kingdoms of South, Cholas, Pandyas, Satyaputras and Kerelaputras.
3.	MRE III	Yuktas and Pradeshikas along with Rajuka shall visit all areas of kingdom once in every 5 years to spread Dhamma. It also talks about generosity with Brahmins.
4.	MRE IV	It gave importance to Dhamma Ghosha (Sound of Dhamma) over Bheri Ghosha (Sound of War). It also emphasised that duty is most important.
5.	MRE V	It talks about appointment of Dhamma Mahamattas to propagate Dhamma and to look after the welfare of the people.
6.	MRE VI	It shows King's desire to get informed about his subject's well-being.
7.	MRE VII	It talks about adoption of the policy of tolerance for all religions.
8.	MRE VIII	It describes Ashoka's first Dhamma Yatras to Bodh Gaya and Bodhi Tree.
9.	MRE IX	It stresses on moral duties of citizens and also condemns popular ceremonies (birth, marriage etc).
10.	MRE X	It stresses on Dhamma and condemns an individual's attempt to fame and glory.
11.	MRE XI	Ashoka explains about the policy of Dhamma and duties towards elders and abstaining from killing animals and liberal behaviour towards friends.
12.	MRE XII	It talks about religious tolerance, particularly about non-Buddhist religions.
13.	MRE XIII	It is the lengthiest of all edicts. It laid paramount importance of Ashoka's policy of Dhamma; mentions about the Kalinga war, Dhamma Victory over kingdoms of far West and South India.
14.	MRE XIV	It talks about engravings of inscriptions in other parts of the territory and purpose of the edicts.

Ashoka's Minor Rock Edicts

1.	Yerraguddi – Andhra Pradesh
2.	Rupnath – Madhya Pradesh
3.	Brahmagiri- Karnataka
4.	Bhabru – Rajasthan
5.	Sidhpur – Karnataka
6.	Ahrora – Uttar Pradesh
7.	Jating Rameshwar – Karnataka
8.	Sasaram – Bihar
9.	Govimath – Karnataka
10.	Panguradia – Madhya Pradesh
11.	Rajul Mandgiri – Andhra Pradesh
12.	Sannati – Karnataka
13.	Maski – Karnataka
14.	Palki gundu – Karnataka
15.	Gurjara – Madhya Pradesh

Ashoka's Kalinga War

- Ashoka's domestic and foreign policies were influenced by the Buddhist ideology. After becoming the emperor, he fought the major war, popularly known as **Kalinga War** in 261 BC.
- Ashoka successfully conquered Kalinga. It became the fifth province of the Magadha along with **Prachaya, Avanti, Uttarpatha** and **Dakshinapatha**.
- According to the Buddhist literature, lakhs of people were killed in this war, lakhs of people were wounded and 1,50,000 people were prisoners of war.
- Ashoka was deeply moved by the large scale massacre in the Kalinga War. He adopted **Dhamma-Ghosha in** place of **Bheri-Ghosha**.

Dhamma Policy of Ashoka

- Ashoka became Buddhist after Kalinga war. He provided immense donations to Buddhists and promoted **Dhamma Yatra**. According to traditional **Anushrutis**, Ashoka organised **third Buddhist Council**.
- Ashoka set a very high ideal for himself i.e., the king being equal to the father.
- Ashoka appointed *Dhamma Mahamattas* to propagate *Dhamma* among different sections of the society including women.
- Ashoka's **Dhamma Policy** was not only religiously motivated, but he consciously tried to use as his state policy as well.
- Ashoka sent his missionaries to promote Buddhism in Sri Lanka and Central Asia. Ashoka used to ask the tribes to follow the path of *Dhamma*.

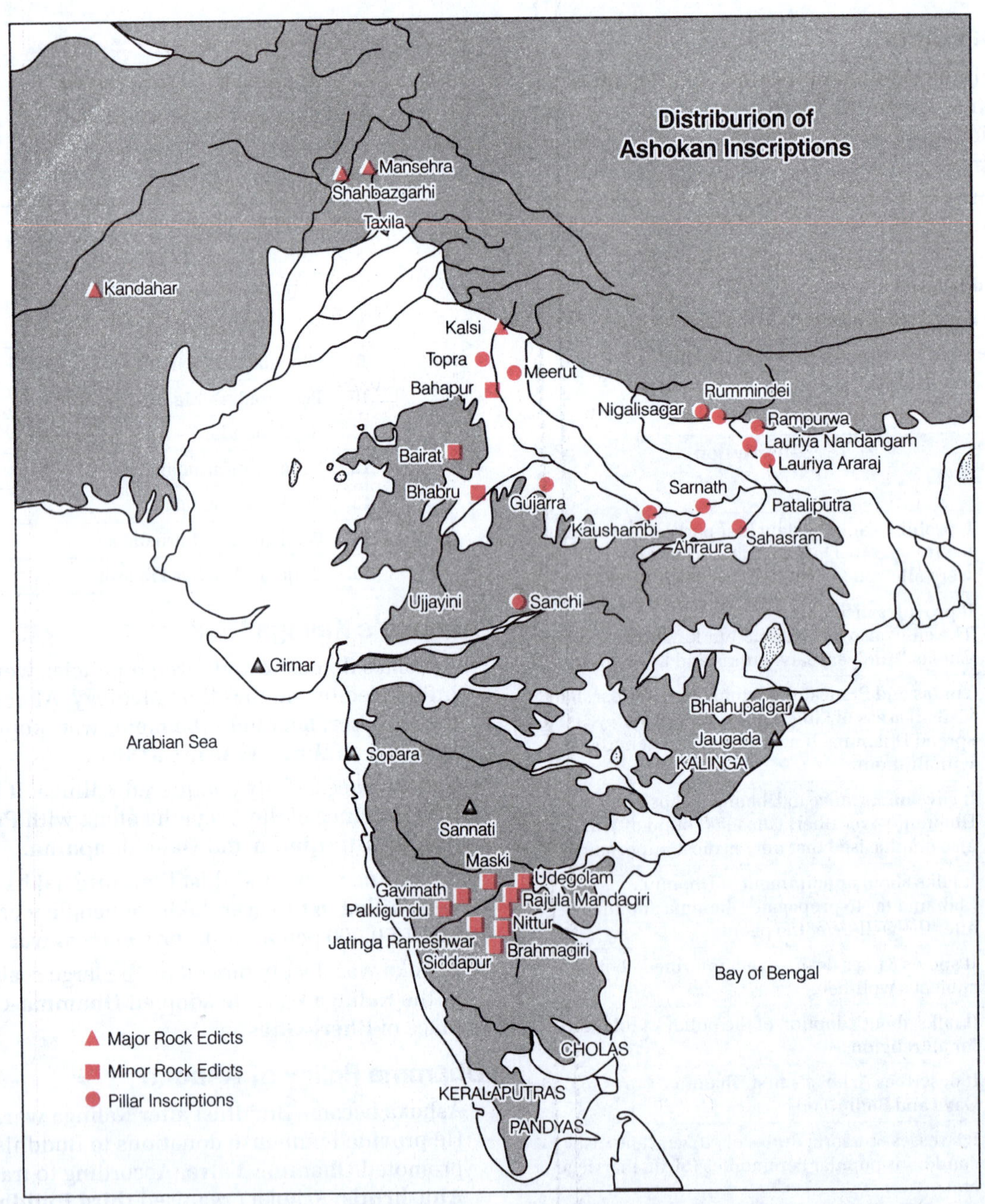

- He also sent messengers to spread ideas about Dhamma to other lands, such as Syria, Egypt, Greece.
- Ashoka appointed officer called **Rajuka** who had the right to reward to save *Dhamma* and punish the subjects if they violate *Dhamma*.
- It is known from the Kandahar inscription that due to the policy of Ashoka's *Dhamma*, the fowlers and fishermen also renounced the violence and lived the life of the farm producers.
- Ashoka opposed rituals and traditions specially prevailed among women. He banned killings of various birds and animals.
- Ashoka taught people the lesson of live and let live. He taught kindness towards living beings and good behaviour towards brothers.
- Before Ashoka, the Egyptian king **Akhnatun** adopted a **Pacifist policy** (Policy of opposing war) in the 14th century BC.

Evaluation of Ashoka

- Ashoka tried to establish pan Indian empire through his ability and spread the fame of the Mauryan empire inside and outside the country.
- Ashoka was successful in uniting the whole country under the principle of one religion, one language and often one script.
- Most of Ashoka's inscriptions are in Brahmi script but in the integration of the country, he respected all scripts like **Brahmi**, **Kharosthi**, **Aramaic** and **Greek**.
- Ashoka's name is immortalised in history for his policy of peace, non-aggression and cultural conquest.
- **Kautilya** adviced the king that he should always try to win by power, but Ashoka adopted the exact opposite i.e., the king should try to win through the means of benevolence.
- During the reign of Ashoka, the Mauryan empire became highly complex which could not survive after the death of Ashoka.
- In 232 BC, after Ashoka's death, the neighbouring kings captured the North-Western frontier of this empire.

Ashoka's Successors

- After Ashoka, the rule of his weak successors continued for the next 50 years.
- After Ashoka, his son **Kunal** became the next emperor, he was called *Dharma Vivardhan* in Divyaavadan.
- According to *Rajatarangini*, the Ruler of Kashmir was **Jaluka** during the rule of Kunal in Magadha.
- The names of **Samprati, Dasharatha, Shalishuka** and **Brihadratha** (last Mauryan ruler) are known as the later Mauryan rulers.

Mauryan Administration System

- The king was the head of the Mauryan administrative system. Kautilya has called the king **Dharma Pravartak** i.e., the 'Operator of the Social System'.
- The top officials in the Mauryan administration were called **Tirthas** (18 in numbers). Most of the officers were paid in cash. Ministers, priests, commanders and princes were of the highest order and were given high salaries.
- The messenger was an important official. He moved from place to place and kept an eye on the activities of the spy officers of the king.
- In the Central Government, there were more than two dozen departments for the administration, which looked after the social and economic activities in the areas adjacent to the capital.

Provincial Administration

- The Mauryan empire was divided into several provinces. Each province was under the control of a prince.
- Provinces were also divided into smaller units. There was a system of administration in both *Gramanchal* and *Nagaranchal*.

Provinces and Capitals during Mauryan Period

Provinces	Capitals
Uttrapath	Taxila
Avantika	Ujjaini
Dakshinapath	Suvarnagiri
Magadh	Pataliputra
Kalinga	Tosali

City Administration

- **Megasthenes** has described the city administration of Pataliputra. Pataliputra city was administered by a group of 30 members. There was a total of six committees in the city and each had five members.
- The head officer of the city was **Astronomoyi** and the head of the district was **Agronomoyi**.

Military Administration

- According to **Megasthenes**, there was a council of 30 members for military administration, which was divided into six sub-committees having five members each.
- These six sub-committees were :

1. Infantry
2. Cavalry
3. Elephant
4. Chariot
5. Boat
6. Transport and provisions

Economic Structure

- According to *Arthashastra*, 27 *Adhyakshas* were appointed in the entire state. They were responsible mainly to regulate economic functions.
- These officers used to control and regulate agriculture, trade and commerce, weight and measurement, mines, spinning and weaving.
- State also provided facilities for irrigation and water distribution and levied tax on the same.
- **Kautilya's** *Arthashastra* mentioned that, there is a system of forced labour in agriculture, which was an important social development.
- However, **Megasthenes** said slavery was not present in Mauryan empire.
- In the Mauryan empire, the state had a monopoly on the sale of mines, alcohol and the manufacturing of weapons.

- Historically slave system came to India with Turkish rulers. However, in the ancient period, it existed in the form of domestic servants and were generally regarded as the members of the master's family.
- The trade routes contributed greatly to the advanced economic system of the Mauryan empire. A popular trade route of this empire was from **Pataliputra** to **Nepal** via **Vaishali** and **Champaran.**
- The **Punch Marked Silver Coins** with peacock, mountain and crescent moon were the valid denomination of the Mauryan empire.

Transportation

- There was also a road in the foothills of the Himalayas. There were major trade centres such as Vaishali, Champaran, Kapilvastu, Kalsi (in Dehradun district), Hazara and Peshawar.
- In the Northern Plains, the Ganges and its tributaries were part of the water transportation.

Tax Structure

- **Kautilya** has described various taxes that were collected from farmers, craftsmen and traders.
- The **Samaharta** was the supreme authority of tax assessment and the **Sannidhata** was the custodian of the state treasury and warehouse.
- The elaborated system of tax assessment was first evident in the Mauryan empire in ancient India.
- In rural areas, there were state warehouses, which indicates that tax was also collected in the form of food grains.
- The taxes collected from farmers ranged from one-fourth to one-sixth of their produce which can be increased at emergency.
- Custom duty was also levied on goods brought for sale in the city.

Mauryan coin with arched hill symbol on reverse

Agriculture

- During Mauryan empire, fallow land has been brought under agriculture. Forced labour and cultivators played an important role in this process. This also increased the revenue of the state.

Mauryan Society

- Society was mainly divided into four Varnas (Brahmin, Kshatriya, Vaishya and Shudra). The Varna system became very rigid and no vertical movement was allowed.
- However, **Megasthenes** divided Mauryan society into seven categories:

1. Philosophers	2. Farmers
3. Soldiers	4. Herdsmen
5. Artisans	6. Magistrates
7. Councillors	

- **Joint family system** was prevalent and family structure was predominantly based on patriarchy.
- Women were allowed to accumulate *streedhan* (property in the form of bride-gift).
- Widows were also given respected position in the society. Any offence against women get punished severely.

Religion During Mauryan Period

- Mauryan period was religiously very active period. It witnessed rise and growth of **Buddhism** and **Jainism** over **Brahmanism.**
- Chandragupta Maurya followed Jainism and went to Shravanabelagola after renouncing the materialistic world.
- Bindusara and his successors were the followers of **Sarmanas** and **Ajivikas.**
- Ashoka was the greatest patron of Buddhism and also convened **Third Buddhist Council** at Pataliputra in 247 BC.
- There was general tolerance prevalent in the society. However, incidents were also mentioned by historians about religious persecution of Brahmins.

Mauryan Art and Architecture

- Stone and wood architectural work began on a massive scale during the Mauryan period. Megasthenes mentioned that the Mauryan palaces at **Pataliputra** were as grand as the palaces built in the Persian empire.
- Fragments of stone pillars and their stubs have been found at **Kumhrar** in modern Patna, which indicate the existence of a huge building with 80 pillars.
- Mauryan pillars made of a single piece of yellow sandstone is also found which was brilliantly polished.
- Carved top with lion and bull are evidenced of unique architectural developments of that time. Mauryan craftsmen also started the tradition of making rock-cut caves for the Buddhist monks. The oldest example of this is the **Barabar Caves.**

- In the Mauryan period, the baked bricks were started using in North-East India. **Baked brick structures** made during this period have been found mainly in Bihar and Uttar Pradesh.
- It is known from the excavations that logs of wood were used to build important water channels and dams to protect against floods and external attacks.
- **Ringed wells** first came into prevalence during the Mauryan period which later spread to the outer provinces of the empire.
- The potteries of Mauryan period was called **Northern Black Polished Ware** (NBPW). It is associated with the second urbanisation in India. These were made of clay with black polish and were highly glazed in appearance.
- In Bangladesh, inscriptions of **Mahasthan** in Maurya Brahmi script have been found in Bogra district and Northern Black Polished Pottery has been found at Bangrah in Midnapore district.

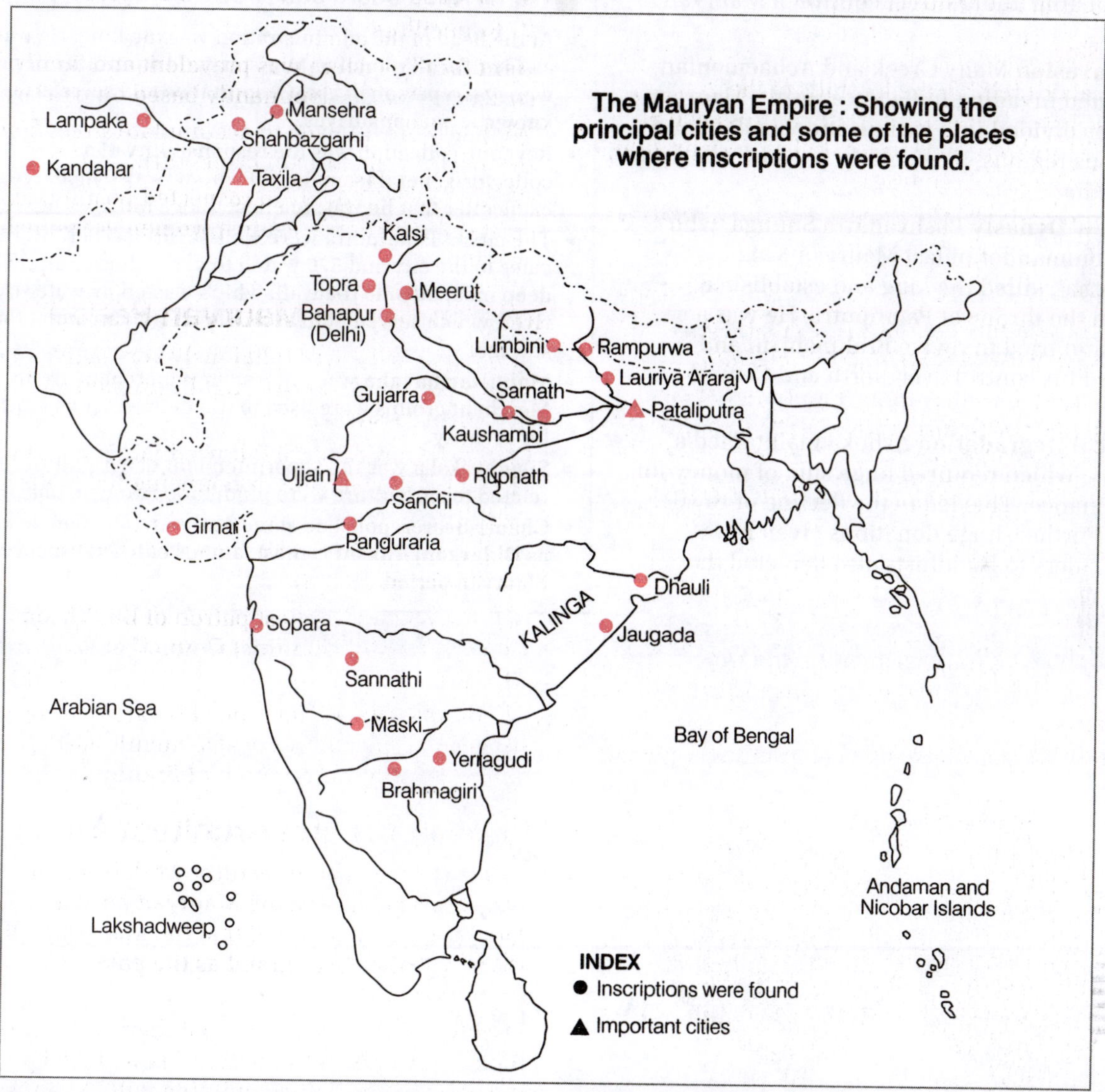

- The settlement of **Shishupalgarh** (Odisha) is believed to be from the third century BC of the Mauryan period. And here, along with the Northern Black Polished Pottery, iron tools and Punch Marked Coins have also been found. Iron tools and weapons of that time have also been found at many places in Andhra Pradesh and Karnataka.
- The art of iron-making spread to some parts of the country through Mauryan contacts. With the spread of iron, some improved methods of clearance of forest and farming began. As a result, conditions for the rise of the Chedi kingdom were created in that region.

Decline of Mauryan Empire

Decline of the Mauryan empire can be attributed to many factors. Not a single reason dominated, rather it was the accumulation of all the reasons that were related by the chain reaction.

These were :

- **Weak and Incapable Rulers** After the death of Ashoka, Mauryan empire was ruled by numerous weak and incapable rulers, which resulted into decrease of area under direct control of Mauryan empire.
- **Foreign Invasion** Many Greek and Achaemenian rulers started invading India. As a result, Mauryan empire was divided into various independent and autonomous regions, particularly in North-Western parts of India.
- **Rise of New Dynasty** Pushyamitra Shunga, who was the Commander of last Mauryan King 'Brahadratha', killed the king and established himself on the throne at Pataliputra. He was a Brahmin and tried to revive Brahmanism and established his control over North and Central India.
- **Economical Degradation** Ashoka maintained a large army, which required huge sum of money for its maintenance. This led to the decline of royal treasury. Further, huge donations given by Mauryan rulers to Buddhists also depleted the treasury.
- **Reaction of Brahmins** Although Ashoka adopted policies of non-violence and prohibition of sacrificial rituals, but it displeased Brahmanical sacrificial order. This resulted into increased support of Brahmins to create displeasure and sense of insecurity against Mauryans (like Pushyamitra Shunga). As a result, many new dynasties emerged during this time, were ruled by Brahmin kings e.g., Satavahana, Shunga, etc.

Extra Facts From Tamil Nadu Board and NIOS

- At the head of the administration was the king. He was assisted by a Council of Ministers and a purohita or priest, who was a person of great importance and secretaries known as mahamatriyas.
- Revenue collection was the responsibility of a collector-general (samaharta) who was also incharge of exchequer that he was, in effect, like a Minister of Finance.
- The city of Pataliputra were well-secured. There were 64 gates to the city and 570 watch towers. There was a wide and deep moat outside the wall, which wasted by water from the river, which served both as a defence and an outlet for sewage.
- **Maha-sarthavaha** was the leader of merchant group. Merchant groups were used to travel together as a caravan for security.
- Sitadhyaksha was the superintendent of agriculture. Taxes related to agriculture were pindikara, Hiranya, bhaga, etc.
- Chauri-Bearer, polished stone sculpture of a female known as **Didarganj Yakshi** is most famous cultural aspect of Mauryan period.

Post-Mauryan Period

[SOURCES]

Class-VI Old NCERT Chap 6 (India from 200 BC to 300 AD), Class-VI Old NCERT Chap 10 (Traders, Kings and Pilgrimages), Class-XI Old NCERT Chap 16 (Central Asian Contacts and Towns), Class-XII New NCERT Chap 17 (The Age of Satvahanas), Class-XII New NCERT Chap 2 (King, Farmers and Towns), Chap 3 (Kinship, Caste and Class), Chap 4 (Thinkers, Beliefs and Buildings) Tamil Nadu Board (Class XI), NIOS

- With the fall of Mauryan empire, **Pushyamitra Shunga** came to the Magadha empire. However, there were many large and small kingdoms which also came up in Indian sub-continent after 185 BC onwards, settled and had deep influence.
- **Indo-Greeks, Parthians, Kushanas and Shakas** came as invaders in North-Western India.
- Indigenous kingdoms like Satavahana, Chola, Chera and Pandya rose in the Deccan and the Southern India.
- The Post-Mauryan period was rich in cultural interaction and emergence of new centres of art and architecture. Increase in trade activities led to economic prosperity in this period.
- The important sources of information about Post-Mauryan period are *Gargi Samhitra* (Sage Garga) and *Mahabhasya* of **Patanjali**, *Malavikagnimitram* of **Kalidasa**, *Harshacharita* of **Banabhatta**, *Milindapanho* of **Nagasena**, etc.
- Works of Greek historians like **Pliny, Plutarch** and **Ptolemy** also throw light on the history of this period.
- Early Tamil literature (the Sangam texts) also mentions different categories of people living in the villages-large landowners or vellalar, ploughmen or uzhavar and slave or adimai.

Indigenous Kingdoms in Post-Mauryan Period

The indigenous kingdoms in Post-Mauryan period are discussed below :

Shunga Dynasty (185-75 BC)

- The founder of this dynasty was **Pushyamitra Shunga**, who was a Commander General in the Mauryan empire. Shunga overthrew the last Mauryan King **Brihadratha.** Vidisha was the capital of Shungas.
- Pushyamitra Shunga followed Brahminism. Some accounts portrayed him as a persecutor of Buddhists and destroyer of stupas but no authoritative evidences have been found so far.
- His successor **Agnimitra Shunga** renovated the Stupas at Sanchi and Barhut. He further beautified the sculptured stone gateway at Sanchi, which was built by king Ashoka.
- He performed Vedic sacrifices such as **Ashvamedha, Rajasuya** and **Vajapeya**.
- Agnimitra reign lasted from about 149 to 141 BC. Agnimitra was the hero of Kalidasa's poem, *Malavikagnimitram*. Agnimitra was succeeded by **Sujyeshtha** and **Vasumitra** respectively.
- The Shunga period witnessed the revival of Brahmanism and growing importance of Bhagvat religion.

- The Shunga ruler Bhagabhadra built the Heliodorus pillar at Vidisha in Madhya Pradesh, which was dedicated to Vasudeva, in Sanskrit inscription, dated around 100 BC.

Kanvas Dynasty (75-30 BC)

- The last Shunga King **Devabhuti** was murdered by one of his ministers **Vasudeva,** who founded Kanva dynasty in 75 BC. Puranas designate the kings of Kanva dynasty as *'Sungabrithyas'* or 'the Servants of Shungas'.
- The empire was divided into parts of Eastern India and Central India. The Kanva dynasty had claimed **Vidisa** as their capital.
- The Kanva kings were Brahmins and they traced their origin to **Rishi Kanva**.
- The last ruler of the Kanva dynasty **Susarman** was killed by the Satavahana rulers..

Satavahana Dynasty (230 BC-220 AD)

- Satavahanas succeeded the Mauryas in the Deccan region.
- In the Puranas, Satavahanas are mentioned as *Andhras*, *Andhrabhiritiya* and *Andhrajatiyah*. According to the Puranas, Satavahanas ruled for around 300 years.
- *Aitreya Brahmana* mention them as the descendants of sage **Vishvamitra**.
- Forest areas were cleared in certain regions for establishing villages. Satavahanas built roads to facilitate better communication in the Northern Deccan, i.e., the Godavari and Krishna Delta regions.

Important Satavahana Kings

The description of important Satavahana kings are given below :

Satakarni I (106 -130 BC)

- Satakarni I was called 'the **Lord of Dakshinapatha**'.
- He conquered Western Malwa, Anupa (Narmada valley) and Vidarbha (Berar).
- After his demise, Sakas attacked Satavahanas and pushed them out of Nashik towards Andhra region.

Hala (20-24 AD)

- The **Matsya Purana** mentions him (Hala) as the 17th ruler of Satavahana dynasty.
- He is famous for compiling *Gaha Sattasai* anthology in Prakrit.
- His Commander-in-Chief **Vijayananda** led a successful campaign in Ceylon.

Gautamiputra Satakarni (106-130 AD)

- Under the leadership of Gautamiputra Satakarni, Satavahanas attacked Sakas and regained Western Maharashtra.
- His kingdom was from Krishna in the South to Malwa and Saurashtra in the North and from Berar in the East to the Konkan in the West.
- In a **Nasik inscription** of his mother **Gautami Balashri,** he is described as the destroyer of the **Sakas**, **Pahlavas** and the **Yavanas** (Greeks). It mentions that he donated 200 *'nivaratanas'* of land to the ascetics.

Vashishtiputra Pulumayi (130-154 AD)

- Vashishtiputra Pulumayi extended Satavahana power upto Krishna and conquered **Bellary**.
- Vasishtiputra Satakarni married daughter of Saka ruler **Rudradaman I**, which is testified from **Kanheri inscription**. The step contained the hostilities between the two kingdoms.
- During his reign, old stupa at Amaravati was repaired.

Yajna Sri Satakarni (165-194 AD)

- He recovered Malwa and Konkan from the Saka rulers.
- Later, with the weakening of the Saka kingdom, Satavahanas also conquered **Kathiawar** in the North and Krishna delta in the South.

Aspects of Material Culture in Satavahana Kingdom

- The people of the Deccan were well-known with the use of iron and agriculture.
- The Satavahanas exploited the rich mineral resources of the Deccan such as iron ores from **Karimnagar** and **Warangal** and gold from **Kolar** fields.
- Coins of lead were mostly issued, which was the main resource found in the Deccan. However, coins of copper and bronze were also issued. There was regular use of fire-baked bricks and use of roof tiles.
- The drains were covered and underground to lead waste water into soakage pits. The Andhra Pradesh in the East Deccan included 30 walled towns, besides numerous villages.

Social Condition in Satavahana Kingdom

- There were four classes in the social hierarchy. **Gautamiputra Satakarni** claimed to have re-established this system.
- Due to increased importance of towns, merchants named themselves after the towns to which they belonged.
- **Mahabhojas, Maharathis** and **Mahasenapati** were the higher strata of the society.

- Merchants gave generous donations to the Buddhist monks.
- Mothers enjoyed a higher status in the Satavahana dynasty as the Kings were named after their mothers. The names **Gautamiputra** and **Vashishthiputra** indicates the importance given to women in the period.
- Satavahana ruling family was patriarchal because succession to the throne passed to the male member.

Religious Life in Satavahana Kingdom

- The Satavahana rulers were **Brahmins**. Vedic customs including Ashvamedha and Vajapeya were performed by the Satavahanas.
- **Vaishnava cults** of **Krishna**, **Vasudeva**, etc were highly worshipped during this period. But, Satavahanas were equally patronised Buddhism as well.
- The **cult of Bodhisattvas** became popular during this period. According to this, any person can attain enlightenment like Buddha, through paths of Buddha.
- Buddhism also flourished under the Satavahanas through granting land and financial aid to the monks. Mahayana Buddhism became popular with the artisan class.
- **Nagarjunakonda** and **Amaravati** in Andhra Pradesh became important Buddhist pilgrimage centres along with Nashik and Junnar areas of Western Maharashtra.

Administration in Satavahana Kingdom

- The Satavahana rulers followed **Dharmashastras** and considered King as the custodian of *Dharma*. The Kings were compared to gods and mythical heroes like **Rama**, **Bhima**, **Arjuna** and so on.
- Many of the administrative mechanisms during the time of Ashoka were retained by the rulers. The districts were called *Ahara* while their officials were known as *Mahamatras* and *Amatyas*.
- The kingdom was divided into administrative units which were ruled by civil and military governors.
- The rural administration was carried out by *Gaulmika* who was the head of a military regiment consisting of nine chariots, nine elephants, 25 horses and 45-foot-soldiers.
- Satavahanas maintained an army of 1,00,000 infantry, 2,000 cavalry and 1,000 elephants.
- The military character of the Satavahana kingdom can be traced from the words like *Kataka* and *Skandhas* that are repeatedly used in their inscriptions.
- Satavahanas granted **tax-free villages** to Brahmanas and Buddhist monks. These areas were free from any administrative interference and were independent within the Satavahana Kingdom.
- The kingdom had **three grades of feudatories**. The highest grade was *Raja* (King), who had the right to mint coins. The second grade was *Mahabhoja*, while the third grade was *Senapati*.

Art and Architecture of Satavahana Kingdom

- Many *Chaityas* (Buddhist place of worship) and *Vihara* (monasteries) were cut out of the solid rock in the North-Western Deccan or Maharashtra.
- **Karle** in Western Maharashtra is the most renowned site of Buddhist architecture. It is about 40 m long, 15 m wide and 15 m high.
- There are three viharas in Nasik and it is believed to have been constructed in the second century AD since, it has the inscriptions of **Nahapana** and **Gautamiputra**.
- The rock-cut architecture is also found in the Krishna-Godavari region in Andhra Pradesh. Some famous Buddhist stupas are in **Amaravati** and **Nagarjunakonda**.
- Amaravati stupa has sculpture that depicts various scenes from the life of Buddha. Its dome measured 53 m across the base and 33 m in height.
- Nagarjunakonda prospered under the patronage of *Ikshvakus*, the successors of Satavahanas.
- Other than Buddhist monasteries, Nagarjunakonda has the earliest Brahmanical brick temples. There are around 24 Buddhist monasteries in Nagarjunakonda.
- Terracottas and their moulds were found from Kondapur, which is 65 kms from Hyderabad. Terracottas were owned by the extremely rich people of the town.
- Indian ivories have been found from Rome and Afghanistan. They are linked to the ivory objects excavated from Satavahana sites in the Deccan.

Language in Satavahana Kingdom

- **Prakrit** was the official language of Satavahanas. All of their inscriptions were in Prakrit written with the **Brahmi script**, just like the **Ashokan inscriptions**.
- Some Satavahana kings have composed Prakrit literary works. One such text *Gathasattasai* is attributed to Satavahana king Hala. It consisted of 700 verses.
- The most celebrated Prakrit poet **Gunadya** had written *Brihat Katha*.

Economic Condition

- Major economic system of Satavahana and other contemporary dynasties were well organised and in systematic manner.
- There was all round development in the field of agriculture, industry and trade during this period.

- **Agriculture** was the main occupation of a large section of the people.
- The paddy transplantation was a well-known art of the Satavahanas. The area between the Krishna and Godavari, formed a **great rice bowl**.
- The *gramakshetra* was protected area by fences and field-watchmen against pests like birds and beasts.
- The entire coast tract from **Kaveripattinam** to **Tamralipti** was the centre of commercial activity. There were silver, copper, lead and potin coins in the Satavahana empire.
- In a village settlement found in **Karimnagar** district (Telangana), carpenters, blacksmiths, goldsmiths, potters, etc lived in separate quarters and agricultural, and other labourers lived at other end.
- Weapons, sickles, balance rods and other equipment were excavated from **Karimnagar** and **Nalgonda** districts.
- **Eighteen types of 'guilds'** were mentioned in the literature. Guilds became an important institution in the economy.
- The guilds implemented and defined rules of work and controlled the quality of the finished product and its prices to safeguard both the artisans and the customers.

Ikshvaku Dynasty

- Ikshvakus were the successors of **Satavahanas** in the Deccan region.
- They ruled in the Eastern Krishna-Guntur region, from their capital at **Vijayapuri** (modern Nagarjunakonda in Andhra Pradesh) during third and fourth centuries AD.
- There are not much historical details available about this dynasty, though **Matsya Purana** mentioned Ikshvakus as **Shriparvatiya Andhras**.
- The Ikshvaku kings were *Shaivites* and performed Vedic rites. Buddhism was also patronised during their reign.

Foreign Kingdoms in Post-Mauryan Period

The Foreign Kingdoms in Post-Mauryan period were :

Indo-Greeks

- The descendants of Greek generals of **Alexander** who ruled Iran and Afghanistan carried out an invasion in India and conquered parts of Punjab and Kabul valley.
- The kingdom started when Graco-Bactrian King **Demetrius** (son of Euthydemus I) invaded India around 180 BC. He conquered Southern Afghanistan and parts of Punjab.
- The most famous Indo-Greek King was **Menander I Soter**, also known as Minedra, Minadra or Milinda (in Pali).
- He was initially a king of Bactria. His empire extended from Kabul river valley in the West to the Ravi river in the East and from Swat valley in the North to Arachosia (Helmand in Afghanistan).
- The Indo-Greek Kings minted coins and these coins help to understand the history of their respective kingdoms. Some of their kings, (e.g. Menander), became Buddhist, others worshipped Lord Vishnu as well.

Sakas (Indo-Scythians)

- In the second century BC, Central Asian nomadic tribes and tribes from the Chinese region invaded the region of present-day Kazakhstan whose inhabitants were Scythians.
- This promoted the Scythians to move towards Bactria and Parthia. After defeating the Parthian king, they moved towards India. Scythians who migrated to India are known as **Indo-Scythians**.
- Sakas came to North-Western India after crossing Hindukush. They ruled Sindh and Saurashtra.
- Sakas were in constant confrontation with the Satavahanas in the South and Kushanas in the North.
- Their most powerful king **Rudradaman I** had resisted the expansion of Satavahana to the North of Narmada.
- He issued the first ever long inscription in chaste Sanskrit known as **Junagarh inscription**.
- Junagadh inscription mentions the Girnar lake, with embankments and water channels, was built by a local governor during the rule of the Mauryas. Rudradaman was ruling in the area, claimed to have got the lake repaired using his own resources, without imposing any tax on his subjects.

Parthians

- The Saka rule in North-Western part of India was followed by the Parthians.
- Parthians had their roots in Iran and from there, they migrated to India.
- Compared with the Sakas and Greeks, they ruled over only a small portion of **North-Western India** in first century AD. The most renowned Parthian king was **Gondophernes**.
- Parthians were noted for the construction of the Buddhist monastery Takht-i-Bahi (UNESCO World Heritage Site) in Mardan, Pakistan.

Kushanas

- The Kushanas were originally from the **Chinese Turkestan** and came to **Afghanistan** in the first century AD.
- Kushanas are considered to be one of the five branches of the **Yuezhi** tribe who lived in the Chinese frontier or Central Asia.
- They displaced Indo-Greeks, Sakas and Parthians and established their kingdom in Taxila and Peshawar.
- Kushanas expanded further and later controlled the entire Punjab plain and Western Ganga plain.
- A large number of Roman gold coins found from this era indicate the prosperity of India at that time and also the growing trade with the Romans.
- Some historians feel that Kushanas considered themselves godlike. Many Kushanas ruler also adopted the title Devaputra or 'Son of God', possibly inspired by Chinese rulers who called themselves son of heaven.

Kujula Kadphises

- **Kujula** was the successor of **Hermaeus**, the last Greek prince of the Kabul valley.
- He minted copper coins, in place of coins. Roman influence can be seen from the coins minted under his kingship.

Vima Kadphises

- Vima was the son of **Kujula**.
- He further expanded the Kushana empire and annexed Taxila and Punjab to his empire.

Kanishka

- Kanishka was the most powerful Kushana king and he adopted the title **Kaiser**.
- He controlled Uttar Pradesh, Punjab, Kashmir, North-Western Frontier Province and Bahawalpur of Northern Sind.
- Under his patronage, the **Fourth Buddhist Council** was organised in Kashmir in 78 AD.

Post-Mauryan Administration

- Sakas were the first to introduce the *Satrapa* system of Government in India. The chief feature of this system was a joint rule by *Mahakshatrapa* (Raja) and *Satrapa* (Yuvaraja).
- Sakas and the Parthians used to govern many of their Indian processions through *Strategoi* and *Satraps*.
- The district officer was known as Merider and the military commandant as *Strategos* under the Greek rulers.
- The general administrative structure did not differ from that of the earlier period. Senior officials were known as *Mahamatras* and *Rajjukas*.

Social Condition in Post-Mauryan Period

- New ideas on religion, culture, art and administration entered into various aspects of Indian life due to foreigners.
- Foreigners were also incorporated into the caste structure. Indian sources referred Greeks as Yavanas.
- Sakas were absorbed to the **Kshatriya caste**, which later in the 9th and 10th century emerged as Rajput clan.
- The growth of arts, crafts and trade resulted in attaining changed social status by the Vaishyas and Shudras.

Religious Condition in Post-Mauryan Period

- In the Post-Mauryan phase, people followed Vedic **Sanantanadharma**, **Buddhism** and **Jainism**.
- Inspite of their personal affiliation to a particular religion or deity, the rulers, they never appear to have made that particular religion as the state religion.
- Along with Vedic ritualism, **Bhagavatism** also flourished during this period.
- Greek ambassador **Heliodorus** had set up a pillar in honour of Vishnu near Vidisha.
- **Mahayana** and **Hinayana** sects emerged from Buddhism.
- Like the Vedic Dharma and Buddhism, Jainism too underwent transformation in this period. It split into **Digambaras** and **Shwetambaras** by the first century AD.

Trade in Post-Mauryan Period

- Massive trade expansion and related activities occurred during this period. The trade between India and Rome increased substantially which is evident from the trade activities that occurred in the South of **Satavahanas**, i.e., Tamil kingdoms.
- Romans mainly imported spices from India, but at the same time, muslin, pearls, jewellery and precious stones were also exported. Some products were also brought in India from China and were later exported to the Eastern part of the **Roman empire**.
- Romans exported wine and various types of pottery to India. **Kushanas** also carried out trade with the Romans.
- A large number of gold coins was exported to India by the Romans. The total number of Roman gold coins found in India during excavations is around 6,000.
- Roman writer **Pliny** had written that Rome was drained of gold due to its trade relations with India.

- Many Roman traders lived in South India during this period and many traders from South India had also settled in Rome.

Coinage in Post-Mauryan Period

- Roman gold coins were largely used for higher transactions. **Indo-Greek rulers** had minted few but finest gold coins, but Kushanas issued gold coins in considerable numbers.
- The **Kushanas** extracted gold from Central Asia. They might have also procured gold from Karnataka and the gold mines of **Dhalbhum** in present Bankura district of West Bengal.
- Kushanas issued **Dinar type gold**, which later became abundant under Gupta rule.
- Day-to-day transactions were carried out using coins made from lead, potin or copper. Kushanas had also issued coins made out of copper.

Art and Architecture in Post-Mauryan Period

- The cultural interaction with Western Asia enriched Indian art.
- Sculptures of **Greek** and **Roman Gods** were brought into the cities of Northern India.
- The new style of sculpturing also interested the Indian artists in Gandhara, which later came to be known as the **Gandhara School of Art**.
- The image of the Buddha emerged during the first and second century AD in India. It was the first time any God-like creation on stone was engraved and started worshipping.
- Another set of artists in Mathura created a new style that was different from the Greek model. This later became **Mathura School of Art**.
- Manufacturing of luxurious handicrafts also became pre-dominant in this period. Many such craft materials were found in Kushana complexes.
- Pre-Mauryan text *Digha Nikaya* mentioned about 24 occupations, while the post-Mauryan text *Mahavastu* mentioned about 36 kinds of workers living in the town of Rajgir.
- *'Milindapanho'* mentions about 75 works, out of which 60 are connected to various types of crafts.
- Eight crafts were associated with gold, silver, lead, tin, copper, brass, iron and precious stones or jewels. Various kinds of brass, zinc, antimony and red arsenic were also mentioned in *Milindapanho*.
- Iron artefacts were found out in large numbers during excavations denoting to Kushana periods.

Literature in Post-Mauryan Period

- Kushana period witnessed development of literature and Sanskrit language. Major Sanskrit texts of the period were written during this time.
- *Buddhacharita* by **Asvaghosha**, *Mahabhibhasha* by **Vasumitra**, *Madhyamika-Sutra* by **Nagarjuna** and Sushruta *Sushruta Samhitha* is some of the important works of this period.
- '*Milindapanho*' by **Nagasena** contained the dialogues between himself and king Menander.
- **Bhasa** wrote thirteen plays including *Svapnavasavadatta*, *Ravanabadh* and *Urubhanga*.

Science and Technology in Post-Mauryan Period

- In the Post-Mauryan Period, much progress was made in the field of metallurgy. The presence of Greek engineers in Kushana court shows an exchange in this field. Engineering skills in the building of dams and irrigation tanks are evident from their remains.
- Geometry seems to have been well-developed and it was applied widely. In the field of astronomy, Greek influence was quite evident from the text *Panch Siddhantika*.
- Indian medicine made remarkable progress during this period. Kanishka's court physician **Charaka** wrote *Charaka Samhita* which is major work on Ayurveda.
- The school at Varanasi specialised in Surgery and *Sushrita Samhita* an encyclopaedia of surgery compiled by **Sushruta**. He also stayed at the court of Kanishka.

Extra Facts From Tamil Nadu Board and NIOS

- Another Indo-Greek king whose name is remembered is **Antialicidas** (or Antialkidas). He is known to us primarily because his emissary. Heliodorus, who was sent to the court of King Bhagabhadra erected a pillar or *garuda-dhvaja* with its capital adorned by a figure of Garuda, in honour of God Krishna.
- The first Saka ruler in India was Maues or Moa/Moga. He occupied Gandhara, driving a wedge into the Indo-Greek Kingdoms. They became assimilated into Hindu society and began to adopt Hindu names and religious beliefs.
- Kushana coins were of the highest equality and conformed to the weight standards of Roman coin. In the coins, Kushana rulers are referred to as 'King of Kings', 'Caesar', 'lord of all lands' and by other such titles.
- Greek astronomers were referred to as Yavanacharya. The knowledge of astronomy has been borrowed from Central Asia.
- **Takht-i-Bahi** inscription recovered from Mardan near Peshawar. It is the source of 'The Parthian' rule.

09

The Age of the Guptas

[SOURCES]

Class-VI New NCERT Chap 9 (New Empires and Kingdoms), Class-VI Old NCERT Chap 7 (The Age of Guptas), Class-XI Old NCERT Chap 20 (The Rise and Growth of the Gupta Empire), Chap 21 (Life in Gupta Age) Tamil Nadu Board (Class XI), NIOS

Gupta Empire

- The disintegration of Kushanas in the North and the Satavahanas in the Deccan paved way for the emergence of several minor powers. Among them, the Guptas laid the foundation of the second empire in Ancient India.
- The Guptas set up their rule over **Anuganga** (the middle Gangetic basin), **Prayag** (modern Prayagraj), **Saketa** (modern Ayodhya) and **Magadha** in 320 AD.
- The Guptas were not only powerful monarchs, but they were also the patrons of learning. The Gupta age is called as the **Classical Age** or the **Golden Age** of India. The Gupta period was defined as the beginning of new creativity, flourishing arts, prominent literature and great scholars.
- There is scarcity of information about the origin of Guptas. It is certain that the Guptas belonged to wealthy family and influencial landowners, who gradually gained control over the Magadha.
- **Srigupta** (240-280 AD) was the founder of the Gupta dynasty. He used the title of 'Maharaja'. The **Poona copper plate inscription** of **Prabhavati Gupta** describes Srigupta as the 'Adiraja of Gupta dynasty'.
- **Ghatotkacha** (280-319 AD) succeeded his father Srigupta. He was also given the title of Maharaja.

Sources of Gupta Empire

Literary sources, inscriptions and numismatic evidences help to reconstruct the history of the Gupta empire.

Literary Sources

- The **Puranas** (Vaya, Vishnu, Matsya, Skanda and Markandeya) give royal geneology of Gupta kings.
- *Devi-Chandraguptam* and *Mudra-Rakshasa* by *Vishakhadatta* give information about rise of the Guptas.
- Kalidasa's *Abhijanasakuntalam, Meghadutam* and *Kumarasambhava* provide reliable information about the governance, society and religion of Gupta age.
- Chinese traveller **Fa-Hien**, who visited India during the reign of Chandragupta II has provided socio-economic and religious condition of the period.

Inscriptions

- These are much reliable sources of Gupta dynasty.
- Important inscriptions are **Allahabad Pillar Inscription** of Chandragupta II and **Junagarh Rock Inscription** of Skandagupta.

Numismatic Evidence

- The Gupta coins, particularly Kumaradevi-type coins of Chandragupta I give valuable information of cultural, religious and political conditions of the Gupta period.

Rulers of Gupta Empire

The rulers of Gupta empire are discussed as follows :

Chandragupta I (319-335 AD)

- The first important king of the Gupta's dynasty was Chandragupta I. He married to a Lichchhavi princess from Nepal, which strengthened his position.
- He accended throne in about 320 AD. He ruled over Saket (the region of Ayodhya), Prayag (Allahabad) and Magadha.
- Chandragupta I was the first Gupta ruler to assume the title **Maharajadhiraja** and issue gold coins.

Samudragupta (335-380 AD)

- Chandragupta I was succeeded by his son Samudragupta who expanded his empire enormously.
- **Allahabad Pillar Inscription**, describes his achievements. This inscription was composed by **Harisena**, a poet at the court of Samudragupta. It was originally a pillar on which emperor Ashoka had an edict inscribed.
- The Allahabad Pillar Inscription also known as Prayag Prashasti. In this inscription, Samudragupta has been described as a Purusha (the Supreme being).
- Samudragupta was known as the **Napoleon of India** as he was undefeated throughout his political life.
- Samudragupta was not merely a conqueror, he was also a poet and musician. In one of his coins, he is shown playing a Veena.

The king who played the Veena

Places Conquered by Samudragupta

The places and the countries conquered by Samudragupta can be divided into five groups :

- **Group One** It includes princes of the Ganga-Yamuna doab, who were defeated and whose kingdoms were incorporated into the Gupta empire.
- **Group Two** It includes the rulers of the Eastern Himalayan states and some frontier states such as princes of Nepal, Assam, Bengal, etc. It also covers some republics of Punjab.
- **Group Three** It includes the Forest Kingdoms situated in the Vindhya region and known as Atavika Rajyas.
- **Group Four** It includes 12 rulers of the Eastern Deccan and South India who were conquered and liberated. The rule of Samudragupta reached as far as Kanchi in Tamil Nadu.
- **Group Five** It includes the Sakas and Kushans; some of them ruling in Afghanistan.

Empire Outside India

- The prestige and influence of Samudragupta spread even outside India.
- According to a Chinese source, **Meghavarman,** the ruler of Sri Lanka, sent a missionary to Samudragupta for permission to build a Buddhist temple at Bodh Gaya. This was granted and the temple developed into a huge monastic establishment.

Ramagupta (380 AD)

- Ramagupta's name does not appear in the official records of the Gupta dynasty, but according to Sanskrit play *Devichandraguptam,* he was emperor of Gupta dynasty.
- The play mentions that Ramagupta surrendered to a Shaka enemy as he was weak ruler. Later, his brother **Chandragupta II** killed the Shaka enemy.
- Some coins discovered in Central India have been attributed to Ramagupta.

Chandragupta II (380-412 AD)

- *Devichandraguptam* of **Vishakhadatta** tells us that Chandragupta II removed and killed his brother Ramagupta and ascended the throne.
- The Gupta empire reached its height in terms of territorial expansion during the reign Chandragupta II.
- He extended the limits of the empire by matrimonial alliances and conquests. He married his daughter **Prabhavati** with Vakataka prince **Rudrasena-II**.
- He conquered Western Malwa and Gujarat, which had been under the rule of the Sakas for about four centuries. The conquest gave Chandragupta the Western Sea coast, famous for trade and commerce.
- Chandragupta II adopted the title of *Vikramaditya*, which had been first used by an Ujjain ruler in 58 BC as a mark of victory over the Sakas.
- It was in Chandragupta's reign that the Chinese pilgrim **Fa-Hien** (399-414 AD) visited India and wrote an elaborate account of the life of its people. He also collected rare Buddhist manuscripts.

Nine Gems of Chandragupta II

- The court of Chandragupta II at Ujjain was adorned by numerous scholars, which were known as *Navratnas* or Nine Gems.
- These were Kalidasa, Vetalabhatta, Varahamihira, Vararuchi, Amarsimha, Dhanvantri, Kahapanaka, Sanku and Harisena.

Kumaragupta (415-455 AD)

- He performed an **Ashvamedha** sacrifice and also issued Ashvamedha type of coins. The epigraphic records show that he organised the administration of vast empire.
- He also laid the foundation of Nalanda University.
- **Bilsada edict** provides information about beginning of his reign.

Nalanda University

Skandagupta (455-467 AD)

- He was one of the greatest rulers of Gupta dynasty. His chief claim to fame in Gupta history rests upon his remarkable defence of the territorial integrity of the Gupta empire, both against foreign invasion as well as internal upheavals.
- He defeated the Huna Armies as indicated by the **Bhittari Stone Inscription**.
- His **Girnar Inscription** mentions the breach at Lake Sudarshana in 455 AD which had been built during Chandragupta Maurya reign and its repair next year within a short period of 2 months.
- With his death in 467 AD, the glory of Gupta empire faded with a rapid pace.

Society and Administration in Gupta Empire

The society and administration in Gupta period was highly centralised. All the powers were concentrated with the king.

Provincial and Local Administration

- The Gupta's organised a system of provincial and local administration.
- The empire was divided into divisions (*Bhuktis*) and each *bhukti* was placed under the charge of an *Uparika*. The *bhuktis* were divided into districts (*Visyas*), which were placed under the charge of *Vishayapati*. In Eastern India, the *Vishyas* were divided into *Vithis*, which again were divided into villages.
- The village headman became more important during this period. He managed the village affairs with the assistance of elders.
- There were Samantas at local level in Gupta period. They maintained themselves through local resources including control over land. They offered homage and provide military support to rulers.
- **No land transactions** could be come into force without the consent of town's leading local elements.
- In the urban administration, organised professional bodies were given considerable share. The artisans, merchants and scribes served on same corporate body.
- The common organisation, artisans and bankers were organised into their own separate guilds.
- **Numerous guilds of artisans** and traders were located at Bhita and Waist. At Mandasor, silk weavers maintained their own guilds and in the district of Bulandshahar in Western Uttar Pradesh, oil-pressers had their own guilds.
- Guild were denoted with the term known as 'Shrenis'. These guilds probably procured raw material, regulated production and marketed the finished product.
- The **representative administration** was prevailed only in North Bengal, Bihar, Uttar Pradesh and some adjoining areas of Madhya Pradesh, which were ruled directly by the officers appointed by the Gupta kings.
- The charters marked with the royal Garuda seal seems to have been issued to the vassals.
- Grant of **fiscal and administrative concessions** to priests and administration became a regular affair in Gupta period.
- Religious functionaries were granted **tax free land** and they were authorised to collect all the taxes from the peasants, which could have otherwise gone to the emperor. The villages granted to the beneficiaries could not be entered by royal agents.
- Abundance of gold coins suggest that higher officials were paid in cash. But many officers may have been paid by land grants as well.

Officers During Gupta Age

Name	Function
Mahabaladhikrita	Commander-in-Chief
Mahadandanayak	Chief Justice
Mahapratihar	Maintenance of Royal Palace
Mahasandhivigrahak	Post-war mediator
Dandapashika	Police Department Head
Bhandagaradhikreta	Head of Royal Treasury
Mahapakshapatalik	Head of Account Department
Vinayasthitisansathapak	Head of Education Department
Sarvadhyaksha	Inspector of all Central Department
Mahashwapati	Controller of Cavalry
Mahamahipilapati	Controller of Elephantry
Vinayapura	Official to present different fiests at the kings's court
Khadyatpakika	Inspector of Royal Kitchen

- *Nagara-shreshthi* was the chief banker and *Sarthavaha* was the leader of the merchant caravans. *Prathama-Kulika* were the chief craftsmen and the head of the *Kayasthas* or *scribe*.

Economy

- The king collected taxes varying from one-fourth to one-sixth of the produce.
- Whenever, the royal army passed through the countryside, the local people had to feed it.
- The peasants had to supply animals, food grains, furniture etc., for the maintenance of royal officers on duty in the rural areas.
- In Central and Western India, the villagers were also subjected to forced labour called **Vishti** for serving the royal army and officials.

Judiciary

- Several law-books were compiled in this period. For the first time **civil** and **criminal law** were clearly defined and demarcated.
- Theft and adultery came under criminal law. Disputes regarding various types of property came under civil law.
- The guilds of artisans, merchants and others were governed by their own laws. Seals from **Vaishali** and from **Bhita** near Allahabad indicate that these guilds were well flourished.

Bureaucracy in Administration

- During the Gupta period, **first signs of bureaucracy** emerged in India.
- The most important officers in the Gupta empire were the *Kumaramatyas*. They were appointed by the king in the home provinces and possibly paid in cash.
- Recruitment was not confined to the upper Varnas only. Several offices were in the hands of the same person and posts became hereditary.

Social Life

- The account of **Fa-Hien** gives information about the social life of Gupta era.
- He informed that Magadha was full of cities and its rich people followed Buddhism and gave ample amount of charities.
- Till 550 AD, India carried on some trade with the Eastern Roman empire, to which it exported silk.
- The striking development of the Gupta period was the emergence of priestly landlords at the cost of local peasants.
- Land grants to the Brahmanas on a large scale suggest that the **Brahmanical supremacy** reached its new height in Gupta times.
- The castes divided into numerous sub-castes as a result of two factors :
  (i) A large number of foreigners were assimilated into the Indian society and each group of foreigners was considered a new kind of Hindu Caste.
  (ii) Another reason was the absorption of many tribal people into Brahmanical society through the means of land grants.
- In some ways, the position of shudras and women improved in this period. They were now permitted to listen to the **epics** and the **Puranas**. They could also worship a new God called **Krishna**.
- During this period, the untouchables increased in number, especially the Chandalas. Fa-Hien informed that the Chandalas lived outside the village and dealt in meat and fisheries.

Trade

- With the increase in trade in the earlier period, towns grew and prospered. In the earlier part of the Gupta period, this prosperity continued.
- There was not only the trade within India itself and with Western Asia, but also with South-East Asia.
- As trade grew, knowledge of sea voyage and ship-building also improved. Larger ships were built than before and many more ships crowded into the ports along the Eastern and the Western coast.
- **Tamralipti** (Tamluk) port in the Ganga delta handled a large part of the trade with countries of South-East Asia, such as **Suvarnabhumi** (Myanmar), **Yavadvipa** (Java) and **Kamboja** (Cambodia).

- Broach, Sopara and Kalyan were the main ports on the West coast and they also sent ships to South-East Asia.
- Indian goods were taken to Mecca, Arabia, Iran and the Mediterranean lands. Caravans of traders and missionaries of religion also travelled over land to Central Asia and China.

Religion

- **Buddhism** no longer received royal patronage and **Hinduism** became a powerful religion during the Gupta era. However, the word 'Hindu' was not used until a later time by the Arabs when they referred to the people of Hind i.e., India.
- The Hindus were worshippers of Shiva, Shakti and Vishnu. **Lord Vishnu** emerged as the God of devotion and he came to be represented as the saviour of the Varna system. A whole Purana called the **Vishnu Purana** was compiled in honour of Lord Vishnu. A law-book called the *Vishnusmriti* was also named after him.
- By the fourth century AD, there appeared the famous **Vaishnava** work *Bhagavad Gita,* which taught devotion to **Lord Krishna**. It emphasised the performance of the functions assigned to each varna.
- It was believed that Vishnu sometimes comes to Earth to help men lead good lives and this is called an *Avatara* or incarnation.
- Many of the older books such as the *Ramayana,* the *Mahabharata* and some of the Puranas were compiled at this time. Now they are treated as religious texts.
- Gupta kings performed religious sacrifices, such as the Ashvamedha but these religious sacrifices were not as frequent as in Vedic times.
- A few Gupta kings were the worshippers of **Shiva**, the 'God of Destruction'. He became prominent God in later phase of Gupta era.
- Idol worship in the temples became a common feature of Hinduism from the Gupta period. The images of Gods were placed in a small room, which was called the *Garbha Griha*.
- The Gupta kings followed a policy of tolerance towards the different religious sects. There is no example of the persecution of the followers of Buddhism and Jainism.

Art and Architecture

- Both **Samudragupta** and **Chandragupta II** were patrons of art and literature.
- For the first time, in the Gupta period images of Vishnu, Shiva and some other Hindu Gods emerged in India.
- The leading God is generally represented large in size, but his subordinate gods were drawn on a smaller scale. This represents a clear social distinction and hierarchy prevailing in that era.
- The early temples were very simple, consisting of one room where the image of the God was kept. The entrance gate to this room was decorated with sculpture.
- Gradually, the number of rooms increased from one to two, three, four and many more. In Deogarh (Jhansi district), there is an example of one earliest Hindu temple in India.
- There are evidence of few temples made of brick in Uttar Pradesh and a stone temple. There are examples of brick temple like Bhitargaon in Kanpur and Bhitari in Ghazipur.
- Over two metre high bronze image of the Buddha of Gupta era is found Sultanganj near Bhagalpur.
- Beautiful images of the Buddha were made at Sarnath and Mathura. But the greatest specimen of Buddhist art is provided by the Ajanta paintings.
- These paintings (known as murals) depict various events in the life of **Gautama Buddha** and the previous life of Buddha. These paintings are lifelike and give the detailed information about cultural and social life.

Literature

- The Gupta period is remarkable for the production of secular literature. In this period, 13 plays were written by Bhasa; the most famous among them was *Urubhanga.*
- **Kalidasa** whole *Abhijnanasakuntalam,* which is considered to be one of the best hundred literary works in the world. He also wrote *Meghadutam* and *Raghuvansham.*
- 'Abhijananashakuntalam' is the story of the love between a king named Dushyanta and a young women named Shakuntala.
- The period also saw the compilation of various Smritis or the law-books written in verse form.
- One of the remarkable grammar work is *Amarakosa* by *Amarsimha,* who was a expert in the court of Chandragupta II.
- The poet Harisena was a *maha-danda-nayaka*, or chief judicial officers. He was a Kumar-amatya, meaning an important minister and a Sandhi-vigrahika, meaning a minister of war and peace.

Science

- There was a tremendous progress in the field of Mathematics, astronomy, astrology and medicine. The decimal system originated in this period during fifth century AD, as testified by a **Gupta inscription** of 448 AD from Allahabad (now Prayagraj).

- **Aryabhatta,** a great mathematician was first astronomer to state more fundamental problems of astronomy in his book *Aryabhatiya*, written in 499 AD.
- **Varahamihira** another great Mathematician and Astronomer also lived in this age. He wrote a major work *Brihatsamhita* and *Panchasiddhantika* in the field of Mathematics.
- **Brahmagupta** was other Mathematician who wrote *'Surya Siddhantika'*.
- In the field of medicine, three great physicians **Charaka, Vagbhata** and **Susruta** belonged to this period.
- The Gupta craftsmen distinguished themselves by their work in iron and bronze. The iron pillar found at Delhi near Mehrauli, which was manufactured in the fourth century AD, has not gathered any rust in the subsequent 15th centuries later.

Decline of the Gupta Empire

The Gupta Empire declined due to variety of reasons as follows :

- The successors of **Chandragupta II** had to face an invasion by the **Hunas** from Central Asia in the second half of the fifth century AD. By 485, Hunas occupied Eastern Malwa and a good portion of Central India. The intermediate regions such as Punjab and Rajasthan also came under their possession.
- **Yasodharman** of Malwa successfully challenged the authority of the Guptas and in 532 AD, set up pillars of the victory commemorating his conquest of almost the whole of Northern India.
- The governors appointed by the Gupta kings in North Bengal and their feudatories in Samatata or South-East Bengal tended to become independent.
- The **Pushyamitras** rose to power in Bihar and Uttar Pradesh and had their capital at Kannauj. It seems that by 550 AD, Bihar and Uttar Pradesh had passed out of reign of Guptas.
- The Guptas also found it difficult to maintain a large professional army on account of the growing practice of land grants for religious and other purposes, which was bound to reduce their revenues.
- The migration of a guild of silk weavers from Gujarat to Malwa in 473 AD and their adoption of non-productive professions show that there was not much demand for cloth produced by them. It shows **lack of economic prosperity**.
- The Gupta kings adopted titles such as **Paramesvara, Maharajadhiraja** and **Paramabhattaraka.** Kingship was hereditary but royal power was limited by the absence of a firm practice of primogeniture (first child receives the property). Slowly, feudalism developed in the empire.
- The king maintained a standing army, which was supplemented by the forces occasionally supplied by the feudatories. Horse archery became prominent in military tactics. They were not matched for facing external and internal enemies.

Extra Facts From Tamil Nadu Board and NIOS

- Mehrauli Iron Pillar Inscription-achievements of Chandragupta I.
- Kamandaka's Nitisara is an important literary source of political system of Gupta period and Sudraka's Mrichakatika also provide details of this period.
- Fahen's account of Mathura and Pataliputra is also an important source of Gupta period. He visited during the rule of Chandragupta II.
- The system of espionage included spies known as Dutakas in Gupta period.
- The officer who maintained records of all the land transaction in the district and the village account was known as Ustapala.
- During the Gupta period the land was classified as detailed below :

Kshetra	Cultivatable land
Khila	Waste land
Aprahata	Jungle or Waste land
Vasti	Habitable land
Gapata Saraha	Pastoral land

Important Taxes During Gupta Period

Tax	Nature
Bhaga	1/6th of the produce paid by cultivators
Bhoga	On periodic supply of froit, firewood
Kara	A periodic tax levied on the villagers
Bali	A voluntary offering by the people to the king
Udianga	Police tax for maintenance of police station
Hiranya	Tax payable on gold coins
Halivakara	A plough tax paid by cultivator
Kulipta and Upakilpta	Sale and purchase of lands

- The invention of the theory of zero and the consequent evolution of the decimal system are to be credited to this period. In the Surya Siddanta, Aryabhatta examined the true cause of solar eclipses. He also deals authored Aryabhattiyam, which deals with arithmetic, geometry and algebra. Varahamihira's Brihat Samhita is an encyclopedia of astronomy, geography, botany, etc.

Post-Gupta Era

(SOURCES)

Class-VI Old NCERT Chap 8 (The Age of Smaller Kingdoms), Class-VI New NCERT Chap 9 (New Empires and Kingdoms), Chap 9 (Traders, Kings and Pilgrim), Class-XI Old NCERT Chap 22 (Spread of Civilisation in Eastern India), Chap 23 (Harsha and His Times), Chap 24 (Formation of New States and Rural Expansion) Tamil Nadu Board (Class XI), NIOS

In the sixth century AD, with the disintegration of Gupta empire, the Northern India, slowly split up into small kingdoms, which were continually fighting with one another.

Magadha and its capital **Pataliputra**, lost importance. After the fall of the Guptas, five major centres of power emerged in North India. These are given below :

- **Maukharis** They held the region of Western Uttar Pradesh around Kannauj had conquered a part of Magadha.
  - **Isanavarman** and his son **Sarvavarman** were powerful rulers of this dynasty and had adopted the title of *Maharajadhiraja*.
- **Maitrakas** They established a kingdom in Saurashtra with Vallabhi as capital. Under the able guidance of **Bhatarka**, Vallabhi not only became a seat of learning and culture, but also a centre for trade and commerce. **Dhruvasena II** was the most important ruler of Maitrakas.
- **Gaudas** They ruled over a territory in Bengal and were quite lesser known as of the four kingdoms. Its most powerful ruler was **Shashanka.**
- Shashank with his ally Devagupta, the king of Malva waged war against Makhauris, killed **Grahavarman** and imprisoned **Rajyasri**. He even murdered her brother **Rajyavardhan**, who was the ruler of Thaneshwar.
- **Hunas** The White raced Hunas established their supremacy over Kashmir, Punjab and Western India from about 500 AD onwards. It was a barbarious race, which came to India from Central Asia.
  - **Toramana** was their oldest ruler and Mihirakula, the most uncultured one.
- **Pushyabhuti Dynasty** The major dynasty that ruled at Thanesar in Haryana and extended its authority over all the other feudatories in northern India.
  - The first ruler of this dynasty was **Prabhakaravardhana**. He assumed the title of 'Paramabhattaraka' and 'Maharajadhiraja'.
  - In *Harshacharita*, he was known as Pratapshila. Harshavardhana belonged to this dynasty.

Harshavardhana (606-647 AD)

- The early history of Harsha's reign is reconstructed from the study of his court poet **Banabhatta**, who wrote **Harshacharita** and **Kadambari**.
- Harsha moved his capital from **Thanesar** to **Kannauj**. He set out on a long campaign and conquered many parts of Northern India including the Punjab, Eastern Rajasthan and the Ganga valley as far as Assam.
- His Southward march was stopped near the bank of the Narmada river by the Chalukyan King **Pulakeshin II**, who ruled over a great part of modern Karnataka and Maharashtra with his capital in Badami in the modern Bijapur district of Karnataka.

Administration under Harshavardhana

- Harsha was an efficient administrator. He personally looked into the affairs of the state and constantly travelled into different parts of his empire.
- He governed his empire on the same lines as the Guptas did, except that his administration had become more feudal and decentralised.
- Harsha's administration was more or less based on the Gupta administration. There was a Council of Ministers to assist Harsha. They were called *Sachiv* or *Amatya*.
- The Chief Ministers of Harsha were — *Mahasandhivigradhikrita* (Minister of war and peace) *and Mahabaladhikrita* (Officer in Supreme Command in the area).
- Watcher of Royal *Harem* was known as *Yamacetis* and superintendent of soldiers barrack was called *Pathi*.
- A new post called **Rajasthaniya** was created, who was the Foreign Secretary.
- He had a standing army with the strength of 1,00,000 horses and 60,000 elephants.
- Land grants continued to be made to priests for special services tendered to the state.
- In addition, Harsha is credited with the grant of land to the officers by charters.
- These grants allowed the same concessions to priests as were allowed by the earlier grants.

Revenue System under Harsha

- The Chinese pilgrim **Hiuen-Tsang** informs us that the revenues of Harsha were divided into four parts :
  (i) One part was earmarked for the expenditure of the king.
  (ii) Second for scholars.
  (iii) Third for the endowment of officials and public servants.
  (iv) Fourth for religious purposes.
- Ministers and high rank officers of the state were endowed with land. The feudal practice of rewarding and paying officers with grants of land seems to have begun under Harsha.

Law and Order Under Harsha

- In the Empire of Harsha, law and order was not so well maintained. The Chinese pilgrim **Hiuen-Tsang** described that he was robbed of his belongings several times.
- Although, he reports that according to the laws, severe punishments were given for crime and the right hand of the robber was ampuated.

Religious Policy of Harsha

- Harsha followed a tolerant religious policy. A **Saivite** in his early years, he gradually became a great patron of Buddhism.
- He used to organise assembly at **Prayag** every 5 years, which was attended by all the tributary princes, ministers, nobles, etc.
- The Buddhists were divided into 18 Sects in the time of the Chinese pilgrim. The most famous centre was **Nalanda**, which maintained a great Buddhist university meant for Buddhist monks. It is said to have had as many as 10,000 students, monks and scholars.
- The monastery at Nalanda was supported from the revenues of 200 villages. Nalanda became a huge monastic establishment in the time of Harshavardhana.

Hiuen-Tsang's Account on Harsha

- The reign of Harsha is vividly described by the Chinese pilgrim Hiuen-Tsang, who left China in 629 AD and travelled all the way to India.
- Hiuen-Tsang described India as a rich and prosperous country. **Brahmanism**, **Buddhism** and **Jainism** were popular religions of India.
- Prayag and Kannauj in the doab had become important.
- The **Brahmanas** and **Kshatriyas** were reported to have led a simple life, but the nobles and priests led a luxurious life.
- He called Shudras as agriculturists, which is very significant information. In the earlier texts, they are represented as serving the three higher Varnas.
- The Chinese pilgrim takes notice of untouchables such as scavengers, executioners, etc. They lived outside the villages and used to consume garlic and onion.
- The dress of the people varied from region to region. He described Indians as simple, humble and honest. Indians were also particular about cleanliness.

Society Under Harsha

- Wealthy Brahmins used to get more revenue from the land. Such grants were called **Agrahara** or **Brahmadeya** grants.
- Brahmins conducted the religious ceremonies and rituals for the king. Some also wrote biographies of the king. A number of Brahmins were also employed as officers.
- People living in the towns were still mainly artisans and traders.
- Shudras were the poorest because most of them were either cultivators or peasants.

- Apart from the Shudras, there were the untouchables who continued to do the work that were considered low in society.

Economy under Harsha

- The king did not have direct control over the revenue. The systems of paying salaries by grants of revenue of land increased during this period.
- As the number of grantees increased, more and more land transferred into the hands of the grantees.
- The officers were now less dependent on the king. Those who had large grants of land often behaved like independent rulers.
- The revenue was being collected by the feudal officers and it was divided between the feudatories and the king.

Harsha Coin

Education and Learning Under Harsha

- The Brahmins were responsible not only for performing the religious ceremonies but also for teaching.
- The schools were held in temples where the higher caste children were taught. Most of them learnt **Sanskrit** and **Mathematics** and read the religious books.
- Sanskrit was still the language of learning and of literature. Perhaps, the most popular work in Sanskrit was the *Katha-Saritasagara*, a collection of stories.
- Biographies of kings were also written such as **Bilhana's** *Vikramanta-deva-charita*. **Kalhana's** remarkable history of Kashmir called the *Rajatarangini* was written in the 12th century.
- The worship of Krishna had increased in Northern India and the story of the love of Radha and Krishna was very popular. Many poems were written on this genere and **Jayadeva's** *Gita Govinda* was one of these.
- In addition to Sanskrit, other languages were developing. They arose out of the **Apabhramsha** languages spoken by the common people.
- The early forms of Marathi and Gujarati were being spoken in Western India and Bengali in Eastern India.
- **Harsha** was a literary figure. He wrote three plays namely *Nagananda*, *Ratnavali* and *Priyadarsika* in Sanskrit.

Spread of Civilisation in Eastern India : Kamarupa Kingdom

- In Eastern India, Kamarupa was the major kingdom that flourished. The modern state of Assam was called **Kamarupa** and **Pragjyotish** in Ancient times.
- There was another kingdom called **Davaka** in this region, which has been mentioned in the Allahabad Inscription of Samudragupta as the border state along with Kamarupa.
- The kingdom of Kamarupa at one time extended up to Northern and Western Bengal, some bordering lands of China as well as Davaka.
- The region was ruled by a single dynasty from the time of Mahabharata upto the middle of the seventh century till **Bhaskaravarman**. The sources of history of this dynasty are the **Dubi** and **Nidhanapur** copper plates of Bhaskaravarman.
- Some other sources include genealogical seals from Nalanda and accounts of **Banabhatta** and **Hiuen-Tsang**.

Ancestors of Kamarupa Dynasty

- According to the epics and the Puranas, this dynasty claims its descent from the **Narakasura** who was the son of Vishnu (in his Varaha incarnation) and Bhumi-Devi (the Earth). Therefore, this dynasty is also called *Bhauma* (i.e. the son of *Bhumi*).
- **Naraka** had a son, **Bhagadatta**, who is said to have taken part in the **Mahabharata** war. The inscriptions of the dynasty claim that king **Bhagadatta** and his successors ruled for about 3,000 years in Kamarupa and then came the king **Pushyavarman**.

Rulers of Kamarupa Dynasty

From the sources, it is evident that thirteen kings ruled Kamarupa:

- **Pushyavarman** (350-374 AD) He became the first king of the dynasty in about 350 AD. The Nalanda seal calls Pushyavarma the 'lord of Pragjotish ' and gives the title of 'Maharajadhiraja' to him.
- **Samudravarman** (374-398 AD).
- **Balavarman** (398-422 AD).
- **Kalyanavarman** (422-446 AD).
- **Ganapativarman** (446-470 AD).
- **Mahendravarman** (470-494 AD).
- **Narayanavarman** (494-518 AD) Narayanavarma and his predecessor performed two horse sacrifices, which shows that he may have become independent of the Gupta empire in the first half of the sixth century.

- **Bhutivarman** (518-542 AD) He is also known as Mahabhutavarman. Under him, Kamarupa became a powerful kingdom.
  - It included the whole of the Brahmaputra valley and Sylhet and extended to the West as far as the Karatoya river which continued to be the traditional boundary of Kamarupa for a long time.
- **Chandramukhavarman** (542-566 AD)
- **Sthitavarman** (566-590 AD) He is said to have performed a horse sacrifice.
- **Susthitavarman** (590-595 AD) Some historians think that this ally of Mahasenagupta was Sasanka of Gauda and not a king of Maukhari dynasty.
- **Supratishthitavarman** (595-600 AD) Gauda king Sasanka defeated and imprisoned Supratishthitavarman and Bhaskaravarman soon after the death of their father Susthitavarman.
  - However, both brothers managed to escape from the prison of the Gauda king and Supratishthitavarman ruled for a short period.
- **Bhaskaravarman** (600-650 AD) After Supratishthitavarman, Bhaskaravarman became king. He was a contemporary of Harshavardhana in the first half of the seventh century.
  - He was an ally of king Harshavardhana. He is described in Harshacharita of Banabhatta. He sent his ambassador **Hamsavega** with presents to have an alliance with Harsha.
  - With the help of Harsha, Bhaskaravarman succeeded in occupying a large portion of Bengal from the kingdom of Sasanka.

Account of Hiuen-Tsang on Bhaskaravarman

- Bhaskaravarman's influence over the Buddhist monastery of Nalanda is also attested by the account of Hiuen-Tsang. He narrates that King Bhaskaravarman sent a messenger to the head of Nalanda monastery, Silabhadra, to send the 'great pilgrim of China' to him.
- The story of Hiuen-Tsang shows that Bhaskaravarman had control over exercises North Bengal and also some influence over Nalanda in Bihar.

Decline of Kamarupa Dynasty

- The dynasty came to an end with the death of Bhaskaravarman in the same way as it happened with the kingdom of Harsha.
- It is indicated by the evidence that the kingdom was occupied by a Mlechchha ruler named Salastambha.

Other Dynasties in Post-Gupta Era

The other dynasties of Post-Gupta Era are discussed below :

Pala Dynasty

- The Province of Bengal, from 650 to 750 AD, after the death of Harsha, was subjected to internal disorder, anarchy and confusion referred to as *Matsya Nyaya* (the rule of strong devouring the weak).
- This gave birth to a revolution by the people, in which the local chief Gopala, the first king of Pala dynasty was elected (*Grahita*) by the leading men of Bengal.

Gopala (750–770 AD)

- He was the son of a warrior named Vapyata and founder of the Pala dynasty. He consolidated his authority over almost the whole of Bengal. He was an ardent Buddhist.
- According to Tibetan Lama, **Taranatha**, Gopala built the celebrated monastery at **Odantapuri** (modern Bihar/sharif Bihar).
- Soon after his accession, Dharmapala got involved in a struggle with the two main powers of the time i.e. the **Pratiharas** and the **Rashtrakutas**.
- He was one of those involved in the Tripartite Struggle (others were **Vatsaraja** of **Pratihara** dynasty and **Dhruva** of **Rashtrakuta** dynasty).
- According to Taranatha, he founded 50 religious institutions and was patron of the great Buddhist author **Haribhadra**.
- He revived the Nalanda University and 200 villages were set apart for meeting its expenses.

Dharampala (770-810 AD)

- He was the son and the successor of Gopala, he extended the kingdom and was a follower of Buddhism.
- He founded the Vikramshila University at Bhagalpur, Bihar.
- He had frequent wars with the Pratiharas and Rashtrakutas.

Devapala (810-850 AD)

- He is considered as the most notable Pala king. A great patron of Buddhism, he constructed Buddhist temples and monasteries in Magadha.
- After a short reign of three to four years, his nephew Vigrahapala sat on the throne.

Narayanapala (850-908 AD)

- He was the son and successor of Vigrahapala. He proved to be weak ruler. The *Bhagalpur Inscription* records that in the 17th year of his reign, he granted **Mudgagiri** (Munghyr) a village in Tira-Bhukti (*Tirhut*), to the shrine of *Shiva* and built one thousand temples in the honour of the same deity.

- Narayanapala was succeeded by weak rulers like Rajyapala, Gopala II and Vigrahapala II.

Mahipala I (988-1036 AD)

- He was the son of Vigrahapala II. He ascended the throne in 988 AD. Rajendra Chola invaded his state and defeated Mahipala I.
- The *Tirumalai Inscription* of Rajendra Chola records the details of his conquests in the North.
- However the invasion did not lead to the establishment of the Chola suzerainty over Bengal.
- **Revolt of Kaivartas** took place during his period. After his death, the Pala power declined due to internal conflicts and external invasions.

Ramapala (1077-1130 AD)

- Ramapala carried out expeditions against the *Kaivartas*—suppressed them and captured their chief. He is mentioned in **Sandhyakara Nandi's book** *Ramcharita*, which is the biography of Ramapala.
- He was succeded by **Kumarapala**, **Gopal III** and **Madanapalle** who were all weak rulers. Thus, by the middle of the 12th century, the Pala power had faded.

Gurjara Pratihara Dynasty

- The Gurjara Pratiharas ruled much parts of the Northern India from the 6th to 11th century AD.
- They find their origin from Ujjain or Mandsaur. Due to the military skills of Gurjara Pratiharas, Arabs were confined to Sind from 7th to 11th century AD.
- The founder of this dynasty was **Harichandra** in sixth century. The successors of Harichandra established Marwar in Rajasthan and built the Temple city of Osian, near Jodhpur.

Nagabhatta I (730-760 AD)

- The first important ruler of this dynasty was Nagabhatta I whose reign was from Mandore (Jodhpur) to Malwa, Gwalior and Bharuch. His capital was Ujjain.
- It was during his times when Junaid, another Arab commander invaded India after Mohammad Bin Qasim.
- Nagabhatta I along with his feudatories such as **Chauhans** and **Guhilots** defended the Western Frontiers but the Arabs were capable of doing a lot of damage to their Western frontiers.
- **Junaid** was defeated and his successor **Tamin** was compelled to run back to Arab. This is known as **Battle of Rajasthan**.

Vatsaraja (780-800 AD)

- He captured Kannauj and came in direct conflict with the Palas of Bengal.
- He defeated **Dharmapala** of Pala dynasty. In 786 AD, the Rashtrakuta king Dhruva defeated him. He died in 805 AD.

Nagabhatta II (795-833 AD)

- Nagabhatta II was initially defeated by Rashtrakuta king Govinda III but later recovered and captured Kannauj.
- He was the most important and powerful rulers of the Gurjara Pratiharas.
- He is best known for rebuilding the Somnath temple in 815 AD, which was destroyed by Arab armies of Junayad in 725 AD.
- This was a large structure of red sandstone, which was again destroyed in 1024 by Mahmud of Ghazni.

Mihir Bhoja (836-885 AD)

- Next important king of this dynasty was Mihir Bhoja who ruled till 885 AD was assumed the title of Adivaraha.
- Mihir Bhoja was one of the great empire builders, who after some initial defeats conquered the territories of modern Rajasthan, Gujarat and Madhya Pradesh. The Teli Mandir at the Gwalior fort built by him.

Decline of Gurjara Pratihara Dynasty

- The beginning of the 10th century brought weakness in the Gurjara Pratiharas. In 912 AD, the Gurjara Pratihara King **Bhoja II** was overthrown by a Pala king **Mahipala I**.
- The feudatories took the advantage of the temporary weakness of the Pratiharas and declared their independence.
- The major feudatories Guhilots captured Chittor and founded the Mewar Kingdom, on the other hand, Chauhans established the Chauhans Kingdom in Ajmer.

Rashtrakuta Dynasty

- **Dr AS Altekar** stated that "The period of Rashtrakuta ascendancy in the Deccan from about 753 AD to 982 AD, constitutes perhaps the most brilliant chapter in the history of India, till the rise of the Marathas as an imperial power in the 18th century."
- Literally, the term '*Rashtrakuta*' means designated officer-incharge of territorial division called *Rashtra*. The Rashtrakutas originally belonged to **Lattalura**, modern **Latur** in the Maharashtra.

- They were of Kannada origin and Kannada was their mother tongue. Initially, they were the feudatories under the Chalukyas of Badami.
- The important Rashtrakutas kings were as follows :

Dantidurga (735-756 AD)

- Dantidurga was the founder of the Rashtrakuta dynasty. He defeated the **Gurjaras** and captured **Malwa** from them.
- Then he annexed the Chalukya kingdom by defeating **Kirtivarman II**. Thus, the Rashtrakutas became a paramount power in the Deccan.

Krishna I (756-773 AD)

- His successor Krishna I was also a great conqueror. He defeated the **Gangas** and the **Eastern Chalukyas** of Vengi.
- He built the magnificent rock-cut monolithic **Kailasa temple** at Ellora. He was succeded by his son **Dhruva** who ruled till 793 AD.

Govinda III (793-814 AD)

- The next important king of this dynasty was **Govinda III.** He achieved victories over North Indian kingdoms.
- He successfully obtained the submission of Gurjara Pratihara **Nagabhatta II, Dharmapala** of Pala empire and other small principalities in Kannauj.

Amoghavarsha I (814-878 AD)

- He ruled for a long period of 64 years. He had lost control over Malwa and Gangavadi. Yet, his reign was popular for the cultural development.
- He was a follower of Jainism. **Jinasena** was his chief preceptor in his reign.
- He was also a patron of letters and he himself wrote the famous Kannada work, **Kavirajamarga**.
- He had also built the Rashtrakuta capital, the city of **Malkhed** or **Manyakheda**.

Krishna III (936- 968 AD)

- Among the successors of Amoghavarsha I, **Krishna III** was famous for his expeditions. He marched against the Cholas and defeated them at **Takkolam**.
- He marched further South and captured **Tanjore**. He went as far as Rameswaram and occupied it for some time.
- He built several temples in the conquered territories including the **Krishneswara** temple at Rameswaram.
- Throughout his reign, he possessed the **Tondaimandalam** region including the capital **Kanchi**. After his death, the power of the Rashtrakutas declined.

Kannauj and the Tripartite Struggle

- The Tripartite struggle, that continued for nearly a century, refers to the struggle among the three important dynasties of the period i.e. the **Gurjara-Pratiharas** of Ujjain/Mandsaur, the **Palas** of Bengal and the **Rashtrakutas** of Manyakheta, Karnataka.
- Kannauj was commercially and strategically very important because it was located on a significant trade route.
- The struggle ultimately ended in favour of the Gurjara-Pratihara ruler **Nagabhata II**, who founded the Gurjara-Pratihara kingdom at Kannauj, which survived for nearly two centuries.

Language and Literature in Post-Gupta Era

- Sanskrit remained the main language and literature of various kinds continued to be written in it. Pali and Prakrit were used for writing the Buddhist and Jain religious literature.
- **Vakapati's Gaudavaho**, a biography of Yashovarman of Kannauj, was the last major work in the older tradition of Prakrit.
- The last stage of Prakrit language is represented by the **Apabhramsha,** which was considered important on account of the fact that the modern languages like Hindi, Gujarati, Marathi and Bangla have all evolved from it.
- During this period, literature shows considerable development. A number of *kavyas* with two fold or even more significance constitutes a special feature of this period.
- The *Ramacharita* of **Sandhyakara Nandi** written during the reign of the Pala king, Mahipal, presents both the story of Rama and the life of King Ramapala of Bengal.
- A large number of treatises were written on poetics. The most important among such works are *Kavyamimamsa* by **Rajashekhara**, *Dasharupa* by **Dhananjaya**, *Saraswati Kanthabharana* by **Bhoja**, *Kavyanushasana* of **Hemachandra**, *Kavikanthabharana* by **Kshemendra**, etc.

Society in Post-Gupta Era

- Apart from four varnas, another important class that emerged as a jati during this period was that of **Kayasthas**, the scribes of the administration, responsible for writing documents and maintaining records.
- Though, the reference of Kayasthas are available from the Mauryan period itself, it appears that by the seventh century they came to be regarded as distinct jati.

- The *Smriti* authorities of this period followed the older marriage rules. The literature also reflects the new ideas and practices regarding remarriges. The words like *Punarbhu* and *Didhishu* meaning a remarried woman is frequently mentioned in the literature.
- The women's right to inherit property was accepted by the authorities. The widow was entitled to succeed to the whole estate of her issueless, deceased husband.

Economic Life in Post-Gupta Era

- During the post Gupta period, the literary and inscriptional evidences show the advanced state of agriculture, trade and economy.
- **Medhatithi** included a group of seventeen articles' (including rice and barley) in the category of grain (dhanya).
- *Abhidhanaratnamala* mentions a large variety of cereals and other food grains with their synonyms. It mentions that soils were classified variously as fertile, barren, fallow, desert, excellent as well as those green with grass or abounding in needs, those which were black or yellow and those which owed their fertility to rivers or rains.
- Irrigation by the *Arahata* (Persian wheel) and by leather buckets are mentioned in the inscriptions.
- The records of this period mention a great variety and qualities of textiles such as woolen and hempen yarns, garments made of silk, deer's hair and sheep and goat's wool. The professions of weavers, dyers and the tailor are mentioned in contemporary literature.
- Some centres of metal industry were famous, such as Saurashtra was famous for its bell industry while Vanga was known for its tin industry, etc.
- Lists of jewels are preserved in various texts, which mention around **33 kinds of gems** and analyse the good qualities of diamond, emerald, ruby, pearls, sapphire, etc.
- The Arab, Chinese and Indian sources mention the flow of trade between East and West *via* India. The best breed of horses were imported from Central and Western Asia.
- The prosperity of the coastal towns of Gujarat, Malabar and Tamil attracted foreign merchants to settle in India.
- The ports along the West coast of India referred to by Arab geographers were **Debal** (in Indus delta) Cambay J'hana, Sopara and Quilon.
- **Medhatithi** mentions both industrial and mercantile guilds. These guilds consisted of people following common profession such as tradesmen, artisans, money lenders, etc.

Religion and Philosophy in Post-Gupta Era

- Both Buddhism and Jainism developed theistic tendencies on the analogy of Shaivism and Vaishnavism.
- During this period, Buddhism witnessed not only decadence of pure **Hinayana** and **Mahayana Buddhism**, but also the appearance of a new phase of the religious philosophy.
- The Jainism gained 'popularity among the trading classes in North and West India and the extensive royal patronage in South India. In the Deccan, it was honoured by the **Gangas**, **Chalukyas** and by **Rastrakuta** rulers.
- During this period, many Jain *Basadis* (temples) and *Mahastambhas* (pillar) were setup in different parts. The colossal image at **Sravanabelgola** was set up during this time.
- Tantricism is another sect which became popular during this time. It had originated in the sixth century but became stronger from the eighth century onwards.
- It was strongest in North-Eastern India and had close ties with Tibet.

Education in Post-Gupta Era

- The system of education which had developed gradually in the earlier centuries continued during this period.
- The later Smiritis introduced a new sacrament called *Vidyarambha* (commencement of education) and *Aksharasvikriti* or *Aksharabhyasa* training in the alphabet.
- Education was imparted in the temple like earlier periods. Students were either taught by the temple priests as in the smaller village temples or else attended the college attached to the larger temples.
- Professional education continued to be maintained through the training given to apprentices in guilds and among the groups of artisans.
- At a more popular level, oral instruction, much simpler than the Sanskrit learning of the colleges was imparted by the saints and elders.
- The numerous mathas and other centres of education in various parts of India enabled ideas to flow freely and quickly from one part of the country to another.
- Education was also available in the Jain and Buddhist monasteries at **Vikramashila, Odantapuri, Vallabhi** and **Nalanda,** which were great centres of higher learning.

Art and Architecture in Post-Gupta Era

- Post-Gupta Era was a fruitful age of the art and architecture as it is be apparent from the numerous temples that are standing for the 1200 years.
- The famous temples of Orissa (Odisha), especially those of **Bhubaneshwar** are magnificent specimens of the Nagar style or North Indian style.
- Another place, where several excellent nagar style temples still stand, is **Khajuraho** in Bundelkhand.
- In the Deccan, the **temples of Vatapi** (Badami) and **Pattadakal** (Bijapur district) are stylistically different. These temples stand on an elaborately decorated base or plinth.
- Some good examples are the **Hoysalesvara temple** at Halebidu, which though incomplete, is unsurpassed by any Indian temple in both its structural and its decorative features.
- Besides free standing temples in the South, temples are also hewn out of solid rock. The Kailas temple at Ellora, dedicated to Shiva excavated during the reign of **Krishna I** of the Rashtrakuta dynasty, is regarded as the architectural marvel.

Extra Facts From Tamil Nadu Board and NIOS

- Key officials during Harshavardhana rule

Avanti	Minister of foreign relation and war
Simhananda	Commander-in-Chief
Kuntala	Chief cavalry officer
Banu	Keeper of records
Sarvagata	Secret Service Department
Mahaprathihara	Chief of the place guard
Skandagupta	Chief commandant of Elephant force

- **Bhaga**, **Hiranya** and **Bali** were the three kinds of taxes collected during Harsh's reign.
- Shilabhadra, a reputed Buddhist scholar, who probably hailed from Assam, was the head of the Nalanda University during.
- The Rashtrakutas made splendid contributions to Indian art. The rock-cut shrines at Ellora and Elephanta Caves located in present-day Maharashtra belong to their period.

11

History of South India

(SOURCES)

Class-XI Old NCERT Chap 18 (The Dawn of History in the Deep South), Chap 24 (Formation of New States and Rural Expansion in the Peninsula), Tamil Nadu Board (Class XI), NIOS

Sangam Age

- **The period between the third century BC to third century AD in South India (the areas of modern Tamil Nadu, Kerala, Karnataka and Andhra Pradesh) is known as Sangam period.**
- It has been named after the Sangam academies held during the period of three great dynasties of **Cheras, Cholas** and **Pandyas**. It flourished under the royal patronage of the **Pandya Kings** of Madurai.
- At the Sangams, eminent scholars assembled and functioned as the board of censors and the literary works were compiled in the form of anthologies.
- These literary works were the earliest specimens of Dravidian literature. According to the Tamil legends, there were **three Sangams** (Academy of Tamil poets) held in the Ancient South India popularly called *Muchchangam*.
  - Mythologically the **first Sangam** is believed to be held at Madurai, attended by Gods and legendary sages. No literary work of this Sangam is available.
  - The **second Sangam** was held at Kapatapuram and the only text during this Sangam that survived was Tolkappiyam.
  - The **third Sangam** was also held at Madurai. A few of the Tamil literary works have survived and are a useful sources to reconstruct the history of the Sangam period.
- The earliest script that the Tamils used was the Brahmi script. It was only from the late ancient and early medieval period, that they started evolving a new angular script, called the **Grantha script**, from which the modern Tamil is derived. The Sangam literature was finally compiled in its present form in 300-600 AD.

Language of Sangam Literature

- The Sangam literature was rightly regarded the age of Tamil literature. **Tamil** is the oldest among the spoken literary languages of South India.
- It deals with secular matter relating to public and social activity like government, war, charity, trade, worship, agriculture, etc. Among the poets and thinkers of the Sangam age, **Tolkappiyar**, **Tiruvalluvar**, **Illango Adigal**, **Sittalai Sattanar**, **Nakkirar**, **Kapilar**, **Paraner**, **Auvaiyar** and **Mangudi Marudanar** are remarkable.
- The Sangam literature can roughly be divided into two groups **narrative** and **didactic**. The nature of Sangam literature is quite unique as it is written in secular nature and its major themes are love, revenge and poetry, etc.

Earliest Tamil Works

- *Tolkappiyam* It is the oldest extant Tamil grammar written by *Tolkappiyar* (one of the 12 disciples of sage Agastya.). It is divided into three major parts, each consisting of nine *Iyals* (sub-parts) and has a total of 1612 *Sutras*.

- *Pattupattu* (Ten poems) The poetry in the *Pattupattu* was divided into two main groups i.e., *Aham* (deals with matters strictly limited to one aspect of subjective experience *viz* love) and *Puram* (deals with matters capable of externalisation of objectification).
- *Murugarruppadai* (by **Nakkirar**), *Sirupanarruppadai* (by **Nattanar**), *Perumbanarruppadai*, *Maduraikkanji* (by **Mangudi Marudam**), *Pattinappalai* (by **Kannan**) and other works, come in the category of *Pattupattu*.
- *Ettutogai* It is a collection of eight anthologies. The eight anthologies were :
  1. *Aingurunuru*, compiled by **Gudalur Kilar**, consists of 500 erotic poems.
  2. *Agananuru*, compiled by **Rudrasarman**, consists of love poems.
  3. *Narrinai* comprises 400 short poems on love.
  4. *Kuruntogai* has 400 love poems.
  5. *Purananuru* consists of 400 poems in praise of kings. The Nandas and Mauryas are referred in one of the poems.
  6. *Kalithogai* comprises love poems.
  7. *Paripadal* has 24 poems in praise of Gods.
  8. *Padirruppattu* is a short collection of 8 poems in praise of the Chera kings.

Pathinenkilkanakku (Eighteen Minor Works)

- These works are called **minor works**, because the poems in these, are shorter in form.
- The most important among these are the *Tirukkural* by **Tiruvalluvar** (known as the Bible of Tamil land), which is a compound of the *Dharmashastra*, the *Arthashastra* and the *Kamasutra*.
- *Pathinenkilkanakku* was translated in English by **Dr. A Dakshinamurthy** in 2010. Most of these books deal with morals and ethics.

The Epics

The epics *Silappadikaram* (The Jewelled Anklet) and *Manimekalai* belong to the early centuries of the Christian era.

- *Silappadikaram* It was written by **Ilango Adigal** (grandson of Karikala, the great Chola king) in the second century AD. It is a tragic story of a merchant, **Kovalan** of Puhar who falls in love with a dancer **Madhavi**, neglecting his own wife **Kannagi**. In the end, Kannagi takes revenge for the death of her husband from the Pandyan king and becomes a Goddess.

  It marks the beginning of Kannagi cult or *Pattini* cult, i.e., the worship of Kannagi as the real wife. There is also a reference to the Ceylonese King **Gajabahu** being present on the occasion of the installation of a Kannagi Goddess in the temple, by Chera King **Senguttuvan**.
- *Manimekalai* It was written by poet **Sattanar**. It is the story of Manimekalai, the daughter of Kovalan and Madhavi, of the earlier epic. The main aim of this epic was to show the excellence of the Buddhist religion through the painful life of Manimekalai due to the loss of the city, Puhar. This epic is the only important ancient work, which gives glimpse of the development of the fine arts in the Sangam age.

Megalith Culture in South India

- The **Megaliths** are the graves encircled by big pieces of stone. They are found in all upland areas of the peninsula, but their concentration seems to be in Eastern Andhra and in Tamil Nadu.
- The people used various types of pottery, but black and red ware popular with them.
- The practice of burying goods in the graves with the dead bodies was based on the belief that the dead would need all these in the next world.
- The **Cholas**, **Pandyas** and **Cheras** mentioned in **Ashokan inscriptions** were probably in the megalithic phase of material culture.
- The Megalithic people in the Southern districts of Tamil Nadu had certain peculiar characteristics. They buried the skeletons of the dead inside urns made of red pottery in pits.
- The practice of urn-burial was different from that of list-**burial** or **pit-burial** surrounded by stone circles, which prevailed in the Krishna-Godavari valley.
- Although, the Megalithic people produced paddy and ragi, apparently the area of cultivable land used by them was very limited, and generally they did not settle on the plains or in the low lands.

Three Early Kingdoms

- The Southern end of the Indian peninsula situated South of the Krishna river was divided into three kingdoms i.e., Pandya, Chola and Chera or Kerala.
- The Pandyas were first mentioned by **Megasthenes**, who said that their kingdom was famous for pearls. He also mentioned that it is being ruled by a woman.
- The Cholas, the Pandyas and the Cheras territories was probably outside the Mauryan empire.

Pandyan Kingdom

- The Pandyan territory occupied the Southernmost and the South-Eastern portion of the Indian peninsula.
- It roughly included the modern districts of **Tirunelveli**, **Ramnad** and **Madurai** in Tamil Nadu.

- It had its capital at Madurai, which became a great cultural centre.
- The Pandyan kings were profited from trade with the Roman empire and sent embassies to the Roman Emperor **Augustus**.
- The Brahmanas enjoyed considerable influence and the Pandyan kings performed Vedic sacrifices in the early centuries.

Chola Kingdom

- The Chola kingdom was called *Cholamandalam* or Coromandal. It was situated to the North-Eastern part of the territory of the Pandyas, between the Pennar and the Velur rivers.
- **Uraiyur** was the chief centre of political power of Cholas. It was a famous place for cotton trade.
- In the middle of the second century BC, a Chola king named **Elara** conquered Sri Lanka and ruled over it for nearly 50 years.
- The Chola kingdom flourished around 100 AD under the rule of famous King **Karikala**.
- He founded **Puhar** and constructed 160 km of embankment along the Kaveri river. Puhar is identical with Kaveripattanam, which was the Chola capital. It was a great centre of trade and commerce. The excavations show that it had a large dockyard.
- One of the main sources of the wealth of the Cholas was trade in cotton cloth. They maintained and efficient navy which sailed as far as the mouths of the Ganga and the Irrawaddy.
- Under **Karikala's** successors, the Chola power rapidly declined and their capital **Kaveripattanam** was also destroyed.

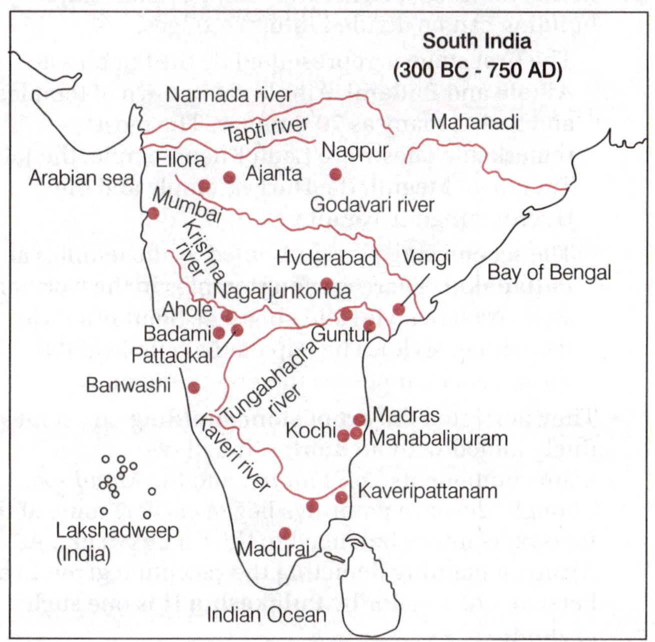

Chera Kingdom

- The Chera or the Kerala country was situated to the West and North of the land of the **Pandyas.** It included the narrow strip of land between the sea and the mountains and covered a portion of the modern Kerala state.
- The Cheras owed its importance to trade with the Romans. The Romans set up two regiments at **Muziris** identical with **Cranganore** in the Chera country to protect their interests.
- The most important event in the political history of the **Cheras** was their fight against the **Cholas** in about 150 AD.
- According to the Chera poets, the greatest king was **Senguttuvan** (Cenkuttuvan), the Red Chera. According to Sangam work *Silappatikaram*, he invaded the North and crossed the Ganga.

Economic Life of the Three Kingdoms

- These states are very much profited from their natural resources and foreign trade. They grew spice especially pepper, which was in great demand in the Western world.
- The sea yielded pearls and their mines produced precious stones. Both of these were sent to the West in good quantity.
- The early Tamil poems also mentioned the wearing of complex patterns on silk. **Uraiyur** was noted for its cotton trade.
- From very early times, the Tamil traders were engaged with the **Greek** or **Hellenistic** kingdom of Egypt, Arabia, Malaya archipelago and China.
- Transit duties were also levied on the merchants who moved with their goods from place to place.
- The land produced paddy, ragi and sugarcane. From the taxes collected from the peasantry, the state maintained a regular army.

Social Life of the Three Kingdoms

- Taxes enabled the king not only to maintain a professional army but also to pay the poets and priets, who were mainly the priest class.
- The Brahmanas first appear in the Tamil land in the Sangam age. Many Brahmanas functioned as court poets and were rewarded by the king.

- The Kshatriyas and Vaishyas do not appear as regular Varnas in the Sangam texts. The class of warriors was also present in the society.
- Captains of the army were given the title of *Enadi* at a formal ceremony. Civil and military offices were held under both the **Cholas** and the **Pandyas** by **Vallalas** or rich peasants.
- The ruling caste was called the *Arasar* and its members had matrimonial relations with the *Vallalas,* who constituted the fourth caste.
- *Vallalas* had vast pasture land and thus constituted the peasantry, divided into the rich and the poor. The rich did not plough the land themselves but employed labourers for this purpose.
- Agricultural operations were generally carried out by women of the lowest class (*Kadaisiyar*), whose status appears to have lower than the slaves.
- There were low class artisans called *Pulaiyans* who used to make rope *Charpaiys* and used animal skins as mats. Several outcastes and forest tribes also existed in the society.

Religious Life of the Three Kingdoms

- The Brahmanical influence was confined to a small part of the Tamil territory and only to the upper levels to Tamil society.
- The chief local deity worshipped by the people was **Murugan**, who was also called **Subramaniya**. The worship of **Vishnu** is also mentioned in the texts.
- People offered paddy to the dead. Cremation was introduced but burial practices of the Megalithic phase was not abandoned.

Organisation of New Kingdoms in Deccan

Between 300-600 AD, many new kingdoms arised to power in Deccan. Some of these are discussed below :

Vakatakas

The Vakataka rulers were the contemporary of the Gupta dynasty. Inscriptions and *Puranas* testify that they dominated the entire country of Bundelkhand, Central Provinces, Berar, Northern Deccan. The Vakatakas were Brahmins and in their inscriptions, they called themselves as *Haritaputras.*

The important rulers of this dynasty were :

- **Vindhyasakti** He was the founder of this dynasty.
- **Pravarasena** Assumed imperial titles such as *Maharajadhiraja* and *Samrat* and also performed *Asvamedha* and *Vajapeya.*
- **Rudrasena I** He faced defeat by Samudragupta.
- **Rudrasena II** He married Prabhavatigupta, (daughter of Chandragupta II) and under her influence became a *Vaishnavite.*
- **Pravarasena II** He built temple of Ramachandra at Pravarapura and composed famous Prakrit poem *Setubandha.* Kalidasa wrote *Meghadutam* in his court.

Chalukyas

- The Chalukyas ruled Deccan from the 6th to 8th centuries AD and again from the 10th to 12th centuries AD. They occupy an important place in the history of the Deccan.
- The Central Government under the Chalukyas of Badami exercised a paternalistic control over the village administration.
- The army of the Chalukyas consisted of a small standing army, but looked after civil administration, whenever the need arised. They patronised education and learning. They promoted both **Sanskrit** and **Prakrit** languages.
- **Gangaraja Durvinita**, a famous Chalukyan feudal lord, wrote a famous book on Grammar known as *Shabavatara.* He also translated the book *Brihatkatha* written by **Gunadhya** into Sanskrit.
- **Udayadeva** wrote a Grammar book known as *Jainendra Vyakarana.* **Vijnanesvara** wrote the *Mitaksara.*
- Though Chalukyas were Brahmin Hindus, they also promoted other religions. For example, Jainism made huge progress under them.
- The Chalukyas developed the Deccan or *Vesara* style in the building of structural temples. The temple building can be divided into two stages.
  - The **first stage** is represented by the temples at **Aihole** and **Badami**. Aihole was a town of temples and had as many as 70 temples. The most remarkable ones were Ladh Khan Temple, the Jain Temple of Meguti, the Durga Temple and the Huchimalligudi Temple.
  - The **second stage** is represented by the temples at **Pattadakal**. There are four temples in the Northern style (Nagara style) and six in the Southern style (Dravidian style). The Papanatha temple and the Virupaksha temple are the prominent ones.
- They perfected the **art of stone building** i.e., stones finely joined without mortar. It had two main components i.e., *Vimana* and the *Mandapa.* Though, the cave paintings began earlier, some of the finest specimens belonged to the Chalukya era. At Ajanta, a painting depicting the reception given to a Persian ambassador by **Pulakeshin II** is one such example.

Pallavas

- The term *'Pallava'* means *creeper* and is a Sanskrit version of the Tamil word *Tondai*, which also carries the same meaning. The Pallavas were possibly a local tribe, who established their authority in the 'Tondai Nadu' (Tondai Mandalam) or the *Land of Creepers*.
- It might have took them some time to be completely civilised and acceptable, because in Tamil the word **Pallava** is also synonym of *robber*.
- **Simha Vishnu** (575-600 AD) was the real founder of this dynasty. His son and successor **Mahendravarman** (600-630 AD) was defeated by the Chalukyan King **Pulakeshin II**. With this, started the great struggle between the Pallavas and the Chalukyas.
- **Narasimhavarman I** (630-668 AD) was the most successful Pallava king. He adopted the title **Vatapikonda**. In 642 AD, he occupied the Chalukyan capital Vatapi and killed Pulakeshin II.
- Many prominent scholars like **Bharavi, Dandin, Dignaga, Mayursarman**, etc achieved a lot in the domain of literature due to the Pallava aid and patronage.
- The Pallava power was wiped out by **Aditya I**, a Chola King, who routed **Aparajitavarman** and annexed the Pallava kingdom.
- **Ghatikas** was the most important medieval Karnataka educational institution of the Pallavas, located near temples.

Conflict between the Chalukyas and the Pallavas

- The main interest in the political history of Peninsular India from the 6th to the 8th centuries AD centres round the long struggle between the **Pallavas** of **Kanchi** and the **Chalukyas of Badami** for supremacy.
- The Pandyas, who were in control of Madurai and Tirunelveli district of Tamil Nadu, joined this conflict as a poor third.
- The Pallavas and the Chalukyas quarrelled with each other for plunder, prestige and territorial resources.
- Both tried to establish supremacy over the land lying between the Krishna and the Tungabhadra.
- The first important event in this long conflict took place in the reign of **Pulakeshin-II** (609-642 AD), the most famous Chalukya king.
- In his conflict with the Pallavas, he almost reached the Pallava capital, but the Pallavas purchased peace by surrendering their Northern provinces to Pulakeshin II.
- Pulakeshin's second invasion of the Pallava territory ended in failure. The Pallava King **Narasimhavarman** (630-668 AD) occupied the Chalukya capital at Vatapi in about 642 AD, when **Pulakeshin II** was probably killed in fight against the Pallavas. Narasimhavarman assumed the title of Vatapi-konda or the Conqueror of Vatapi.
- The Chalukya King **Vikramaditya II** (733-745 AD) attacked Kanchi three times. In 740 AD, he completely routed the Pallavas.

Kadambas

- This kingdom was founded by **Mayursharma** in 345 AD and lasted till 540 AD. It was an ancient royal kingdom that ruled Northern Karnataka and Kanpur area.
- Mayursharma defeated Pallavas for helping native tribes and claimed sovereignty.
- Kadamba power reached its peak during the reign of **Kakusthanarma**.

Western Ganges

- It was an important ruling dynasty from Karnataka from 350 to 750 AD. They began their rule during the time when the Pallava empire was weakening in South India.
- Initially, their capital was **Kolar,** they later moved their capital to **Talakadu** on the banks of Kaveri river in modern Mysore district.

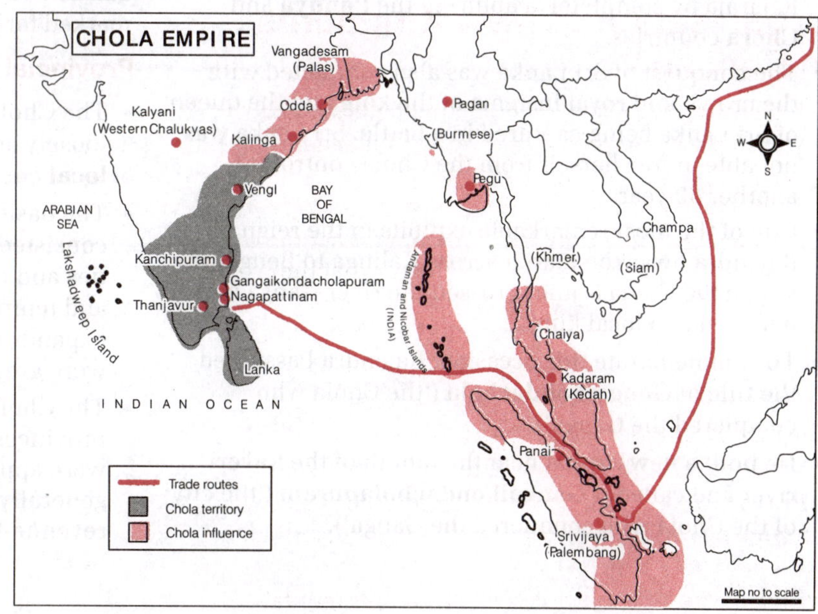

Imperial Cholas

- The founder of the Imperial Chola empire was **Vijayalaya,** who was at first a feudatory of the Pallavas. He captured **Tanjore** in 850 AD. The Cholas had defeated both the Pallavas of Kanchi (Tondaimandalam) and weakened the Pandyas, bringing the Southern Tamil country under their control.
- It was hard for the Cholas to defend their position against the **Rashtrakutas.** This was a serious setback to the Cholas, but they rapidly recovered, particularly after the death of **Krishna III** in 965 AD and the downfall of the Rashtrakuta empire.
- **Rajaraja** and **Rajendra II,** were the most prominent imperial Chola rulers.

Rajaraja (985-1014 AD)

- Rajaraja destroyed the **Chera navy** at **Trivandrum** and attacked **Quilon.** He then conquered Madurai and captured the **Pandyan** king. He also invaded Sri Lanka and annexed its Northern part to his empire.
- The Coromandel coast and Malabar were the centres for India's trade with the countries of South-East Asia. One of his naval exploits was the conquest of the Maldives.
- Rajaraja, annexed the North-Western parts of the Western **Ganga kingdom** in Karnataka and captured **Vengi.**

Rajendra I (1014-1044 AD)

- Rajendra had considerable experience in administration and warfare before his accession to the throne. He carried forward the annexationist policy of Rajaraja by completely capturing the **Pandya** and **Chera** countries.
- The conquest of Sri Lanka was also completed with the crown and royal insignia of the king and the queen of Sri Lanka being captured in a battle. Sri Lanka was not able to free herself from the Chola control for another 50 years.
- One of the most remarkable exploits in the reign of Rajendra I was the march across Kalinga to Bengal in which the Chola armies crossed the river Ganga and defeated two local kings.
- To commemorate this occasion, Rajendra I assumed the title of **Gangaikondachola** ('the Chola who conquered the Ganga').
- He built a new capital near the mouth of the Kaveri river and called it **Gangaikondacholapuram** ('the city of the Chola who conquered the Ganga').
- Another remarkable exploit in the time of Rajendra I was the naval expedition against the **Sri Vijaya empire** in the 10th century. It extended over the Malay peninsula, Sumatra, Java and the neighbouring islands, and controlled the overseas trade route to China.
- The rulers of the **Sailendra dynasty** of the **Sri Vijaya** kingdom were Buddhists and had cordial relations with the Cholas.
- The Sailendra ruler had built a Buddhist monastery at **Nagapatnam** and Rajendra I endowed a village for upkeeping the monastery.

Society Under Imperial Cholas

- In Chola dynasty, the social order was based on the Varna system. Brahmins had many privileges and were exempted from taxation. They also had great influence over the kingdom.
- Chola emperors linked themselves to Solar and lunar dynasties and called themselves *Brahmakshatriyas.*
- Trading communities claimed Vaishya status and called themselves *Kamati*, *Vanijiya* and *Chettiar.*
- The society was also divided in *Sat Sudras* (Higher) and *Asat Sudras* (Lower). Untouchability was prevalent in Chola society.
- The position of women was average. They were allowed to learn Vedas and attend religious ceremonies. However, they were not part of imperial courts. The **Devadasi system** also prevalent.

Administration Under Imperial Cholas

The Chola rulers set up a highly efficient system of administration in the South India. The period was marked for great territorial expansion.

Provincial Administration

- The Chola state included area of **central control** and loosely administered areas under different types of **local control.**
- The basic unit of administration was the *Nadu,* which consisted of a number of villages having close kinship ties and other close associations. Grants to Brahmans and temple authorities increased, which helped in expanding cultivation. In the Chola kingdom, *Nadus* were grouped into *Valanadus.*
- The Chola state was divided into four *Mandalams* or provinces. Sometimes, princes of the royal family were appointed governors of provinces. Officials were generally paid by giving them assignments of revenue-bearing lands.

- The Chola rulers built a **network of royal roads**, which were useful for trade as well as for the movement of the army. **Trade and commerce flourished** in the Chola empire and there were some **huge trade guilds**, which traded in Java and Sumatra.
- The Cholas also **improved irrigation system.** The River Kaveri and other tributaries were used for the purpose. Many tanks for irrigation were also built.
- Some of the Chola rulers carried out an **elaborate survey of land** in order to fix the government's share of the land revenue. In addition to land tax, the Chola rulers drew their income from tolls on trade, taxes on professions, and also from the plunder of the neighbouring territories.

Local Self-Government

- The most important feature of the Chola administration lies in the running of autonomous institutions. Each village had its own general assembly which administered control over all the affairs of the village.
- It was free from the control of the Central Government. It enjoyed all powers regarding the village administration.
- There were two types of institutions working at village level. There were two assemblies, i.e., the **Ur,** and the **Sabha** or **Mahasabha**. The Ur was a General Assembly of the village. This was a gathering of the adult men in the Brahman villages, which were called **Agraharams.**
- The affairs of the village were managed by an executive committee to which educated persons owning property were elected either by drawing lots or by rotation. These members had to retire every three years.
- The Ur consisted of all the taxpaying residents of an ordinary village. The **Alunganattar** was the executive committee and the ruling group of the Ur. The Ur was open to all the adult men but was dominated by the older member of the village.
- The members of the Executive Committee of 'Ur' were called **Shashak Gana** or **Ganam.** Exact number of the committee members or the procedure adopted for their election is not known.
- There were other committees for helping in the assessment and collection of land revenue, for maintenance of law and order, justice, etc. One of the important committees was the tank committee, which looked after the distribution of water to the fields.
- The **Mahasabha** could distribute new lands, and exercise ownership rights over them. It could also raise loans for the village and levy taxes.
- *Eripatti* land was tank land. These were lands registered in the name of particular tank.

Type of Land Gifts in Chola Empire

According to Chola Inscriptions, there were five types of 'land gifts' that Chola kings gave to their people :

- **Vellanvagai,** was land for non-Brahmana, peasant proprietors.
- **Brahmadeya,** was land gifted to Brahmanas.
- **Shalabhoga,** was land for the maintenance of a school.
- **Devadana/Tirunamattukkani,** was land gifted to temples.
- **Pallichchhandam,** was land donated to Jaina institutions.

Education Under Imperial Cholas

- The village assembly would hold its meetings in the temple and business discussed was sometimes recorded on the walls of the temple.
- The priests of the temple were also the local teachers as there was no separate school. The school was held in the temple courtyard.
- The young students, most of whom were Brahmins, learnt their lessons in two languages.
- Much of the religious teachings were in **Sanskrit** since, texts such as the Vedas had to be studied very throughly. The students also learnt **Tamil,** which was widely spoken.
- Many literary and religious works in Sanskrit were re-written in Tamil such as the famous *Ramayana* of **Kamban.**
- Many of the inscriptions of the Chola kings are written in both Sanskrit and Tamil.
- In Andhra region, Telugu was spoken by the local people. There were adaptations of the *Mahabharata* and the *Ramayana* in Telugu. *Naunayya* is remembered for his excellent adaptation of the parts of *Mahabharata*. The adaptation was later added by the poet **Tikkana.**
- In the region around modern Mysore, **Kannada** was the most widely spoken language. The poets **Pampa, Ponna** and **Ranna** are called the **three jewels of Kannada literature.**
- Kannada also became popular because a group of religious teachers called the **Lingayatas** preached in Kannada.

Temple Architecture Under Imperial Cholas

- Temple architecture in the South attained its climax under the Cholas. The style of architecture, which came into vogue during this period is called **Dravida,** because it was confined largely to South India.
- The main feature of this style was the building of many storeys above the *Garbhagriha* (the innermost chamber where the chief deity resides). The number

of storeys varied from five to seven and they had a typical style which came to be called the Vimana.

- The **Kailashnathar temple** at Kanchipuram and **Seven Pagodas** were built in the reign of Narasimhavarman.
- The striking feature of the Kailashnatha temple and Seven Pagodas is that they were carved out of solid rocks. He also built **Mahabalipuram** which was a popular port and shore temple.
- **Rajaraja** and **Rajendra I** marked their victories by erecting a number of Shiva and Vishnu temples at various places. The most famous of these was the Brihadeeshwara temple at Tanjore, which was completed in 1010.
- The Chola rulers adopted the practice of having inscriptions written on the walls of these temples, giving a historical narrative of their victories.

Mahabalipuram Temple

Extra Facts From Tamil Nadu Board and NIOS

- Aihole inscription of Pulakeshin II. The inscription is a *Prashasti* of the Chalukyas especially the reigning king Pulakeshin II, referred to as Sathyasraya. It highlights the history of the dynasty, defeat of all his enemies, especially Harshavardhana.

Category of Minister in Chalukya Dynasty

Category	Departments
Pradhana	Prime Minister
Mahasandhi Vigrahika	Minister of Foreign Affair
Amatya	Revenue Minister
Samaharta	Minister of Exchequer
Grampohis	Village Officials
Mahatras	Village Men
Samantas	Feudal Lords

- Traders founded guilds and called themselves as Sudesi, Nanadesi, Ainurruvar and others. Their main guild functioned at Aihole. These was part of Pallava army.

Chola Empire

- Uttaramerur inscription give details of the process of electing members to various committee that administered the affair of Brahmin settlement in Chola period.
- Kudimai was an important box during Chola reign. It was paid by the cultivating tenants to the government and to the landlords.
- Sambuvarayars were the feudatories. The were found fighting sometimes on the side of their overlord and occasionally against them also. They were chieftain in the North Arcot and Chengalpattu region during the reign of Rajadhiraja and Kulothunga III.

12

Medieval History

Arab and Turk Conquest in India

[SOURCES]

Class-VI Old NCERT Chap 1 (India and the World), Class-XI Old NCERT Chap 5 (The Age of Conflict), Class-XII New NCERT Chap 5 (Through the Eyes of Travellers), Tamil Nadu Board (Class XI), NIOS

- In India, the eighth century AD marked as the end of the ancient period and beginning of medieval period.
- During this time, many aspects of Indian society have changed such as the political and economic aspect as well as social laws, religion, language and art.
- There is more information available about Medieval India than Ancient India such as inscriptions on plates of copper or on stones.
- There are also a great variety of literary sources on paper, as the number of books have survived.

Arabs in India

- In 712 AD, the Arabs conquered Sind in Western India under the leadership of **Muhammad Bin Qasim.**
- In this part of India, that Islam first became an important religion for the first time. He was a military commander of **Al-Hajjaj** and the Governor of **Basna.**
- Arabs established several trading settlements on the West coast of India.
- Here, they lived in peace with the local people, married them and took part in Indian trade with other regions of Asia.

Age of Conflict (1000-1200 AD)

- The period from 1000 to 1200 AD saw rapid changes both in West and Central Asia. Therefore, it paved way to the sudden attack of the Turks into Northern India leading to their rule towards the end of the period.
- The Turkish tribesmen brought along with them the habit of ruthless looting across India. The major attacks were carried out by **Mahmud of Ghazni.**

Ghaznavids

- **Mahmud of Ghazni** ascended the throne (998-1030 AD) as Samanid ruler at Ghazni (Afghanistan).
- Mahmud himself claimed descent from the legendary Iranian king, **Afrasiyab.** He encouraged the Persian language and literature during his reign.
- Mahmud is said to have made seventeen raids into India. The initial raids were directed against the Hindushahi rulers of Peshawar and the Punjab.
- After the death of Mahmud in 1030 AD, a powerful empire, the **Seljuk empire,** came into existence. The Seljuk empire included Syria, Iran and Trans-Oxiana. It contended with the Ghaznavids for the control of Khurasan.
- In a fierce battle, **Masud** (the son of Mahmud) was defeated and had to flee to Lahore for refuge. The Ghaznavid empire was now limited to Ghazni and the Punjab.

Major Invasions of Mahmud Ghazni in India

State/ ruler	Period	Description
Hindushahi Ruler, Jayapala	1001 AD	• Mahmud in his first invasion of India defeated Jayapala in 1001 AD. Peace was made by ceding the territory West of the Indus to Mahmud. • Jayapala killed himself later and his son Anandapala became his successor.
Conquest of Bhera	1003 AD	• Mahmud again appeared on the bank of river Jhelum and invaded Bhera. After his victory, Mahmud plundered Bhera ruthlessly and returned to Ghazni with immense booty.
Sukhpal	1008 AD	• Sukhpal was appointed Governor of Multan by Mahmud because he embraced Islam (Nawasa Shah) but soon he gave up Islam and began to rule as an independent ruler. • Again, Mahmud invaded Multan and Fateh Daud was again appointed the ruler of Multan.
Anandapala (Salt Range)	1009 AD	• Anandapala was defeated and Mahmud plundered his new capital, Nandana, in the Salt Ranges. He captured his fort called Nagarkot (not to confuse with Nagarkot in Himachal).
Lahore/ Kashmir	1015 AD	• In 1015, Mahmud advanced upto Lahore, plundered it and dethroned Anandapala. However, an attack on Kashmir by Mahmud in 1015 AD was failed due to weather conditions.
Kannauj	1018 AD	• During this expedition, Mahmud collected a lot of wealth from the temples of Mathura and Vrindavan. Besides this, he destroyed the temples and broke up the idols.
Plunder of Kalinjar	1022 AD	• In 1022 AD, Mahmud invaded both Kalinjar and Gwalior. Both the kingdoms accepted his supremacy and paid a huge war ransom.
Conquest of Somnath	1026 AD	• In Somnath attack, the objective was also to create a sense of fear and shock among the Rajputs. • The Commander of the city fled at his approach, but the citizens put up a strong resistance. Mahmud broke the Shivalingam and ordered to bring parts of it back with him to Ghazni.
Expedition against Jats	1027 AD	• Mahmud led his last major expedition in 1027 AD against the Jats of Sind. • He plundered the colonies of Jats and set them on fire. He slaughtered the men and enslaved women and children. • This was the last invasion of Mahmud against Hindustan.

Al-Biruni and Kitab-ul-Hind

- Al-Biruni was born in 973 AD, in Khwarizm (present day Uzbekistan). He came to India with **Mahmud of Ghazni**. Al-Biruni's expertise in several languages allowed him to compare languages and translate many Indian texts into Arabic.
- Al-Biruni's **Kitab-ul-Hind** is written in Arabic. It is divided into 80 chapters on subjects such as religion and philosophy, festivals, astronomy, alchemy, manners and customs, social life, laws and metrology (science of measurement).
- Al-Biruni tried to explain the caste system of India. The explained the caste system by looking for parallels in other societies. He noted that in ancient Persia, four social categories were recognised, those of kinghts and princes, monks, fire-priests and lawyers, physicians, astronomers and other scientists, and finally, peasants and artisans.
- Al-Biruni adopted a distinctive structure in each chapter, beginning with a question, following with a description based on Sanskritic traditions and concluding with a comparison with other cultures.
- The term 'Hindu' was derived from an old Persian word, used (sixth-fifth centuries BC to refer to region East of the River Sindhu (Indus)). Arab continued the Persian language and called this region Al-Hind.

Turkish Conquest in India

- After the Ghaznavid conquest of the Punjab, it became common trait of plunder, which resulted in raids into the Gangetic Valley of India.
- The rulers of the Rajput states resisted these raids and became victorious against the Turks on several occasions. Two new powers rose to prominence during this period i.e.,
  - The **Khwarizmi empire** based in Iran,
  - The **Ghurid empire** based in Ghur in North-West Afghanistan.
- The power of the Ghurids increased under Sultan Alauddin who earned the title of the **World Burner** (*Jahan-soz*).

Muhammad of Ghur or Shahabuddin Muhammad

- In 1173 AD, Shahabuddin Muhammad (1173–1206 AD) (also known as Muizzuddin Muhammad bin Sam) ascended the throne at Ghazni.
- Meanwhile, the **Chauhan Rajput** power had been steadily growing in Northern India. The expansion of the Chauhan power brought them into conflict with the Ghurid rulers of the area and several fierce battles were fought.

Major Invasions/Campaigns of Muhammad of Ghor

Years	Places	Ruler/dynasty
1175 AD	Multan	Karmathi dynasty
1178 AD	Gujarat (Battle of Kayadara)	Bhima II
1181 AD	Punjab	Khusru Malik
1186 AD	Punjab	Khusru Malik
1191 AD	First Battle of Tarain	Prithviraj Chauhan
1192 AD	Second Battle of Tarain	Prithviraj Chauhan
1194 AD	Battle of Chandawar	Jaichand
1195 AD	Bayana	Bhima II
1205 AD	Revolt of Khokars	Khokhars

First Battle of Tarain 1191 AD

- The conflict between **Muizzuddin Muhammad** and **Prithviraj Chauhan III** started with rival claims for **Tabarhind**. In the battle, which was fought at Tarain in 1191 AD, the Ghurid forces were defeated.
- Muizzuddin Muhammad's life being saved by a young Khalji horseman. **Prithviraj** conquered **Tabarhind** but he made huge error by not threwing out the Ghurids from the Punjab.

Second Battle of Tarain 1192 AD

- The Second Battle of Tarain in 1192 AD is regarded as one of the turning points in Indian history. Muizzuddin Muhammad had made careful preparations for the contest.
- Prithviraj had fielded a force of 3,00,000 including a large body of cavalry and 300 elephants, but the Turkish army was better organised. Many rajas sent contingents to help him, but **Jaichandra**, the ruler of Kannauj stayed away.
- The superior organisational skill and speed of movements of the cavalry made Turkish power victorious.
- Prithviraj escaped but was captured near **Saraswati** (Sirsa). The Turkish armies captured the fortresses of **Hansi**, **Saraswati** and **Samana** and also captured **Ajmer**.
- Prithviraj might have ruled over Ajmer for some time as coins of that period are found having the date and the legend **Prithvirajadeva** on one side and the words **Sri Muhammad Sam** on the other side.
- After the battle, Tomar ruler of Delhi was dethroned and Delhi was made a base for further Turkish advance into the Ganga valley.

Turkish Conquest of Bihar and Bengal

- Between 1192 and 1206 AD, Turkish rule was extended over the Ganga-Jamuna doab and its neighbouring areas. After the Battle of Tarain, Muizzuddin returned to Ghazni leaving the affairs in India in the hands of one of his trusted slaves, **Qutb-ud-din Aibak**.
- In 1194 AD, Muizzuddin returned to India and battle between Muizzuddin and **Jaichandra** was fought at **Chandawar** near Firozabad. In this battle, Jaichandra was killed by an arrow and his army was totally defeated.
- However, the Turks were more successful in the Eastern India. A Khalji officer, **Bakhtiyar Khalji** made frequent raids into Bihar and had attacked and destroyed some of the famous Buddhist monasteries of **Bihar, Nalanda** and **Vikramashila**.
- Making careful preparations, Bakhtiyar Khalji marched with an army towards Nadia, a pilgrim centre where the Sena ruler, **Lakshmana Sena** was ruling. Lakshmana Sena was scared by the attack and left his capital.
- Bakhtiyar was occupied the Sena capital, **Lakhnauti**, without any opposition.
- Although, Bakhtiyar Khalji was severely defeated by **Magh rulers of Assam** and he was able to come back with a few followers. One of his own *amirs* stabbed him to death.
- Muizzuddin Muhammad led his last campaign into India in 1206 AD in order to deal with the **Khokhar rebellion in Bengal**. On his way back to Ghazni, he was killed by a Muslim fanatic belonging to a rival sect.

Comparison between Muizzuddin and Mahmud of Ghazni

- As a warrior, Mahmud Ghazni was more successful than Muizzuddin, having never suffered a defeat in India or in Central Asia. He also ruled over a larger empire outside India but he had to contend with larger and better organised states in India than Mahmud.
- Though less successful in Central Asia, his political achievements in India were greater. But it was Mahmud's conquest of the Punjab, which paved the way for Muizzuddin's success in North India.
- The political and military motives of the two in India were also different in many respects.
- Hindu officers and soldiers were used by Mahmud as well as by Muizzuddin. But neither hesitated to use the slogan of Islam for their purposes and to justify their plunder of Indian cities and temples in the name of religion.

Causes of Turkish Success

- The most important cause of Turkish success was that they had **superior horses**, which were swifter and stronger than the horses imported into India.
- The Indians were weak in social and organisational areas. The **growth of feudalism**, i.e., rise of the local landed elements and chiefs had weakened the administrative structure and military organisation of the Indian states.
- **Division between Rajput rulers** in India and lack of Central authority in Rajput kingdoms were also led to Turkish success.
- Rajput rulers lacked advance military skills and Turkish army was highly trained.
- The tribal structure of the Turks and the growth of the *Iqta* and *Khalisa* systems, enabled the Turks to maintain large standing armies, which could be kept in the field for a long time. On the other hand, the Indian rulers had to depend more on the various chiefs who rarely acted in coordination.
- In terms of personal bravery, the Turks were inculcated with the **'Ghazi' spirit**. The Rajputs lacked **'strategic vision'**. Once the outer areas of India Kabul and Lahore, had fallen to the Turks, but no concerted attempt was made by the Rajputs to recover them.

Effects of Turkish Invasion

Turkish invasion ended the multiple power centres and build a central authority of Turks. Some of the important effects of Turkish invasion in India were :

- Governance was based on central autocratic system.
- Development of urban economy.
- Development in law systems, Islamic laws stated in justice system.
- Uniformity in revenue system.
- Development of commercial activities and trade.
- Change in military structures, formation and maintenance of standing army.
- Condemnation of caste system.
- Development of Persian language as an official language in India.
- *Iqta* system was introduced for division of areas.
- Development of Hindi.
- Introduction of Turkish architecture, arches, domes, lofty towns or minarets.
- Turks referred to the people East of the Indus as 'Hindu', their land as 'Hindustan' and their language as 'Hindavi'.

Extra Facts From
Tamil Nadu Board and NIOS

- Al-Biruni also translated the Greek word of Euclid into Sanskrit. He transmitted Aryabhatta's magnum opus into Aryabattiyam.
- The important Rajput kingdom during Arab and Turkish invasion were Tomaras (Delhi), Chauhanas (Rajasthan), Solankis (Gujarat), Paramaras (Malwa), Gahadavalas (Kannauj) and Chandelas (Bundelkhand).
- The reason behind the success of Arab and Turkish invasion were the military superiority. Turkish cavalry was more mobile and active than Rajput's military. Turkish horsemen had greater mobility and were skilled in mounted archery while Rajput forces depends more on elephants.

13

Delhi Sultanate

[SOURCES]

Class-VII Old NCERT Chap 3 (Sultan of Delhi), Class-VII New NCERT Chap 3 (Delhi : 12th To 15th Century), Class-XI Old NCERT Chap 6 (Delhi Sultanate I, (1200-1400) Class-XI Old NCERT Chap 7 (Delhi Sultanate II, 1200-1400), Class-XI Old NCERT Chap 8 (Government, Economic and Social Life Under the Delhi Sultanate), Tamil Nadu Board (Class XI), NIOS

Establishment of Delhi Sultanate

- The Turks extended their conquest from the Punjab and Multan into the Ganga valley after the **Battle of Tarain** and even captured Bihar and parts of Bengal. After that, for almost one hundred years these Turkish invaders ruled over the vast part of India and formed the Delhi Sultanate.
- The Turkish rulers were successful in extending their rule over Malwa and Gujarat and penetrate into the Deccan and South India. The effects of the establishment of the Turkish rule resulted in far-reaching changes in society, administration and cultural life of India.
- Dynasties of the Delhi Sultanate are :
  - Mamluk Dynasty (1206-1290 AD)
  - Khilji Dynasty (1290-1320 AD)
  - Tughlaq Dynasty (1320-1414 AD)
  - Sayyid Dynasty (1414-1451 AD)
  - Lodi Dynasty (1451-1526 AD)

1. Mamluk Dynasty (1206-1290 AD)

The earliest rulers of the Delhi Sultanate were Mamluks. They were also known as the **Slave-kings** because many of them were either slaves or many of them were the sons of slaves, who had become Sultans. The first of these kings was Qutb-ud-din Aibak, the general of Muizzuddin (Muhammad Ghori).

Qutb-ud-din Aibak (1206-1210 AD)

- After the death of Ghori, Qutb-ud-din Aibak, became ruler (subordinate of Sultan) in 1206 AD. He had played an important role in the expansion of the Turkish rule in India.
- **Taj-ud-din Yalduz**, the ruler of Ghazni, claimed his rule over Delhi. **Nasir-ud-din Qabacha**, the Governor of Multan and Uch also revolted for independence.
- Aibak was able to win over his enemies. He defeated **Yaldauz** and occupied Ghazni.
- He made Lahore as capital of Delhi Sultanate.
- Qutb-ud-din Aibak was brave, faithful and generous. Due to his generosity, he was known as **Lakh Baksh**.
- He laid the foundation of the 240 ft tall tower Qutub-Minar in Delhi in 1192 AD (named after Sufi Saint **Khwaja Qutb-ud-din Bakhtiyar Kaki**) in Delhi.
- He also built **Adhai Din ka Jhonpra** in 1199 AD in Ajmer.
- In 1210 AD, Aibak died of injuries received in a fall from his horse, while playing Chaugan (Polo). His tomb is in Lahore.

Aram Shah (1210 AD)

- Aram Shah became the second sultan of the Mamluk dynasty of the Delhi Sultanate.
- He briefly held the throne after the unexpected death of Aibak before being dethroned by Iltutmish.

- Some historians were doubtful about his identity however, **Ferishta** and **Al-Badayuni** have written that **Aram Shah** was the son of Qutb-ud-din Aibak.
- Aram Shah was incapable ruler and the Turkish nobles opposed him.
- The weakness of Aram Shah's character became visible soon after his succession, when **Nasir-ud-din Qabacha** rebelled in Sind and besieged the forts of Uch and Multan.

Iltutmish (1210–1236 AD)

- The Turkish chiefs of Delhi invited the then Governor of Badayun, Iltutmish to come to Delhi. Iltutmish defeated Aram Shah and became the Sultan with the name of **Shamsuddin**.
- Iltutmish took up the task of consolidating his position. He defeated Taj-ud-dinYalduz in 1215 AD in the **Third Battle of Tarain**. In 1217 AD, he drove away Qabacha from Punjab.
- In 1220 AD, when **Chengiz Khan** destroyed the Khwarizm empire, Iltutmish realised the political necessity of avoiding a confrontation with the Mongols. When **Jalaluddin Mangbarni**, the son of the Shah of Khwarizm, while escaping from the Mongols, sought shelter at Iltutmish's court, Iltutmish turned him away. Thus, he saved the Sultanate from destruction by the Mongols.
- In 1226–27 AD, Iltutmish sent a large army under his son **Nasir-ud-din Mahmud**, which defeated **Iwaz Khan** and brought Bengal and Bihar back into the Delhi Sultanate.
- He was a generous and able ruler and built many public works. He completed the construction of Qutub Minar in Delhi.
- He shifted capital from Lahore to Delhi. He gave the Sultanate two of its basic coins– the silver 'Tanka' and the copper 'Jittal'.
- To gain greater control over the conquered areas, Iltutmish granted *iqtas* (land assignments in lieu of cash salaries) to his Turkish officers on a large scale.

Turkan-i-Chahalgani (Group of Forty)

- Iltutmish established 'Group of Forty' (*Turkan-i-Chahalgani*). These were Turkish and non-Turkish *amirs* (nobles) who advised and helped the Sultan in administering the Sultanate.
- When Iltutmish died, the balance of power shifted and the Sultan became a puppet of these amirs. For a few years, they decided on the selection of Sultans one after the other. The group was finally eliminated by Balban.

Raziya Sultan (1236–1240 AD)

- Iltutmish considered none of his surviving sons to be worthy of the throne. He finally nominated his daughter, Raziya to the throne. He induced the nobles and the theologians (*ulema*) to agree to the nomination.
- Rule of Raziya Sultan marked the beginning of a struggle for power between the monarchy and the *Turkan-i-Chahalgani*. The nobles wanted to install a puppet ruler on throne whom they could control.
- Iltutmish's *wazir*, **Nizam-ul-Mulk Junaidi**, opposed Raziya's elevation to the throne. He backed and supported a rebellion of nobles against her.
- The Turkish nobles accused her for violating feminine modesty, and being too friendly to an Abyssinian noble, **Yaqut Khan** who was Superintendent of the Royal Stable.
- Rebellions broke out at Lahore and Sirhind. Raziya personally led an expedition against Lahore and compelled the Governor to submit. On the way to Sirhind, an internal rebellion broke out in which Yaqut Khan was killed and Raziya imprisoned at Tabarhind.
- However, Raziya won over her captor, **Altunia**, and after marrying him made a renewed attempt on Delhi. Raziya fought valiantly, but was defeated and killed in a forest by bandits.

Bahram Shah (1240–1242 AD)

- Muiz-ud-din Bahram Shah became the next emperor but merely as the puppet in the hand of Turkish Nobles. **Ikhtiyaruddin Aitigin** used to run the administration of Delhi Sultanate on the behalf of Sultan.
- During his reign, the new post of '*Naib-i-Mamaliqat*' (Deputy of King) was created. He was killed in May 1242 AD by noblemen.

Masud Shah (1242–1246 AD)

- After the death of **Behram Shah**, Turkish Nobles supported and choose Alauddin Masud Shah as next ruler. He was the grandson of **Iltutmish** and son of **Ruknuddin**.
- Due to incompetent sultan, one of the noble and *wazir*, **Hasan Ghori Muhazzabuddin** killed Masud Shah and rose to power.

Nasiruddin Mahmud (1246-1266 AD)

- In 1246 AD, **Ulugh Khan** (Balban) placed the inexperienced and young Nasiruddin (grandson of Iltutmish) on throne and himself assumed the position of Naib (deputy). To further strengthen his position, Ulugh Khan married his daughter to Nasiruddin.
- Sultan Nasiruddin Mahmud died in 1265 AD. According to **Ibn Battuta** and **Isami**, Balban poisoned Nasiruddin and paved way for himself as Sultan.

Balban (1266-1287 AD)

- The struggle between the monarchy and the Turkish chiefs continued, till Balban ascended the throne in 1266 AD.
- Though his methods were often harsh and undesirable, but with his accession to the throne, an era of strong, centralised government began.
- Balban constantly sought to increase the prestige and power of the monarchy. He tried to strengthen his claim to the throne by declaring that he was the descendant of the legendary Iranian King **Afrasiyab**.
- Balban ruled in an autocratic manner and worked hard to elevate the position of the Sultan. He refused to entertain for important government posts anyone who did not belong to a noble family. This virtually meant the exclusion of Indian Muslims from all positions of power and authority.
- Balban broke the power of the *Turkan-i-Chahalgani*. To keep himself well informed, Balban appointed spies in every department.
- He re-organised the Military Department (*Diwan-i-Arz*) and deployed army in different parts of the country to put down rebellion.
- He also organised a strong centralised army, both to deal with internal disturbances, and to push back the **Mongols**, who had well-established themselves in the Punjab and posed a serious threat to the Delhi Sultanate.
- Balban adopted a policy of both force and diplomacy. He repaired the forts of **Tabarhind**, **Sunam** and **Samana** and posted a strong force in order to prevent the Mongols from crossing the river Beas.
- He maintained diplomatic relations with **Halaku Khan**, the Mongol Commander. Balban agreed to leave the major portion of the Punjab under the Mongol control.
- The disturbances in Mewat, Doab, Awadh and Katihar were ruthlessly suppressed by Balban. He also secured control over Ajmer and Nagaur in Eastern Rajputana but his attempts to capture Ranthambore and Gwalior failed.
- In 1279 AD, Governor of Bengal, **Tughril Beg** revolted and assumed the title of Sultan. Balban sent his forces to Bengal and killed Tughril.
- Subsequently, he appointed his own son **Bughra Khan** as the Governor of Bengal.
- Balban was undoubtedly one of the main architects of the Sultanate of Delhi, particularly of its form of government and institutions. He died in 1287 AD.
- After Balban's death, his son, **Bughra Khan**, was invited to rule over the Delhi Sultanate but he preferred to rule over Bengal as Governor.
- The Turkish nobles raised his grandson **Kaiqubad** to the throne. He was soon replaced by his son, **Kaimurs**, who remained on the throne for a little over three months.

Policy of Consolidation by Balban

Balban adopted a Policy of Consolidation rather than expansion. He introduced a new theory of kingship and insisted on the ceremony of *Sijada* (prostration) and *paibos* (kissing of the monarch's feet) in the court. Balban assumed the grand title of '*Zill-i-Ilahi*' means **image of God**. He also introduced Persian new year festival 'Nauroz'.

2. Khilji Dynasty (1290-1320 AD)

- The Khilji rulers were probably of **Turko-Afghan origin**, which replaced Mamluk dynasty in Delhi Sultanate. The Khilji dynasty is termed as 'Khilji Revolution'.

Jalaluddin Khilji (1290-1296 AD)

- After Kaimurs' death **Firoz** ascended the throne under the title of Jalaluddin Khilji and laid the foundation of the Khilji dynasty in 1290 AD.
- He served as *Ariz-i-Mumalik* (Minister of War) during Balban's reign. Some scholars call this event as the **dynastic revolution** of 1290. It brought an end to the slave dynasty.
- Jalaluddin Khilji ascended the throne at the age of 70 years. He ruled only for a short span of six years. He tried to mitigate some of the harsh aspects of Balban's rule.
- He was the first ruler of the Delhi Sultanate to clearly put forward the view that 'the state should be based on the willing support of the people'.
- Jalaluddin tried to win the goodwill of the nobility by a policy of tolerance. He avoided harsh punishments, even to those who revolted against him.
- He not only forgave them but at times even rewarded them to win their support. However, many people considered him to be a weak sultan.

Alauddin Khilji (1296-1316 AD)

- Alauddin Khilji was Jalaluddin's nephew and son-in-law. He had helped his uncle in his struggle for power and was appointed as *Amir-i-Tuzuk* (Master of Ceremonies).
- Alauddin had two victorious expeditions during the reign of Jalaluddin. After the first expedition of **Bhilsa** (Vidisha) in 1292 AD, he was given the *iqta* of **Awadh**, in addition to that of **Kara**.

- He was also appointed *Arizi-i-Mumalik* (Minister of War). In 1294 AD, he led the first Turkish expedition to Southern India and plundered Devagiri.
- In July 1296 AD, he murdered his uncle and father-in-law **Jalaluddin Khilji** and crowned himself as the Sultan.
- Alauddin decided to revive Balban's policies of ruthless governance. He curbed the powers of the nobles and interference of *Ulema* in the matters of the state. He also faced, a few rebellions in succession during the early years of his rule.
- To discourage festive parties, he banned the use of wines and intoxicants. He also instituted a spy services to inform the sultan of all that the nobles said and did.
- Alauddin formulated certain regulations and implemented them in order to prevent the reoccurrence of these rebellions :
  - Families that had been enjoying free land to support themselves, should pay land tax for their holdings. This curbed the excess of wealth owned by some people.
  - The Sultan reorganised the spy system and took measure to make it more effective.
  - The use of liquor and intoxicants was prohibited.
  - The nobles were ordered not to have social gatherings or inter-marriages without his permission.
  - Alauddin established a huge permanent, standing army to satisfy his ambition of conquest and to protect the country from external invasion.
- According to **Barani**, the author of '*Tarikh-i-Firuz Shahi*', Alauddin figured out four reasons for state rebellions:
  (i) Inefficiency of the spy system.
  (ii) The general practice of the use of wine.
  (iii) Social intercourse among the nobles and inter marriage between them.
  (iv) Excess of wealth in the possession of certain nobles.

Amir Khusrau

- Amir Khusrau was the court poet of **Alauddin Khilji** and gave detailed information about Khilji dynasty. He was the renowned Sufi poet and disciple of Nizamuddin Auliya. His major works includes *Tughlaq Nama*, *Wast-ul-Hayat* and *Nuh Sipihr*.
- He introduced many verse forms *viz*. Ghazal, Masnavi, Rubai, etc. Qawwalis, which were originally written in Persian language, also introduced by Khusrau in India.

Agrarian Reforms

- Apart from the control of the market, Alauddin took important steps in the field of land revenue administration. He was the first monarch in the Sultanate, who insisted that in the doab, land revenue would be assessed on the basis of measuring the land under cultivation.
- Alauddin wanted that the landlords of the area—called *khuts* and *muqaddams*, should pay the same taxes as the others. The policy of direct collection of land revenue by the state, based on measurement could only succeed if the amils and other local officials were honest. Alauddin insisted that their accounts should be audited strictly.
- The land revenue reforms of Alauddin marked an important step towards closer relationship with the rural areas. Some of his measures were continued by his successors, and later provided a basis for the agrarian reforms of **Sher Shah** and **Akbar**.
- After the death of Alauddin in 1316 AD, Malik Kafur sat on the throne for a few days, only to be deposed by Qutbuddin Mubarak Shah. He was soon murdered and Khusrau ascended the throne. However, he was defeated and killed by **Ghiyasuddin Tughlaq** in a battle.

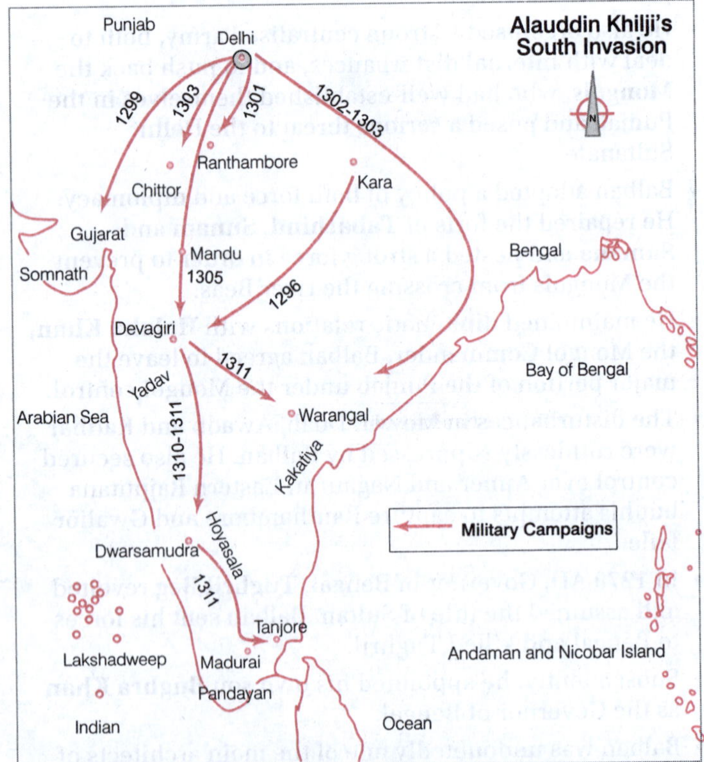

Market Regulations of Alauddin Khilji

- For contemporaries, Alauddin's measures to control the markets was one of the great wonders of the world. Alauddin set up three different markets for different commodities in Delhi. These markets were the grain market (*Mandi*), cloth market (*Sarai Adl*) and the market for horses, slaves, cattle, etc.

- In order to ensure a regular supply of cheap food-grains, he declared that the land revenue in the doab region, that is, the area extending from Meerut near the Yamuna to the border of Kara near Allahabad would be paid directly to the state, i.e., the villages in the area would not be assigned in iqta to anyone.
- To ensure implementation, Alauddin appointed a superintendent (*Shahna-i-Mandi*) who was assisted by an intelligence officer. Alauddin received daily reports of the market from two other independent sources, *barid* (intelligence officer) and *munhiyans* (secret spies).

Expansion of Sultanate

Sultan Alauddin Khilji's major achievement lies in expanding Delhi Sultanate's boundaries across the Rajputana, Deccan and Southern states. Some of his major expeditions are as follows :

Conquests of Alauddin Khilji

States	Native King	Sultanate's Commander (s)	Consequences
Gujarat (1299 AD)	Rai Karan (*Solankis*)	Nusrat Khan and Ulugh Khan	• Plunder of Somnath temple • Nusrat purchased Kafur Hazar Dinari • Alauddin married Chief Queen of Gujarat Kamala Devi
Ranthambore (1301 AD)	Rana Hamir Deva	Alauddin Khilji, Ulugh Khan and Nusrat Khan	• Nusrat Khan died • Fort of Ranthambore taken
Chittor (1303 AD)	Rana Ratan Singh (*Gehlot*)	Alauddin Khilji, Ulugh Khan (Amir Khusrau was eyewitness)	• *Jauhar* ceremony by women (*Rani Padmavati episode*) • Alauddin's son Khizr Khan was given Governorship of Chittor • Chittor renamed as Khizrabad
Deogiri (1307 AD)	Ram Chandra Dev	Malik Kafur	• Ram Chandra Dev was given the title of Rai Rayan
Fortress of Siwana (1308 AD)	Sheetal Dev	Malik Kamal-ud-din	• Sheetal Dev defeated and the fortress of Siwana seised
Warangal (1309 AD)	Pratap Rudra Dev II (*Kakatiya*)	Malik Kafur	• Kohinoor diamond taken away • King agreed to pay annual tribute to Delhi
Dwarasamudra (1310 AD)	Veer Ballal III (*Hoysala*)	Malik Kafur	• King agreed to pay annual tribute to Delhi
Madurai (1311 AD)	Vir Pandya	Malik Kafur	• Devastation of Nataraja temple at Chidambaram
Jalor (1311 AD)	Kanhar Deva	Malik Kamal-ud-din	• Fortress of Jalor seised
Deogiri (1313 AD)	Shankara- deva	Malik Kafur	• Devagiri was annexed and included in Sultanate

3. Tughlaq Dynasty (1320-1414 AD)

- The Tughlaq dynasty was originally Turko-Indian dynasty, which ruled Delhi during the Sultanate period.
- It was mainly ruled by **Ghiyasuddin Tughlaq, Muhammad bin Tughlaq** and **Firuz Shah Tughlaq.**

Ghiyasuddin Tughlaq (1320-1325)

- The founder of the Tughlaq dynasty was **Ghazi Malik** who ascended the throne as 'Ghiyasuddin Tughlaq' in 1320 AD. This dynasty ruled till 1414. Ghiyasuddin rose to an important position in the reign of Alauddin Khilji.
- In 1325 AD, Ghiyasuddin was crushed to death by collapse of stage, while attending an event for his victories in Bengal. Some historians suggest, it was Muhammad Tughlaq who conspired and killed his father.

Muhammad bin Tughlaq (1325-1351 AD)

- Muhammad bin Tughlaq ascended the throne 1325 AD. In contrast to Alauddin Khilji's policy, the Tughlaqs annexed the Deccan region.

- Under the Muhammad's rule the Delhi Sultanate was further consolidated. Many outlying territories were brought under the direct control of the Sultanate.
- Muhammad bin Tughlaq while a prince (called Jauna Khan) led the early expeditions against **Rai Rudra Dev** who was defeated after a prolonged conflict and Warangal was annexed under direct control of the Sultanate.
- **Bhanudeva II**, the ruler of Jayanagar in Orissa had helped Rai Rudra Dev of Warangal in his battle against Delhi Sultans.
- Ulugh Khan led an army against him in 1324 AD. Bhanudeva II was defeated and his territory annexed.
- Muhammad bin Tughlaq was one of the most remarkable rulers of his age. During his religious intercourse, Muhammad conversed not only with the Muslim mystics, but also with the Hindu yogis and Jain saints such as **Jinaprabha Suri**.
- Muhammad bin Tughlaq also welcomed foreigners to the nobility, many whom came to his court. This was not liked by many orthodox theologians, who accused him of being a 'rationalist'.
- Muhammad bin Tughlaq set up a separate department called Diwan-i-amir-i-kohi. The area was divided into development blocs headed by an official whose job was to extend cultivation by giving loans to cultivator.

Ibn Battuta

- Ibn Battuta was born in Tangier (Morocco). He reached Sind in 1333 AD during Muhammad bin Tughlaq's reign. The Sultan appointed him the Qazi (judge) of Delhi.
- Ibn Battuta was appointed as a Qazi or judge of Delhi. He was sent to China in 1342.
- He led campaigns to Kalanaur and Peshawar especially after the Mongol Attack under Tarmashrin Khan in 1326-1327 AD during Tughlaq's reign.
- Ibn Battuta recorded his observations in the book named **Kitab-ul-Rehla** about new cultures, peoples, beliefs, values, etc of Indian subcontinent.
- Ibn Battuta described Indian cities in his book, particularly Delhi and Daulatabad. He mentioned cultural, commercial and social aspect of these cities.
- These cities were connected through communication which was known as **uluq** and **dawa**. The horse post, called Uluq is run by royal horses stationed at a distance of every four miles. The foot-post has three station per mile; it is called Dawa.

Failed Experiments of Tughlaq

- Muhammad took some very bold and strong measures to reform the administration. Though there was nothing fundamentally wrong with Tughlaq's administrative and strategic experiments, but they failed. These are as follows :

Transfer of Capital

- One of the controversial measures of Muhammad bin Tughlaq was that he transferred his capital from Delhi to Deogiri (Daulatabad).
- The Sultan wanted to maintain both Delhi and Daulatabad as his capitals. According to **Barani**, in 1326–27 AD, Sultan decided to shift his capital from Delhi to Deogiri (Daulatabad) in the Deccan because it was more centrally located.
- According to **Ibn Battuta**, the people of Delhi used to write letters containing abuses to the Sultan. In order to punish them, Sultan decided to shift the capital. **Isami** states that Deogir was at a safer distance from the North-West frontier and thus, was safe from the Mongols.
- The entire population was not asked to leave only the upper classes consisting of shaikhs, nobles, ulema were shifted to Daulatabad. No attempt was made to shift the rest of the population.
- Though Muhammad bin Tughlaq built a road from Delhi to Deogir and set up rest houses but the journey was extremely harsh for the people. Large number of people died because of rigorous travelling and the heat.

Expeditions of Khurasan and Qarachil (1329-1330 AD)

- This expedition was launched in the Kumaon hills in the Himalayas. According to a modern historian, the expedition was aimed at Kashmir in order to control the entry of horses from the Chinese side, i.e., Sinkiang.
- However, **Khurasan expedition** never aimed at the conquest of China, as some later historians have suggested. After some success, the armies went too far into the inhospitable region of the Himalayas and suffered a disaster.
- Besides, the Sultan also planned **invasions of Qarachil** region (In present day Himachal Pradesh) and **Qandhar** but it resulted into failure. It is believed from an army of 10,000, only 10 persons returned. However, it seems that the hill rajas accepted the over-lordship of Delhi.

Token Currency

- Another controversial project undertaken by Muhammad bin Tughlaq was the introduction of 'Token Currency'. According to **Barani**, the Sultan introduced token currency because the treasury was empty due to the Sultan's schemes of conquests.
- Muhammad introduced a Copper Coin (**Jittal**) in place of Silver Coin (**Tanka**) and ordered that it should be accepted as equivalent to the Tanka.
- Moreover, **Qublai Khan** of China had already successfully experimented with a token currency. A Mongol ruler of Iran, **Ghazan Khan** had also experimented with it. However, the idea of token currency was new in India and it was difficult for traders and common people to accept it.
- The state also did not take proper precautions to check the initiation of coins issued by the mints. The central administration could not prevent people from forging the new coins and soon the new coins flooded the markets.
- According to **Barani**, the people began to mint token currency in their houses. However, the common man failed to distinguish between copper coin issued by the royal treasury and those, which were locally made. Thus, the Sultan was forced to withdraw the token currency.

Doab Crisis

- Muhammad bin Tughlaq launched a scheme to extend and improve cultivation in the Doab. The area was divided into development blocs headed by an official. He responsibility was to extend cultivation by giving loans to the cultivators and to induce them to cultivate superior crops.
- The scheme failed largely because the men chosen for the purpose proved to be inexperienced and dishonest, and misappropriated the money for their own use. The large sums of money advanced for the project could not be recovered.

Firuz Shah Tughlaq (1351-1388 AD)

- Muhammad bin Tughlaq was succeeded by his cousin Firuz Shah Tughlaq. Under him no new territories could be added to the Sultanate.
- After his accession, Firuz Tughlaq was faced with the problem of preventing the imminent breakup of the Delhi Sultanate.
- The Sultan adopted a policy of trying to appease the nobles. Therefore, he made no attempt to re-assert his authority over South India and the Deccan. He led two campaigns into Bengal but was unsuccessful. Thus, Bengal was lost by the Sultanate.
- Firuz Shah led a campaign against the ruler of Jajpur (Odisha). He destroyed the temples there and gathered a rich plunder but made no attempt to annex Orissa.
- He also led a campaign against Kangra in the Punjab hills. His longest campaign was to deal with rebellions in Gujarat and Thatta (Sind).
- The city **Jaunpur** was founded by Firuz Shah Tughlaq and named in memory of Muhammad bin Tughlaq, whose name was **Jauna Khan**.
- It was during the time of Firuz, that *Jizyah* became a separate tax. Earlier, it was a part of land revenue.
- Firuz refused to exempt the Brahmans from the payment of *Jizyah* since, this was not provided for in the sharia law. Only women, children, the disabled and the indigent who had no means of livelihood were exempt from it.
- Firuz Shah Tughlaq patronised music and despite his orthodoxy, was fond of wine. He was the first ruler who took steps to have Hindu religious works translated from **Sanskrit** into **Persian**, so that there may be a better understanding of Hindu ideas and practices. Many books on music, medicine and Mathematics were also translated from Sanskrit into Persian during his reign.
- Firuz was keenly interested in the economic improvement of the country. He set up a large department of public works, which looked after his building programme.
- Firuz repaired and dug a number of canals. The longest canal was about 200 kilometres, which took off from the river Sutlej to Hansi, another canal took off from the Yamuna. These canals were meant for irrigation purposes.
- Firuz Shah Tughlaq established new towns, these towns were **Hissar-Firuzah** or Hissar (in modern Haryana) and Firozabad (in Modern Uttar Pradesh).
- When Firuz died in 1388, the administrative and political problems, which had to be faced after the death of every Sultan came to the surface. The struggle for power between the sultan and the nobles started once again.
- The governors of provinces became independent, and gradually the Sultan of Delhi was confined virtually to a small area surrounding Delhi. The will of Sultan stated that, 'The dominion of the Lord of the Universe (being the title of the Sultans of Delhi) extends from Delhi to Palam.'

Nasiruddin Mahmud (1390-1394 AD)

- He was the son of Firuz Shah Tughlaq and the last ruler of Tughlaq dynasty. His empire with expanded till Palam of Delhi.
- After his death, **Timur Lang** attacked and ended Tughlaq dynasty.

Timur's Attack of Delhi (1398 AD)

- Timur started his expedition from Kabul in August 1398 AD and reached Delhi in December 1398 AD. On his way to Delhi, he captured and looted all the towns.
- Sultan **Mahmud Shah**, the last Sultan of the Tughlaq dynasty and his Vazir' (Prime Minister) fled from Delhi. Timur ordered a general massacre and plunder, which continued for 15 days.
- Timur also took with him many Indian artisans, such as masons, stone cutters, carpenters, etc. Some of them helped him in putting up many fine buildings in his capital, **Samarqand**.

4. Sayyid Dynasty (1414-1451 AD)

- Sayyid dynasty was the fourth dynasty of Delhi Sultanate, which came to power after Tughlaq dynasty. The ruling family claimed to be Sayyid's or descendants of Prophet Muhammad.

Khizr Khan (1414-1421 AD)

- After defeating the army of Delhi in 1398 Timur appointed Khizr Khan as the ruler of Multan. Khizr Khan defeated **Sultan Daulat Khan** and occupied Delhi and founded Sayyid dynasty. He did not assume the title of Sultan but was comfortable with Rayati-Ala.
- The author of the *Tarikh-i-Mubarak Shahi*, **Yahya Sirhindi** claimed that the founder of the Sayyid dynasty was a descendant of the prophet. Khizr Khan was the most competent Sayyid rule of the dynasty.

Mubarak Shah (1412-1434 AD)

- After Khizr Khan's death Mubarak Shah (1412–1434 AD) and Muhammad Shah (1434–1445 AD) ascended the throne one after another.
- In 1445 AD, Alam Shah ascended the throne and became the Sultan. He proved a totally incompetent Sultan.

5. Lodi Dynasty (1451-1526 AD)

- The Lodis were the last ruling family of the Sultanate period and the first to be headed by the Afghans.

Bahlol Lodi (1451–1489 AD)

- Bahlol Lodi laid the foundation of Lodi dynasty whose rulers were Afghans.
- Sultan Bahlol Lodi was a capable general. The Afghan nobles wanted Sultan to treat them as an equal partner rather than an absolute monarch.
- Bahlol Lodi successfully suppressed the revolts in Mewat and Doab. In 1476 AD, he defeated the Sultan of Jaunpur and annexed it to Delhi Sultanate.

Sikandar Lodi (1489–1517 AD)

- After the death of Bahlol Lodi, Sikandar Lodi ascended the throne. Sikandar Lodi showed little tolerance towards the non-Muslims. He re-imposed *Jizyah* on non-Muslims.
- Sikandar Lodi believed in the superior position of the Sultan vis-a-vis the nobles. He compelled nobles and amirs to show formal respect to the Sultan in darbar and outside and treated them harshly.
- He was contemporary of **Rana Sanga** of Mewar as well as **Mehmud Begrah** of Gujarat. He founded the city in Agra in 1504 AD and made his second capital.
- Sikandar Lodi introduced a new system of land measurement, known as **Gaj-e-Sikandari**.

Ibrahim Lodi (1517-1526 AD)

- Afghan nobles helped Ibrahim Lodi to become Sultan, after the death of Sikandar Lodi in 1517.
- **Daulat Khan** of Bihar and **Rana Sanga** of Mewar sent an invitation to Babur at Kabul to invade India.
- Babur defeated Sultan Ibrahim Lodi in 1526 AD in the historic and decisive **First Battle** at **Panipat**.
- He was the first Sultan of Delhi who was killed in the battle field.

Mongol Invasion in Delhi Sultanate

Mongol invaded India time to time during the reign of different rulers of the Delhi Sultanate.

Mongol Invasion at the time of Iltutmish

- In the year 1218 AD, **Genghis Khan** defeated the Khwarizm empire and destroyed it completely.
- The threat of Mongol invasion of India came in 1221 AD, when Khwarizm crown prince escaped from Mongols and cross Indus river.
- Prince Khwarizm then asked for assylum to Iltutmish, but he denied as Iltutmish do not want the rivalry of Genghis Khan.

Mongol Invasion at the Time of Balban

- After the death of Genghis Khan (1226 AD) his empire divided between his sons.
- The Mongol General **Tair Bahadur** headed towards Lahore and the subedar of Lahore asked for help of Sultan Balban, but Balban did not gave any assistance. Lahore was then captured by the Mongols.
- In the year 1245, Mongol attacked the Sultanate but defeated by **Balban**.

Mongols Invasion during Khiljis

- **Salaluddin Khilji** was the chief defender of North-Western frontiers during the reign of Balban. He fought many battles against the Mongols and was well-known about the fighting skills against Mongols.
- In the year 1292, Mongol commander **Abdullah** attacked Delhi with force of 1,50,000. But **Jalaluddin Khilji** defeated them and a peace treaty was signed due to which 4000 Mongols accepted Islam and settled near Delhi.
- In the reign of **Alauddin**, many battles were fought between Mongols and his army, but Alauddin crushed the Mongols decisively.

Extra Facts From
Tamil Nadu Board and NIOS

- Qutubuddin Aibak captured Ghazni in 1208 AD from Yildiz and in 1197-98 AD Aibak Conquered Badaun and Kannauj from Jaichand's successor **Harishchandra**.
- Through military campaigns, Iltutmish captured **Ranthambore** in 1226 AD and Mandaur, Jalore in 1231 AD; captured Bayana and Gwalior.
- In 1229 AD, Iltutmish received the letter of validity from the Caliph of Baghdad. Alauddin Khilji's title was **Amir-e-Tuzuk** (emperor of festivals) and later he also became **Ariji-e-Mumalik** (Minister of War).
- The commanders of Alauddin's Gujarat campaign were Nusrat Khan and Ulugh Khan and the ruler of Gujarat at that time was Rai Karan.
- Alauddin named Chitand as Khignabad after his son Khinkhon.
- Alauddin Khilji's first Deccan campaign began in 1306-07 AD, while his first campaign in the far South was to Warangal in the Telangana region in 1309 AD.
- **Bhanudev II**, the ruler of Orissa, was defeated by the Tughlaq dynasty. Ulugh Khan was leading the Tughlaq army.
- **Bahlol Lodi** suppressed the rebellion of Doab and Mewat and made Jaunpur a part of Delhi Sultanate.

14

Delhi Sultanate: Administration, Economy, Society and Arts

[SOURCES]

Class-XI Old NCERT Chap 8 (Government, Economic and Social Life under the Delhi Sultanate), Tamil Nadu Board (Class XI), NIOS

The administration during the Delhi sultanate was very systematics, gradually developed into a powerful and highly centralised state.

Administration during the Delhi sultanate was completely dependent on Muslim laws.

Administration in Sultanate Period

The Sultanate had a powerful effect on the Mughal system of administration, which developed in the 16th century.

The Sultan

- Although many of the Turkish sultans in India declared themselves 'lieutenant of the faithful', i.e., of the **Abbasid caliph** at Baghdad, and included his name in the Khutba in the Friday prayers.
- The caliph had only a moral position. By proclaiming his supreme position, the sultans at Delhi were only proclaiming that they were a part of the Islamic world.
- The sultan's office was the most important in the Sultanate and supreme political, military, and even legal authority, was vested in him.
- He was also responsible for the maintenance of law and justice. The sultans dealt with strong manner in dispensing justice. **Balban** didn't spare even his relatives or high officers of state.
- **Muhammad bin Tughlaq** applied this even to the religious classes (*ulema*) who had previously been exempted from harsh punishments.
- No clear law of succession developed among Muslim rulers. The Islamic theory adhered to the idea of the election of the ruler but accepted in practice the succession of any son of a successful ruler.
- However, all the sons of a ruler were considered to have an equal claim to the throne.

Central Administration

- The sultan was assisted by several ministers who were chosen by him and remained in office at his pleasure.
- A definite system of administration developed towards the end of the 13th century AD.

The Wazir

- The key figure in administration was the *wazir*. In the earlier period, the *wazir* were primarily military leaders.
- In the 14th century AD, the *wazir* began to be considered more an expert in revenue affairs and presided over a large department dealing both with income and expenditure.
- A separate Auditor-General for scrutinising expenditure and an Accountant General for inspecting income worked under the *wazir*.

- Muhammad bin Tughlaq paid close attention to the organisation of the revenue department. His *wazir*, **Khwaja Jahan,** was widely respected.
- The rulers of Delhi Sultanate posted intelligence agent called Barids indifferent parts of the empire to keep them informed of what?
- **Khan-i-Jahan**, a converted Tailang Brahman who was deputy to the previous *wazir*, was chosen by Firuz Shah Tughlaq as his wazir.

  His long spell of 18 years as *wazir* is generally considered to be the high watermark of the *wazir's* influence.

Other Important Ministers of Central Administration

- **Barid-i-Mumalik** Head of the State News Agency.
- **Amir-i-Hazib** Officer incharge of the royal court.
- **Sadr-i-Jahan** Officer incharge of religious and charitable endowments.
- **Amir-i-Akhur** Officer commanding the royal horses.
- **Amir-i-Dad** Officer incharge of justice (public prosecutor).
- **Sahna-i-Pil** Superintendent of royal elephants.
- **Shiqdar** Officer incharge of land measuring a '*shiq*'.
- **Amir-i-Majlis** Officer incharge of royal feasts, conference and festivals.
- **Majlis-i-Am or Majlis-i-Khalwat** Council of friends and officers (trusted ministers) consulted on important affairs of state.
- **Kazi-ul-Kazat** Head of the Central Judicial Department.
- **Qazi** Legal officer (dispensed Civil Law based on Muslim Law Shariat).
- **Sadr-us-Sudur** Dealt with the religious matters.
- **Naib Wazir** Deputy Minister.

Major Departments of Delhi Sultanate

- **Diwan-i-Risalat** It dealt with religious matters, pious foundations and stipends to deserving scholars and men of piety. It was presided over by the chief sadr, who was generally the chief *qazi*.
  - The chief qazi was the head of the department of justice. The qazis dispensed civil law based on the Muslim law (*sharia*). The Hindus were governed by their own personal laws.
- **Diwani-i-Arz** The Diwani-i-Arz or the military department was the most important department of state, next to the *wazir*. The head of this department was called the *Ariz-i-Mumalik*.
  - The office came into being the first time under Balban as a separate department. The *Ariz* was not the Commander-in-Chief of the army, but it has responsibilities such as to recruit, equip and pay the army.
- **Diwan-i-Insha** It dealt with state correspondence. There were a number of other departments in addition to these. The rulers posted intelligence agents called barids in different parts of the empire to keep them informed. Only a nobleman who enjoyed the fullest confidence of the ruler was appointed the chief barid.
- **Wakil-i-Dar** Firuz Shah Tughlaq had set up a separate department of slaves, known as *Wakil-i-Dar*, under whom many slaves were employed in royal workshops.
  - He was also responsible for the maintenance of proper decorum at the court, and placing nobles in their proper order of precedence at formal receptions.
- **Diwan-i-Amir-Kohi** The department was related to agriculture, established by Muhammad bin Tughlaq. It was started to improve cultivation in the Doab region, which was facing acute drought and crop failures.

The Army

- The efficiency of Delhi Sultanate's army was the main factor to contain the **Mongol invasions** while at the same time conquering entire North and Deccan. The Turks also maintained a large number of elephants, which were trained for war purposes.
- Balban kept his army in good trim by making it march over long distances on the pretext of undertaking hunting excursions. The Turks and Afghans predominated in the cavalry, which was considered prestigious.
- The Hindus were employed both in the cavalry and the infantry at the time of the Ghaznavids. They continued to be employed but largely in the infantry in the subsequent period.
- Alauddin introduced the branding system (*Dagh*) of the horses so that the soldiers may not bring horses of poor quality. A descriptive roll of each soldier was also maintained.
- Of all the Delhi rulers, **Alauddin Khilji** had the largest standing army. The strength of his army is placed at 3,00,000 by **Barani**, which appears to be an exaggeration.
- Alauddin was also the first sultan who paid his soldiers fully in cash. **Asatvar** (cavalryman) in his time was paid 238 tankas a year or about 20 tangos a month. Earlier, the Turkish soldiers had been assigned several villages in the doab for the payment of their salaries.
- Rather than appointing aristocrats and landed chieftains as governors the early Delhi sultans, especially Iltutmish favoured their special slaves purchased for military services, called Bandagan.

Important Army Officials

Ariz-i-Mumalik	The head of the Diwan-i-Arz department responsible for the recruitment, payment and inspection of troops.
Amir-i-Akhur	Officer commanding royal horses.
Sahna-i-Pil	Superintendent of royal elephants.
Amir-i-Bahr	Officer incharge of police and transport naval port.

Local Administration

- The Turks divided their administration into several tracts called *Iqtas*, which were divided among the leading Turkish nobles. The holders of these offices were called *Muqtis* or *Walis*.
- The *Muqtis* were expected to maintain law and order in their tracts and collect the land revenue due to the government.
- Out of the money they collected, they were expected to meet the salaries of the soldiers and keep the balance.
- These *Iqtas* later became provinces or *subas*. Under Muhammad bin Tughlaq there were twenty-four provinces.
- Below the *iqtas* were the shiqs and these were under control of *Shiqdar*.
- The *pargana* was the next administrative unit. These were grouped into units of 100 to 84 and traditionally called *Chaurasi*. The *Pargana* was headed by the *Amil*.
- The most important persons in the village were the *khut* (landowners) and muqaddam or headman. The village accountant was known as *Patwari*.

Economy in the Sultanate Period

The new system of taxation was based on *Quran*. Four kinds of taxes sanctioned by the *Quran* were imposed namely as *kharaj, zakat, jeziah* and *khums*.

Types of Taxes

- **Zakat** To be paid by well to do Muslims for helping the needy religious tax.
- **Jeziah** Tax levied on non-Muslims in return of which they received protection of life and property and exemption from military services.
- **Kharaj** Land tax, which was equal to 1/10th of the produce of land.
- **Khums** It was 1/6th of the booty captured during war.
- **Abwabs** Excess taxes like house tax, grazing tax, etc.
- **Sharab** Irrigation tax.
- **Ashraf** 1/10th of the gross produce on land held by Muslims.

Types of Lands

- **Khalisa** (Crown Land) It was directly administered by the Central Government. Doab region brought under this.
- **Inam** or **Waqf** It was the land given to the people especially to the Muslim saints and scholars, in gift or charity.
- **Lands of Feudatory Hindu Chiefs** From such lands, the Sultan got annual fixed tributes.
- **Iqta** It is that part of land granted by the Sultan to its military chiefs for the maintenance of a given number of troopers. The land was normally taken back, when the Iqtadars were not in a position to maintain the army.

Currency System

- The sultanate mints generally uttered coins in three mental-gold, silver and billon (copper mixed with very small quantity of silver).
- The main coins were **tanka** and **jital** but some smaller currencies were also in circulation. Barani mentions **Dangs** and **Dirhams** in use at the capital Delhi.

Trade and Industry

- The Sultanate period was marked by the growth of towns and town life. A modern historian states that on the whole 'the Sultanate presents the picture of a flourishing urban economy. **Ibn Battuta** described 'Delhi the largest city in the Eastern part of the Islamic world'.
- The other important cities of the times were **Lahore** and **Multan** in the North-West, **Kara** and **Lakhnauti** in the East and **Anhilwara** (Patan) and **Cambay** (Khambat) in the West.
- Such an economy must have necessitated commerce on a large scale.
- Indian textiles had already established their position in the trade of countries on the Red Sea and the Persian Gulf.
- During this period, fine Indian textiles were introduced to China as well where it was valued more than silk. India imported from West Asia **high grade textiles** (satin, etc.), **glassware** and **horses**.
- Since, India had a favourable trade balance, gold and silver came to India from these countries. India's foreign trade both overland and overseas was truly an international enterprise.
- The royal *karkhanas*, which we have referred to earlier catered to all the needs of the sultan. They manufactured costly articles made of silk, gold and silver ware, etc.

Industries in Sultanate Period

During the Sultanate, various industries were prevailing. The special feature is the combination of Arabic and Persian elements in it. These industries are divided in various categories i.e.,

Royal Industries

- During the Sultanate period, royal industries use to fulfill requirements of Sultan and royal family. Silk, gold, silver and other precious materials and their products are made by these industries.
- Jewellery of diamond, gold, pearl, etc are made in these industries.
- Royal industries were made in the reign of Muhammad bin Tughlaq and it was developed in the reign of Firoz Shah Tughlaq.

Textile Industries

- Invention of Chaluka during Sultanate period boosted the textile industries.
- With the help of sieve, cotton is now cleaned faster.
- **Ziauddin Barani** mentioned about clothes such as Khujkari, Masmesheriuttam, Shirin, Burad, etc.
- **Jyotishwar Thakur** in his text talk about 20 types of clothes during the Sultanate period.
- Muhammad bin Tughlaq use to present clothes to his amins twice a year, these clothes are manufactured in the royal factories. These were usually made up of velvet, damask and wool.
- During this period, India use to trade with countries near Red sea.
- Gujarat and Bengal are two important trade centres for textile trade.
- Raw silk was imported from China and best quality textile was exported to China.

Metal Industry

- Ahmedabad, Delhi and Bengal were important centers for Iron industries during Sultanate period.
- Lahore, Kalinjau, Banaras, Sihalkot and Golconda were famous for sword-making.
- India use to import glass utensils from West Asia and clay utensils from China.
- Utensils of gold and silver are made in metal industries.

Other Industries

- In the Sultanate period, tanning, metallurgy, carpet weaving, wood working, furniture making, stone carving craftmen were famous for their work.
- **Leather industries** of Gujarat was popular.
- Delhi and Multan were important Ivory work centres. Wood Industry of Kashmir was also popular.

Social Life of Sultanate Period

- Several important changes took place in Indian society during this period. One of these was the growing power of a class of people who are variously called *samanta*, *ranak*, *rautta* (rajput), etc.
- Some historians call this type of a society 'feudal', although features of European feudalism, such as vassalge, serfdom and manors did not exist in India.
- Slavery also existed during the period. Prisoners of war, debtors unable to pay their stakes could be sold into slavery.
- During famines, many farmers sold themselves or their wife and children for food.

Caste System

- The caste system continued to be the basis of the society. But there were important changes within the caste system. Thus, there was considerable strengthening of the position of the Brahmans.

Condition of Women

- The omission of all reference to women teachers in the literature written during the period shows the poor state of higher education among women.
- Daughters of high officials and courtesans were also supposed to be highly skilled in various arts, including poetry.
- The practice of *sati* was made obligatory by some writers, but condemned by others.
- According to an Arab writer, **Sulaiman** wives of kings sometimes burnt themselves on the funeral pyre of their husbands.

Literary Works in Sultanate Period

The Delhi Sultanate established a new language and literary style that introduced into the sub-continent. Persian became the official language of Delhi Sultanate and Urdu was mainly the camp language.

Literary Works of Sultanate Period

Author	Book
Al Biruni	Kitab-ul-Hind
Minhaj-us-Siraj	Tabaqat-i-Nasari
Amir Khusrau	Khazain-ul-Futuh, Tughlaqnama
Ziauddin-Barani	Fatwa-i-Jahandari, Tarikh-i-Firoz Shahi
Firoz Shah	Fatwa-i-Firoz Shahi
Hasan Nizami	Taj-ul-Maathir
Abu Bakr	Chach Namah
Ibn Batutta	Kitab-ul-Rehla

Amir Khusrau

- Amir Khusrau was a creative Persian poet (1253-1325 AD) associated with royal courts of more than seven rulers of Delhi Sultanate. Amir Khusrau was a genius of those times. A very versatile person, he was a soldier, a composer of poetry in Arabic, Persian, Urdu and a diplomat, smart in court matters and was also a good musician.
- He innovated *Khayal* (a style of singing), Amir Khusrau wrote *Tarikh-i-Alai* or *Khazain-ul-Futuh*. In this book, he gave an account of conquest of Alauddin. He wrote another book called *Ashiqa*, which contains the love story of Deval Rani and Khizr Khan.
- In his *Nuh-Siphir* or Nine Skies, he gave the story of Sultan **Mubarak Shah**. He also lived in the court of **Ghiyasuddin Tughlaq** and wrote *Tughlaqnama*. Khusrau is also known as *Tuti-e-Hind* or **Parrot of India**.
- He created the fusion of Indian, Arabic and Persian music. He is credited to have invented *tabla*, *sitar* and modified *veena*.

Ibn-Battuta

- Ibn-Battuta belong to Morocco in South Africa.
- He came to India during the reign of **Muhammad bin Tughlaq**. He spent eight years in his court.
- In his arabic work 'The Rihla', he talk about the contemporary social, economic, cultural and religious practices. He also talked about slave trade in India and his experiences during this period.
- He mentions about the seasons in India, the fruits and vegetables, crops, roots, etc. According to him, the soil of India is highly cultivable, in which two crops are grown in one year.
- He talked about village industries, jaggery making, oil extracting techniques and weaving skills of women.
- He mentions in his text about roads, social life, etc.

Architecture of Sultanate Period

- New architectural forms and styles were introduced in India during the Delhi Sultanate. The synthesis of Indian and Islamic architectural features led to emergence of Indo-Islamic architecture.
- The new features were :
  - The arch and dome
  - The use of lime-mortar
  - The development of the true arch
- In the beginning, they converted temples and other structures demolished into mosques.
- For example, the **Quwwat-ul-Islam mosque** near **Qutub Minar** in Delhi was built by using the materials obtained from destroying many Hindu and Jain temples.
- With the arrival of artisans from West Asia the arch and dome began to show up with precision and perfection.
- The **Tomb** of **Balban** was adorned with the first true arch and the **Alai Darwaza** adorned with the first true dome.
- The structures used the combined principle of Slab and Beam method in Sultanate period.
- Architecture during Sayyid and Lodi dynasty developed a new form of Islamic architecture, which was later followed by the Mughals.
- One pattern was based on octagonal plan surrounded by arched walkway with one storey in height and the other one was based on square plan without walkway with two or three storey in height.

Structure and Monuments of Sultanate Period

Structure/ Monument	Built by
Quwwat-ul-Islam Mosque (Delhi)	Qutub-ud-Din Aibak
Adhai Din-ka Jhonpra (Ajmer)	Qutub-ud-Din Aibak
Qutub Minar (Delhi)	Initiated by Qutub-ud-Din Aibak, completed by Iltutmish
Alai Darwaza(Delhi) (the first true dome)	Alauddin Khilji
Jamat Khana Masjid (Delhi)	Initiated by Alauddin Khilji completed by Khizr Khan
Nizamuddin Dargah (Mausoleum)	Muhammad bin Tughlaq
Tomb of GhiyasuddinTughlaq (Delhi)	Initiated by Ghiyasuddin Tughlaq himself, completed by Muhammad Tughlaq
Tomb of Sikandar Lodi Delhi	Ibrahim Lodi

Extra Facts From Tamil Nadu Board and NIOS

- The fiscal claims of hereditary intermediaries (now called Chaudhuris) and the village headman (khots) were drastically curtailed during Sultanate period, particularly in **Lodhi dynasty**.
- Sultan own troops was known as **Hashm-i-qalb**.

15

Vijayanagara and Bahmani Empire

(SOURCES)

Class-XI Old NCERT Chap 1 (The Age of Vijayanagara and the Bahmani's and the Coming of the Portuguese), Class-XI Old NCERT Chap 10 (Struggle for Empire in North India (1400-1525)), Class-XII New NCERT Chap 7 (An Imperial Capital Vijayanagara), Tamil Nadu Board (Class XI), NIOS

- The Vijayanagara and Bahmani Kingdoms emerged in 14th century AD in Deccan region of South India and dominated for more than 200 years. The Vijayanagara was Hindu Kingdom while Bahmani Sultanate was a Persian Sultanate.
- The Vijayanagara and Bahmani kingdoms co-existed and were constantly at war with one another. The Bahmani empire declined towards end of the 15th century AD, and of the Vijayanagara empire ended in 1565 AD in the **Battle of Bannihatti** (The Battle of Rakkasa-Tangadi).

Vijayanagara Empire

- The Vijayanagara Kingdom was founded by **Harihara** and **Bukka** in 1336 AD, who were the feudatories of the **Kakatiyas** of Warangal and later became ministers in the Kingdom of Kampili (Karnataka).
- When Kampili was attacked by Muhammad Tughlaq for giving refuge to a Muslim rebel, the two brothers were imprisoned, converted to Islam. However, **Guru Vidyaranya,** re-admitted both the brothers to Hinduism and they established their capital at Vijayanagara.
- Historians use the term, 'Vijayanagara empire', but the contemporary literature and inscriptions described it as the **Karnataka Samrajyamu.**
- Four dynasties ruled the Vijayanagara empire. These were :
  - (i) Sangam Dynasty (1336-1485 AD) founded by Harihara I and Bukka I
  - (ii) Saluva Dynasty (1485-1505 AD) founded by Saluva Narasimha
  - (iii) Tuluva Dynasty (1505-1570 AD) founded by Vira Narasimha Raya
  - (iv) Aravidu Dynasty (1570-1652 AD) founded by Tirumala II

Sangama Dynasty (1336-1485 AD)

The Sangam dynasty was the first dynasty of the Vijayanagara empire founded by two brothers Harihara and Bukka in 1336 AD. At first, the Vijayanagara Kingdom was a kind of a cooperative commonwealth at first.

Harihara I (1336-1356 AD)

- He was one of the first founders of the empire. He founded 'Vidyanagar' which was later renamed as 'Vijayanagara'. Harihara I made Anagundi his capital.
- He annexed the **Hoyasala** state in 1346 AD and killed **Vir Ballal III**. He also defeated Sultan of Madurai.

Bukka I (1356-1379 AD)

- During his reign, Vijayanagara faced strong confrontation with Bahmani kingdom. In the South, its main rivals were the Sultans of Madurai. He made **Gutti** his royal capital.
- The Vijayanagara empire saw expansion under Bukka I which comprised the whole of South India upto

Rameshwaram, including the Tamil country as well as that of the **Cheras** (Kerala).

Harihara II (1379-1404 AD)

- He was the first ruler to assume legal title as king such as **Raja Parmeshwara** and **Maharajadhiraja**.
- He also led an alliance with the Bahmani kingdom and expansion its territories of Gajapatis and Reddis into Eastern region.
- Victories of Belgaum and Goa from Bahmani kingdom in the Western region considered as greatest achievement of Harihara II. He has sent an expedition to Ceylon (Sri Lanka) as well.

Deva Raya I (1406-1422 AD)

- The reign of Deva Raya I began with a renewed confrontation for the Tungabhadra doab.
- He was defeated by Bahmani Sultan **Firuz Shah** and had to pay huge compensation and gave his daughter in marriage to the Sultan.
- He constructed a dam across Tungabhadra river in 1410 AD.
- Venetian (Italian) scholar and traveller **Nicolo De Conti** visited his court.
- Devaraya I built **Hazar Rama Temple** and **Sri Rangam Inscription** belongs to his reign.

Three Major Areas of Conflict

1. The Tungabhadra doab (Region between the rivers Krishna and Tungabhadra)
2. Krishna-Godavari delta (Region of fertile land and numerous ports)
3. Marathawada (Konkan Region of Western India)

Deva Raya II (1422-1446 AD)

- He assumed the titles *Immadi Devaraya, Proudha Devaraya* and *Gajabetekara*.
- In his reign, the Vijayanagara empire extended to the most distant South and touched the shores of Ceylon (Sri Lanka).
- In order to strengthen his army, he reorganised his army, incorporating in it many features of the armies of the Delhi Sultanate.
- He started recruiting large number of Muslims in his army and starting buying Arab Horses in large numbers.
- The Persian traveller **Abdur Razzaq** and a Portuguese writer **Nuniz**, visited Vijayanagara in the reign of Deva Raya II.
- **Nuniz** states that the Kings of Quilon, Sri Lanka, Pulicat, Pegu and **Tenasserim** (in Burma and Malaya) paid tribute to Deva Raya II.
- Being a great patron of literature Deva Raya II wrote two Sanskrit works **Mahanataka Sudhanidhi** and a commentary on the Brahmasutras of **Bhadrayana**.

Saluva Dynasty (1485-1505 AD)

- After Devaraya II's death, Sangam dynasty declined due to series of civil wars erupted in various parts of the region.
- Therefore, a new dynasty founded known as Saluva dynasty by Saluva Narasimha. He was the **Governor** of **Chandragiri**.

Saluva Narasimha (1485-1491 AD)

- He ended the Civil War and brought peace in Vijayanagara empire.
- He conquered the Western part of Kannada, Honnavan, Bakanur and Bhatkal.
- The later rulers **Timma** and **Imadi Narasimha** were titular kings in the hands of *Narasa Nayak*, a regent of the state.

Tuluva Dynasty (1505-1570 AD)

- After the death of **Narasa Nayak** in 1505 AD, **Vira Narasimha** deposed **Imadi Narasimha** and resumed as new king.
- Krishnadeva Raya was the brother of Vira Narasimha, who became the greatest ruler of Vijayanagara empire.

Krishnadeva Raya (1509-1530 AD)

- In a series of battles lasting seven years, Krishnadeva compelled the ruler of Orissa to restore to Vijayanagara all the territories up to the river Krishna. This led to a hostile alliance between his two main opponents, Bijapur and Orissa.
- Krishnadeva in 1520 AD, completely defeated the Bijapur ruler and briefly captured Bijapur and Belgaum before a truce was made. Babur described him as the **Greatest ruler of Tuluva dynasty**.
- Under Krishnadeva, Vijayanagara emerged as the strongest military power in the South.
- Due to the danger posed by the rise of the Portuguese in trade and commerce he maintained friendly relations with **Albuquerque**, the Portuguese Governor, whose ambassador Friar Louis was a resident of Vijayanagara kingdom.
- He was a gifted scholar in both Telugu and Sanskrit. He wrote *Ushaparinayam* and *Jambavati Kalyanam* in Sanskrit and *Amuktamalya* (Andal's story) in Telugu.
- He took the titles of **Yavanaraja Sthapanacharya** (Restorer of the Yavana kingdom i.e., Bahmani), *Abhinava Bhoja*, *Andhra Pitamaha* and *Andhra Bhoja*.

- The **Vitthalaswamy** and **Tirupati** temple were built during Krishnadeva Raya's reign. Hazara Rama temple was expanded also during his tenure.
- Krishnadeva's court was adorned by the eight poets known as *Ashtadiggajas*. They had composed at least one *Prabandha Kavyamu* (a new form of Telugu literary style).

Ashtadiggajas

Names	Books
Allasani Peddanna (He is considered as Andhra-Pitamah)	Manucharitamu and Harikathasaransamu
Nandi Thimmana	Parijatapaharavamu
Madayyagari Mallana	Raja Shekara Charitamu
Dhurjate	Kalahasti Mahtyamu
Ayyalaraju Ramambhadrudu	Sakalamata Sara Sangrahu
Pingali Suranna	Raghava Pandaviyam and Prabhavati Pradyumanu
Ramarajabhushanudu	Kavyalankara Sangraham
Tenali Ramakrishna	Ponduranga Mahatmyam

Achyuta Deva Raya (1530-1542 AD)

- After the death of Krishnadeva, there was a struggle for succession and Achyuta Deva Raya became the next ruler of Vijayanagara empire.
- During his reign, **Tiruvengalanatha** temple in Hampi was built.
- He ruled for 12 years and later imprisoned by his Chief Minister Rama Raya, with whom he had agreed to share power.

Sadashiva Raya (1543-1567 AD)

- Ultimately, in 1543 AD, Sadashiva Raya, son of Krishnadeva Raya ascended the throne and reigned till 1567.
- The real power was vested in the hands of Rama Raja, who able to play off the various Muslim powers against one another.

Aravidu Dynasty (1570-1652 AD)

- It was founded by Tirumal II, the brother of Rama Raya (ruled as the name of Sadashiva Raya). He has shifted his capital from **Hampi** to **Penugonda**.
- He was succeeded by **Sri Ranga, Venkata II** (1586-1614 AD) and **Sri Ranga III in 1642-1646** AD. Although, the kingdom sustained for almost one hundred more years, but its territories decreased continually and the Raya was no longer counted in the political affairs of South India.

Battle of Bannihatti

- The Battle of Bannihatti popularly known as **Talikota** was fought between Vijayanagara led by **Rama Raja** and confederation of four Muslim Sultanates – **Hussain Nizam Shah I** and **Ali Adil Shah I** of Ahmednagar and Bijapur, **Ali Barid Shah** I of Bidar and **Ibrahim Quli Qutb Shah Wali** of Golkonda in January, 1565.
- Rama Raja was surrounded, taken prisoner and immediately executed. The Battle of Bannihatti is generally considered to mark the end of the great age of Vijayanagara.

Vijayanagara Administration

- The concept of kingship among the Vijayanagara rulers was high. Kingship was based on the principle of absolute monarchy, but with welfare state policy.
- The succession to the throne was hereditary.
- Krishnadeva Raya in his book *Amuktamalyada*, suggests the king that 'with great care and according to his power, should attend to the work of protecting (the good) and punishing (the wicked).'

Central Administration in Vijayanagara Empire

- The king was advised by a Council of Ministers (*Mahapratinidhi*) in Vijayanagara empire, which consisted of the great nobles of the kingdom.
- However, the ultimate decisions were taken by the king himself.
- The king enjoyed absolute authority in executive, judicial and legislative matters.

Provincial and Local Administration

- The kingdom was divided into *Rajyas* or *Mandalam* (provinces) below, which were *Nadu* (district), *Sthala* (sub-district) and *Grama* (village).
- Each province was under a Governor known as '*Mandaleshvara*.'
- The *Gauda* was village headman and basic unit of administration. However, the village self-government concepts were considerably weakened under Vijayanagara rule.

Nayakara and Ayagar System

The Nayakara and Ayagar system were the main components of the Vijayanagara administration.

Nayakara

- The **Nayakara system** was established by the time of **Krishnadeva Raya**. These were a category of officers appointed by the king with rights over land and assigned a piece of land called *Amaram*.

- These chiefs were known as *Palaiyagars* or *Nayaka*. The landholding allocated to the Nayakas was called *Nayakattanam*.
- There were different kinds of *Nayakas* such as *Dannayakas* (military official), *Durga-Dannayakas* (military official in charge of fort) and *Amaranayakas* (*sub-nayaka* who received land from the *Nayaka*).
- In thc popular traditions of Vijayanagara, the Deccan sultans are termed as Ashvapati or lord of horses and the Rayas are called Narapati or lord of men.
- Often the Nayaka gave away a portion of land to temples or some religious institution free of tax. Such grants were called *Manya*.
- The Nayakas were independent in their areas and were non-transferable. In the course of time, it became a major cause of decline of Vijayanagara Empire.
- The Amara-nayakas sent tribute to the king annually and personally appeared in the royal court with gift to express their loyalty. It is likely that many features of this system were derived from the Iqta system of the Delhi Sultanate.

Ayagar

- During the Vijayanagara rule the village administration was organised in the form of the **Ayagar system**. According to this system every village was a separate unit.
- Twelve functionaries, collectively known as *Ayagars* were appointed by the government in each village and once allotted, the office became hereditary.
- The Ayagars could sell or mortgage their office. Tax free lands or manyas were granted to them for their maintenance for perpetuity.

Revenue Administration

- The crown lands were the most important source of revenue. The taxes were collected on the basis of assessment fixed after thorough survey.
- The rates of taxes were as follows:
  - (i) One-third of the produce of *kuruvai* (a type of rice) during winter.
  - (ii) One-fourth of sesame, ragi, horse-gram, etc.
  - (iii) One-sixth of millet and other crops cultivated on dry land.
- In addition to the land tax, there were various other taxes, such as property tax, tax on sale of produce, profession taxes, military contribution (in times of war), tax on marriage, etc.

Society in Vijayanagara Empire

- There was considerable growth of towns and urbanisation under Vijayanagara rule. The Brahmanas held in highest position in the society, religious as well as political matters.
- The position of women was fairly high in the society. They were allowed to access knowledge and many women were employed in royal households. **Allasani Peddana's Manucharitam** gives detailed account of the caste system of the Vijayanagara empire.

Important Terms Associated With Vijayanagara Empire

Terminology	Meaning
Ajamis	Non-Arab lands
Kanikkai	Tax for maintenance of Army
Nadu	Territorial Unit
Nattar	Dominant non-Brahman land holders
Periyanadu	Supralocal (covering multiple regions) assemblies
Sabha	Assembly of Brahmadeya villages
Ur	Assembly of the Nattar

Economic Conditions in Vijayanagara Empire

- Unbounded prosperity prevailed in the Vijayanagara Empire. Agriculture flourished in different parts of the kingdom and the state pursued a wise irrigation policy.
- The principal industries were related to textiles, mining and metallurgy and the most important of the minor industries was perfumery. Craftsmen and merchants guilds played an important part in the economic life of the kingdom.
- Kamala Puram tank, Hiriya canal were the important source for agricultural irrigation in Vijayanagara empire.
- The most remarkable feature in the economic condition of the kingdom was Commerce, Inland, Coastal and Overseas. The most important port on the Malabar coast was **Calicut**.
- It had commercial relations with the islands in the Indian ocean, the Malay Archipelago, Burma, China, Arabia, Persia, South Africa, Abyssinia and Portugal.
- The principal articles of exports were cloth, rice, iron, saltpetre, sugar and spices and the principal imports into the empire were horses, elephants, pearls, copper, coral mercury, China silk and velvet.
- The cheap means of transport for inland trade were *kavadis*, head-load, peak-horses, peck-bullocks, carts and asses.
- Horses were imported from Central Asia, and local traders were known as 'Khudrai Chettis', who controlled the local markets in Vijayanagara empire. Ships were in use for coasting and overseas trade.

- **Alauddin Ahmad II** (1436-1458 AD) During his reign Afghans arrived and their influence increased. There were series of conflicts between Gajpati and Bahmani Kingdom under his rule.
- **Alauddin Humayun** (1458-1461 AD) He was very cruel and barbaric ruler. Mahmud Gawan was made Prime Minister by him in his empire.
- **Muhammad Shah-III** (1463-1482 AD) He was the last ruler of Bahmani Kingdom. During his reign, Russian traveller Nikitin came to Bahmani empire. He made Mahmud Gawan killed after which Bahmani empire declined.

Mahmud Gawan

- During the reign of Alauddin Humayun Shah (1458-1461 AD), Mahmud Gawan rose to prominence and power as Chief or Prime Minister. He was bestowed with the title of 'Malik-ut-Tujjar', and made Tarafdar of Bijapur.
- Mahmud Gawan tried to accommodate Dakhnis and Afaqis in the nobility by giving them important assignments.
- He was the first to introduce gunpowder in India (Babur was first to introduce Artillery in India) during the conflict against Vijayanagara Kingdom at Belgaum.
- He was well versed in Islamic Theology, Mathematics and Persian language. Mahmud Gawan built the Mahmud Gawan Madrasa in Bidar, which was largest library of that time.

Decline of Bahmani Empire

- After the death of Mahmud Gawan, the nobles were divided into the native and long-established **Dakhnis** and the new-comers **Afaqis**, with Iranian origin also called **Gharibs.**
- Though Mahmud Gawan adopted a broad policy of conciliation, but after his death, Bahmani Empire disintegrated and various governors became independent.

Extra Facts From Tamil Nadu Board and NIOS

- The Chief Minister was known as the Mahapradhan. He led a number of lower ranking officer, like Dalavary (Commander), Vassal (guard of the palace), Rayasam (secretary/accountant), Adippam (personal attendant) and Kariya-karta (executive agents).

Terms and their meaning

Commercial centres	Pettai
Merchant	Baliga
Workshop people	Pattadai, Kasaya-vargam

- The Ashtadiggaj as(Eight renowned poet) during Vijayanagara Empire.
- All Asani Peddanna, Nandi Thimmana, Tenali Rama, Dhurjathy, Bhattu Murthy, Puna Vira Bhadra, Malland and Panaji Surana.

16

Rise of Provincial Kingdoms

[SOURCES]

Class-XI Old NCERT Chap 10 (Struggle for Power in North India II), Tamil Nadu Board (Class XI), NIOS

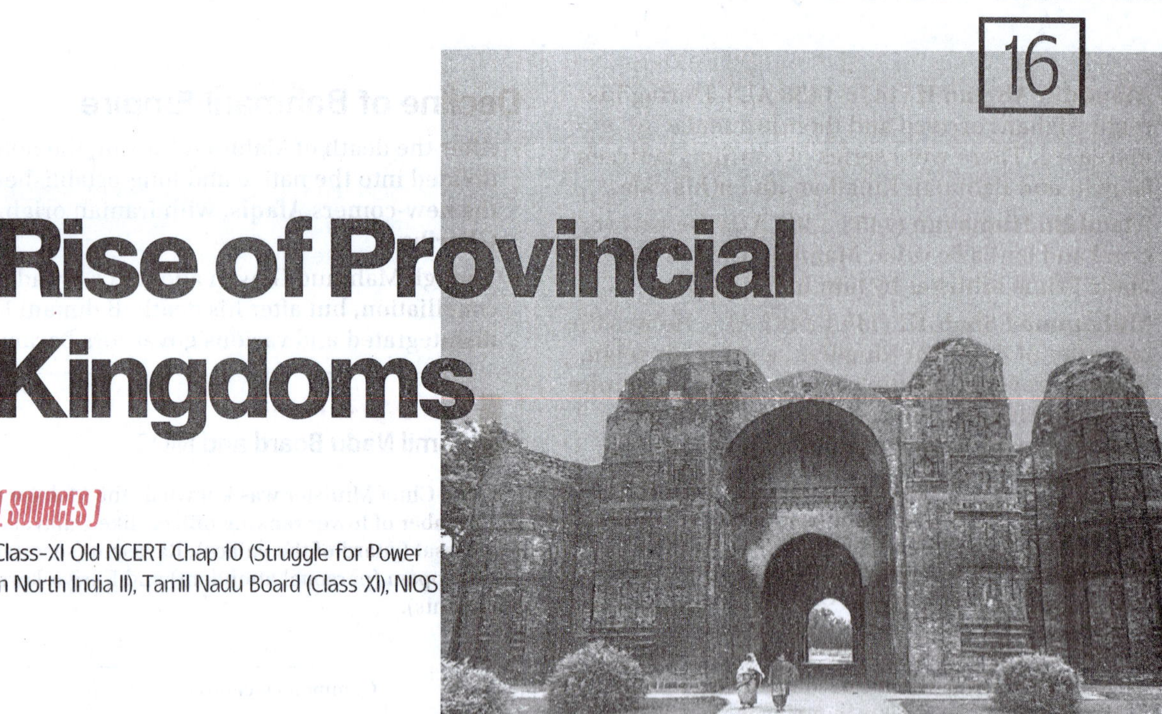

Reasons for the Rise of Provincial Kingdoms

- In 1398 AD, the **attack of Taimur** on Delhi and defeat of Delhi Sultanate showed the administrative weakness of the sultanate. This empowered regional provinces to announce their autonomy from the sultanate.
- Bengal in East to Sind and Multan in West became autonomous from Delhi Sultanate. Subedars of **Gujarat, Malwa** and **Jaunpur** also announced their independence.
- Apart from these, the Rajput dominated provinces of **Malwa, Mewar, Amber** etc also became autonomous.
- There were various regional powers pre-existed and newly emerged in India, during the establishment of the Delhi Sultanate, till its downfall in the 15th century.
- Delhi Sultanate's disintegration helped Bengal, Gujarat, Malwa and Jaunpur to emerge as powerful regional kingdom. Some regional powers also rose into prominence in different regions.

Provincial Kingdoms of Eastern India

In Eastern India, there were three major regional powers i.e., **Bengal, Assam** and **Orissa**. These powers were continuously had conflict with Delhi Sultanate as well as with each others.

Bengal

- Bengal was made a part of Delhi Sultanate by Ikhtiyar-ud-din Muhammad bin Bakhtiyar Khilji 1204 AD. However, it remained a problem area for the Sultans of Delhi due to its distance from the capital.
- In 1345 AD, **Haji Iliyas** became the ruler of Bengal under the title of Sham-ud-din abu Muzaffar Iliyas Shah.
- After Haji Iliyas, his son **Sikandar Shah** succeeded the throne. He ruled Bengal for about 30 years and died around 1390 AD. He was succeeded by his son **Ghiyasuddin Azam Shah** (1390-1410 AD). He sent an ambassador to China. He was also famous for his respect for law and justice. His death was followed by political instability.
- His son, **Saifuddin Hamza Shah** was murdered by his slave. In 1415 AD, a Hindu ruler named **Raja Ganesh** took advantage and assumed power in Bengal. He took the title of 'Danujmardan Dev'.
- After Raja Ganesh, his son **Jadu** converted to Islam and ruled as **Jalal-ud-din Muhammad Shah**. During his reign, Bengali became a court language alongwith Persian. He patronised **Brihaspati Mishra** who wrote commentaries on the *Raghuvansha*, *Meghaduta* and the *Amarakosha*.
- Jalal-ud-din's son, **Shamsuddin Ahmad Shah** was murdered by his slave, **Nasir Khan**, who ascended the throne. The nobles were angry by this act. That's why they killed him and restored the Iliyas Shahi dynasty by

installing **Nasiruddin Mahmood Shah** grandson of **Haji Iliyas** (1442 AD).

- The popularity of Iliyas might have been one of the reason for the failure of Firoz against him.
- He ruled for 17 years and during his reign Bengal was greatly extended. Nasiruddin was succeeded by his son, **Rukunuddin Barbak Shah** but died soon. After Rukunuddin death, some of his slaves created political instability between 1487 to 1493 AD.
- A period of unrest was finally brought to an end when a noble of Arab origin named Sayyid Hussain assumed power (1494 AD) and entitled himself as **Alauddin Hussain Shah**. Thus, the Hussain Shahi dynasty was established.
- Alauddin Hussain Shah ruled between 1494 to 1519 AD and was the most popular ruler of Bengal. It was during his reign, that Bengali language witnessed considerable growth.
- He was succeeded by **Nasiruddin-Nasrat-Shah**. Chaitanya preached Vaishnavism in his reign. He concluded a peace treaty with Babur, but died in 1532 AD.
- He built **Bara Sona** and **Qadam Rasul mosque**. The Portuguese made their first appearance in Bengal during his period.
- He honoured poet **Maladhar Basu**, compiler of *Srikrishna Vijay*, with the title of **Gunaraja Khan**.
- During the rule of Nasrat Shah, the *Mahabharata* was translated in Bengali. After weak successors of Nasrat Shah, Bengal occupied by Sher Shah Suri in 1538 AD.

Assam

- There were two warring kingdoms in Assam at that time. **Kamata** kingdom (Kamrup) was in the West and the **Ahom** kingdom was in the East.
- An attack by Alauddin Hussain Shah of Bengal which was supported by the Ahoms led to the destruction of the city of Kamtapur (in modern Cooch Behar).
- **Suhungmung** (Svarga Narayana), who is considered the greatest Ahom ruler, not only repulsed the Muslim attack, but also extended his kingdom in all directions. The Vaishnavite reformer **Shankaradeva**, belonged to his time.

Orissa

- The **Ganga dynasty** was ruled over Orissa and its nearby region during the Delhi Sultanate period, which made frequent made attempts to annex Bengal.
- **Firuz Shah Tughlaq** attacked Orissa in 1340 AD and destroyed the Jagannath temple of Puri when it was under the rule of the Ganga dynasty King **Bhanudeva III**.
- The Eastern Ganga dynasty ruler Anantavarman Chodganga Deva and Narsimhadeva I were built Jagannath temple at puri and Sun temple at Konark respectively.
- Gajapati dynasty was established by Kapilendra Deva in 1434 AD.
- Krishnadevraya invaded Udaygiri in 1513 AD.
- Quli Qutub Shah who was the general of Sultan Mahmud Shah of Bahamani kingdom, invaded Orissa in 1522 AD and was defeated by Prataprudra Deva.

Provincial Kingdoms of Western India

These three were other most important regional powers in India, which gave stiff resistance to Delhi Sultanate time-to-time.

Gujarat

- The real founder of the kingdom of Gujarat was **Ahmad Shah I**. He shifted the capital from Patan to the new city of Ahmedabad, the foundation laid in 1413 AD.
- He was a great builder and drew on the rich architectural traditions of the Jains style of building. The Jama Masjid in Ahmedabad and the Teen Darwaza built during his time.
- The most famous sultan of Gujarat was **Mahmud Begarha** (1459-1511 AD), who ruled over Gujarat for more than 50 years.
- Mahmud Begarha besieged Girnar with a large force. Though, the raja had only a few guns in the fort, he resisted gallantly, but to no avail.
- He was called **Begarha** because he captured two of the most powerful forts (garhs), Girnar and Champaner in one day. His court poet was **Udayaraja** who composed many texts in Sanskrit.
- He formed a naval alliance with the Sultans of Turkey and Egypt and defeated the Portuguese in the **Battle of Chaul** (1508 AD), but got defeated the next year in the **Battle of Diu**.
- Malik Ghori was his Chief Minister and his court poet was **Udayraja**. The Italian traveller, **Barthema** and Portuguese traveller **Barbosa** visited his court.

Other Rulers of Gujarat

- **Muzaffar Shah I** (1407-1411 AD) After Taimur's invasion of Delhi in 1398 AD, Gujarat became independent under its Governor, Zafar Khan.
  He named himself Muzaffar Shah I. He was appointed as Governor of Gujarat by Nasir-ud-din Muhammad bin Tughlaq IV in 1391 AD.
- **Shihab-ud-din Ahmed** (1411-42 AD) He founded the city of Ahmedabad and shifted the capital from Patan

to Ahmedabad. He also built the *Jama Masjid* and *Teen Darwaja* at Ahmedabad.

Muslim historians argue that he was an idol breaker. He imposed *Jizya* for the first time in Gujarat on Hindus. The Hindu pilgrimage centre, Sidhpur was destroyed.

But, he also appointed Hindu officials, **Manikchand** and **Motichand** into the government.

- **Muzaffar Shah II** (1511-37 AD) He fought against Rana Sanga of Mewar. He restored Mahmud Khilji II of Malwa to this throne. He was considered by Babur to be one of the five great rulers of Hindustan.
- **Bahadur Shah** (1526-37 AD) He annexed Malwa in 1531 AD. He was the last able ruler of Gujarat.

  He imposed a humiliating treaty on Chittor, so Humayun attacked in 1534-35 AD, whereupon Bahadur Shah sought help from Portuguese and had to surrender Bassein and Diu to Portuguese.

  He recaptured Gujarat from **Humayun**, but was killed by the Portuguese. Emperor Akbar finally captured Gujarat in 1572-73 AD.

Malwa

- During the 15th century, the kingdom of Malwa remained at the height of its glory. The capital was shifted from Dhar to Mandu. This place was highly defensible.
- During the Medieval period, the kingdom of Malwa remained at the height of its glory. One of the early rulers of Malwa, **Hushang Shah**, adopted a broad policy of religious toleration. Many Rajputs were encouraged to settle in Malwa.
- Hushang Shah was the first ruler of Deccan who extended his patronage to the Jains. Nardeva Soni, was one of his advisors. **Lalitpur temple** was built during Hushang Shah's period.

Mewar

- Mewar was an old principality of minor importance under the rule of the **Guhilot dynasty**, with its capital Nagada. Although Alauddin Khilji captured **Chittor**, the Capital of Mewar, in 1303 AD, it was soon restored by **Rana Hamir**, who established the rule of Sisodiya dynasty.
- **Rana Kumbha** (1433-68 AD) The greatest ruler of the Sisodiya dynasty, carried out continuous warfare against Gujarat and Malwa. The first great ruler of medieval Mewar was Rana Kumbha.

  Some contemporary inscriptions and a literary work Ekling Mahatmya speaks of his military success.

  He wrote commentaries on **Jayadeva's** *Gita- Govinda* and *Chandisatakam.*

  The greatest architectural monument of his reign was the Kirtistambha built by him at Chittor. He was murdered by his son, Uda, to gain the throne. He was famous for Kirtistambha or the **Tower of Fame**.
- **Rana Sanga** (1509-28 AD) His real name was Rana Sangram Singh. He defeated Mahmud Khilji II of Malwa and also Ibrahim Lodhi of Delhi at Ghatoli. He was defeated by Babur in the **Battle of Khanwa** in 1527 AD.

Provincial Kingdoms of North-West and North India

These two important provincial kingdoms not only expanded territorially but also encouraged art and cultural development prominently in their respective states.

Jaunpur

- Jaunpur was a prosperous province in the Eastern part of India. **Malik Sarwar**, a prominent noble during Firuz Shah Tughlaq's period became ruler of Jaunpur.
- In 1402 AD, **Ibrahim Shah Sharqi** became the Sultan, who was a scholar, well versed with music and fine arts. A distinctive architecture evolved during this period known as the Sharqi style of architecture. Its capital **Jaunpur** was called the '**Sheraz of India**'.

Kashmir

- A Muslim adventurer from Swat, **Shah Mirza** had entered into the service of the Hindu prince of Kashmir in 1315 AD. The Hindu prince died shortly afterwards and Shah Mirza seized the throne. He kept aside the claims of descendants of the Hindu prince and himself assumed the title of the king.
- He died in 1349 AD and was succeeded by his four sons, one after another who ruled for a total period of 46 years.
- After the death of the fourth son **Qutb-ud-din** (1394 AD), his son **Sikandar** ascended the throne.
- Sultan **Zainul Abidin** (1420-1470 AD) was the greatest Muslim ruler of Kashmir. He was highly enlightened, liberal and benevolent, for which he was known as the **Akbar of Kashmir**. He abolished *Jizya* and withdrew *Sati.*
- He abolished cow slaughter, because of his liberal approach, he was called *Badshah* i.e. great king.
- He had translated *Mahabharata* into Persian. Two famous scholars **Johraja** and **Srivara** extended Kalhana's *Rajatarangini* to the 15th century under the patronage of Zainul Abidin.

- He created *Zaina Lanka*, the artificial island on the Wular lake.
- After Zainul Abidin death, an anarchy under the rule of the nominal kings arised who ascended the throne.
- **Haidar Shah** was a fairly competent ruler, but his successors were incompetent and in 1540 AD, a relative of Babur, **Mirza Haidar**, conquered Kashmir.
- Later, Akbar annexed Kashmir into the Mughal empire in 1588 AD.

Other Regional Kingdoms

- **Marwar** Rao Chunda, who ruled from 1404 to 1421 AD, was succeeded by Jodha. Jodha built the fort of Jodhpur. Bikaner was founded by Bika, Malwa ruler and one of the sons of Jodha in 1465 AD.
- **Amber** or **Amer** Dullah Rao was the founder of the **Kachhawaha dynasty**, which ruled Amber or Amer during this period. **Hammir Deva** was the most famous ruler of this dynasty.

Extra Facts From Tamil Nadu Board and NIOS

- After the demise of Firozshah Tughlaq in 1338 AD, provincial subedars started operating as independent powers.
- Bihar declared itself independent during the reign of Ibrahim Lodhi, while Punjab's Governor Daulat Khan rebelled and invited Babur to attack India in 1526 AD.
- Kashmir was ruled by Shaiva rulers in 11th century. Alberuni has mentioned this in his book **Kitab-ul-Hind.**
- The rulers of Kashmir lost public support due to not facing the Mongol invasion properly and in 1339 AD Shamsuddin Shah deposed the shaivite rulers.
- Persian Literature was patronised during the reign of Bengal ruler Ghiyassudin Azam. He had trade relations with China. The port of Chittagong was an important centre of commodity exchange. On the demand of the Chinese ruler. Azam had sent Buddhist monk to China.
- In 1538 AD, Sher Shah Suri annexed Bengal into his kingdom and in 1586 AD, Akbar made it a 'suba'.
- Foreign traveller Duarto Barbosa has written about Gujarat ruler Mahmud Begdha that he was fed poison in his childhood. In 1507 AD, he led the campaign against the portuguese.

17

Bhakti and Sufi Movements

[SOURCES]

Class-VII New NCERT Chap 6 (Devotional Paths to the Divine, Class-VII Old NCERT Chap 5-Life of the People), Class-VIII Old NCERT Chap 8 (Changes in Religious Beliefs and Devotional Texts), Class-XI Old NCERT Chap 1 (Cultural Development in India From the Thirteenth to the Fifteenth Century), Class-XII New NCERT Chap 6 (Bhakti Sufi Traditions), Tamil Nadu Board (Class XI), NIOS

- The medieval period in India saw the rise and growth of the Bhakti and Sufi Movements. The two movements brought a new form of religious expression amongst Muslims and Hindus.
- The Sufi and Bhakti saints played an important role and made religion accessible and meaningful to the common people.

Bhakti Movement

- The word **Bhakti** is derived from a Sanskrit word '**Bhuj**', which means **coordination and charity**. The roots of Bhakti first found in the Vedas. It stresses the Union of the individual with God as well as one's personal devotion to God.
- Bhakti movement originated in South India between the 7th and the 12th centuries AD. The **Shaiva** and **Vaishnava** saints during the rule of **Pallavas** began the Bhakti movement. It also received patronage of the **Chola rulers**.
- According to the saints of Bhakti movement, an individual could realise God through devotion and personal efforts.
- The saints of Bhakti movement gave three means or margas for attainment of Moksha or salvation, which were
  - (i) **Gyan Marga** Salvation through Learning and Understanding
  - (ii) **Karma Marga** Through good deeds like service of mankind
  - (iii) **Bhakti Marga** Through unconditional love and total surrender to God

Causes for the Emergence of Bhakti Movement

- The common people were no longer satisfied with a religion, which only emphasised ceremonies and forms.
- The Bhakti saints believed that salvation can be achieved by all.
- Their ideas were drawn from both Hindu and Islamic traditions and were aimed at bridging the gulf between the Hindus and the Muslims.
- Improvement in the economic conditions of the lower classes and the impact of Islam's Doctrine of Monotheism and Equality also were important cause of the emergence of Bhakti movement.
- Emergence of great reformers was also the cause of the emergence of Bhakti movement.

Features of Bhakti Movement

- Open mindedness about religious matters.
- They rejected caste discrimination and believed in equality of all humans.
- Bhakti saints use local or regional language for preaching.
- Condemnation of rituals, ceremonies and blind faith.

- An important contribution of Bhakti saints was towards the development of music. Jayadeva of Bengal composed the Gita Govinda in Sanskrit, each song composed in a particular raga and tala.

Nayanars and Alvars

- The seventh to ninth centuries saw the emergence of new religious movements in India, led by the **Nayanars** (worshippers of **Shiva**) and **Alvars** (worshippers of **Vishnu**) who came from all castes including those considered 'untouchable' like the **Pulaiyar** and the **Panars.**
- They disregarded the rigidities of the caste system and also disregarded the austerities of the Jains and the Buddhists. They drew upon the ideals of love and heroism from Sangama literature and both **Alvars** and **Nayanars** used Sanskrit and Tamil languages in their hymns.

Nayanars

- They are devotees of Shiva.
- The Tamil Nayanar saints were total 63 in number. **Nambiyandar Nambi** gives detailed information about these 63 Nayanar saints in **Tiruktatotar Tiruvantati**.
- There are two sets of compilations of Nayanar saints' songs i.e., **Tevaram** and **Tiruvacakam.**
- Some of the important Nayanar saints called as '**Samyacharya**' were as follows
  1. **Appar** He was known as 'Tirunavukarrashu'.
  2. **Tirugyansamnbandar** He was famous as 'Dravida Shishu'
  3. **Sundarmurti** He was regarded as 'saint of the saints'.
  4. **Mannikavachkar** Known as Tiru-vadvur.
- *Tirumarai* is the compilation of hymns of *Nayanars* by Nambiyandar Nambi.

Alvars

- Alvars or Vaishnavites also emerged during the Pallava rule in South India. The total numbers of Alvara saints were 12 and their combined anthology is known as the **Nalayira Divyaprabandham** ('Four Thousand Sacred Compositions')
- By the tenth century, the compositions of the 12 Alvars were compiled in this anthology known as the **Nalayira Divyaprabandham.**
- Other devotional literature such as Appar, Sambandar and Sundarar form the Tevaram, a collection that was compiled and classified in the tenth century on the basis of the music of the songs.
- Some of the prominent Alvar saints were as follows
  1. **Nammalvar** The greatest among all Alvar saint. His works termed as 'Four Vedas of South'.
  2. **Thirumangai** His poetries considered as 'Six Vedangas of Tamil'.
  3. **Andal** The only female Alvar saint and considered as 'Mirabai of South India'.
  4. **Vishnuchitta** 'Amuktamalyada' of Krishnadeva Raya based on his life.
  5. **Poigai** Considered as the last Alvar saints.

Bhakti Saints

Some of the significant Bhakti saints with distinct schools of philosophy emerged. They were as follows

Shankaracharya (788-820 AD)

- Shankaracharya was one of the most influential philosophers of India, was born in Kerala in **788 AD.**
- He advocated *Advaita* (doctrine of the oneness) of the individual soul and the Supreme God (the Ultimate Reality). He considered the world as an illusion or maya.
- He preached renunciation of the world and adoption of the path of knowledge to understand the true nature of Brahman and attain salvation.
- His greatest work known as *Brahmasutrabhasya* and greatly emphasised on the study of the Upanishads to gain self-liberating knowledge.
- Shankaracharya established four Mathas at **Dwarka** (Sharda Peeth) in the West, **Puri** (Goverdhan Peeth) in the East, **Sringeri** in the South and **Badrinath** in the North. These four mathas were headed by his four main disciples.

Ramanujacharya (1017-1137 AD)

- Born in Tamil Nadu in the 11th century AD. Ramanujacharya was deeply influenced by the Alvars.
- He propounded the doctrine of **Vishishtadvaita** or qualified oneness. There exist a plurality and distinction between *Atman* (soul) and *Brahman* (metaphysical). According to him, the best means of attaining salvation was through intense devotion to Vishnu.
- His major works include *Vedarthasangraha, Sri Bhashya* (commentary on the Brahma Sutras) and Gita Bhashyam.
- He founded the **Shrivaishnava Sampradaya,** which greatly inspired the new strand of Bhakti in North India.

Nimbarkacharya (1130-1200 AD)

- Nimbarkacharya, a Telugu Vaishnavite was in Andhra Pradesh in 11th century AD but spent most of his life in Mathura. He was the chief proponent of Dvaitadvaita (dualistic–non-dualistic).
- He referred five ways of salvation such as
  1. *Karma* (Righteous Action)
  2. *Vidya* (Knowledge)
  3. *Dhyana* (Meditation)
  4. *Prapatti* (Complete Surrender to God)
  5. *Gurupassatti* (Devotion for the Guru)

Madhvacharya (1238-1317 AD)

- Madhvacharya was born in 1238 AD at Udupi, Karnataka. He was a chief proponent of the Dvaita (dualism) school of Vedanta (Divine is separate from human soul). He called his philosophy **Tattvavada** (Arguments from a realist viewpoint).
- Madhva's greatest work was *Anu-Bhashya,* a philosophical supplement composed with a poetic structure. He founded **Brahma Sampradaya** and proclaimed himself to be an avatar of Vayu.
- He played a major role in spreading the worship of Radha-Krishna cult and founded **Nimbarka Sampradaya**, one of four main traditions of Vaishnavism.

Note *Nimbarkacharya was the contemporary of Madhvacharya.*

Vallabhacharya (1479-1531 AD)

- Vallabha was born in a Telugu Tailang Brahmin family and spent his entire life in Varanasi.
- Vallabha rejected asceticism and monastic life, suggested that through loving devotion to God Krishna, anyone could achieve salvation.
- He founded the Krishna-centred **Pushti-Marg** sect of Vaishnavism in the Braj region and the philosophy of **Shuddadvaita** (Pure Non-dualism).
- He was the prominent saint of Rudra Sampradaya out of the four traditional Vaishnava Sampradayas.

Note *Vallabhacharya was contemporary of Krishnadeva Raya and received the title 'Jagadguru'.*

Virashaiva Tradition

- A new form of tradition and movement emerged in Karnataka in 12th century AD by **Basavanna** (1106-68 AD), who was a minister in the court of Kalachuri dynasty.
- His followers worship Shiva as a linga and were known as **Virashaivas** (heroes of Shiva) or **Lingayats** (wearers of the *linga*).
- Virashaivas believe that on death the devotee will be united with Shiva and will not return to this world. They also questioned the theory of rebirth.
- The source of Virashaiva tradition is compiled as '*Vachanas*' composed in Kannada.
- The Virashaivas argued strongly for the equality of all human beings and against Brahmanical ideas about caste and the treatment of women. They were also against all forms of ritual and idol worship.

Nirguna Saints

- Nirguna saints believed in invisible formless God and God without attributes.
- Some of the important Nirguna saints are :

Dadu Dayal (1544-1603 AD)

- He was born in Ahmedabad, Gujarat in 1544 AD. He founded the **Brahma Sampradaya**. His teachings were compiled in the book named *'Dadudayal ki Bani'*. Much of the imagery used is similar to that used by Kabir.
- He believed that devotion to God should transcend religious affiliation and the one should become non-sectarian or *Nipakh*.
- Dadu Dayal's compositions in Braj language were recorded by his disciple **Rajjab** and are known as the *Dadu Anubhav Vani*, a compilation of 5,000 verses.

Kabir (1440-1510 AD)

- There is uncertainty about the early life of Kabir. According to legend, he was the son of a Brahman widow and was brought up in the house of a Muslim weaver living at Kashi.
- He was the disciple of **Ramananda** from whom he adopted **Vedanta Philosophy**.
- Kabir, who is generally placed in the 15th century AD, emphasised the unity of God whom he calls by several names, such as Rama, Hari, Govinda, Rahim, etc.
- He strongly denounced idol-worship, pilgrimages, bathing in holy rivers or taking part in *Namaz*.
- The mission of Kabir was to preach a religion of love, which would unite all castes and creeds.
- Kabir strongly denounced the caste system, especially the practice of untouchability and emphasised the fundamental unity of man.

Bijak

Sayings of Kabir were compiled in a book named *Bijak*. It is the holy Scripture for followers of the **Kabirpanthi religion**. The Bijak is one of the earliest of the major texts in modern **Bagheli**.

Guru Nanak (1469-1539 AD)

- Guru Nanak was born in a Khatri family in Talwandi (Nankana, Pakistan) in 1469 AD.
- He composed hymns and sang them along with his faithful attendant, **Mardana**.
- It is said that Nanak undertook wide tours all over India and even to Sri Lanka and Mecca and Medina.
- Guru Nanak laid great emphasis on the purity of character and conduct as the first condition of approaching God, and the need of a guru for guidance.
- He advocated a middle path in which spiritual life could be combined with the duties of the householder.
- Baba Guru Nanak organised his followers into a community. He set up rules for congregational worship (*sangat*) involving collective recitation.
- He appointed one of his disciples, Angad, to succeed him as the preceptor (*guru*) and this practice was followed for nearly 200 years.
- **Guru Arjan,** the fifth guru, compiled Baba Guru Nanak's hymns along with his four successors and religious poets like **Baba Farid, Ravidas** (also known as Raidas) and **Kabir** in the **Adi Granth Sahib.** These hymns, called 'gurbani', are composed in various languages.
- In the late 17th century the tenth preceptor, Guru Gobind Singh, included the compositions of the ninth guru, Guru Tegh Bahadur and this scripture was called the Guru Granth Sahib.
- **Guru Gobind Singh** also laid the foundation of the Khalsa Panth (army of the pure) and defined its five symbols: uncut hair, a dagger, a pair of shorts, a comb and a steel bangle.

Comparison between Kabir and Nanak

- Like Kabir, Nanak laid emphasis on the one God, by repeating whose name and dwelling on it with love and devotion one could get salvation without distinction of caste, creed or sect.
- Guru Nanak, like Kabir, strongly denounced idol-worship, pilgrimages and other formal observances of the various faiths. Nanak had no intention of founding a new religion.
- Guru Nanak's approach aimed at bridging distinctions between the Hindus and the Muslims, in order to create an atmosphere of peace, goodwill and mutual give and take. This was also the aim of Kabir.
- In course of time, the ideas of Nanak gave birth to a new creed, Sikhism, while the followers of Kabir shrank into a sect, the Kabir Panthis. The fundamental teachings of these two great saints are reflected in the religious ideas and policies of Akbar in a remarkable manner.

Saguna Saints

Saguna Bhakti Saints believed in God with forms and attributes. Some of the important Saguna saints are :

Ramananda (1299-1411 AD)

- He was a 14th century Vaishnava devotional poet saint and spent most part of his life in Kashi. He was the founder of the **Ramanandi Sampradaya**; the largest monastic community all time.
- Saint Ramananda developed his philosophy and devotional themes through inspired by Ramanuja and by Nathpanthi and Siddhas ascetics' school of philosophy.
- An early social reformer, he accepted disciples without discriminating anyone by gender, class.
- His twelve disciples included later Bhakti movement poet-saints such as **Kabir**, **Ravidas**, **Pipa** and others.
- Ramananda composed his works and discussing spiritual themes in vernacular Hindi, stating that this makes knowledge accessible to the masses. His verse is mentioned in the Sikh scripture Adi Granth.

Twelve Disciples of Ramananda

Kabir	Muslim Weaver
Raidas	Cobbler
Pipa	Rajput Prince
Dhanna	Jat Peasant
Sena	Barber
Narhariyananda Sursurananda Sukhananda Bhavananda Anantananda	All were Brahmins/Priests
Padmavati Surasari	Female Disciples

Tulsidas (1544-1623 AD)

- He was a poet and saint belonged to Ram Bhakti sect. He spent most of his life in the city of Varanasi. He was a contemporary of **Akbar** and his works include *Ramcharitamanas, Kavitawali, Gitawali, Parvati Mangal, Janki Mangal, Vinaya Patrika*, etc.

Nabhadas (1537-1643 AD)

- He wrote *Bhaktmal* in the Braj language, which gives short biographies of more than two hundred devotees. He belonged to the tradition of Ramananda.
- He was born on 8th April, 1537 at Bhadrachalam on the bank of Godavari River in Khammam district of Telangana.
- Guru Nabhadas belonged to Dumna community now known as 'Nabhadassia'.

Difference Between Nirguna and Saguna Saints

Nirguna	Saguna
Believed in 'Formless existence of God'.	Believed in the 'Personification of God'.
Formless idea of God with his omnipresence.	Deities were lord Vishnu as Rama and Krishna.
Liberal in social matters, against of caste system and rituals.	Rigid in social matters.
Saints- Kabir, Nanak, Ravidas, Dadudayal, etc.	Saints- Ramananda, Surdas, Tulsidas and Chaitanya Mahaprabhu.

The Vaishnavite Movement

The Bhakti movement in North-Eastern India developed as the Vaishnavite movement with the worship of **Rama** and **Krishna**.

They used the love between Radha and Krishna in an allegorical manner to depict the relationship of love, in its various aspects, between the individual soul and the supreme soul.

Narsi Mehta (1414-1481 AD)

- Also known as **Narsi Bhagat**, he was a 15th century poet of Gujarat.
- He was disciple of **Saint Dadu Dayal**.
- He has written the famous Bhakti Bhajan **'Vaishnavajan'**.
- He highly contributed in the development of Gujarati literature and spread of Bhakti movement in Gujarat.

Chaitanya Mahaprabhu (1483-1533 AD)

- He was the most popular Bhakti reformer from Bengal.
- He was born at Nabadwip (Bengal). He was also known as **Gouranga** and **Vishwambar**. He preached Vaishnavism in Bengal and Odisha.
- According to Chaitanya, worship consisted of love, devotion, song and dance. These produce a state of ecstasy in which the presence of God (Hari), could be realised. Such a worship could be carried out by all, irrespective of caste or creed.
- He was also the first to introduce *Kirtans* in Bhakti movement. The form of Vaishnavism that he preached came to be called as **Goudia Vaishnavism**.

Surdas (1478-1583 AD)

- Disciple of Vallabhacharya, a blind poet from Agra. He sang the glory of Krishna in his *Sursagar*.
- He belonged to the Saguna saints–Krishna Bhakti sect.
- He was an ardent devotee of Krishna. His compositions, compiled in the Sursagara, Surasaravali and Sahitya Hahari, express his devotion.

Mirabai (1498-1546 AD)

- Rathor princess of Merta and daughter-in-law of **Rana Sanga** of Mewar (husband–Bhoja Raja). She wrote the verse *Padavali*. She was devotee of Lord Krishna and she devoted her life to Lord Krishna.

Shankaradeva (1449-1568 AD)

- In the late 15th century, Shankaradeva emerged as one of the leading proponents of Vaishnavism in Assam.
- His teachings are often known as the *Bhagavati dharma* because they were based on the **Bhagavad Gita** and the **Bhagavata Purana**. They focused on absolute surrender to the supreme deity, in this case Vishnu.
- He emphasised the need for *naam kirtan*, recitation of the names of the lord in *satsanga* or congregations of devotees.
- He also encouraged the establishment of *satra* or monasteries for the transmission of spiritual knowledge and *naam ghar* or prayer halls.
- Many of these institutions and practices continue to flourish in the region. His major compositions include the *Kirtana-ghosha*.

Raidas

- Raidas is also known as **Ravidas**. He was one of the most renowned saints of the North Indian Bhakti movement.
- He was born in a low caste family of untouchable leather-working class. His poems and songs often revolve around social inequality and hierarchy.
- He preached self-devotion to God.

Vidyapati (1352-1448 AD)

- Vidyapati was a Sanskrit writer and Maithili poet who was referred to as **Maithil Kavi Kokil** (meaning the poet cuckoo of Maithili).
- Vidyapati mainly propagated Vaishnavism in his region that was initiated by Ramanuja. It advocated liberation through direct love of God Krishna. His works included Bhu-Parikrama, Varsaktrya and Danavakyavali, etc.

Bhakti Movement in Maharashtra

- From the 13th to the 17th centuries, Maharashtra saw a great number of saint-poets, whose songs in simple Marathi continue to inspire people.
- The most important among them were **Dnyaneshwar** (*Gyaneshwar*), **Namdev**, **Eknath** and **Tukaram** as

well as women like **Sakhubai**. This regional tradition of Bhakti focused on the **Vitthala** (a form of Vishnu) temple in Pandharpur, as well as on the notion of a personal god residing in the hearts of all people.

Nathpanthis, Siddhas and Yogis

- The Nathpanthis, Siddhacharas and Yogis advocated renunciation of the world.
- The path to salvation to them lay in meditation on the formless **Ultimate Reality** and the **Realisation of Oneness with it.**
- To achieve this, they advocated intense training of the mind and body through practices like yogasanas, breathing exercises and meditation.
- They criticised the ritual and other aspects of conventional religion and the social order, using simple, logical arguments.
- These groups became particularly popular among 'low' castes.

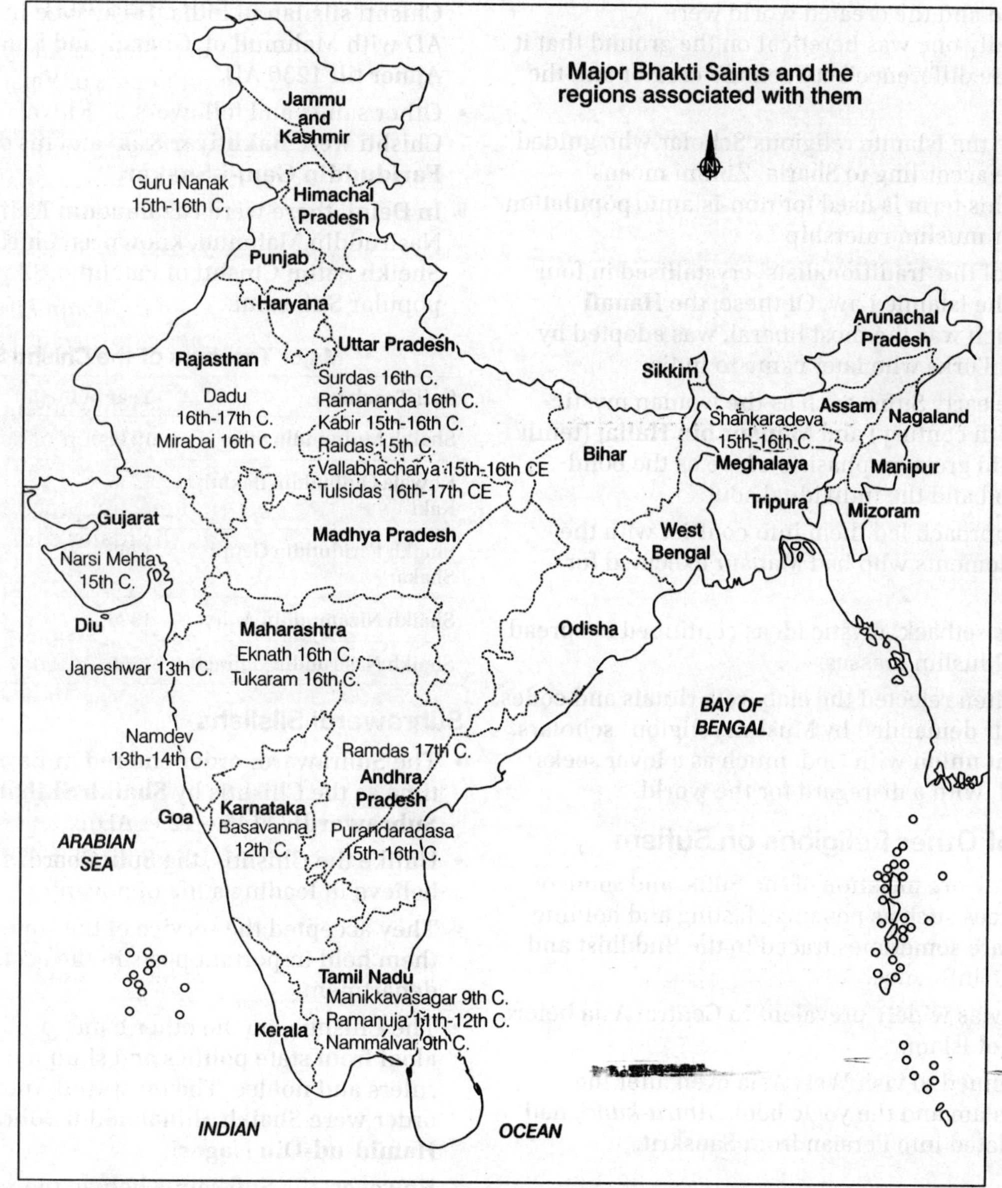

Sufi Movement

- The tenth century AD is important in Islamic history for variety of reasons; first, it marks the rise of the Turks on the ruins of the **Abbasid Caliphate**, as well as important changes in the realm of ideas and beliefs.
- In the realm of ideas, it marks the end of the domination of the *Mutazila* or rationalist philosophy. It marks the rise of orthodox schools based on the Quran and Hadis (traditions of the Prophet and his companions) and rise of the Sufi mystic orders.
- The 'rationalists' argued that their philosophy of monism God and the created world were fundamentally one was heretical on the ground that it abolished the difference between the creator and the created'.
- Ulama were the Islamic religious Scholar who guided ruler to rule according to Sharia. Zimmi means protected, this term is used for non-islamic population living under muslim rulership.
- The works of the 'traditionalists' crystallised in four schools of the Islamic Law. Of these, the **Hanafi School**, which was the most liberal, was adopted by the Eastern Turks who later came to India.
- Some of the early Sufis, such as the woman mystic **Rabia** (eighth century) and **Mansur bin Hallaj** (tenth century), laid great emphasis on love as the bond between God and the individual soul.
- But their approach led them into conflict with the orthodox elements who had Mansur executed for heresy.
- Despite this setback, mystic ideas continued to spread among the Muslim masses.
- The sufis often rejected the elaborate rituals and codes of behaviour demanded by Muslim religious scholars. They sought union with God, much as a lover seeks his beloved, with a disregard for the world.

Influence of Other Religions on Sufism

- The monastic organisation of the Sufis, and some of their practices such as penance, fasting and holding the breath are sometimes traced to the Buddhist and Hindu yogic influence.
- Buddhism was widely prevalent in Central Asia before the advent of Islam.
- Yogis continued to visit West Asia even after the advent of Islam and the yogic book, *Amrit-kund*, had been translated into Persian from Sanskrit.

Twelve Sufi Silsilahs

- Around this time, the Sufis were organised in 12 orders (or Silsilahs). A Silsilah was generally led by a prominent mystic who lived in a *Khanqah* along with his disciples.
- The link between the teacher or pir and his disciples or murids was a vital part of the Sufi system. Every pir nominated a successor or wali to carry on his work.
- The Sufi saints and many modern thinkers trace the Sufi ideas to the *Quran*.
- Irrespective of origin, there were many similarities in the ideas of the Sufis and the Hindu yogis and mystics.

Chishti Silsilahs

- Sufi saint **Khwaja Moinuddin Chishti** introduced the Chishti silsilah in India. He arrived in India in 1161 AD with Mahmud of Ghazni and found a base in Ajmer till 1236 AD.
- Other saints and followers of Khwaja Moinuddin Chishti were **Bakhtiyar Kaki** and his disciple **Fariduddin Ganj-i-Shakar**.
- In Delhi, there were Nizamuddin Auliya and Shaikh Nasiruddin Mahmud, known as 'Chirag-i-Delhi'. Sheikh Salim Chishti of Fatehpur Sikri was another popular Sufi saint.

Major Teachers of the Chishti Silsilah

Sufi Teacher	Year of Birth	Location
Shaikh Muinuddin Sijzi	1235	Ajmer (Rajasthan)
Khwaja Qutbuddin Bakhtiyar Kaki	1235	Delhi
Shaikh Fariduddin Ganj-i-Shakar	1265	Ajodhan (Pakistan)
Shaikh Nizamuddin Auliya	1325	Delhi
Shaikh Nasiruddin Chiragh-I	1356	Delhi

Suhrawardi Silsilahs

- The Suhrawardi order entered India at about the same time as the Chishtis by **Shaikh Shihabuddin Umar Suhrawardi** (1145 – 1234 AD).
- Unlike the Chishtis, the Suhrawardi saints did not believe in leading a life of poverty.
- They accepted the service of the state, and some of them held important posts in the ecclesiastical department.
- The Chishtis, on the other hand, preferred to keep aloof from state politics and shunned the company of rulers and nobles. The most well-known saints of the order were Shaikh Shihabuddin Suhrawardi and **Hamid-ud-Din Nagori**.
- However, the Sufi saints helped the rulers in their own way by creating a climate of opinion in which people belonging to different sects and religions could live in peace and harmony.

- While Mecca remained the holy of holies, the rise of popular saints provided a useful point of veneration and devotion to the mass of Muslims within the country.

Qadiri Silsilahs

- This order was founded by Abdul-Qadir Gilani (1078-1166 AD). It is popular among the Muslims of South India. **Sheikh Niamatullah** was the first important *Qadri* to come to India.
- **Nasir-ud-din Muhammad Jilani** was the most important *Qadri,* who effectively organised the *Qadiri* order.

  This order was dominant in Sindh and Lahore. Shahjahan's eldest son **Dara Shikoh** was a follower of the *Qadiri* order.

Naqshbandi Silsilahs

- This order was founded by Baha-ud-din Naqshband Bukhari (1318-1389 AD), born in Bukhara. Mughal emperor Babur was a follower of Ubaidullah Ahrar who was a *Naqshbandi.*
- **Sheikh Ahmad Sirhindi** was a contemporary of Akbar and Jahangir. He was against the liberal policies of Akbar which he criticise as **un-Islamic**. Sirhindi wanted to remove Hindu influences on Islam. He was also opposed to the Shias.
- His work *Maktubat* is compiled into three volumes called *Durr-al- Ma'rifat, Noor-al-Khallaq* and *Ma'rifat-al-Haqa'iq,* in which he systematised the doctrine of the *Wahadat-ul-Wujood.*

Firdausi Silsilahs

- This order was popular in Bihar. It was popularised by **Sheikh Sharfuddin Yahya**, who was a disciple of Khwaja **Nizamuddin Firdausi**, prominent saints of this order were Badruddin Samarqandi and Sheikh Sharfuddin Maneri.
- They practiced ascetic practice in forests and believed in the philosophy of *Wahadat-ul-Wujood.*

Shattari Silsilahs

- This order was introduced in India in the 15th century by **Abdullah Shattari**.
- Other prominent saints were Sharaf Wajihuddin of Gujarat and Shah Pir of Meerut. The saints of this order claimed direct contact with God.

Important Sufi Saints

Important Sufi Saints are discussed as follows

Moinuddin Chishti

- He is the most famous saint of the *Chishti* order. He was born in 1141 AD and died in 1236 AD. He became a disciple of the *Chishti* Saint Usman Harooni. He reached Ajmer along with Mu'izz ad-Din Mohammad and settled down.
- It was during the reign of Akbar that Ajmer emerged as one of the most important centre of pilgrimage. Moinuddin Chishti written several books including *Anis al-Arwah* and *Dalil al-Arifin*, both of which deal with the Islamic law of living.

Qutubuddin Bakhtiyar Kaki

- He was a renowned Muslim Sufi mystic, saint and scholar of the *Chishti* order. He was a disciple of **Moinuddin Chishti.**
- He played a major role in establishing the order securely in Delhi, which was earlier confined to Ajmer and Nagaur. He was followed by the first Delhi Sultan, **Qutubuddin Aibak,** who started the construction of Qutub Minar.

Nizamuddin Auliya

- He was a famous *Sufi* saint of *Chishti* order. He was born in 1238 AD in Badayun, Uttar Pradesh.
- His biography finds mention in **Ain-i-Akbari,** a 16th century document written by Mughal emperor Akbar's *Wazir*, **Abu'l Fazl.**
- One of the kings of the Delhi sultanate during Nizamuddin Auliya lifetime was **Qutub-ud-din Mubarak Shah**, the last ruler of Khilji dynasty.

Baha-ud-Din Naqshband Bukhari

- He was born in 1318 and was the founder of what would become one of the largest and most influential *Sufi* Muslim order, the Naqshbandi.

Sheikh Rukn-ud-Din Abul Fateh

- He was commonly known by the title *Rukn-e-Alam* (pillar of the world) or *Shah Rukne Alam* and was among the important *Sufi* saint from Multan.
- He was the grandson and successor of Sheikh **Baha-ud-din Zakariya.**

Baba Sain Mir Muhammed Sahib

- He was popularly known as **Mian Mir** and was a famous Sufi saint, who resided in Lahore, specifically in the town of Dharampura (in present day Pakistan). He belonged to the *Qadiri* order of *Sufism.*
- He is famous for being a spiritual instructor of **Dara Shikoh**, the eldest son of Mughal emperor Shahjahan. He is identified as the founder of the *Mian Khail* branch of the *Qadiri* order.

Mullah Shah Badakhshi

- He was popularly known as Mullah Shah. He was a 17th century Muslim Sufi and spiritual successor of the famous Sufi saint Mian Mir (1550-1635 AD).

- He belonged to the Qadiri order of sufism. He was the spiritual mentor of the Mughal prince **Dara Shikoh Qadri** (1615-1659 AD) and his sister princess **Jahanara Begum**.

Burhanuddin 'Gharib'

- He studied under Nizamuddin Auliya. Burhanuddin succeeded the Sultan-ul-Mashaikh as caliph.
- He allowed music and joy in the religious exercises at his convent. He remained for sometime at Daulatabad and then left for Roza (Khuldabad), where he died.

Sources used to reconstruct the History of sufi traditions

A wide range of texts were produced in and around sufi khanqahs. These included:

- Treatises or manuals dealing with sufi thought and practices – The Kashf-ul-Mahjub of Ali bin Usman Hujwiri (died c. 1071) is an example of this genre. It enables historians to see how traditions outside the subcontinent influenced sufi thought in India.
- Malfuzat (literally, "uttered"; conversations of sufi saints) – An early text on malfuzat is the Fawa'id-al-Fu'ad, a collection of conversations of Shaikh Nizamuddin Auliya, compiled by Amir Hasan Sijzi Dehlavi, a noted Persian poet. Source 9 contains an excerpt from this text. Malfuzats were compiled by different sufi silsilas with the permission of the shaikhs; these had obvious didactic purposes. Several examples have been found from different parts of the subcontinent, including the Deccan. They were compiled over several centuries.
- Maktubat (literally, "written" collections of letters); letters written by sufi masters, addressed to their disciples and associates – While these tell us about the shaikh's experience of religious truth that he wanted to share with others, they also reflect the life conditions of the recipients and are responses to their aspirations and difficulties, both spiritual and mundane.
- Tazkiras (literally, "to mention and memorialise"; biographical accounts of saints) – The fourteenth-centurySiyar-ul-Auliya of Mir Khwurd Kirmani was the first sufi tazkira written in India. It dealt principally with the Chishti saints. The most famous tazkira is the Akhbar-ul-Akhyar of Abdul Haqq Muhaddis Dehlavi (d. 1642). The authors of the tazkiras often sought to establish the precedence of their own orders and glorify their spiritual genealogies.

Extra Facts From Tamil Nadu Board and NIOS

- According to the popular Tazkirah-i-Auliya-i-Hind (Lives of Muslim Saints), Kabir was a disciple of the Muslim sufi, Shaikh Taqi.
- Ramananda was the first to preach his doctrine of devotion in Hindi. Among his twelve disciples the famous were Ravidas, Kabir and two women.
- Tuka Ram believed in a formless God. According to him, it was not possible to enjoin spiritual joy with worldly activities. He stressed on all-pervasive God. He rejected vedic sacrifices, ceremonies, pilgrimages, idol-worship, etc.

Terms	Meanings
Qurbat	Divine proximity
Hulul	Infusion of the divine spirit
Fana	Self-annihilation
Maqamat	various stages
Wahdat al Wujud	Unity of being
Ziyarat	The practice of visiting tombs

18

The Mughal Empire and Its Decline

[SOURCES]

Class-VII New NCERT Chap 4 (The Mughals 16th to 17th Century), Class-VII Old NCERT Chap 7 (The Coming of the Mughals and the Europeans), Class-VII Old NCERT Chap 1 (The Age Magnificence), Class-XI Old NCERT Chap 12 (Struggle for Empire in North India-II (Mughals and Afghans 1525-1555), Class-XI Old NCERT Chap 1 (Consolidation of the Mughal Empire (Age of Akbar), Class-XI Old NCERT Chap 14 (The Deccan and South India), Class-XI Old NCERT Chap 15 (India in the First Half of the Seventeenth Century), Class-XI Old NCERT Chap 1 (Climax and Disintegration of the Mughal Empiere-I), Class-XII New NCERT Chap 8 (Peasants, Zamindars and the State), Tamil Nadu Board (Class XI), NIOS

- The Mughal empire which lasted for more than 300 years (1526-1857 AD), was a period of national integration with stability. It was a period of flourishing art and culture in medieval India.
- The name 'Mughal' derives from Mongol, though Mughal rulers claimed from 'Timurids' lineage. Historically, the Mughals were descendants of two great lineages of **Genghis Khan** and **Timur**. Babur was the founder and first emperor of Mughal Dynasty.

Rulers of Mughal Empire

The important rulers of Mughal empire were

Babur (1526-1530 AD)

- Zahir-ud-Din Muhammad Babur, the eldest son of **Umar Sheikh Mirza**, ascended the throne of Fergana (Transoxiana, Central Asia) in 1494 AD at the age of 12. He tried to conquer his homeland, the city of Samarkand; however, he faced stiff resistance from Uzbeks chief **Shaibani Khan**.
- Babur forced to move towards Northern India where he defeated Ibrahim Lodi in **First Battle of Panipat** (1526 AD) with the use of gunpowder, firearms and field artillery, first to do so.

First Battle of Panipat

- First Battle of Panipat (21st April, 1526) was fought near a small village of Panipat (Haryana) between the **Babur** and the Delhi Sultanate emperor **Ibrahim Lodi**.
- As per the historical sources, Babur forces numbered around 15000 with two dozen pieces of field artillery. The forces of Ibrahim Lodi were much larger, estimated around 40,000 men and 1000 elephants.
- Babur's army used gunpowder and artillery which proved to be decessive in the battle.
- Two of Babur's artillery men's **Ustad Ali** and **Mustafa** played important role in it.
- Ibrahim Lodi died in the battlefield and Babur became victorious. This laid the foundation of Mughal empire in Delhi.

Major Wars Won by Babur

Battle	Year	Between
First Battle of Panipat	20th April, 1526 AD	Babur and Ibrahim Lodi
Battle of Khanwa	17th March, 1527 AD	Babur and Rana Sanga
Battle of Chanderi	29th January, 1528 AD	Babur and Medini Rai
Battle of Ghaghra	6th May, 1529 AD	Babur and Eastern Afghan Confederates

Significance of Babur's Advent

- With the advent of Babur, for the first time since the downfall of the **Kushan empire**, Kabul and Qandahar (now in Afghanistan) became integral parts of India.
- The control of **Kabul** and **Qandahar** strengthened India's foreign trade since these two towns were the starting points for caravans meant for China and Mediterranean.
- Babur introduced new modes of warfare in India through gunpowder and skilled combination of artillery and cavalry.
- Babur was deeply learned in Persian and Arabic. His famous memoirs, *Tuzuk-i-Baburi*, is considered one of the classics of world literature written in now extinct Chagtai Turkish language.
- He laid out a number of formal gardens including **Bagh-e-Babur** in Kabul where he was buried.

Humayun (1530-1540 AD), (1555-1556 AD)

- Humayun succeeded Babur in December, 1530 AD at the young age of 23.
- He had to deals with a number of problems left behind by Babur. Immediately, after the death of his father, Humayun divided his empire, giving Mewat to **Hindal**, Sambhal to **Askari** and; Punjab, Kabul and Qandahar to **Kamran**.

Humayun's Expeditions

Humayun's famous expeditions may be listed as follows :

- **Expedition of Kalinjar** (1531 AD) Six months after his accession, Humayun besieged the powerful fort of Kalinjar in Bundelkhand. This fort, along with Bayana, Gwalior and Dholpur, formed the chain of forts protecting Agra from the South. The Chandela ruler surrendered Kalinjar to Humayun after a siege of a month. He was allowed to keep the fort in return for accepting Humayun's suzerainty and giving 12 tonnes of gold.
- **Battle of Dauhariya** (1532 AD) Humayun defeated Mahmood Lodi, the Afghan of Bihar in this battle.
- **Siege of Chunar** (1532 AD) Humayun seized the fort of Chunar which was under Sher Shah Suri. It was also known as **Gateway of Eastern India**. But instead of following up his success by crushing the routed Pathans, Humayun accepted the submission of Sher Shah, who promised to be loyal to the Mughals and sent one of his sons to Humayun as a hostage.

  Thus, the fort was returned to Sher Shah Suri. The abandoning of Chunar siege was actually induced by the fear of the Bahadur Shah, who was aiming at the conquest of Delhi.
- **Wars with Bahadur Shah** (1535-36 AD) Humayun waged wars with Bahadur Shah from 1535-36 AD and conquered the provinces of Sarangpur, Mandesar, Fort of Mandu, Champaner and Diu. With the conquest of Gujarat, Humayun completed his conquest in Central India.
- **Battle of Chausa** (1539 AD) The battle was fought between Humayun and Sher Shah Suri in which Humayun was defeated. It facilitated Sher Khan to march on to Delhi and Agra and occupied them.
- **Battle of Kannauj** (1540 AD) Sher Shah Suri defeated Humayun in the Battle of Kannauj. After the battle, Humayun fled to Iran and Sher Shah occupied Delhi. Humayun lost the battle because none of his brother supported him.

Restoration of Humayun (1555-1556 AD)

- With the death of last Sur ruler **Ismail Shah**, Humayun got the opportunity to regain its kingdom in India. In two closely contested battles in 1555 AD, he defeated the Afghans and recovered Delhi and Agra.
- However, he did not live long to enjoy the victory as he died from a fall from the first floor of the library building in 1556 AD at Delhi.

Sur Empire (1540-55 AD)

- Sher Shah and his successors ruled for 15 years. This period is known as the period of second Afghan Empire.

Sher Shah

- Sher Shah ascended the throne of Delhi at the age of 54. His original name was **Farid** and his father was a small *jagirdar* at Jaunpur. The title of **Sher Khan** was given to him by his ruler of Bihar for killing a lion.
- Sher Shah's empire extended from Bengal to the Indus, excluding Kashmir. In the West, he conquered Malwa and almost the entire Rajasthan.

Major Battles of Sher Shah

Battle	Date	Between	Result
Battle of Chausa	26th June, 1539 AD	Sher Khan and Humayun	• Mughal army defeated and Humayun fled to Agra.
Battle of Bilgram	17th May, 1540	Sher Khan and Humayun	• Sher Khan defeated the Mughal army for the second time. • Humayun took shelter at the court of the Iranian king Tahmasp.
Battle of Kalinjar	22nd May, 1545 AD	Sher Khan and Raja Kirat Singh	• The fort of Kalinjar was taken by Afghan forces but, Sher Shah died due to cannon burst.

Contribution of Sher Shah

Amongst the foremost contributions of Sher Shah was his re-establishment of law and order across the length and breadth of his empire. His major reforms in different areas were as follows :

Central Administration

- Sher Shah continued the strong central machinery of administration.
- A number of villages comprised a pargana. The pargana was under the charge of the shiqdar, for law and order and general administration, and the munsif or amil looked after the collection of land revenue.
- Above the pargana was the shiq or sarkar under the charge of the *shiqdar-i-shiqdaran* or *faujdar* and a *munsif-i-munsifan*.

Important Officials

- *Diwan-i-Wizarat* – Revenue and Finance.
- *Diwan-i-Ariz* – In charge of Army.
- *Diwan-i-Rasalat* – Foreign Minister.
- *Diwan-i-Insha* – Minister of Communication.
- Barid – Intelligence.

The Army

- Sher Shah set up a strong army in order to administer his vast empire. He recruited soldiers directly. Every soldier had his **descriptive roll** (*chehra*) recorded and his horse branded with the imperial sign.
- Sher Shah set up cantonments in different parts of the empire and a **strong garrison** was posted in each of them.

Judicial System

- Sher Shah gave immense importance to the judicial system in empire.
- *Kazis* were appointed in different places to deliver justice.
- But like old traditions in village, civil and criminal matters were managed by Panchayats or landlords.

Land Revenue System

- Sher Shah insisted on measurement of the sown land. The produce of land was no longer to be based on guess work. A crop rate (*ray*) was drawn up, laying down the state's share of the different types of crops.
- The share of the state was one-third of the produce. The peasants were given the option of paying in cash or kind, though the state preferred cash. All the details were written down on a paper called *patta*.
- He started land assessment every year.
- Land survey was carefully done and he introduced a schedule of crop rates.
- Revenue officials called *Amils* and *Qanungo* were the officials incharge of maintaining revenue record.
- All cultivable land were classified into three categories i.e., good, middle and bad. The state's share was one-third of the average produce and it was paid in cash or crop.
- Land was measured using **Sikandari gaz** (32 points).

Roadways

- Sher Shah paid great attention to the fostering of trade and commerce and the improvement of communications in his kingdom.
- He restored the old imperial road called the **Grand Trunk Road**, from the river Indus in the West to Sonargaon in Bengal.
- He also built a road from Agra to Jodhpur and Chittor, evidently linking up with the road to the Gujarat seaports. He built a third road from Lahore to Multan.

Sarai

- For the convenience of travellers, Sher Shah built a total 1700 *sarai* at a distance of every two *kos* (about eight km) on these roads.
- Every *sarai* had several watchmen under the control of a *shahna* (custodian). His roads and sarais have been called **'the arteries of the empire'**.

Trade and Commerce

- Sher Shah also promoted the growth of trade and commerce. He directed his governors and *amils* to treat merchants and travellers well in every way, and not to harm them at all.
- Sher Shah made the local village headmen (*muqaddams*) and zamindars responsible for any loss that a merchant suffered on the roads.
- The currency reforms of Sher Shah also helped in the growth of commerce and handicrafts. His silver rupee remained a standard coin for centuries after him.
- He introduced *Rupaya* (a silver coin) and *Dam* (a copper coin).

Art and Architecture

- Sher Shah was also a great builder. The tomb which he built for himself at **Sasaram** is regarded as one of the masterpieces of architecture.
- Sher Shah also built a new city on the bank of the Yamuna near Delhi known **Old Fort** (Purana Qila) and the fine mosque within it.
- One of the finest works in Hindi, the *Padmavat* of **Malik Muhammad Jayasi**, was completed during Sher Shah's reign.

Akbar (1556-1605 AD)

- Akbar, the greatest of the Mughal rulers, was born at 1542 AD at Amarkot (Sindh, Pakistan).
- Abul Fazl placed Mughal kingship as the highest station in the hierarchy of object receiving light emanating from God (*Farr-i-Izadi*). Abul Fazl was the court historian of Akbar.
- When Humayun died, Akbar was at Kalanaur in the Punjab. He was crowned there in 1556 AD at the young age of 13 years and 4 months.
- It was Akbar's tutor **Bairam Khan,** who served the Mughal emperor and even commanded the **Second Battle** of Panipat to consolidate the Mughal empire in India.
- The battle between the Mughals and the Afghan forces led by **Hemchandla Vikramaditya,** took place once again at Panipat (Second Battle of Panipat) on 5th November, 1556 AD. Bairam Khan of Mughal army decisively defeated Afghan forces. Hemu was captured and executed.

Regent of Bairam Khan

- Bairam Khan emerged as the most powerful noble and became very arrogant. By this time, Akbar also wanted to assume full control.
- Akbar removed Bairam Khan as *Wakil* and asked him to retire to Mecca for pilgrimage, though he was killed by an Afghan near Ahmedabad.
- Bairam Khan's son later became an influential noble under Akbar as **Abdur Rahim Khan-i-Khana**.

The Nine Gems (Navratnas) of Akbar

1. **Raja Man Singh** He was the Chief of Staff of the Mughal Army.
2. **Miyan Tansen** A renowned singer in Mughal court who composed many ragas.
3. **Mulla Do-Piyaza** Minister of Home Affairs in Akbar's court.
4. **Raja Birbal** Foreign Minister and the only Hindu to convert to Din-i Ilahi.
5. **Abul-Fazl** Grand Wazir or Prime Minister.
6. **Faizi** Minister of Education and mentor of royal Princes.
7. **Fakir Aziao-Din** Minister of Religious Affairs.
8. **Abdul Rahim Khan-i-Khana** Defence Minister, wrote numerous Dohas in Hindi.
9. **Raja Todar Mal** Finance Minister; he was famous for framing Dahsala system.

Akbar's Military Campaigns

Against	Details
Malwa (1561 AD)	• The expedition against Malwa was led by Adham Khan, son of Akbar's foster-mother, Maham Anaga. Baz Bahadur was badly defeated on 1561 AD.
Garh-Katanga (1564 AD)	• The kingdom of Garh-Katanga (Northern Madhya Pradesh) was under Sangram Shah. • Mughal Governor of Allahabad Asaf Khan defeated the Gonds decisively.
Chittor (1568 AD)	• A major step in his campaign against the Rajput states was the siege of Chittor ruled by Rana Udai Singh. • Chittor fell on 1568 AD after a gallant siege of six months. In honour of the gallant Jaimal and Patta, two stone statues erected by Akbar at the gate of fort of Agra.
Battle of Haldighati (1576 AD)	• In 1572, Rana Pratap succeeded Rana Udai Singh in Mewar. Many embassies were sent by Akbar to accept Mughal suzerainty but failed. • In 1576, under Raja Man Singh Mughal forces defeated Mewar.
Gujarat (1572 AD)	• In 1572, At Surat, Akbar assaulted the Mirzas with the help of Man Singh and Bhagwant Das of Amber. The Mirzas were defeated and Gujarat came under Mughal control.
Bengal (1576 AD)	• The Afghans under Daud Khan had continued to dominate Bengal and Bihar. • For the first time, Akbar advanced with a strong flotilla of boats and in a stiff battle in Bihar in 1576 AD, Daud Khan was defeated by the Mughals.
Ahmad Nagar (1596 AD)	• The Mughal invasion was led by Prince Murad, who was the Governor of Gujarat and by Abdur Rahim Khan-i-Khana against Chand Bibi. • The two sides in the end came to an agreement in 1596 AD. Mughal suzerainty was also recognised.
Khandesh (1601 AD)	• The fort of Asirgarh in Khandesh was reputed to be the strongest fort in the Deccan. After a tight siege, it surrendered on 1601 AD to Mughals. • Prince Daniyal, the youngest son of Akbar, concluded a peace with Murtaza Nizam Shah II.

Rajput Policy of Akbar

- To win over the friendship of Rajput rulers and using their loyalty and bravery to strengthen his own position were the twin pillars of the Rajput Policy of Akbar.
- Akbar developed special relationship with the Rajput rulers. Rajputs became the important supporters and strength of the Mughal empire.
- As the relationship grew, Rajputs were assigned by position of responsibilities. Akbar made the Rajputs not only his friends, but also took many Rajput princess as his bride.
- He established matrimonial alliances with the Royal families of the Rajput states of Amber, Bikaner and Jaisalmer. **Raja Bharmal Kachhwaha** of Amber married his eldest daughter to Akbar.

- **Raja Bhagwan Das** (Raja Bharmal's heir) and Man Singh, son of Bhagwan Das were subsequently given senior positions in the imperial hierarchy. They were given 5000 and 7000 *Zat* ranks respectively.
- *Ain-i-Akbari*, one of the most important chronicles, which talks about Mughal empire's socials, political and religious life. It had had been written by Abul Fazl.
- Soon other, *Rajput* rulers also followed the *Kachhwahas* and established friendly relations with Akbar. This included Rathore of Jodhpur, Bhatis of Jaisalmer, Hadas of Ranthambore, etc.
- Only the **Sisodias of Mewar** refused to accept Mughal paramountcy and kept on struggling for its survival as a fully sovereign state under its rulers like **Udai Singh**, **Rana Pratap**, etc.

Religion and Social Reforms

- One of the first actions which Akbar took, after he had taken power in his own hands, was to abolish the poll tax or *jizyah*. At the same time, Akbar abolished the pilgrim tax as well. He also abolished the practice of forcibly converting prisoners of war to Islam.
- Akbar's initiated a policy of religious harmony named *Sulh-i-Kul* or 'peace to all'. According to which, a true ruler solely depended on divine illumination (*farr-i-izadi*). Hence, no one could stand between God and a true ruler.
- Akbar also set up a new religion *Din-i-Ilahi* or *Tauhid-i-Ilahi* which literally means **Divine Monotheism**. However, many leading nobles, except **Birbal**, declined to join. The number of this group was eighteen only.

Ibadat Khana

- In 1575, Akbar built a hall called *Ibadat Khana* or the Hall of Prayer at his new capital, **Fatehpur Sikri**. To this, he called selected theologians to discuss religious and spiritual topics with them.
- The proceedings, at first, were confined to the Muslims. Later, he opened Ibadat Khana to Christians, Zoroastrians, Hindus, Jains, even atheists.
- Akbar invited **Purushottam** and **Devi** to explain the doctrines of Hinduism, and **Maharaji Rana** (Meherji Rana) for Zoroastrianism.
- Akbar also sent an embassy to Goa and two Christian missionaries *Aquaviva* and *Monserrate* came to Akbar's court. Jain saint of Kathiawar, *Hira Vijaya Suri* participated in *Ibadat Khana*.
- The debates in the *Ibadat Khana* had not led to a better understanding. Hence, in 1582 AD, Akbar discontinued the debates in the *Ibadat Khana*.

Din-i-Ilahi

- The *Din-i-Ilahi* was a syncretic religion propounded by Akbar in 1582 AD. He wanted to merge the best elements of the religions of his empire.
- The elements were primarily drawn from **Islam** and **Hinduism**, but some others were also taken from **Christianity**, **Jainism** and **Zoroastrianism.**
- The basic purpose of the formulation of *Din-i-Ilahi* was *Sul-i-Kul* or universal harmony which governed all public policies of Akbar.

Tenets of Din-i-Ilahi (1582)

- It could be adopted on Sunday by performing *paibos* (the emperor placed his feet on the head of the initiated), following which Akbar gave *Shat* (formula).
- The initiated had to express greeting in the form of *Allah-O-Akbar* and *Jalle-Jalaluhu.*
- He had to abstain from eating meat and had to give alms. There were no scriptures or priests.
- *Tauhid-i-Ilahi* had four grades of devotion in the ascending order sacrifice of property, life, honour and religion.
- **Birbal**, **Abul Fazl** and **Faizi** joined the order. **Badauni** believed that Akbar was creating a new religion but contemporary historians believe that he was only trying to attain the status of *Insaan-i-Kamil.*

Jahangir (1605–1627 AD)

- Jahangir, the eldest son of Akbar, succeeded in 1605 AD to the throne. Under his reign, the Mughals played a key role in stabilising India's relations with neighbouring such as Iran, the Uzbeks and the Ottoman Turks.
- The main achievement of Jahangir, was the settlement of the outstanding dispute with Mewar. He launched three successive campaigns and in 1613 a peace treaty was accorded by **Prince Khurram** (later Shah Jahan) to Mewar.
- Jahangir was the first Islamic emperor to introduce the fashion of men wearing costly jewels in their ears after piercing them.
- Jahangir after killing **Nur Jahan's** first husband, Sher Afghan, married to her in 1611 AD. Her father, **Itimaduddaula**, had been made joint diwan by Jahangir.

Nur Jahan

- Nur Jahan along with her father **Itmad-ud-Daula** and brother **Asaf Khan**, and in alliance with Khurram, formed a group or *junta*.
- Coins were issued in her name and she was given the title of Badshah Begum.
- Under Mughal rule, no woman had reached such an important position earlier.
- She lived a retired life till her death and was buried at Lahore.

Rebellion of Prince Khurram and Mahabat Khan

- Towards the end of Jahangir's reign, a struggle for power took place between prince **Khurram** and prince **Shahryar**, Jahangir's youngest son and the son-in-law of Nur Jahan.
- Prince Khurram captured Bihar and Bengal. **Asaf Khan** supported Khurram in the civil war which lasted for more than three years. The royal forces recaptured Bengal and Bihar and Khurram had to seek shelter in Deccan.
- Khusrau was imprisoned and blinded to disqualify him as an emperor. One of Khusrau's well-wishers, **Guru Arjan Dev** (5th Guru of the Sikhs), was beheaded.
- Finally, Khusrau died at Burhanpur in 1621 AD. Another revolt was led by **Mahabat Khan** who had been deprived of his office.
- Crossing the river Jhelum, on the way to Kabal, Mahabat Khan attacked Jahangir and his royal party in 1626 AD. However, the diplomacy of Nur Jahan saved the situation.

Shah Jahan (1628–1658 AD)

- Jahangir breathed his last at Lahore on 1627 AD and Shah Jahan became next Emperor with all his rivals were murdered by his order.
- In the areas of Art and Architecture, Shah Jahan's reign is considered as '**Golden Era in Medieval India**'.
- The reign of Shah Jahan marked as successful conquest of Deccan with the treaties with Bijapur and Golconda in 1636 AD. It helped Mughals could expand their area of dominance to large parts of Southern India.
- Shah Jahan's reign also marked with continuous struggle with **Safavid** (Iran) empires for the territory of **Qandahar** (Afghanistan). However, despite of various attempts, the Mughals failed to capture Qandahar.
- The Mughals lost more than 5000 lives during their successive invasions between 1638 AD and 1647 AD. Shah Jahan became more realistic and stopped dreaming of ruling over his former ancestral lands.
- The Badshah Nama, an important chronicles during Mughal period, was revised by Sadullah Khan, Shah Jahan's wazir. The Badshah Nama is the official history in three volumes (daftars) of ten lunar years each. Lahori wrote the first and second daftars comprising the first two decades of the emperor's rule.

Conquests by Shah Jahan

- **Bundelas and Afghans** In the first year of his reign, Shah Jahan had to overcome the revolts of the Bundelas at Bundelkhand and the Afghan noble named **Khan Jahan Lodhi**, an ex-viceroy of Deccan.
- During Jahangir's reign, Bir Singh Bundela had become the emperor's favourite by assassinating Abul Fazl. After his death, his son Jujhar Singh succeeded him. **Jujhar** and his son, **Vikramajit**, rebelled against the Mughals, but the imperialist forces pursued them relentlessly and eventually murdered them.
- **Ahmednagar** (1633 AD) Shah Jahan pursued the Mughal designs of the complete conquest of the Deccan. However, it could not be completed during Shah Jahan.
- After the death of Malik Ambar, his son, Fateh Khan failed to get the cooperation of the Nizam Shahi nobles and consequently surrendered to the Mughals. Ahmednagar was annexed to the empire in 1633 AD.
- **Other Deccan States** Next Shah Jahan forced the kingdoms of Bijapur and Golconda to accept his overlordship. Both Bijapur and Golconda signed a treaty with the emperor in 1636 AD.
- Khandesh, Berar, Telangana and Daulatabad were made into four Mughal provinces. This brought 20 years of peace to the Deccan, till war broke out again in 1656 AD.
- **Marathas, Portuguese and Kamarup** Shah Jahan lured some Maratha leaders into his service. The most influential among them was **Shahji Bhonsle**.

  Shah Jahan also expelled the Portuguese from Hooghly, as they were abusing their trading privileges and indulging in piracy and slave-trade. **Kamarup** was also annexed.
- **Central Asia Kandahar and Transoxiana** Shah Jahan's policy towards Central Asia was to secure a possession of Kandahar, which the Persians had re-occupied during the Jahangir's reign. He had recovered Kandahar in 1638 AD, only to lose it in 1649 AD. But his three expeditions to regain it were without success.

Thus, Kandahar was forever lost to the Mughal empire. Shah Jahan, wanting to conquer Badakshan and Balkh, sent his forces there in 1646 AD, but the campaign proved a failure.

The Mughal inability to fight prolonged wars in mountains frustrated Shah Jahan's ambitions to conquer Transoxiana, his ancestral lands.

Wars of Succession

- The last years of Shah Jahan's reign were surrounded by a bitter war of succession among his sons. Shah Jahan rallied in favour of his eldest son **Dara Shikoh** as his successor (*wali-ahd*) and gave the title-**Shahzada-e-Buland Iqbal** (Prince of High Fortune).

Dara Shikoh 'Most Learned Prince'

- Dara Shikoh was the most learned Prince of Mughal empire.
- Dara Shikoh wrote *Majma-ul-Bahrayn* (The Meeting Place of the Two Seas), a famous book about the similarities between Islam and the monotheistic streak of Hinduism.
- He also had the Upanishads translated in Persian text called *Sirr-i Akbar* (The Greatest Secret).

Three Major Wars of Succession

Battle	Date	Result
Battle of Dharmat (District Indore, Madhya Pradesh)	1658 AD	Both Raja Jaswant Singh and Shuja were defeated by Aurangzeb.
Battle of Samugarh (near Agra, Uttar Pradesh)	29th May, 1658 AD	Aurangzeb defeated Dara Shikoh Shah Jahan besieged in fort of Agra by Aurangzeb.
Battle of Deorai (near Ajmer, Rajasthan)	March, 1659 AD	The last major battle between Dara and Aurangzeb. Dara was defeated and executed along with his son, Sulaiman Shikoh in 1661 AD.

Aurangzeb (1658-1707 AD)

- During Aurangzeb's long reign of 49 years, the Mughal empire reached its territorial climax, more than as it was during Akbar's reign.
- Aurangzeb proved to be a hardworking ruler and a strict disciplinarian who did not spare his own sons.
- In 1686 AD, he imprisoned prince **Muazzam** on a charge of intriguing with the ruler of Golconda and kept him in prison for 12 long years.
- Unlike his predecessors, Aurangzeb did not like extravagant lifestyle.

  His personal life was marked by simplicity. In course of time, he began to be regarded as a *Zindapir* or **a living saint**.

Rajput Policy of Aurangzeb

- Aurangzeb gave immense importance to friendship with Rajput. To gain more support of Maharana of Mewar, he increased his position from 5000 *zat* to 6000 *zat*.
- **Rathore** ruler of Marwar, **Sisodiya** ruler of Mewar and Ajmer were the close allies of Aurangzeb.
- **Jai Singh**, until the death of Aurangzeb in 1707 AD.
- **Jaswant Singh** was given the responsibility of suppressing revolts in Afghanistan.
- Aurangzeb has the most Rajput officials in his court than any other Mughal ruler.

Aurangzeb's Religious Policy

- It is believed that he reversed Akbar's policy of religious toleration and thus undermined the loyalty of the Hindus to the Empire.
- A compendium of Aurangzeb's rules and regulations had been collected in a work called '*Zawabit-i-Alamgiri*'.
- His prohibitive steps were as follows :
  - Discontinuation the *kalma* on coins.
  - Discontinuation of the festival of *Nauroz*.
  - Official department of history-writing discontinued.
  - Aurangzeb discontinued the practice of *jharoka-darshan*.
  - Appointment of *Muhtasibs* to check and promote the *Sharia* laws.
  - Ban on singing and dancing in the court.

Steps against Hindus

- During his reign, Aurangzeb ordered in 1665 AD order to demolish many temples including temple of Somnath at Gujarat, temple of Vishwanath at Banaras and the temple of Keshava Rai at Mathura.
- Aurangzeb re-introduced *jizyah* or the poll tax, which was abolished by Akbar.

Revolts During Reign of Aurangzeb

Revolt	Cause/Description
Cooch- Behar and Ahom	The first ten years of Aurangzeb's rule were militarily and politically a great success. By 1661 AD, Mughal Governor of Bengal, **Mir Jumla**, seized Cooch-Behar and marched up the Brahmaputra. Next year, he entered Garhgaon (near Guwahati), the Ahom capital. The Ahom army was defeated, but Mughals failed to suppress the feelings of regional independence, among the people of Ahom kingdom. Finally, Mir Jumla made peace with the Ahom Raja. After Mir Jumla's death, Aurangzeb appointed Shaista Khan as Governor of Bengal.
Afghan Revolt	In 1667 AD, Afghans revolted under leadership of Bhagu. It was suppressed by Mughal Subedar Amir Khan. In 1672 AD, Afghans again revolted under leadership of Akmal Khan Afridi.
Satnami Peasants of Punjab	The revolt by the *Satnami* peasants of Punjab in 1672 AD was sparked off by a minor dispute between a *Satnami* peasant and a Mughal foot soldier. *Satnamis* established an independent government, but the imperial army crushed the rebellion.
Bundelkhand	The *Bundelas* under the leadership of Champat Rai and Chhatrasal Bundela in Bundelkhand revolted against the reactionary policies of Aurangzeb. Chhatrasal attacked imperial troops and began collecting *Chauth* (tax) from the neighbouring tracts of the Mughal empire.
Jat Revolt	The cruelty committed by Abd-un-Nabi, the *faujdar* of Mathura, aroused the Jats around Mathura and Agra to rise in Revolt in 1699-70 AD. Gokula, a *zamindar* of Tilpat, became the Jat leader and killed the *faujdar*. The emperor himself marched to the area and put down the rebellion temporarily by capturing and executing Gokula (1669 AD).
Sikh Revolts	**Guru, Tegh Bahadur**, opposed the religious policy of Aurangzeb openly and resented against it, in a public meeting. Aurangzeb arrested him and forced him to accept Islam. Guru's refusal led to his torture and finally his execution. In 1675 AD, Guru Tegh Bahadur was beheaded on the orders of the *Qazi* of Delhi. **Guru Gobind** the tenth guru of the Sikhs, reinterpreted the Sikh ideologies to justify military action and created *Khalsa* (the army of pure). After the death of Gobind Singh, the *Khalsa* rose in revolt against Mughals, under the leadership of Banda Bahadur.
North- Western India (Marwar)	The most serious revolt against Aurangzeb, however, was done by *Rajputs* of Jodhpur. This begun when Maharaja Jaswant Singh died in the North-Western tribal region in 1678 AD. He had no heirs, but one of his pregnant queens gave birth to his son Ajit Singh.

Decline of Mughal Empire

- The Mughal empire had become highly centralised and too large to be controlled by any ruler from one centre i.e. Delhi. The Great Mughals till the reign or Aurangzeb) were efficient and exercised control over administration and army; however the later Mughals were weak and lacking foresightedness.
- During the last years of Aurangzeb's reign, the number of jagirdars appointed had risen to such a great number that there was a serious shortage of *paibaqi* land (land earmarked to be given as jagirs). This created huge crisis in jagirdari system among nobles and the Mughal Emperor.
- **Aurangzeb Deccan Policy** was another cause of downfall of the Mughal dynasty. His religious persecution against the Shia kingdoms of Bijapur and Golconda and waged a long, endless war against the Marathas inflicted disagreement among his own nobles and *mansabdars*.

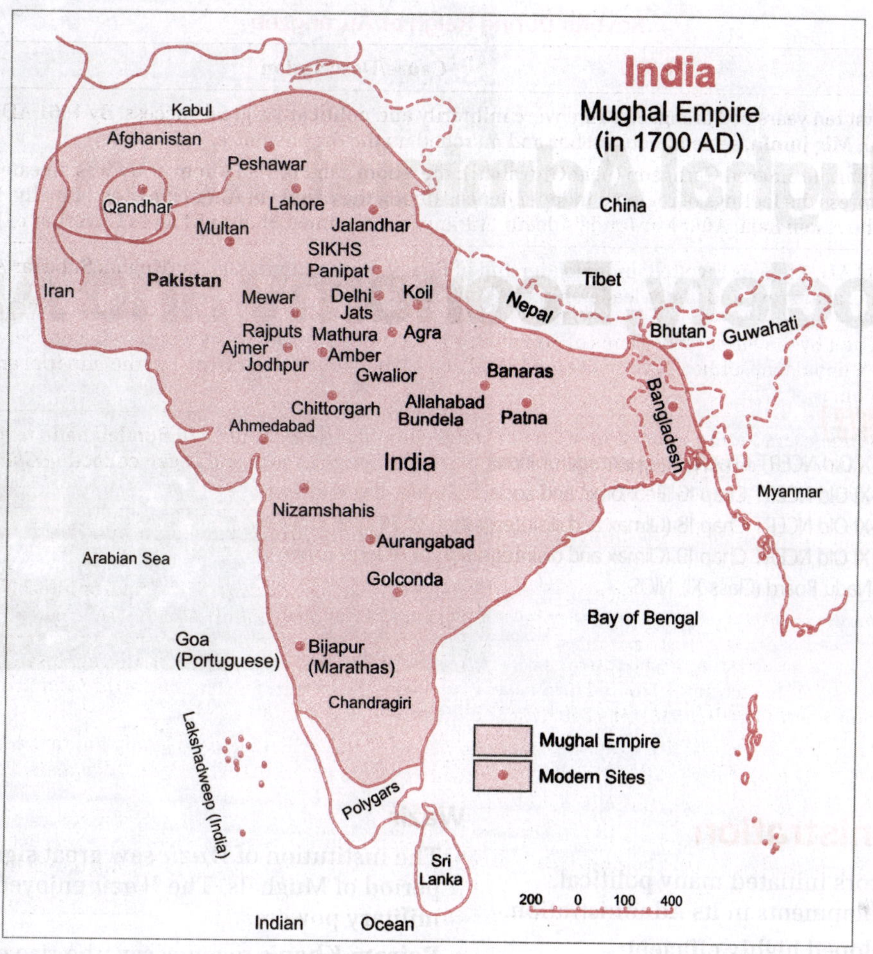

Extra Facts From Tamil Nadu Board and NIOS

- Babur's memoris **Tuzuk-i-Baburi** (Baburnama) is considered a world classic. Babur found nothing admirable either in the Afghan who ruled India for some time but his description of India is delightful.
- Jaipur, Gwalior, Ajmer and Kabul were the powerful, however, Akbar's rule saw the expansion of the Mughal empire and controlled these region very soon.
- Malwa was conquered in 1562, Gondwana region was annexed in 1564 and Gujarat was conquered in 1573 by Akbar.
- Akbar defeated Mirza Hakim of Kabul with the help of Raja Man Singh and Bhagwan Das. He conquest Kashmir in 1586 and Sindh in 1591.
- Akbar was interested to learn about the doctrine of all religions and propagated a Philosophy of Sudh-i-Kul (peace of all). He established Ibadat Khana.
- Jahangir's reign witnessed the visit of two Englishmen-William Hawkins and Sir Thomas Roe. While, the former could not get the consent of the emperor for establishing a factory, the latter, sent as ambassador by King James I, succeeded in securing permission to established a British factory at Surat.
- A contemporary of Louis XIV of France, Shah Jahan ruled for thirty years. In his reign, the famous peacock throne was made for the king.
- Bernier, Tavernier, Mandelslo and Manucci visited India during the reign of Shah Jahan and left behind detailed accounts of India.

Mughal Administration, Society, Economy and Arts

[SOURCES]

Class-X Old NCERT Chap 1 (The Heritage of India),
Class-XI Old NCERT Chap 16 (Economic and social life under the Mughals)
Class-XI Old NCERT Chap 18 (Climax and disintergration of Mughal Empire-I),
Class-XI Old NCERT Chap 19 (Climax and disintegration of Mughal Expire-II),
Tamil Nadu Board (Class XI), NIOS

Mughal Administration

- The Mughal Emperors initiated many political, administrative developments in its Administration.
- They not only developed highly efficient governance but also ensured effective working of both at the central as well as provincial levels.

Central Administration

- The Mughal administrative structure was highly centralised in nature.
- This centralisation is manifested in the efficient working of land revenue system, *mansab* and *jagir*, uniform coinage, etc.
- In spite of the vast range of powers enjoyed by the Central ministers, the Mughals prevented any minister or officer from gaining unlimited powers through a system of checks and balances.

The Emperor

- The concept of **supreme leader** traditions had always special feature of the Mughal Empire.
- The Mughal king considered as of divine origin among the Indian people. With that reason, all officers in Mughal administration owed their position and power to the Emperor, which were subject to the ruler's personal preferences.
- The position of emperor was hereditary.

Wazir

- The institution of *Wazir* saw great significance during the period of Mughals. The *Wazir* enjoyed both the civil and military powers.
- **Bairam Khan's** regency saw the rise of the *wakil-wazir* with unlimited powers. Akbar took away the financial powers of the *wakil* and entrusted it into the hands of the *Diwan-i-Kul* (Finance Minister).

Important Officials in Central Administration

- **Diwan-i-Kul** His duty was to supervise the imperial treasury and check all accounts. Akbar entrusted the revenue powers to the Diwan. The entire revenue collection and expenditure machinery was under his charge.
- The central revenue ministry had many sub-departments such as *Diwan-i-Aalisa*, *Diwan-i-Tan* (For cash salary), *Diwan-i-Jagir*, *Diwan-i Buyutat* (Royal household), etc.
- **Mir Bakhshi** He was the head of the military administration and also incharge of intelligence gathering. Intelligence officers (*barids*) and news reporters (*waqia-navis*) were appointed under him. Recommendations for military appointments and promotions to the Emperor were also done by him.
- **Mir Saman** The Mir Saman was the officer in-charge of the royal *karkhanas*. He was also known as *Khan-i-saman*. He was responsible for the purchase of all kinds of articles and their storage for the royal household.

He also used to supervise the manufacture of weapons of war and articles of luxury. Under the Mir Saman, there was *Tahsildar* (Cash keeper).

- **Sadr-us Sudur** The Sadr-us Sudur was the head of the religious department. His chief duty was to protect the laws of the shariat. He was also connected with the distribution of charities – both cash (*Wazifa*) and land grants (*Suyurghal, in'am, madad-i ma'ash*).
- **Qazi-ul-Quzzat** He was the head of the judiciary and was known as *Qazi-ul-Quzzat*. His principal duty was to administer the shariat law both in civil and criminal cases. In the capacity of the chief *qazi*, he looked into the appointment of the *qazis* in the *suba*, *sarkar*, *pargana* and town levels. There was a separate *qazi* for army also.

Provincial Administration

Mughal rulers also paid great attention to the organisation of the provincial governments. The Mughal Empire divided into **15 subas**. These were -Bengal, Bihar, Allahabad, Awadh, Agra, Delhi, Lahore, Multan, Kabul, Ajmer, Malwa, Gujarat, Ahmednagar, Khandesh and Berar.

- **Subedar** (Provincial Governor) The governor of a *suba* (Subedar) was directly appointed by the Emperor. Usually the tenure of a subedar was around three years. He looked after the welfare of the people and the army. He was responsible for the general law and order problem in the suba. He was supposed to take up welfare activities like construction of *sarais*, gardens, wells, water reservoirs, etc.
- **Diwan** He was the head of the revenue department in the suba. The provincial diwan was appointed by the Emperor. He supervised the revenue collection in the suba and maintained accounts of all expenditure incurred in the suba. A *Roznamcha* (Daily register) was maintained by the diwan which carried entries of amount that was deposited in the royal treasury.
- **Bakhshi** The *Bakhshi* was appointed by the imperial court at the recommendation of the *Mir Bakhshi*. He was responsible for checking and inspecting the horses and soldiers maintained by the *mansabdars* in the suba. He issued the paybills of both the *mansabdars* and the soldiers. It was his duty to prepare a list of deceased mansabdars. To facilitate his work, he posted his agents in the parganas and various important offices.
- **Darogha-i-Dak** At every *suba* headquarters, *Darogha-i-Dak* was appointed for communication network purpose. A number of dak chowkis were also maintained throughout the Empire where postal runners (*Mewras*) were stationed who carried the post to the next *chowki*. His duty was to pass on letters through the postal runners to the court. Horses and boats were also used to help in speedy delivery.

Local Administration

At the local level in the Mughal Empire, it was known as the *Sarkar*, *Pargana* and *Mauza* (village) levels.

Sarkars (Districts)

- In Mughal administration, provinces were further divided into *Sarkars* (Districts).
- Important officials of *Sarkars* were :
  - **Faujdar** He was the executive head of the Sarkar. His duty was mainly to take care of rebellions, and law and order problems. His jurisdiction was decided according to the needs of the region. In special circumstances, he was to help the Amalguzar in matters of revenue collection.
  - **Amalguzar** The most important revenue collector was the Amil or Amalguzar. His primary duty was to assess and supervise the revenue collection through other subordinate officials. Daily receipts and expenditure reports were sent by him to the provincial diwan.
  - **Qazi** The office of Qazi was responsible for judicial administration in Sarkars (Districts). He provides justice in both civil and criminal matter where one or both parties were Muslim.

Pargana

- Parganas were the administrative units below Sarkar. The *Shiqdar* was the executive officer of the Parganas.
- Important officials of Pargana were :
  - **Shiqdar** He was the executive officer of the Pargana and assisted the Amils in revenue collection.
  - **Amil** He looked after the revenue collection at the Pargana level also. His duties were similar to those of the Amalguzar at the sarkar level.
  - **Qanungos** He kept all the records pertaining to the land in his area. He was to take note of different crops in the Pargana.
  - **Faujdar** He used to be the treasure of Pargana. It was his responsibility to protect treasury of Parganas.
  - **Karkun** He used to be the clerk of Pargana, his responsibility is to keep the records of revenue and expenditures.

Mauza

- During the Mughal period, villages were known as Mauza.
- Important officials of villages were :

- **Patwari** He keeps all the records of land in a village and get the commission of 1 cp in every land sale or purchase. He is the lowest rank of treasury department.
- **Muqaddam** He was the village headman and he was responsible for the welfare of village.

Other Important Departments of Local Administration

Post	Details
Kotwal	His primary duty was to safeguard the life and property of townsmen.
Qiladar	In-charge of the fort
Mutasaddi	Governor of the port

Judicial System

- Mughal justice system was Islamic justice system, the basis of which is *Quaran*, *Hadith* and *Shariya*.
- According to **Abul-Fazal**, the emperor use to protect four rights of his citizens and they were-life, property, honour and religious faith.
- Mughal emperor use to be the supreme judge of all matters in justice system.
- Civil matters of Hindus were dealt according to Hindu Personal laws and matter of Muslims by Muslim Personal laws. But, if one party is Muslim and another is Hindu in the matter then Islamic laws is used for judicial process. In the criminal matters only Islamic laws are used.
- Matters other than religious are heard by *Mir-e-adal.*

Monetary System

- **Babur** in Kabul started silver **Shahrukhi** and **Baburi** named coins in Kandhar.
- **Akbar** started various gold, silver and copper coins of different weights and values. Akbar also introduced a gold coin named Asharafi.

Akbar coin

- Akbar introduced practice of inscribing Persian poetry praising the ruler on coins.
- Akbar began dating his coins as per new '*Illahi era*'.
- **Nisar** named silver coin stated by **Jahangir**.
- **Aurangzeb** started inscribing *Kalma* (prayer) on coins.

Revenue Administration

- During Mughal period, land revenue and other taxes were major source of income. *Zakat* tax to be collected from Muslim (2.5% of property) and *Jaziya* tax on Hindu's are also included in revenue.
- Apart from this, *Khums* (booty of war) was also a part of revenue.

Land Revenue Administration

In Mughal period particularly Akbar, paid personal attention to the land revenue system. He adopted **Sher Shah's** system, by which the cultivated area was measured and a crop rate (*ray*) was drawn up.

- **Zabti system** of measuring land was used during Mughal period. According to size of land, its total land revenue is estimated.
- The office of diwan was responsible for supervising the fiscal system of the empire-Amil-Gozar were the revenue collector.
- Akbar implemented land measurement system in every part of his kingdom.
- During the reign of Akbar, there were two other land revenue systems that is *'Galla-Bakshi'* and *'Batai'*. These systems fixed the division of crop between the farmers and empire.
- Another important procedure of deciding land revenue was called as *Kankut*. Under this system, prediction of revenue was made on the basis of crop.

The Dahsala System

- Akbar instituted **Dahsala** system in 1580 AD with the help of **Todar Mal**. Under this system, the average produce of different crops as well as the average prices prevailing over the last ten (*Dah*) years was calculated. One-third of the average produce was the state share and stated in cash.
- *Dahsala* calculation was done on the basis of a schedule of average prices over the past ten years. The state always used to modify it time to time.
- The *Dahsala* system was a further development of the *Zabti* system. In fact it was the system of measurement and the assessment. It is sometimes called Todar Mal's Bandobast.

Batai/Ghalla-Bakhshi

- Indo-persian sources of Mughal period used the term Raiyat (Plural, Riaya) or Muzarian to denote a peasants.
- Another system of assessment under Akbar was called *batai* or *ghallabakhshi*. In this system, the produce was divided between the peasants and the state in fixed proportion.
- Under *batai*, the peasants were given the choice of paying in cash or kind.

Nasaq

- A third system which was widely used in Akbar's time was *Nasaq*. It was a rough calculation on the basis of what peasant had been paying in the past. It is also called *Kankut* or estimation.

Classification of Land

Land was classified into following four types :

- **Polai** Continuously cultivated and very fertile.
- **Parauti** Left fallow for a year or two to recover its productivity.
- **Chachhar** Left fallow for 3-4 years.
- **Banjar** Uncultivable land.

The Army

- Cavalry and elephantry were the main basis of the Mughal army including artillery.
- The contingents were mixed group of Mughal, Pathan, Hindustani and Rajput. Akbar also kept an efficient collection of war boats.
- There is a new Methodology adopted in the Mughal army by Akbar that was *Dagh* and *Chehra*. For this purpose, the soldier's horse was branded with the imperial marks, called the **dagh system.** With the requirement of best and competitive soldiers, a **descriptive roll** (*Chehra*) of the soldier was included.

The Ahadis : Most Trusted Troops

- Mughal emperors used to carry the individual troopers, called *ahadis*. They received much higher salaries and highly trusted corps, being recruited directly by the emperors.
- The Mughal Emperors also maintained a corps of royal bodyguards (*Walashahis*). The footmen (*Piyadgan*) formed a miscellaneous body of troops.

Mansabdari System

- Mughal Emperor **Akbar** introduced Mansabdari system in Mughal Empire. The word '*Mansab*' is of Arabic origin meaning rank or position. The origins of the Mansabdari system related with **Genghis Khan.**
- Under the Mansabdari system, every officer was assigned a rank (*Mansab*). The lowest rank was 10 and the highest upto 7000 for the nobles. Princes with blood relations always received higher *Mansabs*.
- The **Mansab System** developed gradually under Akbar. At first there was only one rank (*Mansab*) but from 1594-95 AD, the ranks were divided into two—*zat* and *sawar*.
- The word *zat* means personal. It fixed the personal status of a person, and also the salary due to him.
- The *sawar* rank indicated the number of cavalrymen (*sawars*) a person was required to maintain.
- The salary of the Mansabdars generally not paid in cash, but by assigning them a *jagir*. The Manasabdari system was further moved forward by **Jahangir** and **Shah Jahan** with minor modifications.

Du-Aspah and Sih-Aspah

- Jahangir introduced a system whereby selected nobles could be allowed to maintain a large quota of troopers, without raising their **zat rank.**
- This was the *du-aspah* (a trooper with two horses) or *sih-aspah* (a trooper with three horses) system.

Jagirdari System

- The Jagirdari system can be defined as system of land ownership. Mansabdars who were paid through land (*Jagirs*) were called *Jagirdars*.
- The Jagir assignment to *Mansabdars*, initiated by Akbar, was only meant to give rights to collect revenue. Later Rajput Mansabdars were given more extensive rights of residence within their own homeland.

Types of Jagir

Types	Nature	Meaning
Tankha Jagirs	Transferable	It is given in lieu of salaries.
Mashrut Jagirs	Transferable	It is given on certain conditions.
Watan Jagirs	Hereditary and Non-Transferable	It is assigned to Zamindar or Rajas in their local dominions.
Al-Tamgha Jagirs	Hereditary and Transferable	It is given to Muslim nobles in their place of birth.

Note *In Mughal period, only Autonomous Rajas were allowed to continue with their traditional land revenue system in their territories.*

Society During Mughal Period

- Society during Mughal phase was feudal and majority of its population is dependent on agriculture.
- There were high influential elites in provinces and center, who were wealthy.
- Farmers, workers, servants, slaves, beggars etc came under lower middle class and middle class.
- In North India, people use wheat, dal and vegetables and in Southern and East India rice and fish was consumed more.
- Banjaras were important trader class of medieval era.
- Artisans and merchant belong to both higher class and middle class.

Economy During Mughal Period

- India had a large class of rich traders and merchants, some of them being amongst the richest merchants of the world in the medieval times.
- The Indian trading classes were large in numbers, spread out all over the country, well organised and highly professional.
- Some traders specialised in long distance, inter-regional trade and were called *Seth, Bohra, Modi,* and *Beoparis* or *Banik*. There was a special class of traders, the Banjaras, who specialised in carrying bulk goods, such as textiles, silks, etc.
- Boat traffic on waterways, and coastal trade along the seashore was highly developed during this period.
- The movement of trade across the region was made possible through agents (*Gumashtas*) and commission agents (*Dalals*).

Major Centres of Trade

- **Bengal** Sugar and rice as well muslin and silk.
- **Coast of Coromandel** Textile production.
- **Gujarat** Fine textiles and silks (Patola), Entry point of foreign goods.
- **Burhanpur and Agra** Nodal points of trade in North India.
- **Malabar** Pepper and spices.

Hundi System

- The Hundi was a letter of credit payable after a period of time at a discount. Movement of goods was facilitated and done through the use of *Hundis*.
- The *Hundis* often included insurance which was charged at different rates on the basis of value of the goods, destination, etc.
- The *sarrafs* (*Shrofs*) who specialised in changing money also specialised in dealing with Hundis. They also acted as private banks.
- The *sarrafs* helped in supplementing the money in circulation during this period.

The Spread of Tobacco

- The Tobacco first arrived in the Deccan, spread to Northern India by the Portuguese.
- Akbar and his nobles came across tobacco for the first time in 1604. However it became a major article of consumption, cultivation and trade all over India.

Famous Merchants in Medieval Period

- **Virji Vohra** He set up agency houses across the Asia and reputed to be amongst the wealthiest men of his time.
- **Abdul Ghafur Bohra** He left 55 lakh rupees in cash and goods and a fleet of 17 sea-going ships at the time of his death in 1718 AD.
- **Malay Chetti, Kashi Viranna and Sunca Rama Chetti** They were extremely wealthy of Coromandel region with extensive network in India and abroad.

Major Towns through the Eyes of Travellers

- **According to Ralph Fitch**, an English Merchant and traveller, Agra and Fatehpur Sikri were larger than London, then one of the biggest town in Europe.
- **Anthony de Montserrat**, the Jesuit priest of Portugal who came to Akbar's court, stated that Lahore was second to none of the cities in Europe or Asia.
- **Francois Bernier**, a French Physician, who wrote in the middle of the 17th century, says that Delhi was not less than Paris and that Agra was bigger than Delhi.

Mughal Paintings

- The Mughals made distinctive contribution in the field of painting.
- They introduced new themes depicting the court, battle scenes and the chase, and added new colours and new forms.
- Under Akbar, European painting was introduced at the Mughal court by the Portuguese priests. Under their influence, many new features were adopted. **Daswant** and **Basawan** were two of the famous painters of Akbar's court.
- Under the rule of Jahangir, special progress was made in portrait painting and paintings of animals. **Mansur** was the great name in this field.

Mughal Paintings

Literature During Mughal Period

Mughal Rulers were great patrons of literature and laureates. During this period, many significant biographies, memoirs and history texts were written. Some of the important literary works were as follows :

- **Baburnama** It is an autobiography Babur written in Chagtai Turkish language. Babur has given detailed information about political, natural, economic and environmental condition of India. He also mentioned about the types of farming and crops cultivated in India.
- **Humayunama** It was written by Gulbadan Begum in 1523 AD. The book is divided into two parts the first part consists of the life history of Babur and the second part consists of information about Humayun's rule.
- **Akbarnama** It was written by Abul Fazl. Divided in three volumes, the book is the official chronicle of the reign of Akbar. Ain-i-Akbari was the last volume of this book.
- The Ain is made up of five books (daftars), of which the first three books describe the administration. The first book called Mazil-abadi, concerns the imperial household and its maintenance. The second book, Sipah-abadi, covers the military and civil administration. The third book, mulk-abadi, is the one which deals with the fiscal side of the empire. The fourth and fifth book (daftars) deal with the religious.
- **Tuzuk-i-Jahangiri** It is an autobiography of Jahangir and the primary source of his era.
- **Padshahnama** It is the first official document of Jahangir and gives detailed information about his rule.
- **Tarikh-i-Shahjahani** It was written by Sadik Khan and gives detailed information about the rule of Shah Jahan.
- **Futuhat-i-Alamgiri** The book was written by Isardas Nagar. It tells about the relation of Aurangzeb with the Rajputs.

Music in Mughal Period

- In *Ain-i-Akbari*, **Abul Fazal** suggests that there were 36 musicians of high grade in the Mughal court of Akbar.
- Tansen was also one among the **eight Maharatnas** of Akbar court, who is considered as greatest musician of Indian history.
- **Tansen** said to have invented many *rages*.
- Mughal emperors patronised music and music grown during their period.
- At the court of Akbar, Hind and Islamic music mingled and became one. Music was also a part of culture in society during Mughal period.

Mughal Art and Architecture

The establishment of Mughal Empire in India revolutionalised Indo-Islamic form of architecture and techniques that they brought from Central Asia and Persia. Babur, Humayun, Akbar, Jahangir, and especially Shah Jahan were personally interested in literature, art and architecture.

Main characteristics of Mughal Architecture were bulbous domes, slender minarets, large halls, massive vaulted gateways, delicate ornamentation, etc.

Bagh-e Babur (Kabul)

- Babur was very fond of gardens and Bagh-e Babur was one of the earliest surviving Mughal gardens built by him.
- After his death, Babur was buried in this garden in 1544 AD.

Mughal Architecture

Reign	Monuments	Description
Akbar The common use of sandstone arches (mainly in a decorative form) and the decoration by brightly coloured patterns on the interiors increased during Akbar's reign.	Humayun's Tomb	• It was commissioned by Humayun's wife Bega Begum and completed by Akbar in 1558 AD. • It was the first garden-tomb on the Indian subcontinent.
	Agra Fort	• Built in 1565-73 AD in red sandstone by Akbar, this massive fort is first building to have many magnificent gates.
	Fatehpur Sikri	• A palace-cum-fort complex, Fatehpur Sikri built in 1572 AD by Akbar. • It is based in Gujarat style of Architecture.
	Buland Darwaza	• It is located inside the complex of Fatehpur Sikri. • It is completed in 1575 AD to commemorate Akbar's victory over Gujarat.
	Panch Mahal	• The Panch Mahal 'Five-level Palace' located inside the Fatehpur Sikri. • It was used for entertainment and relaxation purposes by royal woman.

Reign	Monuments	Description
Jahangir During his reign Red sandstone was replaced by Marble and beginning of Pietra dura style of work in monuments.	Tomb of Itmad-ud-Daulah	• This is the tomb of Mirza Ghiyas, father of Nur Jahan. • Important aspect of this tomb is its ornamentation in geometrical designs and mosaic techniques of Pietra-Dura. It is often regarded as a draft of the Taj Mahal.
	Begum Shahi Mosque	• The Begum Shahi Mosque is an early 17th century mosque situated in Lahore, Pakistan. The mosque is in the style of the Persian Char Taq (four arches).
Shah Jahan Mughal architecture reached its zenith during his reign and is best remembered as the golden age of Mughal period.	Red Fort	• Its massive, 2.5-km-long enclosing walls are made of red sandstone. The fort was completed in 1643 AD. It was originally named Qila-i-Mubarak.
	Jama Masjid	• Jama Masjid of Delhi is the largest mosques in India. It was built by between 1650 and 1656.
	Taj Mahal	• This magnificent piece of art built by Shah Jahan in memory of his wife Mumtaz Mahal in 1649 AD. It consists of a symmetrical building with an iwan (an arch-shaped doorway) topped by a large dome and finial. Pietra Dura and Jali work.
Aurangzeb In this period, squared stone and marble were replaced by brick and rubble with stucco ornamentation.	Bibi ka Maqbara	• It was built by Aurangzeb in 1660 AD in memory of his wife, Dilras Bano Begum in Aurangabad (Maharashtra).
	Moti Masjid	• The mosque was built by Aurangzeb at the Red Fort for his second wife Nawab Bai in the year 1659-1660 AD. • The mosque was originally covered in gilded copper.

Extra Facts From Tamil Nadu Board and NIOS

- In Mughal administration, the chief Diwan was called '*Diwan-i-Kul*', which was called as **Diwan-e-Aala** during the reign of Akbar.
- **Daroga-e-Dak-Chouki** appointed at the provincial level.
- The Elite class who provided their services to the government were entrusted with the responsibility of collecting revenue of a particular area. This system was called **Jagirdari System**. It was not a hereditary system.
- During the reign of Akbar, the entire revenue land was divided into two parts-**Khalisa land** (revenue received in royal treasury) and Jagir land for Jagirdars.
- Revenue distribution of crops was done in three ways-**Galla** or **Fasal Batai** (after receiving the grains), **Khet Batai** (sharing of standing crops) **Lang Batai** (after harvesting the crops without separating the grains).
- Another method of revenue crop distribution was called Kankun, in which measurement of land was important. After measurement of land, revenue was determined by assessing crop production.
- Agriculture expanded during the Mughal period. The reason tax expansion of agriculture during this period was deforestation, while large network of rivers contributed to expansion of Agriculture in Punjab.
- During the Mughal period, apart from the local market, trade was also done through periodic markets, which were called 'Haat' or 'paith'.
- 'Hundi' or 'bill of exchange' was a Medieval trading activity.
- Akbar appointed Humayun's painter **Mir Sayyid Ali** and **Abdus Samad** for the interpretation of **'Hamjannama'** manuscript.
- Jahangir art style is an example of **Rupvadi style**.
- Akbar's architecture includes Jama Masjid, Akbar's tomb, Itmad-ul-Daula's tomb was commissioned during the reign of Jahangir.
- The architecture of Shahjahan period includes Red Fort of Delhi, Moti Masjid of Agra, Jama Masjid of Delhi, Red Fort of Agra.
- In the medieval period, the use of ornamental style in palaces, tomb etc was a new experiment in architecture, which included calligraphy, depiction of leaves, drawing etc.
- Fathullah Shirazi was a skilled engineer of Akbar's era. The art of binding papers developed during this period.
- One approach to trade convenience was the **Dadni system** in which the trader purchased goods from the artisans.
- It provided raw and necessary infrastructure for that production, due to which small artisans were saved from financial burden.
- The trading communities of the Mughal period were Khatri (Punjab), Komati (Golkanda), Chaiti (South India), Kaling (Coromandel to Orissa) Bohra etc.
- Ali Kul Salem and Abu Talib Kalim were the main poets of Shahjahan's time. Abu Talib Kalim composed **Badshahnama**.

Emergence of Maratha Empire

(SOURCES)

Class-VII Old NCERT Chap 1 (Climax and Disintegration of the Mughal Empire-II), Class-VII New NCERT Chap 8 (Eighteenth-Century Political Formation), Tamil Nadu Board (Class XI), NIOS

Rise of Marathas

- The rise of the Marathas in the 17th century AD is a significant and far-reaching event in the history of Medieval India.
- This rise of Maratha power is primarily due to **Shivaji** who shaped the Marathas into a superb guerilla fighting force. The Marathas fought for the defence of their religion and territory against Mughal rulers.
- The emergence of Maratha power can be asserted as a 'Hindu' reaction against the communal policies of Mughal Emperor **Aurangzeb**.

Causes for the Rise of Marathas

- **Geographical Location** The geographical location of the Marathwada (modern Maharashtra) region was one important factor, which gave rise to Maratha power.

  The region was encircled through Sahayadri, Satpura and Vindhya mountain range. So, many chieftains of this region developed a sense of autonomy.
- **Role of Bhakti Movement** The spread of the Bhakti Movement in Western India inculcated the spirit of oneness among the Marathas.

  Many saints such as Jnaneshvar, Namdev, Tukaram, and Samarth Ramdas played a significant role in providing the Marathas a cultural identity as well.
- **Internal Conflicts** There was struggle for control over land among regional landlords such as deshmukhs, mirasis and the uparis (outsiders). There was mal-administration everywhere. The common people were tired of this oppression.
- **Misrule of Deccan Sultans** The major factor that helped to the rise of Marathas was the misrule of Deccan Sultans.

  A large portion of Marathwada was under the rule of the Nizam Shahis of Ahmednagar and the Adil Shahis of Bijapur.

  They constantly fought each other and due to which common people suffered a lot.
- **Shivaji's Charismatic Personality** Shivaji's own personality played a great part in the rise of the Maratha power.

  He united different Maratha Chiefs and filled them with the feelings of self-respect and faith. He was not only the maker of the Maratha nation, but also a brilliant leader of medieval India.

Maratha Rulers

Shahji Bhonsle, Shivaji, Shambhaji, Rajaram I and Shahu were important maratha rulers.

Shahji Bhonsle

- Shahji Bhonsle was the father of Shivaji Maharaj. He acquired practical experience of war and tactics under his father **Maloji** and **Malik Ambar** of Ahmednagar.
- Shahji also joined the Mughals during the reign of **Shah Jahan** but later rebelled.
- Shahji acted as the kingmaker in Ahmednagar and settled number of Maharashtrian Brahmins and Marathas in his Poona *jagir*. He acquired great fame and was renowned as a capable administrator.

Shivaji : The Great Maratha

- Shivaji born at **Shivneri** on 19th Feb, 1630 was the youngest son of **Shahji** and **Jija Bai**.

(**Note** : *As Per NCERT Shivaji's tenure was 1627-1680)*

- After Shahji's death, Shivaji was raised under the guardianship of **Dadaji Konddev** and **Guru Samarth Ramdas** was his spiritual guru.
- At the age of 18, Shivaji attacked a number of hill forts of Poona, Rajgarh, Kondana and Torna.
- After **Dadaji Konddev's** death in 1647 AD, Shivaji became the sole in-charge of his Poona jagir as Shahji's successor.
- Shivaji wanted to occupy all the possessions of Shahji, as a matter of legitimate right.

Military Expeditions of Shivaji

- Shivaji showed his military tactics for the first time in 1645 AD as a teenager. He successfully got control of the Torna fort which was under Bijapur.

Battles fought by Shivaji

Battle	Date	Detail
Battle of Pratapgarh	10th November, 1659 AD	• Between the forces of Shivaji and the Adilshahi general Afzal Khan. The Marathas defeated the Adilshahi forces despite being outnumbered.
Battle of Pavan Khind	13th July, 1660 AD	• Shivaji, managed to escape from the battlefield. It resulted in losing the Panhala fort of Maratha to Adilshahi rulers.
Battle of Umberkhind	2nd February, 1661 AD	• Between Shivaji and Uzbek General Kartalab Khan of Mughals. Shivaji was well-prepared and defeated the Mughal forces.
Battle of Purandar	2nd June, 1665 AD	• It was fought between the Mughal Empire under Jai Singh and Shivaji. Mughal army killed Maratha General Murarbaji, Shivaji surrendered and treaty of Purandar was signed.
Battle of Sinhagad	4th February, 1670 AD	• It was fought to occupy Sinhagad fort, between Tanaji Malusare of Maratha and Udaybhan Rathore of Mughal army. • Maratha forces occupied the Sinhagad fort but with the loss of Tanaji. Shivaji renamed the fort as 'Sinhagad' (Earlier 'Kondhana fort').
Battle of Sangamner	1679 AD	• The war the last battle in which the Maratha King Shivaji fought against Mughal Empire. The Mughals attacked Shivaji with a large force and defeated. However Shivaji escaped to Raigad.

Relations with Aurangzeb

- The relation between the Mughals and Marathas were always been competitive in the Deccan region.
- Mughal Emperor Aurangzeb launched a full-fledged campaign against the Marathas under the leadership of **Shaista Khan**, who occupied Poona in 1660 AD. However, in return, Shivaji made a night strike and killed all sons of Shaista Khan and forced him to escape.
- After the failure of Shaista Khan, Aurangzeb deputed **Raja Jai Singh** of Amber to deal with Shivaji. Jai Singh decided to strike at the heart of Shivaji's territories 'Fort Purandar'. After long period, Shivaji opened negotiations and treaty of Purandar was signed.

Shivaji's Visit to Agra

- **Jai Singh** persuaded Shivaji to visit Mughal emperor at Agra, which proved a disaster.
- Shivaji felt insulted when he was put in the category of mansabdars of 5000—a rank which had been granted earlier to his minor son.
- Shivaji walked off angrily and refused imperial service. He was later detained in the **Agra fort**, from where he escaped on 1666 AD.
- Shivaji's Agra visit proved to be the turning point in Mughal relations with the Marathas.

Coronation and Grand Title

- Shivaji was crowned as the King of Marathas on 6th June, 1674, at **Raigad Fort** and founded the Maratha Empire. He also assumed titles of *Chhatrapati, Shakakarta, Kshatriya Kulavantas* and *Haindava Dharmodhhaarak*.

- The Maratha Kingdom founded by Shivaji grew larger over time and became the dominant Indian power in the early 18th century.

Major Forts of Shivaji

Forts	Location
Sinhagad Fort	Pune (Earlier known Kondhana)
Raigad Fort	Mahad (Raigad District) (Coronation of Shivaji)
Shivneri Fort	Pune (Birthplace of Shivaji)
Vijaydurg Fort	Devgad (Sindhudurg District)
Sindhudurg Fort	Malvan (Sindhudurg District) (Most Strongest Fort)
Rajgad Fort	Pune
Pratapgad Fort	Satara
Lohagad Fort	Pune

Administrative Structure

The Maratha administration was essentially derived from the Deccani Sultanate structure of rule and Mughal institutions.

Central Administration

- The nature of Maratha polity was essentially a centralised and autocratic monarchy one but with the elements of benevolence. The king was at the head of the affairs its chief objective was the happiness and prosperity of his subjects (*Raja Kalsya Karnaam*).

Ashta-Pradhana System

To assist the king, there was a council of state ministers known as Ashta-Pradhana, which was devised by Shivaji. These offices were neither hereditary nor permanent. These were :

- **Peshwa** (Prime Minister) Head of both Civil and Military Affairs.
- **Mazumdar** (Auditor) He looked into the income and expenditure of the state.
- **Waqia-Navis** In charge of King's Private Affairs.
- **Dabir** (Sumant) Foreign Secretary
- **Shurunavis** (Superintendent) He used to take care of all the official correspondences.
- **Panditrao** Ecclesiastical (Priestly) Head
- **Sar-i-Naubat** (Senapati) Commander in Chief
- **Nyayadhish** Chief Justice

- Next to *Ashtapradhan* was **Chitnis** (secretary), who dealt with all diplomatic correspondences and wrote all royal letters. The letters of commanders of forts was responded by the **Fadnis**.
- On the other hand, the **Potnis** looked after the income and expenditure of the royal treasury, while the **Potdar** was an assessment officer.

Provincial Administration

- The Maratha Empire was divided into *Mauzas, Tarfs* and *Prants*. Among these, *Mauza* was the lowest unit.
- The provinces were known as Prants under the rule of *Subedar, Karkun* (Mukhya Deshadhikari).
- Under Shivaji, none of the officers was permanent and hereditary. All officers were liable to frequent transfers. But under the Peshwas, many offices became permanent.

Other Important Posts Under Maratha Rule

- **Deshmukh** Village Headman
- **Jamadar** Treasurer
- **Mamlatdar** Subedar of bigger provinces
- **Kamavisdar** Subedar of small provinces
- **Sarsubedar** Supervisor of the work of Subedars

Military Administration

- Military organisation of Shivaji was largely based on Fort system. During his life, Shivaji constructed around 250 forts and not a single officer was entrusted sole charge of a fort. Instead every fort there was a **Havaldar, Sabnis** and **Sarnobat**.
- The *Havaldar* was the in-charge of the keys of the fort. The Sabnis controlled the muster-roll and dealt with all government correspondences of the fort. The Sarnobat was the in-charge of the garrison.
- Besides, there was *Karkhanis* who used to take care of grain stores and other material requirements. There was good system of checks and balances was applied by Shivaji to keep them under control.
- Shivaji's cavalry consisted of *Bargirs* and the *Siledars*. The bargir troopers were supplied horses and arms by the state while the siledars had to bring their horses and arms.
- Shivaji maintained light cavalry and light infantry trained in guerilla and hilly warfare. The *Mevalis* and the *Hetkaris* were his most excellent troopers.
- Later, under the **Peshwas**, the **Pindharis** who were robbers and plunderers were also allowed to accompany the Maratha army.
- The groups of highly mobile, peasant pastoralists (Kunbis) provided the backbone to the Maratha Army.

Maratha Navy

- Shivaji also built a strong navy. His fleet was equipped with **Ghurabs** (gunboats) and **Gallivats** (row boats with 2 masts).
- Shivaji used his naval power to check both Siddis and European trade powers.
- **Robert Orme**, an English Historian mentions that Maratha Navy was led by Admiral Dariya Sarang and Mai Naik Bhandari.

Revenue Administration

- Shivaji introduced **Ryotwari system**, replacing Jagirdari system in Maratha kingdom. He changed the position of hereditary revenue officials. Shivaji also strictly supervised the *Mirasdars* who had hereditary rights in land.
- The revenue system was patterned on the **Kathi system** of **Malik Amber** in which every piece of land was measured by Kathi or stick.
- Other sources of income were **Chauth** and **Sardeshmukhi**. Chauth amounted to 1/4 of the standard which was paid to Marathas as a safeguard in Non-Maratha territories. Sardeshmukhi was an additional levy of 10% demanded from areas outside of the Maratha kingdom.

Judiciary

- The King was the supreme and last authority in the judicial matters in Maratha empire. Next to the king were the *Nyayadhish* and the *Pandit Rao*, appointed by him and accountable to him.
- Along with the king and his *Nyayadhish*, the *Huzur Hazir Majlis* or *Dharmasabha* (Central Judicial Assembly) played an important part in the administration of justice.
- The village official was *Patel* who had administrative revenue and judicial responsibilities.
- He was the main link between the village folk and the Maratha's bureaucracy. The post of **Patel** was hereditary in nature.

Successors of Shivaji

- **Shambhaji** After the death of Shivaji, his son from first wife, Sambhaji became the king of Marathas in 1681 AD. He continued the attacks on Mughal territories. Mughal emperor Aurangzeb with all his capacity waged war against Marathas. Sambhaji was captured and executed in 1689 AD. His infant son Sahuji imprisoned.
- **Rajaram I** He was the second son of Shivaji and half-brother of Sambhaji. His reign (1689-1700 AD) marked with a constant struggle against the Mughals. After Rajaram's death in 1700 AD, his widow, Tarabai proclaimed her son, Shivaji II as the Chhatrapati and ruled as his regent.
- **Shahu** He was the son of Sambhaji and as a child, was taken prisoner along with his mother in 1689 by Mughals. In 1707 AD, Mughal Emperor Bahadur Shah I released Shahu. Thereafter, with his aunt Tarabai, Shahu fought a brief war and gained the Maratha throne in 1708 AD.

Rise of the Peshwas

After Shivaji's death, effective power in the Maratha state was wielded by a family of Chitpavan Brahmanas who served Shivaji's successors as Peshwa : Poona became the capital of the Maratha kingdom.

During the reign of Shahu, Balaji Vishwanath became a prominent Peshwa.

Over the next fifty years, the Peshwas expanded Maratha power in all directions of the Indian sub-continent. Important Peshwas were :

Balaji Vishwanath (1713-1720 AD)

- Better known as **Peshwa Balaji Vishwanath** was the first of a series of hereditary Peshwa gained effective control of the Maratha Empire.
- Balaji Vishwanath assisted a young Maratha Emperor Shahu to consolidate his grip on Maratha kingdom. He was called **the Second Founder of the Maratha State.**

Baji Rao I (1720-1740 AD)

- He was a General of the Maratha Empire before serving as the Peshwa. **Baji Rao I** is credited with expanding the Maratha Empire in India.
- In his 20 years reign, **Baji Rao I** never lost a single battle. In 1713 AD, Nizam ul Mulk of Hyderabad was defeated by Baji Rao I in **Battle of Palkhed**. The Nizam accepted the Maratha suzerainty.

Balaji Baji Rao (1740-1761 AD)

- Also known as **Nana Saheb**, he was appointed as Peshwa in 1740 AD. Balaji Baji Rao was not a great military leader as like his father.
- During his tenure, the Maratha king was reduced to a mere figurehead.

Madhav Rao I (1761-1772 AD)

- After the death of Balaji Bajirao, his son Madhav Rao succeeded him as Peshwa. Madhav Rao defeated **Hyder Ali** of Mysore.
- He established the Maratha supremacy of the Marathas in the North India again. After his death, Peshwa power decreased in rapid pace.

Anglo-Maratha Wars

- **First Anglo-Maratha War** (1775-82 AD) Favouring the cause of Raghunath Rao (Raghoba) for Peshwaship, English (Hasting) came in conflict with the Marathas. On being defeated, the British had to sign the Convention of Wadgaon (1779 AD), later signed the Treaty of Salbai (1782 AD).
- **Second Anglo-Maratha War** (1803-06 AD) It was the conflict between British East India company and the Maratha empire in India. The Maratha Peshwa signed the Subsidiary Alliance Treaty of Bassein (1802).
- **Third Anglo-Maratha War** (1817-18 AD) Lord Hasting was determined to proclaim British Paramountacy in India. He moved against Pindaris. It was the final and decisive conflict between the British East India Company and the Maratha empire in India.

Narayan Rao (1772-73 AD)

- Narayan Rao was the fifth Peshwa of the Maratha empire from November, 1772 till his death by murder in August, 1773.

Sawai Madhav Rao (1774-95 AD)

- He is also known as Sawai Madhav Rao or **Madhav Rao II Narayan**. He was the posthumous son of Narayan Rao Peshwa. Madhav Rao's death was a suicide.

Peshwa Baji Rao II (1796-1818 AD)

- After the death of Madhav Narayan Rao (1795 AD), the son of Raghunath Rao, Baji Rao II became the Peshwa.
- He was an incompetent ruler. He signed the **Treaty of Bassin** with British in December 1802, in which British agreed to reinstate Baji Rao II as Peshwa. The treaty was done in return of stationing of a permanent resident of British at Poona and 6000 British troops will be stationed in Maratha territory. **Hoolkars** and **Sindhi** as resisted this treaty, which resulted in **Second Anglo-Maratha war** (1803-1805).
- The British defeated the Marathas, due to internal intrusion in Marathas and they were forced to surrender much of their territories to British.
- During the 1817-1818 AD, **Third Anglo-Maratha war** took place, which ended in defeat of Marathas and Baji Rao II was forced to sign an agreement renouncing claims on Gaekwar's revenues and ceding large swarth territory to the British.

Third Battle of Panipat

- The effective image of the Marathas was dented through the defeat in Third Battle of Panipat in **1761 AD** by Ahmed Shah Abdali.
- Thereafter, the Maratha started transforming into a confederacy.

Maratha Confederacy

The major four Maratha states or confederacy that emerged and became powerful were as follows :

- **Bhonsle of Nagpur** It was the first independent state that emerged in Maratha confederacy. Raghuji Bhonsle (1727–55 AD) was the founder, who expanded Maratha kingdom into Bengal and Bihar.
- **The Gaikwads of Baroda** The state became a leading power in Maratha confederacy. The founder of the dynasty was Damaji I who had risen to power by 1740 and made a leading power in Maratha confederacy. Sayajirao Gaekwad III is remembered for reforming much of his state during his rule.
- **Holkars of Indore** On 29th July ,1732, Peshwa Bajirao I granted Holkar State to Malhar Rao Holkar, the founder ruler of Holkar dynasty. The greatest ruler Ahilyabai Holkar (1767–1795 AD) of this dynasty was a great pioneer and builder of Hindu temples.
- **Scindia of Gwalior** Peshwa Bajirao I made Ranoji Shinde as a Sardar in the Gwalior region. He was instrumental in re-establishing the Maratha supremacy and prestige in North India after the Maratha defeat at Panipat.

Decline of Maratha Empire

Several factors have been assigned for the defeat of the Marathas against the English.

Some of them were as follows :

- **Internal Weakness** The empire of the Marathas was not a central empire under one chief. The nominal unity of the Marathas remained only up to the period of the rule of Peshwa Madhav Rao I. After him, the Peshwa could not control his subordinate chiefs, who pursued against each other's interest.
- **Lack of Political Foresight** The Marathas lacked political wisdom and farsightedness. When they had become the strongest power in India, they simply desired to control the Mughal emperor. They therefore, failed to achieve political unity of India.
- **Corrupt Jagirdari System** During the later Maratha period, Maratha chiefs distributed jagirs to their officers for facilitating collection of Chauth and Sardeshmukhi which led to the growth of corrupt

jagirdari system. This system weakened Maratha chiefs in all respects.

- **Military Weakness** The primary cause of the decline of Maratha power was due to its military weakness. They adopted European means of warfare but failed to perfect them.

  The same way, the Maratha soldiers trained by the French in European methods did not achieve perfection in their training.

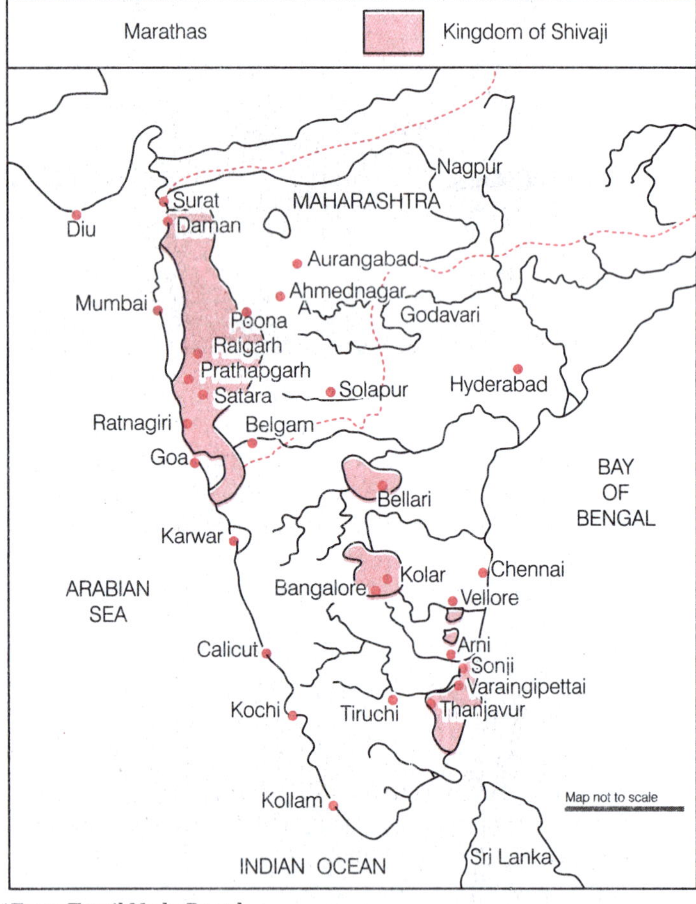

*From Tamil Nadu Board

Important Treaties of Maratha

Treaties	Importance
Treaty of Purandar (1665)	Signed between Commander of Mughal Empire Jai Singh I and Shivaji. By this treaty Shivaji surrendered 23 out of 35 forts.
The Treaty of Surat (1775)	Between British East India Company and Peshwa Raghunathrao.
Treaty of Wadgaon (1779)	Signed between the British and Raghunathrao Peshwa.
Treaty of Salbai (1782)	Signed between East India Company under Warren Hastings and Mahadaji Shinde.
Treaty of Seringapatam (1792)	Signed between the British (Lord Cornwallis), the Marathas, Hyderabad and Tipu Sultan.
Treaty of Deogaon (1803)	Between Raghuji Bhonsle II, the Maratha Raja of Berar and the British East India Company.
Treaty of Surji-Anjangaon (1803)	Between the Maratha Chief Daulat Rao Sindhia and the British.
Treaty of Rajpurghat (1805)	Between the Marathas under Holkars and English East India Company.
Treaty of Mandsaur (1818)	Between Malhar Rao Holkar of Maratha and the British.

Extra Facts From Tamil Nadu Board and NIOS

- In 1676, Shivaji began his career of conquests in the South. A secret treaty was signed with the Sultan of Golkonda.
- He captured Senji and Vellore and annexed the adjoining territories which belonged to his father Shahji.
- In 1670, Shivaji captured Surat, the most important port on the Western coast. In 1672, the Marathas imposed chauth or one fourth of the revenue as annual tribute on Surat.

21

Modern History

Later Mughals (18th Century)

[SOURCES]

Class-VIII New NCERT Chap 2 (From Trade to Territory), Class-VIII Old NCERT Chap 2 (India in the Eighteenth Century), Class-XII Old NCERT Chap 1 (India in the Eighteenth Century), Tamil Nadu Board (Class XI), NIOS

Disintegration of Mughal Empire

- The death of **Aurangzeb** in 1707 resulted into rapid decline of the Mughal Empire. The Mughal court became site of fighting among the nobles and provincial governors began to act in an independent manner.
- The Mughal Emperors who came to the throne after the death of Aurangzeb are called the **Later Mughals**. The real power under these rulers passed into the hands of nobles.
- The weakness of the empire was proclaimed to the world when **Nadir Shah** imprisoned the Mughal Emperor and looted the Delhi in 1739.
- In 1803, Delhi was occupied by the British Army and the Mughal Emperor was reduced to the status of a pensioner of a foreign power.
- On Aurangzeb's death, his three sons fought among themselves for the throne in which 65 year-old **Bahadur Shah**, emerged victorious.

Bahadur Shah I (1707-1712)

- During his brief reign, Bahadur Shah tried to restore the goodwill of the Mughal Empire by conciliating the Marathas and the Rajputs.
- He reversed the narrow-minded policies and measures adopted by **Aurangzeb** and adopted a more tolerant attitude towards the Hindu chief and *rajas*.
- In order to exercise greater control over the Rajput states, he replaced **Jai Singh** by **Vijai Singh** at Amber and forced **Ajit Singh** of Marwar to submit to the Mughal authority.
- Under his reign, an attempt to garrison the cities of Amber and Jodhpur was met with firm resistance.
- After realising his mistake, he restored the Kingdom of **Raja Jai Singh** and **Ajit Singh**, however, their demand of high *mansab* and *subedarship* of important provinces was not accepted.
- He made a half-hearted conciliation regarding Maratha Sardars. He granted the *Sardeshmukhi* of Deccan to them but their demand of *chauth* was rejected.
- He released *Shahu*, the grandson of *Shivaji* but didn't recognise him as the rightful Maratha king. It resulted into struggle for supremacy between **Tara Bai** and **Shahu** and a situation of disorder arised in the Deccan.
- He firstly tried to conciliate the rebellious elements by making peace with the **Guru Gobind Singh** and giving him a high *mansab*. But after the death of the Sikh Guru, he led a campaign against the rebellious elements headed by the **Banda Bahadur**.
- He succeeded in capturing some important Sikh strongholds including the Lohgarh fort built by Guru Gobind Singh, North-East of Ambala. But the Sikhs could not be crushed and in 1712, they recovered the fort of Lohgarh.

- He made peace with **Chhatarsal**, the Bundela chief and the Jat chief **Churaman**, who joined him in the campaign against Banda Bahadur.
- Due to his reckless grants of *Jagirs* and promotions, the position of state finances became worse. An amount of some ₹ 13 crore exhausted from the royal treasure in 1707. In 1707, after the death of **Bahadur Shah I**, the empire once again entered into civil war.

Jahandar Shah I (1712-13)

- During this phase of Mughal rule, a new element entered the Mughal politics in which the nobles became owner of power and used princes as mere puppets to capture the seat of authority.
- Thus, after the death of **Bahadur Shah I**, Jahandar Shah emerged victorious, as he was supported by the **Zulfiqar Khan**, the most powerful noble of that time.
- Jahandar Shah was a weak prince who was wholly devoted to pleasure. During his brief reign, the administration was virtually in the hands of his *wazir*, Zulfiqar Khan who was extremely capable and energetic.
- In order to strengthen his own position at the court and to save the Mughal Empire, he tried to establish friendly relations with the Rajput *rajas*, Maratha chiefs and other Hindu chieftains.
- In his reign, *Jizyah* was abolished. **Raja Jai Singh** of Amber was accorded the status of **Mirza Raja Sawai** and appointed the Governor of Malwa. **Ajit Singh** of Marwar was awarded the title of Maharaja and appointed as Governor of Gujarat.
- Zulfiqar Khan also confirmed the arrangement between his deputy in the Deccan **Daud Khan Panni** and the Maratha King **Shahu** in 1711.
- He granted the *Chauth* and *Sardeshmukhi* to the Marathas with a condition that it would be collected by the Mughal officials.
- He also pacified **Churaman** Jat and the **Chhatarsal Bundela**. But the old policy of suppression was carried towards the Sikhs under the leadership of **Banda Bahadur**.
- In order to improve the finances of the empire, he made an attempt to check the reckless growth of *jagirs* and offices. He compelled the *Mansabdars* to maintain their official quota of the troops.
- He introduced the *Ijarah* system. In this system, the Government contracted the revenue farmers and middleman to pay the Government a fixed amount of money while they were free to collect whatever they could from the Peasant.

Farrukhsiyar (1713-1719)

- He was nephew of **Jahandar Shah I** and defeated him in 1713 at Agra. The two Sayyid brothers – **Abudullah Khan** and **Husain Ali Khan** supported the Farrukhsiyar in the war of succession. And after victory, they were rewarded with the offices of *Wazir* and *Mir Bakshi* respectively.
- As Farrukhsiyar was incapable and cruel, the two Sayyid Brothers acquired the dominant control over the affairs of the state.
- The Sayyid brothers adopted the policy of religious tolerance and abolished *jizyah*.
- In order to strengthen their own position they provided high positions to Rajput princes, made an alliance with **Churaman**.
- They also made an agreement with **Shahu** by providing him the right to collect the *Chauth* and *Sardeshmukhi* of the six provinces.
- In return, Shahu agreed to support them in Deccan with 15,000 mounted soldiers.
- In 1719, the Maratha Peshwa, **Balaji Vishwanath** accompanied Sayyid Hussain Ali Khan to Delhi and helped the Sayyid Brothers in overthrowing Farrukhsiyar.
- On the other hand, Farrukhsiyar in order to exercise his personal authority intrigued against the Sayyid Brothers which ultimately resulted into desposition and execution of Farrukhsiyar.
- Finally, Sayyid Brothers selected **Muhammad Shah** the Emperor of India.

Downfall of Sayyid Brothers

- Sayyid Brothers' attempts to save the empire from administrative disintegration failed because of constant political rivalry amongst the nobility.
- Gradually, they were looked upon as traitors and the powerful members of nobility including **Nizam-ul-Mulk** (Chin Qilich Khan)and his fathers' cousin **Muhammad Amin Khan** began to conspire against them.
- These factions of nobility were supported by Emperor Muhammad Shah and ultimately in 1720, they succeeded in assassinating the Husain Ali Khan and the elder brother **Abdullah Khan** was defeated near Agra. These two brothers are known in Indian history as the '**King-makers**'.

Muhammad Shah (1719-48)

- He was weak-minded ruler and over-fond of a life of ease and luxury. During his reign, the conflict between the different groups of nobles weakened the authority of Central Government.

- He neglected the affair of the state and instead of giving full support to able *wazirs* such as **Nizam-ul Mulk**, he fell under the influence of corrupt and worthless nobles and conspired against his own ministers.
- Thus, Nizam-ul-Mulk (who was appointed *wazir* in 1722) decided to leave the Emperor due to his suspicious nature.
- He founded the state of Hyderabad in the Deccan and it marked the physical break-up of the Mughal Empire.
- Gradually, hereditary *Nawabs* owing nominal allegiance to the Emperor of Delhi arose in many part of the country i.e., in Bengal, Awadh, Hyderabad and Punjab.
- In many parts, *Zamindars, Rajas* and *Nawabs* raised the banner of rebellion and independence. The Maratha Sardars also began their Northern expansion and captured Malwa, Gujarat and Bundelkhand.
- This situation alongwith weak central leadership led to the invasion of **Nadir Shah.**
- During the reign of Muhammad Shah, significant progress in Hindustani music was observed. During his reign, the semi-independent state of Rohilkhand rose to power.

Invasion of Nadir Shah (1738)

- The visible weakness of the Mughal Empire in addition to near bankruptcy condition attracted Nadir Shah (the ruler of Persia) to attack Mughal Empire.
- The years of neglect of North-Western frontier and factions among nobles led to the crushing defeat of Mughals in **Battle of Karnal** on 13th February, 1739.
- The Emperor Muhammad Shah was imprisoned and **Nadir Shah** marched to Delhi.
- He took possession of royal treasury and plundered wealth having estimated value of 70 crores of rupees. He also carried away the famous *Koh-i-Noor* diamond and Jewel studded peacock throne of **Shah Jahan.**
- He also compelled Muhammad Shah to cede him all the provinces of the Empire West of Indus.

Ahmad Shah (1748-1754)

- He was son of Muhammad Shah and inherited the that was filled with mutual jealousness among the nobility.
- His reign is marked by series of plundering raids by the Afghan ruler **Ahmad Shah Abdali,** who invaded North India five times between 1748 and 1761.
- During his reign, the Marathas successfully annexed the Mughal territories of Malwa and Bundelkhand.
- He was imprisoned and blinded by his own *wazir*, **Imad-ul-Mulk.**

Alamgir II (1754-59)

- After desposition of Ahmad Shah, **Imad-ul-Mulk** raised Alamgir II as the Emperor of Mughal Empire.
- During his reign, the Mughal Empire witnessed repeated attacks of **Ahmad Shah Abdali. The Battle of Plassey** (1757) was also fought during his reign.
- He was murdered by his own *wazir*, **Imad-ul-Mulk.**

Shah Alam II (1759-1806)

- Shah Alam II, who ascended the throne in **1759**, spent the initially years as an Emperor wandering from place to place far away from his capital as, he feared his own *wazir*.
- During his reign, the **Third Battle of Panipat (1761)** was fought between the Marathas and Ahmad Shah Abdali, the General of Nadir Shah. It resulted into defeat of Marathas.
- The battle and the subsequent defeat gave a big blow to the Maratha ambition of controlling the Mughal Emperor and thereby dominating the country.
- Meanwhile in 1764, Shah Alam II joined **Mir Qasim** of Bengal and **Shuja-ud-Daula** of Awadh to fought British East India Company in the **Battle of Buxar** (1764).
- After defeat in this battle, he lived for several years at Allahabad as a pensioner of the East India Company. In 1772, he returned to Delhi under the protective arm of Marathas.
- The Britishers secured the *Diwani* or the right to collect revenues of Bihar, Bengal and Orrisa from Shah Alam II.
- During his reign, the British occupied Delhi in (1803). Thus, he is regarded as the last sovereign Mughal Emperor to rule Delhi.

Akbar II (1806-37)

- He is regarded as the first Mughal Emperor to rule India under the Britishers.
- In 1830s, he gave the title of *Raja* to the great social reformer **Ram Mohan Roy** and also sent him as the envoy of the Mughal Emperor to England.

Bahadur Shah II (1837-58)

- He was the last Mughal Emperor, although at that time the post of Mughal Emperor had became titular head only.
- He was well-versed in Urdu poetry and wrote poems under the pen name of *Zafar*. He was contemporary of the famous Urdu poet **Mirza Ghalib.**

- The Governor-General **Lord Dalhousie** in 1848, announced that the successor to **Bahadur Shah** would have to abandon the historic Red Fort.
- In 1856, the Viceroy **Lord Canning** announced that after Bhadur Shah's death the Mughals would lost the title of Kings and would be known as mere princess.
- During the **Revolt of 1857**, he was recognised as the Emperor of India by the rebel soldiers and *Zamindars*.
- On 20th September, 1857, British captured Delhi and the aged Bahadur Shah was taken as the prisoner. The Royal princess were mercilessly captured and killed.
- The Bahadur Shah was tried and exiled to Rangoon where he died in 1862.

Causes for the Decline of the Mughal Empire

The causes for the decline of the Mughal Empire are as follows:

- **Aurangzeb's intolerant religious policy**, spoiled relations with Jats, Marathas and Rajputs and the suspicious nature of Aurangzeb led to the fall of empire.
- Aurangzeb's religious policies was discriminatory and most prominent example of this is the tax imposed on Hindus called *Jizyah* that led to dissatisfaction among public as well as Hindu rulers.
- His **Deccan Policy** was also a reason for the decline of Mughal Empire.
- Invasions of **Nadir Shah** and **Ahmed Shah Abdali** were also the cause of downfall.
- One of the major reasons for the fall was financial crisis. The Royal treasury was almost empty by the 18th century because of the maintanence of military affairs.
- Worthless and negligent later Mughal emperors were also the cause of downfall.
- Absence of a definite law of succession lead to the instability of the government. The growth of partisanship at the cost of patriotism existed.
- A heterogeneous and **non-hereditary nobility** was proxminent that was divided in factions.
- Vast expansion of the empire made it difficult for the weak rulers to control it, after Aurangzeb's death.
- Deterioration of the army revolts of Rajputs, Sikhs, Jats and Marathas due to Aurangzeb's religious policy.

Extra Facts From
Tamil Nadu Board and NIOS

- Aurangzeb, the last of the 'great Mughals' died in 1707. One of the major development following his death was the establishment of what have been called 'successor states'.

22

Arrival of European Powers in India

(SOURCES)

Class-VIII New NCERT Chap 2 (From Trade to Territory), Class-VIII Old NCERT Chap 3 (The Rise and Growth of British Rule in India), Class-XII Old NCERT Chap 2 (European Penetration and the British Conquest of India), Class-XII New NCERT Chap 9 (Colonialism and Country Side), Tamil Nadu Board (Class XI), NIOS

Advent of Europeans in India

- The old trading routes between East and West came under Turkish control after the Ottoman conquest of **Asia Minor** and the capture of **Constantinople** in 1453.
- The West European states including **Spain** and **Portugal** were denied any share in the trade through old routes by the merchants of **Venice** and **Genoa** who had monopolised these routes.
- In order to break the Arab and Venetian trade monopolies and to bypass Turkish hostilities, West European states and merchants began to search for new and safer sea route to India and Indonesia.
- These state were able to find sea routes due to great advancement in ship-building and the science of navigation in 15th century.
- The first steps were taken by **Portugal** and **Spain** whose seamen, sponsored and controlled by the governments, began a great era of geographical discoveries.
- In 1498, **Vasco-da-Gama** of Portugal discovered a new all-sea route from Europe to India. He sailed Africa around **Cape of Good Hope** and reached Calicut.

Portuguese

- Before the arrival of **Vasco-da-Gama**, Portuguese under their ruler **Dom Henrique** (also known as Henry the Navigator) made significant attempts to search out a sea route to India.
- From 1418, **Prince Henry** sent two or three ships every year to explore the sea route. He was motivated by the two objectives
  - To oust the Arabs as well as European rivals.
  - To counter the growing power of Turks and Arabs by converting indigenous population of Asia and Africa to Christianity.
- In 1487, **Bartholomew Diaz** rounded the Cape of Good Hope and laid the basis of direct trade links between Europe and India.
- When Vasco-da-Gama landed at Calicut in 1498, he met with stiff resistance from Arab merchants, who had established their colony on the Malabar Coast.
- However, the Hindu ruler, **Zamorin** welcomed the Portuguese and allowed them to trade.
- He returned on his ship with a cargo which was sold for 60 times the cost of his voyage. In 1502, he established a factory at Cochin.

- Since the 16th century, Portuguese enjoyed a virtual monopoly of the highly profitable Eastern trade for nearly a century.
- Under the Viceroyalty of **Alfonoso de Albuquerque,** they established their domination over the entire Asian coast from Hormuz in the Persian Gulf to Malacca in Malaya and the Spice Islands in Indonesia.
- They were successful in maintaining their possessions in India for a century due to naval superiority and absence of strong enemy as Mughals in the South India.

Important Portuguese Governors in India

- **Francisco de Almeida** (1505-09) He defeated the combined naval fleet of Sultan of Egypt and Ruler of Gujarat in 1509. He pursued Blue Water Policy in order to strengthen the Portuguese hold in Indian sub-continent and build forts at Anjediva, Cannanore and Cochin.
- **Afonso de Albuquerque** (1509-15) He is considered as real founder of Portuguese power in India. He captured Goa from Bijapur in 1510. He encouraged Portuguese to marry natives and abolished the practice of Sati in his dominion.
- **Nuno da Cunha** (1529-38) He transferred his capital from Calicut to Goa in 1530 and annexed Diu and Bassein in 1534 from Bahadur Shah of Gujarat.
- **Alfonso de Souza** (1542) He succeded Nuno da Cunha. During his reign, famous Saint, Francisco Xavier came to Goa.

Contribution of Portuguese

- Portuguese traded pepper, arms and ammunition and war horses with royal monopoly.
- They opened up India's trade with Japan from which copper and silver were obtained.
- They introduced the **first printing press at Goa** in 1556.
- Furthermore, they were instrumental in starting the cultivation of vegetables like tomatoes, potatoes and chillies in India. Fruits like, pineapple and papaya were also introduced by the Portuguese.
- The cultivation of tobacco and maize also started under the Portuguese rule in India.
- They are also credited with the first scientific work on Indian medicinal plants.

Important European Companies in India

Company	Year of Establishment	First Factory	Headquarters
Portuguese East India Company	1498	Calicut (1503)	Initial- Calicut Final- Goa
English East India Company	1600	Surat (1605)	Initial- Surat Final-Calcutta
Dutch East India Company (Netherlands)	1602	Masulipatnam (1605)	Indonesia
Danish East India Company (Denmark)	1616	Tranquebar (1620)	Initial- Tranquebar (Tamil Nadu) Final-Serampore (West Bengal)
French East India Company	1664	Surat (1668)	Initial- Surat Final- Pondicherry

Key Battles Fought by Portuguese in India

- **Battle of Chaul** (1508) It was a naval battle fought between the Portuguese and the combined forces of *Mamluk* Sultan and the sultan of Gujarat. It resulted in defeat of Portuguese.
- **Battle of Diu** (1509) It was also a naval battle fought between the Portuguese forces on one side and the combined forces of the Sultan of Gujarat, Zamorin of Calicut and *Mamluk* sultan of Egypt. It resulted in decisive victory of Portuguese.
- **Battle of Swally** (1612) It was fought between the British and Portuguese colonial powers. In this battle, Portuguese lost Surat to the British.
- **Battle of Vasai** (1739) It was fought between the Marathas and the Portuguese forces. It resulted in victory of Marathas.

Decline of Portuguese

- The Portuguese power began to decline during the second half of the 16th century mainly due to intense competition among European powers.
- By the early 18th century, the position of Portuguese was undertaken by the **English** and the **French.**
- They lost Surat to the English in 1612 and eventually the Dutch also won the entire Portuguese fort on the Malabar coast.
- In 1662, the Portuguese gave the island of Bombay to **King Charles II** of England as dowry for marrying Portuguese princess. Thus, the Portuguese lost all their possessions in India except Goa, Diu and Daman.
- The emergence of powerful Marathas in Maharashtra and areas surrounding Konkan coast also led to the downfall of the Portuguese power in India. They captured **Salsette** and **Bassein** from Portuguese in 1739.

The Dutch

- In 1602, the Dutch East India Company was formed. The Dutch States General (the Dutch Parliament) gave it a charter. This charter empowered it to wage wars, conclude treaties, acquire territories and build fortresses.
- The main interest of the Dutch was not in India but in the Indonesian Island of **Java**, **Sumatra** and the **Spice Islands** where spices were produced.
- They soon turned out the Portuguese from the Malay Straits and in 1623, defeated the English attempts to establish themselves there. The first Dutch mission to India was led under the leadership of **Corneliss de Houtman.**
- The Dutch established themselves at Masulipatnam, obtaining a *farman* from the ruler of Golconda in 1606.
- As their main interest lied in the spice trade, they quickly realised that spices could be obtained most easily against Indian textiles. Thus, they alongwith English were instrumental in exporting Indian textiles to the West.
- They spread South from Masulipatnam to the Coromandel coast, obtaining Pulicat from the local ruler and making it base of their operations.
- They also established trading depots at Surat, Broach, Cambay and Ahmedabad in Gujarat in West India and Cochin in Kerala, Nagapattinam in Madras, Masulipatnam in Andhra, Chinsurah in Bengal, Patna in Bihar and Agra in Uttar Pradesh.
- Later, they defeated Portuguese and annexed their key forts on Malabar coast. In 1658, they also conquered Sri Lanka from the Portuguese. The English Company fell out with the Dutch company over division of the spice trade of the Indonesian Islands.
- The intermittent war in India between the two powers, began in 1654 and ended in 1667, when the English gave up all claims to Indonesia while the Dutch agreed to leave the English settlements in India.

Contribution of Dutch

- They helped in development of new markets for Indian products in Europe. **Calicos** (Cotton textiles), Indigo and **Salt petere** was the main item of the export.
- In order to expand their trade, they developed **Coromandel coast** and established **Pulicat** as the base of their operations in India.
- As their trade flourished, they established mints at Cochin, Masulipatnam, Nagapattinam, Pondicherry and Pulicat. They issued gold coins depicting an image of **Lord Venkateswara** (God Vishnu) from Pulicat mint.

Factories established by Dutch in India

Centre	Year
Pulicat	1610
Surat	1616
Chinsurah	1653
Kasim Bazar	1659
Patna	1659
Nagapattinam	1659
Cochin	1663

The English

- An English Association or Company to trade was formed in 1599 by a group of merchants known as the **Merchant Adventurers.**
- The Governor and Company of Merchants of London trading into East India, (popularly known as the East India Company), was granted a royal charter and exclusive privilege to trade in the East by **Queen Elizabeth** on 31st December, 1600.
- With this charter, the Company could venture across the oceans, looking for new lands from which it could buy goods at a cheap price and carry them back to Europe to sell at higher prices.
- This charter granted to the East India Company exclusive privilege of trading East of the **Cape of Good Hope** for a period of 15 years.

Expansion of East Indian Company

- East India Company had established factories at Surat, Bharuch, Ahmedabad, Agra and Masulipatnam till 1623 AD.
- The situations in the Deccan were favourable for Britishers as there were no powerful kingdom.
- Company established one of its factories in the Eastern India at Orissa in 1633 AD.
- The Britishers threw out Portuguese and Dutch rivals by the end of 17th century, but France still was the main rival of Britishers for the supremacy in India. Britishers fought French for about 20 years from 1744 to 1763 AD.

Expansion in Western Coast

- **William Hawkins** journeyed from Surat and arrived at the **Jahangir's court** in 1609 AD, but failed to get permission to erect a factory at Surat.
- However, the victory of English under captain best over Portuguese fleet at **Swally** (near Surat) in 1612 AD broke the tradition of Portuguese naval supremacy.

- A *Farman* was issued by **Jahangir** permitting the English to establish a factory at Surat 1613 AD.
- **Sir Thomas Roe** was the royal ambassador from **King James** I to the Mughal Emperor. He succeeded in getting two *Farmans* by 1618, one of the Mughal **Emperor Jahangir** and the other of the Prince **Khurram** granting the permission to trade and erect factories in different parts of the empire.
- **Surat** was one of the chief centres of maritime trade, it is from Surat that the English extended their inland trading operations and by 1616 built subordinate factories at Ahmedabad, Baroda, Bharuch and Agra.
- Finally, **Bombay** was declared as headquarters of the company on the West coast in 1687AD.

Gerald Aungier

He was the **first Governor of Bombay** 1669 to 1677 AD. Under Aungier, Bombay became a safe asylum for all merchants and manufacturers. He established vigorous and strict discipline over all the inhabitants of the city and allowed every community to enjoy the free exercise of its religion.

Expansion in Eastern Coast

- The English were permitted to trade in Masulipatnam in 1611 AD and in 1630 AD secured the '**golden farman**' from the Sultan of Golconda 1632 AD, which ensured safety and prosperity of their trade.
- In 1639 AD, **Francis Day** obtained the site of Madras from the **Raja of Chandragiri** with permission to build a fortified factory, which was named **Fort St. George**.
- The position of the English on the Eastern coast became strong and permanent with the foundation of Madras by the English in 1639. They arrived at Hughli in 1650 AD and establish a factory at **Balasore** in North Orissa.
- Madras soon replaced Masulipatnam as the headquarters of the English on the Coromandel coast.
- In 1641 AD, all the English settlements in Eastern India (Bengal, Bihar and Orissa) and the Coromandel were placed under the control of the President and Council of Fort St. George.

Expansion in Bengal

- In 1633 AD, the Mughal Governor of Orissa gave the English merchants permission to establish factories at Hariharapur (near the mouth of Mahanadi), Balasore and Pipli.
- The English also succeeded to establish their factory at Hughli in 1651 AD, followed by those at Patna, Dacca and Kasim bazar.
- In 1667 AD, **Aurangzeb** gave the English a *farman* for trade in Bengal and 5 years later, in 1672 AD, the Mughal Governor, **Shaista Khan**, issued an order confirming all the privileges already acquired by the English.
- The rebellion of **Sobha Singh**, a *Zamindar* in the district of Burdwan, gave an opportunity to the English to fortify their settlement at Sutanuti in 1696 AD.
- They were permitted by **Azimuth Shah** Governor of Bengal, to purchase the *Zamindari* of the three villages of **Sutanuti**, **Kalikata** and **Govindpur** on payment of ₹ 1200 to the old proprietors.
- In 1700 AD, the directors constituted Bengal as a separate presidency independent of Madras and nominated **Sir Charles Eyre** as its first President.
- Aurangzeb's death in 1707 AD made the English at Calcutta fear that their growing trade would be swept away by the coming tide of civil war and anarchy.
- After protracted negotiations, the English got confirmation of their privileges from the new emperor **Shah Alam** and the *de facto* ruler of Bengal **Murshid Quli Khan**.
- The most important event in the history of the Company during these years was the diplomatic mission led by **John Surman** in 1715 AD to the court of the Mughal Emperor **Farrukhsiyar**.
- It resulted in the granting of three famous *farmans* addressed to the officials in Bengal, Hyderabad and Gujarat.
- The *farmans* gave the Company many valuable privileges, which are as follows
  - In **Bengal**, it exempted the Company's imports and exports from additional customs duties, excepting the annual payment of ₹ 3000 as settled earlier. The Company was allowed to rent additional lands around Calcutta.
  - In **Hyderabad**, the Company's old privileges of freedom from dues in trade was retained and it had to pay only the existing rent for Madras.
  - In **Gujarat**, the Company was exempted from the levy of all duties for its exports and imports in lieu of an annual payment of ₹ 10000 and the coins of the Company minted at Bombay were to have currency throughout the Mughal empire.
  - In the subsequent years, the English East India Company began to extend its territorial claims. It defeated **Battle of Bedara**, 1759 (Dutch) and **Battle of Wandiwash**, 1760 (French). By the end of the 18th century, it succeeded in establishing its Paramountacy.

Important Terms related with European Rule in India

- **Cartaz System** It was a naval pass issued by the Portuguese, which was compulsorily required by any contingent passing through their territories.
- **Factories** It was developed by the European powers in India to store commodities which were later exported. Here Company's officials resided and it was fortified to defend against the adversaries.
- **Feitorias** It was an unfortified trading post developed by the Portuguese on strategic locations.
- **Farman** It was a royal order issued by Mughal authority usually to the European trading companies.
- **Mercantile** A business enterprise that makes profit primarily through trade, buying goods cheap and selling them at higher prices.

The Danes (Danish)

- The Danes came from Denmark to India in 1616 AD and established their first factory at **Tranquebar** (Tamil Nadu) in 1620 AD. Later, they established their second factory and its headquarters in **Serampore** in Bengal.
- At Serampore, they established a printing press in 1800 and a college in 1818.

Clash of European Companies with Each Other in India

- Until the first decade of the 17th century, all major European trading companies had strengthened their position in India. And all the companies were interested in buying the same things, i.e. fine qualities of cotton and silk.
- Competition amongst the European companies inevitably pushed up the prices at which these goods could be purchased and this reduced the profits that could be earned. The only way of trading companies could flourish was by eliminating rival competitors. Therefore, the urge to secure markets led to fierce battles between the trading companies.

The French

- The French East India Company was founded in 1664. It was firmly established at **Chandernagore** near Calcutta and **Pondicherry** on the East coast.
- The French Company also had some other factories at several ports on the East and West coasts. It had also acquired control over the islands of Mauritius and reunion in the Indian ocean.
- It was heavily dependent on the French Government, which helped it by giving it treasury grants, subsidies and loans.
- Consequently, it was largely controlled by the government which appointed its directors after 1723.
- The state control of the company proved quite harmful to it as the French state of the time was autocratic, semi-feudal and unpopular.

Carnatic Wars

- For nearly 20 years from 1744 to 1763, the French and the English were in conflict for control over the trade, wealth and territory of India.
- The area where conflict first erupted between the French and the English companies was the **Mughal Suba of Caranatic Arcot** situated between Madras and Pondicherry was the capital town of Carnatic.
- In order to control the Southern regions of India and expand their empires in India, they fought three crucial battles in India, known as Carnatic wars.

First Carnatic War (1746-48)

- In 1742, war broke out in Europe between France and England over the Austrian succession. It was continued in India where two companies fought to secure and expand its positions.
- **Dupleix**, the French Governor-General started recruiting India soldiers and giving them training in modern methods of warfare.
- In 1745, the English navy captured French ships off the South-East coast of India and threatened Pondicherry. However, under the leadership of Dupleix French retaliated and occupied Madras in 1746.
- The **Nawab of Carnatic** was alarmed at growing power of the French in his province and sent an army against them.
- In 1748, peace was concluded in Europe between the British and the French with the treaty of **Aix-La Chapelle**. The victorious French restored Madras to the British.

Joseph François Dupleix

He was the Governor-General of the French possessions in India from 1742 to 1754. He devised few mechanism of statecraft which was later used by the British to conquest whole India.

He evolved the strategy of using the well-disciplined, modern French army to intervene in the mutual quarrels of the Indian princes and by supporting one against the other, securing monetary, commercial or territorial favours from the **Victor**.

Through the resources and armies of the native princess and later making them their satellite, he tried to serve the interests of the French Company and to expel the English from India. This strategy was fully conceptualised in the form of **Subsidiary Alliance** by the Britishers.

Second Carnatic War (1749-54)

- The second Carnatic war was mainly fought because of the two rival companies supported different claimants to the posts of the Nizam of Hyderabad and the Nawab of the Carnatic.
- The French helped **Muzaffar Jang** and later when he died raised Salabat Jang as the Nizam of the Hyderabad.
- In return, the Nizam granted the areas in Andhra Pradesh known as Northern Sarkars.
- The French supported **Chanda Sahib** to become the Nawab and the English sent **Robert Clive** with a small army to install **Muhammad Ali** as the Nawab of Arcot in 1751.
- In the war that followed French forces were repeatedly defeated and **Chanda Sahib** was captured and killed.
- In the end, the French Government, due to heavy expenses of the war in India and fearing the loss of its American colonies, initiated peace negotiations. In 1754, it agreed to the English demand for the recall of Dupleix from India.

Third Carnatic War (1756-63)

- The temporary peace between the two companies ended in 1756, when another war between England and France broke out.
- In the very beginning of the war, the English managed to gain control over Bengal. The rich resources of Bengal turned the scales decisively in favour of the English.
- Even though the French Government made a determined attempt this time to oust the English from India and sent a strong force headed by **Count de Lally**, it was all in vain.
- The decisive battle of the war was fought at **Wandiwash** on 22nd January, 1760, when the English General **Eyre Coot** defeated the French Governor-General **Lally**.
- Salabat Jung, the Nizam of Hyderabad, without fighting a battle signed an agreement with the British. The Nizam transferred Masulipatnam and northern circas from French to English.
- The war ended in 1763 with the signing of the **Treaty of Paris**. The French factories in India were restored but they could no longer be fortified or even adequately garrisoned with troops.
- The English emerged as the undisputed colonial power in India, changing from a trading company into that of a territorial power.

Significance of Anglo-French Struggle

This struggle freed English of all its European rivals and they embarked a new era of territorial expansion in India. But more importantly they learnt few lessons, which helped them in consolidating their empire in India.

- **Firstly**, that in the absence of nationalism in the country, they could advance their political schemes by taking advantage of the mutual quarrels of the Indian rulers.
- **Secondly**, the Western trained infantry, European or Indian, armed with modern weapons and backed by artillery could defeat the old- style Indian armies with ease in pitched battles.
- **Thirdly**, it was proved that the Indian soldiers trained and armed in the European manner made as good a soldier as the European. And since, the Indian soldier too lacked a feeling of nationalism, he could be hired and employed by anyone.

Extra Facts From Tamil Nadu Board and NIOS

- The English acquired the islands of Bombay in 1668 and set up their headquarter in Bombay in 1687. Their primary objective was to develop Bombay as an alternate base for their operations.
- The English got a piece of land further South from the local chief, Damarla Venkatadri Nayak on which they built Fort St. George in 1639. Damarla was an Nayak of Vijayanagra empire.
- Cotton fabrics were the most important exports from all parts of India to the rest of the world.
- Under the Cartaz system, the Portuguese exacted money from the traders as price for protection against what they termed as piracy.
- **Berber**, a French agent in India obtained a farman on 4th September, 1666 from Aurangzeb and the first French factory was established at Surat in December, 1668.
- The French secured Mahe in 1725 and Karaikal in 1739.

Rise of New and Autonomous States

(SOURCES)

Class-VII New NCERT Chap 8 (Eighteenth Century Political Formations), Class-VIII New NCERT Chap 2 (From Trade to Territory), Class-VIII Old NCERT Chap 2 (India in the Eighteenth Century), Class-XII Old NCERT Chap 1 (India in the Eighteenth Century), Tamil Nadu Board (Class XI), NIOS

- By 1761, the Mughal empire was just a symbolic authority. Due to its weaknesses, the local powers asserted their independence.
- The new states did not directly challenge his authority and constantly sought his sanction to legitimise their rule.
- Therefore, the emergence of these states in the 18th century, represented a transformation rather than collapse of the polity.
- Following the disintegration of Mughal empire, there were number of autonomous or independent states that emerged.
- During the first half of the 18th century, the boundaries of the Mughal empire were reshaped by the emergence of a number of kingdoms such as **successor states, independent kingdoms and new states.**

Successor States

Successor states were the Mughal provinces that turned into states after breaking away the empire.

Important successor states are as follows

Hyderabad

The important rulers of the erstwhile Hyderabad state were

Asaf Jah (1724-1748 AD)

- Hyderabad was founded by **Nizam-ul-Mulk Asaf Jah** in 1724. His real name was **Chin Qilich Khan.**
- He played a leading role in overthrowing **Sayyid Brothers.**
- From 1720 to 1722, he consolidated his hold over the Deccan by suppressing all opposition to his viceroyalty and organising the administration on efficient lines.
- From 1722 to 1724, he was the *wazir* of the empire. But he soon got disgusted with that office as the Emperor **Muhammad Shah** frustrated all his attempts at reforming the administration.
- So, he decided to go back to the Deccan where he could safely maintain his supremacy. Here, he laid the foundations of the Hyderabad state which he ruled with a strong hand.
- **Asaf Jah** never openly declared his independence from the Central Government, but in practice he acted like an independent ruler.
- The state of Hyderabad was constantly engaged in a struggle against the Marathas to the West and with independent Telugu warrior chiefs (*nayakas*).
- He waged wars, concluded peace, conferred titles and gave *jagirs* and offices without reference to Delhi. He followed a tolerant policy towards the Hindus. For example, a Hindu, **Puran Chand** was his *Diwan*.
- He consolidated his power by establishing an orderly administration in the Deccan on the basis of the *jagirdari* system on the Mughal pattern.

- He forced the big, turbulent *zamindars* to respect his authority and kept the powerful Marathas out of his dominions.
- Asaf Jah also made an attempt to rid the revenue system of its corruption. But after his death in 1748, Hyderabad fell a prey to the same disruptive forces as were operating at Delhi.

Nasir Jung (1748-1750 AD)

- He ascended throne in 1748 AD.
- He was defeated and murdered by **Muzaffar Jung** (son of Nasir's sister and grandson of Nizam-ul-Mulk).

Muzaffar Jung (1750-1751 AD)

- He ascended the throne with the help of the French in 1750 AD.
- In 1751 AD, his rule came to an abrupt end with his accidental death.

Salabat Jung (1751-1760 AD)

- He was the third son of **Nizam-ul-Mulk**. He came to the throne with the help of the French in 1751 AD.

Carnatic

- The Carnatic was one of the *subahs* of the Mughal Deccan and came under the Nizam of Hyderabad's authority.
- The Nizam had become independent of Delhi alongwith the Deputy Governor of the Carnatic, known as the **Nawab of Carnatic**.
- He had freed himself from the control of the Viceroy of the Deccan and made his office hereditary.
- Thus, *Nawab* **Saadatullah Khan** of Carnatic had made his nephew **Dost Ali** his successor without the approval of his superior, the Nizam.
- Later, after 1740, the affairs of the Carnatic deteriorated because of the repeated struggles for its **nawabship**.
- This provided an opportunity for the European trading companies to directly interfere in Indian Politics.

Bengal

Owing of the growing weakness of the Central authority, **Murshid Quli Khan** and **Alivardi Khan** made Bengal virtually independent.

Following were the main Rulers/Nawabs of Bengal

Murshid Quli Khan

- Murshid Quli Khan (1717-1727 AD) was appointed as the **Diwan of Bengal** in 1700 and was made **Governor of Bengal** in 1717.
- He soon freed himself from central control though he regularly sent a large tribute to the emperor.
- He established peace by freeing Bengal of internal and external danger. Bengal was now also relatively free of major uprisings by *zamindars*.

Trade and Finance in Bengal in Murshid Quli Khan

- Murshid Quli Khan affected economies in the administration and reorganised the finances of Bengal by transferring large parts of *jagir* lands into *Khalisah* lands by carrying out a fresh revenue settlement and by introducing the system of revenue-farming. He recruited revenue farmers and officials from local *zamindars* and merchant-bankers.
- He also granted agricultural loans (**taccavi**) to the poor cultivators to relieve their distress as well as to enable them to pay land revenue in time.
- Murshid Quli Khan and the succeeding *Nawabs* gave equal opportunities for employment to Hindus and Muslims.
- They filled the highest civil posts and many of the military posts with Bengalis, mostly Hindus.
- In choosing revenue farmers Murshid Quli Khan gave preference to local *zamindars* and Mahajan's (money-lenders) who were mainly Hindus. He thus, laid the foundations of a new landed aristocracy in Bengal.
- Moreover, even though Khan demanded only the standard revenue and forbade illegal cesses, he collected the revenue from the *zamindars* and the peasants with utmost cruelty.
- Another result of his reforms was that many of the older *zamindars* were driven out and their place was taken by upstart revenue-farmers.
- They also provided for the safety of roads and rivers from thieves and robbers by establishing regular *thanas* and *chowkis*.
- The *Nawabs* of Bengal neglected to build a strong army and paid a heavy price for it.
- In 1756-1767 AD, the English East India Company declared war on Siraj-ud-Daula, the successor of Alivardi, the absence of a strong army contributed much to the victory of the British.

Sarfaraz Khan (1739-1740 AD)

- He was the son of Shuja.
- He took the title of **Alam-ud-Daula Haider Jung**.
- He was defeated by Alivardi Khan, Governor of Bihar in the **Battle of Giriya** (1740 AD) and was murdered.

Alivardi Khan (1740-1756 AD)

- In 1741 AD, Alivardi Khan, the Deputy Governor of Bihar, killed the *Nawab* of Bengal **Sarfaraz Khan in a** battle.
- He certified his own position as the new *Subahdar* of Bengal by paying a large sum of money to the Mughal Emperor, **Muhammad Shah.**
- Alivardi Khan ruled for 15 years, during which he fought with the Marathas. But he died in April, 1756 and was succeeded by his grandson, **Siraj-ud-Daula.**

Siraj-ud-Daula (1756-1757 AD)

- He had a rival in his cousin, the *Nawab* of Purnea, Shaukat Jang; his aunt, *Ghasiti Begum* and a rebellious commander of the army, **Mir Jafar.**
- There was a dominant group in his court comprising **Jagat Seth, Omichand, Rai Ballabh, Rai Durlabh** and others who were opposed to him.
- To these, internal rivals were added the threat to Siraj's position from the ever-growing commercial activity of the English company.
- Impulsive by nature and lacking experience, Siraj felt insecure and this prompted him to act in ways which proved counterproductive.

> **Black Hole Tragedy** (20th June, 1758)
> Siraj-ud-Daula, is believed to have imprisoned with 146 English persons who were lodged in a very tiny room due to which 123 of them died due to suffocation. This incident is referred as Black Hole Tragedy.

Important Events in Reign of Siraj-ud-Daula

Important events in reign of Siraj-ud-Daula were

Battle of Plassey, 1757

- **Robert Clive** forged a secret alliance with the traitors of the *Nawab*—**Mir Jafar, Rai Durlabh, Jagat Seth** (an influential banker of Bengal) and **Omichund.** Due to the conspiracy of the nawab's officials, Siraj was defeated by Clive's forces in Battle of Plassey on 23rd June, 1757.
- Siraj-ud-Daula was captured and murdered by the order of Mir Jafar's son, **Miran.** The Battle of Plassey had political significance for it laid the foundation of the British empire in India.

Mir Qasim to Power

- After the death of Miran, the son of Mir Jafar there was a tussle over authority of Bengal between Mir Qasim, the son-in-law of **Mir Jafar** and Miran's son.
- **Vansittart**, the new Governor of Calcutta agreed to support Mir Qasim's claim after a treaty between Mir Qasim and the East India Company was signed in 1760.
- Mir Qasim was the ablest nawab among the successors of **Alivardi Khan.** After assuming power, Mir Qasim shifted the capital from Murshidabad to Munger in Bihar.

Battle of Buxar

- The combined armies of **Mir Qasim**, the Nawab of Awadh and **Shah Alam II** were defeated by the English forces under **Major Hector Munro** at Buxar on 22nd October, 1764 in a closely contested battle. The English campaign against Mir Qasim was short but decisive.
- The importance of this battle lay in the fact that not only the Nawab of Bengal but also the Mughal Emperor of India was defeated by the English.
- The victory made the English a great power in Northern India and contenders for the supremacy over the whole country.

Dual Government in Bengal (1765-1772 AD)

- After the **Battle of Buxar, Robert Clive** introduced the Dual System of Government, i.e., the rule of the two (the Company and the Nawab) in Bengal.
- In this both the *Diwani*, i.e., collecting revenues and *Nizamat*, i.e., police and judicial functions, came under the control of the Company.
- The Company exercised diwani rights as the *diwani* and the *nizamat* rights through its right to nominate the Deputy subahdar. The Company acquired the *diwani* functions from the emperor and *nizamat* functions from the *subahdar* of Bengal.

Najm-ud-Daulah (1765-1772 AD)

- He was the son of **Mir Jafar.**
- He was made the Nawab in 1765 AD and remained a puppet in the hands of the British during the period of 'Dual System of Government' under **Robert Clive.**

Awadh

- The subah of Awadh was extended from Kannauj district in the West to the River Karmnasa in the East.

Saadat Khan Burhan-ul-Mulk (1722-1739 AD)

- He was the founder of the autonomous kingdom of Awadh. He was appointed Governor of Awadh in 1722.
- At the time of his appointment, many rebellious *zamindars* refused to pay the land tax, organised their own private armies, erected forts and defied the **Imperial Government.**
- For years Saadat Khan had to wage war upon the *zamindars*. He succeeded in suppressing lawlessness and disciplining the big *zamindars* and thus, increasing the financial resources of his government.

- Saadat Khan also carried out a fresh revenue settlement in 1723.
- He is said to have improved the lot of the peasant by levying equitable land revenue and by protecting them from oppression by the big *zamindars*. He also continued the *jagir* system.
- Like the Bengal *nawabs*, Saadat Khan too did not discriminate between Hindus and Muslims. Many of his commanders and high officials were Hindus.
- His troops were well paid, well armed and well trained. His administration was efficient.
- He was succeeded by his nephew **Safdar Jang**, who was simultaneously appointed the *wazir* of the empire in 1748 and granted in addition the province of Allahabad.

Safdar Jang (1739-1754 AD)

- Safdar Jang gave a long period of peace to the people of Awadh and Allahabad before his death in 1754.
- He suppressed rebellious *zamindars*, won over others and made an alliance with the **Maratha Sardars**. He was able to win the loyalty of **Rajput chieftains** and *Shaifyizadas*.
- He carried on warfare against the **Rohillas** and the **Bangash Pathans**. In his war against the Bangash Pathans in 1750-1751 AD, he secured the help of Maratha Military.
- Safdar Jang entered into an agreement with the Peshwa by which the Peshwa was to help the Mughal empire against **Ahmad Shah Abdali** and to protect it from such internal rebels as the Indian Pathans and the Rajput *rajas*.
- In return the Peshwa was to be paid ₹ 50 lakhs, granted the *Chauth* of the Punjab, Sindh and several districts of Northern India and made the Governor of Ajmer and Agra. But the agreement failed.
- Safdar Jang organised an equitable system of justice. He adopted a policy of impartiality in the employment of Hindus and Muslims.
- The highest post in his government was held by a Hindu Maharaja **Nawab Rai**. The prolonged period of peace and of economic prosperity of the nobles under the government of the *nawabs* resulted in time in the growth of a distinct Lucknow culture around the Awadh court.
- Lucknow, for long had been an important seat of the Awadh Nawabs. After 1775, Delhi rivalled in its patronage of the arts and literature. It also developed as an important centre of handicrafts. Crafts and culture also percolated to towns under the patronage of local chieftains and *zamindars*.

Shuja-ud-Daula (1754-1775 AD)

- He was the son of Safdar Jang. **Ali Gauhar** (*Shah Alam*), the heir apparent of the puppet Mughal emperor **Alamgir II** was provided protection at his court.
- He was driven out of Delhi by Turani Wazir, **Imad-ul-Mulk**. He was an ally of the Afghan invader **Ahmad Shah Abdali.**
- He concluded the **Treaty of Banaras** (1773 AD), with **Warren Hastings** whereby Kara and Allahabad were sold to the Nawab and British troops were stationed at Awadh to protect the Nawab, for which he had to pay a subsidy to the British.
- He defeated the Rohillas with the help of the British and annexed Rohilkhand to Awadh in 1774 AD.

Asaf-ud-Daula (1775-1797 AD)

- He signed the **Treaty of Faizabad** (1755 AD) with the British. He transferred his capital from Faizabad to Lucknow in 1775 AD.
- He is also known for promoting Lucknow culture and built important monuments like **Imambara** and **Rumi Darwaza.**

Saadat Khan (1798-1840 AD)

- He was elder brother of Asaf. He ascended the throne in 1798 AD with the help of the British.
- He signed a **subsidiary Alliance** with **Lord Wellesley** in November, 1801 AD. By the treaty, the *Nawab* was deprived of about half of his territory for the maintenance of the subsidiary troops.

Wajid Ali Shah (1841-56 AD)

- He was the **last Nawab of Awadh**. During his reign, **Lord Dalhousie** annexed Awadh under the infamous 'Doctrine of Lapse' on the grounds of bad governance.

Independent Kingdoms

They came into existence primarily due to the destablisation of the Mughal control over the Provinces. E.g., 'Mysore and Rajputs Kingdoms'.

Mysore

Next to Hyderabad, the most important power that emerged in South India was Mysore under **Haider Ali.** The kingdom of Mysore had preserved its independence ever since, the end of the Vijayanagara empire.

Mysore maintained a limited association with Mughal empire. It became independent under Hindu **Wodeyar dynasty** in 1565 after the fall of Vijayanagar empire.

Some of the important rulers of Mysore were as follows

Haider Ali (1761-1782 AD)

- He was born in 1721 and started his career as a petty officer in the Mysore army. Though uneducated, he possessed a keen intellect and was a man of great energy, daring and determination. He was also a brilliant commander and a diplomat.
- Haider Ali soon found his opportunity in the wars which involved Mysore for more than 20 years. Cleverly, using the opportunities that came his way, he gradually rose in the Mysore army.
- He soon recognised the advantages of Western military training and applied it to the troops under his own command.
- He established a modern arsenal in **Dindigul** in 1755 with the help of French experts.
- He was responsible for introducing the Mughal administrative and revenue system in his dominions.
- Haider Ali took over Mysore when it was a weak and divided state. Soon, made it one of the leading Indian powers.
- He practiced religious tolerance and his first Diwan and many other officials were Hindus.
- Almost from the beginning of the establishment of his power, Haider Ali was engaged in wars with the **Maratha sardars**, the **Nizam** and the **British**. In 1769, he repeatedly defeated the British forces and reached the walls of Madras.
- Haider Ali died in 1782 in the course of the **Second Anglo-Mysore War** and was succeeded by his son Tipu.

Tipu Sultan (1782-1799 AD)

- Tipu Sultan ruled Mysore from 1782 to 1799. He was the eldest son of **Haider Ali**.
- His desire to change with the times was symbolised in the introduction of a new calendar, a new system of coinage and new scales of weights and measures.
- His personal library contained books on such diverse subjects as religion, history, military science, medicine and mathematics.
- He showed a keen interest in the **French Revolution**. He planted a **Tree of Liberty** at in Srirangapatnam and he became a member of a **Jacobin Club**.

Economic Changes Under Tipu Sultan

- Tipu Sultan tried to do away with the custom of giving jagirs and thus increase state income.
- He also made an attempt to reduce the hereditary possessions of the poligars and to eliminate the intermediaries between the state and the cultivator.
- However, his land revenue was as high as that of other contemporary rulers—it ranged up to one-third of the gross produce.
- But he checked the collection of illegal cesses and he was liberal in granting remissions.

Miliatry Under Tipu Sultan

- Tipu's troops remained disciplined and loyal to him to the last while there was general indiscipline among Indian armies.
- His infantry was armed with muskets and bayonets in the European fashion which were manufactured in Mysore.
- Tipu Sultan also made an effort to build a modern navy after 1796. For this purpose, he established two dockyards, the models of the ships being supplied by the Sultan himself.

Modern Industrialisation Under Tipu Sultan

- Tipu Sultan made some attempts to introduce modern industries in India by importing foreign workmen as experts and by extending state support to many industries.
- He sent emissaries to France, Turkey, Iran and Pegu, Myanmar to develop foreign trade. He also traded with China.
- He even tried to set up a trading company on the pattern of European companies and thus sought to imitate their commercial practices.
- He tried to promote trade with **Russia** and **Arabia** by setting up state trading institutions in the port towns.

Religious Policies of Tipu Sultan

- Tipu was orthodox in his religious views. He was tolerant and enlightened in his approach towards other religions.
- Tipu gave money for the construction of the image of **Goddess Sarda** in the **Sringeri Temple** after, it was looted by Maratha horsemen in 1791.
- Tipu regularly gave gifts to this temple as well as several other temples. The famous temple of **Sri Ranganath** was situated barely a hundred yards from his palace.
- But while he treated the vast majority of his Hindu and Christian subjects with consideration and tolerance, he was harsh on those Hindus and Christians who might directly or indirectly aid the British against Mysore.

Anglo- Mysore Wars

- **First Anglo-Mysore War** (1767-1769) It was concluded by Treaty of Madras.
- **Second Anglo-Mysore War** (1779-1784) It was concluded by Treaty of Mangalore.
- **Third Anglo-Mysore War** (1790-1792) It was concluded by Treaty of Srirangapatnam.
- **Fourth Anglo-Mysore War** (1799) It was concluded by British forces.

The Rajputs

- The principal Rajput states took advantage of the growing weakness of Mughal power to virtually free themselves from central control while at the same time increasing their influence in the rest of the empire.
- In the reign of **Farrukhsiyar** and **Muhammad Shah**, the rulers of Amber and Marwar were appointed governors of important Mughal provinces such as Agra, Gujarat, and Malwa.

Raja Sawai Jai Singh II (1699-1743 AD)

- Jai Singh was a distinguished statesman, law-maker and reformer. He was a man of science in an age when Indians were oblivious of scientific progress.
- He founded the city of **Jaipur** and made it a great seat of science and art. Jaipur was built upon strictly scientific principles and according to a regular plan. Its broad streets are intersected at right angles.
- Jai Singh was above everything a great astronomer. He erected observatories with accurate and advanced instruments, some of them of his own invention, at Delhi, Jaipur, Ujjain, Varanasi and Mathura.
- He drew up a set of tables, entitled **Zij Muhammad Shahi,** to enable people to make astronomical observations.
- He had **Euclid's** 'Elements of Geometry' translated into Sanskrit as also several works on trignometry and **Napier's** work on the construction and use of logarithms.
- Jai Singh was also a social reformer. He tried to enforce a law to reduce the lavish expenditure which the Rajputs had to incur on their daughters' weddings.
- This had given rise to the evil practice of female infanticide. This remarkable prince ruled Jaipur for nearly 44 years from 1699 to 1743.

The Sikhs

- The Sikhism religion was founded at the end of the 15th century by **Guru Nanak**, this religion spread among the Jat peasantry and other lower castes of the Punjab.
- The transformation of the Sikhs into a militant, fighting community was begun by **Guru Har Gobind**.
- It was, however, under the leadership of **Guru Gobind Singh**, the tenth and last Guru of Sikhs, that they became a political and military force.
- After Guru Gobind Singh's death, Banda Bahadur rallied together the peasants and the lower.
- Castes of the Punjab and carried on a vigorous though unequal struggle against the Mughal army.
- However, he failed because Mughal centre was still strong and the upper classes and castes of Punjab joined forces against **Banda Bahadur** for his championship of the lower castes and rural poor.
- The invasion of **Nadir Shah** and **Ahmad Shah Abdali** and the consequent dislocation of Punjab administration gave the Sikhs in opportunity to rise once again.
- With the withdrawal of Abdali from the Punjab, they began to fill the political vacuum. Between 1765 and 1800 they brought the Punjab and Jammu under their control.
- But at this stage, power in the Sikh polity became more horizontally structured, as misls or combinations based on kinship ties, now held territories as units.
- The political authority in Punjab remained decentralised and more horizontally dispersed during this whole period until **Ranjit Singh**, the chief of the **Sukerchakia misl**, tried to raise a more centralised Sikh state at the end of the 18th century.

Punjab

The kingdom of Punjab was founded by Maharaja Ranjit Singh.

Maharaja Ranjit Singh (1780-1839 AD)

- He captured **Lahore** in 1799 and **Amritsar** in 1802.
- He soon brought all Sikh chiefs West of the Sutlej under his control and established his own kingdom in the Punjab. Later, he conquered Kashmir, Peshawar and Multan.

Economic System Under Maharaja Ranjit Singh

- Ranjit Singh did not make any changes in the system of land revenue promulgated earlier by the Mughals.
- The amount of land revenue was calculated on the basis of 50% of the gross produce.

Military Under Maharaja Ranjit Singh

- Ranjit Singh built up a powerful, disciplined and well equipped army along European lines with the help of European instructors.
- His new army was not confined to the Sikhs. He also recruited Gorkhas, Biharis, Oriyas, Pathans, Dogras and Punjabi Muslims.

- Ranjit Singh set up modern industries to manufacture cannon at Lahore and employed Muslim gunners to use them. He possessed the second-best army in Asia, the first being the army of the English East India Company.

Administration Under Maharaja Ranjit Singh

- Ranjit Singh had great capacity for choosing his ministers and officials. His court was full of outstanding men.
- He was tolerant and liberal in religious matters. He patronised not only Sikh but also Muslim and Hindu holy men. Many of his important ministers and commanders were Muslims and Hindus.
- The most prominent and trusted of Maharaja Ranjit Singh's ministers was **Fakir Aziz Uddin**, while his Finance Minister was **Dewan Dina Nath**.
- The Sikh peasants were as much oppressed by Sikh chiefs as was the Hindu or Muslim peasant. In fact, the structure of the Punjab as a state under Ranjit Singh was similar to the structure of the other Indian states of the 18th century.

British Conquest of Punjab

- The process of decline of Sikh empire began with the death of Ranjit Singh in 1839.
- Plans and counter plans of various groups to capture the throne of Lahore provided an opportunity for decesive action by the English.
- The **First Anglo-Sikh War** started in 1845 AD, the Britishers were led by **Hughe Gough**. Lord Hardinge was the Governor-General of India at that time.
- Sikh army was led by **Raja Lal Singh** and **Teg Singh**.
- The end of the First Anglo-Sikh war forced the Sikhs to sign a humiliating treaty in 1846, which included war indemnity of more than one crore rupee to the English.
- Since, the Sikhs were not able to pay entire was indemnity, Kashmir including Jammu was sold to **Gulab Singh**.
- After the defeat of Sikhs in **Second Anglo-Sikh War** (1848-1849), Punjab fell into the hands of English.
- **Lord Dalhousie** was the Governor-General of India at that time.

The Marathas

- They were another powerful regional kingdom to arise out of a sustained opposition to the Mughal Rule.
- The **Maratha Confederacy** was a dominating power in many regions of India during the 18th century. The rule of Marathas presented perhaps the most formidable challenge to Mughal Rule both in Deccan and in the North.
- When **Aurangzeb** died after 40 years of futile warfare in the Deccan, the Marathas still remained to be subjugated and after his death Shivaji's grandson Shahu was released by Bahadur Shah.
- The **Maratha Kingdom** was, however, certainly weakened and the process was further worsened due to the civil war between **Shivaji's** grandson **Shahu** at Satara and his aunt **Tarabai** at Kolhapur who had carried out an Anti-Mughal struggle since, 1700 in the name of her son **Shivaji II**.
- The contest with the Tarabai faction was settled later in the **Treaty of Warna** in 1731, which gave the state of Kolhapur to **Shivaji II**.
- In 1719, **Balaji Vishwanath**, as the head of Maratha force accompanied **Sayyid Hussain Ali Khan**.
- They helped the Sayyid Brothers in overthrowing **Farrukhsiyar** in Delhi. After that Peshwa secured a Mughal *Sanad* (imperial order) recognising Shahu's right to *Chauth* and *Sardeshmukhi* (one-fourth and one-tenth respectively) in six Mughal provinces of Deccan, **Chauth** of Malwa and Gujarat and independent status in Maharashtra.
- After Maratha civil war was brought to an end, the control of the state gradually passed on from the line of **Shivaji** to that of the Peshwas.
- After Balaji Vishwanath died in 1720, he was succeeded as Peshwa by his 20 year old son **Baji Rao I**.
- By 1740, when Baji Rao died, the Marathas had won control over Malwa, Gujarat and parts of Bundelkhand.
- The Maratha families of Gaekwad, Holkar, Scindia and Bhonsle came into prominence during this period in the short period of 20 years.
- In the crucial **Third Battle of Panipat**, the Maratha forces under **Sadashiv Rao Bhao** were routed by **Abdali** and this marked the beginning of the decline of Maratha power.

Kerala

At the beginning of the 18th century Kerala was divided up among a large number of feudal chiefs and *rajas*. The four most important states were those of Calicut, under the Zamorin, Chirakkal, Cochin and Travancore.

Following are the two most prominent kings that ruled over Kerala

King Martanda Varma

- The kingdom of **Travancore** rose into prominence after 1729 under King Martanda Varma, one of the leading statesmen of the 18th century.
- He subdued the feudatories, conquered **Quilon** and **Elay Adam** and defeated the Dutch, thus ending their political power in Kerala.

- He organised a strong army on the Western model with the help of European officers and armed it with modern weapons. He also constructed a modern arsenal.
- He used his new army to expand Northwards and the boundaries of Travancore soon extended from Kanyakumari to Cochin. He undertook many irrigation works, built roads and canals to encourage foreign trade.
- By 1763, all the petty principalities of Kerala had been absorbed or subordinated by the three big states of **Cochin**, **Travancore** and **Calicut**.
- **Haider Ali** began his invasion of Kerala in 1766 and in the end annexed Northern Kerala up to Cochin, including the territories of the Zamorin of Calicut.

Rama Varma

- Rama Varma was successor of Martanda Varma. He was a poet, scholar, musician, renowned actor and a man of great culture.
- He conversed fluently in English. He took a keen interest in European affairs and regularly read newspapers and journals published in London, Calcutta and Madras.

> **Malyalam Literature in 18th Century**
> The 18th century saw a remarkable revival in Malayalam literature. This was due in part to the *rajas* and chiefs of Kerala who were great patrons of literature. Trivandrum, the capital of Travancore, became a famous centre of Sanskrit scholarship in the second half of the 18th century.

The Jats

- The agriculturists Jat settlers living around Delhi, Mathura and Agra had revolted against the oppressive policies of **Aurangzeb.** However, the Mughal Emperor Aurangzeb suppressed the revolt but the area remained disturbed.
- Though originally a peasant uprising, the Jat revolt was led by *zamindars*. Sooner, it became predatory. The Jat state of Bharatpur was set up by **Churaman** and **Badan Singh**. Jat power reached its highest glory under **Suraj Mal** (1756-1763).
- Some important leaders of the community were as follows

Gokla

- He was the *zamindar* of Tilpat, who provided leadership to the Jat uprisings in 1669 AD. The uprising was suppressed by the Mughal Governor, **Hasan Ali Khan.**

Rajarama (1670-1688 AD)

- He was the *Zamindar* of Sinsani. He provided leadership to the Jat uprisings in 1685 AD, which was suppressed by **Raja Bishan Singh Kachwaha** of Amber.

Churaman (1690-1721 AD)

- He obtained *Mansab* from the Mughal ruler **Bahadur Shah I** and established the State of Bharatpur. He served in Bahadur Shah's campaign against **Banda Bahadur.**

Badan Singh (1722 -1756 AD)

- He was the nephew of **Churaman.**
- **Ahmad Shah Abdali** gave him the title of *Raja*. He may be regarded as the real founder of the Jat States of Bharatpur.

Suraj Mal (1756-1763 AD)

- Suraj Mal compelled the Mughal authorities to recognise him by successfully withstanding a siege by Abdali's army. He supported the Marathas in the **Third Battle of Panipat.**
- He tried to lay the foundation of an enduring state by adopting the Mughal revenue system.
- But after his death in 1763, the Jat state declined and was split up among petty *zamindars* most of whom lived by plunder.

Rohilakhand

- **Muhammad Khan Bangash** and Afghan adventurer established his control over the territory around Farrukhabad (between what are now Aligarh and Kanpur).
- During the collapse of administration following Nadir Shah's invasion, **Ali Muhammad Khan** carved out a separate principality, known as Rohilakhand in 1741, at the foothills of the Himalayas between the Ganga in the South and the Kumaon hills in the North.
- The Rohilas clashed constantly with Awadh, Delhi and the Jats.

Later Mughal States and their Rulers

States	Rulers	Years
Hyderabad	Nizam-ul-Mulk Asaf Jah	1724
Karnataka	Saadutullah Khan	1720
Bengal	Murshid Quli Khan	1719-20
Awadh	Saadat Khan Burhan-ul-Mulk	1722
Mysore	Haider Ali	1761
Rohilakhand	Muhammad Khan Bangash	1741

Socio-Economic Conditions During 18th Century

- In 18th century India failed to make progress economically, socially or culturally, at an adequate pace.
- The common people remained impoverished, backward and oppressed, the rich and the powerful enjoyed a life of luxury and lavishness.

Agriculture

- Though agriculture was technically backward, it was worked by the hard labour of peasants. It was backward and stagnant.
- The state, *zamindars* and *jagirdars* and revenue farmers tried to extract maximum amount of farmer's produce from him. It was common across all the autonomous states.

Trade and Industry

- On account of being self-sufficient in handicrafts and agricultural products, India did not import foreign goods on a large scale.
- On the other hand, its industrial and agricultural products were in good demand in foreign markets.
- Hence, its exports were more than its imports; trade was balanced by import of silver and gold. India was known as a **sink of precious metals.**
- Textile industry flourished during 18th century important centres of Textile industry- Dacca, Murshidabad, Patna, Surat, Ahmedabad, Haruch, Chanderi, Burhanpur, Jaunpur, Varanasi, Lucknow, Agra, Multan, Lahore, etc.

Items of Import

- **From the Persian Gulf Region** Pearls, raw silk, wool, dates, dried fruits and rose water
- **From Arabia** Coffee, gold, drugs and honey
- **From China** Tea, sugar, porcelain and silk
- **From Tibet** Gold, musk and woolen cloth
- **From Africa** Ivory and drugs
- **From Europe** Woolen cloth, copper, iron, lead and paper

Items of Export

Cotton textiles, raw silk and silk fabrics, hardware, indigo, saltpeter, opium, rice, wheat, sugar, pepper and other spices, precious stones and drugs.

Status of Education

- The education imparted in 18th century India was still traditional, which could not match with the rapid developments in the West.
- The knowledge was confined to literature, law, religion, philosophy and logic and excluded the study of physical and natural sciences, technology and geography.
- Elementary education among the Hindus and the Muslims was quite widespread.
- The Hindu and Muslim elementary schools were called *pathshalas* and *maktabs* respectively. The education was confined to reading, writing and arithmetic. Children from the lower caste sometimes attended the schools, but female presence was rare.

Social Conditions

- The society of 18th century India was characterised by traditional outlook and stagnation. Though there existed a certain degree of broad cultural unity, people were divided by caste, religion, region, tribe and language.
- The family system was primarily patriarchal and caste was the central feature of the social life of the Hindus. Religious conversions occurred and caste proved to be a major divisive force and element of disintegration in 18th century India.

Position of Women in Society

- In the **patriarchal family system** in India, women possessed little individuality of their own. While upper class women remained at home, lower class women worked in fields and outside their homes supplementing the family income.
- Certain outdated and exploitative social customs and traditions such as the *purdah*, *sati*, **child marriage**, **polygamy** did exist in 18th century.

Condition of Slaves

- European travellers and administrators, who came in the 17th century, reported the widespread prevalence of slaves in India.
- It is believed that some people were compelled to sell their offspring due to economic distress, famines, natural calamities and extreme poverty. Generally higher classes of Rajputs, Khatris and Kayasthas kept women slave for domestic work.

Development of Art and Architecture During 18th Century

- The decline of the imperial Mughals forced talented people to seek the patronage of newly established state courts like Hyderabad, Lucknow, Jaipur, Murshidabad, Patna, Kashmir, etc.
- At Lucknow, **Asaf-ud-Daula** built the **Bada Imambara in 1784**. In the first half of the 18th century, in the South, in Kerala, the **Padmanabhapuram Palace**, was constructed they were famous for its architecture and mural paintings. New schools of painting were born and achieved distinction. The paintings of the **Rajputana** and **Kangra schools** became prominent and revealed new vitality and taste.
- A distinct feature of the literary life of the 18th century was the growth of Urdu language and poetry. It was the period of Urdu poets like **Mir, Sauda, Nazir** and **Mirza Ghalib (19th century).**
- **Kanchan Nambiar** was a noted Malayalam poet. The Tamil language was enriched by sittar poetry.
- **Thayumanavar** (1706-1744 AD), one of the best exponents of Sittar poetry, protested against the abuses of temple rule and the caste system.
- **Heer-Ranjha**, the romantic epic in Punjabi literature, was composed by **Warris Shah**.
- In Sindhi literature, **Shah Abdul Latif** composed *Risalo*, a collection of poems. These are just some examples of literary works in regional languages.

Extra Facts From
Tamil Nadu Board and NIOS

- In South India, Martanda Varma and Rama Varma of Travancore Kerala strengthened their position by using sea and ports.
- Mysore state gained significance during the reign of rulers of Wadiyar dynasty, Kandiraya and Chikka Deva Raya. Later Hyder Ali deposed the Wadiyar dynasty and consolidated and organised Mysore state.
- Under the leadership of Nawab of Awadh, first Faizabad and later Lucknow become a competitive state of Delhi in the field of art, literature and crafts. As a result of cultural harmony, the development of Kathak dance style is seen.
- Amritsar was the centre of Sikh activities from 1720 to 1730 AD. Jassa Singh Ahluwalia laid the foundation of Kapurthala state.
- Jaipur in Eastern Rajasthan (formerly Amber) was under the control of Kachhwaha clan.
- In 1720 AD, Gujarati port Surat lost its prominence while ports like Bombay, Madras and Calcutta became significant.
- Family was the centre and basis of society. Except kerala, society was Patriarchal. Society was Matriachal in Kerela.

24

Administrative and Economic Policies Under British Rule

(SOURCES)

Class-VIII New NCERT Chap 2 (From Trade to Territory), Chap 3 (Ruling the Country Side), Chap 6 (Civilising the 'Native', Educating the Nation), Class-VIII Old NCERT Chap 4 (Administrative Structure, Policies and Impact of British Rule), Class-XII Old NCERT Chap 3 (The Structure of Government and Economic Policies of the British Empire of India, 1757-1857), Tamil Nadu Board (Class XI), NIOS

- **British** rule in India can be divided into two phases: (i) **Phase One** 1773-1857 (The Company Rule) and (ii) **Second Phase** 1857-1947 (The Crown Rule).
- This is a popular classification because it was the year 1857 that completely changed the way British governed in India.
- They received a major jolt in the form of **Revolt of 1857**, that compelled them to bring about some drastic changes in their administrative, economic and social structure.
- Revolt of 1857, is also stated as **First War of Independence** by **VD Savarkar**. It was a cumulative effect of British expansionist policies, economic exploitations and administrative innovation over years. It had an adverse effect on all sections and classes of Indian society. Hence, people actively revolted against the government.
- It was an unexpected revolt from India which had shaken the Britishers. Hence, it became inevitable to bring changes in the administrative, economic and social structure in the country.
- The nature and objective of these changes were to serve the British imperial ideology but unintentionally they introduced elements of the modern State into India's political and administrative system.

Acts and Amendments Under British Rule

Major Acts and Amendments of British Era are described below :

Phase 1 The Company Rule (1773-1857)

- After the Battle of Buxar in 1764, the East India Company got the Diwani (right to collect revenue) of Bengal, Bihar and Orissa.
- An annual subsidy was to be paid to the Mughal Emperor, **Shah Alam II** and an annual pension to the Nawab of Awadh, Shuja-ud-Daula.
- The Company appointed two Indians as the Deputy Diwans—**Mohammad Reza Khan** for Bengal and **Raja Shitab Rai** for Bihar.
- In 1767, British for the first time attempted to intervene in economic affairs and demanded 10% share in the plunder amounting to 4 million pounds annually.
- From the year 1765 to 1772, the dual system of government continued, where the Company had the authority but no responsibility and its Indian representatives had all the responsibility but no authority.

- This period was characterised by :
  - Widespread corruption among servants of the Company who made full use of private trading to enrich themselves.
  - Excessive revenue collection and oppression of peasantry.
  - The Company's bankruptcy, while the servants were flourishing.
- By now the British Government decided to regulate the Company to bring some order into its business. From now, there would be a gradual increase in controlling laws.

Regulating Act of 1773

- The Governor of Bengal was designated as the Governor- General of Bengal and he was nominated as Governor- General for all the three Presidencies of Bengal, Madras and Bombay.
- **Executive Council** of four members was created to assist Governor-General in the administration.
- **Supreme Court at Calcutta** was established in 1774. It comprised of one Chief Justice and three other judges.
- Court of Directors (governing body of the Company) had to report on its revenue, civil and military affairs in India to British Government.

Amending Act of 1781 (Act of Settlement 1781)

- This Act was passed in order to rectify the loopholes in the **Regulating Act of 1773**. It was also known as **Act of Settlement**.
- The activities of the Governor-General, his Executive Council and the servants of the Company were exempted from the jurisdiction of the Supreme Court.
- Supreme Court had to consider religious and social customs of Indians while administering the law.
- Act laid down that the appeals from the Provincial Courts could be taken to the Governor- General in Council and not to the Supreme Court.

Pitt's India Act of 1784

- The Act made distinction between commercial and political functions of the Company.
- **Board of Control** was created to manage the political affairs of the Company.
- Board of Control were empowered to manage political affairs and the civil and military government or revenues of the British possessions in India. Court of Directors was empowered to manage commercial affairs.
- System of **Dual Government** was also established.

Act of 1786

- **Lord Cornwallis** was appointed as Governor-General of Bengal in 1786 and the Act was enacted to endorse his demands.
- He demanded power to supersede decision of his council and would operate as Commander-in-Chief.

Charter Act of 1793

- Governor-General of Bengal was given more power over governments of Bombay and Madras and trade monopoly of the Company was extended for another twenty years.
- Board of Control and their staff were to be paid out of Indian revenues.

Charter Act of 1813

- The Act abolished the trade monopoly of the East India Company in India and asserted sovereignty of British Crown over Company's territories in India.
- It provided for spread of Western education in India and permitted Christian missionaries to come to India.
- Local Governments were authorised to impose taxes.

Charter Act of 1833

- The Act made Governor-General of Bengal as **Governor-General of India** with all civil and military powers. (First Governor-General of India- **Lord William Bentinck**).
- Governor-General of India was given all legislative powers. Laws that were made by this act were known as Acts, where as previously were known as **regulations**.
- Activities of East India Company as a commercial body were ended.
- Competition for selection of Civil Servants was introduced in which Indians could also participate without any discrimination.

Charter Act of 1853

- Legislative and Executive functions of Governor-General's Council were separated and established Governor-General's Legislative Council known as Indian Central Legislative Council.
- **Macaulay Committee** was appointed on Indian Civil Services was appointed in 1854 for recruitment and selection of Civil Servants.
- Local representation of in Central Legislative Council was introduced. Four members were appointed from governments of Bengal, Madras and Agra.

Phase II Crown Rule (1858-1947)

After the Revolt of 1857, Britishs were compelled to bring about some drastic change in administrative, economic and social structure.

Government of India Act, 1858

- This Act was passed due to Revolt of 1857. It was also known as **Act of Good Governance of India.**
- The Act also abolished the East India Company and transferred all its powers and possessions to the Crown.
- Power was now to be exercised by **Secretary of State** for India aided by a Council. Secretary was a member of British Cabinet and was responsible to British Cabinet.
- System of Dual Government was put to an end by abolishing Board of Control and Court of Directors.
- Designation of Governor-General of India was changed to **Viceroy of India** (direct representative of British Crown).
- Governor-General was to have an Executive Council member who were to act as heads of different departments and their position was similar to that of Cabinet Ministers.

Indian Councils Act, 1861

- It enlarged Governor-General's Council for purpose of making laws known as **Imperial Legislative Council.**
- It was authorised to add six to twelve members out of which at least half were to be Indians and it only acted as an advisory body.
- It provided that the Viceroy should nominate some Indians as non-official members of his expanded council.
- In 1862, **Lord Canning**, the then Viceroy, nominated three Indians to his Legislative Council–the **Raja of Banaras**, the **Maharaja of Patiala** and **Sir Dinkar Rao.**
- It initiated the process of decentralisation by restoring the legislative powers to the Bombay and Madras Presidencies.
- It created New Legislative Councils for Bengal, North-Western Provinces and Punjab in 1862, 1886 and 1897 respectively.

Indian Councils Act, 1892

- Under this Act, number of non-official members were increased but maintained official majority in them.
- Functions of Legislative Council were increased and was conferred power to discuss budget and asking questions to executive.
- Under this Act, system of elections were introduced.

Indian Councils Act, 1909

- It is also known as **Morley-Minto Reforms.**
- It increased the size of both Central (from 16 to 60) and Provincial Legislative Council and retained official majority in the Central Legislative Council, but allowed the Provincial Legislative Councils to have non-official majority.
- For the first time, it provided for the association of Indians with the Executive Councils of the Viceroy and Governors.
- **Satyendra Prasad Sinha** became the first Indian to join the Viceroy's Executive Council. He was appointed as the 'Law Member'.
- It introduced a system of communal representation for Muslims by accepting the concept of 'separate electorate'. Thus, the Act 'legalised communalism' and **Lord Minto** came to be known as the **Father of Communal Electorate.**

Government of India Act, 1919

- It is also known as **Montagu-Chelmsford Reforms.**
- The Central and Provincial Legislatures were authorised to make laws on their respective list of subjects.
- Dyarchy System of Government was introduced. It divided the provincial subjects into two parts– **transferred and reserved.**
- The transferred subjects - administered by the Governor with the aid of Ministers responsible to the Legislative Council.
- The reserved subjects - administered by the Governor and his Executive Council without being responsible to the Legislative Council.
- **Bicameralism** and **direct elections** were introduced in the country. Indian Legislative Council was replaced by a Bicameral Legislature consisting of an **Upper House** (Council of State) and a **Lower House** (Legislative Assembly). The majority of members of both the Houses were chosen by direct election.
- A **Central Public Service Commission** was set up in 1926 for recruiting civil servants.

Government of India Act, 1935

- It provided for the establishment of an **All India Federation** consisting of Provinces and Princely States as units.
- The Act divided the powers between the Centre and units in terms of three lists– **Federal List** for Centre, with 59 items, **Provincial List** for provinces, with 54 items, **Concurrent List** for both, with 36 items. Residuary powers were given to the Viceroy.
- It **abolished dyarchy** in the provinces and introduced 'provincial autonomy' in its place.

- **Bicameralism** was introduced in six out of eleven provinces., the legislatures of Bengal, Bombay, Madras, Bihar, Assam and the United Provinces were made bicameral.
- The Act provided for setting up of following institutions in India :
  - Reserve Bank of India
  - Federal Public Service Commission and Provincial Service Commission and Joint Public Service Commission
  - Federal Court (1937)

Indian Independence Act, 1947

- The British rule in India came to an end and India was declared as an independent and sovereign state from 15th August, 1947.
- India was partitioned of India independent dominions of India and Pakistan were created.
- It Act abolished the office of the Secretary of State for India and transferred his functions to the Secretary of State for Commonwealth Affairs.
- It Act designated the Governor-General of India and the Provincial Governors as constitutional (nominal) Heads of the States.

Provincial Administration

- For the administrative convenience, the British had divided India into provinces three of which – Bengal, Madras and Bombay were known as **Presidencies**.
- They were administered by a Governor and his three Executive Councils, who were appointed by the Crown.
- The Central Government exercised authoritarian control over the provincial expenditure. But this system proved quite wasteful in practice.
- In 1870, **Lord Mayo** had taken the first step in the direction of separating central and provincial finances.
- Lord Mayo's scheme was enlarged in 1877 by Lord Lytton who transferred to the provinces certain other heads of expenditure such as Land Revenue, Excise, General Administration and Law and Justice.
- The financial arrangements between the centre and the provinces were to be reviewed every five years.

Local Bodies

- There were many factors which made it necessary for the British Government in India towards establishing local bodies such as
  - Financial difficulties faced by the Government due to over centralisation, made decentralisation imperative.
  - The utilisation of local taxes for local welfare could be used to counter any public criticism of British reluctant to draw upon an already overbourdened treasury or to tax the rich upper class.
- Local bodies were first formed in the period between 1864 and 1868, but in most cases consisted of nominated members and were headed by District Magistrates.
- In 1882, the Government of **Lord Ripon** desired the provincial government to apply the same principle of financial decentralisation in case of local bodies implemented by **Lord Mayo's** Government. For his contributions, Lord Ripon is called **'Father of Local-self Government in India'**.

Rule of Law

- In India, British implemented the rule of law. That means their administration was guided by laws and rules not by the wish or direction of the ruler.
- The law classified the rights of citizens, their responsibilities and special privileges.

Economic Policies of British

- The major difference between the British colonists in India and earlier invaders was that none of the earlier invaders made any structural changes in Indian economy or drained away India's wealth as tribute.
- British rule in India caused a transformation of India's economy into a colonial economy, i.e., the structure and operation of Indian economy were determined by the interests of the British economy.
- The economic policies of British can be broadly divided into three phases which are as follows:

Phase 1 of Mercantilism

- This phase was based on two basic objectives :
  (i) To acquire a monopoly of trade with India, against other English or European merchants or trading companies as well as against the Indian merchants;
  (ii) To directly appropriate or take over governmental revenues through control over State power.
- This phase consisted of large-scale **drain of wealth** from India.
- There was no large-scale import of British manufactures into India but increase in export of Indian textiles.

Phase 2 of Mercentalism /Free Trade/ Industrial Capitalism

- Free entry was also granted to the British capitalists to develop tea, coffee and indigo plantations, trade, transport, mining and modern industries in India.

- The **Permanent Settlement** and the **Ryotwari system** in agriculture were introduced to transform traditional agrarian structure into a capitalist one.
- The taxation and the burden on peasant rose sharply due to economic transformation and costly administration (civil as well as military).

Phase 3 of Mercentilism/Financial Capitalism

- The third stage is often described as the **Era of Foreign Investments** and **International Competition** for Colonies.
- Britain's industrial supremacy was challenged by several countries of Europe, the United States and Japan.
- The strengthening of colonial rule over India was meant to keep out the rivals as well as to attract British capital to India and provide it security.
- As a result, a very large amount of British capital got invested in railways, loans (to the Government of India), trade and to a lesser extent, in plantations, coal mining, jute mills, shipping and banking in India.

Land Revenue System

In order to have an effective control over economy, British introduced many Land Revenue systems in different areas, which are as follows :

Permanent Settlement

- The system of Permanent Settlement was introduced in Bengal, Bihar and Orissa, districts of Banaras and Northern districts of Madras by **Lord Cornwallis** in 1793.
- According to the Permanent Land Revenue Settlement, the *Zamindars* were recognised as the permanent owners of the land and acted as the agents of the government.
- Zamindars controlled numerous villages while jotedars were the rich ryot, trader and money-lender.
- 1/11th of the revenue could be retained by *zamindars* while 10/11th was to be submitted to the Company.
- The estate of the landlord was to be treated as his property and was divisible among his dependents upon his death.
- This system strengthened feudalism in upper sections and slavery in lower sections of society.
- Due to fixation of land revenue, the income of government through land revenue could not increase even if the cost of agricultural land and production increased.
- Most of the *zamindars* had their focus on collection of maximum revenue rather than focusing on betterment of agricultural land, which degraded the condition of farmers.
- *Zamindars* started shifting to the cities, which gave rise to **Absentee Landlordism**.
- **Sunset Law** was introduced in 1794 according to which if a *zamindar* fails to submit the revenue from his land by the sunset of the fixed date, his estate would be confiscated and auctioned.
- 'Fifth report', it ran into 1002 pages, of which over 800 pages were appendices which includes petitions of zamindars and ryots, reports of collectors from different districts and statistical tables on revenue returns. This report was presented in British Parliament in 1813.

Ryotwari System

- It was introduced in the territories of the Company by **Thomas Munroe** and **Captain Reed** in 1820.
- Ryots (or Raiyyats) were recognised as owners of the land they cultivated and the revenue was to be collected directly from them.
- The farmers had to pay revenue between 45%-55% to the Company. The system was revised and improved by **Wingate** and **Goldsmith** after 1836.
- Revenue was not fixed so that government can increase revenue in case of more production. Also, the settlement was not fixed and could be revised between 20 to 30 years when the revenue demand was usually raised.

Mahalwari System

- This system was devised after Permanent Settlement and Ryotwari System. Mahalwari system was formally launched in 1822 based upon the regulation of East India Company Secretary **Holt Mackenzie.**
- It was used in 30% area of British India (North-West provinces, parts of Central India, Punjab and Ganga valley).
- Under this system, revenue was fixed on the basis of assessment of production of the complete village (*mahal*) and was fixed collectively for all the landowners.
- This revenue settlement was done with the landlords who collectively claim to be the landlords of the village.
- Mahalwari system was basically a dual system in which settlement was done collectively with the whole community and also with the individual landlords. The revenue was periodically revised in this system.

Taluqdari System

- The term *taluqdar* has different meanings in different parts of India. In Awadh, *taluqdar* is a great landholder. But in Bengal, a taluqdar is next to *zamindar* in extent of land control and social status.

- Government made an agreement with the *taluqdar* for period of 30 years. He collected the revenue from the villages under his charge. Then, he deposited with revenue the government after deducting cost of collection and his own remuneration.

Banking System Under British Rule

The banking system in India is not a new phenomenon and its earliest evidence can be traced back to the Vedic civilisation.

But the evolution and development of the modern banking system can be traced back to the British era. The first modern bank set up in India was **Bank of Hindustan** in 1770.

The development of the Indian banking system can be segregated into two phases :

- Pre independence era (1786 to 1947)
- Post independent era (after 1947)

Pre-Independence Era of Banking System (1786 to 1947)

- The roots of the modern banking system can be traced back to the establishment of the **Bank of Calcutta** in 1786. Later on, the British set up Presidency Banks at Bengal, Bombay and Madras.
- The **Bank of Calcutta** was set up on 2nd June, 1806. The **Bank of Bombay** was set up on 15th April, 1840 and the **Bank of Madras** was established on 1st July, 1843.
- These three Presidency banks were merged in 1921 and a new bank was formed which was named as the **Imperial Bank of India**. Later on, in 1955 the Imperial Bank of India was nationalised by the Government and was renamed as the **State Bank of India.**
- **Allahabad Bank**, established in 1855 was the first Indian-owned Bank. The **Punjab National Bank** was set up in 1895. The **Bank of India** was established in Mumbai in 1906.
- Between 1906 and 1913, many commercial banks including Indian bank, **Central Bank of India, Bank of Mysore, Canara Bank** and **Bank of Baroda** were set up under the Indian ownership.
- **Reserve Bank of India** (RBI) was established in 1935, on the recommendations of Hilton Young Commission, the Royal Commission on Indian currency and Finance set up by the British Government.
- The RBI started functioning as the Central Bank of the country. It is a statutory body established through RBI Act, 1934.
- During this phase, the development of banking system in India was very slow and it experienced periodic failures. The banking system neglected the rural and agricultural sector and was mostly concentrated in the urban areas.

Evolution and Reforms in Civil Services

- The **Regulating Act of 1773**, brought the Company's management under the control of British Government.
- **Lord Cornwallis** after becoming the Governor-General of India in February, 1786, brought about a series of legal and administrative reforms.
- He enacted the **Cornwallis Code** in 1793 to improve overall governance of East India Company in India and separated revenue administration and judicial administration by establishing the Cornwallis Code.
- He is also referred to as **Father of Civil Service in India** as he reformed and reorganised administration for the Company.
- To check rampant corruption among Company servants, Lord Cornwallis debarred civil servants from taking presents, bribes, etc.
- He even raised their salaries and debarred private trade for such servants.
- Governor-General **Wellesley** established Fort William College for training of new recruits, which was later disapproved by the Directors of Company.

Progress Made Under Lord Macaulay

- **The Charter Act of 1833**, allowed native Indians to be part of administration in British India.
- The Charter set up India's **First Law Commission** under the Chairmanship of **Lord Macaulay** which recommended codification of the Penal Code, the Criminal Procedure Code and other legal provisions.
- The concept of a merit based modern Civil Service in India was introduced in 1854 after submission of Lord Macaulay's Report of the **Select Committee** of British Parliament. The Report recommended that patronage-based system of East India Company should be replaced by a **Permanent Civil Service** based on a merit-based system with entry through competitive examinations.
- Recommendations of Lord Macaulay (in the backdrop of **Charter Act of 1853**, along with Queen's Proclamation of 1858) led to the enactment of **Indian Civil Services Act, 1861**. It allowed Indians to compete at par with the Britishers in an open merit-based recruitment.
- In 1864, **Satyendra Nath Tagore** became the first Indian to succeed at the exam.

Reforms Under Lord Dufferin

- Formation of **Indian National Congress** in 1885, led to a growing demand for simultaneous examination both in India and London including the demand for raising the upper age limit.
- On the basis of these rising demands by the Moderate faction of Indian National Congress, **Lord Dufferin** appointed **Aitchison Committee** on Public Services in 1886. It aimed to investigate into the problems of civil services in India.
- The Commission rejected the idea of simultaneous examination but rather proposed setting up of provincial civil service. The members of this service would be separately recruited in every province either by promotion from lower ranks.
- The recommendations of Aitchison Committee were accepted and the covenanted civil service came to be known as **Civil Service of India**. The provincial service was called after the particular province.

Royal Commission on the Superior Civil Services in India : Lee Commission, 1923

- The next major development in the permeation of civil services in Indian roots was the appointment of **Royal Commission** on the Superior Civil Services in India. It was also known as **Lee Commission**.
- The Commission was appointed by the British Government in 1923 to consider the ethnic composition of the superior Indian public services of the Government of India. It had equal numbers of Indian and British members.
- Earlier, **Islington Commission** (1917) in its report of 1917 had recommended that 25% of the higher government posts should go to the Indians.
- The Lee Commission examined the recommendations of the Islington Commission report and reviewed the existing position of two groups of services i.e., **All India Services** and the **Central Services**. The Provincial Services were not considered as they had already come under the control of the provincial governments.
- On the basis of Islington Commission's report, the Lee Commission proposed in 1924 that 20% of the superior posts should be filled by promotions from provincial civil services. The out of remaining 80%, 40% should be British and 40% should be directly recruited Indians.
- The Lee Commission, in its report in the year 1924, recommended that the statutory Public Service Commission contemplated by the **Government of India Act, 1919**, should be established without delay.
- So, on 1st October, 1926, for the first time the **Public Service Commission** was set up in India.

Police System Under British Rule

The **Indian Councils Act of 1861**, created a professional police bureaucracy in India and it developed over the years under different Governors.

Cornwallis System

- With the rise of the Company's authority, a need was felt for the creation of a police force which maintained the law and order.
- The new system of *Faujdars* being replaced by *English Magistrates* as police functions proved to be inadequate in bringing down the crime rate. Hence, **Lord Cornwallis** realised the need for police reforms and he made many changes in the police organisation.
- Lord Cornwallis denied the *Zamindars* of their policing powers, divided the district into *thanas* or units of police jurisdiction of 20 to 30 miles.
- Each unit was under an officer known as the *Darogas* who was appointed by the Magistrates and placed under their supervision.
- *Darogas* came to be seen as the medium of the Company's power and control over the rural areas. This came to be known as the **Cornwallis System.**

Changes Made in the 19th Century

- The *Daroga* system was formally abolished in 1812.
- The *Tehsildars* were deprived of their police duties much earlier in 1807. The **District Collector** was made incharge of the village police.
- This led to an extreme concentration of power in the office of Collector since, he was responsible for revenue, police and magisterial functions.

Sind Model

- The existing system hardly produced satisfactory results in terms of upholding law and order throughout the empire.
- Then a new model was experimented within Sind after it was conquered by **Sir Charles Napier** in 1843.
- The previous practice of trying to adopt the indigenous systems to the needs of the colonial state was discarded.
- A separate police department with its own officers was established on the lines of **Royal Irish Constabulary** which was found to be ideally suited for colonial conditions.
- The Sind model was extended to Punjab in 1849, Bombay in 1853 and Madras in 1859; but with various modifications.

Indian Police After, 1857

- The **Revolt of 1857**, had shaken the foundations of British Empire and made them more conscious about the need to have an effective machinery for collection of information and for policing the Empire's territories.
- The **Police Commission** appointed in 1860 had provided a basic structure for the police establishment needed by the Empire. It led to the enactment of the **Police Act of 1861**.
- In the new organisation, **Military Police** were eliminated and the **Civilian Police** were organised on a provincial basis.
- The entire police organisation was placed under the control of the civilian authorities. For a long time, the positions of the inspector general were filled by civil servants.
- The district superintendents were to be incharge of rural police and the *Daroga* became the sub-inspector. The new system had solved the age-old problem of integrating the rural police into the imperial structure.
- The **Police Commission of 1902**, had provisions for the appointment of educated Indians to the position of officers but below the rank of European officers.
- The police under the colonial rule gradually became successful in reducing major crimes such as dacoit. They were also able to prevent the organisation of a large-scale conspiracy against the colonial rule.

Judicial Policies Under British Rule

- The Judicial System in India was neither adopted proper procedures nor had the proper organisation of the law court from the ancient India to Mughal India.
- The beginning of a common law system, based on recorded judicial precedents, can be traced to the establishment of **Mayor's Courts** in Madras, Bombay and Calcutta in 1726 by the East India Company.
- With the Company's transformation from a trading company into a ruling power, new elements of judicial system replaced the existing Mughal legal system.
- Various Governor-Generals introduced various reforms in Judicial systems. Some of them are as follows :

Reforms Under Warren Hastings

- District *Diwani Adalats* were established in districts to solve civil disputes. These *adalats* were placed under the Collector and had Hindu law applicable for Hindus and the Muslim law for Muslims and District Fauzdari Courts were set up to try criminal disputes.
- Under the **Regulating Act of 1773**, a Supreme Court was established at Calcutta.

Reforms Under Cornwallis

- The District Fauzdari Courts were abolished and instead, **Circuit Courts** were established at Calcutta, Dacca, Murshidabad and Patna.
- The District Diwani Adalat was now designated as the district, city or the Zila Court and placed under a district judge.

Reforms Under William Bentinck

- The four **Circuit Courts** were abolished and their functions transferred to Collectors under the supervision of the Commissioner of revenue and circuit.
- *Sadar Diwani Adalat* and a *Sadar Nizamat Adalat* were set up at Allahabad for the convenience of the people of Upper Provinces.
- In 1860, it was provided that the Europeans can claim no special privileges except in criminal cases and no judge of an Indian origin could try them.
- In 1865, the Supreme Court and the *Sadar Adalats* were merged into three **High Courts** at **Calcutta, Bombay** and **Madras**.
- In 1935, the **Government of India Act**, provided for a **Federal Court** (set up in 1937), which could settle disputes between governments and could hear limited appeals from the High Courts.

Transport and Communication System Under British Rule

- Upto the middle of the 19th century, the means of transport in India were backward. They were confined to bullock-cart, camel and packhorse.
- The British rulers soon realised that a cheap and easy system of transport was a necessary if British manufactures were to flow into India on a large-scale.
- The British rulers introduced steamships on the rivers and also improved the roads. Work of the **Grand Trunk Road** from Calcutta to Delhi began in 1839 and completed in the 1850s. Efforts were also made to link by road the major cities, ports and markets of the country.

Development of Railways

- The first railway engine designed by **George Stephenson** was put on the rail in England in 1814. Railways developed rapidly during the 1830s and 1840s.
- In 1831, the earliest suggestion to build a railway in India was made in Madras. But the wagons of this railway were to be drawn by horses.
- Construction of steam-driven railways in India was first proposed in 1834 in England. It was given strong

political support by England's railway promoters and mercantile houses trading with India.

- The first railway line running from **Bombay to Thane** was opened in 1853.
- **Lord Dalhousie**, who became Governor-General of India in 1849, was an advocate of rapid railway construction.
- Dalhousie proposed a network of four main trunk lines which would link the interior of the country with the big ports and inter-connect the different parts of the country.
- The railway lines were laid primarily with a view to link India's raw material producing areas in the interior with the ports of export. The Britishers neglected the needs of Indian industries regarding their markets and their sources of raw materials.
- Moreover, the railway rates were fixed in a manner so as to favour imports and exports and to discriminate against internal movement of goods.
- Several railway lines in Burma and North-Western India were built at high cost to serve British imperial interests.

Development of Post and Telegraph System

- The British also established an efficient and modern postal system and introduced the telegraph.
- The first telegraph line from **Calcutta to Agra** was opened in 1853.
- **Lord Dalhousie** introduced postage stamps. Previously, cash payment had to be made when a letter was posted. He also cut down postal rates and charged a uniform rate.

Impact of Economic Policies of British in India

- Indian goods were purchased at cheap rates and sold in high prices in England. Cheap and machine-made imports flooded the Indian market after the **Charter Act of 1813**, allowing one-way free trade for the British citizens. On the other hand, Indian products found it more and more difficult to enter the European markets.
- The newly introduced rail network helped the European products to reach the remotest corners of the country. Thus, from being a net exporter, India became a net importer.
- The loss of traditional livelihood was not accompanied by a process of industrialisation in India.
- **By 1815, half of the total land in Bengal had passed into new hands—merchants and moneylenders. Increase in number of intermediaries to be paid gave rise to absentee landlordism and increased the burden on the peasant.**
- **The cultivator had neither the means nor any incentive to invest in agriculture. The *zamindar* had no roots in the villages, while the Government spent little on agricultural, technical or mass education. All these were significant cause of low level of productivity.**
- **Regular famines became a common feature in India. These famines were not just because of food grain scarcity, but were a direct result of poverty imposed by colonial forces in India.**

Commercialisation of Agriculture

- **The later half of the 19th century, saw the emergence of the commercialisation of agriculture. Now, agriculture began to being influenced by commercial considerations.**
- **Certain specialised crops began to be grown not for consumption in the village but for sale in the national and even international markets.**
- **For the Indian peasant, commercialisation seemed a forced process. There was hardly any surplus for them to invest in commercial crops.**
- **Commercialisation linked Indian agriculture with international market trends and their fluctuations.**
- **Forcible growing of commercial crops proved hazardous for peasants because they had to buy food grains at high prices and sell cash crops at low prices.**
- **Commercialisation of agriculture resulted in reduced area of cultivation of food crops due to substitution of commercial non-food grains instead of food grains.**
- **This had a devastating effect on rural economy and got manifested in the series of famines.**
- **The devastating effects of 1876-78 famine compelled the British Government to do something substantial to check the recurrence of famines in India. Hence, they formed three Famine Commissions in 1878, 1897 and 1900 respectively**

Destruction of Traditional Indian Industries

- **Indian industry such as ship-building and steel industries were crushed. The development of railways was not coordinated with India's industrial needs and it demanded in a commercial rather than an industrial revolution. Such developments were considered more for benefits of British rather than Indians.**
- **It was only in the second half of the 19th century that modern machine based industries started coming up in India.**

- In 1854, the first cotton textile mill was set up in Bombay by **Cowasjee Nanabhoy Davar** and the first jute mill came up in 1855, in **Rishra** (Bengal). Most of the modern industries were foreign owned and controlled by British managing agencies.
- The basic assertion of these early intellectuals was that India was poor and growing poorer due to British imperialism.
- Since, the causes of India's economic backwardness were man-made, they were explainable and removable. The problem of poverty was seen as a problem of raising productive capacity and energy of the people or as a problem of national development.

Impact of Powerful Class of Manufacturers

- The class of manufacturers began to attack the monopolisation of the Company rule. They discouraged imports of manufacturers from India and encouraged exports of its own products to India.
- From 1793 to 1813, they launched a powerful campaign against the Company and its commercial privileges. In 1813, they finally succeeded in abolishing its monopoly of Indian trade.
- The Government of India now followed a policy of free trade of British goods. However, this free trade imposed on India was one-sided. Indian handicrafts were exposed to the unequal competition of the machine-made products of Britain and gradually faced extinction.
- Indian hand-made goods were unable to compete against the much cheaper products of British mills.
- These mills were rapidly improving their productive capacity by using inventions and a wider use of system power.
- Instead of exporting manufactured products, India was now forced to export raw materials like raw cotton and raw silk, plantation products like Indigo, tea or foodgrains, which were in short supply in Britain.

Extra Facts From Tamil Nadu Board and NIOS

- Charles Trevelyan to a select committee of the House of common in 1840 made the following observation "The peculiar kind of silky cotton formely grown in Bengal, from which the Dacca muslins used to be made is hardly ever seen."
- The Torture commission, appointed by the Company government in Madras in its report presented in 1854 exposed the atrocities perpetrated by the Indian revenue and police official in the process of collecting land tax from the cultivator.
- **Madras famine of (1876-1878)** The failure of two successive monsoon caused a severe famine in the Madras Presidency during 1876-1878.
- R.C. Dutt estimated that during the last decade of the reign of queen Victoria (1891-1901) of the total income 647 million pounds, 159 million pounds drained to England. This worked to 44% of the total income of the country.

25

Civil Uprisings, Peasant, Tribal & Labour Movements

(SOURCES)

Class-VIII New NCERT Chap 3 (Ruling the Countryside), Chap 4 (Tribals, Dikus and the Vision of a Golden Age), Class-XII New NCERT Chap 11 (Mahatma Gandhi and the Nationalist Movement), Class-XII Old NCERT Chap 13 (Struggle For Swaraj (1927-1947)), Tamil Nadu Board (Class XI), NIOS

- Although the **Revolt of 1857**, is considered as the first major uprising against the British, but it is considered as an amalgamation of many civil and tribals that took place before the revolt.
- There was a building resentment against the British rule which manifested itself in several sessions of resistance by different groups of people in different regions of India.
- Erosion of the traditional forms of authority and increased economic pressure were two basic reasons for these uprisings.
- The rebellions in pre 1857 period can be divided into following categories:
  1. Civil and Peasant Uprisings
  2. Tribal Movements

Civil and Peasant Uprisings in India

Important civil and peasant uprisings in India are discussed as follows:

Sanyasi Revolt (1763-1800)

- The disastrous famine of 1770 and government restriction on people from visiting holy places provoked **Sanyasis in Eastern India**. This led to the rebellion against the government.
- They were joined by farmers, evicted landlords, disbanded soldiers.
- **Majnu Shah Fakir** was the leader of the revolt. Focal point of the revolt was Rangpur to Dhaka.
- Sanyasis defeated a Company of sepoys and killed the commander. They captured some districts, virtually running a parallel government. This rebellion continued till the end of the 18th century.
- Governor-General **Warren Hastings** launched a military campaign against Sanyasis.
- **Chirag Ali, Musa Shah, Bhawani Pathak** and **Debi Chaudhurani** were important leaders of the revolt.
- **Debi Chaudhurani's** participation is an important feature as it showed the active participation of the women in early resistances against the British.
- **Bankim Chandra Chattopadhyay** wrote Anandamath, a semi-historical novel which is based on the Sanyasi Revolt.

Peasants Uprising of Rangpur (1783)

- The **Rangpur Dhing** (rebellion) erupted in the district of Rangpur and Dinajpur in Bengal in 1783.
- It was a protest by the peasants and the *zamindars* against the very high demands of revenue by the government and revenue contractors.
- At that time, the **Ijaradari system** was prevalent according to which the *ijardar* (revenue farmer) was contracted by the Company to pay revenue that was fixed either annually or every 5 years on a piece of land.

- The *ijardar* was not interested in the welfare of the farmers who cultivated the land under him or in the development of the land.
- One such revenue contractors, **Debi Singh** practiced extremely harsh measures against the peasants.
- When the peasants sent a petition to the Company asking for relief, it did not pay any heed to the farmers' grievances. This led to the farmers taking things into their own hands.
- They elected **Dirhinjanarayana** as their leader and attacked local kutcherries, tore houses of crops of local agents of the contractors and government officials. Both Hindus and Muslims fought side by side in the rebellion.
- Ultimately, the government's armed forces took control of the situation and suppressed the revolt.

Poligar Revolt (1795-1805)

- The poligars (or palayakkarargal) of South India gave a stiff resistance to the British between 1795 and 1805.
- The main centres of these strong uprisings were Tinneveli (or Thirunelveli), Ramanathapuram, Sivaganga, Sivagiri, Madurai and North Arcot.
- The problem started in 1781, when the **Nawab of Arcot** gave the management and control of Tinneveli and the Carnatic Provinces to the East India Company.
- This arrangement caused resentment among the poligars who had, for long considered themselves as independent sovereign authorities within their respective territories.
- **Kattabomman Nayakan,** the poligar of Panjalankurichi, led the insurrection between 1795 and 1799.

Velu Thampi Revolt (1808-1809)

- In 1808-09, **Velu Thampi**, the Dewan of Travancore, rose up in rebellion against the British attempt to remove him from the Diwanship.
- He opposed the heavy burden imposed on the state through the **Subsidiary Alliance System.**
- In one of the protests Velu Thampi was injured and died in forest. However, even though dead, he was publicly hanged as an example to the fate of those who rose against the British.

Paika Rebellion (1817)

- The **Paiks of Odisha** were the traditional landed militia (foot soldiers) and enjoyed rent free land tenures for their military service and policing functions on a hereditary basis.
- The oppressive land revenue policy of the Company caused resentment among *zamindars* and peasants alike. Common masses were affected by the rise in prices of salt due to taxes imposed on it, abolition of **cowrie currency** and the requirement of payment of taxes in silver, etc.
- The leader of the rebellion was **Bakshi Jagabandhu Bidyadhar**. He along with support of **Mukunda Deva**, the last Raja of Khurda and other *zamindars* of the region led an army of Paikas. It forced the East India Company forces to retreat. The rebellion came to be known as the **Paika Bidroh** (rebellion).

Revolt of Mysore (1830-31)

- After the defeat of **Tipu Sultan** and imposition of the subsidiary alliance, the financial pressure from the Company on the Mysore ruler increased.
- It compelled him to increase revenue demands from the *zamindars*. The increasing burden of revenue ultimately fell on the cultivators.
- The corruption and extortion of local officials added to the existing miseries of the peasants.
- The growing discontent of the peasants broke out into an open revolt in the province of Nagar, one of the four divisions of Mysore.
- Peasants from other provinces joined the rebellious peasants of Nagar and the rebel peasants were led by **Sardar Malla**, the son of a common ryot of **Kremsi.**
- The peasants defied the authority of the Mysore ruler. The British force regained control of Nagar from the rebel peasants after strong opposition and ultimately the administration of the country passed into the hands of the British.

Moplah Rebellion (1835-1921)

- The Moplah rebellions of Malabar, South India, were not only directed against British but also the Hindu landlords. The relations of the Arabs traders with the Malayali society can be traced back to the ninth century.
- The traders helped the local Hindu chieftains and were granted concessions. Many of the Arab traders settled in Malabar marrying mostly Nayar and Tiyar women; and the subsequent descendants came to be known as **Moplahs.**
- Their numbers also increased with the conversion of Hindus from the lower castes, especially the **Cherumars** who were slave labourers and hoped to gain better social status upon conversation.
- The Moplahs were settled, became agriculturalists and joined the ranks of landless labourers, cultivating tenants, fishermen and petty traders.
- In the traditional Malabar land system, the *Jenmi* held land by birthright and were mostly high caste Hindus and let it out to others for cultivation.

- The other main sections of the Malabar society were the **Kanamdar,** who were mostly Moplahs, the **Verumpattamdar** (cultivators) and agricultural labourers. The peasants were mostly the Muslim Moplahs.
- The land was given by the ruling raja to **Namboodiri** Brahmins whose obligation was to look after the temple and related institutions and the chieftains (mostly Nayars), who provided martial aid when needed.
- Traditionally, the net produce of the land was shared equally between the three. But, during the reign of **Haider Ali** and **Tipu Sultan,** Namboodiri Brahmins and Nayar Chiefs fled and the subsequent vacuum was filled by the **Moplahs**.
- The conflict arose in 1792, after Malabar's cession to the British. After the return of the exiled Namboodiri Brahmins and Nayars, the government re-established and acknowledged their landlord rights.
- The British by recognising the **Jenmis** as the absolute owners of the land gave them the right to evict the tenants at will. This reduced the other two groups to the status of tenants and leaseholders.
- The courts and the law officers sided with the Jenmis. The law court and the police started tightening their hold and demands on the subordinate classes. Thus, the Moplah peasantry rose up in revolt.
- According to **Dhanagare,** the first outbreak occurred in 1836 and during the period of 1834-1854, there were 22 uprisings, out of which uprising of 1841 and 1849 were quite serious.
- The faithful sacrificed their lives in the belief that as **Ahadis** would go straight to heaven.
- The **second phase of the revolt** was recorded in 1882-1885, while another uprising occurred in 1876.

Gadkari Revolt (1844)

- The revolts in and around Kolhapur region of Maharashtra state were led by Gadkaris. They were hereditary servants attached to Maratha forts, that were disbanded.
- There was a revolt led by **Daji Krishna Pandit** and occupied the Samangarh and Bhudargarh forts. Similarly, the discontent among people caused a revolt in **Savantvadi** areas.

Indigo Revolt (1859-1860)

- Under the **ryotwari system**, the planters forced the ryots to sign a contract, an agreement (*satta*).
- In April 1860, all the farmers in the Barasat division of the districts Nadia and Pabna went on a strike and refused to grow indigo.
- In March 1859, thousands of ryots in Bengal refused to grow indigo in Nadia district of Bengal. As the rebellion spread, ryots refused to pay rents to the planters and attacked indigo factories armed with swords and spears, bows and arrows.
- Women turned up to fight with pots, pans and kitchen implements. Those who worked for the planters were socially boycotted and the *gomasthas* – agents of planters – who came to collect rent were beaten up.
- Farmers were led by the **Biswas brothers of Nadia, Rafiq Mondal of Malda** and **Kader Molla of Pabna.** The revolt also received support from many *zamindars* notably **Ramrattan Mullick of Narail**.
- The play *Nil Darpan* (The Mirror of Indigo) by **Dinabandhu Mitra** written in 1858-1859 portrayed the farmers' situation accurately.
- It showed how farmers were coerced into planting indigo without adequate payment.
- The play became a talking point and it urged the Bengali intelligentsia to lend support to the indigo revolt.

Pabna Rebellion (1873-1875)

- In larger parts of Eastern Bengal, landlords forcefully collected rents and land taxes, often enhanced for the poor peasants.
- The peasants were also prevented from acquiring **Occupancy Rights under Act X of 1859**.
- In May 1873, an **Agrarian League** was formed in the **Yusuf Shahi Pargana** of Pabna district, Patna (East Bengal). It raised funds to meet litigation expenses. It organised mass meetings in which villagers were called by the sounding of buffalo horns, drums and night.
- Rent strikes were organised, funds were raised and the struggle spread throughout Patna and to other districts of East Bengal. The struggle was mainly legal resistance and little violence.
- The discontent continued till 1885 when the Government by the **Bengal Tenancy Act of 1885**, enhanced the occupancy rights.
- The Pabna revolt and similar movements in other districts evoked sharply varied reactions among the Bengali educationists.
- The *zamindar* dominated British Indian Association was bitterly hostile and its organ Hindu Patriot tried to portray the Pabna movement as a communal agitation of Muslim peasants against Hindu landlords.
- Though the bulk of the peasants in Pabna happened to be Muslim and their *zamindars* mostly Hindus, the communal element was as yet virtually absent.

- The three principal leaders of the agrarian league were the petty landholder **Ishan Chandra Roy**, the village headman **Shambhu Pal** (both caste Hindus), and the Muslim jotedar **Khoodi Mollah**.
- The struggle was supported by **Bankim Chandra Chatterjee, RC Dutt** and the Indian Association under **Surendranath Banerjee**.

Deccan Riots (1874-75)

- The Deccan Riots took place in the Ryotwari areas of Pune and Ahmednagar of Maharashtra.
- The main reasons for the revolt were that the land revenue was very high and farmers had to pay land Revenue even during bad seasons.
- Sahukars, those who lent money to farmer were loyal to company. They lent farmer with minimum interest rate but after the end of American Civil War, they asked farmers to return the money with higher interest rates.
- During **American Civil War** in 1860, there was a cotton boom but in 1864, ended of war led to the decline in cotton boom and government raised land revenue.
- Farmers had taken loans from moneylenders, but now they were unable to repay them. As a result, moneylender took away their land, cattle, jewelry and property.

Eka Movement (1921)

- Peasant discontent began to resurface in the United Province by the end of 1921, mainly in the Northern districts of Hardoi, Bahraich, Sitapur.
- The issues they raised included excessive rents which were 50% higher than the recorded rates, the oppression by *thekedars* who were incharge of revenue collection and the practice of share-rents.
- Eka or the Unity Movement was under the leadership of **Madari Pasi**.
- Its meetings symbolised a religious ritual in which the peasants who had assembled took the vows to pay the rent on time. Only the recorded rent was refused to leave when they get evicted and not surrender to forced labour.
- In Uttar Pradesh, the revolt began under the leadership of the Fiji-returned indentured labourer **Baba Ramachandra**, who operated independently but against the backdrop of the **Non-Cooperation** and the **Khilafat Movement**.
- The **Kisan Sabha Movement** under **Baba Ramachandra** was basically a tenant and small *zamindars* movement against big landlords and *taluqdars*.
- Inspired by the Non-Cooperation Movement, the Eka organisers added three important demands to the original charter:
  - Fight for self-rule; adoption and promotion of Swadeshi
  - A pledge to avoid the British judicial system
  - Resolution of all conflicts at the local Panchayat level, thereby directly bringing it in confrontation with the British Raj.
- The increasingly militant movement threatened to destroy the feudal-colonial order in the region and prompted government to pass **Awadh Rent (Amendment) Act, 1922**.

Peasant Movements

Movements/ Organisations	Location	Leaders
Pagal Panthis (1825-35)	Bengal (*now in Bangladesh*)	Karam Shah, Tipu Shah (*Hajong and Garo tribes*)
Sambhalpur Uprisings (1840)	Sambhalpur	Surendra Sai
The Kuka Revolt (1840)	West Punjab	Bhagat Jawahar Mal and Baba Balak Singh
Gadkari Rebellion (1844-45)	Kolhapur	Gadkaris
Indigo Revolt (1860)	Nadia district of Bengal	Digambar Biswas, Bishnu Biswas, Harish Chandra Mukherjee (*Editor of newspaper Hindu Patriot*)
Poona Sarvajanik Sabha (1870)	Pune	MG Ranade
Pabna Agrarian Uprising (1873)	Pabna district of Bengal	Shah Chandra Roy, Shambhu Pal
Ramosis Uprising (1877-87)	Ramosis, Maharashtra	Vasudev Balwant Phadke
Bijolia Movement (1905, 1913, 1916, 1927)	Rajasthan	Sitaram Das, Vijay Pathak Singh
Champaran Satyagraha (1917)	Bihar	Gandhiji, Dr Rajendra Prasad, Raj Kumar Shukla
Kheda Satyagraha (1918)	Uttar Pradesh	Gandhiji
United Province Kisan Sabha (1918)	Uttar Pradesh	Gauri Shankar Mishra, Indra Narayan Dwivedi,
Uttar Pradesh Kisan Sabha (1918)	Uttar Pradesh	Indra Narayan Dwivedi, Madan Mohan Malaviya
Awadh Kisan Sabha (1920)	Oudh	Jawaharlal Nehru, Baba Ramachandra
Eka (1921)	Awadh	Madari Pasi
Moplah Rebellion (1835-1921)	Malabar region (*Kerala*)	Sayyid Ali, Sayyid Fazi

Movements/ Organisations	Location	Leaders
Andhra Ryots Association (1928)	Andhra Pradesh	NG Ranga
Bardoli Satyagraha (1928)	Bardoli (*Gujarat*)	Vallabhbhai Patel
All India Kisan Sabha (1936)	United Province	Swami Sahajanand
Tebhaga Movement (1946)	Tebhaga (*Bengal*)	Leaders of Bengal Kisan Sabha
Telangana Movement (1946-51)	Hyderabad	Praja Mandal and Communist Party of India

Tribal Movements in British India

Important tribal movments are as follows :

Khasi Uprising (1793-1833)

- British occupied the hilly region between Garo and Jaintia hills with and intention of building a road linking the Brahmaputra valley with Sylhet passing through the Khasi domain.
- Khasis in 1793 revolted under the leadership of **Tirut Singh**, a Khasi chief in order to protest against mobilisation of workers for road construction and Garos joined them in their revolt.
- By 1833, the superior English military force had suppressed the revolt.

Bhil Uprising (1819)

- The Bhils were mostly concentrated in the hill ranges of Khandesh. The British occupied Khandesh in 1818 which agitated the Bhils because they were suspicious of outsiders' incursion into their territory.
- Moreover, it was believed that **Trimbakji**, rebel minister of **Baji Rao I**, instigated the Bhils against the British occupation of Khandesh.
- There was a general insurrection in 1819 and the Bhils in several small groups ravaged the plains.
- There were similar types of insurrection quite often by the Bhil chiefs against the British.
- The British Government used its military force to suppress the rebels and at the same time tried to win them over through various conciliatory measures. But the British measures failed to bring the Bhils to their side.

Ramosi Uprising (1822, 1825-1826)

- The Ramosis, the hill tribes of the Western Ghats, had not reconciled to British rule and the British pattern of administration.
- They resented the policy of annexation. After the annexation of the Maratha territories by the British, the **Ramosis**, who had been employed by the Maratha administration, lost their means of livelihood.
- They rose under **Chittur Singh** in 1822 and plundered the country around Satara.
- In 1825-1826, they again rose up in rebellion under the banner of **Umaji** on account of acute famine and scarcity in Pune. For three years they ravaged the Deccan.
- Finally, the British Government pacified them not only by condoning their crimes but also by offering them land grants and recruiting them in the Hill Police.
- Ramosis again rose later from 1877 to 1887 against the British failure to take up anti-famine measures. It was led by **Vasudev Balwant Phadke**.
- It was protested in the violent manner and not in the peaceful manner.

Pagal Panthi Revolt (1825-35)

- The main reason behind the revolt was the *zamindari* oppression in North Bengal.
- Pagal Panthi was as semi-religious sect founded by **Karam Shah**. It consisted of **Hajong** and **Garo tribes**. The revolt was organised under the leadership of Karam Shah's son **Tipu Shah**.
- Initially, British agreed to Pagal Panthi demand, made arrangement to protect the cultivators from *zamindar*. But later, massive military operation to suppress Pagal Panthis was carried out by the Government.

Ahom Revolt (1828-1833)

- The Ahom revolt sparked off in 1828, under the leadership of **Gomdhar Konwar**.
- The British had the commitment to leave Assam after the First Burma war (1824-26).
- But, after the war, instead of leaving, the British attempted to integrate the Ahom's territories in company's dominion.
- Finally, the company decided to accept the policy and gave Upper Assam to **Maharaja Purandar Singh Narendra** and part of the kingdom was restored to the Assamese King.

Kol Uprising (1831-1832)

- The Kols of Singhbhum for long centuries enjoyed independent power under their chiefs.
- As a result, when British occupied Singhbhum and the neighbouring territories, a large number of people from outside began to settle in this area. This resulted in transfer of tribal lands to the outsiders.
- The transfer of tribal lands and coming of merchants, money-lenders and the British law in the tribal area

posed a great threat to the hereditary independent power of the tribal chiefs.

- This led to popular uprisings against the outsiders in the tribal area. The rebellion spread over Ranchi, Hazaribagh, Palamau and Manbhum. The target of attack was the settlers from other regions whose houses were burnt and property was looted.
- The uprising was inhumanly suppressed by the British militia. The government crushed *zamindari* forces and **Dadu Miyan** was imprisoned.

Khond Uprising (1837- 56)

- The Khonds lived in vast hill tracts stretching from Tamil Nadu to Bengal and covering central provinces.
- Their uprisings from 1837 to 1856, were directed against the British. the movement was led by **Chakra Bisoi** in the name of the Young Raja.

Santhal Rebellion (1855-56)

- Santhal rebellion occurred in **Raj Mahal hills** of Santhal region.
- The Santhals were given land and persuaded to settle in the foothills of Rajmahal. By 1882 a large area of land was demarcated as Damin-i-Koh. This was declared to be the land of the Santhals.
- 'Damin-i-Koh' is a Persian term that means 'skirt of the hills'. Damin-i-Koh is in the area of Sahebganj, Pakur and Godda district in the Jharkhand.
- It primarily happened due to the oppression of police, atrocities of landlords and moneylenders, ill-treatment of small farmers by land revenue officials. Government banned shifting cultivation in forest areas.
- Leaders of the uprising were **Sidhu** and **Kanhu.** Under them the Santhals proclaimed an end to Company rule and declared the area between Bhagalpur and Rajmahal as autonomous. The rebellion was suppressed by 1856.
- The government pacified these Santhals and created a separate district of Santhal Parganas by passing the **Santhal Parganas Tenancy Act.**

Munda Uprising (1899-1900)

- In the Mundas, in the region South of Ranchi rose under **Birsa Munda.**
- The **Ulgulan** (Chhota Nagpur Plateau) was one of the most significant tribal uprisings in the period 1860-1920.
- The rebellion which began as a religious movement gathered political force to fight against introduction of feudal, *zamindari* tenures and exploitation by money-lenders and forest contractors.
- Birsa wanted to drive out missionaries, moneylenders, Hindu landlords and the government and set up a **Munda Raj** with Birsa at its head.
- The movement identified all these forces as the cause of the misery the Mundas were suffering.
- They attacked police stations, churches and raided the property of moneylenders and *zamindars.* They raised the white flag as a symbol of Birsa Raj.
- In 1900, Birsa died of *cholera* and the movement faded out.
- However, the movement was significant in atleast two ways:
  - **First** It forced the Colonial Government to introduce laws so that the land of the tribals could not be easily taken over by dikus. (outsiders)
  - **Second** It showed once again that the tribal people had the capacity to protest against injustice and express their anger against colonial rule.

Rampa Rebellion (1922)

- A unique example of tribal militancy came from the Rampa region North of Godavari which had witnessed various uprisings in the 19th century.
- Their grievances were against moneylenders and forest laws.
- The movement was led by an outsider, **Alluri Sitarama Raju**, claiming astrological and healing powers, who has become a folk hero in Andhra Pradesh.
- He was inspired by the **Non-Cooperation Movement** and admired Gandhiji, though he considered violence necessary to win tribal goals. The revolt came to an end after the execution of Raju in May, 1924.

Tribal Rebellions

Tribe	Year	Leader	Cause
Chuar	1798-99	Raja Jagannath	Excess revenue demand and Bengal famine
Bhil	1817	Sewaram	Agrarian hardship
Ho	1820-27	Ganga Narain	British occupation of Singhbhum
Ramosi	1822-26	Chittur Singh, Pratap Singh, Dattatraya Patkar	British rule
Koli	1824		Dismantle of forests
Ahom	1828-33	Gomadhar Kunwar	British occupation

Tribe	Year	Leader	Cause
Khasi	1829-32	Tirut Singh	British occupation
Kol	1831-32	Buddha Bhagat	Land transfer to outsiders
Santhal	1855-56	Sidhu and Kanhu	British rule
Naikda	1858	Rup Singh	For Dharma Raj against Ban Joria Bhagat on grazing and timber
Bhuyan and Juang	1867-68 1891	Ratna Nayak Dharani Nayak	Installation of British protege on throne
Kacha Naga	1882	Sambhuden	British intervention
Munda (*Ulgulan*)	1899	Birsa Munda	Land system, missionary activity and forced labour
Bhils	1913	Govind Guru	A temperance and purification movement
Oraons (*Tana Bhagat*)	1914	Jatra Bhagat and other Bhagats	Religious reason, a millenarian movement
Chenchu	1921-22	Hanumanthu	British control of forests
Koyas/ Rampa	1922-24	Alluri Sitarama Raju	British rule
Naga	1905-31	Jadunag and Rani Gaidinliu	A reformist movement later directed against excess of British rule

Movement of Working Class (1899)

- The Indian working class suffered from the same kind of exploitation witnessed during the industrialisation of Europe and the rest of the West.
- They were distressed with low wages, long working hours, unhygienic and hazardous working conditions, employment of child labour and the absence of basic amenities.
- The earlier attempts to improve the economic conditions of the workers were in the nature of the philanthropic efforts.
- In 1899, the first strike by the great Indian Penisular Railways took place and it got widespread support by **Bal Gangadhar Tilak** and other leaders.

The AITUC

- The All India Trade Union Congress (AITUC) was founded on 31st October, 1920. **Lala Lajpat Rai** was elected as the first President of AITUC.
- Swarajist Leader **CR Das** who presided over the third and fourth sessions of AITUC advocated that the Congress should take up the workers and peasant's cause.
- It urged to incorporate them in the struggle for swaraj or else they would get isolated from the movement.

Major Farmer's Association

Association	Year	Founder
Uttar Pradesh Kisan Sabha	1918	Gauri Shankar Mishra, Indranarayan Dwivedi
Awadh Kisan Sabha	1920	Baba Ramchandra
Bihar Kisan Sabha	1929	Sahajananda Saraswati
Krishak Praja Party	1929	Abdul Rahim/Fazlul Haq
Akhil Bhartiya Kisan Sabha	1936	Sahajananda Saraswati, NG Ranga

Important Factory Acts

Act	Viceroy	Important Facts
Factory Act, 1881	Lord Ripon	Children less than 7 years of age were prohibited from working.
Factory Act, 1891	Lord Lansdowne	Children less than 9 years of age were prohibited from working, work hours 11/days, one day leave in a week.
Factory Act, 1911	Lord Hardinge	Work hours for male workers fixed to 12 hours.
Factory Act, 1934	Lord Willingdone	Classification of weather and non-weather factories, facility of treatment and rest for the workers.
Factory Act, 1944	Lord Wavell	Facility of canteen, if number of workers is more than 200.

Major Strikes by Labourers

Year	Strike
1877	Strike in Nagpur Mill
1895	Weaver's strike against the Ahmedabad Mill Owners Union.
1899	Strike in Great Indian Peninsular Railway.
1908	Strike by Textile Mill workers in Mumbai because of the arrest of Tilak.
1918	Strike in Bombay Textile Mill.
1922	TISCO, Jameshedpur strike.
1922	Strike in Surat Textile Mill.
1928	Bombay Textile Mill strike (longest strike 6 months)

Extra Facts From Tamil Nadu Board and NIOS

- The poligars of Malabar and coastal Andhra Pradesh in South India revolted in the late 18th century.
- The Moplah Rebellion was an important peasant rebellion in the Malabar region. Moplahs are the descendants of Arab castes who was converted to Hinduism.

26

Socio-Religious Reform Movements in India

[SOURCES]

Class-VIII New NCERT Chap 7 (Women, Caste and Reform), Class-XII Old NCERT Chap 5 (Social and Cultural Awakening in 19th Century), Chap 10 (Rise of New India), Tamil Nadu Board (Class XII), NIOS

- With the onset of British rule in India came modern thoughts, Western education, modern means of communication and Western culture.
- With the advent of Modern Western education, people started questioning the basis and infallibility of age-old customs and traditions.
- How, the age-old customs and traditions started to be questioned. Due to printing of newspapers, magazines, all kinds of issues – social, political, economic and religious – could now be debated and discussed by men (and sometimes by women as well) in the new cities.
- Many defects and ills of Indian society began resurfacing and Indian intellectuals such as **Raja Ram Mohan Roy**.
- They not only began questioning the customs but also took measures to eradicate them. Some of these measures and reforms are discussed in this chapter.

Social Reform Movements

Prominent social reform movements are discussed as follows :

Brahmo Samaj

- Raja Ram Mohan Roy founded the **Brahmo Sabha** in August, **1828**. It was later renamed Brahmo Samaj.
- Its purpose was to purify Hinduism and preach monotheism. E.g., worship of one God.
- The new society was based on reason and Upanishads and Vedas. The main theme was **Nirgunsapna** (formless worship).
- Brahmo Samaj led emphasis on human dignity, opposed idolatry and *Sati*.
- It focused on prayers, meditation and reading of the scriptures. It believed in the unity of all religions.
- It was the first intellectual reform movement in modern India. It led to the emergence of rationalism and enlightenment in India, which indirectly contributed to the nationalist movement.
- Prayers, meditation and readings of the Upanishads were considered as the forms of worship and no image, statue or sculpture, carving, picture, portrait, etc were allowed in the Samaj buildings.
- Samaj weres tolerant towards all religions as it tried to incorporate teachings of other religions.

Raja Ram Mohan Roy

- He is greatly regarded as **Father of Indian Renaissance** and the **Father of Bengal Renaissance**.
- During his early education, Raja Ram Mohan Roy studied Persian and Arabic at Patna. Here, he read the *Quran*, the works of Sufi mystic poets and the Arabic translation of the works of **Plato** and **Aristotle**.
- In Banaras, he studied Sanskrit and read Vedas and Upanishads. At the age of sixteen, he wrote a **rational critique of Hindu idol worship**.

- He possessed a great love for his country and people and worked for their social, religious, political and intellectual upliftment.
- He wrote **Gift to Monotheists** (1809) and translated into Bengali. The Vedas and the five Upanishads to prove his conviction that ancient Hindu texts support monotheism.
- In 1814, he set up the **Atmiya Sabha** (or society of friends) in Calcutta to propagate the monotheistic ideals of the Vedanta and to campaign against idolatry, caste rigidities, meaningless rituals and other social ills.
- Although he had great love for his Indian culture and traditions, he believed that Western education alone can help to regenerate the society.
- Ram Mohan Roy was given the title of **Raja** by the titular Mughal Emperor of Delhi, **Akbar II** whose grievances the former was to present before the British king.

Contributions of Raja Ram Mohan Roy Towards Social Reforms

- Raja Ram Mohan Roy organised a crusade against practice of *Sati*. He visited the cremation grounds, organised vigilance groups and filed counter petitions to the Government during his struggle against *Sati*.

Sati, Painted by balthazar Solvyn, 1813

- His efforts were rewarded by the Government Regulation in 1829, which declared the practice of Sati a crime under **Lord William Bentinck.**
- He condemned polygamy and demanded the right of inheritance and property for women.
- He assisted **David Hare** in forming **Hindu College** and in 1825, he established **Vedanta College.**
- He was also a pioneer in Indian Journalism and brought out various journals, newspapers in Bengali, Persian, Hindi and English.

Keshub Chandra Sen and Brahmo Samaj

- Brahmo Samaj was revived with new enthusiasm under Keshub Chandra Sen when he was made **Acharya by Debendranath Tagore.**
- Many branches of the Samaj were opened outside Bengal like United Provinces, Punjab, Bombay, Madras and other towns.
- **Debendranath Tagore** did not like some ideas of Sen. He was dismissed from post of Acharya in 1865.
- Keshub and his followers founded the Brahmo Samaj of India in 1866, while Debendranath Tagore's Samaj came to be known as the Adi Brahmo Samaj.

Prarthana Samaj

- It was founded by **Atmaram Pandurang** with the help of **Keshub Chandra Sen** in 1867.
- A precursor of the Prarthana Samaj was the **Paramahansa Sabha**, something like a secret. It was like a society to spread liberal ideas and encourage the breakdown of caste and communal barriers.
- Some of the prominent members of this organisation were **Mahadev Govind Ranade, RG Bhandarkar, NG Chandavarkar.** It was connected to Bhakti cult in Maharashtra.
- Prarthana Samaj had point social agenda, these are
  - disapproval of caste system
  - women's education
  - widow remarriage
  - raising the age of marriage for both males and females

Justice Ranade and Prarthana Samaj

- Justice Mahadev Govind Ranade was the most influential member of the Samaj.
- Under his guidance **Widow Remarriage Association** was formed in 1861.
- He worked for the spread of education among widows. He was one of the promoters of **Sharada Sadan** whose motive was spreading education among the widows.
- He founded girls's college in 1861 in Poona and **'Deccan Education Society'**.

Arya Samaj

- The first Arya Samaj unit was formally set up by **Swami Dayanand Saraswati** at Bombay in 1875, whereas its headquarters was established at Lahore.
- Following are the ten guiding principles of Arya Samaj :

1. God is the efficient cause of all true knowledge and all that is known through knowledge.

2. God is existent, intelligent and blissful. He is formless, omniscient, just, unborn, endless, unchangeable, omnipresent, immortal, fearless, eternal. He alone is worthy of being worshipped.
3. The Vedas are the scriptures of all true knowledge. It is the paramount duty of all Aryas to read them, teach them, recite them and to hear them being read.
4. One should always be ready to accept truth and to abandon untruth.
5. All acts should be performed in accordance with Dharma that is, after deliberating what is right and wrong.
6. The prime object of the Arya Samaj is to do good to the world, that is, to promote physical, spiritual and social good of everyone.
7. Our conduct towards all should be guided by love, righteousness and justice.
8. We should dispel Avidya (ignorance) and promote Vidya (knowledge).
9. No one should be content with promoting his/her good only on the contrary, one should look for his/her good in promoting the good of all.
10. One should regard oneself under restriction to follow the rules of society calculated to promote the well being of all, while in following the rules of individual welfare all should be free.

- The Samaj also worked during the times of calamities such as earthquakes, famines and floods. It also worked for promoting education.
- Education was an all-important field for the samaj. The **Dayananda Anglo Vedic** (DAV) College was established in Lahore in 1886 .

Swami Dayanand Saraswati

- The **Arya Samaj** was founded by Dayanand Saraswati or Mulshankar (1824-1883).
- He was born in the old Morvi state in Gujarat and belonged to a brahmin family.
- His famous work is *Satyarth Prakash* where he expressed his views.
- He was inspired by the Vedas and considered them to be **India's Rock of Ages**.
- He gave the slogan **"Back to the Vedas"**.

Ramakrishna Mission

- Named after **Ramakrishna Paramhansa**, Swami Vivekananda's guru, the Ramakrishna Mission emphasised the ideal of salvation through social service and selfless action.
- **Swami Vivekananda** was the first Indian in modern times, who re-established the spiritual pre-eminence of the **Vedanta philosophy** on a global scale. But his mission was not simply to talk about religion.
- He was convinced that many of the problems facing the mankind could only be overcome if the nations of the world come together on an equal footing.
- He united youth on the basis of a common spiritual heritage.

Swami Vivekananda

- Swami Vivekananda (1863-1902), whose original name was **Narendra Nath Dutta**, combined the simple teachings of Sri Ramakrishna with his well founded modern outlook and spread them all over the world.
- He was extremely pained at the poverty and the misery of his countrymen.
- He firmly believed that any reform could become successful only by uplifting the condition of the masses.

Young Bengal Movement

- Young Bengal Movement was an intellectual, radical movement among the youth of Bengal.
- **Henry Vivian Derozio** (1809-1831), a young Anglo-Indian was its leader.
- He taught at the **Hindu College** from 1826 to 1831 and was inspired by **French Revolution**.
- Derozio inspired his followers to think freely and rationally, question all authority, love, liberty, equality and freedom and oppose in moral customs and traditions.
- However, the Derozians failed to have a long-term impact. Derozio was removed from the **Hindu College** in 1831 because of his radicalism.
- There was no support from any other social group or class. The Derozians lacked any real link with the masses.

Theosophical Society

- **Madame HP Blavatsky** and **Colonel MS Olcott**, founded the Theosophical Society in New York City, United States in 1875.
- In 1882, they shifted their headquarters to Adyar in the outskirts of Madras.
- It recognised the Hindu beliefs in reincarnation and *karma* and was inspired by the philosophy of the Upanishads and Samkhya, yoga and **Vedanta schools of thought**.
- Its objective was to work for universal brotherhood of humanity without distinction of race, creed, sex, caste or colour.
- In India, the theosophical society gained momentum after the election of **Annie Besant**.
- The society did an extensive work in field of education.

Annie Besant

- Annie Besant arrived in India in 1893. She laid the foundation of the **Central Hindu College** in Banaras in 1898.
- College curriculum included both Hindu religion and Western scientific subjects. The college became the basis for the formation of **Banaras Hindu University** in 1916.
- Annie Besant took enormous efforts towards the cause of the education of women.

Satyashodhak Samaj

- **Jyotiba Phule** (1827-1890), born in Satara, Maharashtra, belonged to the mali (gardener) community, organised a powerful movement against upper caste domination and brahminical supremacy.
- Phule founded the Satyashodhak Samaj (Truth Seeker's Society) in 1873, it had a leadership of the samaj belonged to the backward classes, malis, telis, kunbis, saris and dhangars.
- The main objective of the movement were :
  - social service
  - spread of education among
  - women and lower caste people.
- Phule's works, *Sarvajanik Satyadharma* and *Gulamgiri* were sources of inspiration for the masses.
- Phule, firmly believed in gender equality and was a pioneer in women's education. He with the help of his wife, **Savitribai** opened a girl's school at Poona.
- He was a pioneer of **widow remarriage movement** in Maharashtra and also opened a home for widows in 1854.
- Phule was awarded the title 'Mahatma' for his social reform work.

Satnami Movement (1820)

- Guru Ghasidas started the Satnami Movement in 1820, in present day Chhattisgarh.
- He preached a code of ethical and dietary self-restaint and social equality.
- The satnami sect challenged political and religions authority by rallying around and understanding of god as Satnam.

Servants of Indian Society

- Servants of Indian Society was formed by **Gopal Krishna Gokhale** in 1905 for the expansion of Indian education.
- The society trained people to be selfless workers so they could work for the common good of the people.
- The aims of the organisation were as follows :
  - To train national missionaries for the service of India.
  - To promote true interest of all Indians by all constitutional means.
  - To prepare a cadre of selfless workers for the service to the country in a religious spirit.

Social Service League

- It was founded by **Narayan Malhar Joshi** in Bombay.
- Aim of the league was to secure for the masses better and reasonable conditions of life and work.
- They organised many schools, libraries, reading rooms, day nurseries and cooperative societies.
- Activities of the league included police court agents' work, legal aid and advice to the poor and illiterate. These also included excursions for slum dwellers, facilities for gymnasia and theatrical performances, sanitary work, medical relief and boy's clubs and scout corps.
- Joshi also founded the **All India Trade Union Congress** (1920).

Indian Social Conference

- It was found by **MG Ranade** and **Raghunath Rao**.
- It was virtually the social reform cell of the **Indian National Congress**.
- Its first session was held in Madras in December, 1887.
- The Conference advocated inter-caste marriage and opposed *Kulinism* and polygamy.
- It launched the famous **Pledge Movement** to inspire people to take an oath to prohibit child marriage.

Prominent Social Reformers

In 19th century, many social reformers were born in India who guided the society with many important reforms. Few of them are as follows :

Ishwar Chandra Vidyasagar

- He was one of the great reformers of 19th century.
- Used the ancient texts to suggest that widows could remarry. His suggestion was adopted by British officials and a law was passed in 1856 permitting **widow remarriage**.
- In 1850, he became the principal of **Sanskrit College**.
- He was determined to break the priestly monopoly of scriptural knowledge and for this he opened the Sanskrit College to break the self-imposed isolation of Sanskritic learning. He evolved a new technique for learning Sanskrit.
- He raised his powerful voice and thoroughly supported the cause of widow remarriage and devoted his entire life for his agitation for legalising widow remarriage.

- **First lawful Hindu widow remarriage** among the upper caste in India was celebrated under the inspiration and supervision of Vidyasagar.
- Through his endeavours nearly 25 widow remarriages were solemnised between 1855-1860
- For his advocacy of widow remarriage, he had bitter opposition from Orthodox Hindu class.
- In 1850, he protested against child marriage and all his life he campaigned against polygamy.

Balshastri Jambhekar

- He is also known as **father of Marathi Journalism** for his efforts in starting journalism in Marathi language with the first newspaper in the language named **Darpan**.

Gopal Hari Deshmukh

- He was the famous social reformer of Maharashtra. He was also known as **Lokhitawadi**. He started the publishing of a magazine named *Prabhakar* in 1848 AD.
- He was related to the **Theosophical Society** and **Arya Samaj**. He authored a book named **Jatibhed** in Marathi.

Shri Narayan Guru

- He started reform movement in Kerala.
- He proclaimed the ideals of unity for his people.
- According to him, all humankind belonged to the same caste.
- His famous statement was : "oru jati, oru matam, oru daivam manushyanu" (one caste, one religion and one god for humankind).

Pandita Ramabai

- Pandita Ramabai was a great scholar of Sanskrit. She felt that Hinduism was oppressive towards women and wrote a book about the miserable lives of upper-caste Hindu women.
- She established a widow's home at Poona to provide shelter to widows who had been treated badly by their husband's relatives. Here women were trained so that they could support themselves economically.

Tarabai Shinde

- She was educated at home at Poona.
- She published a book Stripurushtulna (a comparison between women and men).
- She criticised the social differences between men and women.

Religious Reform Movements

Prominent religious reform movements are discussed as follows :

Swami Narayan Sect

- Swami Narayan Sect was launched by **Swami Sahajanand** (1781- 1830) in Gujarat.
- This sect was a sort of protest against the luxurious practices of **Vaishnavism**.
- The sect advocated vegetarianism and adviced people to shun liquor and drugs.
- The sect preached monotheism. It emphasised on the importance of a pure and simple life and social unity.
- The sect attacked the restrictions on widow remarriage, the institution of Sati and the practice of female infanticide.

Radha Swami Movement

- Radha Swami Movement was founded in 1861 by **Tulsi Ram**.
- Tulsi Ram was also popularly known as **Shiv Dayal Saheb** or **Swamiji Maharaj**.
- The Radhaswamis believed in one supreme being, the supremacy of the Guru.
- They also believed in the company of the 'pious people' (*Satsang*) and simple social life.
- They were of the view that there is no need to renounce the worldly life for spiritual attainments.

Deva Samaj

- Deva Samaj was founded by **Shiv Narain Agnihotri**, in 1887 at Lahore.
- The teachings of the Samaj were compiled in book form in **Deva Shastra**.
- The teachings of the Deva Samaj emphasised the supreme being, eternity of the soul, the supremacy of the Guru and need for good action.
- The Samaj prescribed ideal, social, conduct and moral ethics, such as not accepting bribe, abstaining from gambling, intoxicants, non-vegetarian food and violence.

Wahabi Movement

- Wahabi Movement was a revivalist response to Western influences and the degeneration.
- It was the teachings of **Abdul Wahab** of Arabia and the preaching of **Shah Walliullah** that inspired the movement.
- The movement stress was to condemn any change into the original Islam and return to its true spirit.

- The movement was led by **Syed Ahmed Barelvi.**
- India was considered to be *Dar-ul-Harb* (land of the Kafirs) and it needed to be converted to *Dar-ul-Islam* (land of Islam).
- Initially, the movement was directed at the Sikhs in Punjab but after the British annexation of Punjab (1849), the movement was directed against the British.
- During the **Revolt of 1857**, the Wahabi's played an important role in spreading anti-British feelings.
- The Wahabi Movement dissolved out in 1870s.

Aligarh Movement

- **Sir Syed Ahmed Khan** was one of the important Muslim reformers of India. He interpreted *Quran* in the light of modern rationalism and science.
- His greatest achievement was the establishment of the **Mohammedan Anglo Oriental College** (Also known as Aligarh Muslim University) at Aligarh in 1875.
- In course of time, this college became the most important educational institution of Indian Muslims. It provided for education in humanities and science throughout English medium.
- The movement of Muslim awakening associated with Syed Ahmed Khan and Mohammedan Anglo Oriental College came to be known as **Aligarh Movement**.
- He appealed to the Muslims to return to the original Islamic principles of purity and simplicity.
- He advocated English education for the regeneration of Muslims in India.
- He worked towards improving the position of women through better education and by opposing purdah and polygamy, advocating easy divorce and condemning the system of *piri* (mystic *fakirs* being treated as teachers and *gurus*) and *muridi*(disciple).

Faraizi Movement

- Faraizi Movement was founded by **Haji Shariatullah** in the year 1818. The movement seeked to purify the religion by out casting all practices and preaching that are not in line with Islamic beliefs.
- Under the leadership of Haji's son, **Dudu Mian**, the movement turned to become revolutionary from 1840 onwards.

Ahmadiya Movement

- The Ahmadiya movement was launched by **Mirza Ghulam Ahmad of Qadiyan** in 1889.
- It described itself as the standard-bearer of **Mohammedan Renaissance** and based himself on the principles of universal religion of all humanity and opposed **jihad** (sacred war against non- Muslims).
- The **Ahmadiya community** is the only Islamic sect to believe that the Messiah had come in the person of Mirza Ghulam Ahmad to end religious wars and bloodshed and to reinstate morality, peace and justice.
- They believed in separating the mosque from the State as well as in human rights and tolerance.

Deoband Movement

- Deoband Movement was founded in 1867 by two theologians, **Muhammad Qasim Nanautavi** (1837-80) and **Rashid Ahmad Gangohi.**
- The movement had two important objectives :
  - Popularising the teachings of Kuran and Hadis.
  - To initiate Jihad against foreign rule.
- The aim of the Deoband Movement was moral and religious regeneration of the Muslim community.
- The instruction imparted at Deoband was in original Islamic religion.
- The modern awakening among the Muslims led to a decline in the practice of polygamy and widow remarriage was encouraged.

Nirankari Movement

- **Baba Dayal Das** (1783-1855) was the founder of this movement. This movement consisted of purification and return.
- In the 1840s, he called for the return of Sikhism to its origin and emphasised the worship of one God and *nirankar* (formless).
- Such an approach meant a rejection of idolatry and also prohibition of eating meat, drinking liquor, lying, cheating, etc.
- It laid emphasis on **Guru Nanak** and on Sikhism before the establishment of *Khalsa* by **Guru Gobind Singh** at Anandpur. This separated them from the *Namdharis*.

Namdhari Movement

- It was founded by **Baba Ram Singh** (1816-1885) in 1857.
- The movement was founded on a set of rituals modeled after **Guru Gobind Singh's** founding of the *Khalsa*. Its followers were required to wear the five symbols but instead of the sword the followers were supposed to carry a stick.
- The movement required the followers to abandon the worship of gods, idols, tombs, trees, snakes, etc. And abstain from drinking, stealing, falsehood, slandering, backbiting, etc.
- Further the consumption of beef was strictly forbidden as protection of cattle was important.

Singh Sabha Movement

- Reform organisations of the Sikhs, the first **Singh Sabhas** were formed at Amritsar in 1873 and at Lahore in 1879.
- The Sabhas sought to rid Sikhism of superstitions, caste distinctions and practices seen by them as non-Sikh.
- They promoted education among the Sikhs, often combining modern instruction with Sikh teachings.

Akali Movement

- Before 1920, the Sikh Gurdwara were governed by the **Udasi Sikh mahants**, who treated the Gurdwara offerings and other income of the Gurdwaras as their personal income.
- The British Government supported these mahants as a counterpoise to the rising tide of nationalism among the Sikhs.
- Matter came to such a pass that the priest of the golden temple issued a *hukamnama* (injunction) against Ghadarites, declaring them renegades.
- Then honoured **General Dyer**, the butcher of Jallianwala massacre with a *saropa*.
- The Gurdwara Reform Movement launched an agitation for freeing the Gurdwaras from these corrupt mahants and for handing over the Gurdwaras to a representative body of Sikhs.
- Under the growing pressure of the nationalist and Gurdwara agitators, the Gurdwaras came under the control of an elected committee known as the **Shiromani Gurdwara Prablandhalk Committee**, in November, 1920.
- The movement for liberation of Gurdwaras soon turned into Alkali movement, which later on got divided into three streams, namely **moderate nationalist reformers**, **pro-government loyalists** and **political organ of Sikh communalism**.

Reforms in Parsi Community

- The earliest attempts to reform Parsi community were started in the 19th century.
- To revive and transform the social situation of Parsi community, Religious Reform Association was formed.
- **Rehnumai Maj Daysan Sabha** was the name of this reform association.
- **Dadabhai Naoroji** and **SS Bengali** were the main founders of the League.

Lower Caste/Caste Movements and Organisation

Movements/Organisations	Years	Places	Founders
Satya Shodhak Samaj	1873	Maharashtra	Jyotiba Phule
Aruvippuram Movement	1888	Aruvippuram, Kerala	Shri Narayan Guru (1856-1928)
Shri Narayan Dharma Paripalana Yogam or SNDP Movement	1902-03	Kerala	Shri Narayan Guru, Dr. Palpu and Kumaran Asan
The Depressed Class Mission Society	1906	Bombay	Vitthal Ramji Shinde
Bahujan Samaj	1910	Satara, Maharashtra	Mukundrao Patil
Justice (*Party*) Movement	1915-16	Madras (*Tamil Nadu*)	C. Natesa Mudaliar, Taravath Madhavan Nair and P. Tyagaraja Chetti
Depressed Class Welfare Institute (*Bahishkrit Hitkarni Sabha*)	1924	Bombay	Dr. Bhimrao Ramji Ambedkar
Self-Respect Movement	1925	Madras (*Tamil Nadu*)	EV Ramaswami Naicker Periyar
Harijan Sevak Sangh	1932	Pune	Mahatma Gandhi
Dravida Munnetra Kazhagam	1944		Conjeevaram Natarajan Annadurai and Ramaswami Naicker

Socio-Religious Reform Movements and Organisations

Movements/Organisations	Years	Places	Founders
Swaminarayan Sampraday	1781	Gujarat	Swami Sahajanand (*original name Ghanshayama*)
Atmiya Sabha *(later Brahmo Samaj)*	1815-28	Calcutta	Raja Ram Mohan Roy
Dharma Sabha	1830	Calcutta	Radha Kanta Deva
Namdhari/Kuka Movement	1841-71	NWFP and Bhaini (*Ludhiana district, Punjab*)	Bhai Balak Singh and Ram Singh
Rahnumai Mazdayasnan Sabha	1851	Bombay	SS Bengali, Naoroji Fundonji, JB Nacha etc
Indian Reform Association	1870	Calcutta	Keshub Chandra Sen
Deccan Education Society	1884	Pune	Mahadev Govind Ranade, VG Chibdonkarm and Gopal Ganesh Agarkar, etc
Seva Sadan	1885	Bombay	Behramji M Malabari
Indian National Social Conference	1887	Bombay	Mahadev Govind Ranade and Raghunath Rao
Deva Samaj	1887	Lahore	Shiv Narayan Agnihotri
Madras Hindu Association	1892	Madras	Viresalingam Pantalu
Bharat Dharma Mahamandal	1902	Varanasi	Pandit Madan Mohan Malaviya and Pandit Din Dayal Sharma
The Servants of Indian Society	1905	Bombay	Gopal Krishna Gokhale
Poona Seva Sadan	1909	Pune	GK Devadhar and Ramabai Ranade (*wife of Mahadev Govind Ranade*)
Nishkama Karma Math *(The monastery of disinterested work)*	1910	Pune	Dhondo Keshav Karve
The Bharat Stree Mandal	1910	Allahabad	Sarala Devi Chaudhurani
Social Service League	1911	Bombay	Narayan Malhar Joshi
Seva Samiti	1914	Allahabad	Pandit Hridyanath Kunzru
The Women's Indian Association	1917	Madras	Annie Besant
Khudai Khidmatgar Movement	1929	NWFP	Khan Abdul Ghaffar Khan

Extra Facts From Tamil Nadu Board and NIOS

- In 1864, a Tamil journal titled Tathuva Bodhini was started for the cause of the Brahmo Samaj.
- The National Social Conference organised at the initiative of MG Ranade met each year immediately after the Indian National Congress 1885 annual session.
- In 1875, he founded the Arya Samaj and published his major work the Satyarth Prakash.

27

Development of Education and Press During the British Rule

[SOURCES]

Class-XII Old NCERT Chap 6 (Administrative Organisation and Social and Cultural Policy), Class-VIII New NCERT Chap 6 (Civilising the 'Native', Educating the Nation) Tamil Nadu Board (Class XII), NIOS

- Initially, the **British East India** Company was not concerned with the development of the education system because their prime motive was trading and profit-making.
- Modern education began in India under British rule. Before the British, India had its own educational systems like the **Gurukuls** and the **Madrasas**.
- The East India Company, during their first 60 years of rule didn't care much for the education of those they ruled in India.
- The development of education under British can be divided into two phases:
  - Development of education under East India Company.
  - Development of education under Crown rule.

Development of Education Under East India Company

- East India Company took hardly a few measures to promote and develop education in India. In 1781, **Lord Warren Hastings** set up Calcutta Madrasa for Muslims law and related subjects.
- In 1783, a person named William Jones arrived in Calcutta.
- He was enthusiastic about Indian culture, tradition and language. He started Asiatic Researches and set up the Asiatic Society of Bengal.
- **Jonathan Duncan** started **Sanskrit College** at Varanasi for studying Hindu Law and Philosophy.
- **Fort William College** was set up by **Wellesley** in 1800 for training of civil servants of the Company in languages and customs of Indians.
- Enlightened Indians and missionaries started exerting pressure on the government to promote modern, secular, Western education. They believed that Western education was the remedy for social, economic and political ills of the country.
- Missionaries thought that modern education would destroy the faith of Indians in their own religions and they would take to Christianity. **Serampore missionaries** were very enthusiastic about spread of education.

Charter Act of 1813

- The Charter Act of 1813, incorporated the principle of encouraging learned Indians and promoting knowledge of modern sciences in the country.
- The Act directed the Company to sanction one lakh rupees annually for this purpose.
- However, even this small amount was not made available till 1823.
- Enlightened Indians such as **Raja Ram Mohan Roy** worked relentlessly and a grant was sanctioned for **Calcutta College** set up in 1817 by educated Bengalis, imparting English education in Western humanities and sciences.

- The government also set up three Sanskrit colleges at Calcutta, Delhi and Agra.

Orientalist-Anglicist Controversy

- Within the General Committee on Public Instruction, the Anglicists argued that the government should spend exclusively on modern education. The Orientalists said while Western sciences and literature should be taught to prepare students to take up jobs, emphasis should be placed on expansion of traditional Indian learning.
- Even the Anglicists were divided over the question of medium of instructions :
  - One faction was for English language as the medium.
  - The other faction was for Indian languages (vernaculars) for the purpose.

Lord Macaulay's Minutes

- The famous Lord Macaulay's Minutes favoured Anglicists views. The limited government resources were dedicated to teaching of Western sciences and literature through the medium of English language.
- English was made the medium of instruction in schools and colleges and alongside a few schools and colleges were also opened instead of elementary schools and thus neglected mass education.
- The British planned to educate a small section of upper and middle classes who would act as interpreters between the government and masses.
- They would also enrich the vernaculars by which knowledge of Western sciences and literature could reach the masses. This was called the **'Downward Filtration Theory'**.

Wood's Despatch (1854)

- In 1854, Charles Wood prepared a despatch on an educational system for India which was considered the **'Magna Carta of English Education in India'**.
- This document was the first inclusive plan for the spread of education in India.
- The despatch instructed the Government of India to undertake responsibility for education of the masses, and thus rejected the **'downward filtration theory'**, at least on paper.
- It organised the hierarchy of education in the following manner :
  - Vernacular primary schools in villages at bottom.
  - Followed by Anglo-Vernacular High Schools.
  - Followed by an affiliated college at the district level.
  - And affiliating Universities were set up in the Presidencies of Calcutta, Bombay and Madras.
- It recommended English as the medium of instruction for higher studies and vernaculars at school level.
- The despatch emphasised on female and vocational education, teachers' training and insisted that the education imparted in government institutions should be secular.
- It recommended a system of grants-in-aid to encourage private enterprises.

Development of Education Under Crown Rule

After the Revolt of 1857, the East India Company was abolished and Crown rule was started in India. Hence, many new reforms came into education which were as follows:

Hunter Education Commission (1882-1883)

- In 1882, the Government appointed a commission under the Chairmanship of **WW Hunter** to review the progress of education in the country since, the Despatch of 1854.
- The Hunter Commission mostly limited its recommendations to primary and secondary education. The following recommendations of the Commission were :

(i) Emphasised that state's special care is required for extension and improvement of primary education, and that primary education should be imparted in a vernacular language.

(ii) The Commission recommended transfer of control of primary education to newly set up district and municipal boards. It also recommended that secondary (High School) education should have two divisions :
  - **Literary** Leading up to university
  - **Vocational** For commercial careers

(iii) The Commission also paid attention to inadequate facilities for female education, especially outside the presidency towns and made recommendations for its spread.

- For the next two decades, there was a rapid growth and expansion of secondary and college education with the participation of Indians.
- Universities were set up like the **Punjab University** (1882) and the **Allahabad University** (1887).

Indian Universities Act, 1904

- In 1902, **Raleigh Commission** was set up to study the conditions of universities in India and to suggest measures for improvement in their structure and working.
- The Commission did not report on primary or secondary education.
- Based on its recommendations, the **Indian Universities Act** was passed in 1904.
- Following are the recommendations of the Act :
  - Study and research were more encouraged in the universities.
  - The number of fellows of a university and their period in office were reduced and most fellows were to be nominated by the Government.
  - Government could have power to exercise veto universities' senate regulations. It could amend or pass these regulations on its own.
  - Conditions for affiliation of private colleges were to be made stricter and five lakh rupees were to be sanctioned per annum for five years for improvement of higher education and universities.

Government Resolution on Education Policy, 1913

- In 1906, the progressive state of Baroda introduced compulsory primary education throughout its territories. National leaders urged the government to do so for British India.
- In its **Resolution on Education Policy, 1913**, the government refused to take up the responsibility of compulsory education, accepted the policy of removal of illiteracy.
- It urged Provincial Governments to take early steps to provide free elementary education to the poorer and more backward sections.
- Private efforts were to be encouraged for this and the quality of secondary schools was to be improved.
- A university, was to be established in each province and teaching activities of universities were to be encouraged.

Sadler University Commission (1917-1919)

- The purpose of the commission was to study and report on problems of **Calcutta University**. Although its recommendations were applicable to other universities also.
- It also studied the entire arena from school education to university education and stated the view that, for the improvement of university education and improvement of secondary education were a necessary pre-condition.

Observations of the Commission

- All the teaching resources in Calcutta should be organised so that Calcutta University may entirely become a teaching university.
- A separate board of secondary and intermediate education was to be set up for administration and control of secondary and intermediate education. A full time Vice-Chancellor should be appointed as the head of university.
- There should be less rigidity in framing university regulations and university should function as centralised, unitary residential-teaching autonomous body, rather than as scattered, affiliated colleges.
- Female education, applied scientific and technological education, teachers' training including those for professional and vocational colleges should be extended.
- Provisions should be made for instructions in engineering, law, agriculture and technology.
- From 1916 to 1921, seven new universities came up at Mysore, Patna, Banaras, Aligarh, Dacca, Lucknow and Osmania.

Hartog Committee (1929)

The Hartog Committee was set up to report on development of education. Its main recommendations were as follows :

- Emphasis should be given to primary education but there need to be no hasty expansion or compulsion in education.
- It also recommended selective system of admission to universities and diversified courses leading to industrial and commercial careers.
- Only deserving students should go in for high school and intermediate stage, while average students should be diverted to vocational courses after Standard VIII.
- For improvements in standards of university education, admissions should be restricted.

Sergeant Plan of Education

- The Sergeant Plan (Sergeant was the educational adviser to the Government) was worked out by the **Central Advisory Board of Education** in 1944. It recommended following points :
  - Pre-primary education for 3-6 years age group.
  - Free universal and compulsory elementary education for 6-11 years age group.
  - High school education for 11- 17 years age group for selected children.

- A university course of 3 years after higher secondary and high schools were to be of two types i.e., Academic or Technical and Vocational.

- It provided for adequate technical, commercial and arts education and abolition of intermediate course.
- The Plan also advocated for liquidation of adult illiteracy in 20 years.
- Teachers' training, physical education, education for the physically and mentally handicapped was stressed upon.

Wardha Scheme of Education (1937)

- Wardha Scheme of Basic Education (1937) is also known as **Nai Talim / Buniyadi Talim** was the outcome of thinking of **Mahatma Gandhi**. He considered education as an effective instrument of national reconstruction.
- **Indian National Congress** had been pleading for free and compulsory universal education. When Congress Ministries were elected in the provincial elections of 1937, it became the duty of Congress to implement it into action.
- However, it required huge amount of funds which was lacking. To solve this problem, Mahatma Gandhi put forward his scheme of self-supporting education. He placed his basic education system in the Wardha Conference of 1937.
- A committee was appointed under the Chairmanship of **Dr. Zakir Hussain** to formulate the scheme of basic education in India.
- The report submitted by the committee and published in March, 1938, came to be known as Wardha scheme of education.
- To discuss the proposed new education scheme, an **All-India Education Conference** was held in Wardha on 22nd and 23rd October, 1937.

Features of Wardha Scheme

- Free and compulsory education was to be given for 8 years (from 6 to 14 years). It was to be given in two stages, the junior stage covering 5 years and senior stage for 3 years.
- The idea behind the scheme was to provide education through some form of craft or productive work. It was to relieve the child from the tyranny of purely academic and theoretical instruction and to break down the existing barriers of prejudice between manual and intellectual work.
- Scheme aimed to provide such kind of education which can be self-supporting in later life. It would also ensure the dignity of labour along with livelihood for the students after leaving school.
- **Zakir Hussain Committee** had proposed that proper teaching in the mother tongue should be the foundation of all education. Mother tongue would have helped to speak, read and write correctly and effectively and to develop precision of thought and clarity of ideas.
- Various subjects were introduced like the basic craft, mother tongue, mathematics, social studies, painting, music and sports, etc. English was not included in the curriculum.

Development of Technical Education

During the British rule, there was some focus on the development of technical education in the form of setting up of new colleges and courses which are described as follows:

- The **Engineering College at Roorkee** was set up in 1847; the Calcutta College of Engineering came up in 1856.
- In 1858, **Overseers' School at Poona** was raised to the status of Poona College of Engineering and affiliated to Bombay University. Guindy College of Engineering was affiliated to Madras University.
- Medical training started with establishment of a Medical College in Calcutta in 1835.
- **Lord Curzon** worked to broaden the whole basis of professional courses—medicine, agriculture, engineering, veterinary sciences, etc.
- He established an Agriculture College at Pusa, which acted as a parent institution of similar institutions in other provinces.

Developments in Indian Education Post Independence Era

The following developments took place in the field of education after India's independence :

Radhakrishnan Commission

- For the improvement of education in India, the Radhakrishnan Commission was appointed in November, 1948. It gave a report on university education in India.
- The Radhakrishnan Commission submitted its report in August, 1949. Recommendations of this education commission in independent India on the teaching standards.

- Commission recommended for 12 years of **Pre-University education** before entry into universities.
- The Committee gave three major objectives for the higher education:
  - Central education
  - Liberal education
  - Occupational education
- The Committee recommended for diverting the students after 10 to 12 years of Pre- University education to different vocational subjects in large number of occupational institutes.
- It was an important step to promote vocational education by this education commission in independent India.
- This education commission in independent India recommended for increasing the number of working days for a minimum of 180 days in a year.
- It recommended for three terms of about 11 weeks each.
- It recommended to raise the standard of education in universities and university education was to be placed in the Concurrent List.
- It recommended for setting up the **University Grants Commission** (UGC) to look after the universities in India.
- Recommendations of this education commission in independent India on professional education were made by the commission.
- This education commission in independent India recommended to divide the professional education into 5 aspects i.e., agriculture education, commercial education, engineering and technology, medical education and the Legal education.
- For finance, the Central Government was given the responsibility to promote higher education in India. University Grant Commission was given the responsibility for allocation of grants to the universities and promote education in India.
- UGC was constituted in 1953 and was given statutory status in 1956 by an Act of Indian Parliament.

Kothari Education Commission (1964-1966)

- The **Indian Education Commission**, popularly known as Kothari Education Commission (1964-1966) was set up by the Government of India on 14th July, 1964, under the Chairmanship of **Dr. DS Kothari**.
- The objective of the Kothari Education Commission (1964-1966) was to examine the different aspects of the education system in India.
- The recommendations of the Kothari Commission education reforms became part of national policy on education in 1968. The Commission was assisted by experts from countries like UK, USA, USSR, UNESCO.

Recommendations of Kothari Education Commission

- To provide free and compulsory education for children between 6 to 14 years.
- To provide adequate and satisfactory service conditions for the teachers along with proper qualifications and responsibilities.
- The adoption of three language formula i.e., Hindi, English and a regional language (mother tongue).
- Provision of educational facilities in the rural and backward areas.
- The adoption of a common school system in India.
- Emphasis on the education of girls to promote social justice and social transformation.
- Development of education among backward classes and tribal people.

University Grants Commission (UGC)

- The UGC was established in 1953 based on the recommendations of **Radhakrishnan Committee** and was made into a statutory organisation with the UGC Act in 1956.
- UGC is responsible for coordinating, determining and maintaining standards of higher education.
- The University Grants Commission provides recognition to universities in India and disburses funds to such recognised universities and colleges.

Development of Press in India

- Press in India started with the first newspaper, The **Bengal Gazette** or **Calcutta General Advertiser**, by **James Augustus Hicky** in 1780.
- Press in its initial phase was primarily an outspoken critic of the misdeeds of British administration and its officers.
- The Indian press (both Vernacular and English language) played a major role in National awakening and mobilising public opinion and fighting for freedom of India.
- Some examples of early newspapers are: '*Payam-e-Azadi*' or the Message of Freedom (1857) by **Nana Saheb Peshwa**, the Hindu and Swadesamitran by **G Subramania Iyer**.

- The Bengalee by Surendranath Banerjee, Voice of India by **Dadabhai Naoroji**, Kesari (in Marathi) and Maharatta (in English) under **Bal Gangadhar Tilak**.

Censorship of Press Act, 1799

- This Act was enacted **Lord Wellesley** while anticipating French invasion of India.
- It imposed almost wartime press restrictions including pre-censorship but were relaxed under **Lord Hastings**, who had progressive views and in 1818, press censorship was dispensed with.

Licensing Regulations, 1823

- It was enacted by the **John Adams**. According to this regulation, press without licence was a penal offence.
- The restriction was directed mainly to Indian language newspapers or those edited by the Indians.

Press Act of 1835 or Metcalfe Act

- **Metcalfe** (Governor-General – 1835-36) repealed the obnoxious 1823 ordinance and was named, **liberator of the Indian press**.
- The new **Press Act** (1835) required a printer/publisher to give a precise account of premises of a publication and cease functioning, if required by a similar declaration. The result of a liberal press policy was a rapid growth of newspapers.

Licensing Act, 1857

- This Act imposed licensing restriction and the right to stop publication and circulation of book, newspaper or printed matter reserved with the government.
- This Act was mainly introduced due to the emergency caused by the Revolt 1857, this Act imposed licensing restrictions in addition to the already existing registration procedure laid down by **Metcalfe Act**.

Registration Act, 1867

- This Act relaxed the restrictions put by Metcalf's Act of 1835 and hence, states that government acts as regulatory not restrictive body. As per the Act :
  - Every book/ newspaper was required to print the name of the printer and the publisher and the place of the publication.
  - A copy was to be submitted to the local government within one month of the publication of a book.

Vernacular Press Act, 1878

It was constituted for 'better control' of the vernacular press and effectively punished and repressed seditious writing. The provisions of the Act are given below:

- The District Magistrate was empowered to call upon the printer and publisher of any vernacular newspaper to enter into a bond with the government.
- By undertaking not to cause disaffection against the government or antipathy between persons of different religions, caste, race through published material.
- The printer and publisher could also be required to deposit security, which could be seized if the offences re-occurred.
- The magistrate's action was final and no appeal could be made in a court of law.
- A vernacular newspaper could get an exemption from the operation of the Act by submitting proof to a government censor.

Newspaper (Incitement to Offences) Act, 1908

- This Act empowered the magistrates to confiscate press property which published objectionable material.
- These material would likely to cause incitement to murder/acts of violence against the Extremist nationalist activity.

Indian Press Act, 1910

- This Act was a revision of the **Vernacular Act** that empowered the local government to demand a security at registration from the printer/publisher and forfeit/deregister if it was an offending newspaper.
- The printer of a newspaper was required to submit two copies of each issue to local government.

Press During and After the First World War

- Defence of India Rules were imposed for repression of political agitation and free public criticism during the First World War.
- In 1921, on the recommendations of a **Press Committee** chaired by **Tej Bahadur Sapru**, the Press Acts of 1908 and 1910 were repealed.

Indian Press (Emergency Powers) Act, 1931

- This Act gave powers to provincial governments to suppress propaganda for Civil Disobedience Movement.
- It was further amplified in 1932 to include all activities calculated to undermine government authority.

Press During the Second World War

- Under the Defence of India Rules, pre-censorship was imposed and amendments made in Press Emergency Act and Official Secrets Act.
- At one time, publication of all news related to Congress activity was declared illegal.

Development of Press in India After Independence

- In March 1947, a **Press Enquiry Committee** was established to analyse the various existing laws and regulations and to modulate them in accordance with the Fundamental Rights proposed by the Constituent Assembly.
- The Committee recommended to repeal the Indian Emergency Powers Act of 1931, modification in Section 124(A) and Section 153(A) of the Indian Penal Code, Amendments to the Press and Registration of Books Act.

Extra Facts From Tamil Nadu Board and NIOS

- English education in India began in the 18th century with the education of children in Anglo-Indian schools in **Calcutta**, **Madras** and **Bombay** by some charity schools.
- On the basis of **Wood's Dispatch Scheme**, Department of Public Instruction was established in 1855 AD. The Wood's Dispatch (1854) also emphasised on vocational education.
- Punjab University and Allahabad University was established in **1882 AD** and **1887 AD** respectively.
- Among the newspapers, Calcutta Chronicle was published in **1786 AD**, Madras Courier in **1788 AD** and Bombay Herald was published in **1789 AD**.
- During the period of Wellesley in **1799 AD**, strict restrictions were imposed on the press by the censorship of Press Act. In which the pre-censorship was removed after giving some relaxation in **1818 AD** (during the period of Lord Hastings).

28

The Revolt of 1857

[SOURCES]

Class-VIII New NCERT Chap 5 (When People Rebel 1857 and After), Class-XII New NCERT Chap 10 (Rebels and the Raj : The Revolt of 1857 and its Representations), Class-VIII Old NCERT Chap 5 (Revolts against British Rule), Class-XII Old NCERT Chap 6 (The Revolt of 1857)

- The revolt of 1857 was one of the most important moments in Indian Freedom Struggle. The policies of the East India Company before 1857 had started to affect different section of people.
- Kings, queens, peasants, landlords, tribes and soldiers were all affected in different ways. People began resistance against such policies and actions that were harming their interests or were going against their sentiments, which culminated into this moment.

Causes of the Revolt

Variety of causes i.e., political, social, administrative, economic, military, etc were responsible for the outbreak of the Revolt of 1857. Important causes of the Revolt of 1857 are as follows :

Political Causes

- East India Company being ignored the interests and pleas of kings, nawabs, etc.
- **Rani Lakshmibai** of Jhansi wanted her adopted son as the heir to the kingdom after the death of her husband. **Nana Saheb**, the adopted son of **Peshwa Baji Rao II**, wanted his father's pension. But both were refused by company.
- Right to succession was denied to Hindu princes. Doctrine of Lapse and Subsidiary Alliances were used to subjugate states and take away their powers.
- Awadh provided around 75,000 sepoys to the company. It was annexed by **Lord Dalhousie** in name of 'misgovernance'. This act sent a wave of discontent among sepoys.
- The company also brought the Mughal dynasty to an end. The name of the Mughal king was removed from the coins minted by the company.
- In 1849, Governor-General Dalhousie announced that after the death of **Bahadur Shah Zafar**, the family of the king would be moved out of the Red Fort and given another place in Delhi to reside in. He would be last king and next would be called princes.

Subsidiary Alliance and Doctrine of Lapse

- **Subsidiary Alliance** It was devised by Lord Wellesley in 1798.
- Following were condition under this system which had to be accepted by those who entered into such an alliance.
  - The British would be responsible for protecting their ally from external and internal threats to their power.
  - In the territory of the ally, a British armed contingent would be stationed. He was known as resident.
  - The ally would have to provide the resources for maintaining this contingent.
  - The ally could enter into agreement with other rulers or engage in warfare only with the permission of the British.
- **Doctrine of Lapse** was an annexation policy followed by Dalhousie who ruled from 1848-1856. According to it any ruler under this if did not have male heir would be annexed by company. And any adopted son would only inherit his father's personal property and assets.

Administrative Causes

- The phase from Battle of Plassey 1757 to the Revolt of 1857 was not of peace. It had different uprisings against Britishers by tribes and peasants. **Sanyasi Revolt** in Bihar and Bengal, from 1763 to 1800 was one of such revolts. **Fairazi**, a Muslim sect also rose against Zamindar and British, in Faridpur in 1838.
- British policies did not make neither Zamindar nor peasant happy. Zamindar still understood problems of peasants and was kind, but Britishers were focused on their fixed revenue collections.
- Zamindars were dissatisfied with Britishers, as often their lands were taken away and were made to feel inferior.
- **Revenue settlement policies** did not satisfy new Zamindar and made peasants go through tough collections, brutalities of officials.
- In addition, common people were hit hard by the prevalence of corruption at the lower levels of administration. The police, petty officials and lower law courts were corrupt.
- Officials lost no opportunity of enriching themselves at the cost of the Ryots and Zamindars. The complex judicial system enabled the rich to oppress the poor. Torture and jailing of the cultivators for rent or land revenue or interest on debt were quite common.

Socio-Religious Causes

- The Britishers felt they were superior and they had right to 'civilised' Indian society. The abolition of the custom of *Sati*, the **legalisation of widow remarriage** and the opening of Western education to girls were seen as interference.
- An important factor in turning the people against British rule was fear of destroying their religion.
- This fear was due to the **activities of the Christian missionaries** who came in the schools, the hospitals, the prisons and at the market places.
- These missionaries tried to convert people and made violent **public attacks on Hinduism and Islam**. They openly criticised the long-cherished customs and traditions of the people.
- Religious sentiments were also hurt by the policy of taxing lands belonging to temples and mosques and to their priests or the charitable institutions which were not taxed by earlier rulers.
- Rumours and prophecies played important role in moving people into action in the revolt. Rumours such as British had mixed the bone dust of cows and pigs into the flour that was sold in the market. Prophecy that British rule would come to an end on the centenary of the Battle of Plassey, on 23rd June, 1857.

Economic Causes

- The most important cause of the popular discontent was the economic exploitation of the country by the British. The complete destruction of its traditional economic fabric impoverished the vast mass of peasants, artisans and handicraftsmen as also a large number of traditional Zamindars and chiefs.
- British policies destroyed local rulers and their courts who were patrons of handicrafts and artisans, which in turn led to destruction of local craftsmen and artist.
- British also favoured the items which came from West and tried to dumped them India, as they were cheaper and Indian commodities could not compete with them. Both of these led to impoverishment of people.
- This led to pressure on agricultural lands and discontent among rural areas which also affected sepoys who came from these areas.

Military Causes

- The Indian sepoys in the employ of the company also had reasons for discontent. They were unhappy about their pay, allowances and conditions of service. Some of the new rules. Moreover, violated their religious sensibilities and beliefs.
- In 1824, the sepoys were ordered to go to Burma by the sea route to fight for the company, when they refused, they were punished. Later, they agreed to go by the land route.
- In 1856, **Lord Canning's** Government **Service Entitlement Act** declared that every new person, who took up employment in the company's army had to agree to serve overseas if required.
- There was already discrimination in army between British and Indian soldiers in payments and promotions.
- And the foreign allowance *Bhatta* was withdrawn paid to sepoys which added to their wounds.

Immediate Cause

- The pre-existing discontent among sepoys was fuelled by newly introduced enfield rifle, whose cartridge was supposedly made of **cow and pig fat.** It was supposed to be bitten by mouth before use.
- Both of these issues became end points in their growing dissatisfaction for the sepoys. They felt it was done to destroy their religion and convert them into Christianity.
- Both Hindu and Muslim sentiments were hurt by these actions and no steps were taken to allay these fears.

Outside Influence on Revolt of 1857

- The period of the growth of discontent among the people coincided with certain events which shattered the general belief that British are unbeatable.

- They encouraged the people to believe that the days of the British regime were over.
- Britishers suffered setbacks in different battles in India as well as outside India. **Santhal uprising** (1855-57), **First Afghan War** (1838-42), **Punjab War** (1845-49) and the **Crimean War** (1854-56), provided a sense of belief that they can be challenged and won over.

Beginning and Course of Revolt

- On 8th April, 1857, **Mangal Pandey** was hanged to death for attacking his officers in **Barrackpore**.
- Some days later, some sepoys of the regiment at **Meerut** refused to do the army drill using the new cartridges, which were suspected of being coated with the fat of cows and pigs.
- Eighty-five sepoys were dismissed from service and sentenced to ten years in jail for disobeying their officers. This happened on 9th May, 1857.
- The response of the other Indian soldiers in Meerut was quite extraordinary. On 10th May, the soldiers marched to the jail in Meerut and released the imprisoned sepoys. They attacked and killed British officers.
- They captured guns and ammunition and set fire to the buildings and properties of the British and declared war on the Firangis. The soldiers were determined to bring an end to their rule in the country.
- The soldiers chose the Mughal Emperor **Bahadur Shah Zafar** as the leader of the rebellion. And with this, it turned into a widespread revolt all over not just military camps.
- Civilians began to join the unrest, particularly in North-Western and Awadh. It compassed of peasants, zamindars, religious leaders and civil servants.
- The Azamgarh Proclamation, 25th August, 1857, is one of the main sources of our knowledge about the rebel. The objectivity of this proclamation was to maintain unity against the British.
- Delhi was captured back by British on 20th September, 1857, **Bahadur Shah** was taken prisoner and sent to Rangoon (Myanmar). He died in 1862.
- Most of the leaders of rebellion were defeated. **Nana Saheb** lost Kanpur and escaped to Nepal in 1859. **Rani Lakshmibai** died on battlefield in June 1858.
- In the end by 1859, revolt had been suppressed and British had to bring more supplies and resources to re-establish their governance.
- Maulvi Ahmadullah Shah was one of the many maulvis who played an important part in the Revolt of 1837. He was popularly known as Dankashah. He was an leading personality from Faizabad (Awadh region).

Centres of Revolts and Leaders

Places	Indian Leaders	British Leaders	Dates
Delhi	General Bakht Khan	John Nicholson, Lieutenant Willoughby	11th May, 1857
Lucknow	Begum Hazarat Mahal	Colin Campbell, Henry Lawrence	4th June, 1857
Bihar	Kunwar Singh	William Taylor	27th July, 1857
Kanpur	Nana Saheb, Tantia Tope	Colin Campbell	4th June, 1857
Bareilly	Khan Bahadur Khan	—	4th June, 1857
Faizabad (Ayodhya)	Maulavi Ahmadullah	—	4th June, 1857
Jhansi	Rani Lakshmibai	Sir Hugh Rose	4th June, 1857
Allahabad (Prayagraj)	Liyaqat Ali	Colonel Neil	5th June, 1857
Barout, Uttar Pradesh	Shah Mal (Jat leader)	—	—
Kheri, Madhya Pradesh	Rani Avantibai	—	—

Weakness of Revolt and Failure

- Revolt was limited to Northern states; Southern, Western and Eastern were missing from the revolt.
- Some classes did not join the revolt and some Indian rulers even actively helped British officials.
- East India Company had modernised weapons (Guns, telegraph) by which they could easily tell about movements of rebels. Peasants and most of Indians fought with swords, spears and few had guns.
- Revolt was not very well-coordinated and was fought mostly independently without any strategy while British commanders experienced men like Lawrence brothers, **John Nicholson**, **James Outram**, etc.
- Revolt also did not have a forward looking outlook, even if they won an area did not know what to do with it.
- These rebel came from different sections of society and class and a feeling of unity or nationalism was missing.

Causes of the Failure of the Revolt

The poor organisation and lack of coordination among the rebels was perhaps the most important cause of its failure. Some other causes were as follows :

- The stronghold area of the revolt remained limited enabling the English to concentrate and utilise their strength, effectively against the rebels in the limited area.
- The English had better resources, **modern weapons** and materials of war.
- The **Telegraph** kept Commander-in-Chief well informed about the movement of rebels.
- There was **lack of unity** among Indians. Many natives actively helped the British to suppress the revolt. They were the *Scindhia* of Gwalior, the *Holkar* of Indore, the *Nizam* of Hyderabad, *Raja* of Jodhpur and other rulers of Patiala, Nabha, Jind and Kashmir and many other ruling chiefs and big *zamindars*.
- The modern educated Indians also did not support the revolt. They were repelled by the rebels' appeals to superstitions and their opposition to progressive social measures.
- Neither the leaders nor the sepoys were inspired by any high ideals of patriotism and nationalism.

Views of Historians on Nature of Revolt

- The Revolt of 1857 is difficult to be seen as most of the documents related to revolt were destroyed by rebels or were burnt by British officials. British did not want people to know rebels.
- Some consider it to be as **Sepoy Mutiny**; other as National Struggle or **First War of Independence**.
- **SB Chaudhary** describes as, "First War of Independence it certainly was, as in the whole canvas of the recorded history of India it would be difficult to find a parallel to this gigantic anti-foreign combine of all classes of people and of many provinces of India.
- There was never a war in India lasting continuously for more than a year and simultaneously in all the regions which had for its objective the abasement and ejectment of the alien ruling power."
- **Dr. K Datta** considers the Revolt of 1857 to have been "mainly a military outbreak, which was taken advantage of by certain discontented princes and landlords, whose interests had been affected by the new political order."
- **VD Savarkar** in his book, First War of Indian Independence described it as a "planned war of national independence."
- **RC Mazumdar** did not consider it as national struggle, and said, "It is difficult to avoid the conclusion that the so-called First National War of Independence of 1857 is neither First, nor National, nor War of Independence."

Significance of the Revolt

- Revolt was significant as it was not communal in character and Hindu-Muslim, both fought together. And it took from mutiny of soldiers and became a rebellion against Britishers.
- Another important thing to come out of revolt was new sense of a modern nationalism.

Impact of Revolt of 1857

- Revolt of 1857 was unprecedented and made Britishers feel seriously threatened which led to changes in administration and policies.
- The British Parliament passed a new Act in 1858 and transferred **East India Company** to the **British Crown** in order to ensure a more responsible management of Indian affairs.
- A member of the British Cabinet was appointed Secretary of State for India and made responsible for all matters related to the governance of India. He was given a Council to advice him, called the **India Council**.
- The Governor-General of India was given the title of Viceroy, i.e., a personal representative of the crown.
- Through these measures, the British Government accepted direct responsibility for ruling India.
- The change of responsibility to British crown was announced at *darbar* at Allahabad by **Lord Canning** in '**Queen's Proclamation**' on 1st November, 1858. So rule of East India Company came to an end.
- As Britishers came to realise they had antagonised and made enemy of native rulers, they tried to win over them by promising them autonomy and respect to their rights.
- Indian annexed states and provinces were brought under a **single British paramountancy**.
- The British officials found army to be main cause of such revolt and to prevent such reoccurrence, reorganised it.
- The domination of the army by European branch was fixed. The share of Europeans in army was increased and fixed at 1 to 2 in Bengal and 2 to 5 in Madras and Bombay armies.
- The old policy of excluding Indian sepoys from officer ranks was still maintained.

Indian National Movement : First Phase (1885-1915)

(SOURCES)

Class-VIII New NCERT Chap 8 (The Making of the National Movement : 1870s-1947),
Class-XII New NCERT Chap 11 (Mahatma Gandhi and the Nationalist Movement),
Class-XII Old NCERT Chap 9 (Growth of New India- The Nationalist Movement, 1858-1905);
Chap 10 (Nationalist Movement, 1905-1918: (Growth of Militant Nationalism)
Tamil Nadu Board (Class XI), NIOS

- The second half of the 19th century witnessed the emergence of national political consciousness and growth of organised National Movement in India.
- A new feeling of oneness and belongingness to the same nation also arised. It gave a new and different path to the movement for independence **Swaraj**.

Emergence of Nationalism in India

Consciousness of a common nation began to be clearly stated by the political associations formed after 1850, especially those that came into being in the 1870s and 1880s. Most of these were led by English-educated professionals such as lawyers.

Causes and Rise of Nationalism

Different causes that led to the rise of nationalism in India are as follows :

Differences in Interests of Indians and Britishers

- The root problem of British rule was its selfish interest which was totally different from Indian people. They ruled over India and always prioritised their interests over Indian welfare. Indians realised that their interests were being sacrificed over British manufacturers.
- Educated Indians were also dissatisfied with acquired knowledge about economic and political exploits by the British.
- The ruin of Indian economic conditions was also due to this very fact, India was dumped with cheaply made products from machines that destroyed Indian handicrafts. And at the same place nothing was done in respect of industrialisation in India.
- The peasants also realised that they were suffering due to foreign rule, who took away large part of their produce as revenue, and the police, courts, favoured and protected the *Zamindars* and landlords, who took heavy rents and exploited them.
- They realised **British capitalism** was not going to modernise Indian economic systems and British policies were meant to help British capitalists.
- Heavy tariffs, taxation and transport policies didn't help Indian capitalists, who were competing against industries favoured by the British.

Administrative and Economic Unification

- The sentiments of the nation grew among people after 1857 as India was unified and sense of nationalism emerged during the 19th and 20th centuries.
- The British gradually introduced a uniform system and modern system of government throughout the country and in this way unified it administratively.
- As an economic unit, the country had become a unit and the destruction of the local self-sufficient and rural economy interlinked the economic life of different parts of the country. If one area was under drought or famine others also felt shortages of food and prices fluctuations.

- **Introduction of telegraph, railways** and **unified postal system** had also brought different areas of India together and increased mutual contacts among Indians, particularly among the leaders.

Development of Press, Newspapers and Literature

- The main medium through which the Indian people of nationalist mindset spread their message of patriotism and modern ideas, thoughts, about social, economic conditions was the press.
- Many newspapers with nationalist thoughts emerged during the second half of the 19th century.
- They criticised British policies, perspectives of Indians were put forward, people were involved to unite and work for national betterment.
- Ideas of self-government, democracy and industries were brought in popular mass discussion by the press and newspapers. It also brought people living in different parts of the country together and helped them exchange their views.

Prominent Nationalist Writers of the Period

- Many novels, essays, patriotic poetry were written by writers like Bankim Chandra Chatterjee, Rabindranath Tagore in Bengali, Laxminath Bezbaruah in Assamese, Vishnu Shastri Chiplunkar in Marathi, Subramaniyam Bharti in Tamil.
- **Bharatendu Harishchandra** (the first writer in Hindi) and **Altaf Husain Hali** (Urdu writer) were famous in this period. They helped in arousing feeling of patriotism and national consciousness in country through their writings.

Modern Western Education and Thoughts

- In the 19th century, many Indians who were educated in Western education learnt and adapted a rational, secular, democratic and nationalist political viewpoint. They admired and had inspirations from contemporary nationalist movements of European nations.
- These educated people assumed the leadership of the national movement and gave it democratic and modern direction.
- English language also provided a certain uniformity and community among educated Indians and helped the speed of ideas between these people.

Effects of Contemporary World Movements

- Modern educated Indians found their political guide in **Rousseau, Paine, John Stuart Mill** and other Western thinkers.
- They had their political heroes in **Mazzini, Garibaldi,** and Irish nationalist leaders. These movements in Italy, South American nations where new states were being established provided a dream to Indian leaders of a free Indian nation.

Cultural and Historical Invocation of India's Past

- People of India had lost confidence in their own potential of self-government. British officials and some British thinkers constantly wrote about this.
- Nationalist writers, like **RG Bhandarkar, RL Mitra** and later **Swami Vivekananda** helped form a new picture and encouraged people to respect their own self and countered this propaganda.
- Nationalists pointed to Indian heritage of culture and rules of **Ashoka, Chandragupta Maurya, Akbar** etc. They helped people to have faith, think of self-government and throwing away chains of British rule over India.

Socio-Religious Reform Movements

- In light of Western and modern education, a new temperament developed through which religious, social, and other traditions were relooked and reformed were promoted.
- Steps were taken by new organisations that were established in the country, e.g., **Brahma Samaj, Paramhans Mandali, Prarthana Samaj, Arya Samaj** and **Mohammedan Literary Society**, etc.

Apathetic Attitude and Reactionary Policies of Lytton

- There was an attitude of racial superiority by Britishers and deliberate discrimination against Indians was done.
- Indians felt disgusted by such treatment and actions of officials.
- Lytton who served as Viceroy from 1876-1880, reduced the age limit of **Indian Civil Service** (ICS) examination from 21 years to 18 years to make it difficult for Indians to join in 1876.
- He held **Delhi Darbar** in 1877 which was heavily criticised as India was reeling under famine that time.
- Major Acts such as the **Vernacular Act, Arms Act** both passed in 1878 instigated a new front of opposition in the country.

Ilbert Bill Controversy (1883-1884)

- During the period of **Lord Ripon** (1880-1884) who came after **Lytton**, had the controversy of introducing Ilbert Bill. The Bill was supposed to end the 'judicial disqualification on the basis of race differences' but it was shelved because of opposition by Europeans.
- Thus, Bill's original purpose was gone as it was modified to keep the favour in place of Europeans.

- This made it clear to nationalist leaders that fairness and justice could not be expected from British empire and it made it clear that only united they could fight against the British.
- They also learnt how to agitate, put forth demands by agitations of Europeans who were against the Bill.

Political Organisations before Congress

- In the 1870s, Indian nationalism had gathered enough strength and momentum to appear as a major force on the Indian political scene. The **Indian National Congress,** founded in December, 1885, was the first organised expression of the **Indian National Movement** on an all-India scale. However, it had many predecessors.
- **Raja Ram Mohan Roy** was the first Indian leader to start an agitation for political reforms in India. Many public associations were started in different parts of India after 1836. Most of these were dominated by rich and aristocratic people and they were regional or local in nature.
- These usually worked for reforms in administration, association of Indians in administration and spread of education and were usually dealing with petitions being sent to the British Parliament with demands of Indians.

Names	Founders	Objectives
Bangabhasha Prakasika Sabha (1836 in Bengal)	Associates of Raja Ram Mohan Roy	Welfare of Society, it asked for attention of Britishers on problems of Indians and measures.
Zamindari Association or The Landholders' Society (1838)	Dwarkanath Tagore, Radhakant Deb, Prasanna Tagore, etc	Safeguarding interests of landlords.
Bengal British India Society (1843)	George Thompson	Collection and distribution of information about condition of people in British India.
British Indian Association (1851) **Note :** Its demand was accepted in the Charter Act of 1853- addition of six members to the Governor-General's Council was accepted.	Radhakant Deb	Separate legislature, separation of executive and judiciary, reduction of salary of higher officials, abolition of various duties.
East India Association (1866 in London)	Dadabhai Naoroji (known as Grand Old Man of India)	Influenced public in England to promote Indian welfare.
Indian League (1875)	Sisir Kumar Ghosh	Spreading political education
Indian Association of Calcutta or Indian National Association (1876) **Note :** Its first All India Conference in 1883 was attended by 100 delegates and it later merged with Indian National Congress in 1886.	Surendranath Banerjee, Anand Mohan Bose	Creating public opinion on politics, Unifying Indians in a common political process.
Poona Sarvajanik Sabha (1876)	SH Chiplunkar, Ganesh Vasudev Joshi, MG Ranade	Acting as a bridge between government and people.
Bombay Presidency Association (1885)	Badruddin Tyabji, Pherozeshah Mehta, KT Telang	Posting of Indians in jobs and organising ICS examination in India.
Madras Mahajan Sabha (1884)	M Viraraghavachari, B Subramaniya Aiyer, P Ananda Charlu	Organising local association works.

Formation of Indian National Congress

- Many Indian people have been planning for an All India Organisation of political nature for workers and activists. It was **AO Hume,** a retired English Civil Servant who founded the Indian National Congress in 1885.
- AO Hume got in touch with famous Indian leaders of that time and with their support the First Session of Indian National Congress (INC) was held at Bombay in December, 1885.
- First President of INC was **WC Bonnerjee** and the First Session of Congress was attended by 72 delegates.
- From here, each Congress Session was held every year in December in different states of the country each time. **Dadabhai Naoroji** was the President of Congress three times. **Badruddin Tyabji, Pherozeshah Mehta, Romesh Chandra Dutt, Gopal Krishna Gokhale** were other leaders who became President of INC in its early phase.

- Before this, two sessions of the Indian National Conference were held in **1883** and **1885** which had representatives from all over India.

Purpose and Objectives of INC

In the First Session of Indian National Congress, President **WC Bonnerjee** declared these to be its objectives :

- Training and organisation of public opinion in the country.
- Promotion of friendly relations between nationalist political workers from different parts of the country.
- Development and consolidation of the feeling of national unity irrespective of caste, religion or province
- Formulation of popular demands.
- Presentation of these demands before the British Government.

Safety Valve Theory

- Various safety valve theorists states that **AO Hume** founded Indian National Congress. He encouraged it to give a '**safety valve**' or a safe path to vent out the increasing discontent and dissatisfaction among educated Indians.
- He was the one who convinced **Lord Dufferin** not to hinder the formation of Congress.
- The 'Safety Valve Theory' is partially correct, as modern historians disagrees with it. They say that Congress represented thoughts of Indian political leaders. They knew, if such an organisation is founded, it would have met with stiff opposition from the British Government.
- According to **Bipin Chandra**, Indian leaders cooperated with Hume whose ideas were not evil and had love and respect for India and its poor people.

Attitude of British Power Towards Congress

- British officials were hostile to the rising nationalist movement and had become suspicious of the National Congress. Dufferin tried to persuade Hume to devote Congress to only social work and not political affairs.
- After Congress leaders refused to limit themselves only to social affairs, British Officials realised Congress had become a tool in hands of Indian leaders. It was the focus of Indian nationalism and they began to criticise it openly and its leaders.
- British officials from 1887 in Madras Presidency became totally against Congress. Dufferin labelled nationalist leaders as **disloyal babus**, **seditious brahmins** and **violent villains**. He termed the congress as a **Factory of sedition**.
- As Congress was uniting people and country, British officials used the policy of 'divide and rule'. They encouraged **Sayyid Ahmed Khan, Raja Shiva Prasad** of Benaras and other pro-British individuals to start an **Anti-Congress Movement**.
- British also tried to start a communal divergence by putting Hindu and Muslim interests. They offered concessions to one and repressed the other to put down nationalism.
- However, these efforts failed to limitise the growth of the national movement.

Moderate and Extremists Phase of Congress

First phase of Indian National Movement's can be further divided into two phases on the basis of policies and actions of Congress.

1. Moderate Phase (1885 to 1905)

- In the beginning of the Congress, there was dominance of leaders like **Dadabhai Naoroji, MG Ranade, Gopal Krishna Gokhale, WC Bonnerjee, SN Banerjee, Pherozeshah Mehta**, etc. They were firm believers in liberalism and a 'moderate' way of struggle.
- Moderates organised a powerful agitation against nearly all important official economic policies based on colonial structure.
- They opposed the British attempt to develop in India, making it supplier of raw materials, a market for British manufacturers and a field of investment for foreign capital.
- Moderates also complained of growing poverty and economic backwardness. They considered British exploitation the reason behind the failure of modern industry and low agricultural productivity to grow.
- Early moderates complained of the wealth of India being drained and demanded reduction of land revenue in order to lighten the burden of taxation on the peasants.
- Moderates in the early phase were not in favour of direct attack on the British Government and chose to work under such a system, but criticised the administration and policies.

Methods of Political Work of Moderates

- Early moderates as they believed that if public opinion was created and organised.
- They presented popular demands to the authorities through petitions, meetings, resolutions and speeches. The authorities would concede these demands gradually and step by step. They used **3Ps- Petitions, Protests** and **Prayers** for these demands.

- They published newspapers, wrote articles, and showed how British rule was leading to the economic ruin of the country.
- They criticised British rule in their speeches and sent representatives to different parts of the country to mobilise public opinion.
- They felt that the British had respect for the ideals of freedom and justice, and so they would accept the just demands of Indians.
- Therefore, it was necessary to express these demands and make the government aware of the feelings of Indians.

Propaganda of Moderates in England

- To persuade the British Government and public opinion in England in Indian favour, many steps were taken by **AO Hume, Dadabhai Naoroji** and **William Wedderburn**.
- For this, many newspapers, magazines were started and associations were set up in England.
- In 1887, Dadabhai Naoroji established the **Indian Reform Committee** in England.
- In 1888, with the association of William Digby, Dadabhai Naoroji set up the **Indian Political Agency** to hear the grievances of Indians. In 1889, British Committee of Congress was set up, which also published a monthly magazine named India.
- In 1890, a **Committee of Representatives** was sent to England by Congress to make representation of Indians in British Parliament. Members of this committee were **Surendranath Banerjee, WC Bonnerjee** and **AO Hume**.
- With the efforts of moderates in England, a sympathy was generated towards Indians. In 1879, **Lalmohan Ghosh** was sent to England to demand the posting of Indians in Civil Services.
- In the 1889 Session of Congress, a Member of British House of Commons, **Charles Bradella** was present.

Demands of Moderates

- In the early phase of Congress, moderate leaders did not ask for independence from British rule but demanded concessions, and presented their grievances which they hoped would be addressed.
- They asked for reforms in the following fields :
  - Legislatures and its expansion,
  - Posting of Indians in higher offices, exams in India and England for Indians in Civil Services and its Indianisation,
  - Removing the bans on press, newspapers and speeches,
  - Demand for inquiry by Royal Commission on Indian Administration,
  - Removal of taxes on salt,
  - Other industrial reforms and their promotion and
  - Repeal of the Arms Act.

Contributions of Moderates in Indian National Movement

- According to critics, not much was achieved by early moderates and Congress, as very few reforms were introduced of the demands made by them.
- It is partially true, but it cannot be said the early phase of moderate and Congress was a failure.
- It succeeded in creating awareness of the feeling of belonging to a common nation among people.
- It showed how politically, socially and economically their interests were intertwined.
- It trained people in political work and popularised among people the idea of democracy, liberty, nationalism and secularism.
- They exposed the true character of British rule, by showing how they used the economic resources of India for them.
- Their economic critique of imperialism served as a main base for coming years of national movement against British rule.
- It laid the foundation for national struggle which was to grow and it provided a political and economic programme on which later political struggle could be based.

2. Extremists Phase (1905-1919)

- Over the years, the trend of radical thoughts grew and an extremist approach to national movements started to grow from the 1890s. By 1905 onwards, it took a concrete shape.
- Leaders of this school of thought included Raj Narain Bose, Aswini Kumar Datta, Aurobindo Ghose, Bipin Chandra Pal in Bengal, and Vishnu Shastri Chiplunkar and Tilak in Maharashtra.

Reasons for Growth of Extremism

- When the British Government was not conceding to important demands, many of the political leaders started to feel that only an Indian Government could bring India on a path of progress attracted more and more people.
- In the years between 1896 and 1900, over 90 lakhs died because of severe famines. Bubonic plague affected large areas of Deccan, the British Government failed to provide major relief and help in these areas.
- The British did not pay attention to people in distress, leaders in the **Indian National Congress** (INC) felt politically disappointed.

- Spread of education among the masses led to increased awareness. The rising unemployment among the educated led their attention to poverty and underdevelopment under British rule.
- International events in the 19th century encouraged extremists in India also. Progress made by Japan after 1868 and its emergence as an industrial power opened the eyes of Indians.
- They realised that economic progress was possible even by an Asian country without any external help.
- The defeat of the Italian army by **Ethiopians** (1896), the **Boer Wars** (1899-1902) where the British forces defeated and Japan's victory over Russia (1905) demolished myths of European invincibility.
- Also, the nationalists were inspired by the nationalist movements worldwide in Ireland, Russia, Egypt, Turkey, Persia and China.
- The Indians realised that a uniform spirit of people with will to make sacrifices could take on the mightiest of empires.
- Reacting to increasing Westernisation, the new leadership felt the stranglehold of excessive Westernisation and sensed colonial designs to submerge the Indian national identity in the British empire.
- The intellectual and moral inspiration of the new leadership was Indian intellectuals like **Swami Vivekananda, Bankim Chandra Chatterjee** and **Swami Dayanand Saraswati**.
- They inspired many young nationalists with their forceful and articulate arguments, painting India's past in brighter colours than the British ideologies had.

Major Events that Shaped Nationalist Growth

Years	Significance
1892	Indian Council Act was passed, it failed to satisfy extremists leaders as it did not fulfill all demands.
1897	The Natu Brothers were deported without trial and Tilak and others were charged with sedition.
1898	Repressive laws in IPC Section 124 (A) were made more stringent with addition of new provisions under Section 156 (A).
1899	In Calcutta Corporation number of Indian members was reduced.
1904	Official Secret Act was brought to curb the freedom of press.
1904	Indian Universities Act was brought to bring more control over universities so that it can exercise power over activities and discussions of national movement there.

Partition of Bengal, 1905

- On 16th October, 1905, **Lord Curzon** had divided Bengal into Eastern Bengal (with Assam) and the rest of Bengal. The decision had come after Lord Curzon claimed that Bengal was too large to be governed effectively.
- The partition separated the largely **Muslim Eastern areas** from the largely **Hindu Western areas.** It was definitely the 'divide and rule' policy for the Indians and the national leaders outraged about the fact that the British Government turning native population against itself in order to rule.
- Bengali Hindus were at the forefront of political agitation. Following the partition, an **Anti-British Movement** began. This involved non-violent and violent protests and boycotts. The Indian National Congress began the **Swadeshi Movement**.

Swadeshi and Boycott Movement

- The main reason for partition of Bengal was to weaken the political struggle whose centre was in Bengal.
- **Lord Curzon** tried to favour the Muslims by announcing that Dacca (Dhaka) would be new capital of Muslim majority province.
- With the announcement of partition on 7th August, 1905, a **Resolution of Boycott** was announced in Calcutta town hall and the formal proclamation of **Swadeshi Movement** was made.
- On 16th October, 1905, the partition came into force, this day was observed as a day of mourning throughout Bengal. People bathed in Ganga and walked barefoot singing **Vande Mataram** which became the theme song of the movement.
- People tied rakhis on each other's hand as a symbol of unity. **Surendranath Banerjee** and **Anand Mohan Bose** addressed the gathering.

Other Movements and their Leaders

Regions	Leaders
Poona and Bombay	Bal Gangadhar Tilak
Punjab	Lala Lajpat Rai and Ajit Singh
Delhi	Syed Haider Raza
Madras	Chidambaram Pillai

Position of Congress

- Under the Presidentship of **Gopal Krishna Gokhale,** Congress in 1905, condemned partition and supported Anti-Partition and Swadeshi Movement.

- In 1906, under the Presidentship of **Dadabhai Naoroji,** the goal of Congress was declared as the 'self-government' or **Swaraj.**

Movement Under Extremist Leadership

- Under extremist leaders, boycott of foreign goods, public meetings and processions were organised.
- Samiti or corps of volunteers generated awareness. They tried to arise the sentiments of the public by songs, lectures, training in Swadeshi crafts and organising courts.
- Self-reliance or *Atma Shakti* was encouraged, emphasis was placed on national dignity, honour, and social and economic regeneration of villages.
- A Swadeshi Programme on National Education was planned. **Bengal National College** was set up in 1906 (Aurobindo Ghosh as its Principal), inspired by Tagore's **Shantiniketan.**
- On 15th August, 1906, National Council of Education was set up **Satish Chandra Mukherjee** to organise National Education - literary, scientific and technical. Education was to be imparted in the vernacular medium. Bengal Institute of Technology was set up for technical education.
- Swadeshi (indigenous) Enterprises such as : Swadeshi textile mills, soap and match factories, tanneries, banks, insurance companies, shops, etc were set up. **VO Chidambaram Pillai** set up the **Swadeshi Steam Navigation Company** at Tuticorin.
- **Rabindranath Tagore** wrote *Amar Sonar Bangla,* **Subramania Bharati** wrote *Swadesha Geetham* to arouse national sentiments.
- **Tilak** used **Ganapati** and **Shivaji** festival as a medium of propagation of nationalist ideas. In Bengal, traditional folk theatres were used for this purpose.

Participation of Masses

- There was mass participation of students, and women in the Swadeshi Movement. Labour unions organised strikes in Bengal, Punjab and Tamil Nadu. So, the social base of the movement had increased.
- Muslim of upper and middle caste didn't participate in the movement. People like Nawab **Salimullah** of Dacca supported the Bengal partition.

Suppression of the Movement

- The British Government adopted a harsh attitude towards the agitators. Indigenous activists were prosecuted and jailed.
- To end the participation of students in the **Swadeshi Movement**, the British Government, on 22nd October, 1905, the **Carlyle Circular** was implemented.
- Under this, grants and scholarships given to educational institutions were to be stopped. The students were even given corporal punishment.
- In December 1908, 9 leaders of Bengal were expelled from the country by the police at the Bengal Provincial Conference held at Barisal in April, 1900. Among them were **Krishna Kumar Mitra** and **Ashwini Kumar Datta.**
- After the riots in Punjab, **Lala Lajpat Rai** and **Ajit Singh** were expelled from the country.
- The movement failed to create an effective organisation or a party structure. The movement was rendered leaderless with most of the leaders either arrested or deported by 1908 and with **Aurobindo Ghosh** and **Bipin Chandra Pal** retiring from active politics.
- Internal differences among leaders, magnified by the **Surat Split** (1907) also affected the movement.
- The movement aroused the people but did not know how to use the newly released energy or how to find new forms to give expression to popular resentment.

Establishment of Muslim League (1906)

- Partition of Bengal became the biggest reason for the split between Hindu and Muslim communities in India.
- The Muslim delegation under the leadership of **Aga Khan** met the then Viceroy **Lord Minto** and demanded a special status for Muslims.
- In the year 1906, **Muslim League** was established in Dhaka under the leadership of **Salimulla Khan** and **Aga Khan**. The first President of the League was **Waqar-ul-Mulk Mustaq Hussain.**
- Between the years 1905 to 1907, the mutual differences of extremist and liberal ideas grew.
- Moreover, the leaders of the Extremist Party did not believe in the ability of the Moderates to negotiate with the British Government.
- In the year 1905, in the Banaras Session of the Congress, both the parties reached the edge of split over the post of President.
- In the conference, Tilak wanted to make **Lala Lajpat Rai** the President and **Bipin Chandra** Pal wanted to make Tilak the President. This possibility was averted with **Dadabhai Naoroji** becoming the President.

Surat Split (1907)

- In 1907 Surat session, the two main objectives placed by the extremists were that

  (i) Demand for resolution of swaraj

  (ii) Tilak or Lala Lajpat Rai to be made the president of INC.

- These two demands were not acceptable to the moderates. Thus instead of Lala Lajpat Rai or Tilak, the moderates supported the idea of Rash Behari Ghosh as the president. This was the first time that there was to be an election in the INC presidentship held.
- In between the election, the extremists were expelled from the INC and the moderates had complete command over the affairs of the INC. Rash Behari Ghosh became the president of Surat session.

Delhi Darbar

- The Delhi Darbar was an Indian imperial style mass assembly organised by the British to mark the succession of an Emperor or Empress of India. It was held three times i.e., in 1877, 1903 and 1911.
- The Darbar of 1877 was called **Proclamation Darbar**. It's organisation was undertaken by **Thomas Henry Thornton**.
- It was held to proclaim Queen Victoria as Empress of India by the British. It was attended by the first **Earl of Lytton** (Viceroy of India), many Princely States and intellectuals.
- This was the culmination of transfer of control of British India from the East India Company to the crown.
- The Darbar in December 1911 was held to commemorate the coronation of **George V** and **Mary of Teck** and to allow their proclamation as Emperor and Empress of India.
- In this Darbar, annulment of partition of Bengal and the transfer of India's capital from Calcutta to Delhi were announced.

First Phase of Revolutionary Activities (1907-17)

The beginning of revolutionary ideology and activities in Indian were the result of internal and external factors.

Revolutionary Programme

The revolutionaries did not adopted a violent mass revolution throughout the country at this stage.

Instead, they opted to follow in the footsteps of **Russian** or the **Irish nationalists**.

This methodology involved individual heroic actions, such as:

- Organising assassinations of unpopular officials, traitors and informers among the revolutionaries themselves.
- Conducting *Swadeshi* dacoities to raise funds for revolutionary activities (during the First World War), organising military conspiracies with expectation of help from the enemies of Britain.

Emergence of Revolutionary Movement

- Disappointed with the outcomes of the work of moderates of Congress, extremists emerged which gave birth to the movement.
- They were inspired by **Western ideology**. They used to publish literature for the promotion of their ideas. The major centres of early phase of revolutionary movement was in Bengal, Maharashtra, Punjab, Uttar Pradesh and almost entire parts of East India.

Objectives of the Movement

- The idea was to strike terror in the hearts of the rulers.
- Arouse people and remove the fear of authority from their minds.
- The revolutionaries intended to inspire the people by appealing to their patriotism, especially the idealistic youth.

Revolutionary Activities

The description of revolutionary activities in different parts of India is given below :

Bengal

- By the 1870s, Calcutta's student community was mixed with secret societies, but these were not as active.
- The first revolutionary groups were organised in 1902 in Midnapore, in Bengal under **Jnanendranath Basu**, and in Calcutta.
- The **Anushilan Samiti** was founded by **Promotha Mitter** and including Jatindranath Banerjee, Barindra Kumar Ghosh and others.
- Activities of these societies were limited to giving physical and moral training to the members and were not that significant till 1907.
- In April 1906, an inner circle within Anushilan with **Barindra Kumar Ghosh, Bhupendranath Dutta** started the weekly magazine *Yugantar*.
- In 1906, **Rash Behari Bose** and **Sachin Sanyal** organised a secret society covering Punjab, Delhi and United Province. **Hemachandra Kanungo** went abroad for military and political training.
- The **Yugantar group** made an attempt on the life of a very unpopular British official, **Sir Fuller** (the first Lt. Governor of the new province of Eastern Bengal and Assam).
- They attempted to derail the train on which the Lieutenant-Governor, Sir Andrew Fraser, was travelling.
- **Dacca Anushilan** under **Pulin Das** did **Barrah dacoity** to raise funds for revolutionary activities.

Alipore Bomb Conspiracy Case (1908)

- The 'Alipore Bomb Conspiracy Case' was related to the assassination attempt against **Douglas Kingsford**, who was an unpopular British Chief Magistrate. He was the target of the bomb thrown at Muzaffarpur (Northern Bihar).
- Two young revolutionists **Prafulla Chaki** and **Khudiram Bose** threw bomb. However, the carriage at which the bomb was targeted not contained Kingsford, but two British women, who died in the attack.
- The British Government arrested **Sri Aurobindo, Barindra Ghose** and many young revolutionaries. They were charged with 'Conspiracy' or 'waging war against the King'. They were all members of the Anushilan Samiti in Calcutta.
- Chaki committed suicide while Bose, then only 18 years of age, was caught and sentenced to death by hanging. Aurobindo Ghose was released due to lack of evidence and others served life-terms in prison.

Maharashtra

- Revolutionary activities here was the organisation of the **Ramosi Peasant Force** by **Vasudev Balwant Phadke** in 1879.
- It aimed to remove the British using an armed revolt by and breaking communication lines. It hoped to raise funds for its activities through dacoities. It was stopped at the very start.
- During the 1890s, **Tilak** began a spirit of militant nationalism, through Ganapati and Shivaji festivals and his journals **Kesari** and **Maharaita**. Two of his disciples– the Chapekar brothers, **Damodar** and **Balkrishna** murdered the Plague Commissioner of **Poona, Rand** and one **Lt. Ayerst** in 1897.
- Savarkar and his brother organised **Mitra Mela**, a secret society, in 1899 which merged with **Abhinav Bharat** (imitating Mazzinni's Young Italy) in 1904. With this, Nashik, Poona and Bombay became centres of bomb-making.
- In 1909, **Jackson**, the District Magistrate of Nashik, was killed by **Anant Lakshman**; who was a member of Abhinav Bharat.

Punjab

- Reason of Extremism in Punjab was due to issues of frequent famines and rise in land revenue, and irrigation tax, practice of 'begar' by *zamindars*, and by the events in Bengal.
- Leaders like, **Lala Lajpat Rai** brought out *Punjabee* (with its motto of all help at any cost) and Ajit Singh (Bhagat Singh's uncle) who organised the extremist **Anjuman-Mohisban-Watan** in Lahore with its journal, *Bharat Mata*.
- **Ajit Singh's** group turned to extremism and was active in urging non-payment of revenue and water rates among Chenab colonists and Bari Doab peasants.
- Other leaders included **Aga Haider, Syed Haider Raza, Bhai Parmanand**. The radical Urdu poet, **Lalchand Falak** joined the movement.
- The British Government in May 1907 banned political gathering and Lala Lajpat Rai and Ajit Singh were deported and the movement died down here.

Revolutionary Activities Abroad

- The need for shelter, possibility of bringing out revolutionary literature that would not be under Press Acts, and search for arms took revolutionaries abroad.
- **Shyamji Krishnavarma** started India House, in 1905 in London, it was a student resident for radical youth students. **VD Savarkar** and **Lala Hardayal** became members of **India House**.
- **Madanlal Dhingra** assassinated India Office bureaucrat **Curzon Wylie** in 1909.
- **Madam Bhikaji Cama**, started Indian **Home Rule Movement** in 1916 in **Belgavi** and established a centre in France and brought out **Vande Bharat** newspaper. It was operated by Ajit Singh.
- **Virendranath Chattopadhyay** did his activities from Berlin in 1909. Alongwith him, **Bhupendranath Dutta, Lala Hardayal** and others, the **Berlin Committee for Indian Independence** was established in 1915.
- It was helped by German officials and was known as the **Zimmerman Plan**. It was to use and mobilise Indians in Foreign countries and arms, and send volunteers to India for rebellion against the British.

The Ghadar

- It was a revolutionary group organised around a weekly newspaper, **The Ghadar** with its headquarters at San Francisco and branches along the coast of USA and in the far East. **The Ghadar** was established in **1913**.
- The Ghadar Programme intended to organise assassinations of officials, publish revolutionary and anti-imperialist literature, work among Indian troops abroad, procure arms and bring about a revolt in all British colonies.
- The revolutionaries included mainly ex-soldiers and peasants who had migrated from the Punjab to the USA and Canada in search of better employment opportunities.
- Pre-Ghadar revolutionary activities were carried out by **Ramdas Puri, GD Kumar, Taraknath Das, Sohan Singh Bhakna** and **Lala Hardayal** from 1911.

- **Swadesh Sevak Home** was set up in Vancouver, and 'United India House' at Seattle.
- Prominent Ghadar leaders were Lala Hardayal, Ramchandra, Bhagwan Singh, Kartar Singh Sarabha, Barkatullah and Bhai Parmanand.
- **Defence of India Act, 1915** was the chief and most draconian instrument used by the British to counter the Ghadar Movement.

Komagata Maru Incident

- In the year 1914, Komagata Maru- a ship chartered from Singapore carrying Sikh and Punjabi Muslims were denied entry into Canada and forced to return to India.
- The British Government tried to detain the immigrants at Calcutta, in order to transport them to Punjab.
- The immigrants refused to give in. A tussle ensued in which 22 immigrants lost lives.
- The Ghadar leaders were angry by this incident. They planned to launch a violent attack to expel the British.
- **Kartar Singh Sarabha, Raghubar Dayal Gupta, Rashbehari Bose** and **Sachin Sanyal** were the prominent leaders involved in the attack.
- 21st February, 1915 was fixed as the date of attack. However, the British got to know about the attack, made pre-emptive arrests and suppressed the movement.

Decline of Revolutionary Activities

There was a temporary decline in revolutionary activities due to various seasons. These were as follows :

- Release of prisoners held under the Defence of India Rules, after the World War I.
- Montagu's statement of August, 1917 offered some conciliations to Indians.
- Entry of Gandhiji in the freedom struggle and his new methods of struggle.

World War I and Nationalist's Response

- In **First World War** (1914-1919), Britain allied with France, Russia, USA, Italy and Japan against Germany, Austria Hungary and Turkey.
- Nationalists leaders responded to British participation in war in three ways:
  - Moderates were in favour of offering support to Britishers in war as a matter of duty.
  - Extremists including Tilak supported the war in misbelief that the British Government would provide self-government to Indians as payback.
  - The revolutionaries groups decided to use the opportunity to wage a war on the British and free the country.
- Indians failed to realise while supporting Britishers in war efforts that the British were fighting only to safeguard their colonies and investments and markets.

Revolutionary Activities Done in War Times

- Ghadar Party carried activities mainly in North America.
- **Berlin Committee** in Europe sent missions to Baghdad, Persia, Turkey, Kabul to work among Indian prisoners of war and to incite anti-British sentiments.
- **Raja Mahendra Pratap Singh, Mohammed Barkatullah** and **Ubaidullah Sindhi** went to Kabul to establish a 'Provisional Indian Government' with the help of Prince Amanullah in 1915.
- Indian soldiers in Singapore revolted against the British Government on 15th February, 1915. It's leaders were **Jamadar Chisti Khan, Jamadar Abdul Gani** and **Subedar Daud Khan**.

Extra Facts From Tamil Nadu Board and NIOS

- Following factors were also responsible for rise of nationalism in India.
  - Laissez faire policy and De-industrialisation : Impact on Indian Artisans.
  - The commodification of land and commercialisation of agriculture.
  - Racial discrimination, the English followed a policy of racial discrimination.
- Both Moderates and the radicals (Extremists) were of the same view when it come to accepting the fact that they needed to fulfill the role of educators. They tried to instill nationalist consciousness through various means including press.
- Dadabhai Naoroji founded and edited two journals called Voice of India and Rastgoftar.
- Gopal Krishna Gokhale said, "the Swadeshi Movement is not only for the improvement of our industry but for an allround enhancement of our national life".
- Swadeshi means of one's own country. The origin of the idea can be traced to 1872 when Mahadev Govind Ranade, in a series of lectures in Poona, popularised the idea of Swadeshi.

30

Indian National Movement : Second Phase (1915-1935)

[SOURCES]

Class-VIII New NCERT Chap 8 (The Making of the National Movement: 1870s-1947), Class-XII New NCERT Chap 11 (Mahatma Gandhi and the Nationalist Movement), Class-XII Old NCERT Chap 11 (Nationalist Movement, 1905-1918; Growth of Militant Nationalism), Class-VIII Old NCERT Chap 10 (Struggle for Swaraj)

- In the second phase of the Indian National Movement, Indian leaders, after providing support to the British Government in **World War I** expected returns from them, and planned further movement accordingly.
- This phase also marked the entry of **Mahatma Gandhi** into the Indian Freedom Struggle.

Lucknow Pact (1916)

- The **Lucknow Session** (1916) was presided by a moderate leader **Ambika Charan Majumdar**. This session witnessed two important events i.e.,
  - **First,** Extremists led by Tilak were readmitted in Congress fold.
  - **Secondly,** Muslim League and Congress joined each other and presented their demands together to the British Government.
- Joint demands made by Congress and Muslim League were; Self-Government, Representative Assemblies, reforms in Viceroy's Council, Secretary of State to be paid by British treasury.
- Extremists were readmitted in Congress as differences of past opinions had become meaningless. Political inactivity created by extremists because of the split were realised by both moderates and extremists.
- **Annie Besant** and **Tilak** made efforts for reunion of extremists and moderates to strengthen the movement.
- Death of two main moderates **Gopal Krishna Gokhale** and **Pherozeshah Mehta** also led to further closeness among two sections.

Reasons behind shift in Muslim League's Stand and Lucknow Pact were :

- Britain's refusal to help Turkey during World War I.
- Annulment of Bengal's partition.
- Refusal by British Government to set up University at Aligarh with powers to affiliate colleges.
- Rise of younger members in the league, who were more anti-imperialistic like **Maulana Azad** (through his work *Al Hilal*) and **Mohammad Ali** (by his work *Comrade*) helped Muslim League to change its stand.
- Congress agreed to the League's demand for a separate electorate. Muslims were granted a fixed proportion of seats at all-India and provincial levels.

Evaluation of Lucknow Pact

- Though bringing together of Congress and Muslim League was a grand vision but the acceptance of separate electorates by Congress led to establishment of **Two-nation Theory**. Efforts of bridging the gap between masses of two communities were not done.
- Acceptance of separate electorates helped in allaying fears of minority community.
- This pact generated a new wave of enthusiasm and hope in people because of reunion.

- This pact also led the British Government to declare to grant self-government to Indians in **Montagu's August 1917** declaration, seeing unity among various factions Congress and also with league.

Home Rule League Movement

It was an Indian response to the **First World War**, inspired by the **Irish Home Rule League**. The Indian National Movement at this time was influenced by various factors which led to formation of Home Rule Leagues.

These were :

- Nationalists believed that popular pressure was required to attain concessions from the government.
- The moderates were disillusioned with the **Morley-Minto Reforms**.
- People were feeling the burden of wartime miseries caused by high taxation and a rise in prices and were ready to participate in any aggressive movement of protest.
- It was an imperialist war that exposed the myth of white supremacy.
- **Bal Gangadhar Tilak**, after his release in 1914, was ready to assume nationalist leadership. He was inspired by the Irish Home Rule League.
- **Annie Besant** began to take active part in Nationalist movement.

Objectives of the Home Rule League

- The main objective of the movement was **self-rule**.
- Self-rule was to be achieved through political education and discussion.
- It can be done by collecting funds, organising social work and participating in local government activities.

Branches of Home Rule League

- **Tilak** and **Besant** set up separate leagues to avoid friction. Tilak's league was set up in April, 1916 and it's activities covered Maharashtra (except Bombay), Karnataka, Central Provinces and Berar.
- It has six branches. Its demands were Swarajya, formation of linguistic states and education in vernacular languages.
- **Annie Besant** set up her league in September, 1916 in Madras and covered the rest of India (this included Bombay also).
- It had 200 branches, was loosely organised as compared to Tilak's League and **George Arundale** was it's organising secretary. **BP Wadia** and **CP Ramaswamy Aiyar** also worked closely with these leagues.

Major Leaders in Leagues

- Leaders like Motilal Nehru, Jawaharlal Nehru, Bhulabhai Desai, Jinnah, Tej Bahadur Sapru, Lala Lajpat Rai, CR Das, Madan Mohan Malviya joined leagues.
- **Servants of India Society** also joined the movement. It was formed by **Gopal Krishna Gokhale**.
- Muslims and Non-Brahmins from South India did not join as they were under the impression that leagues were a Hindu majority and dominated by high castes.

Response of British Government to Home Rule Leagues

- The British Government dealt with high hands with leagues. Annie Besant and her companions, **BP Wadia** and **George Arundale** were arrested in June, 1917.
- Opposing the arrest, **Sir Subramaniya Aiyar** renounced his Knighthood and **Tilak** began passive resistance against this action of the government.

Decline of Home Rule Leagues

- There was not effective organisation in leagues, they were loosely formed.
- Communal riots witnessed during 1917-1918 weakened the movement.
- The moderates were pacified by method of reforms.
- The extremists kept the moderates away from activity from September, 1918 onwards.
- The **Montagu-Chelmsford Reforms** which became known in July, 1918 further divided leaders.
- League main leaders like Tilak and Annie Besant moved army, Tilak went abroad and Annie Besant in response to proposed reforms resorted to passive movements.

Achievements of Home Rule League Movement

- These leagues shifted base from educated people to masses. The link was established between villages and towns this movement created new cadre of nationalists this phase paved the way for next stage of movement of Gandhi phase.
- Home Rule League leaders helped bridge the gap between moderate and extremists by **Lucknow Pact 1916**.
- **August Declaration of 1917**, by Montagu was direct result of these movements.

Gandhian Era of Indian National Movement

- The emergence of **Mohandas Karamchand Gandhi** in the National Movement played a pivotal role in the history of Indian Nationalism.
- Gandhiji relied on the tools of *Ahimsa* and *Satyagraha* to fight the British regime.

Gandhi's Activism in South Africa

- The first twenty years that Gandhiji spent in South Africa, had a decisive influence on his later life. His political ideologies, his greatest contribution to Indian politics, took shape in South Africa.
- Gandhiji relied on sending petitions and memorials to authorities in South Africa and Britain. To unite different sections of the population, Gandhiji setup **Natal Indian Congress** and started newspaper *Indian Opinion*.

Satyagraha/Campaign of Gandhiji in South Africa

- **Satyagraha against Registration Certificate** New legislation made it mandatory to carry registration certificates for Indians. Indians under Gandhiji's leadership started Satyagraha against this discriminatory practice.
- **Campaign against Restrictions on Indian Migration** New legislation imposed restrictions to migration, Indians defied by crossing over from one province to other.
- **Campaign against Poll Tax and Invalidation of Indian Marriages** A poll tax of 3 Pounds was imposed on all ex-indentured Indians, abolished of poll tax and demanded for invalidation of Indian marriages.

Arrival of Mahatma Gandhi in India

- Gandhiji returned to India in 1915. During his starting days, he spent his time at the **Sabarmati Ashram** in Ahmedabad.
- At this time, Gandhiji sought guidance from **Gopal Krishna Gokhale** in assuming his political stance. It was Gokhale's advice to Gandhiji that he should first study in detail the socio-political scenario prevalent in the country and then act accordingly.
- Gandhiji attended first major public appearance at BHU, Varanasi in 1916.

Initial Movements in India

After spending time at Ashram and roaming the country, Gandhiji led different movements, some of the initial movements are as follows :

Champaran Satyagraha, 1917

- It was the **first Civil Disobedience Movement** in India.
- During the 31st congress session in Lucknow in 1916, Gandhiji met Rajkumar Shukla, who requested him to come and see the miseries of Indigo ryots in Champaran.
- Peasants were forced to grow indigo on 3/20th part of the land, which was known as the **Tinkathia System.**
- European planters demanded high rents and illegal dues to maximise their profits.
- A committee was constituted to look into the issue and Gandhiji was a member of that committee.
- The *Tinkathia System* was abolished and 25% of the compensation was provided.
- Other leaders related to this movement were **Rajendra Prasad, Mazhar-ul-Haq, Mahadeo Desai, Narhari Parekh, JB Kripalani**, etc.

Ahmedabad Mill Strike, 1918

- In March, 1918, there was a strike in the cotton mills under the leadership of Gandhiji. In this strike Gandhiji used Hunger strike first time in Indian National movement.
- Dispute between cotton mill owners and workers over the issue of discontinuation of **plague bonus.**
- Workers were demanding a raise of 50% in wages.
- Gandhiji demanded for a 35% hike and took a fast unto death.
- **Anusuya Sarabhai** was a social worker who invited Gandhiji to fight for these mill workers.

Kheda Satyagraha, 1918

- It was the **first Non-Cooperation Movement** by Gandhiji.
- In Kheda district of Gujarat crops had failed but the administration was still hell bent on retrieving the taxes.
- Though there was a remission clause in case of failure of produce, British administrators didn't give remission.
- Leaders associated with Kheda Satyagraha were **Sardar Vallabhbhai Patel, Narhari Parekh, Mohanlal Pandya**.

Rowlatt Act, 1919

- In March 1919, the British Government passed the Rowlatt Act, despite every single Indian member of the **Central Legislative Council** being opposed to it.
- This Act authorised the Government to imprison any person without trial and conviction in a court of law.

- So, it enabled the Government to suspend the right of Habeas Corpus which had been the foundation of civil liberties in Britain.
- The Act was officially called the **Anarchical and Revolutionary Crimes Act**.
- It recommended imprisonment of activists without trial for two years. Gandhiji called for a mass protest at all India levels.

Anti-Rowlatt Satyagraha

- Before the protests which was supposed to start on 6th April, 1919, there were large scale violent, anti-British demonstration in major cities.
- It was the first all India protest movement on a mass level.
- He organised **Satyagraha Sabha** and roped in youths of Home Rule Leagues and Pan Islamists.
- They form of protest finally chosen included observance of a nationwide hartals.
- These hartals were accompanied by fasting and prayer and Civil Disobedience was against specific laws, etc.

Jallianwala Bagh Massacre

- The Jallianwala Bagh Massacre (also known as the Amritsar Massacre), took place on 13th April, 1919.
- Against the **Rowlatt Act**, there were protests by Indians and repression was on peak by British Officials.
- Troops of the British Indian Army under the command of Acting **Brig-Gen Reginald Dyer** fired rifles into a crowd of people who had gathered in Jallianwala Bagh, Amritsar and Punjab.
- The civilians had assembled for a peaceful protest to condemn the arrest and deportation of two national leaders, **Satya Pal** and **Saifuddin Kitchlew**.
- This incident shocked **Rabindranath Tagore** (First Asian Nobel Laureate) to such an extent that he stated whilst returning his 'Knighthood' and said "such mass murderers aren't worthy of giving any title to anyone".
- Gandhiji also surrendered his title '*Kaiser-e-Hind*' bestowed upon him by the British.

Khilafat Movement, 1919

- During the **First World War**, Turkey, which was a German ally, had fought against the British. After Turkey's defeat, the **Ottoman Caliphate** was proposed to be dissolved.
- The Khilafat Movement was launched by Muslims in India to persuade the British Government not to abolish the **Caliphate**.
- The **Treaty of Sevres** with Turkey had completely dismembered Turkey.
- And due to this, Indian Muslims like other Muslims, all over the world for whom Sultan of Turkey was a spiritual leader, **Khalifa** showed their sympathies.
- The leaders of this movement accepted the **Non-Cooperation Movement** of Gandhiji and led a joint protest against the British.
- In 1919, a **Khilafat Committee** was formed under the leadership of Ali brothers (Shaukat and Muhammad), Maulana, Ajmal Khan. Gandhiji headed the **All India Khilafat Committee**.

Non-Cooperation Movement (NCM)

From 1919-1922, the British were faced with two movements whose bases were masses—**Khilafat** and **Non-Cooperation**.

Causes of the Non-Cooperation Movement

- There was resentment against the British after the War.
- Indians thought that they would be rewarded by autonomy in return for the extensive support of manpower and resources they had provided to Britain during the **First World War**.
- But the Government of India Act, passed in 1919, was dissatisfactory. In addition, the British also passed repressive acts like the Rowlatt Act, which further angered many Indians who felt betrayed by the rulers despite their wartime support.
- The **Home Rule Movement** started by Annie Besant and Bal Gangadhar Tilak set the stage for the Non-Cooperation Movement.
- The extremists and moderates of the INC were united and the **Lucknow Pact** also showed solidarity between the **Muslim League** and the **Congress Party**. The return of the extremists gave the INC a militant character.
- Due to **World War I**, prices of goods began to rise and this affected the common man.
- Peasants also suffered because the prices of agricultural products did not increase. All this led to resentment against the government.
- The repressive **Rowlatt Act** and the **Jallianwala Bagh Massacre** had a profound effect on the Indian leaders and the people.
- Their faith in the British system of justice was broken. The whole country rallied behind its leaders who were pitching for a more aggressive and firm stand against Britishers.
- **Khilafat Movement** also gave an encouragement to Non-Cooperation Movement as they merged their movement in it.

Congress Nagpur Session, 1920

- In this session, the **Non-Cooperation Movement** was endorsed.
- Attainment of *Swaraj* through peaceful and legitimate means, thus commitment for extra constitutional mass struggle was made.
- **Congress Working Committee** was set up to lead the Congress.
- Provinces on linguistic basis and ward committees were also set up.

Features of Non-Cooperation Movement (NCM)

- NCM was essentially a peaceful and non-violent protest against the British Government in India.
- People were asked to resign from their government jobs, withdraw children from government schools, boycott foreign goods, boycott elections and not to serve in the British army.
- The INC also demanded Swaraj or self-government.
- The Non-Cooperation Movement was a decisive step in the Independence Movement because for the first time, the INC was ready to forego constitutional means to achieve self-rule.
- In Bengal, a movement was started against Union board taxes.
- **No Tax Campaign** was started in Andhra Pradesh.
- The movement aroused popular resentment among the Moplah against their Hindu landlords **Akali Movement** was also started as a part of this movement.
- Labour in tea plantations of Assam also went on strike during this movement.
- Gandhiji had assured that *Swaraj* would be achieved in a year if this movement was continued to completion.
- Louis Fischer was an American Biographer. He was an important personality during non-Cooperation Movement.

Response of Masses in NCM

- The NCM was led by the middle class, business classes supported it as nationalist emphasised on *Swadeshi*.
- Massive participation of peasants, students and women, also played a dominant role.
- Communal unity could also be seen at this time in movement.
- Gandhiji was under increased pressure to launch a **Civil Disobedience Movement** (CDM).
- Gandhiji threatened to launch CDM on February 1922, if political prisoners were not released and press controls were not removed. It was abruptly brought to an end because of the **Chauri-Chaura incident**.

Chauri-Chaura Incident, 1922

- In **Chauri-Chaura**, (Gorakhpur, Uttar Pradesh), police had allegedly beaten up the group of volunteers who were protesting against liquor sale and high food prices.
- Violent mob set fire to a police station killing 22 policemen during a clash between the police and protesters of the movement. This happened on 5th February, 1922.
- Gandhiji called off the movement saying people were not ready for revolt against the British Government by **Ahimsa** (Non-violence).
- Congress working committee in 1922 at the **Bardoli Session** passed a resolution to stop the Non-Cooperation Movement.
- Most of the leaders like **CR Das**, **Subhash Chandra Bose**, **Jawaharlal Nehru** and **Motilal Nehru** were not in favour of stopping the movement. They were surprised by the decision to stop it.
- In March, 1922, Gandhiji was arrested and sentenced to jail for 6 years.
- Justice CN Broomfield made a remarkable speech while pronouncing his sentence during the trial of Gandhiji. He said "If the course of events in India should make it possible for the government to reduce the period and release you, no one will be better pleased than I".

Evaluation of the Non-Cooperation Movement

- The NCM movement brought a new form of struggle to the **Indian National Movement**.
- Though the movement was not successful in achieving its goal of *Swaraj*, it mobilised masses.
- Lakhs of Indians participated in the open protest against the government through peaceful means. The movement reached common people in villages and far flung corners of the country.
- As use of *Khadi* was promoted the Indian merchants and mill owners enjoyed good profits during this period as a result of the boycott of British goods.
- This movement also established Gandhiji as a leader of the masses.
- It drew many Muslims towards the movement.
- Although most Congress leaders remained firmly behind Gandhiji, the determined broke away. The Ali brothers later become fierce critics.

Other Contemporary Movements

Movements	Years	Related facts
Flag Satyagraha (Jabalpur, Nagpur)	1923	It aimed at exercising the right and freedom to hoist the nationalist flag.
Borsad Satyagraha (Gujarat)	1923	To Boycott 'Docoit Tax'
Guru Ka Morcha (Punjab)	1922-23	To emancipate Gurdwara Sahib from stronghold of Mahant Sunder Singh.
Vaikom Satyagraha	1924	It was led by Mannathu Padmanabhan against untouchability and caste discrimination.

Formation of Swaraj Party

- When the Non-Cooperation Movement suddenly came to an end due to the **Chauri-Chaura incident**, there was debate and difference of opinion on what to do during the transition period.
- One section led by **CR Das, Motilal Nehru** and **Ajmal Khan** wanted to end the boycott of Legislative Councils, and demanded entry into Councils. These groups were called **Swarajists.**
- Swarajists thought entering the Councils would help the Non-Cooperation Programme.
- It would enthuse masses and keep up their morale at a time of political vacuum.
- Councils can be used as an arena of political struggle.
- Other sections led by **C Rajagopalachari, Vallabhbhai Patel, Rajendra Prasad** and **MA Ansari** came to be known as '*No-Changers*'.
- Council entry would lead to political corruption and loss of revolutionary zeal.
- They also thought constructive work done would prepare masses for the next phase of **Civil Disobedience**.
- *Ashrams* were brought up empowering tribals and low castes.
- Hindu-Muslim unity was promoted and programmes to remove untouchability, boycott of foreign cloth and liquor, flood relief were done.
- Promotion of *Charkha* and *Khadi* was done to establish a sense of self-sufficiency.
- Gandhiji saw the Charkha as a symbol of a human society that would not glorify machine and technology. The spinning wheel, moreover, could provide the poor with supplementary income and make them self-reliant.
- National schools and colleges were setup to promote education.
- Swarajists were further divided into, **responsivists** and **non-responsivists**.
- **Lala Lajpat Rai, Madan Mohan Malviya** and **NC Kelkar** advocated for cooperation with the government and holding office and also to protect the Hindu interest.
- Finally in 1930, they walked out as a result of the **Lahore Congress Session** resolution and beginning of Civil Disobedience Movement.

Achievements of Swarajists

- **Vithalbhai Patel**, (Speaker of the Central Legislative Assembly), gave a powerful speech.
- Defeat of **Public Safety Bill**, 1928 through which the Government could deport undesirable and subversive foreigners, etc.

Drawbacks of Swarajists

- Swarajists could not form a uniform coalition and their differences led to weakening of Swarajists outfit.
- Swarajists failed to resist perks and privileges offered by the British officials. They were attracted towards privileges which later became the communal divide in the Indian National Movement.
- They also failed to raise and support the peasant cause and to support the work done by no-changers in masses and villages.

Simon Commission (1927-1928)

- The **Indian Statutory Commission**, (commonly referred to as the Simon Commission), was a group of seven British Members of Parliament under the Chairmanship of **Sir John Simon**. The commission arrived in British India in 1928.
- The Government of India Act, 1919, had a provision of appointment of a commission to enquire into the act and provide reforms.
- The Government of Britain appointed the commission after two years in fear that the next Government might appoint liberal and pro-India commission.
- The British Government appointed the Simon Commission to report on India's constitutional progress for introducing constitutional reforms.
- The Commission was strongly opposed by many in India for a number of reasons.
- The commission was seen as racist and colonialist as it had seven British members of the British Parliament and no Indian members.

Recommendations of Simon Commission

- It proposed the abolition of dyarchy and the establishment of representative government in the provinces.
- It rejected parliamentary responsibility at the centre. The Governor-General was to have complete power to appoint the members of the Cabinet.

- It recommended that separate communal electorates be retained. It accepted the idea of federalism but not in the near future.
- It suggested that a **Consultative Council of Greater India** should be established which should include representatives of both the British Provinces as well as Princely States.
- It also suggested that the Indian army should be Indianised, though British forces must be retained.

Anti-Simon Agitation

- The British action was seen as a violation of the principle of self-determination (strike) and a deliberate insult to the self-respect of the Indians.
- On 3rd February, the day the Commission reached Bombay, an all India *hartal* strike was organised. Wherever, the Commission went, it was greeted with *hartals* and black-flag demonstrations under the slogan **"Simon Go Back"**.
- The Government used brutal suppression and police attacks to break the popular opposition. **Lala Lajpat Rai** died because of brutal *Lathi* Charge while leading the **Anti-Simon** protests.
- In Madras Session (1927), presided over by **Dr. Ansari**, the National Congress decided to boycott the Commission at every stage and in every form.
- The Muslim League and the **Hindu Mahasabha** decided to support the Congress decision.
- **Muslim League** even accepted the principle of joint electorate, if seats were reserved for the Muslims.
- All important Indian leaders and parties also tried to meet the challenge of the Simon Commission by getting together. They tried to evolve an alternative scheme of constitutional reforms.
- Many conferences and joint meetings of leading political workers were held. The end result was the **Nehru Report** named after **Motilal Nehru.**

Nehru Report, 1928

- The Nehru report was prepared by a committee headed by Motilal Nehru. The committee includes Tej Bahadur Sapru, Subhash Chandra Bose, MS Aney, Mangal Singh, Ali Imam, Shuaib Qureshi and GR Pradhan as its members.
- It was done in response to a challenge posed by the Simon Commission and **Lord Birkenhead.**
- Major recommendations of Nehru Report were as follows :
  - Dominion status on lines of self-governing dominions.
  - Rejection of separate electorates.
  - Joint electorates with reservation of seats for Muslims at the centre and in provinces where they were in minority.
  - Linguistic provinces were demanded.
  - Nineteen Fundamental Rights including equal rights for women, right to form unions and Universal Adult Suffrage.
  - Responsible government at the centre and in provinces. Full protection of the cultural and religious interests of Muslims.
  - Complete dissociation of state from religion.
- At **all Party Conference** in Calcutta in December 1928, Nehru Report was considered upon, here Jinnah on behalf on Muslim League wanted Amendments to Nehru Report. These demands of Jinnah are known as **Fourteen Points.**

Jinnah's Fourteen Points, 1929

Fourteen demands were made by **Mohammad Ali Jinnah** in 1929, which are popularly known as Jinnah's fourteen points.

Following were fourteen demands of Jinnah :

- Federal Constitution with residual powers to provinces
- Provincial autonomy
- No constitutional amendment without state concurrence in Indian Federation
- Adequate representation in Legislative Bodies
- Adequate representation of Muslims in self-governing bodies and in the services
- 1/3rd representation in Central Legislative Assembly
- 1/3rd representation in Cabinet, Separate Electorates
- No bills without 3/4th minority consideration
- Territorial distribution not to affect Muslim majority in Punjab, Bengal and North-Western Frontier Provinces (NWFP)
- Full religious freedom to all communities
- Protection of Muslim rights in religion, culture education and language
- Separation of Sindh from Bombay
- Constitutional reforms in the NWFP and Balochistan
- Separate electorates

Lahore Session of Congress and Poorna Swaraj

- At the **Calcutta Session** of Congress (1928), the Nehru Report was approved. Motilal Nehru was the President of Congress at this session. The first All India Youth Congress also came into being in this session.

- Younger leaders like **Jawaharlal Nehru, Subhash Chandra Bose** and **Satya Murthy** expressed dissatisfaction at the goal of dominion status.
- The government was given a one year period to accept this goal. It was stated that if the government did not accept a Constitution based on dominion status by the end of the year, the Congress would demand complete independence. It would also launch a Civil Disobedience Movement to attain its goal.
- Calcutta Session paved the way for the Lahore Session in 1929. **Jawaharlal Nehru** was nominated as the President for the Lahore Session of the Congress (December 1929) mainly due to Gandhi's backing.
- The following major decisions were taken at the Lahore Session :
  - The **Round Table Conference** was to be boycotted.
  - Complete independence was declared as the aim of the Congress.
  - **Congress Working Committee** was authorised to launch a programme of Civil Disobedience including non-payment of taxes and all members of legislatures were asked to resign their seats.
  - On 31st December, 1929 at midnight on the banks of Ravi river, the newly adopted tricolour flag was hoisted by **Jawaharlal Nehru.**
  - On 26th January, 1930 was fixed as the first independence, **Swarajya Day** was to be celebrated everywhere.

Civil Disobedience Movement

- The Indian National Congress authorised Gandhiji to start the Civil Disobedience Movement.
- Gandhi presented eleven demands to the government and gave an ultimatum of 31st January, 1930 to accept or reject these demands.
- Demands made by Mahatma Gandhi to **Lord Irwin** were opposed by **Jawaharlal Nehru.**

Gandhiji's Eleven Demands

1. Prohibit intoxicants and liquor
2. Change the ratio between the rupee and the sterling.
3. Reduction in the rate of land revenue,
4. Abolition of salt tax
5. Reduce the military expenditure,
6. Reduce expenditure on civil administration,
7. Impose custom duty on foreign cloth,
8. Accept the Postal Reservation Bill,
9. Abolish the CID Department,
10. Release all Political prisoners and
11. Issue licenses of arms to citizens for self-protection.

Salt Satyagraha : Dandi March

- As there was no positive response from the British Government, Gandhiji decided to launch the Civil Disobedience Movement by making **Salt Satyagraha** its main theme.
- Salt was made an issue, because the government controlled the sale of this indispensable commodity and imposed a tax on it, which was felt mostly by the poor.
- Gandhiji, along with a band of seventy-eight members of **Sabarmati Ashram,** was to march from his headquarters in Ahmedabad through the villages of Gujarat for 240 miles on 12th March, 1930 to 6th April, 1930.
- On reaching the coast at Dandi, the Salt Law was to be violated by collecting salt from the beach.
- Further actions were planned as Gandhi gave the directions wherever possible Civil Disobedience of the Salt Law should be started.
- Foreign liquor and cloth shops can be picketed, non-payment of tax, boycott court, resign from government service were to be done.

Spread of Salt Disobedience

- Gandhi's arrest came on 4th May, 1930 when he had announced that he would lead a raid on Dharasana Salt Works on the West coast.
- After Gandhi's arrest, the **Congress Working Committee** sanctioned Non-payment of revenue in Ryotwari areas; No-*chowkidari*-tax campaign in *Zamindari* areas; Violation of forest laws in the Central Provinces.
- Different forms of mobilisation like Prabhat Pheris, *Vanar Senas, Manjari Senas,* Secret Magazines and Magic Lanterns shows were done.
- Women and students participated in huge numbers in Salt Satyagraha.
- Merchants and traders were enthusiastic and supported the movement.
- There was an active participation of tribals, workers and peasants.
- But in the Salt Satyagraha, Muslim participation was least in comparison to Non-Cooperation Movement (NCM) 1920-1922.

Satyagraha at Different Places

- In **Tamil Nadu** C. Rajagopalachari organised a march from Tiruchirapalli to Vedaranyam on the Tanjore coast.
- In **Malabar** Kelappan known for Vaikom Satyagraha organised salt march.

- In **Andhra** Sibirams were organised.
- **Orissa** Gopal Bandhu Chaudhuri organised in Balasore, Cuttack organised marches.
- **Bihar** Non-tax payment was planned.
- In **Peshawar** Badshah Khan also known as Abdul Gaffar Khan organised **Khudaikhidmatgars (Red Shirts)** which organised a march.
- In **Maharashtra, Sholapur**, Sarojini Naidu led the protests.
- Defiance of forest laws in Karnataka, Maharashtra and Central Provinces was done.
- In Manipur and Nagaland, Rani Gaidinliu at the age of 13 years raised the banner against the British.

Gandhi-Irwin Pact

- In July, 1930, the Viceroy **Lord Irwin,** suggested a **Round Table Conference** and reiterated the goal of dominion status.
- In August 1930, **Motilal** and **Jawaharlal Nehru** were taken to Yeravada jail to meet Gandhiji and discuss the possibility of a settlement.
- The Nehrus and Gandhiji unequivocally reiterated the demands of :
  - Right of secession from Britain.
  - Complete National Government with control over defence and finance.
  - An independent tribunal to settle Britain's financial claims.
- On 14th February, 1931 pact was signed it is also known as **Delhi Pact**. It placed the Congress on equal footing with the British Government.
- Irwin on behalf of British Government agreed on release of political prisoners.
- Remission of fines, return of land, right to make salt etc. were granted.
- Public inquiry into police excesses was not accepted.
- And commutation of punishment to Bhagat Singh and his comrades' death sentence to life sentence was also not accepted.
- Gandhi on behalf of Congress agreed to suspend the Civil Disobedience Movement to participate in the next Round of Table Conference.

Karachi Session of Congress in 1931

- The Karachi Session of Congress was presided by **Vallabhbhai Patel.**
- In this Congress Session, Gandhi-Irwin Pact was endorsed.
- A resolution admiring the courage, bravery and sacrifice of three martyrs–**Bhagat Singh, Sukhdev** and **Rajguru** was passed. They were executed on 23rd March, 1931.
- Two resolutions– one on Fundamental Rights and other on the National Economic Programme were adopted.

Round Table Conferences

The Round Table Conferences were a series of Peace Conferences organised by the British Government and Indian National Movement leaders to discuss constitutional reforms in India. Total three Round Table Conferences were organised from 1930–1932.

First Round Table Conference
(November 1930, January 1931)

- The First Round Table Conference was a stage where for the first time British and Indian leaders met as an equal.
- Congress boycotted the conference. British representatives–Labour, Conservative and Liberal. Muslim League was represented by **Aga Khan** and **Jinnah**. It was also attended by Indian princes of states. British India representatives were **Ambedkar** and **Sapru.**
- In this, All India Federation was accepted which was responsible government at provinces and Internal sovereignty to Princely States was promised.
- The British Prime Minister in this conference urged the Indian National Congress to attend the next round of conference.

Second Round Table Conference
(September-December 1931)

- The Second Round Table Conference was attended by Congress as they had agreed in the Delhi Pact. It was attended by Mahatma Gandhi as representative of INC. Other participants of the First Round of Conference were also present.
- **Sarojini Naidu** participated as a representative of Indian women. Gandhiji in this conference claimed Congress to be only representative of political India.
- And Muslim and Untouchables should not to be treated as minority as it will divide the Indians and fade the movement.
- **Ramsay McDonald** headed the **National Government** in Britain at this time. As the conference failed, the second phase of Civil Disobedience Movement was resumed.

Third Round Table Conference (November-December 1932)

- The Third Round Table Conference was called on 17th November, 1932. The Congress boycotted it. Only 46 delegates attended the session.
- The prominent members were **Tej Bahadur Sapru** and **Bhimrao Ramji Ambedkar** (the only persons to attend all Three Round Table Conferences).
- The conference lasted till 24th December, 1932. The discussion of this conference led to the formulation of the Government of India Act, 1935.

Civil Disobedience Movement : Second Phase

- Gandhiji went to England in September 1931 to attend the **Second Round Table Conference**. But inspite of his powerful advocacy, the British Government refused to concede to the demand of immediate grant of **Dominion Status**.
- In the meanwhile, peasant unrest had developed in several parts of the country as peasants found the fall in the prices of agricultural products because of world depression.
- In December 1931, the Congress started a **no-rent, no-tax campaign**.
- On his return to India, Gandhiji had no choice but to resume the Civil Disobedience Movement.
- The Government, headed by the new **Viceroy Lord Willingdon**, believed that a major error had been made in signing a truce with the Congress.
- He was fully determined and prepared to crush the Congress this time.
- The government's response was to arrest **Jawaharlal Nehru** on 26th December. On 24th December, their leader **Khan Abdul Ghaffar Khan** was arrested.
- In April 1934, Gandhiji decided to withdraw the Civil Disobedience Movement as there was no momentum left in to keep the movement going.
- And masses were also not prepared for a fresh movement.

Communal Award, 1932

- The Communal Award was announced by the British Prime Minister, **Ramsay McDonald**, on 16th August, 1932. The Communal Award was based on the findings of the Indian Franchise Committee (also called the Lothian, Committee).
- It established separate electorates and reserved seats for minorities (Muslims, Europeans, Sikhs, Indian Christians, Anglo-Indians) including the depressed classes.
- Gandhiji saw the **Communal Award** as an attack on Indian unity and nationalism.

Poona Pact, 1932

- It was signed by **BR Ambedkar** on behalf of the depressed classes on 24th September, 1932 with Gandhiji.
- The Poona Pact abandoned the idea of separate electorates for the depressed classes.
- But the seats reserved for the depressed classes were increased from 71 to 147 in Provincial Legislatures and to 18% of the total in the Central Legislature.
- The Poona Pact was accepted by the government as an amendment to the **Communal Award**.

Revolutionary Activities in Second Phase

The sudden withdrawal of the Non-Cooperation Movement made many nationalists question the strategy of nationalists and their emphasis on non-violence.

- New communist groups emerged with their emphasis on marxism, socialism and proletariat.
- They were inspired by the **Russian Revolution** (1917) and the success of the young soviet state.
- There was also the influence of journals, the articles on self-sacrifice of revolutionaries, such as *Atmashakti, Sarathi* and *Bijoli*.
- *Bandi Jeewan* by **Sachin Sanyal,** *Pather Dabi* by Sarat Chandra Chatterjee became popular.

Hindustan Republic Association (HRA)

- It operated in areas of Punjab, United Provinces and Bihar.
- It was founded in October, 1924 in Kanpur.
- **Ramprasad Bismil, Jogesh Chandra Chatterjee** and **Sachin Sanyal** were its founders.
- Their objectives were to organise armed rebellion to overthrow the colonial government and to establish the Federal Republic of the United States of India.
- It was later renamed as Hindustan Socialist Republic Association.
- The members of HRA looted the official railway cash at **Kakori**, Lucknow in 1925.
- Ramprasad Bismil, Ashafaqullah, Roshan Singh and Rajendra Lahiri were hanged in this case.

Hindustan Socialist Republic Association (HSRA)

- It was formed under the leadership of **Chandra Shekhar Azad.**
- Its participants were **Bhagat Singh Sukhdev, Bhagwati Charan Vohra, Bejoy Kumar Sinha** etc.
- It decided to work under a collective leadership and adopted socialism as its official goal.
- Saunders who had ordered *Lathi* Charge in Lahore was shot dead by **Bhagat Singh, Azad** and **Rajguru** in December, 1928.
- To protest against the **Public Safety Bill** and **Trade Dispute Bill** which were restrictive in nature. Bhagat Singh and Batukeshwar Dutt threw bombs in the Central Legislative Assembly on 8th April, 1929.
- **Chittagong Bengal Armoury** was done by the Indian Republican Army in April, 1930. It was led by **Surya Sen.**
- The plan was to occupy two main armouries in Chittagong to seize and supply revolutionaries to arms.
- The raid was successful and Sen hoisted the National Flag and proclaimed a provisional revolutionary government. But later, they got arrested.

Hindustan Socialist Republican Association (HSRA Army)

- On 9th and 10th September, 1928 revolutionaries of Northern India met at Ferozshah Kotla Ground in Delhi and changed the name of the party of Hindustan Socialist Republican Association (HSRA) and accepted socialism as their official goal.
- Unlike early revolutionaries who believed in individual heroic action, HSRA favoured the idea of mass-based armed struggle.
- But with the death of **Lala Lajpat Rai**, subsequent to *Lathi* charge while he was leading a demonstration against the **Simon Commission**, the revolutionaries decided to avenge the same.
- On 17th December, 1928, **Bhagat Singh**, **Chandra Shekhar Azad** and **Rajguru** assassinated Saunders at Lahore, a police official involved in a brutal *Lathi* Charge.
- In April 1929, a bomb was thrown in the Central Legislative Assembly at New Delhi by Bhagat Singh and BK Dutta.
- In December 1929, there was an attempt to blow up the special train in which the Viceroy Lord Irwin was travelling to Delhi.
- **Bhagat Singh** and **BK Dutta**, who had been arrested for the bomb incident in the Central Assembly, were prosecuted. They were also figured in the Lahore Conspiracy.
- One of the conspiracy case prisoners, **Jatin Das** died on 13th September, 1929, on the sixty-fourth day of the fast. He was fasting against the harsh conditions of political prisoners in jail.
- Bhagat Singh, Rajguru and Sukhdev were executed on 23rd March, 1931.

Revolutionary Books and Newspapers

Name	Newspaper/ Journal	Year	Founder
Bande Mataram	English language newspaper	1905	Aurobindo Ghose
Bhawani Mandir	English political pamphlet	1905	Aurobindo Ghose
Bharat Mata	English journal	1907	Sardar Ajit Singh
Bombay Chronicle	English -language newspaper	1910	Pherozeshah Mehta
Comrade	Weekly english newspaper	1911	Maulana Mohammad Ali
New India	English-language daily newspaper	1914	Annie Besant
Mook Nayak	Marathi weekly	1920	BR Ambedkar
Bandi Jeevan	Autobiography	1922	Sachindra Nath Sanyal
Free Hindustan	Journal	1936	Tarak Nath Das
Hindustan Dainik	Hindi newspaper	1936	MM Malviya

Major Revolutionary Organisations (India)

Organisations	Place	Year	Founder
Vyayam Mandala	Poona	1896-1897	Chapekar Brothers
Mitra Mela	Nasik (Later Poona)	1901	Savarkar Brothers
Anushilan Samiti	Midnapur	1902	Pramath Nath Mitra
Abhinava Bharata	Poona	1904	Vikram Damodar (VD) Savarkar
Swadesh Bandhav Samiti	Barisal	1905	Ashwini Kumar Dutta
Anushilan Samiti	Dacca	1907	Pulin Bihari Das
Bharat Mata Society	Punjab	1907	Ajit Singh, Sufi Amba Prasad
Hindustan Republican Association Army (HRA)	Kanpur	1924	Sachindra Nath Sanyal
Bharat Naujawan Sabha	Lahore	1926	Bhagat Singh
Hindustan Socialist Republican Association/Army (HSRA)	Delhi	1928	Chandra Shekhar Azad

Indian Revolutionary Organisations (Abroad)

Organisations	Place	Year	Founder
India Home Rule Society (India House)	London	1904	Shyamji Krishna Verma
Abhinav Bharat	London	1906	Vikram Damodar Savarkar
Indian Independence League	California (USA)	1907	Tarak Nath Das
Gadar Party	San Francisco	1913	Lala Hardayal
Indian Independence League	Berlin (Germany)	1914	Lala Hardayal and Virendra Nath Chattopadhyaya
Indian Independence League and Government	Kabul	1915	Raja Mahendra Pratap

Major Conspiracy Cases During British Rule

Case	Year	Related Facts
Alipur Conspiracy Case	1908	Khudiram Bose and Praffula Chaki threw bomb on Chief Presidency Magistrate DH Kingsford of Muzaffarpur.
Delhi Conspiracy Case	1912	Headed by Ras Bihari Bose to assassinate the then Viceroy of India, Lord Hardinge. Basant, Kumar Biswas, Master Amichand and Avadh Behari were convicted and executed.
Lahore Conspiracy Case	1928-31	This case was against Bhagat Singh, Rajguru and Sukhdev who killed Saunders mistakenly as the real target was, James Scott, who was responsible for the *Lathi* Charge that killed Lala Lajpat Rai. Three were found guilty and executed.
Kanpur Bolshevik Conspiracy Case	1924	A significant case against the leaders of the Non-cooperation Movement in India to supress revolutionary political activism.
Peshawar Conspiracy Case	1922-1927	It was a trial against the Mujahirs, who had tried to enter in India from Russia to start a Communist Movement in India.
Kakori Conspiracy Case	1925	It was a train robbery against the British Indian Government that was organised by Hindustan Republican Association. Death sentences were awarded to Ramprasad Bismil, Ashfaqullah Khan, Thakur Roshan Singh and Rajendra Lahiri. Sachindra Bakshi and Sachindra Nath Sanyal were deported to Cellular Jail for life term.
Meerut Conspiracy Case	1929	Several Communists including three Eglishmen were arrested for organising an Indian railway strike.

Indian National Movement : Third Phase (1935-1947)

(SOURCES)

Class-VIII New NCERT Chap 8 (The Making of the National Movement 1870-1947), Class-XII New NCERT Chap 11 (Mahatma Gandhi and the Nationalist Movement), Class-XII Old NCERT Chap 13 (Struggle for Swaraj-II), Class-VIII Old NCERT Chap 10 (Struggle for Swaraj)

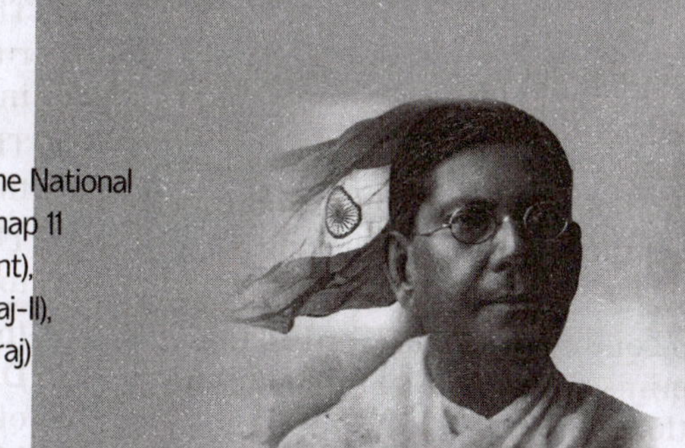

- The Third Phase of Indian National Movement was set by the mass movements like **Civil Disobedience Movement, Salt Satyagraha**, which had shaken the roots of struggle in people of India.
- Third phase began with passing of the **Government of India Act, 1935** and lasted till 1947 when India got its independence.

Government of India Act, 1935

In the backdrop of Indian Political leaders being in jail in 1932, the **Third Round Table Conference** was held without participation of Congress, which led to the formulation of Government of India Act, 1935.

Government of India Act, 1935 was passed in August, 1935 in the British Parliament.

Following were the main provisions of the Act :

- An **All India Federation** was to be established. The federation was to be based on a union of the provinces of British India and the Princely States.
- Powers were divided between centre and states, Princely States in three lists- **Federal, Provincial** and **Concurrent lists**. Residuary powers were given to Viceroy.
- This federation never came into being because of two conditions– **first** states comprising 52% seats in Council should agree to join the federation and **second**, total population of these states should be 50% of all Indian states. These conditions were not met as the Princely States had refused to join the federation.
- A new system of government for the provinces on the basis of provincial autonomy was also promised. The **dyarchy was abolished** in provinces.
- The Dyarchy was introduced at centre and federal subjects were divided into reserved and transferred subjects. This part did not come into operation.
- There was to be a bicameral federal legislature in which the states were given disproportionate weightage.
- The representatives of the states were not to be elected by the people, but appointed directly by the rulers.
- Only 14% of the total population in British India was given the right to vote.
- The legislature, in which the princes were once again to be used to check and counter the nationalist elements, was denied any real power.
- **Defence and Foreign affairs** remained outside legislative control, while the Governor-General retained special control over the other subjects.
- The Governor-General and the Governors were to be appointed by the British Government and were to be responsible to it.
- In the provinces, local power was increased. Ministers responsible to the provincial assemblies were to control all departments of provincial administration.

- The Governors were given special powers. They could veto legislative action and legislate on their own. They kept full control over the civil service and the police.
- It provided for the establishment of the **Reserve Bank of India**.
- This Act also abolished the **Council of India** and provided the Secretary of State for India with Advisers.
- It also established Federal, Provincial and Joint Public Service Commissions.
- A **Federal Court** was also set up in 1937, through this Act.
- The Act could not satisfy the nationalist aspiration for both political and economic power, which continued to be concentrated in the hands of the British Government.
- Foreign rule was to continue as before; only a few popularly elected ministers were to be added to the British administration.

Provincial Elections

In its **Lucknow** and **Faizpur Sessions** of Congress (1936), it decided to contest the elections under the new Act of 1935.

Election Manifesto of Congress

Congress manifesto for elections of 1937 promised following :

- Total rejection of Government of India Act, 1935 was reiterated.
- Release of prisoners held by the British administration.
- Removal of discrimination based on Gender and caste.
- Transformation in agricultural system
- Reduction of rent, revenue and rural debts
- Credit on discounted rate
- Right to form trade unions and to strike

Results of Elections 1937

- The election campaign of the Congress met with massive popular response, even though Gandhiji did not address a single election meeting.
- The elections, held in February 1937, showed that a large majority of Indian people supported the Congress, which swept the polls.
- Congress Ministries were formed in July 1937 in seven out of eleven provinces.
- Later, Congress formed coalition governments with two others.
- Only Bengal and Punjab provinces had non-Congress Ministries.
- Punjab was ruled by the **Unionist Party** and Bengal by a coalition of **Krashak Praja Party** and **Muslim League**.

Congress Ministries in Office (1937-1939)

- In the 28 months of Congress rule in the provinces, Congress Ministries tried to improve the condition of people in what limited power they had.
- The Congress Ministers reduced their salaries to 500 rupees per month. They travelled third or second class in the railways.
- They promoted civil liberties, repealed restrictions on the press and radical organisations.
- They permitted trade unions and Kisan organisations to function and to grow police powers were curbed.
- In Bombay, land confiscated during the **Civil Disobedience Movement** were restored. Pensions of officials associated with the Civil Disobedience Movement were also restored.
- Measures for welfare of Harijans were taken up temple entry, use of public facilities, etc.
- Support was given to *Khadi* and other village industries through subsidies and other measures.
- Education at primary and secondary level was given attention. The technical and higher education was also promoted.

Resignation of Congress Ministries

- In September 1939, the **Second World War** broke out and Britain declared India's support for war without consulting Indians.
- Congress' response was moderate and well measured looking at the aim of war as it was being fought against fascist nations.
- At the **Wardha Congress Working Committee** meeting in September 1939, Gandhi's stand was unconditional support to British war efforts.
- Other leaders like Subhash Chandra Bose wanted to take advantage of Britain's and start a mass movement.
- **The Congress Working Committee** (CWC) decided to not support Britain's war efforts and also asked for the Government's aim of war.
- **Lord Linlithgow's** statement declared the aim of war to stop the aggression and also declared that all interested parties would be consulted to modify the **Government of India Act, 1935**. A consultative Committee was immediately formed.
- He also had an ulterior motive of using Muslims League and Princes of states against Congress.

- **Defence of India Ordinance** had been enforced on the same day the war was declared. Thus civil liberties were restricted.
- In May 1940, a top secret **Draft Revolutionary Movement Ordinance** had been prepared, aimed at launching a crippling pre-emptive strike on the Congress.
- Congress was totally dissatisfied by this response and decided not to support the war and Congress Ministries resigned from the Provinces at CWC meeting in October, 1939.

Tripuri Session and Forward Bloc (1939)

- Gandhiji retired fròm Congress in 1934 and Congress came under leadership of Pt. **Jawahar Lal Nehru.**
- At the same time Subhash Chandra Bose was chosen the President of Congress unanimously in February, 1938 congress session held at **Haripura.**
- Due to differences between Gandhi and Bose, Gandhiji nominated **Pattabhi Sitaramayya** as Presidential Candidate. But he was defeated and Bose re-elected.
- Later, Bose stepped down from the Presidency in Tripuri Session and he formed **Forward Bloc** in 1939 within the Congress.

August Offer, 1940

The events of World War II turned in favour of Hitler. Thus, the British Indian Government under Viceroy came up with the August Offer:

- **Dominion status** as the objective for India.
- Expansion of the **Viceroy's Executive Council,** which would have a majority of Indians (who would be drawn from major political parties).
- Setting up of a **Constituent Assembly** after the war where mainly Indians would decide the Constitution.
- This decision would be according to their social, economic and political conceptions.
- No future Constitution was to be adopted without the support of consent of minorities.

Reaction to August Offer

- Congress rejected the August offer as there was no offer to form a National Government.
- **Nehru** rejected it saying, "Dominion Status concept is dead as a doornail".
- **Muslim League** also didn't respond positively and declared that partition was the only way forward.
- For the first time accepted **Dominion status** was explicitly offered, Indian's request to form a Constituent Council to frame Constitution for themselves was also accepted.
- In July 1941, the **Viceroy's Executive Council** was enlarged to give the Indians a majority of 8 out of 12 for the first time, but the British remained in charge of defence, finance and home.
- The **National Defence Council** was set up with purely advisory functions.

Individual Satyagrahas

The objectives of launching individual Satyagraha were:

- To show that nationalist patience was not due to weakness.
- To express people's feeling that they were not interested in the war and that they made no distinction between **Nazism** and the double autocracy that ruled India.
- To give another opportunity to the government to accept Congress' demands peacefully.
- The demand of the *Satyagrahi* would be the freedom of speech against the war through an anti-war declaration. They were supposed to march towards Delhi to convert the movement into **Delhi Chalo Movement.**
- **Vinoba Bhave** was the first to offer the Satyagraha and Nehru, the second.

The movement generated little enthusiasm in people as there were differences among the Congress about how to take forward the struggle and about participating in the **Second World War.** Thus, it was suspended.

Parallel Governments

Ballia

- **Tenure** One week, August, 1942.
- **Leadership** Chittu Pandey
- All the powers of district officials were taken away and all the Congress leaders in jail were released.

Tamluk

- **Tenure** December, 1942 to September, 1944.
- **Leadership** Satish Samant, Matangini Hazara
- Jatiya Sarkar came into existene. It undertook cyclone relief work, gave grants to schools and organised an armed **Vidyut Vahini.**

Satara

- **Tenure** August, 1943 to May, 1946.
- **Leadership** Nana Patil, VB Chavan, Achyut Patwardhan
- Nyayadan Mandals or People's court were set up and justice dispersed.

Cripps Mission, 1942

- In March 1942, a mission headed by **Stafford Cripps** was sent to India with constitutional proposals to seek Indian support for the war. Following were the reasons for sending Cripps Mission to India :

- Japan's invasion was at India's door so India's support was important and even **Allied powers** (USA, USSR) were pressuring the British for the same.
- Indian nationalists had agreed to support the Allied cause if substantial power was transferred immediately and complete independence given after the war.

- Main clauses of the Cripps Mission were as follows:
  - Dominion status to India and permission to opt out of Common wealth and free to join any international bodies, including the United Nations.
  - After the end of the war, a **Constituent Assembly** would be convened to frame a new Constitution. Members of this assembly would be partly elected by the Provincial Assemblies through proportional representation and partly nominated by the princes.
  - The British Government would accept the new Constitution subject to two conditions:
    (i) Any province not willing to join the Union could have a separate Constitution and form a separate Union.
    (ii) The new Constitution making body and the British Government would negotiate a treaty to effect the transfer of power and to safeguard racial and religious minorities.
- In the meantime, defence of India would remain in British hands and the Governor-General's powers would remain intact.
- The proposals differed from those offered in the past in many respects :
  - The making of the Constitution was to be solely in Indian hands now (and not mainly in Indian hands-as contained in the **August Offer**).
  - A concrete plan was provided for the **Constituent Assembly**.
  - Option was available to any province to have a **separate Constitution**–a blueprint for India's partition.

Failure of Cripps Mission

The Cripps Mission was a big failure. The **Congress Working Committee** on 11th April, 1942 rejected the Cripps Mission. Reasons for its failure were:

- The Congress objected to dominion status and demanded full transfer of powers.
- Right of Provinces to secede was not favourable for the Indian Union to come up.
- Retention of Governor-General supremacy
- No immediate transfer of power
- **Nehru** and **Maulana Azad** were the official negotiators for the Congress. The Muslim League objected to idea of a single Indian Union
- Muslim League did not like the machinery for the creation of a Constituent Assembly.
- Pakistan not being explicitly offered also disappointed **Muslim League** leaders.
- An important reason for the failure of the negotiations was the incapacity of Cripps to bargain and negotiate. He had been told not to go beyond the Draft Declaration.
- **Winston Churchill, Amery** (the Secretary of State), Linlithgow (the Viceroy) and **Wavell** (the Commander-in-Chief), did not want Cripps to succeed. They constantly opposed his efforts to accommodate Indian opinion.
- Congress insisted that if it was to help the British defend India from the Axis power, then the Viceroy had first to appoint an Indian as the Defence member of his Executive Council. This was also the reason for failure of Cripps Mission.

Quit India Movement, 1942

After the failure of Cripps Mission, Gandhiji formulated a resolution and put forward a call for withdrawal of British and non-violent, Non-Cooperation Movement against Japanese invasion.

The **Congress Working Committee** at Wardha on 14th July, 1942 accepted this idea of resolution.

Reasons for CWC to accept this course of struggle were following :

- The **failure of the Cripps Mission** embittered the people of India. While, they still fully sympathised with the anti-fascist forces, they felt that the existing political situation in the country had become intolerable.
- Discontent was further fuelled by **war-time shortages** and rising prices.
- The period from April to August, 1942 was one of daily heightening tension with Gandhiji. More and more militant as Japanese forces moved towards India and the spectre of Japanese conquest began to haunt the people and their leaders.
- The Congress now decided to take active steps to compel the British to accept the Indian demand for independence.
- Leadership Movement also wanted to prepare the masses for a possible Japanese invasion.

Course of the Movement

- The **All India Congress Committee** met at Bombay on 8th August, 1942. It passed the famous '**Quit India Resolution**' and proposed the starting of a non-violent mass struggle under Gandhi's leadership to achieve this aim.

- The resolution declared:

...the immediate ending of British rule in India is an urgent necessity, both for the sake of India and for the success of the cause of the United Nations....

- Demand was made for an immediate end to British rule in India and declare commitment of free India to defend itself against all types of Fascism and imperialism.
- Demand for the formation of a provisional Government of India after British withdrawal a sanction to Disobedience Movement against British rule was also given.
- Gandhiji had built the tempo of movement by **Individual Satyagraha**, revamping the organisations, and continuous propaganda against British rule.
- But on 9th August, all the top leaders of Congress were arrested and taken to unknown locations.
- After this major activities took place without leaders, these were as follows:
  - The general public attacked symbols of authority and hoisted national flags forcibly on public buildings.
  - Bridges were blown up, railway tracks were removed and telegraph lines were cut.
  - Most intense activities were in Eastern United Provinces and Bihar.
  - Students responded by going on strike in schools and colleges, participating in processions, writing and distributing illegal news sheets (*patrikas*) and acting as couriers for underground networks.
  - In 1943, some of the younger leader in the Satara district of Maharashtra set up a parallel government (Prati Sarkar), with volunteer corps (*Seba dals*) and village units (*Tufan dals*).
  - Workers went on strike in Ahmedabad, Bombay, Ahmednagar, Poona and Jamshedpur.
  - The participants in these activities were the socialists, forward members, Gandhi ashramites, revolutionaries in Bombay, Poona, Satara, Baroda and other parts of Gujarat, Karnataka, Kerala, Andhra, United Provinces, Bihar and Delhi.
  - The underground activity taking up were Ram Manohar Lohia, Jayaprakash Narayan, Aruna Asaf Ali, Usha Mehta, Biju Patnaik, Chhotubhai Puranik, Achyut Patwardhan, Sucheta Kripalani and RP Goenka.
  - **Usha Mehta** started an underground radio in Bombay.
  - This phase of underground activity was meant to keep up popular morale by continuing to provide a line of command and guidance to distribute arms and ammunition.
  - **Parallel governments** were set up at different places.
  - Prohibition campaigns were carried on and 'Gandhi marriages' were organised.

Participation in Quit India Movement

- **Youth** the students of schools and colleges, remained in the forefront.
- **Women** especially school and college girls, actively participated, and included Aruna Asaf Ali, Sucheta Kripalani and Usha Mehta.
- **Workers** went on strikes and faced repression
- **Peasants** of all strata were at the heart of the movement. Even *zamindars* participated. There was a complete absence of anti-*zamindar* violence.
- **Government officials** especially those who belong to lower levels in police and administration, participated. This resulted in erosion of government loyalty.
- **Muslims** helped by giving shelter to underground activists. There were no communal clashes during the movement.
- **Communists** did not join the movement; in the wake of Russia being attacked by Nazi Germany, the communists began to support the British war against Germany and the **Imperialist War** became the **'People's War'**.
- **Muslim League** opposed the movement, fearing that if the British left India at that time, the minorities would be oppressed by the Hindus.
- The Hindu Mahasabha boycotted the movement. The Princely States showed a low-key response.

Suppression of Quit India Movement

- The Government on its part went all out to crush the 1942 Movement.
- The press was completely censored. The demonstrating crowds were machine-gunned and even bombed from the air.
- Prisoners were tortured and the military took over many towns and cities. Over 10,000 people died in police and military shootings.
- Rebellious villages had to pay huge sums as punitive fines and the villagers had to undergo mass floggings.
- India had not witnessed such intense repression since, the Revolt of 1857.
- Gandhiji commenced a fast on 10th February, 1943 in jail. He declared the fast would last for 21 days.
- Groups of people secretly reached Poona to offer Satyagraha outside the Aga Khan Palace, where Gandhiji was being held in detention.

Subhash Chandra Bose and Indian National Army

- Subash Chandra Bose was born on 23rd January, 1897 in Cuttack, Bengal Presidency.
- He passed the **Indian Civil Services** Examination but resigned in 1921 to join the struggle for freedom by becoming a member of the INC.
- His political mentor was **Chittaranjan Das.** Chittaranjan Das was the Mayor of Calcutta in 1924-25 and Subhas Chandra Bose was the Mayor of Calutta in 1930-31.
- He presided over the Haripura Session of INC in the year 1938. Bose chose his own path, because of the ideological and strategic differences with INC and party leaders.
- He formed a **Forward Bloc Party** in the year **1939**.

Formation of Indian National Army (INA)

- **Mohan Singh** created an army of retreating soldiers from Malaya and Prisoners of war from Japan. By the end of 1942, fourty thousand persons were ready to join the INA.
- INA would go into action only on the invitation of the **Indian National Congress** and the people of India. The step to form this army has been seen as a check against the misconduct of the Japanese against Indians in South-East Asia and as a bulwark against a possible future Japanese invasion in of India.
- After the **Quit India Movement**, Mohan Singh wanted to launch an invasion on India with the help of the Japanese with larger Indian troops. However, differences emerged over the role to be played by INA. Finally, Mohan Singh was imprisoned by the Japanese.

Active Phase of INA

- In June 1943, **Subhash Chandra Bose** met the Japanese Prime Minister in Tokyo and secured permission for INA.
- **Rash Bihari Bose** fled to Japan in 1915 due to failed revolutionary activities in India and became a naturalised citizen of Japan.
- He made a lot of effort in getting the Japanese interested in the Indian Independence Movement. He had created the **Indian Independence League** (IIL) in 1942, in Tokyo.
- After the formation of INA, he decided to fly to Singapore and place INA under the Indian Independence League.
- After Subhash Chandra Bose reached Singapore, he met Rashbihari, who transferred the control and leadership of the Indian Independence League and the INA to Subhash in July, 1943.
- On 21st October, 1943, Subhash Chandra Bose formed the **Provisional Singapore**, Government for Free India at Singapore.
- The famous slogan-"Give me blood, I will give you freedom" was given here.
- This Provisional Government declared war on Britain and the United States and was recognised by the Axis powers.
- A women's regiment called the **Rani Jhansi Regiment** was also formed.
- On 6th November, 1943, Andaman and Nicobar islands were given by the Japanese army to the INA.
- The INA headquarters was shifted to Rangoon (in Burma) in January, 1944 and the war **"Chalo Delhi"** became a famous cry.
- On 6th July, 1944, Subhash Chandra Bose addressed Mahatma Gandhi as '**Father of Nation**' from the Azad Hind Radio.
- The **Azad Hind Fauj** crossed the Burma border and stood on Indian soil on 18th March, 1944 then advanced up to Kohima and Imphal.
- On 14th April, **Colonel Malik** of the Bahadur Group hoisted the INA flag for the first time on the Indian mainland at Moirang, in Manipur.
- The INA met the same fate as the Japanese and all brigades began their withdrawal on 18th July, 1944.

Indian National Army (INA) Trials

- Trial of Indian National Army prisoners is sometimes described as **edge of volcano**.
- The British initially decided to hold trials of several hundreds of INA prisoners.
- The first trial was held at Red Fort in November, 1945 putting on dock together a Hindu, **Premkumar Sehgal**, a Muslim, **Shah Nawaz Khan** and a Sikh, **Gurbaksh Singh Dhillon**.
- Indian National Army Day is celebrated on 12th November since, 1945. INA week is observed from 5th to 11th November. Indian National Army agitation spread all over the country and witnessed participation of diverse social groups.

Course of Events for Independence

There were various plans and proposals were prepared and drafted for the amicable solution for avoidance of partition of India and granting independence.

Rajagopalachari Formula (March 1944)

C. Rajagopalachari proposed a formula for Congress and Muslim League Cooperation. It was a tacit acceptance of the League's demands for Pakistan and Gandhi supported the formula.

Main points of the CR Plan were as follows:

- Muslim League to endorse Congress demand for the independence.
- The League was to cooperate with the Congress in forming a Provisional Government at centre.
- It was to be decided by plebiscite for the Muslim majority areas, whether or not to form a separate sovereign state.
- In case of partition, agreement to be made jointly for safeguarding defence, commerce, communications, etc.
- Jinnah wanted the Congress to accept the **Two Nation Theory** demand.
- He wanted only Muslims to vote in plebiscite in the Muslim majority areas.

Desai-Liaqat Pact, 1945

Bhulabhai Desai who was the leader of Congress Party in Central Legislative Assembly with Deputy Leader of Muslim League in the Assembly came up with a proposal for the formation of interim government at the centre.

Major features were as follows :

- An equal number of representatives for both the Muslim League and the Congress in the Central Executive and 20% seats were to be reserved for minorities.
- No final settlement could be reached with this proposal also.

Wavell Plan (Shimla Conference June 1945)

The elections in England necessitated a sincere effort on reaching a solution.

A conference was convened by the Viceroy **Lord Wavell**, at Shimla in June 1945.

The main proposals of the Wavell Plan were as follows:

- With the exception of Governor-General and Commander-in-Chief all other members in the Executive Council are to be Indians.
- Both Hindus and Muslims were to have equal representation.
- The reconstructed Council was to function as an interim government.
- Governor-General was to exercise his veto on the advice of ministers.
- Congress objected to the plan as it reduced the Congress as a pure caste Hindu Party.
- Muslim League wanted all Muslim members to be league nominees.

Royal Indian Naval Ratings Revolt

- On 18th February, 1946 in Bombay, the Royal Indian Navy Ratings went on a strike to protest the racial discrimination, abuse by senior officers and use of the Indian troops in Indonesia, etc.
- Other naval branches also joined them later. They hoisted the tricolour flags and went around Bombay in cars. They threatened the policemen and Europeans.
- They became a symbol to people and supported the cause of freedom. They cheered for them on roads and offered food and drinks.

Cabinet Mission Plan (March 1946)

- In 1946, Secretary of State **Pethick Lawrence** in **Attlee Government** personally led a three man cabinet deputation to New Delhi with the hope of resolving the Congress–Muslim League deadlock. He wanted to transfer British power to a single Indian administration.
- The Cabinet Mission was sent as the British withdrawal became imminent by 1946:
  - Success of nationalist forces in struggle for hegemony.
  - Demoralisation among bureaucracy and loyalists.
  - Limitation of conciliation and repression strategy of the British.
  - **Royal Indian Naval Ratings Revolts** also shook the British Government and official rule seemed impossible.
- Major recommendations of the Commission were
  - The subcontinent was to be divided into three major groups of provinces: Sections A, B and C.

    Section A Madras, Bombay, Central Provinces, United Provinces, Bihar and Orissa, which were of Hindu Majority.

    Section B Punjab, North-West Frontier Province and Sind, these were Muslim majority areas.

    Section C Bengal and Assam Muslim majority areas.
  - Rejection of a full-fledged Pakistan.
  - Provincial to have autonomy and residual powers. Common centre for defence, communications and external affairs.
  - Three-tier Executive and Legislature at Province, Princely States and Union level.
  - Local Provincial Governments were to have the choice of opting out of the group in, which they found themselves should a majority of their populace vote to do so.
  - A Constituent Assembly was to be formed by proportional representation, which will form the interim government.

Composition of Constituent Assembly

- The proposed Constituent Assembly was to consist of 292 members from British India and 93 from the Indian states.
- The British India members were to be divided into 210 General, 78 Muslims and 4 Sikh seats.
- In the preliminary meeting, the assembly was to elect not only a chairman and other office bearers but also an **Advisory Committee**.
- The elected members were divided into three Sections A, B and C.
- All these sections were to have the authority to draw up it's Constitution and set up Provincial Legislature and Executives.
- After the first general election, a province could come out of a group. After 10 years a province could call for reconsideration of the Group or Union Constitution.

Elections of 1945-1946

- The failure of the **Shimla Conference**, once again revived with the coming to power of the Labour Party in Britain.
- An important initiative taken by the Labour Government was the declaration that elections to the Central and Provincial Assemblies in 1945 and 1946.
- The main parties in the contest were the Congress and the **Muslim League**. The elections were particularly important for the League in its quest for Pakistan.
- The **Indian National Congress** emerged as the largest party, winning 59 of the 102 elected seats.
- The Muslim League's biggest success was in Bengal where out of 119 seats for Muslims, it won 113.
- The elected members later formed the Constituent Assembly of India. These were the last general elections in British India; consequent election was held in 1951 in India.

Direct Action Day (16th August, 1946)

- This happened, when the Viceroy **Lord Wavell**, invited the Congress to form an interim government, still hoping that details could be worked out later.
- **Nehru** formed a cabinet, which included two Muslims, but **Jinnah** was convinced that the Hindus could not be trusted to treat the Muslims fairly.
- He called for a **day of Direct Action** in support of a separate Pakistan.
- The League decided that 16th August, 1946 would be observed as Direct Action Day throughout the country.
- Thus, began India's bloodiest year of Civil War since, the mutiny nearly a century earlier.
- The Hindu-Muslim rioting and killing started in Calcutta sent deadly sparks of fear to every corner of the subcontinent, as all civilised restraint seemed to have had disappeared.

Interim Government

On 12th August, 1946, the Viceroy **Lord Wavell** invited Congress to form the government under the leadership of **Jawaharlal Nehru**, which finally came into being on 2nd September, 1946. Following are important events related to formation of interim government:

- The Muslim League kept out initially.
- The interim government was composed of 12 members including 3 Muslims nominated by the Congress.
- It was for the first time since, the coming of the British that the Government of India was in Indian hands.
- In 13th October, the Muslim League decided to join the interim government. On 26th October, five nominees of the league joined the government.
- Congress appointees resigned to make room for the league nominees (two seats were already vacant, while. **Mr Sarat Bose, Sayyid Ali Zahir** and **Sir Shafat Ahmed Khan** resigned).
- Out of the portfolios of the composite 14 member government, the first nine represented the Congress, while the last five belonged to the League.
- The Muslim League joined the interim government not to work sincerely and cooperate with the Congress, but to block the functioning of the new government.
- **Liaquat Ali** used his position as Finance Minister in the interim government to fulfil this aim of the league. This strategy of the league effectively brought the business of the government to a virtual standstill.

Interim Government (1946)

Members	Portfolios Held
Pt. Jawaharlal Nehru	External Affairs and Commonwealth Relations
Sardar Vallabhbhai Patel	Home, Information and Broadcasting
Dr. Rajendra Prasad	Food and Agriculture
Dr. John Mathai	Industries and Supplies
Jagjivan Ram	Labour
Sardar Baldev Singh	Defence
CH Bhabha	Works, Mines and Power
Liaquat Ali Khan	Finance
Abdur Rab Nishtar	Posts and Air
Asaf Ali	Railways and Transport
C. Rajagopalachari	Education and Arts
Ibrahim Ismail Chundrigar	Commerce
Ghazanfar Ali Khan	Health
Jogendra Nath Mandal	Law

Attlee's Statement (20th February, 1947)

- On 30th June, 1948, a deadline for transfer of power irrespective of any situation in India was set.
- The British would relinquish power either to some form of Central Government or in some areas to the existing Provincial Governments, if the Constituent Assembly was not fully representative, i.e., if the Muslim majority provinces did not join.
- British powers and obligations vis-a-vis the Princely States would lapse with transfer of power, but these would not be transferred to any successor government in British India.
- **Mountbatten** would replace **Wavell** as the Viceroy.
- The statement contained clear hints of partition and even Balkanisation of the country into numerous states and was, in essence, a reversion of the Cripps offer.
- The date was fixed by the government to prevent any further escalation of the constitutional crisis and to portray the British's sincerity.
- The INC was fine with the transfer of power to more than one centre as it meant the current government could work for its Constitution.
- However, emboldened by this provision, Muslim League launched **Civil Disobedience Movement** in Punjab to overthrow coalition government in Punjab.
- On April 1947, the **Indian National Congress** was ready for partition. Bengal and Punjab were to be divided in a fair manner.

The Mountbatten Plan (June 3rd Plan)

- **Lord Mountbatten**, India's last Viceroy, released a plan on the country's independence from the British on 3rd June, 1947. The plan, famously known as the Mountbatten Plan. It was the 'Last Plan for Independence' of India.
- The June 3rd Plan announced that India would be splitting into two nations after its independence. India and Pakistan. The division came into effect on 15th August, 1947.
- The plan included the principles of partition and gave autonomy and sovereignty to both India and Pakistan. It also gave the nations the right to form their own Constitution.
- The plan was accepted by both the Congress and the Muslim League.
- Under this plan, the Princely States, such as Jammu and Kashmir, were given a choice to either remain independent or join India or Pakistan.
- The **Indian Independence Act of 1947**, which was passed in the British Parliament and received the royal assent on 18th July, 1947, was drafted based on the Mountbatten Plan.
- Until the formation of new Constitutions, the Governor-General was made a constitutional head. He was made responsible for assenting to laws passed by the Constituent Assemblies of the nations as part of this plan.
- Thus, the League's demand was conceded to the extent that Pakistan would be created and the Congress' position on unity was taken into account to make Pakistan as small as possible. Mountbatten's formula was to divide India but retain maximum unity.

Disapproval of the Plan by Nationalist Leaders

- **Khan Abdul Ghaffar Khan** wanted an independent Pathan state in North-Western Frontier Provinces (NWFP).
- **Suhrawardy** and **Abul Hasan** were for an independent united Bengal.
- The **Hindu Mahasabha** too opposed the partition.
- The non-Muslim majority areas in Punjab and in Bengal, as also the entire province of Assam (except a part of Sylhet) remained within the boundaries of India.
- Khan Abdul Ghaffar Khan regarded the partition as treachery on the part of the Congress and felt that 'the *Khudai Khidmatgars* were being thrown to the wolves.' They even boycotted the referendum held in NWFP.

Indian Independence Act, 1947

On 5th July, 1947 the British Parliament passed the Indian Independence Act, which was based on the **Mountbatten Plan**.

The Act was implemented on 15th August, 1947. Provisions of the Act are:

- The creation of two independent dominions– India and Pakistan.
- A Governor-General for each dominion for the effective operation of the Act.
- The Constituent Assembly of each new dominion was to exercise the powers of the legislature of that dominion and the existing Central Legislative Assembly and the Council of States were to be automatically dissolved.
- Till formation of new Constitution both dominions to Act in accordance with Government of India Act, 1935.
- **MA Jinnah** became the first Governor-General of Pakistan and Mountbatten of India.

Partition of India

The Indian nationalists accepted partition not because there were two nations in India - a Hindu nation and Muslim nation but because of following reasons :

- The historical development of communalism, both Hindu and Muslim, over the past 70 years or so had created a situation where the alternative to partition was mass killing of lakhs of innocent people in senseless and barbaric communal riots.
- Riots had not been confined to one section of the country that Congress leaders could have curbed them.
- **Two Nation Theory** was actively promoted by Jinnah.
- Foreign Government also tried to further these divisions, take advantage and encouraged these riots.

Radcliffe Boundary Commission

- A Consultative Committee in July 1947 recommended how the Punjab and Bengal regions of the Indian subcontinent were to be divided between India and Pakistan.
- The Commission appointed by **Lord Mountbatten**, consisted of four members from the Indian National Congress and four from the Muslim League and was chaired by **Sir Cyril Radcliffe.**
- The commission's mandate was to draw boundaries in the two regions that would keep intact as much as possible, the most-cohesive Hindu and Muslim populations within Indian and Pakistani territory, respectively.

Integration of Princely States After Independence

- Nehru presided over the All India State People's Conference Sessions in **Udaipur** (1945) and **Gwalior** (April 1947).
- He declared that the states refusing to join the Constituent Assembly would be treated as hostile.
- In July 1947, Vallabhbhai Patel took charge of the new States Department and skillfully incorporated all the states in the following two phaser.
  - **Phase-I** On 15th August, 1947, all states except Kashmir, Hyderabad and Junagadh had signed an instrument of accession with the Indian Government, acknowledging central authority over defence, external affairs and communication.
    The princes agreed to this fairly easily because
    (i) they were 'surrendering' only what they never had and
    (ii) there was no change in the internal political structure.
  - **Phase-II** It involved a much more difficult process of 'integration' of states with neighbouring provinces or into new units like the Kathiawar Union, Vindhya and Madhya Pradesh, Rajasthan or Himachal Pradesh along with internal constitutional changes in states. For some years, they retained their old boundaries (Hyderabad, Mysore, Travancore-Cochin). This phase was accomplished within a year.
- The principal bait offered was a generous privy purse while some princes were made Governors and **Rajpramukhs** in free India.
- This rapid political unification of the country after independence was Patel's greatest achievement.

32

Governors, Governor-Generals and Viceroys

[SOURCES]

Class-VIII New NCERT Chap 8 (The Making of the National Movement [1870s-1947]), Class-XII New NCERT Chap 11 (Mahatma Gandhi and the Nationalist Movement), Class-XII Old NCERT Chap 13 (Struggle for Swaraj-II), Class-VIII Old NCERT Chap 10 (Struggle for Swaraj)

- .The East India Company was run by the **Governor of Bengal till 1772 AD**. Madras and Bombay presidencies also had separate Governors.
- After 1772 AD, through **Regulating Act of 1773**, Governor of Bengal was made Governor-General. This setup continued till 1833 AD. **Warren Hastings** was the first Governor-General.
- **Lord William Bentick** was the **First Governor-General of India** as from 1833 to 1857. Governor-General of Bengal was called Governor-General of India.
- In Government of India Act, 1857, the name of Governor-General was changed to Viceroy. **Lord Canning** was the first Viceroy of India.
- The **Government of India Act, 1935**, changed the post of Viceroy to Governor-General of India again, this system continued till, 1950.

Governors of Bengal (1757-1774)

East India Company built an administrative system in Bengal and top official in hierarchy was the Governor of Bengal.

Robert Clive (1757-1760 and 1765-1767)

- The victory in **Battle of Plassey** in 1757 led to Clive becoming Governor of Bengal. After the Battle of Buxar, Clive was again made the Governor of Bengal in 1765. In this period, he brought the **Policy of Dual Government** in Bengal, which continued till 1772.
- **Clive and Warren Hastings** are said to be the chief instruments of laying the foundation of British power in India.
- Clive is also criticised for his policies, which led to famine in Bengal. In 1770 AD, Clive established the **Society for Trade**. It was meant as a monopoly but was not allowed by the East India Company.

Governors of Bengal After Clive

- **John Zephaniah Holwell** was a temporary Governor of Bengal in 1760. He survived the **Black Hole Incidence of Calcutta in June 1757**.
- **Henry Vansittart** was Governor of Bengal from 1760-1965. In his Governorship, **Battle of Buxar** was fought.
- **Harry Verelst** was Governor of Bengal from 1767-1769, at this time Bengal was put under the Dual Government rule.
- **John Cartier** was Governor of Bengal from 1769-1772. During his time, the first famine of Modern India occurred in 1770.
- **Warren Hastings** was made the Governor of Bengal in 1772 and continued till 1773. He abolished the Dual Government System.

Governor-Generals of Bengal (1773-1833)

Between 1773 and 1833, the following **Governor**-Generals were appointed in Bengal :

Warren Hastings (1773-1784)

- The **first Governor-General of India** was Warren Hastings from 1773 to 1784. He was impeached in 1784 for corruption and was acquitted in 1795 and was made a **Privy Councillor**.
- He joined the British East India Company in 1750 as a clerk. In 1757, he was made the British Resident (administrative incharge) of Murshidabad.
- He was appointed to the **Calcutta Council** in 1761, but went back to England in 1764. He returned to India in 1769 as a member of the **Madras Council**.
- Hastings took measures to contain the Rohillas though they could not be prevented from capturing Agra.
- Hastings concluded treaties with various rulers and sought alliances against the powerful forces of **Haider Ali** of Mysore.
- However, in order to wage these wars, Hastings borrowed heavily from the **Begum of Awadh** and **Raja Chait Singh** of Banaras.
- Warren Hastings brought out a large number of reforms as follows :

Administrative Reforms

- Warren Hastings put an end to the Dual System of Government in Bengal, established by **Robert Clive** in 1768. Due to which the company took responsibility for revenue collection.
- He also stopped the payment of ₹ 26 lakh given to the Mughal Emperor.

Revenue Reforms

- A **Board of Revenue** was established in Calcutta to supervise the collection of revenue.
- In 1772, Calcutta was made capital and the treasury was shifted from Murshidabad to Calcutta.
- English collectors were appointed in each district, who were helped by native officials.
- Warren Hastings made the account of revenue simple, intelligible and made many provisions for the protection of *Ryots*.

Judicial Reforms

- Warren Hastings carried reforms in the Judicial system. A **Civil Court** and **Faujdari Adalat** (Criminal Court) in each district was to be established.
- A Supreme Court was also established in 1774 under the **Regulating Act of 1773**, during the tenure of Warren Hastings.

Social Reforms

- The **Asiatic Society of Bengal** was established in 1784 AD by Hastings.
- He established a madarsa in Calcutta for the development of Muslim education.
- In 1791,a **Sanskrit School** was established in Banaras by **Jonathan Duncan**.
- Hastings strengthened the British power in India by signing the **Treaty of Banaras** (1773) and the **Treaty of Faizabad** (1775).
- This increased the influence of the English in the state of Awadh and made the *Nawab* dependent on the company.

Lord Cornwallis (1786-1793)

After Hastings, **Sir John Jefferson** was made acting Governor-General for one year from (1785-1786) and then Lord Cornwallis came to India as next Governor-General of India.

Cornwallis was again made the Governor of India in 1805. In the meantime, he died in Ghazipur in 1805. His tomb is situated in Jaipur.

Following are the main reforms taken out by Cornwallis:

- Cornwallis is called **'the father of civil service in India'**. He started the civil services for administration in British India.
- He was the first person to codify laws in 1793. The code separated the revenue administration from the administration of justice. This is known as **Cornwallis Code**.
- He also created the post of **District Judge**.
- The *Zamindari* system was introduced by Lord Cornwallis in 1793 by Permanent Settlement. It fixed the land rights of the *zamindars* in perpetuity without any provision for fixed rent or occupancy rights for actual cultivators.
- The share of the government in the total land revenue collected by the *zamindars* was at 10/11th and the rest went to *zamindars*.
- According to the Permanent Land Revenue Settlement, the *zamindars* were recognised as the permanent owners of the land.
- In his period, the **third Anglo-Mysore War** took place in which defeat of **Tipu Sultan** led to the **Treaty of Seringapatam**, in 1792.
- In his period, Europeanisation of administrative machinery was done.

Sir John Shore (1793-1798)

- The British Parliament passed the **Charter Act of 1793**, in the time of Sir John Shore.
- The period of Shore's rule as Governor-General was comparatively uneventful. His policy was attacked as balancing and timid.
- His rule saw the **Battle of Kharda** between Nizam and Marathas in 1795.

Lord Wellesley (1798-1805)

- Lord Wellesley vigorously applied the policy of subsidiary alliance to achieve British Paramountcy in India. The first **Subsidiary Alliance** was made with *Nizam* of Hyderabad in 1798.
- Through the Subsidiary Alliance, princely rulers were stopped from making any negotiations and treaty with any other Indian ruler without informing the Company officials.
- They were also not supposed to maintain any standing armies.
- They were instead to be protected by the troops of the European companies and Princely rulers had to pay for upkeep of the British Army stationed at them. A British resident was also kept at the court of the native ruler.
- He also founded the **Board of Trade**.
- He sent a British envoy **Mehdi Ali Khan** to the Court of Shah of Persia. Later, he sent **John Marshall**.
- Wellesley passed a regulation for controlling the press. No newspaper was to be published at all, until the manuscript of the whole paper was submitted to and approved by the government.
- Christian missionaries established a printing press at **Serampore**.
- Wellesley founded **Fort Williams College**. **Sir John Gilchrist** was appointed as head of Hindustani Language Department.
- **Fourth Anglo-Mysore War** (1799) was fought in his rule, resulting in the defeat and death of Tipu and the annexation of many parts of Mysore.
- Wellesley took the administration of Tanjore on 25th October, 1799, of Surat in March, 1800 and Carnatic on 1st July, 1801.
- In his rule, the **Treaty of Bassein** (1802) was signed and the **Second Anglo Maratha War** (1803-05) resulted in the defeat of the Scindia, the Bhonsle and the Holkars.
- The **Madras Presidency** was formed under his Governorship.

Sir George Barlow (1805-1807)

- In his Governorship, the **Vellore Mutiny** of sepoys took place in 1806 AD. Main grievances of the sepoys were related to uniform, hair cuts, etc.
- It was suppressed by Governor of Madras, at that time it was William Bentinck.

Lord Minto I (1807-1813)

- The main event in his Governorship was the **Treaty of Amritsar in** 1809 with Ranjit Singh. On this treaty **Charles Metcalfe** signed on behalf of the British administration.
- The **Charter Act of 1813**, was also passed during his tenure.

Lord Hastings (1813-1823)

- The **Nepalese War of 1814-1816** occurred during his Governorship. The Gorkhas accepted the **Treaty of Sagauli** in March 1816.
- He participated in the **Pindari War** (1817-1918), which resulted in the suppression of the Pindaris.
- He fought the **Third Maratha War** from 1817 to 1818 wherein Maratha power was finally crushed. Peshwaship was abolished and all his territories were annexed.
- Bombay Presidency was created out of the Maratha regions in 1818.
- The **Ryotwari settlement** was introduced in the Madras Presidency by Governor **Thomas Munro** in 1820.
- This was the primary land revenue system in South India. Major areas of introduction include Madras, Bombay, parts of Assam and Coorg provinces of British India.
- In the **Ryotwari System**, the ownership rights were handed over to the peasants. The British Government collected taxes directly from the peasants.
- The revenue rates of the Ryotwari System were 50% where the lands were dry and 60% in irrigated land.
- Though ownership of land was vested with the farmers, excessive tax impoverished them. Furthermore, the tax rates were frequently increased.
- The **Bengal Tenancy Act** was passed in 1822. Coffee plantation was started in Bengal and Assam region during his tenure.

Lord Amherst (1823-1828)

- He fought the **First Burmese War** 1824-26.
- During his tenure, **Barrackpore Mutiny** took place in 1824.
- The Malay Peninsula was also added to British territories in his reign.
- Capture of territories of Bharatpur was done in 1826 by him.

Governor-Generals and Viceroys of India (1828-1950)

By Charter Act of 1833, the post of Governor-General of India was made and territories of Bengal, Madras, Bombay and other territories, placed under his control.

Lord William Bentinck (1828-1835)

- Bentinck was the last Governor-General from 1828 to 1833 of Bengal and the first Governor-General of India from 1833 to 1835.
- He is regarded as one of the liberal and enlightened Governor-General of India. He is said to be **'the Father of Modern Western Education in India'**.
- In his tenure, annexation of Mysore in 1831 took place.
- He concluded a treaty of perpetual friendship with **Ranjit Singh** (1831).
- The **Charter Act of 1833**, was passed during his reign. It provided that no Indian subject of Company was to be debarred from holding an office on account of his religion, place of birth, descent and colour. So the removal of distinction in recruitment to public services was removed.
- Following were the reforms measures taken by him:
  - He abolished *Sati* and other cruel rites in 1829. Regulation of 1829 was brought in for abolition of *Sati* first in Bengal and then extended to Madras and Bombay Presidency in 1830.
  - Suppression of *thugi* was another reform undertaken by him in 1830.
  - In education, Bentinck brought the **Macaulay Minute** and English was made the official language of the British Indian administration. It helped the growth of higher education in India.
  - In judicial reforms, the provincial courts of appeal and circuit court were abolished. Their duties were transferred to Magistrates and Collectors under the supervision of the Commissioner of Revenue and Circuit.
  - For the convenience of the public of Upper Province (present-day UP) and Delhi, a separate **Sadr Nizamat Adalat** and a **Sadr Diwani Adalat** were set up at Allahabad.
  - The residents of these areas were no longer under the necessity of travelling long distance to file their appeals at Calcutta.
  - Persian was so far the court language. Bentinck gave the suitors the option to use vernaculars in filing their suits. In higher courts, Persian was replaced by English language.
  - Qualified Indians were appointed in junior judicial capacities of Munsiffs and could rise to the position of Sadr Amins.
- William Bentinck followed the policy of non-interference into the affairs of Indian states as far as possible.
- At the request of the new Nizam, **Nasir-ud-Daula,** who succeeded his father to *gaddi* 1829, the British officers were removed from Hyderabad.
- A similar policy of non-intervention followed towards the states of Jodhpur, Bundi, Kota and Bhopal.
- However, Bentinck, departed from the policy of non-intervention and annexed Mysore (1831), Coorg (1834) and central Cachar (November 1834) on the plea of misgovernance.

Sir Charles Metcalfe (1834-1836)

- Charles Metcalfe is known for freeing the press in India.
- He passed the famous **Press law**, which removed the restrictions placed on press.

Lord Auckland (1836-1842)

- The most important event of his reign was the **First Afghan War** (1831–125), in which the British suffered heavy losses.
- This defeat was a blow to the prestige of British power in India.
- Due to this, a **Tripartite Treaty** was made in **1858** AD between Shah Shuja, Ranjit Singh and the British for Afghanistan.
- **Shah Shuja** was to be seated on the Afghan seat, but later **Ranjit Singh** withdraw from this treaty.
- In his tenure, the construction of a road from Delhi to Calcutta was started in 1839 and during this time, Sher Shah Suri Marg was renamed as **Grand Trunk Road** (GT Road).

Lord Ellenborough (1842-1844)

- In his two years of tenure, he brought an end to the Afghan war. Sind was annexed in 1843 in the leadership of **Charles Napier**.
- He brought the **Indian Slavery Act, 1843,** which aboished slavery in India.

Lord Hardinge I (1844-1848)

- The main event to have occurred in his reign was **Anglo-Sikh War**. This war started in 1845 and four battles were fought at Mudki, Sobraon, Feroz Shah and Aliwal. War came to an end with the **Treaty of Lahore** in 1846.
- He also took steps to abolish female infanticide and human scarifice.

Lord Dalhousie (1848-1856)

- Lord Dalhousie became India's Governor-General in 1848 at the age of 36. He did a lot of important work by expanding the British Empire on the basis of war and **Doctrine of Lapse**.
- During the time of Dalhousie, the **Second Anglo-Sikh War** was fought in 1840, in which the Sikhs were defeated and Punjab was annexed to the British Empire in 18 days.
- In Dalhousie's time, the **Second Anglo-Burmese War** in 1852 took place. In this war, Burmese lost and Lower Burma or Pegu were dissolved in the British Empire.
- Sikkim was merged with the British India in 1850 AD.
- A major **revolt by Santhals** in 1856 AD took place in his tenure, which was suppressed.

Doctrine of Lapse

- Using the doctrine of lapse, Satara in 1848, Jaitpur and Sambhalpur in 1849, Baghat in 1850, Jhansi in 1853, Udaipur in 1852 and Nagpur in 1854 were merged with the British Empire.
- In 1856, Awadh was annexed by Dalhousie and merged with the British Empire on the basis of 'misgovernance'.

Reforms undertaken by Dalhousie

- Dalhousie appointed a Lieutenant-Governor for Bengal to ease the work of Governor-General of India under administrative reforms.
- Territories, which had recently been annexed to the British Empire were put in a system of a centralised control, in which a commissioner was appointed in the territory who reported directly to the Governor-General.
- This was known as the **Non-regulation system.**
- In Military reform, he raised the **Gurkha regiment**.
- Dalhousie also emphasised the reduction of Indians in the British army, which he saw as a danger. The Gurkha regiment helped in the suppression of the revolt of 1857.
- In Educational Reforms, he recommended the **Thomsonian System** of Vernacular education for the whole of the North-Western Provinces (1853).
- Wood's Education Despatch of 1854 and opening of **Anglo-Vernacular Schools** and **Government Colleges** came in his tenure.
- An **Engineering College** was established at Roorkee.
- **Public Works** like the first railway line connecting Bombay with Thane was started in 1853.
- **Electric telegraph** services also began in his reign.
- He also laid the basis for the modern postal system in 1854. A separate **Public Works Department** was set up for the first time.
- He also worked on the construction of the **Grand Trunk Road** and developed the harbours of Karachi, Bombay and Calcutta.

Lord Canning (1856-1862)

- **Canning** was the last Governor-General of India and became the first Viceroy of India with the passage of the **Government of India Act, 1858.**
- The Government of India Act, 1858 ended the rule of the East India Company and Indian territory came in direct control of the British monarch.
- In his tenure, the **Widow Remarriage Act**, was passed on 25th July, 1856.
- The **Revolt of 1857**, took place in his Governorship.
- He withdraw the policy of Doctrine of Lapse.
- The Indian Councils Act of 1861, was passed, it proved to be a landmark in the constitutional history of India.
- The Indian **Penal Code of Criminal Procedure** (1859, and the Indian High Court Act (1861) were enacted.
- Income Tax was introduced for the first time in 1858 in his tenure.
- On the recommendation of **Wood's Despatch,** Universities of Calcutta, Bombay and Madras were founded in 1857. The Indigo riots in Bengal (1860) took place in his Governorship.

Lord Elgin I (1862-1863)

- The **Wahabi Movement**, which was a Pan-Islamic Movement, began in his period. It was suppressed by the Britishers.
- He died in Dharmshala in 1863, which was in Punjab at that time.

Sir John Lawrence (1864-1869)

- Lawrence adopted the **Policy of Non-Intervention** in the case of Afghanistan. He was also a friend of the ruler of Afghanistan, **Sher Ali**.
- In his tenure, the region of Odisha, Bundelkhand and Rajputana fell under severe famine. A **Famine Commission** was set up under **George Campbell** to deal with the famine.
- Telegraphic communication was opened with Europe through sea in his tenure. High courts were established at Calcutta, Bombay and Madras in 1865 and reorganised the native judicial service.
- He expanded canal works and railways.
- **The Bhutan War** (1865) took place in his reign.
- He also created the **Indian Forests Department**.

Lord Mayo (1869-1872)

- Under his tenure, the system of state railways began.
- Establishment of colleges for the education and political training of the Indian Princes was done.
- **Rajkot College** in Kathiawar and the **Mayo College** at Ajmer were established.
- The **Organisation of Statistical Survey** of India under **WW Hunter** was done and the first census of India was taken in 1872.
- Department of agriculture and commerce was established.
- He initiated the process of financial decentralisation in India in 1870.
- He took the first step in the direction of separation of central and provincial finances.
- In 1872, **Sher Ali Afridi**, an Afridi Pathan, a convict in the Andamans assassinated Mayo. He was the only Viceroy to be murdered in office.

Lord Northbrook (1872-1876)

- **Kuka Movement** of Punjab took place in 1872, in his tenure.
- The **Prince of Wales** (King Edward Seventh) also visited in 1875 while he was Viceroy.
- He donated ₹ 10000 to **Mohammedan Anglo Oriental College**.

Lord Lytton (1876-1880)

- Lord Lytton was a great writer and talented administrator. He wrote with the pseudonym Owen Meredith for writing poetry.
- In his tenure, the **Second Anglo-Afghan War** (1878-1880) was fought. He adopted an aggressive policy towards Afghanistan.
- Under the chairmanship of **Richard Strachey,** a commission was formed under his tenure. This commission had advised the Constitution of the Famine Fund in each province.
- During his reign, **Delhi Darbar** was organised on 1st January, 1877, in which Queen Victoria was honored with the title of *Kaiser-e-Hind*. This was organised while the country was under severe famine.
- It was during Lytton's time that the **Vernacular Press Act** was passed in 1878. Newspapers were banned in the Indian language because of this Act. This act was also known as the **Galaghont** Act.
- He is also criticised for free trade and abolition of duties on manufacturing goods in India, which led to drain of wealth.
- He also lowered the maximum age limit from 21 to 19 years.

Lord Ripon (1880-1884)

- He repealed the Vernacular Press Act, in 1882 and introduced the **First Factory Act, 1881** for improving the conditions of workers in factories.
- During his tenure, **Census** began to take place regularly from 1881.
- The introduction of **Local Self-Government** began in 1882 with the Resolution for Local Self-government.
- That's why, he is called the **Father of Local Self-Government in India.**
- He formed the **Hunter Commission** in 1882, which worked to improve primary education in India.
- **Ilbert Bill Controversy** took place during his time in 1883. This bill tried to do away with discrimination by allowing Indian Jurists to try Europeans.
- But the bill had to be amended because of protests by Europeans. He resigned after this.

Lord Dufferin (1884-1888)

- An important event of Dufferin's rule was the **Third Anglo-Burmese War** (1885 - 1888 AD). Burma was defeated in this war. This led to annexation of Lower and upper Burma in 1885.
- In his rule, the **Tenancy Act**, was passed in Bengal in 1885, according to which the landlords could no longer snatch the land of the farmers as per their wish.
- It was during Dufferin's time that the **Indian National Congress** was established in 1885.
- **Allahabad University** was established in 1887 AD during his tenure.

Lord Lansdowne (1888-1894)

- In the time of Lansdowne, the **Second Factory Act** was passed in 1891 AD. Also the **Indian Council Act, 1892** was passed in his tenure.
- It was during this very period that the boundary line between India and Afghanistan was determined. India-Afghanistan border line is known as **Durand line.**

Lord Elgin II (1894-1899)

- During the tenure of Lord Elgin, between 1896 to 1898 there was a severe famine in Uttar Pradesh, Madhya Pradesh, Bihar and Punjab.
- In 1898, a **Famine Commission** was appointed under the chairmanship of James Lyall to investigate these.
- In the time of Elgin itself, an **Opium Commission** was constituted in 1893. The **Munda Uprising** from 1899 took place under his regime.
- Two British officials **Rand** and **Amherst,** were assassinated by **Chapekar Brothers** in 1897 in his tenure.

Lord Curzon (1899-1905)

Lord Curzon had accomplished many important works in India. During his time as Viceroy, Lord Curzon created the territory of Eastern Bengal and Assam. **Partition of Bengal** was also planned in his tenure.

Some of the major reforms done by him in India were as follows :

- **Foreign Policy** Curzon United the new North-West Frontier. He started interference in Tibet by accusing the Dalai Lama of his inclination towards Russia. In the year 1903, under the leadership of Colonel Young husband, the army went to sign a treaty with Tibet.
- **Education** Curzon established Indian University Commission- under Thomas Raleigh in 1902. The Indian Universities Act was passed in the year 1904 on the basis of the recommendation of the Commission.
- **Police Reform** Lord Curzon set up a Police Commission under the chairmanship of Sir Andrew Fraser in 1902. In the year 1903, CID (Criminal Investigation Department) was established in the Police Department.
- **Constitution of Famine Commission** During the reign of Lord Curzon, a Famine Commission was appointed under the chairmanship of Anthony McDonnell. Its function was to make recommendations in the matter of running the system of famine assistance efficiently.
- **Agriculture** During his reign, the Agricultural Research Institute was established at Pusa (New Delhi).

  In the year 1901, an Irrigation Commission headed by **Sir Colin Scot Moncrieff** was set up to study the problem of irrigation in India.

Lord Minto II (1905-1910)

- The anti-partition and Swadeshi Movement against the Bengal partition were one of the main events to occur in his tenure.
- **Muslim League** was founded in 1906 by **Aga Khan** in his tenure.
- Congress announced its goal of Swaraj in the Calcutta Session in 1906.
- **Split in Congress** took place in its annual session of Surat in 1907.
- In his tenure in 1908, **Khudiram Bose** was sentenced to death and **Bal Gangadhar Tilak** was sent to prison for six years.
- **Indian Council Act, 1909,** known as **Morley-Minto Reforms** were announced in 1909. It widened the gulf between Hindus and Muslims by announcing separate electorates.

Lord Hardinge II (1910-1916)

- The **Delhi Darbar** was organised in 1911 during the reign of Lord Hardinge-II. **King George V** and **Queen Mary** of Britain came for coronation and visited the Darbar.
- The partition of Bengal was cancelled at the time of King George V and Queen Mary's Delhi Darbar and the transfer of capital to Delhi from Calcutta, was announced in 1911.
- On 23rd December, 1912, Hardinge was hit by a bomb while entering Delhi in which he got injured.
- **World War I** began during Hardinge's tenure.
- In 1916, Lord Hardinge gave his permission to open the **Banaras Hindu University**.

Lord Chelmsford (1916-1921)

- The **Home Rule League** was formed in 1916 during the time of Lord Chelmsford. At the same time, Women University was established in Poona.
- **Lucknow Pact** was signed between Congress and Muslim League in 1916 and Moderates and Extremists also came back together in the same year. The **Sadler Commission** on Education was appointed in 1917.
- It was during this period, that the **Rowlatt Act of 1919,** was passed, during this time the **Jallianwala Bagh** massacre took place on 13th April, 1919 and the **Government of India Act, 1919**, was passed.
- During the reign of Chelmsford, the **Khilafat Movement**, Non-cooperation Movement from 1920 to 1922 took place. The **Third Anglo-Afghan War,** 1919 took place in his tenure.

Lord Reading (1921-1926)

- He was the only Jewish Viceroy to come to India.
- During his reign, on the recommendation of the **Acworth Committee**, the Railway budget was separated from the General budget.
- **Moplah Rebellion** took place in Kerala in 1921 in his tenure.
- The **Swaraj Party** was founded in December 1922, during the time of Reading.
- On 5th February, 1922, after the incident at **Chauri-Chaura**, the Non-cooperation Movement was stopped.
- Civil Services exams began to be held in Delhi and London simultaneously from 1923.
- It was at the time of Reading that the **Lee Commission** for the Public Service was established in the year 1924.
- On 19th August, 1925, at the time of the **Kakori Incident**, Reading was the Viceroy of India.

Lord Irwin (1926-1931)

In the tenure of Lord Irwin, the Simon Commission came to India. Under his tenure, the following important events took place :

- The **Nehru Report** in 1928 was published under the chairmanship of **Motilal Nehru**. Against the Nehru report **Jinnah** put his 14 points.
- The **Royal Commission** related to agriculture was appointed in 1928 in his tenure.
- On 31st December, 1929, **'Declaration of Purna Swaraj'** in the Lahore session was made.
- On 26th January, 1930, Independence Day was organised in the entire country.
- Civil Disobedience was launched by Gandhiji on 12th March, 1930. In it Dandi March also took place.
- The **First Round Table Conference** was held in London in 1930.
- Gandhi-Irwin Pact took place in March 1931.

Lord Willingdon (1931-1936)

- The **Second Round Table Conference** was organised in London, 1931.
- It was during Willingdon's time that **Ramsay MacDonald** announced the **Communal Award** in 1932.
- Individual Civil Disobedience Movement were launched in his tenure.
- The **Third Round Table Conference** (1932) was held.
- The Government of India Act, 1935 was passed.
- India was separated in 1935 from Burma.
- In 1936, **All India Kisan Sabha** was formed.

Lord Linlithgow (1936-1944)

- In his tenure, the first general elections were conducted and Congress attained absolute majority. Congress formed Ministries in the majority of the provinces (1937).
- He decided unanimously that British India would participate in Second World War in 1939 without consultation of Congress or any other political party.
- Congress Ministries resigned in 1939 after the outbreak of the **Second World War**.
- **Subash Chandra Bose** was elected as Congress President in 1938 and later resigned and formed the forward Bloc in 1939.
- The **August Offer** was proposed by Viceroy in 1940 and it was rejected by the Congress.
- The **Cripps Mission** also came in 1942.
- On 7th August, 1942, Congress Session passed the Quit India Resolution (8th August, 1942) and launched the Quit India Movement.

Lord Wavell (1944-1947)

- **CR Formula** was evolved by C. Rajagopalachari in 1944 and **Gandhi-Jinnah** talks based on it took place in 1944. In the winter of 1945-1946 provincial election were held in India.
- On 25th June, 1945, **Shimla Conference** took place to discuss the Wavell Plan.
- On 28th January, 1946, Wavell announced the government's intention to set up an **Executive Council** of political leaders.
- On 18th February, 1946, **Mutiny of the Indian Naval Ratings** occurred in Bombay.
- The INA Trial began in 1946.
- On 15th March, 1946, Attlee announced the **Cabinet Mission,** under Pethick Lawrence, Stafford Cripps and AV Alexander, arrived in Delhi on 24th March, 1946.
- It's proposal was accepted by Congress.
- The **Direct Action Day** in August, 1946 was observed by Muslim League.
- Elections were held for the Constituent Assembly and an interim government was formed by Congress in September 1946. The Great Calcutta killing was took place in August, 1946.
- Prime Minister of England **Clement Attlee** announced the end of British rule in India on 20th February, 1947.
- The Objective Resolution was passed by Pt. Jawaharlal Nehru in 13th December, 1946.

Lord Mountbatten (1947-1948)

- He announced the 3rd June, 1947 plan, which is known as **Mountbatten Plan.**
- The **Indian Independence Bill** was introduced in the House of Commons in his tenure on 4th July, 1947.
- As per the Bill, two independent Nations—India and Pakistan were to be formed.
- Two Boundary Commissions under **Sir Cyril Radcliffe** were appointed for the partition of Punjab and Bengal.
- Pakistan got independence on 14th August, 1947 and India on 15th August, 1947.
- After Independence, Mountbatten became the first Governor-General of free India.

C. Rajagopalachari (June 1948-January 1950)

- He was the **last Governor-General of free India** and only Indian Governor-General.
- In his tenure, the Constitution was adopted on 26th November, 1949 and enacted on 26th January, 1950.

33

India After Independence

(SOURCES)

Class-VIII New NCERT Chap 10 (India After Independence), Class-XII Old NCERT Chap 14 (Understanding Partition), Class-XII New NCERT Chap 12 (Framing the Constitution-The Beginning of a New Era)

Challenges for Newly Independent India

When India became independent in August 1947, it faced a series of challenges. Some of which were as follows :

- As a result of partition, **8 million refugees** had come into the country from what was now Pakistan. These people had to be found, homes and jobs.
- There was the problem of the **Princely States**, almost 500 of them, each ruled by a *maharaja* or a *nawab*, each of whom had to be persuaded to join the new nation.
- In the longer term, the new nation had to adopt a **political system** that would best serve the hopes and expectations of its population.
- India had to adopt a Constitution and build a consensus on which ideals the Constitution would be based.
- India was left with a **colonial legacy**- which had drained the country of its economic wealth, industries.
- It had impoverished the masses, agricultural lands were heavily burdened and were concentrated in hands of few.

Making of the Constitution

- In the situation of challenges, the Constituent Assembly pondered and discussed the making of the Constitution of India.
- The members of the Constituent Assembly were not elected on the basis of **Universal Franchise**.
- In 1945-1946, **provincial elections** were held in India. The Provincial Legislatures then selected the representatives to the Constituent Assembly.
- The Constituent Assembly that came into being was dominated by one party the **Congress**.
- The Congress swept the general seats in the provincial elections, and the **Muslim League** captured most of the reserved Muslim seats.
- Muslim League chose to boycott the Constituent Assembly, pressing its demand for Pakistan with a separate Constitution.
- Though the Constituent Assembly was dominated by Congress, views of its members differed on critical issues.
- Some members were inspired by **socialism** while others were defenders of **landlordism**. Some were close to **communal parties** while others were **assertively secular**.
- The Constituent Assembly had 300 members. Of these, six members played particularly important roles.
- Three were representatives of the Congress, namely, **Jawaharlal Nehru, Vallabhbhai Patel and Rajendra Prasad**.
- And the other three were lawyers- **BR Ambedkar, KM Munshi** from Gujarat and **Alladi Krishnaswamy Aiyar** from Madras.
- During the period of British rule, Ambedkar had been a political opponent of the Congress, but on the advice of

Mahatma Gandhi, he was asked at independence to join the Union Cabinet as **Law Minister**.

Important Facts

- Dr. **BR Ambedkar** served as Chairman of the Drafting Committee of the Constitution.
- He was given assistance by two civil servants
  - **BN Rau**, Constitutional Advisor to the Government of India.
  - He prepared a series of background papers based on a study of the political systems in other countries.
  - The Chief Draughtsman, **SN Mukherjee**, who put complex proposals in clear legal language.
- **Hansa Mehta** from Bombay demanded social, economic and political justice for women in the Constituent Assembly.

- **Jawaharlal Nehru** moved the resolution proposing that the **National Flag of India** be a 'horizontal tricolour of saffron, white and dark green in equal proportion', with a wheel in navy blue at the centre.
- In 13th December, 1946, Jawaharlal Nehru introduced the **Objectives Resolution** in the Constituent Assembly.
- The Objective Resolution outlined the defining ideals of the Constitution of Independent India. It provided the framework within which the work of Constitution-making was to proceed.
- Pt. Jawaharlal Nehru mentioned that the objective of the Indian Constitution would be to fuse the liberal ideas of democracy with the socialist idea of economic justice, and re-adapt and re-work all these ideas within the Indian context.
- The Constitution of India was framed between December, 1946 and November 1949. During this time, it's drafts were discussed clause by clause in the Constituent Assembly of India.
- The Constituent Assembly held **eleven sessions,** with sittings spread over 165 days. In between the sessions, the work of revising and refining the drafts was carried out by various committees and sub-committees.
- The constitution of India was adopted on 26th November, 1949 and finally enforced on 26th January, 1950.
- The Indian Constitution, which came into effect on **26th January, 1950**, the longest in the world.
- One feature of the Constitution was its adoption of **universal adult franchise.** All Indians above the age of 21 would be allowed to vote in state and national elections.
- A second feature of the Constitution was that it guaranteed **equality before the law** to all citizens, regardless of their caste or religious affiliation.
- After a long debate, the Constituent Assembly also recommended that a certain percentage of seats in legislatures as well as jobs in government be reserved for members of the lowest castes.
- The Constitution sought to **balance the power** of the Central Government and States by providing three lists of subjects a **Union List**, a **State List** of subjects and a **Concurrent List**. The Constitution declares India, that is, Bharat, a Union with federal features.
- Major debate in the Constituent Assembly took place concerning language. Many members believed that the English language should leave India with the British rulers. According to them, Hindi should take place of English.
- A compromise was made that Hindi would be the 'official language' of India, English would be used in the courts, the services and communications between one state and another.
- **First General Election** was held in 1951-1952 on the basis of universal adult franchise and those above 21 years were eligible to vote.

Timeline

1945	
26th July	Labour Government comes into power in Britain
December-January	General Elections in India
1946	
16th May	Cabinet Mission announces its constitutional scheme
16th June	Muslim League accepts cabinet Mission's constitutional scheme
16th June	Cabinet Mission presents scheme for the formation of an Interim Government at the Centre
16th August	Muslim League announces Direct Action Day
2nd September	Congress forms Interim Government with Nehru as the Vice-President
13th October	Muslim League decides to join the Interim Government
3-6th December	British Prime Minister. Attlee, Meets some Indian Leaders; talks fail
9th December	Constituent Assembly begins its sessions
1947	
29th January	Muslim League demands dissolution of Constituent Assembly
16th July	Last meeting of the Interim Government
11th August	Jinnah elected President of the Constituent Assembly of Pakistan
14th August	Pakishtan Independence, celebrations in Karachi
14-15th August	At midnight India celebrates Independence

1949	
December	Constitution adopted
1950	
January	Constitution enforced

Integration of Princely States

- **Indian Independence Act of, 1947** ended the British paramountcy on India states and the princely were given the choice of either merging with India or Pakistan or remain independent.
- On 15th June, 1947, **All India Congress Committee** decided that it will not accept independence of any province within the territory of India and will neither allow any integral part of India to succeed from India.
- To resolve the issues of provinces, a **Department of Indian Provinces** was established on 5th July, 1947, which is headed by the then Home Minister **Sardar Vallabhbhai Patel.**
- By the time of 15th August, 1947, majority of states get merged into India, but only three states-**Junagarh, Hyderabad** and **Kashmir** retained their autonomy.

Junagarh

- The population of Junagarh was almost 7 lakhs and had a Hindu majority population of 80%, but the ruler was a Muslim *Nawab*, **Mahawat Khan.**
- On September 1947, the Nawab announced the **merger of Junagarh into Pakistan**, but the majority of population wanted to live in India.
- Due to the resistance of people in Junagarh, the *Nawab* flee to Pakistan.
- A plebiscite (voting) was held in Junagarh where majority of people voted for merger with India.
- On 8th November 1947, the Diwan of Junagarh, **Sahanavaz Bhutto** sent a letter integration to Government of India.

Kashmir

- The Kashmir problem was different from that of two other princely states. The majority of population was Muslim and the ruler was a Hindu king.
- Kashmir decided neither to integrate with Pakistan nor with India and remain independent. But Pakistan attacked Kashmir with help of tribes of mountain areas.
- To protect the territory of Kashmir, **Raja Hari Singh** requested Indian military for help and integration with India.
- Indian government accepted the request and on 26th October, 1947 sent army in Kashmir.
- India approach **UN Security Council** with regards to the Pakistan attack in Kashmir. It lead to the ceasefire, but the original status was not established.
- In the year 1954, the Constituent Assembly of Jammu and Kashmir confirmed integration of Kashmir with India.

Hyderabad

- Hyderabad was the biggest princely state in India. It was surrounded from all sides from Indian territory. The *Nawab* of Hyderabad was **Miz Usman Ali Khan.**
- *Nawab* wanted to integrate with Pakistan but the majority of population was Hindu.
- Hyderabad signed a standstill agreement with India in November 1947, to retain the same status as it had before 15th August, 1947.
- Hyderabad did not remain loyal with the agreement, it started building military strength and weaponising its army.
- By military action in September 1948, the Hyderabad was integrated into India.

Integration of European Colonies

- After India's independence, **Portuguese** and **French** colonies existed in India. Portuguese included Goa, Daman and Diu, Dadra and Nagar Haveli and French colonies included Pondicherry, Karikal, Yanam, Mahe and Chandranagar.
- In 1954, a treaty was sign between India and France; according to which all the French colonies were liberated by France.
- In 1961, **Daman** and **Diu and Goa** were merged into the Republic of India, after attaining independence from Portuguese rule.

Formation of States and Linguistic Problem

- In the 1920s, the **Indian National Congress** had promised that once the country won independence, each major linguistic group would have its own province.
- But after independence, both Prime Minister **Nehru** and Deputy Prime Minister **Vallabhbhai Patel** were against the creation of linguistic states.
- The Kannada, Malayalam, and Marathi speakers, had all looked forward for having their own state.
- However, the strongest protests, came from the Telugu-speaking districts of what was the Madras Presidency.
- When Nehru went to campaign there during the general elections of 1952, he was met with black flags and slogans demanding "We want Andhra".
- In October, 1952, a veteran Gandhian named **Potti Sriramulu** went on a hunger strike demanding the

formation of Andhra state to protect the interests of Telugu speakers. On 15th December, 1952, 58 days into his fast, Potti Sriramulu died.

- Thus, on 1st October, 1953, the new state of Andhra came into existence, which subsequently became Andhra Pradesh.
- A **States Reorganisation Commission** was set up, which submitted its report in 1956, recommending the redrawing of district and provincial boundaries to form compact provinces of Assamese, Bengali, Oriya, Tamil, Malayalam, Kannada and Telugu speakers respectively.
- The Hindi-speaking region of **North India** was broken up into several states.
- In 1960, the bilingual state of **Bombay** was divided into separate states for Marathi and Gujarati speakers.
- In 1966, the state of **Punjab** was also divided into Punjab and Haryana on linguistic basis. The Punjab was for the Punjabi languages speakers who were also mostly Sikhs. The Haryana was for the rest who spoke not Punjabi but versions of Haryanvi or Hindi.

Tribal Integration and National Consolidation

- Tribals in India are a heterogeneous community and they were gradually integrated in India.
- **Manipur** was a monarchy at the time of independence, it was merged into India in September 1949.
- In 1969, **Meghalaya** was made another state within **Assam,** and later a full state in 1972.
- **Nagaland** came into being with India in 1963 after a violent rebellion with **Dr Imkongliba** accepting the Indian offer of a separate state.
- **Mizoram** became a full state in 1987 with **Laldenga** as its first Chief Minister after years of insurgency.
- In the case of Jharkhand, **Jharkhand Mukti Morcha** and **Shibu Soren** led the demand and got statehood in the year 2000.

Development and Planning

- In 1950, the government set up a **Planning Commission** to help design and execute suitable policies for economic development.
- A 'mixed economy' model was adopted in which both the State and the private sector play roles in increasing production and generating jobs.
- In 1956, the **Second Five Year Plan** focused strongly on the development of heavy industries such as steel, and on the building of large dams.
- Focus was also put on Science and Higher Education. **Indian Council of Scientific Research** (ICSR) and **Indian Institutes of Technology** were established.
- The **Atomic Energy Commission** under **Homi Jehangir Bhabha** for development of nuclear energy was set up in 1948.
- Rural upliftment was done by two Programmes- **Community Development** (CDP), 1952 and **Panchayati Raj**, 1959.

Banking Sector Reforms

- After independence, the government of India made many banking sector reforms.
- On 1st April, 1949, the **Reserve Bank of India** was nationalised.
- On 1st July 1955, the **Imperial bank** was nationalised and made the **State Bank of India**.
- The government of India made banking one of the branches of social sector reforms and expanded into services into social sector.

Foreign Policy

- India gained freedom soon after the **Second World War**. The **United Nations** formed in 1945 was in its infancy. The 1950s and 1960s saw the emergence of the **Cold War**- conflicts between the USA and the USSR, with both countries creating military alliances.
- Prime Minister **Jawaharlal Nehru**, who was also the Foreign Minister of newly independent India, developed free India's foreign policy in this context. Non-alignment formed the bedrock of this foreign policy.
- It was led by statesmen from **Egypt**, **Yugoslavia**, **Indonesia**, **Ghana** and **India**. The Non-aligned Movement urged countries not to join either of the two major alliances.
- But this policy of staying away from alliances was not a matter of remaining 'isolated' or 'neutral'.
- Non-aligned countries such as India played an active role in mediating between the American and Soviet alliances. They tried to prevent war — often taking a humanitarian and moral stand against war.
- The **Panchsheel Agreement** was signed between India and China in 1954 over the issue of Tibet.

Panchsheel Agreement

- The Panchsheel or five principles of peaceful coexistence was first formally signed on 29th April, 1954 between India and China. The agreement was signed between the then Prime Minister of India **Jawaharlal Nehru** and China's first Prime Minister **Chou En-Lai**.

- The main points of Panchsheel agreement were
  - Peaceful co-existence
  - Mutual respect for each other's territorial integrity and sovereignty.
  - Mutual non-interference
  - Mutual non-aggression
  - Equality and Mutual benefits

Non-Aligned Movement (NAM)

- The First Prime Minister of India **Jawaharlal Nehru** with **Nkrumah** from Ghana, **Nasser** from Egypt, **Sukarno** from Indonesia and **Tito** from Yugoslavia (now Serbia) had a meeting of non-aligned nations in New York (USA) in October, 1960. These five comprised the core leadership of the Non-Aligned Movement (NAM).
- Free India's foreign policy reflected all these concerns in the period immediately after independence. Apart from these factors at the global level, India had its own share of concerns.
- As a nation born in the backdrop of the World Wars, India decided to conduct its foreign relations with an aim to respect the sovereignty of all other nations and to achieve security through the maintenance of peace.
- This aim is derived from the **Directive Principles of State Policy.**
- Just as both internal and external factors guide the behaviour of an individual or a family, both domestic and international environment influence the foreign policy of a nation.
- Since independence, **Cold War** was just beginning and the world was getting divided into these two camps. The foreign policy of a nation reflects the interplay of domestic and external factors. Therefore, the noble ideals that inspired India's struggle for freedom influenced the making of its foreign policy.

Bandung Conference

- The **Afro-Asian Conference** held in the Indonesian city of Bandung in 1955 is commonly known as the Bandung Conference. It marked the zenith of India's engagement with the newly independent Asian and African nations. The Bandung Conference later led to the establishment of the NAM.
- The **First Summit** of the NAM was held in Belgrade in September 1961. Nehru was a co-founder of the NAM.

PL 480 Agreement

- In the year 1959, the President of America **Dwight D. Eisenhower** visited to India. After he visited in the year 1960, he made a four year PL 480 agreement between both countries.
- According to which, the USA will fill the food demand in India by exporting food grains.
- In the year, 1964, USA helped India to overcome heavy food shortage in India by exporting huge amount of food grain to India.
- This agreement also impacted India negatively as India became dependent on USA for food security.
- During the year 1965, USA stopped supply of food grains to India as an effect of India-Pakistan war.
- This event made the government realise to became self-sufficient in food production.

An Evaluation of the Ideals of Our Country

- India is united and it is still democratic.
- Many foreign observers like **Churchill** had felt that India could not survive as a single country, that it would break up into many parts, with each region or linguistic group seeking to form a nation of its own.
- Others believed that it would come under military rule. However, since independence, is united despite of several internal conflicts and factions.
- There is a free press, as well as an independent judiciary.
- Finally, the fact that people speak different languages or practice different faiths has not come in the way of national unity.
- Though deep divisions persist despite constitutional guarantees. The Constitution recognises **equality before the law**, but in real life some Indians are more equal than others.

Indian Paintings

[SOURCES]

Class-VI NCERT Chap 2 (On The Trail of the Earliest People), **Class-XI NCERT** (All Chapters) (An Introduction to Indian Art-Part-I), **Class-XII NCERT** (All Chapters) (An Introduction to Indian Art-Part-II)

Origin of Indian Paintings

- Painting as an art form has flourished in India from pre-historic times (around 5000 BC), in the rock-shelters and caves as a form of **Rock Arts**.
- **Bhimbetka** and **Lakhudiyar** rock paintings have the earliest pre-historic paintings in India.
- The first discovery of rock paintings was made in India in 1867–68 AD by English archaeologist, **Archibald Carlyle** and **John Carkburn** at rock shelters in **Sohagighat** (Mirzapur district, Uttar Pradesh).
- **Percy Brown** (1917) is credited for combining pre-historic paintings with the origins of Indian paintings in the 1st edition of his book '*Indian Painting*'.
- The paintings of Indian subcontinent can be divided into two categories- **mural and miniature paintings**. The mural paintings can be defined as any piece of artwork that painted or applied directly on a wall or ceiling.
- On the other hand, miniatures are small sized colourful paintings with complex and gentle brush work on materials like palm leaves, paper, wood, marble and cloth.
- The cave paintings of post-Mauryan and Gupta period at **Jogimara**, **Ajanta** and **Ellora**, represent the mural art forms in India.
- In the medieval period, miniature paintings emerged as a new art form, in which book illustrations or albums of paintings were dominant feature.
- During 19th and 20th century, Indo-European style of paintings, referred as the **Company style** started by European and Indian artists. Apart from that, many regional folk paintings were also predominantly existed in many parts of India.

Development of Indian Paintings

The development of Indian paintings can be divided into following two phases :

1. Prehistoric Rock Paintings
2. Painting of Historical Age

Pre-historic Rock Paintings

- The pre-historic period is commonly known as the Old Stone Age or the Palaeolithic Age in the early development of human civilisations. Pre-historic paintings in rock shelters and walls of caves show early life and activities of human society.
- Pre-historic paintings have been found in many parts of India. Remnants of rock paintings have been found on the walls of the caves situated in several districts of Madhya Pradesh, Uttar Pradesh, Andhra Pradesh, Karnataka and Bihar.

Subjects/ Material/Characteristics

- Hunting scenes are the main theme of pre-historic paintings in India.
- The hunting scenes depicted people hunting in groups, armed with barbed spears, pointed sticks, arrows and bows.
- The hunters are shown wearing simple clothes and ornaments. Sometimes, men have been decorated with elaborate head-dresses and masks as well.
- Elephant, bison, tiger, boar, deer, antelope, leopard, panther, rhinoceros, fish, frog, lizard, squirrel and some times birds are also depicted in these paintings.
- Though these animals were painted in a naturalistic style, humans were depicted only in a stylistic manner.
- There are paintings of people gathering fruit or honey from trees and of women grinding and preparing food.
- In many of the rock-shelters hand prints, fist prints and dots made by the fingertips are found. Community dances also provide a common theme.

Bhimbetka Cave Paintings

- The caves of Bhimbetka were discovered in 1957–58 by eminent archaeologist **VS Wakankar**. The themes of paintings found here are of great variety, ranging from events of daily life in those times to sacred and royal images.
- These events included hunting, dancing, music, horse and elephant riders, animal fighting, honey collection, decoration of bodies and other household scenes.
- The paintings of the caves of Bhimbetka are representations in green and dark red colours of huge animal figures, such as bisons, elephants, tigers, rhinos and boars besides stick-like human figures. Most of the paintings are filled with **geometric patterns**.
- The artists of Bhimbetka used many colours, including various shades of white, yellow, orange, red ochre, purple, brown, green and black. But white and red were their favourite colours.

Bhimbetka Cave Paintings

Lakhudiyar Cave Paintings

- Located in the Almora district of Uttarakhand, the Lakhudiyar (literally means one lakh caves) cave is another important rock shelters having pre-historic paintings.
- The paintings here can be divided into three categories: man, animal and geometric patterns in white, black and red ochre.
- Humans are represented in stick-like forms. A long-nose animal, a fox and a multiple legged lizard are the main animal motifs. One of the interesting scenes depicted here is of hand-linked dancing human figures.

Painted Earthenware of Indus Valley Civilisation

- Found in different sites of Indus Valley Civilisation, the painting decorations consist of chequers, leaf patterns, lattice work and peepal trees etc.
- Birds, fishes and different animals are also shown.Simplistic in form, these Earthen-wares has maximum polishing touch.

Paintings of Historic Age

Paintings of Historic age can be divided in the following four categories :

1. Paintings of Classical Age (3rd century BC to 9th century AD)
2. Early medieval Paintings (9th-13th century AD)
3. Medieval Paintings (13th to 18th century AD)
4. Paintings of Colonial Age (18th century to 1947)

1. Paintings of Classical Age

- The Classical age of painting is referred to as the Buddhist cave paintings related to Post-Mauryan period (Around 200 BC) till Post-Gupta period (fifth century AD).
- The unique emerged features of such cave paintings were ample use of fresco and tempera style of paintings with vibrant use of colours on the walls and on the ceilings as well.

Jogimara Cave Art

- Jogimara caves are located in the Surguja district in the State of Chhattisgarh. These caves are dated back to around 300 BC and are among the **oldest surviving cave paintings** in India.
- The doorway of Jogimara cave is ornamented with seven paintings, primarily picturing a couple in love, singers, dancers, fish and elephant figures. Each painting is painted on the white **base plaster with a red outline**.

Ajanta Cave Paintings

- The most famous cave site is **Ajanta**, which is located in **Aurangabad district of Maharashtra.** It has **29 caves**, which were built in three phases.
- The first group starting around the second century BC, while the second and third group of caves built around 400–650 AD.
- On 28th April, 1819, **John Smith**, the Madras Presidency officer of **East India Company**, accidentally discovered the Ajanta caves.

Ajanta Cave Paintings

- Paintings of Ajanta caves have a lot of typological and stylistic variations, as different guilds of artisans have worked on painting of these caves. Many caves of Ajanta have double-storeyed layers.
- The caves of the early phase includes **Cave No. 9** and **10** of Ajanta. They belong to the first century BC. The figures are broad with heavy proportion and arranged in the picture space in a linear way. Lines are sharp, colours are limited and there is no over-stylisation.
- The second phase of paintings is of the images of the Buddhas painted on the walls and pillars of same Cave No. 10 and 9. These Buddha figures are different from the figures painted in the fifth century AD.
- Cave No. 10, 9, 12 and 13 belong to the early phase, Cave No. 11, 15 and 6 upper and lower and Cave No. 7 belong to the phase earlier than late fifth century AD. The rest of the caves belong to late fifth century AD. The Chaitya Cave No. 19 and 26 are elaborately carved.
- The third phase of development observed in Ajanta paintings are mainly in the paintings of **Cave No. 16, 17, 1 and 2.** Various skin colours have been used in the paintings, which represents a multi-coloured population during that time.
- The themes of the Ajanta paintings are the events from the life of the Buddha, the Jatakas and the Avadanas. Some paintings such as **Simhala Avadana, Mahajanaka Jataka** and **Vidhurpundita Jataka** cover the entire wall of the cave.
- The **Chaddanta Jataka** has been painted in the entire Cave No 10. The other important paintings are the famous **Padmapani** and **Vajrapani** in cave No. 1.
- The **Third Khanda** (Chapter) of the *Vishnudharmottara Purana*, a fifth century text has a chapter **Chitrasutra**, which is considered as a source book of Indian art in general and specifically in painting. It talks about the art of an image making called *Pratima Lakshana*, which are the canons of painting.

Ellora Caves

- Another important cave site is located in Aurangabad district of Maharashtra is Ellora. It is located at about 100 kilometres from Ajanta and has thirty-four Buddhist (Caves 1-12), Brahmanical (Caves 13-29) and Jain caves (Caves 30-34). It is also unique in terms of **stylistic eclecticism**, i.e., confluence of many styles at one place.
- Buddhist caves are big in size and are of single, double and triple storeys (Cave No. 12). All the caves were plastered and painted but few are left uncounted. The caves of Ellora have images of **Tara**, **Avalokiteshvara**, **Manushi Buddhas**, etc.
- The most numerous and best preserved Jain paintings at Ellora are found in one of the smaller Cave No. 19, which is part of the largest Jain cave complex, the **Indra Sabha.** The paintings are found in the ceiling in the main hall and on the walls along with the ceiling of the inner sanctum.

Ellora Caves

Bagh Caves

- The Bagh caves situated at the Vindhyas in **Bagh** town of **Dhar district**, in Madhya Pradesh are a group of nine rock-cut monuments, which were built in the fifth to sixth century AD.
- These paintings are materialistic rather than spiritualistic. Characteristics of Bagh cave paintings are similar to those of Ajanta caves.
- The paintings on the wall and ceilings in **Cave No. 3** and **Cave No. 4** of the Bagh caves, were executed through tempera method (use of permanent fast-drying painting medium). **Cave No. 2** is the best preserved cave of Bagh, known as **'Pandava Cave'**.

Badami Cave Paintings

- Badami caves are located in the state of Karnataka. The Chalukya king, **Mangalesha** patronised the excavation of the Badami caves as it was the capital of the early Chalukyan dynasty, which ruled the region from 543 to 598 AD. The paintings of Badami represents an extension of the tradition of mural painting from Ajanta to Badami in South India.
- However, only fragments of painting have survived on the vaulted roof of the front Mandapa. Paintings in this cave depict the palace scenes. The **Cave No.4** is popularly known as the **Vishnu cave**.
- The curving drawn lines, fluid forms and compact composition exemplify the proficiency and maturity, the artists had achieved in the sixth century AD. The gracefully drawn faces of the king and the queen resembles the Ajanta paintings. Their eye-sockets are large, eyes are half-closed, and lips are very unique.

Sittanavasal Art Form

- The Sittanavasal cave is a rock-cut temple also known as **Arivar Koil**. It is part of second century complex of Jain temples located in the Sittanavasal village of **Pudukkotai** district of Tamil Nadu.
- The temple is famous for its magnificent mural paintings dating back to Pallava era of sixth century AD, which lasted till ninth century AD of early Pandyan reign.
- The painting technique used here is Fresco and the murals are painted on surfaces that first have been covered with lime plaster. The ceilings have depiction of natural looking images of men, animals, flowers, birds and fishes representing the Samavasarana faith of Jainism.

2. Early Medieval Period Paintings

- The period of later Pallavas and Cholas in South India is considered as the beginning of art forms in the early medieval India.
- Apart from that Pala School of Bengal, Gujarat School and other regional art forms also developed during the early medieval period.

Chola Art Forms

- Paintings of Chola period are found in the **Natyakuran** of the **Brihadeeswara** temple of Thanjavur. These paintings are the examples of Murals or the tempera technique. It shows continuation of the style and methods of the Ajanta style.
- The paintings show narrations and aspects related to Lord Shiva, Shiva in Kailash, Shiva as Tripurantaka, Shiva as Nataraja, a portrait of the patron Rajaraja and his mentor Kuruvar, dancing figures, etc.
- Chola paintings have brilliantly executed the colour treatment and different sizes of the images that are painted and also remark about the judgements of the artists. The walls that bear the paintings are usually 8 ft high and 40 ft wide. The paintings have adopted the complex method of the Fresco style.

Pala School of Art

- The **Palas rulers of Bengal** and Bihar patronised Pala School of Art form during 9th till 12th century AD, which is considered as an earliest example of miniature painting in manuscripts. Almost all illuminations were inspired by **Vajrayana Buddhism.**
- The Pala School used natural colours for painting human skin. They developed pictures on paper manuscripts, wooden covers and palm leaf. Flat heads, curving finishing lines, attention on mostly lone human figure, paintings with no name are the features of this school of painting.
- A fine example of a Pala Buddhist palm leaf manuscript is **Astasahasrika Prajnaparamita** or the **Perfection of Wisdom**, written in 8000 lines.
- During the Muslim attacks, the Buddhist monasteries were destroyed, which led to the abrupt end of the **Pala School of miniature painting**. Although some of the artists and monks escaped to Nepal and assisted in strengthening the prevailing art tradition there.

Apabhramsa School of Art/Western School of Paintings

- Painting activity that developed largely in Western parts of India is known as the **Apabhramsa** or **Western School of Painting**. Gujarat is the most prominent centre of this school Southern parts of Rajasthan and Western parts of Central India are the other centres.
- The word 'apabhramsa' means corrupt or mixed. So, it can be observed a much stylistic difference between the early and later phases through **Apabhramsa School of Art**.

Jain School of Painting

- Jain painting received impetus because the concept of *shaastradaan* (donation of books) gained favour in the community, where the act of donating illustrated paintings to the monastery's libraries, called **bhandars** (repositories) was glorified as a gesture of charity, righteousness and gratitude.
- Early Jain paintings were traditionally done on palm leaves before paper was introduced in the 14th century and the earliest surviving palm leaf manuscript from the Western part of India dates back to the 11th century.
- Among the most widely illustrated canonical text in the Jain tradition is **Kalpasutra**. It has a section, reciting events from the lives of the 24 Tirthankaras.

- Jain paintings developed a schematic and simplified language for painting. Thin and wavy lines predominate the composition and three-dimensionality of the face is attempted with an addition of a further eye.

Pre-Mughal/Pre-Rajasthani

- A large group of works, portraying Hindu and Jain subjects, such as the **Mahapurana**, **Chaurpanchashika**, **Aranyaka Parvan** of the **Mahabharata**, **Bhagvata Purana**, **Gita Govinda**, etc are representative of this indigenous style of painting in early medieval period in India. This phase and style is also referred to as pre-Mughal or pre-Rajasthani, which is largely synonymous with the term 'indigenous style'.
- A particular figure type evolved with an interest in depicting transparency of fabrics known as—*odhnis* i.e., 'ballooned' over the head of heroines and draped with stiff and standing edges. Different kind of hatchings evolved for depiction of water bodies and particular ways of representing the horizon, flora and fauna, etc., got formalised.

3. Paintings in Medieval Period

- During the early part of 13th century, Vijayanagara and Deccan Sultanate were the patrons and under them developed various forms of paintings, among which Vijayanagara kingdoms were significant. Apart from that, Kerala murals were also developed in the same period.

The Vijayanagara Paintings

- With the decline of power of the Chola Dynasty in the 13th century, the Vijayanagara Dynasty brought under its control the region from Hampi to Trichy and many paintings were made in different temples.
- The paintings at **Tiruparakunram**, near Trichy, done in the 14th century represents the early phase of the Vijayanagara style. In Hampi, the **Virupaksha temple** has paintings on the ceiling of its *mandapa* narrating events from dynastic history and episodes from the Ramayana and the Mahabharata.
- In **Lepakshi**, present in Andhra Pradesh, there are glorious examples of Vijayanagara paintings on the walls of the Shiva temple. The faces are shown in profile and figures and objects two-dimensionally. Lines become still but fluid, compositions appear in rectilinear compartments.
- In keeping with the tradition, the Vijayanagara painters evolved a pictorial language wherein the faces are shown in profile and figures and objects two-dimensionally.

Murals of Kerala

- Kerala painters (during the period from the 16th to the 18th century) evolved a pictorial language and technique of their own while discriminately adopting certain stylistic elements from Nayaka and Vijayanagara schools.
- The painters evolved a language taking clues from contemporary traditions, like **Kathakali** and **Kalam ezhuthu** (ritual floor painting of Kerala), using vibrant and luminous colours, representing human figures in three-dimensionality.
- More than sixty sites have been found with mural paintings in three palaces—**Dutch palace** in Kochi, **Krishnapuram palace** in Kayamkulam and **Padmanabhapuram palace**.

Murals of Kerala

The Deccani Schools of Painting

- **The Deccani style of Painting** was placed under the **Indo-Persian** art for long. It was considered to be Middle Eastern, Safavid, Persian, Turkish and even Mughal in origin.
- The kingdoms of **Bijapur**, **Golconda** and **Ahmednagar** developed highly sophisticated and distinct school of court painting.

Ahmednagar School of Painting

- The earliest examples of Deccani painting are in a volume of poems, celebrating the reign of **Hussain Nizam Shah I** of Ahmednagar (1553–1565).
- One of the detailed paintings, has depiction of the queen and her marriage with gorgeous colours. The woman represented in it belongs to the Northern tradition of pre-Mughal painting.
- The women in the paintings of Ahmednagar wear a modified Northern costume with *choli* **(bodice)** and long braided pigtails, ending in a tassel. Only a long scarf, passing round the body below the hips, is a Southern fashion, which is seen in the Lepakshi painting.

Bijapur School of Painting

- Paintings from Bijapur in the 16th century have a richly illustrated encyclopedia known as the **Nujum-al-Ulum** dated 1570 AD. **The school of Bijapur** was patronised by

Ali Adil Shah I (1558–1580 AD) and his successor **Ibrahim II** (1580–1627 AD), both patrons of art and literature.

- The theme of one of the Bijapuri painting is **Yogini**—one who believes in yoga, leads a disciplined life of physical and emotional training, pursues spiritual and intellectual explorations and is famous for renunciation of worldly attachments.

Golconda School of Painting

- Golconda became an independent state in 1512 AD. By the end of the 16th century, it was the wealthiest of the Deccan kingdoms.
- Golconda's art became popular as Dutch merchants carried the portraits of sultans in the late 17th century to Europe.
- The earliest five miniatures, identified as Golconda work, were bound up in **Diwan of Hafiz**, dated 1463 AD.
- These paintings represent court scenes of a young ruler, who is depicted seated enthroned, holding a typically long and straight Deccani sword, in the centre of one of the painting folios.

Mughal School of Miniature Painting

- Mughal painting is the style of miniature painting that developed in the Northern Indian subcontinent in the 16th century.
- It continued till the mid–19th century in various art forms and contributed towards enhancing the status of art, viz., calligraphy, painting, bookmaking, book illustration projects, etc. The development of mughal school of Miniature painting under different rulers is stated below :

Babur

- In 1526, Babur, the first Mughal Emperor had a dynamic taste for a variety of arts. Babur's detailed accounts in *Baburnama*, his autobiography, are narratives of the emperor's political carrier and artistic passion.
- The books and albums that were produced in the royal ateliers were not only calligraphic but also painted. **Bihzad** was the prominent artist who find mention in Babur's memoirs.
- He was a master artist from the Persian school of painting, **Herat** (now in present day Afghanistan) and was known for his sophisticated compositions and colour tints. Another artist, **Shah Muzaffar** (painter), excelled in the representation of hairstyle.

Humayun

- Babur was succeeded by his son Humayun in 1530 AD and during his exile in Shah Tahmasp's court in Iran, Humayun witnessed the magnificent artistic tradition of miniature paintings and manuscripts.
- Humayun brought back with him the master artists when he regained power in India. He invited two Persian artists—**Mir Sayyid Ali** and **Abd-us-Samad** to establish a studio in his court and carry out royal paintings.

Akbar

- The tradition and fascination for painting started by Humayun was carried forward by his illustrious son Akbar (1556–1605 AD). The Emperor took great interest in both pictorial narrative, as well as, recitation of **Hamza Nama**.
- The base surface is cloth with paper at the back, on which the narrative text is written to help the narrator known as gouache technique, which is water based and in opaque colours.
- The Persian translation and illustrated version of the Hindu epic Mahabharata done this period came to be known as **Razm Nama** by **Daswant** in 1589 AD. This manuscript was scribed in ornate calligraphy and contained 169 paintings. Artists like **Govardhan** and **Miskin** were popular for their visuals of court scenes.
- **Madonna and Child (1580)** by **Basawan**, was painting is an important early work of the Mughal School of Painting during Akbar's reign. Madonna, here, is an extraordinary theme, which brings the Byzantine art, the European classical and its Renaissance to the Mughal atelier.

Jahangir

- The Mughal miniature style and set standards were further taken to new heights by Jahangir (1605–1627). Jahangir employed **Aqa Riza**, a well-known Iranian painter and his son **Abul Hasan** to achieve unparalleled sophistication in painting. *Tuzuk-i-Jahangiri*, the memoirs of Jahangir, tells about his great interest in arts.
- Jahangir was presented with paintings and decorative objects, depicting high arts from Europe.Therefore, European art sensibilities started overtaking into the prevalent Indo-Iranian style, thereby, making the Jahangir school of art more impressive and vibrant.
- Jahangir in Darbar from *Jahangirnama*, attributed to Abul Hasan and Manohar (1620 AD) is an excellent painting. Jahangir is at the highest level in the centre, where the stunning white pillars surrounded by sparkling clear colours and brilliantly framed overhead canopy.
- In the painting, Jahangir enthroned on an **Hourglass** (1625 AD), symbolism is creatively applied by the court painter, **Bichitra**. Portrait that resemble the Ottoman Sultan, **King James I** of England also stands on the right hand with gifts for the mighty emperor.

Shah Jahan

- The son of Jahangir, Shah Jahan encouraged the artists in the atelier to create magnificent works that were a blend of imagination and documentation. Idealisation and great stylisation were preferred over naturalistic rendering and accurate depiction.
- One of the exceptional painting of Shah Jahan was the titled **Dara Shikoh with Sages in a Garden** was created by Bichitra in 1635 AD.
- The artworks produced under his supervision concentrated on superficial qualities and extreme beautification, which was created by the use of jewel-like colours and intricate fine lines.
- *Padshahnama* (The Chronicles of the King) is one of the most extensive painting projects undertaken by his court ateliers.

Later Mughal Painting

- After **Shah Jahan**, Mughal painting declined drastically under Aurangzeb. Although some masterworks were produced during the periods of **Muhammad Shah Rangila**, **Shah Alam II** and **Bahadur Shah Zafar**, but these were mere in declined state of the Mughal miniature style.

Rajasthani Rajput Schools of Painting

- The Rajasthani Schools of Painting' prevailed in the princely kingdoms. They constitute Rajasthan and parts of Madhya Pradesh in the present time, such as Mewar, Bundi, Kota, Jaipur, Bikaner, Kishangarh, Jodhpur (Marwar), Malwa, Sirohi etc.
- The pictorial styles that emerged and evolved in these kingdoms were significantly diverse in terms of compositional elements, modes of narration, or on extreme mannerism.
- Scholar **Anand Coomaraswamy** in 1916 coined the term 'Rajput Paintings' to refer to these as most rulers and patrons of these kingdoms were Rajputs.

Malwa School of Painting

- The Malwa School flourished between 1600 and 1700 AD and is most representative of the Hindu Rajput courts.
- Its two-dimensional simplistic language appears as a consummation of stylistic progression from the Jain manuscripts to the **Chaurpanchashika** manuscript paintings.
- A large number of Malwa paintings discovered from the **Datia Palace** of Bundelkhand defy an obvious Mughal influence, which is contrary to the works on paper that are stylistically inclined towards indigenous two-dimensional simplicity.

Mewar School of Painting

- Mewar is a significant early centre of painting in Rajasthan, from where, hypothetically, one would have been able to formalise a continuous stylistic tradition of painting.
- The reign of **Jagat Singh I** (1628–1652) is recognised as the period when pictorial aesthetics got reformulated under great artists **Sahibdin** and **Manohar**.
- Sahibdin painted the famous **Yuddha Kanda** of Ramayana (1652 AD). **Manohar's** most significant work is that of **Bal Kanda** of Ramayana (1649). Mewar artists, generally prefer a bright colour palette with prominent reds and yellows.

Bundi School of Painting

- A prolific and distinct school of painting flourished in Bundi in the 17th century, which is remarkable for its unblemished colour sense and excellent formal design. The Bundi School began under the reign of **Bhoj Singh** (1585–1607 AD).
- The Bundi School blossomed under the patronage of **Rao Chattar Sal** (1631–1659 AD), who was made the Governor of Delhi by Shah Jahan and his son **Rao Bhao Singh** (1659–1682 AD). Baramasa is a popular theme of Bundi paintings, an atmospheric description of the 12 months by **Keshav Das**.
- Bundi's earliest phase of painting, Bundi Ragamala bears an inscription in Persian that dates back to 1591 mentions names of its artists-Shaykh. Hasan, Shaykh Ali and Shaykh Hatim, who introduced themselves as pupils of master artist, Mir Sayyid Ali and Khwaja Abddus Samad of the Mughal court.

Kota School of Painting

- In the early period, the paintings of Bundi and Kota cannot be distinguished for several decades as Kota painters borrowed from the Bundi collections.
- During the course of time, artists had passionately enlarged their inventory to a large variety of subjects in their compositions.
- Bundi and Kota were parts of the same kingdom till 1625 AD when **Jahangir** divided the Bundi Empire into two.
- Kota paintings are characteristically spontaneous and calligraphic in execution. They emphasise on marked shading, especially, the double–lid eye. Artists of the Kota School excelled in providing animals and combat.

Bikaner School of Painting

- As a result of long association with the Mughals, Bikaner developed a distinctive language of painting that was influenced by the Mughal elegance and subdued colour palette. In the reign of **Anup Singh**, **Ruknuddin** was the master artist, whose style was an amalgamation of the Deccani and Mughal conventions.

- The custom of having portraits of artists is unique to the Bikaner School and most of them are inscribed with information regarding their ancestry. In some cases, even the place of production and occasions for which the works were commissioned.

Kishangarh School of Painting

- The most stylised of all Rajasthani miniatures, Kishangarh paintings are distinguished by their eyebrows, lotus petal shaped eyes, having drooping eyelids, a sharp slender nose and thin lips.
- A distinctive style of delicate human form, making lavish use of green and panoramic landscapes had evolved.
- The most celebrated and outstanding artist was **Nihal Chand** who worked for **Sawant Singh** at Kishangarh. His most renowned work is known as **Bani Thani**, where Radha is unique in her deeply curved eyes, arch of the eyebrows, pointed nose, thin lips and pronounced chin.

Jodhpur School of Painting

- With the political presence of Mughals since the 16th century, influence of their visual aesthetics made its way in the style of Jodhpur School of Painting. A productive period of painting was under **Maharaja Jaswant Singh** (1638–1678 AD).
- He was the follower of Vallabha cult of Shrinathji, and patronised many Krishna related themes with **Bhagvata Purana** as the most prominent one.
- The last phase innovative of Jodhpur painting was during the reign of **Man Singh** (1803–1843 AD) under whom **Dhola-Maru** (1804) painting was created.

Jaipur School of Painting

- The Jaipur School of painting originated in its former capital Amer. **Sawai Jai Singh** (1699–1743 AD), an influential ruler, established a new capital city Jaipur named after him in 1727 and shifted from Amer.
- He was drawn to the Vaishnavite sect and commissioned numerous paintings on the theme of Radha and Krishna. Artists during his reign, painted sets based on **Rasikapriya**, **Gita Govinda**, **Baramasa** and **Ragamala**, where the hero's figure is in striking resemblance with the king.

Pahari Schools of Painting

- Pahari Schools of Painting includes towns, such as Basohli, Guler, Kangra, Kullu, Chamba and others in the hills of Himalayas, which emerged as centres of painting from 17th to 19th century.
- The emergence of the Pahari School mainly initiated by the artists who migrated from the Mughal atelier to the hills.

Basohli School of Painting

- Basohli painting is a traditional art form that originated in Basohli town of Jammu and Kashmir, known for its rich cultural heritage.
- From 1678 to 1695 AD, under **Kirpal Pal**, an enlightened prince, Basohli developed a distinctive and magnificent style.
- It is characterised by a strong use of primary colours and warm yellows—filling the background and horizon, stylised treatment of vegetation etc.

Guler School of Painting

- The first quarter of the 18th century saw a complete transformation in the Basohli style, initiating the Guler–Kangra phase.
- This phase first appeared in Guler, a high-ranking branch of the Kangra royal family, under the patronage of **Raja Govardhan Chand** (1744–1773).

Kangra School of Painting

- Painting in the Kangra region blossomed under the patronage of a remarkable ruler, **Raja Sansar Chand** (1775–1823). The Kangra style is by far the most poetic and lyrical of Indian styles marked with serene beauty and delicacy of execution.
- Characteristic features of the Kangra style are delicacy of line, brilliance of colour and minuteness of decorative details. **Bhagvata Purana** paintings is one of the greatest achievements of Kangra artists. It is best-known for its effortless naturalism and vivid details of figures that portray dramatic scenes.

Painting in Colonial Age

- With the colonial rule, many English officers commissioned local artists to paint scenes around them to get a better idea of the natives.
- The local artists had to rely more on close observation, a striking feature of the **European art**, rather than memory and rule books, as seen in traditional art.
- It is the mixture of traditional and European style of painting that came to be known as the **Company School of Painting**.

Academic Style of Painting

- The academic style of oil painting that used a European medium to depict Indian subject matter, however, flourished in the art schools set up by the British.
- The most successful examples of this can be seen in the works produced by self-taught artist, **Raja Ravi Verma** of the Travancore Court in Kerala.

- By imitating copies of European paintings popular in Indian palaces, he mastered the style of academic realism and used it to depict scenes from popular epics like the **Ramayana** and **Mahabharata**. Many of his paintings were copied as oleographs (printed on cloth to imitate an oil painting) and even entered people's homes as calendar images.

Bengal School

With the rise of nationalism in India by the end of the 19th century, the Bengal School emerged as an art movement and a style of painting that originated in Calcutta, the centre of British power, but later influenced many artists in different parts of the country, including Shantiniketan.

Abanindranath Tagore (1871-1951 AD)

- The Bengal School of Painting was spearheaded by **Abanindranath Tagore** who enjoyed the support of British administrator and principal of the Calcutta School of Art, **EB Havell** (1861–1934).
- Both Abanindranath and Havell were critical of colonial Art Schools and firmly believed in creating a new type of painting that was Indian not only in subject matter but also in style.
- For them, Mughal and Pahari miniatures were more important sources of inspiration, rather than either the Company School of Painting taught in the Colonial Art Schools. Both Abanindranath Tagore and Havell had established **Government Art School**, Calcutta (now, **Government College of Art and Craft**, Kolkata).

Nandalal Bose

- Nandalal Bose, a student of Abanindranath Tagore, was a prolific early modernist painter, who was invited by Rabindranath Tagore to head the painting department in the newly established **Kala Bhavana** (India's first National Art School) at **Shantiniketan**.
- **Mahatma Gandhi** invited him to paint panels that were put on display at the Congress session at Haripura in 1937. Famously called the **Haripura Posters**, they depicted ordinary rural folks busy in various activities — a musician drumming, a farmer tilling, a woman churning milk and so on.

Modern Indian Art

- By mid and late 19th century, art schools were established in major cities like Lahore, Calcutta, Bombay and Madras.
- These art schools influenced Indian artists like **Gaganendranath** and poet–painter **Rabindranath Tagore**, who welcomed international trends of **Cubism** and **Expressionism**.
- Rabindranath Tagore often make patterns out of doodles and developed a unique, calligraphic style out of crossed out words.

Gaganendranath Tagore (1869-1938)

- Paintings by Gaganendranath Tagore, brother of Abanindranath Tagore, the influence of modern **Western style of paintings** can be clearly seen.
- He was one of the earlier Indian painters, who made use of language and syntax of **Cubism** to render his ideas.
- **City in the Night** is a watercolour painting made by Gaganendranath Tagore in 1922.
- He visualised the mysterious world of his imaginary cities like **Dwarka** (Lord Krishna's legendary abode) or **Swarnapuri** through multiple viewpoints, multi-faceted shapes and jagged edges of Cubism.

Jamini Roy (1887-1972)

- Jamini Roy was called the **Father of the folk Renaissance** in India, who created an alternative vision of modern Indian identity.
- In the mid–1920s, he travelled to the countryside of Bengal to collect folk paintings (pats) and learn from folk artisans.
- In his painting, a mother and her child created in 1940 are with bold simplifications and thick outlines with sweeping brush strokes.
- Figures are coloured in dull yellow and brick-red background.
- The two-dimensional nature of the painting is derived from pat paintings and his search for simplicity and pure form is visible.
- Roy used the notion of village community as a weapon of resistance to colonial rule and a political act of making local signify national spirit.

Benode Behari Mukherjee

- Benode Behari Mukherjee was **Nandlal Bose's** most creative student, who gave a lot of thought as how to understand the world.
- Rather than making paintings around well-known epics like **Ramayana** and **Mahabharata**, Benode Behari Mukherjee was drawn to the lives of medieval saints.
- On the walls of **Hindi Bhavana** in **Shantiniketan**, he made a mural called Medieval Saints, in which he charts a history of medieval India through the lives of **Tulsi Das**, **Kabir** etc., and focuses on their humane teachings.

Ramkinkar Baij

- He was an artist given to the celebration of nature. Ramkinkar developed his own unique style of art that could capture not only their immediate environment like *flora* and *fauna* but also those who lived there. Almost all his sculptures and paintings are created as response to his environment.
- His Santhal Family, made as an outdoor sculpture within the **Kala Bhavana** compound. The daily activity of a Santhal family setting out for work are presented in the form of a life size piece of art.

Amrita Shergill (1913–1941)

- Amrita Shergill half Hungarian and half Indian, emerges as a unique female artist, who contributed immensely to modern Indian art through the 1930s.
- Unlike others, she was trained in Paris and had a first-hand experience in **European modern art** trends such as **Impressionism** and **post–Impressionism**.
- After deciding to make India her base, she worked to develop art with Indian themes and images. Amrita Shergill assimilated miniature and mural traditions of Indian art with European modernism. She died young, leaving behind a remarkable collection of work.

Progressive Artists' Group

The desire for political as well as, artistic freedom soon spread widely among young artists, who witnessed independence from the British Raj.

- In Bombay, a set of artists formed a group, called **The Progressives** in 1946 with **Francis Newton Souza** as the leader of the group, they included **MF Husain** and **SH Raza** and others. They wanted to question and challenge the traditional sense of beauty and morality.
- **Francis Newton Souza** (1924-2002) he was one of the first painters to achieve international recognition from a newly independent India. He was a leading figure of the progressive artists group. As a result of his time spent abroad, Souza's style drew heavily from Expressionism and often referred to as the **Indian Picasso**.
- **MF Husain** (1915-2011) Maqbool Fida Husain, known as MF Husain, was most eminent artist of India. He attended JJ School of Arts in Bombay. Using freehand drawing and vibrant colour, he depicted Indian subject matter in the style of contemporary European art movements, particularly Cubism.
- **SH Raza** (1922-2016) One of the most distinguished artists of the Indian subcontinent, Sayed Haider Raza is famous for his usage of rich colours in all his portrays. The paintings of SH Raza revolved mainly around nature and its various facets. Over the years, his paintings transformed into abstract ones such as the *Bindu* (dot).

Living Art Traditions of India

- Our country has always been a repository of indigenous knowledge, which has been transferred from one generation to another.
- Artists in each generation have created the best of works out of available material and technology.
- Among the many popular traditions of painting, Mithila or Madhubani painting of Bihar, Warli painting of Maharashtra, Phad from Rajasthan etc., are famous.

Mithila Painting

- Among the most known contemporary painterly art forms is Mithila art that derives its name from Mithila. Also called **Madhubani painting** after the nearest district capital, it is a widely recognised folk art tradition.
- These paintings, characterised by bright colours, are largely painted in three areas of the house— various armed gods and animals or images of women at work like carrying waterpots or winnowing grain, etc., are vividly portrayed in the outer central courtyard.

Warli Painting

- The Warli community inhabit the West coast of Northern Maharashtra around the North Sahyadri range with a large concentration in the district of Thane. Married women play a central role in creating their most important painting called **Chowk** to mark special occasions.
- The central motif related scenes of everyday life, portraying acts of hunting, fishing, farming, dancing, mythological stories of animals, where the tiger is conspicuously visible and busy urban life of Mumbai.

Gond Painting

- Paintings of Gonds of Mandla (Madhya Pradesh) and its surrounding regions have been transformed into a colourful depiction of animals, humans and flora.
- The delicate paintings are geometric drawings done on the walls of huts, portraying **Krishna** with his cows surrounded by *gopis* with pots on their heads.

Pata Painting

- Done on fabric, palm leaf or paper, scroll painting is another example of art form practised in different parts of the country, especially, Gujarat and Rajasthan in the West and Odisha and West Bengal in East. It is also known as **Pachedi**, **Phad**, etc.

- **Bengal Patas** comprise the practice of painting on cloth (pata) and storytelling in regions of West Bengal. It is the most receptive oral tradition, constantly seeking new themes and formulating novel responses to major incidents in the world.
- The vertically painted pata becomes a prop used by a patua (performer) for performance. Patuas, also called *Chitrakars*, belong to communities largely settled around Midnapore, Birbhum and Bankura regions of West Bengal, parts of Bihar and Jharkhand.
- Puri Patas or paintings evidently acquire their claim to recognition from the temple city of Puri in Odisha. It largely comprises the pata (initially, done on palm leaf and cloth but now done on paper as well).
- A range of themes are painted, such as the daily and festival veshas (attires) of Jagannath, Balabhadra and Subhadra.

Living Art Traditions of India

Phads of Rajasthan

- Phads are long, horizontal, cloth scrolls painted to honour folk deities of pastoral communities inhabiting the region around **Bhilwara** in Rajasthan. Designated by the broad term **bhomia**, these heroes are honoured, worshiped and remembered for their acts of martyrdom.
- Illustrating the valorous tales of these bhomias, the phads, are carried by bhopas, the wandering bards. Phads, however, are not painted by the bhopas. They have traditionally been painted by a caste called **Joshis** who have been painters in the courts of the kings of Rajasthan.

Kalamkari Painting

- Kalamkari is an ancient style of hand painting done on cotton or silk fabric with a pen, using natural dyes.
- The word 'Kalamkari' is derived from a Persian word where 'kalam' means pen and 'kari' refers to craftsmanship.
- This art involves 23 steps of dyeing, bleaching, hand painting, block printing, starching, cleaning and more.

Kalamkari Painting

- Kalamkari art and printing is concentrated primarily in **Kalahasti** and **Machilipatnam** districts of Andhra Pradesh.
- In the Machilipatnam, motifs are essentially printed with hand-carved traditional blocks with complex detailing painted by hands. On the other hand, **Srikalahasti** style of painting draws inspiration from the Hindu mythology.

Extra Facts From Tamil Nadu Board and NIOS

- **Pre-historic Painting of India** Panchmarhi rock painting It is located in Madhya Pradesh. Panchmarhi literally means group of five caves. Here collective pictures of cows in a row had been made. Soil and mineral powder had been used to make pen, which were saffron and red in colour.
- **Painting of Indus Valley Civilisation** Animals on the utensils of Indus Valley Civilisation. The figures generally depicted are those of types bull, deer and fish.

  The utensils were well cooked, shiny and dark red in colour. The bottom part of almost all the utensils is painted black. The painted vessels were generally used for storages. The size of utensils have been made in proper proportion. Some of the pets depicts geometric fish motifs. These are considered to be from third century BC. It has been made obtained from Mehrgarh. The shape of a peacock with its feathers spread has been depicted on some utensils.
- **Thanjavur Painting Style** The origin of this style is considered to be Tanjore city of Tamil Nadu. It developed between the 16th and 18th centuries under the patronage of Nayak and Maratha rulers. Its subject Matter is mainly Hindu Gods and Goddesses, kings and princely states, mythological characters, etc. These paintings are made by pasting cloth on wooden boards.

  This is the reason why these paintings are called Palamai Padani in Tamil, which means painting made on woods. Panchmukhi Anjneya is the most famous painting of this painting style.
- **Mysore Painting Art** This art style developed in Mysore city of Karnataka during the 18th century. Its subject mater has been Hindu God and Goddesses and stories related to them. These were also depicted in manuscripts. The most famous picture of this style is Matsya avatara.
- **Kalighat Painting Style** The origin of this art is Kalighat of Calcutta. This was the result of social and cultural upheavals taking place in 19th century Calcutta. Its subject matters was Hindu Gods and Goddesses, a satire on social, evils, a donor, a musician, a woman combing her hair, an obese women holding red rose in her hand. The most famous depiction of this style of painting is depiction of *Sita* and *Luv-Kush*.

35

Sculpture Art of India

[SOURCES]

Class XI New NCERT Chap 3 (Fine Arts , Arts of the Mauryan Period),
Chap 4 (Post-Mauryan Trends in Indian Art and Architecture),
Chap 7 (Indian Bronze Sculpture),
Class XII New NCERT Chap 1 (Bricks, Beads and Bones)
Tamil Nadu Board (Class XI), NIOS

- Beginning of sculpture art in India is primarily attributed to **Indus Valley Civilisation** where first evidence of sculpture art, found in different variations and in mass scale.
- The artists of Harappan Civilisation had fine artistic sensibilities and a vivid imagination.
  In the **Mauryan period** and later phases, sketches of human and animal figures were made in a highly realistic nature with extremely careful manner.
- From **Medieval period**, some notable sculpture art forms from Vijayanagara empire can be found.

Art Forms of Harappan Civilisation

- The arts of the Indus Valley Civilisation emerged during the second half of the third millennium BC. The forms of art found from various sites of the civilisation include sculptures, seals, pottery, jewellery, terracotta figures, etc.
- The Harappan people had constructed mainly three types of buildings-dwelling houses, pillared halls and public baths.
- The most important featur_s of Harappan art forms were as follows

Stone Statue of the Priest King

- The statue is made of steatite and it was found in Mohenjodaro.
- He is wearing an armlet in right arm, short beard, half closed elongated eyes (meditative posture). He is recognised as the 'priest king'.

Priest King

- The figure is draped in a shawl coming under the right arm and covering the left shoulder.

The Dancing Girl

- The world's first bronze sculpture of a dancing girl has been found in **Mohenjodaro**. This exquisite casting depicts a girl whose long hair is tied in a bun.
- Approximately four-inch-high copper figure has bangles on her left arm, a bracelet and an amulet or bangle adorn her right arm and a cowry shell necklace is seen around her neck. Her right hand is on her hip and her left hand is clasped in a traditional Indian dance gesture. This figure is full of expression and bodily vigour and conveys a lot of information.

The Male Torso

- The Male Torso of Harappa is a fine example of the earliest Harappan work. It is made of red limestone. Its legs, arms and head are broken, its belly is also heavy.
- There are three socket holes made on this torso where the head and arm can be attached. It indicates that the people of the Indus Valley Civilisation knew to make such sculptures that can bend their neck and arms.

Mother Goddess

- The Mother Goddess figures are usually crude standing female figures adorned with necklaces hanging over and wearing a loin cloth and a girdle.
- The fan-shaped head-dress with a cup-like projection on each side is a distinct decorative feature of the Mother Goddess figures of the Indus Valley.

Terracotta

- The Indus Valley people made terracotta images also. They are more realistic and the most important among the Indus figures are those representing the mother Goddess. A terracotta figure of a male in a yogic posture has also been excavated.

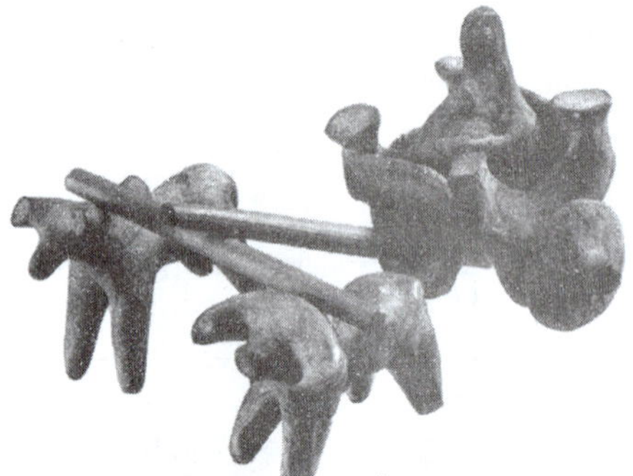

A Terracotta Cart

- In terracotta, we also find a few figurines of bearded males with coiled hair, their posture rigidly upright, legs slightly apart and the arms parallel to the sides of the body.
- The repetition of this figure in exactly the same position would suggest that he was a deity. A terracotta mask of a horned deity has also been found. Toy carts with wheels, whistles, rattles, birds and animals, gamesmen and discs were also rendered in terracotta.

Seals

- Archaeologists have discovered thousands of seals, mostly made of steatite. The purpose of producing seals was mainly commercial. The standard Harappan seal was a square plaque 2×2 square inches, made from **steatite.** Every seal is engraved in a pictographic script which is yet to be deciphered.
- The most remarkable seal is identified as the **Pashupati Seal.** This seal depicts a human figure seated cross-legged. An elephant and a tiger are depicted to the right side of the seated figure, while on the left a rhinoceros and a buffalo are seen. In addition to these animals two antelopes are shown below the seat.

Pottery

- A large quantity of pottery excavated from the sites, enable us to understand the gradual evolution of various design motifs as employed in different shapes, and styles.
- **Plain pottery** is more common than painted ware. Plain pottery is generally of red clay, with or without a fine red or grey slip. It includes knobbed ware, ornamented with rows of knobs.
- The **black painted** ware has a fine coating of red slip on which geometric and animal designs are executed in glossy black paint.
- **Polychrome pottery** is rare and mainly comprises small vases decorated with geometric patterns in red, black, and green, rarely white and yellow.

Mauryan Sculpture

Sculptures of the Mauryan empire mainly involve Ashoka's edicts carved on pillars and sandstone rocks, which represent the earliest stone sculpture of India.

Mauryan Pillars

- Stone pillars were erected by Ashoka, which have found in the entire Mauryan empire with inscriptions engraved on them.
- The top portion of the pillar was carved with capital figures like the bull, the lion, the elephant, etc.
- The tradition of constructing pillars was prevalent in the Achamenian empire of Persia as well. But the Mauryan pillars are different from the **Achamenian pillars.**
- They carved single rock-cut pillars thus displaying the carver's skills. The Achamenian pillars are constructed in pieces by a mason.
- All the capital figures are vigorous and carved standing on a square or circular abacus. Abacuses are decorated with stylised lotuses. Some of the existing pillars with capital figures were found at Basarah-Bakhira, Lauriya-Nandangarh and Rampurva in Bihar, Sankisa and Sarnath in Uttar Pradesh.
- The **Mauryan pillar capital** found at Sarnath popularly known as the **Lion Capital** is the finest example of Mauryan sculptural tradition.

- It is also our national emblem. This pillar capital symbolising *Dhammachakrapravartana* (the first sermon by the Buddha).

Lion Capital at Sarnath

Yakshas and Yakhinis

- Large statues of Yakshas and Yakhinis are found at many places like Patna, Vidisha and Mathura.
- These monumental images are mostly in the standing position. One of the distinguishing elements in all these images is their polished surface.

Didarganj Yakshi

- One of the finest examples is a Yakshini figure from Didarganj, Patna, which is tall and well-built. It shows sensitivity towards depicting the human physique. The image has a polished surface.
- Almost 2000 years old, it stands five feet four inches and is carved out of a single stone.
- The chauri is held in the right hand whereas the left hand is broken. The image shows sophistication in the treatment of form and medium.

Mathura, Sarnath and Gandhara Schools of Art

- The first century AD onwards, Gandhara (now in Pakistan) and Mathura in Northern India emerged as important centres of art production.
- In this period, another important school of sculptures at Sarnath emerged in Northern Indian fifth century AD, and used chunar sandstone and localised around Sarnath.
- Many Buddha images in Sarnath can be attributed with the plain transparent drapery covering both shoulders and the halo around the head has very little ornamentation.

Gandhara School of Art

- The region extending from Punjab to the borders of Afghanistan known as the Gandhara region was an important centre of **Mahayana Buddhism** upto the fifth century AD.
- The region became famous throughout the world since, a new school of Indian sculpture known as the **Gandhara school** developed during that period.
- Owing to its strategic location, the Gandhara school imbibed all kinds of foreign influences like **Persian**, **Greek**, **Roman**, **Saka** and **Kushana**.
- The origin of the Gandhara art can be traced to the Greek rulers of **Bactria Parthia** and North-West India. But, it was during the reign of **Kanishka**, that the art received great patronage.

Contribution of Gandhara School

- The Gandhara School of Art is also known as the **Graeco-Buddhist School of Art** since, Greek techniques of art were applied to the Buddhist subjects. The most important contribution of the Gandhara School of Art was the evolution of beautiful images of the **Buddha** and **Bodhisattavas**, which were executed in black stone and modelled on identical characters of **Graeco-Roman pantheon**. Hence, it is said, 'the Gandhara artist had the hand of a Greek, but the heart of an Indian.'
- The most characteristic trait of Gandhara sculpture is the depiction of Lord Buddha in the standing or seated positions. The seated Buddha is always shown cross-legged in the traditional Indian way.
- Another typical feature of the Gandhara art is the rich carving, elaborate ornamentation and complex symbolism. The best specimens of Gandhara art are from **Jaulian** and **Dharmarajika** stupa at Taxila and from Hadda near Jalalabad in modern Afghanistan.

  The tallest rock-cut statue of Lord Buddha is also located at **Bamiyan** in modern Afghanistan and dates back to the third and fourth centuries AD.
- Gandhara Art lost its pre-eminence and newer schools of sculpture evolved, the finest example being the beautiful Buddhist statue of Sarnath. A few other such wonderful specimens are the **Manjushree Avalokiteshwar** statue at Sarnath, the Bodhisattava at Sanchi and the bronze statue of Buddha found at Mathura.

Characteristics of Gandhara School of Art

Below are some characteristics of Gandhara School of Art

- Moulding human body in a realistic manner with minute attention to physical features like muscles, moustache and curly hairs.

- Thick drapery, with large and bold fold lines.
- Rich carving, elaborate ornamentation and symbolic expressions.
- In Early Gandhara School, blackish grey sandstone was used and in later school mud and lime plaster was used.
- The main theme was the Mahayana Buddhism.

Mathura School of Art

- The Mathura School of Art flourished at the holy city of Mathura during the reign of Kushana especially between first and third centuries AD.

Contribution of Mathura School

- It established the tradition of transforming the Buddhist symbols into the human form. Buddha's first image can be traced to **Kanishka's** reign (about 78 AD).
- The earliest sculptures of Buddha were made keeping the Mathura Style **yaksha** prototype in mind. They were depicted as strongly built with the right hand raised in protection and the left hand on the waist.
- The figures produced by this school of art do not have moustaches and beards as in the Gandhara Art. These figures can be seen in the museum of Mathura.
- The standing Buddha figures resembles the *yaksha* figures and indicates the Kushana influence. The seated figures are in the *padmasana* posture. Here statues were made with delighted facial expressions and graceful postures.
- The Mathura School not only produced beautiful images of the Buddha, but also of the Jain Tirthankaras and Gods and Goddesses of the Hindu pantheon.
- Many scholars believe that the Mathura School of Art, although of indigenous origin, was greatly influenced by the Gandhara School of Art. The Guptas adopted the Mathura School of Art and further improvised and perfected it.

Sculpture of Mathura School

Characteristics of Mathura School of Art

Below are the some characteristics of Mathura School of Art

- The Buddha image exhibit the spiritual feeling on his face which was largely absent in the Gandhara school.
- The Mathura school also carved out the images of Shiva and Vishnu along with their consorts Parvati and Lakshmi.
- The female figures of *yakshinis* and *apsaras* of the Mathura school were beautifully carved.
- Earliest statues of Buddha were made in Mathura School of Art.

Indian Bronze Sculpture

- Bronze sculptures and statuettes of Buddhist, Hindu and Jain icons have been discovered from many regions of India. Most of these were used for ritual worship and are characterised by exquisite beauty and aesthetic appeal.
- The **cire-perdu** or 'lost-wax' process for casting was learnt as long ago as the **Indus Valley Culture**. Perhaps, the 'Dancing Girl' from Mohenjodaro is the earliest bronze sculpture dates back to 2500 BC.

The Lost-wax Process

- The Lost-wax process is a technique used for making objects of metal, especially in Himachal Pradesh, Odisha, Bihar, Madhya Pradesh and West Bengal.
- The Lost-wax process involves several different steps and made by hand of pure beeswax.

- Interesting images of Jain Tirthankaras have been discovered from Chausa, Bihar, belonging to the Kushana Period during second century AD. In Buddhist centres like **Nalanda**, a school of bronze-casting emerged around the ninth century during the rule of the **Pala dynasty** in Bihar and Bengal regions.
- Among the Pallava Period, bronze sculptures of the eighth century is the icon of Shiva seated in *ardhaparyanka asana* (one leg kept dangling). The right hand is in the achamana mudra gesture, suggesting that he is about to drink poison.

Avalokitesvara

- A remarkable bronze is of a four-armed **Avalokitesvara**, which is a good example of a male figure in graceful **tribhanga posture**.
- Worship of female Goddesses was adopted which is part of the growth of the **Vajrayana** phase in Buddhism.

- Images of **Tara** became very popular. Seated on a throne, she is accompanied by a growing curvilinear lotus stalk and her right hand is in the *abhaya-mudra*.

The Nataraja

- The well-known dancing figure of Shiva as Nataraja was evolved and fully developed during the Chola Period and since, then many variations of this complex bronze image have been modelled. This bronze image of Nataraja is in the **chatura-tandava** pose.
- The three-eyed and four-armed Shiva is dancing with his right foot placed on the demon of ignorance, Apasmara. The rear right hand holds the damaru and the front right hand is in *abhaya-mudra*, with a serpent coiled around the forearm.

Portrait of Krishnadeva Raya

- During the 16th century, at Tirupati, life-size standing portrait statues were cast in bronze, depicting Krishnadevaraya with his two queens, **Tirumalamba** and **Chinnadevi**.
- The sculpture has combined the likeness of the facial features with certain elements of idealisation. The standing king and queens are depicted in praying posture, that is, both hands held in the namaskara mudra.

Extra Facts From Tamil Nadu Board and NIOS

- The size of the stone statue of a Yogi bust or priest of the Harappan period is 145 × 11 cm.
- It has been preserved in Karachi National Museum, Pakistan.
- The specially carved beard of this statue shows that people of this period had an understanding of fashion. The priests of the temples of Babylon also used to wear clothes decorated with this tifulia.
- The Harappan bronze dancer figurine has been made using the lost-wax techniques.
- In this technique, first of all a wax idol was made, then a paste of soil/dung was applied on it. When, this paste dried, the wax was heated and taken out and the wax was poured into the empty space and given the shape of a statue.
- The statue of Nagmatadevi is a better example of this among the Harappan period clay sculptures. These were constructed for the purpose of religious worship. Mother Goddess was worshipped in the form of Mother Earth. It was constructed in 2500 BC. It has been obtained from Mohenjodaro. Its size is 85 × 34 cm. It is preserved in National Museum, New Delhi.
- Mauryan period sculpture Chavar Dharini Yakshini-Height of this statue is 1622 cm.

Indian Architecture : Styles & Development

[SOURCES]

Class-XI New NCERT Chap 1 (Fine Arts, Prehistoric Rock Paintings), Chap 3 (Arts of Mauryan Period), Chap 4 (Post-Mauryan Trends in Indian Art and Architecture), Chap 5 (Later Mural Traditons), Chap 6 (Temple Architecture and Scultpture), Chap 8 (Some aspects of Indo-Islamic Architecture)

- Art and architecture forms an important part of Indian culture. The earliest and most remarkable evidence of Indian architecture is found in the cities of the **Harappan Civilisation**, which boast of a unique town planning.
- In the post Harappan period, architectural styles have been classified as Hindu, Buddhist and Jain. The medieval period saw the synthesis of **Persian** and indigenous styles of architecture. Thereafter, the colonial period brought the influence of Western architectural forms to India.

Harappan Architecture

- The most unique feature of the Harappan architecture was the development of the Great Bath and the planned drainage system.

The Great Bath

- The Great Bath found in **Mohenjodaro** (modern day Pakistan) was a large rectangular tank in a courtyard surrounded by a corridor on all four sides.
- There were two flights of steps on the North and South leading into the tank, which was made water-tight by using a mortar of gypsum.
- There were rooms on three sides, in one of which was a large well.
- Water from the tank flowed into a huge drain. Across a lane to the North lay a smaller building with eight bathrooms, with drains connecting to a common drain that ran along the corridor.

Mauryan Architecture

- By the fourth century BC, the **Mauryan empire** established their power and under **Ashoka**, a large part of India was under Mauryan control.
- Rock-cut architecture and construction of stupas and *viharas* as part of monastic establishments became part of the Mauryan traditions of architecture.

Rock-Cut Monuments

- The rock-cut elephant cave at Dhauli in Odisha belonged to Mauryan period is a fine example of exemplary piece of monument with linear rhythm.
- It also has Ashokan rock-edict. The rock-cut cave carved at **Barabar hills** near Gaya in Bihar is known as the **Lomas Rishi cave**.
- The facade of the cave is decorated with the semi-circular *chaitya* arch as the entrance. The interior hall of this cave is rectangular with a circular chamber at the back. The entrance is located on the side wall of the hall. The cave was donated by Ashoka for the **Ajivika sect**.

Pillars

- The pillars built by Ashoka furnish the finest remains of the Mauryan art. The pillars with Ashoka edicts inscribed on them were placed either in sacred enclosures or in the vicinity of towns.
- The pillars were made of two types of stone, the spotted red and white sandstone from the region of Mathura and the buff coloured fine grained

hard sandstone usually with small black spots quarried in Chunar near Varanasi.

- The palace of **Chandragupta Maurya** excavated in **Kumrahar** near Patna is an example of high level of stone art. The stone was transported from Mathura and Chunar to the various sites where the pillars have been found and here the stone was cut and carried by craftsmen.
- Each pillar had three parts, the **prop** under the foundation, the **shaft** or the Column and the **capital**. The Prop is buried in the ground. The Shaft made of a single piece of sandstone supports the Capital made of another single piece of sandstone.
- The thin–round and slightly tapering shaft is highly polished and very graceful in its proportions. The capital, which is the third part of the pillar, consists of some finally executed animal figures such as the lion or the elephant.

Stupas

- Stupas were built of huge mounds of mud, enclosed in carefully burnt small standard bricks. Built by the Mauryan kings, **Buddha's burial mounds** and places of major events in his life became important landmarks of the significant architectural buildings in the country.
- Due to the popularity of **Buddhism** and **Jainism**, stupas and *viharas* were constructed on a large scale. Stupas consist of a cylindrical drum with a circular and a harmika and a chhatra on the top.
- In the subsequent century, stupas were elaborately built with certain additions like the enclosing of the circular path with railings and sculptural decoration.
- There were numerous stupas constructed earlier but expansions or new additions were made in the second century BC.
- Apart from the circular path, gateways were added. Thus, with the elaborations in stupa architecture, there was ample space for the architects and sculptors to plan elaborations and to carve out images.
- During the early phase of Buddhism, Buddha is depicted symbolically through footprints, stupas, lotus throne, *chakra*, etc.
- Gradually, narrative became a part of the Buddhist tradition. Thus events from the life of the Buddha, the Jataka stories, were depicted on the railings and torans of the stupas. Mainly **synoptic narrative**, **continuous narrative** and **episodic narrative** are used in the pictorial tradition.

Sanchi

- The great stupa at Sanchi was built with bricks during the time of Ashoka and later it was covered with stone and many new additions were made.
- Stupa-1 at Sanchi has upper as well as lower pradakshinapatha or circular path. It has four beautifully decorated toranas depicting various events from the life of the Buddha and the Jatakas.
- Figure compositions are in high relief, filling up the entire space. Heads have considerable projection in the picture space.
- Stupa-1 is presumed to have the relics of the Buddha, Stupa-2 has the relics of ten less famous *arhats* belonging to three different generations. Stupa-3 has the relics of *Sariputta* and *Mahamougalayana*.

Sanchi Stupa

Viharas

- The viharas are excavated in all the cave sites of Ajanta and Ellora caves. The plan of the viharas consists of a veranda, a hall and cells around the walls of the hall. Some of the important vihara caves are **Ajanta cave, Bedsa cave, Nashik cave**.
- Many of the early vihara caves are carved with interior decorative motifs like *chaitya* arches and the vedica designs over the cell doors of the cave.
- Facade design in **Nashik cave** became a distinct achievement.
- The vihara caves at Nashik were excavated with front pillars carved with **ghata-base** and **ghata-capital** with human figures.
- One such *vihara* cave was also excavated at Junnar in Maharashtra, which is popularly known as **Ganeshleni** because an image of Ganesha belonging to a later period was installed in it.

Post-Mauryan Architecture

- From the second century BC onwards, various rulers established their control over the vast Mauryan empire. There are numerous sites dating back to the second century BC in India.

- Some of the prominent examples of the finest sculpture are found at Vidisha, Bharhut, Bodhgaya, Mathura, Khandagiri-Udayagiri of Odisha and others.

Amaravati Stupa

- Amaravati Stupa site belong to Vengi in Andhra Pradesh, which has many stupa sites. The Amaravati School developed under the patronage of the **Satavahanas**. A great stupa was built at Amaravati in the lower Godavari region.

Amaravati Stupa

- Like the Sanchi Stupa, the Amaravati Stupa also has *pradakshinapatha* enclosed within a *vedika* on which many narrative sculptures are depicted. The domical stupa structure is covered with relief stupa sculptural slabs which is a unique feature.
- There are a number of **Jataka scenes** that have not been completely identified. In the depiction of the birth event, the queen is shown reclining on a bed surrounded by female attendants. A small-sized elephant is carved on the upper frame of the composition showing the dream of **Queen Mayadevi**. In another relief, four events related to the **birth of the Buddha** are shown.

Bharhut Stupa

- Bharhut sculptures are tall and similar to the images of **Yaksha** and **Yakhshini** in the Mauryan period.
- In the relief panels depicting narratives, illusion of three-dimensionality is shown with tilted perspective. Clarity in the narrative is enhanced by selecting main events.
- Narrative reliefs at Bharhut show how artisans used the pictorial language very effectively to communicate stories. In one such narrative, showing **Queen Mayadevi's** (mother of Siddhartha Gautama) dream, a descending elephant is shown.
- On the other hand, the depiction of a **Jataka story** is very simple-narrated by clubbing the events according to the geographical location of the story. Such Jataka stories became part of stupa decoration.

Cave Tradition in Western India

- In Western India, many Buddhist caves dating back to the second century BC onwards have been excavated. Mainly three architectural types were executed
  (i) apsidal vault-roof *chaitya* halls (found at Ajanta, Pitalkhora, Bhaja).
  (ii) apsidal vault-roof pillar-less hall(found at Thana, Nadsur in Maharashtra).
  (iii) flat roofed quadrangular hall with a circular chamber at the back (found at Kondivite in Maharashtra).
- The front of the *chaitya* hall is dominated by the motif of a semi-circular *chaitya* arch with an open front, which has a wooden facade and in some cases, there is no dominating *chaitya* arch window such as found at **Kondivite**. In all the *chaitya* caves a stupa at the back is common.

Karla Chaitya Hall

- The Chaitya griha at Karla is the biggest of its type in the whole of India.
- The cave consists of an open courtyard with two pillars, a stone screen wall to protect from rain, a veranda, a stone-screen wall as facade, an apsidal vault-roof *chaitya* hall with pillars and a stupa at the back.
- Karla *chaitya* hall is decorated with human and animal figures. They are heavy in their execution and move in the picture space.

Cave Tradition in Eastern India

- Like in Western India, Buddhist caves have also been excavated in Eastern India, mainly in the coastal region of Andhra Pradesh and in Odisha.
- One of the main sites in Andhra Pradesh is Guntapalle in Eluru district and the Udayagiri-Khandagiri caves in Bhubaneswar, Odisha. The caves have been excavated in the hills along with the structured monasteries.

Guntupalli Chaitya Cave

- The Guntupalli Chaitya cave is circular with a stupa in the circular hall and a *chaitya* arch carved at the entrance.
- The cave is relatively small when compared to the caves in Western India. The main *vihara* caves, despite the small dimensions, have been decorated with *chaitya* arches on the exterior.
- They are rectangular with vaulted roof and are carved single-storeyed or double-storeyed without a large central hall. These excavations date back to the second century BC.

Udayagiri-Khandagiri Caves

- The rock-cut cave tradition also existed in Odisha. The earliest examples are the Udaigiri-Khandagiri caves in the vicinity of **Bhubaneswar**. These caves are scattered and have inscriptions of **Kharavela**, a Jain king.

Udayagiri-Khandagiri Caves

- According to the inscriptions, the caves belongs to **Jain monks**. There are numerous single-cell excavations. Some have been carved in huge independent boulders and given the shape of animals. The figures in this cave are voluminous and are an excellent example of qualitative carving.

Temple Architecture

- The beginning of Gupta period marks the beginning of the construction of Brahmanical/ Hindu temples. It had a central shrine or garbhagriha where the image of the deity was placed. Each temple had a principal image of a God.
- The shrines of the temples were of three kinds
  (i) **Sandhara** type (without pradakshinapatha)
  (ii) **Nirandhara** type (with pradakshinapatha)
  (iii) **Sarvatobhadra** (which can be accessed from all sides)
- Some of the important temple sites of this period are **Deogarh** in Uttar Pradesh, Eran, **Nachna-Kuthara** and **Udayagiri** near **Vidisha** in Madhya Pradesh. These temples are simple structures consisting of a *veranda*, a hall and a shrine at the rear.

Basic Forms of the Hindu Temple

- The basic form of the Hindu temple comprises the following
  (i) The **sanctum** (*garbhagriha*), which was a small cubicle with a single entrance and grew into a larger chamber in time.
  (ii) The **entrance** to the temple, which incorporates space for a large number of worshippers and is known as a mandapa.
  (iii) The **shikhar** in North India and a pyramidal tower, called a *vimana*, in South India.
  (iv) The **vahan**, i.e., the mount or vehicle of the temple's main deity.
- Two broad orders of temples in the country are known— **Nagara** in the North and **Dravida** in the South. At times, the **Vesara** style of temples as an independent style created through the selective mixing of the Nagara and Dravida orders.
- As temples grew more complex, more surfaces were created for sculpture through additive geometry, i.e., by adding more and more symmetrical walls and niches, without breaking away from the fundamental plan of the shrine.

Nagara Temple Style

- The style of temple architecture that became popular in Northern India is known as **Nagara**. In North India, it is common for an entire temple to be built on a stone platform with steps leading up to it.
- Unlike in South India, it does not usually have elaborate boundary walls or gateways. While the earliest temples had just one tower or *shikhara*, later temples had several.
- The *garbhagriha* is always located directly under the tallest tower.
- There are many sub-divisions of Nagara temples depending on the shape of the *shikhara*. The *shikhara* which is square at the base and whose walls curve or slope inward to a point on top is called the **latina** or the *rekha-prasada* type of *shikara*.
- The second major type of architectural form in the Nagara order is the *Phamsana*. *Phamsana* buildings tend to be broader and shorter than **latina** ones.
- Their roofs are composed of several slabs that gently rise to a single point over the centre of the building, unlike the latina ones, which look like sharply rising tall towers.

Nagara Temple Style

- The third main sub-type of the Nagara building is what is generally called the *valabhi* type. These are rectangular buildings with a roof that rises into a vaulted chamber.
- The edge of this vaulted chamber is rounded, like the bamboo or wooden wagons that would have been drawn by bullocks in ancient times. They are usually called **wagon-vaulted buildings**.

Temples of Nagara Style

Important temples of Nagara style are discussed as follows

Dashavatara Vishnu Temple, Deogarh

- Dashavatara Vishnu temple in Deogarh (in Lalitpur district, Uttar Pradesh) was built in the early sixth century AD belongs to Gupta period. The temple is in **Panchayatana style** of architecture where the main shrine is built on a rectangular plinth with four smaller subsidiary shrines at the four corners.
- The tall and curvilinear *shikhara* also corroborates this date. The presence of this curving latina or *rekha-prasada* type of *shikhara* also makes it clear that this is an early example of a classic Nagara style of temple.
- There are three main reliefs of Vishnu on the temple walls – **Sheshashayana** on the South, **Nara-Narayan** on the East and **Gajendramoksha** on the West. The temple is West-facing, which is less common, as most temples are East or North-facing.

Lakshmana Temple, Khajuraho

- The Lakshmana temple of Khajuraho, dedicated to Vishnu, was built in 954 AD by the Chandela king, **Dhanga**. It is placed on a high platform accessed by stairs.
- There are four smaller temples in the corners and all the towers or shikharas rise high upward in a curved pyramidal fashion. This emphasise the temple's vertical thrust ending in a horizontal fluted disc called an **amalak** topped with a **kalash** or vase.

Kandariya Mahadev Temple, Khajuraho

- Kandariya Mahadeo temple at Khajuraho is the epitome of temple architecture in Central India.
- Its sculptures are highly stylised with typical features i.e., they are in almost full relief, cut away from the surrounding stone, with sharp noses, prominent chins, long slanting eyes and eyebrows.

Chausath Yogini Temple, Khajuraho

- Chausath Yogini temple is the tenth century AD. This is a temple of small, square shrines of roughly-hewn granite blocks, each dedicated to goddesses associated with the rise of Tantric worship after the seventh century AD.
- Several such temples were dedicated to the cult of the *yoginis*. They were built between the seventh and tenth centuries AD, but few have survived.

Sun Temple, Modhera

- The Sun temple at Modhera in Gujarat, dates back to early 11th century and was built by **Raja Bhimdev I** of the **Solanki Dynasty** in 1026 AD. There is a massive rectangular stepped tank called the **Surya kund** in front of it. This 100 sq metre rectangular pond is perhaps the grandest temple tank in India.
- A 108 miniature shrines are carved in between the steps inside the tank. A huge ornamental arch-torana leads one to the *sabha mandapa* (the assembly hall), which is open on all sides, as was the fashion of the times in Western and Central Indian temples.

Kamakhya Temple, Assam

- Kamakhya temple, a shakti peeth, is dedicated to Goddess Kamakhya and was built in the 17th century.
- The style that came with the migration of the Tais from Upper Burma mixed with the dominant Pala style of Bengal and led to the creation of what was later known as the **Ahom style** in Guwahati.

Siddheshwar Mahadeva Temple, Bengal

- The Siddheshwar Mahadeva temple in Barakar in Burdwan district of Bengal belongs to Pala dynasty of 9th century AD.
- The style of the sculptures during the period between the ninth and eleventh centuries in Bengal (including Bangladesh) and Bihar is known as the Pala style.
- While the Palas are celebrated as patrons of many Buddhist monastic sites, the temples from that region are known to express the local **Vanga style**. The temple shows a tall curving *shikhara* crowned by a large *amalaka* and is an example of the early Pala style.

Surya/Sun Temple Konark, Odisha

- The Surya or Sun temple is built in stone around 1240. Its *shikhara* was a colossal creation said to have reached 70m, which fallen in the 19th century.
- The vast complex is within a quadrilateral shape which the *Jagamohana* or the dance-pavillion (mandapa) has survived.
- The Sun temple is set on a high base, its walls covered in extensive, detailed ornamental carving.
- These include twelve pairs of enormous wheels sculpted with spokes and hubs, representing the chariot wheels of the Sun god, rides a chariot driven by seven horses.

Unique Temple Style of Odisha

- The main architectural features of Odisha temples are classified in three orders, i.e., **rekhapida**, **pidhadeul** and **khakra**.
- The temples of Odisha constitute a distinct sub-style within the Nagara order. In general, here the *shikhara*, called deul in Odisha and *mandapas* called *Jagamohana*.

Pandrethan Temple, Kashmir

- The **Karkota period** of Kashmir is the most significant in terms of architecture, who built the Pandrethan temple in eighth and ninth centuries, possibly dedicated to Shiva.
- In keeping with the tradition of a water tank attached to the shrine, this temple is built on a plinth built in the middle of a tank.
- The architecture of this temple is similar to the age-old Kashmiri tradition of wooden buildings. Due to the snowy conditions in Kashmir, the roof is peaked and slants slowly outward.

Dravida or South Indian Temple Style

- Unlike the Nagara temple, the Dravida temple is enclosed within a compound wall. The front wall has an entrance gateway in its centre, which is known as a *gopuram*. The shape of the main temple tower known as *vimana* in Tamil Nadu is like a stepped pyramid that rises up geometrically rather than the curving *shikhara* of North India.
- In the South Indian temple, the word *shikhara* is used only for the crowning element at the top of the temple. It is usually shaped like a small *stupika* or an octagonal *cupola*— this is equivalent to the *amlak* and *kalasha* of North Indian temples.
- It is common to find a large water reservoir or a temple tank, enclosed within the complex. Subsidiary shrines are either incorporated within the main temple tower or located as distinct, separate small shrines beside the main temple.

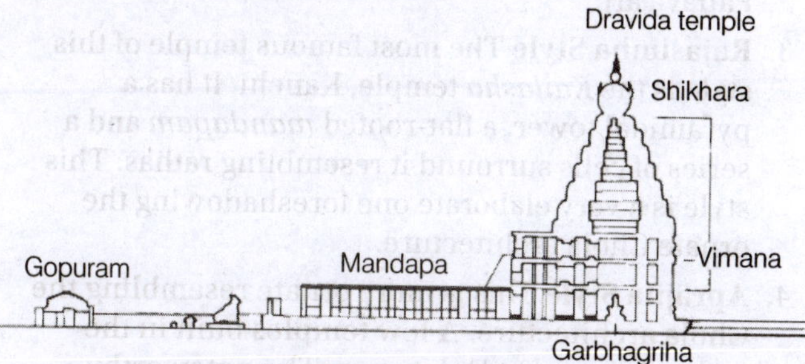

Temple architecture and sculptors

- The most sacred temples in South India, the main temple in which the *garbhagriha* is situated has one of the smallest towers. This is because it is usually the oldest part of the temple.

Temples of Dravida Style

Important temples of Dravida style are discussed as follows

- The most sacred temples in South India, the main temple in which the *garbhagriha* is situated has one of the smallest towers. This is because it is usually the oldest part of the temple.

Shore Temple, Mahabalipuram

- The Shore temple is the icon of the ancient monuments of Mahabalipuram. The sculptural excellence symbolises the heights of **Pallava architecture** under the rule of King **Narasimha Varman I** during seventh century AD.
- Erected on a 50 feet square platform, the temple is a pyramidal structure rising to the heights of 60 feet. As a characteristic specimen of Dravidian temple architecture, the Shore temple has three shrines, devoted to **Lord Shiva** and **Lord Vishnu**.
- The main temple is a five-storeyed structure sculpted out of granite dedicated to Lord Shiva. The pyramidal structure is 60 feet (18m) high and sits on a 50 feet (15 m) square platform. In the shrine, Lord Vishnu is seen reclining on the *Sheshnag*.

Brihadeeshwarar Temple, Thanjavur

- The magnificent **Shiva temple of Thanjavur**, called the **Rajarajeshwara** or Brihadeeshwarar temple, was completed around 1009 by **Rajaraja Chola**. It is the largest and tallest of all Indian temples.
- This temple's pyramidal multi-storeyed *vimana* rises a massive, 70 metre (230 ft. approx) structure topped by a monolithic *shikhara*, which is an octagonal dome-shaped *stupika*.
- It is in this temple that one notices for the first time two large *gopurams* (gateway towers) with an elaborate sculptural programme, which was conceived along with the temple. Huge Nandi-figures are at the corners of the *shikhara* and the *kalasha* on top by itself is about 3 m and 8 cm in height.
- Hundreds of figures decorate the *vimana*. The main deity of the temple is Shiva, who is shown as a huge *lingam* set in a two-storeyed sanctum. The walls surrounding the sanctum have extended mythological narratives, which are depicted through painted murals and sculpture.

Vesara Temple Style

- Many different styles of temple architecture influenced by both North and South Indian temples were used in regions like Karnataka.
- A hybridised style that seems to have become popular after the mid-seventh century, is known in some ancient texts as *vesara*.

Temples of Vesara Style

Important temples of Vesara style are discussed as follows

Kailashnath Temple, Ellora

- The Kailashnath temple at Ellora is a complete Dravida building with a Nandi shrine since the temple is dedicated to Shiva. It has as *gopuram* like gateway, surrounding cloisters, subsidiary shrines, staircases and an imposing tower or *vimana* rising to 30 m.
- Importantly, all of this is carved out of living rock. One portion of the monolithic hill was carved patiently to build the Kailashnath temple. The sculpture of the Rashtrakuta phase at Ellora is dynamic, the figures often larger than life-size figures.

Virupaksha Temple, Pattadakal

- The hybridisation and incorporation of several styles was the hallmark of Chalukyan buildings. The most elaborate of all Chalukyan temples at Pattadakal is Virupaksha temple made in the reign of **Vikramaditya II** (733-44) by his chief queen **Loka Mahadevi**.
- The Virupaksha temple is a large complex consisting of a tall *vimana* with axial mandapas and peripheral sub-shrines round the court, enclosed by a wall with gopura-entrances in front and behind.
- The temple is notable for its range and quality.

Hoysaleswara Temple (Lord of the Hoysalas) Halebidu

- The Hoysaleswara temple (Lord of the Hoysalas) at Halebidu in Karnataka was built in dark schist stone by the Hoysala king in 1150 AD. Hoysala temples are sometimes called hybrid or *vesara* as their unique style seems neither completely Dravida nor Nagara.
- They are easily distinguishable from other medieval temples by their highly original star-like ground plans and a profusion of decorative carvings.
- Dedicated to Shiva as Nataraja, the Halebid temple is a double building with a large hall for the *mandapa* to facilitate music and dance.
- A Nandi pavilion precedes each building. From the central square, plan cut-out angular projections create the star effect decorated with the carvings of animals and deities.

Pallava Art

- The Pallava architecture shows the transition from the rock-cut architecture to the stone built temples.
- The earliest examples of the Pallava art are the rock-cut temples of the seventh century AD, while the later examples are of the structural temples built in the eighth and the ninth centuries.
- The rock-cut reliefs of the Pallavas are the earliest surviving royal portraits after the Kushana images.
- **Mahendravarman** I introduced the rock-cut temples. This style of Pallava temples are seen at places like Mandagapattu, Mahendravadi, Mamandur, Dalavanur, Tiruchirappalli, Vallam, Siyamangalam and Tirukkalukkunram.
- The five rathas, popularly called as the **Panchapanadava rathas**, signifies five different styles of temple architecture. The *mandapas* contain beautiful sculptures on its walls. The most popular of these *mandapas* are *Mahishasura Mardini Mandapa*, *Tirumurti Mandapa* and *Varaha Mandapa*.
- The Pallava architecture is known for their four specific styles
  1. **Mahendra Style** The influence of the cave style of architecture is to be seen in an ancient pillar engraved in the Ekambaranatha (Kanchipuram) temple.
  2. **Mamalla Style** The seven Pagodas are small temples, each of which is chop-out of a single rock boulder. They lie near Mahabalipuram, founded by Narasimhavarman.
     These monolithic temples are complete with all the details of an ordinary temple and stand as an undying testimony to the superb quality of the Pallava art.
  3. **Rajasimha Style** The most famous temple of this style is the *Kailasha* temple, Kanchi. It has a pyramidal tower, a flat-roofed *mandapam* and a series of cells surround it resembling rathas. This style is a very elaborate one foreshadowing the ornate Chola architecture.
  4. **Aprajita Style** This is more ornate resembling the Chola architecture. A few temples built in the style are found at Dalavanur. The noteworthy feature of some shrines is that they are adorned by beautiful life-like images of Pallava kings and their queens.

Important Pallava Temples

- **Mandagapattu Temple** This is the first Pallava rock-cut temple, built by **Mahendra** I in the early seventh century. An inscription on the temple calls it the Laksitayatna and dedicates it to Brahma, Isvara and Vishnu. The facade of the rectangular *mandapa* has four massive pillars and is flanked by niches containing large *dvarpalaka* images carved in relief.
- **Kailasanatha of Kanchipuram** The temple is credited to the initiative and enterprise of the Pallava ruler **Narasimhavarman II** or **Rajasimha** who reigned between 690 to 728 AD. The Kailasanatha temple is the finest structural project of the Pallavas. It looks as if a chariot from heaven has descended on the Earth.
- **Vaikuntha Perumal Temple** This temple is situated at Kanchipuram in Tamil Nadu and was built in the eighth century AD. It was built by the Pallava emperor, **Nandivarman** Pallavamalla in the eighth century AD.
- This temple is famous for its unique architectural grandeur and religious importance.

  This temple is one of the 108 *Divya Desam* dedicated to the Lord Vishnu. This temple is also called the **Tiru Parameswara Vinnagaram**.
- **Shore temple** This temple at Mamallapuram was built during the reign of the Pallava King **Rajasimha** (700 to 728 AD). Its three sanctuaries are dedicated to Vishnu and Shiva.
- This temple is also acknowledged for being the first stone structure made by the Pallavas. Before this, the monuments used to be carved out of the rocks or stones. This group of temple is an UNESCO World Heritage Site.
- **Seven Pagodas** This term is closely associated with the **Shore Temple** of **Mahabalipuram**. According to a popular belief, once upon a time six other temples stood along with the now famous Shore temple on the shores of Mahabalipuram's rock strewn beaches.
- In the late 2004, during the tsunami that struck the coast, the sand deposits of around 500 m from the Shore temples were gulped by the sea. During this time, tourists and residents were reported to have seen a long, straight row of large rocks emerge from the water just before the waters rushed back again.
- The tsunami also made some immediate, lasting changes to the coastline, which left a few previously covered statues and small structures uncovered on the shore like the large stone lion left sitting uncovered on Mahabalipuram's beach.

Chalukyan Temple Architecture

- The structural temples of the Chalukyas exist at **Aihole, Badami** and **Pattadakal**. Cave temple architecture was also famous under the Chalukyas. Their cave temples are also found in Ajanta, Ellora and Nasik.
- The best instance of Chalukya paintings can be seen in the **Badami cave temple** and in the **Ajanta caves**. The reception given to a Persian embassy by **Pulakesin II** is depicted in a painting at Ajanta.
- The Chalukya temples may be divided into two stages
  - The **first stage** is represented by the temples at Aihole and Badami. Among the seventy temples found at Aihole, four are important
    1. Lad Khan temple is a low, flat-roofed structure consisting of a pillared hall.
    2. Durga temple resembles a Buddha Chaitya.
    3. Huchimalligudi temple at Aihole.
    4. The Jain temple at Meguti.
  - The **second stage** is represented by the temples at Pattadakal. There are ten temples here, four in the Northern style and the remaining six in the Dravidian style.
- The **Papanatha temple** is the most notable in the Northern style. The Sangamesvara temple and the Virupaksha temple are famous for their Dravidian style.
- The **Virupaksha temple** is built on the model of the Kailasanatha temple at Kanchipuram. It was built by one of the queens of **Vikramaditya II**.
- Sculptors brought from Kanchi were employed in its construction. It is located in Hampi, Karnataka on the banks of the Tungabhadra river.

Rashtrakuta Art

- The rulers of the Rashtrakuta dynasty were great patrons of art and architecture and were great builders and a half century of the Rashtrakuta rule, witnessed a very high achievement in the fields of sculpture and architecture.
- The **Ellora** and **Elephanta caves** provide splendid examples of that era which excelled in carving out huge monuments and monolithic sculptures.
- In Ellora (Maharashtra), rock-cut cave temples of all faiths are found that are flourishing in India i.e., Buddhist, Jain, Shaiva and Vaishnava.
- Out of the 34 caves, 12 are Buddhist, (in the South) 17 are Hindu (Vaishnava, Shaiva and Shakta) and 5 caves on the Northern side are Jain.

Chola Art

- Many temples had been built by the Chola kings throughout their kingdoms. The temples of the early Cholas are found in large number in the former Pudukkottai region.
- These Chola temples reveal the gradual evolution of the Chola art and architecture. The Chola kings earlier built brick temples. Later, they built stone temples.
- The *dvarapalas* or guardian figures, at the entrance to the *mandapa* or hall which started from the Pallava period became an unique feature of the Chola's temples.
- The Dravidian style got fully developed after a transition from the rock-cut structures of the Pallava period.
- Important Temples of Chola art are Brihadeeswarar Temple and Temple of Gangaikonda Cholapuram.

The Temple of Gangaikonda Cholapuram

It was built by **Rajendra** I and was completed in 1035. Its 53m *vimana* (sanctum tower) has recessed corners and a graceful upward curving movement, contrasting with the straight and severe tower at Thanjavur. It has six pairs of massive, monolithic dvarapalas statues guarding the entrances and bronzes of remarkable beauty inside.

Buddhist and Jain Architectural Developments

- Buddhist and Jain architectural developments were equally vibrant from the fifth to fourteenth centuries. Sites such as **Nalanda** and **Mahabodhi** temple were built during this time.
- When the Gupta empire crumbled in the sixth century AD, this Eastern region of Bihar and Bengal, historically known as Magadha, appears to have remained unified under the **Pala rulers.**

Mahabodhi Temple, Bodhgaya

- The Mahabodhi temple at Bodhgaya is an important architectural monument. The first shrine here, located at the base of the Bodhi tree.
- It is said to have been constructed by King Ashoka, the *vedika* around it is said to be **post-Mauryan**, of about 100 BC. Many of the sculptures in the temple are dated to the eighth century **Pala period.**
- The actual Mahabodhi temple itself as it stands now is largely a **Colonial period** reconstruction of the old seventh century design.
- The design of the temple is unusual. It is neither Dravida nor Nagara style.
- It is narrow like a Nagara temple, but it rises without curving, like a Dravida one.

Nalanda University

- The monastic university of Nalanda is a *mahavihara* as it is a complex of several monastries of various sizes.
- Most of the information about Nalanda is based on the records of **Xuan Zang** (Hiuen Tsang). The foundation of a monastery was laid by **Kumargupta I** in the fifth century AD.
- The sculptural art of Nalanda, in stone and bronze, developed out of a heavy dependence on the Buddhist Gupta art of Sarnath, characterised by distinctive facial features, body forms and treatment of clothing and jewellery.
- The characteristic features of Nalanda art can be distinguished by its consistently high quality of workmanship.
- Its sculptures are also usually not flat in relief but are depicted in three-dimensional forms. The back slabs of the sculptures are detailed and the ornamentations are delicate.

Lakshmana Temple, Sirpur

- The Lakshmana temple Sirpur in Chhattisgarh is an early-Odisha style site belonging to the period between 550 and 800 AD, with both Hindu and Buddhist shrines.
- In many ways, the iconographic and stylistic elements of the Buddhist sculptures here are similar to that of Nalanda.

Lord Bahubali, Gomateshwara

- The Gomateshwara temple at Shravanabelagola, Karnataka is the most renowned Jain pilgrimage in South India. The place is famous for its Gomateshwara temple also known as **Bahubali temple.**
- The Bahubali statue is a 57 feet high monolithic statue built in around 983 AD by **Chamundaraya**, the General-in-Chief and Prime Minister of the Ganga Kings of Mysore.

Jain Temples, Mount Abu

- The Jain temples at Mount Abu were constructed by **Vimal Shah.** Dilwara Jain temples is one of the finest Jain temple for its extraordinary architecture and marvellous marble stone carvings.

- Notable for a simplistic exterior in contrast with the marble interiors, their rich sculptural decoration with deep undercutting creates a lace-like appearance.
- The temple is famous for its unique patterns on every ceiling and the graceful bracket figures along the domed ceilings.

Indo-Islamic Architecture

- The Indo-Islamic architecture began in the early 13th century AD in India with large scale building activity begun under the Delhi Sultanate, established after the Turkish conquest of Northern India.
- In the field of architecture, a mix of many structural techniques, stylised shapes and surface decorations came about through constant interventions or modification of architectural elements.
- The study of Indo-Islamic architecture is conventionally categorised into the Imperial Style (Delhi Sultanate), the Provincial Style (Mandu, Gujarat, Bengal and Jaunpur), the Mughal Style (Delhi, Agra and Lahore) and the Deccani Style (Bijapur and Golconda).

Typologies of Structures

- In Sultanate and Mughal era, architectural buildings were constructed over a period of time for religious and secular necessities. These were mosques for daily prayers, the Jama Masjids, tombs, dargahs, minars, hammams, formally laid out gardens, madrasas, sarais or caravanserais, Kos minars, etc. These were additions in the existing types of buildings in the sub-continent.
- In spite of the obvious **Saracenic**, **Persian** and **Turkish** influences, Indo-Islamic structures were heavily influenced by prevailing sensibilities of Indian architectural and decorative forms.
- Although religion and religiosity were very important to people of medieval India, as elsewhere, they borrowed architectural elements liberally.

Architectural Influences

- Amongst provincial styles, the architecture of Bengal and Jaunpur is regarded as distinct. Gujarat was said to have a markedly regional character for patrons borrowed elements from regional temple traditions. These traditions were *toranas*, lintels in *mihrabs*, carvings of bell and chain motifs and carved panels depicting trees, for tombs, mosques and dargahs.
- The 15th century white marble dargah of **Shaikh Ahmad Khattu** of **Sarkhej** is a good example of provincial style and it heavily influenced the form and decoration of Mughal tombs.

Materials For Construction

- The walls in all buildings were extremely thick and were largely constructed of rubble masonary, which was easily available. These walls were then cased over with chunam or limestone plaster or dressed stone.
- A range of stones were utilised for construction such as quartzite, sandstone, buff, marble, etc. Polychrome tiles were used to great advantage to finish the walls.
- From the beginning of the 17th century, bricks were also used for construction and these imparted greater flexibility to the structures. In this phase, there was more reliance on local materials.

Decorative Forms

- These forms included designing on plaster through stucco (fine cement) designs were either left plain or covered with colours. Motifs were also painted on or carved in stone. These motifs included varieties of flowers, both from the sub-continent and places outside, particularly Iran.
- In the 14th, 15th and 16th centuries tiles were also used to surface the walls and the domes. Popular colours were blue, turquoise, green and yellow. Subsequently, the techniques of tessellation (mosaic designs) and pietradura were made use of for surface decoration particularly in the dado panels of the walls. At times, *lapis lazuli* was used in the interior walls or on canopies.
- Other decorations included calligraphy and high and low relief carving and a profuse use of jalis. The high relief carving has a three-dimensional look. The arches were plain, squat and sometimes high and pointed.
- The roof was a mix of the central dome and other smaller domes, *chatris* and tiny minarets. The central dome was topped with an inverted lotus flower motif and a metal or stone pinnacle.

Forts

- Building monumental forts in medieval times, often symbolised the seat of power of a king. Some examples of strong, complex architecture which still amaze the visitor are the forts of Chittor, Gwalior, Daulatabad, earlier known as Devgiri and Golconda.
- Commanding heights were utilised to construct forts. These heights provided a good perspective of the region and strategic advantage for security.
- Other complexities woven into such topography were concentric circles of outer walls as in Golconda, so that the enemy had to breach these at all stages before getting in.
- **Daulatabad Fort** had several strategic devices to deals with the enemy, such as staggered entrances so that gates could not be opened even with the help of elephants.

- It also had twin forts, one within the other but at a higher elevation and accessed by a complex defence design arrangement. One wrong turn in the labyrinth or complex pathway could lead to the enemy soldier going in circles or falling to his death several hundred feet below.
- The **Gwalior Fort** was invincible because its steep height made it impossible to scale. It had many habitations and usages. Babur, who did not find much merit in many things he saw in Hindustan, was said to have been overawed at the sight of the Gwalior Fort.
- **Chittorgarh Fort** bears the distinction of being the largest fort in Asia and was occupied for the longest length of time as the seat of power. It has many types of buildings including stambhas or towers to signify victory and bravery. It was replete with numerous water bodies.
- Innumerable acts of heroism have been associated with the principal people in the fort, forming the substance of many a legend. An interesting aspect associated with forts is that within the palace complexes, stylistic and decorative influences were absorbed most liberally.

Structures for Common People

- One of the architectural features of medieval India was also a coming together of styles, techniques and decorations in public and private spaces of non-royal sections of the society.
- These included buildings for domestic usage, temples, mosques, khanqahs (hermitage of Sufi saints) and dargahs, commemorative gateways, pavilions in buildings and gardens, bazaars, etc.

Minars

- Another form of stambha or tower was the minar, a common feature in the sub-continent as Indo-Islamic art form. Two most striking minars of medieval times are the **Qutub Minar** in Delhi and the **Chand Minar** at Daulatabad Fort. The everyday use of the minar was for the azaan or call to prayer.
- Qutub Minar's phenomenal height, however, symbolised the might and power of the ruler. It is associated revered saint of Delhi, **Khwaja Qutub-ud-din Bakhtiyar Kaki**. The Qutub Minar, built in the 13th century, is a 234 feet high tapering tower divided into five storeys.
- The minar is a mix of polygonal and circular shapes. It is largely built of red and buff sandstone with some use of marble in the upper storeys. It is characterised by highly decorated balconies and bands of inscriptions intertwined with foliated designs.
- **Chand Minar**, built in the 15th century, is a 210-feet-high tapering tower divided into four storeys. It has bold bands of Quranic verses. Although it looked like an Iranian monument, it was the combined handiwork of local architects with those from Delhi and Iran.

Tombs

- Monumental structures over graves of rulers and royalty was a popular feature of medieval India. Some well known examples of such tombs are those of **Ghiyasuddin Tughlaq**, **Humayun**, **Abdur Rahim Khan-i-Khanan** in Delhi, **Akbar** and **Itmad-ud-Daula** in Agra. These includes *khanqahs* (hermitage of Sufi saints) and *dargahs*.
- Beginning with the introduction of Quranic verses on the walls, the tomb was placed within paradisiacal elements such as a garden or near a body of water. The case of the Humayun's tomb and the **Taj Mahal**, follows the *charbagh* style.

Sarais

- An interesting feature of Indo-Islamic architecture was the sarais, which ringed cities. Sarais were largely built on a simple square or rectangular plan. They were meant to provide temporary accommodation to Indian and foreign travellers, pilgrims, merchants, traders, etc.
- In effect, sarais were public domains, which thronged with people of varied cultural backgrounds. This led to cross-cultural interaction, influences and syncretic tendencies of the times and at the level of the people.

Regional Architectural Style

The provincial style of architecture encompasses the architectural trends and developments noticed in different provincial capitals in India, but specifically in the following Architectural form

Bengal Architecture

- The **Adina** and **Pandua** mosques are the earliest architectural examples in Bengal.
- The tomb of **Akhi Serajuddin**, the **Kotwali Darwaza**, the **Dakhil Darwaza** and the tomb of **Sultan Jalaluddin Muhammed Shah** (1414-1431 AD), known as the **Eklakhi Tomb**, served as prototypes for the subsequent Islamic architecture of Bengal.
- The other important buildings of Bengal include Tantipara Masjid (1475 AD), Chamkatti Masjid (1475 AD), Lotan Masjid (1480 AD), and Chota Sona Masjid (1510 AD).

Jaunpur Architecture

- Under the **Sharqi dynasty**, Jaunpur became a great centre of art, culture and architectural activity. During the rule of **Shamsudin Ibrahim** (1402-1436 AD) several palaces, mosques, tombs and other buildings came up, the most prominent being the Atala Masjid built in 1378.
- Later, other important buildings were produced that include a Khalis Mukhlis Masjid (1430 AD), Jahangiri Masjid (1430 AD), Lal Darwaja Masjid (1450 AD) and the Jama Masjid (1470 AD).

Malwa Architecture

- This is a very unique and adaptive architecture form of 15th century. They used stones and marbles of different colours in their buildings and decorated with arches and pillars.
- They used locally available materials. Few important features of their architecture are presence of large windows, use of artificial reservoirs and no use of minars.
- Some of their prominent buildings are **Jahaz Mahal, Raani Roopmati Pavillion**, etc.

Bijapur Architecture

- This style developed under **Adil Shah**, one of the prominent kings of Bahamani dynasty/kingdom. He built various tombs, palaces and mosques.
- Some important features of their buildings are bulbous dome, use of cornice, three arched facade and use of iron clamps for providing support to the ceilings. Some of the prominent buildings are **Gol Gumbaj, Bijapur Fort**, etc.

Mughal Architecture

- The art and architecture of this period have a characteristic of **Indo-Islamic-Persian style** that flourished on the Indian sub-continent during the Mughal empire (1526-1857).
- This new style combined elements of Islamic art and architecture, which had been introduced to India during the Delhi Sultanate (1192–1398). Many great monuments are made in this style such as the Qutub Minar, with features of Persian art and architecture. Mughal monuments are found chiefly in Northern India, but there are also many remains in Pakistan.

Babur

- The Mughal dynasty was established with the crushing victory of Babur at Panipat in 1526.
- During his short five-year reign, Babur took considerable interest in erecting buildings, though few have survived. He constructed the mosque at Rohilakhand and Panipat.

Humayun

- Humayun's era was very turbulant even then he built some famous buildings like Mosques of Agra and Fatehabad and most importantly **Din-Panah city** which is also known as **Fifth Delhi.**

Akbar

- In architecture, the first great Mughal monument was the **Mausoleum** of **Humayun**, erected during the reign of Akbar (1556–1605).
- The tomb, which was built in the 1560s, was designed by a Persian architect Mirak Mirza Ghiyas. It was set in a garden at Delhi and has an intricate ground plan with central octagonal chambers, joined by an archway with an elegant facade and surmounted by **Cupolas, Kiosks** and **Pinnacles**. At the same time, Akbar was building his fortress-palace in his capital, Agra.
- Native red sandstone was inlaid with white marble and all the surfaces were ornately carved on the outside and sumptuously painted inside. Akbar went on to build the entire city of **Fatehpur Sikri** (City of Victory) in which extensive use was made of the low arches and bulbous domes that characterise the Mughal style.
- Built in 1571, the choice of the site of Sikri reflected Akbar's gratitude to a Muslim saint at Sikri for the birth of his son. Courtiers soon followed suit and built homes surrounding the palace and mosque. The new city became the capital of the empire, but in 1585 it was abandoned.

Jahangir

- Though, Jahangir was more interested in paintings. Under his reign more emphasis was given to album and individual portrait than illustrated manuscript. Some important buildings were made during his rule.
- First of such buildings is **Mausoleum of Akbar** in Sikandara near Agra, which does have a dome and has features of Buddhist architecture.
- It was started by Akbar himself. Another important building is tomb of **I'timad-ud-Daulah** built by **Noorjahan**, in this building for first time Pietra Dura style was used.

Shahjahan

- It was Shahjahan (1628–1658) who perfected Mughal architecture and erected at Agra, its most noble and famous building, the tomb of his favourite wife, which is known as the **Taj Mahal**.
- A huge white marble building of simple, symmetrical plan, it is inlaid with colourful semiprecious materials and is set in an equally beautiful and symmetrical garden.

- The Taj Mahal continues the tradition of Mughal garden tombs, of which Humayun's tomb was the first. Shah Jahan established (1638) Delhi as his capital and built there the famous **Red Fort**, which contained the imperial Mughal palace. Paintings also flourished during Shah Jahan's reign. Portraiture was most highly developed at his sophisticated court and ink drawings were of high quality.

Aurangzeb

- Under the orthodox Aurangzeb (1659–1707) the decline of the arts began, although his ornate **Pearl Mosque** (1662) at Delhi is worthy of mention. During his reign, the Mughal academy was dispersed.
- Many artists then joined the Rajput courts, where their influence on Hindu painting is clearly evident. He was not so aspiring to spend time and resources to erect huge buildings and therefore he has the credit of constructing very few buildings such as **Bibi Ka Maqbara** (Rabia Durani). It is an imitation of Taj Mahal at Aurangabad, Maharashtra.
- Apart from this, the **Badshahi Mosque** at Lahore and the **Moti Masjid** at Lal Quila, Delhi are other two specimens of his contribution towards Mughal architecture.

Colonial Architecture

- The colonial influence can be seen in the architecture buildings of Europeans who started coming from 16th century AD constructed many churches and other buildings.
- Portuguese built many churches at Goa, the most famous of these are **Basilica Bom Jesus** and the chruch of Saint Francis.
- The British also built administrative and residential buildings, which reflect their imperial glory. Some Greek and Roman influence can be observed in the colonnades or pillared buildings. **Parliament House** and **Connaught Place** (now Rajiv Chowk) in Delhi are good examples.
- The architect Lutyens, designed **Rashtrapati Bhavan**, formerly the Viceroy's residence. It is built of sandstone and has design features like canopies and *jaali* from Rajasthan. The **Victoria Memorial** in Calcutta, the former capital of British India, is a huge edifice in marble. The British also left behind impressive railway terminals like the **Victoria Terminus** (now Chatrapati Shivaji Terminus) in Mumbai.

37

Music, Dance and Theatre Craft

[SOURCES]

Class-X Old NCERT (The Story of Civilisation Volume II), Chap 14 (The Heritage of India), Class-XII NCERT Chap 8 (The Living Art Traditions of India Fine Arts)

- The history of Indian music and dance is deep rooted from the period of Vedic Age, where the earliest tradition of Indian music found mentioned in **Sama Veda**, which contained the *shlokas* related to music.
- The detailed information is found in **Bharatmuni's Natyashashtra** (compiled during second century BC to second century AD).

Indian Classical Music

- The Indian classical music is broadly based on two traditions, the Hindustani form prevalent in North India and the Carnatic music form in South India. Both have some features in common.
- However, their *ragas* and their articulation are usually distinctive.

Hindustani Classical Music

- Hindustani classical music may be traced back to the period of the **Delhi Sultanate** and to **Amir Khusrau** (1253-1325 AD) who encouraged the practice of musical performance with particular instruments. He is believed to have invented the *sitar* and the *tabla* and is said to have introduced new ragas.
- The *gharanas* functions as guru-shishyaparampara, that is, disciples learning under a particular guru, transmitting his musical knowledge and style, will belong to the same *gharana*.

Styles of Hindustani Music

Different style of Hindustani music are :

- **Dhrupad** This style of singing is traditionally performed by men with a *Tanpura* and *Pakhawaj*. The lyrics sung in *Dhrupad* are in a medieval form of Hindi and typically heroic in theme or in praise of a particular deity. *Dhrupads* are sung in four styles called *Bansi Gaurhar, Dagur, Khandhar* and *Nauhar*, initially named after the language or dialect in which the verse was written. Pandit Uday Bhawalkar, Pandit Ritwik Sanyal and the Umakant Gundecha and Ramakant Gundecha (Gundecha Brothers) are some famous *Dhrupad* vocalists.
- **Khayal** It consists of about 4-8 lines of lyrics set to a tune. The performer uses these few lines as the base for improvisation. Generally, the theme of Khayal is romantic in nature. They sing about love, even if they are related to the divine creatures.
- One of the most important/unique features of Khayal is the use of taan in the compositions. The *Khayal* form of Hindustani classical music is ascribed to **Hussain Shah Sharqui**, the 15th century ruler of the Sharqui dynasty. It was made popular by the 18th century Mughal ruler **Mohammad Shah**. Some of the modern day vocalists are late Bhimsen Joshi, Nagaraja Havaldar, Kishori Amonkar, Ulhas and Kashalkar, Prabhakar Karekar, Pandit Jasraj, etc.

- **Dhamar** These compositions are similar to *Dhrupad*, but are chiefly associated with the festival of Holi. Here, the compositions are specifically in praise of Lord Krishna. This music, sung in the Dhamar Tal is chiefly used in festivals like Janmashtami, Ramnavami and Holi.
- **Tarana** Another vocal form of the *Hindustani* music is *Tarana*. *Tarana* are songs that are used to convey a feel of joy and are usually performed towards the end of a concert.
- **Thumri** It is an informal vocal form of *Hindustani* classical music and is said to have begun with the court of *Nawab* Wajid Ali Shah, the *Nawab* of Oudh. The compositions are either devotional or romantic in nature. It was inspired by Bhakti Movement. It is mainly used in Hindi dialects like Awadhi or *Braj Bhasha*.

Carnatic Music

- The compositions in Carnatic music may be attributed collectively to three composers who lived between 1700 and 1850 AD.
- They were Shyam Shastri, Thyagaraja and Muthuswami Dikshitar. Thyagaraja is reversed both as a saint and an artist. He epitomises the essence of Carnatic music. Purandara dasa was another great composer of Carnatic music.
- The main compositions are known as kriti and are devotional in nature. The Carnatic alapana is similar to alap in Hindustani classical as well as Tilana in Carnatic resembles Tarana of Hindustani. Both lay stress on tala or talam.

Styles of Carnatic Music

Styles of Carnatic Music are as follows :

- **Varnam** It is a composition usually sung or played at the beginning of a recital and reveals the general form of the *raga*. The two halves are almost equal in length. The *Varnam* is made up of two parts which are as follow :
  1. The *Purvanga* or first-half.
  2. The *Uttaranga* or second-half.
- **Kriti** It is a highly evolved musical song set to a certain *raga* and fixed *tala* or rhythmic cycle.
- **Ragam** It is a melodic improvisation in free rhythm played without *mridangam* accompaniment.
- **Tanam** It is another style of melodic improvisation in free rhythm.
- **Pallavi** This is a short pre-composed melodic theme with words and set to one cycle of *tal*. Here, the soloist improvises new melodies built around the word *Pallavi*.
- **Trikalam** It is the section where the *Pallavi* is played in three tempos keeping the *tal* constant.
- **Swara-Kalpana** It is the improvised section performed with the drummer in medium and fast speeds.
- **Ragamalika** This is the final part of the *Pallavi*, where the soloist improvises freely and comes back to the original theme at the end.

Gharanas of Classical Music

Some of the popular Gharanas of Indian Classical music are as follows :

Gwalior Gharana

- This is the oldest among all the *Khayal Gayaki* (vocal) styles. The distinctive feature of this style of singing has been noted for its lucidity and simplicity.
- Its founders were **Ustad Hassu Khan, Ustad Haddu Khan, Ustad Nathu Khan**.
- Prominent exponents of the gharana are Bal Krishna Ealchal Karanjikar, Vishnu Digambar Paluskar, Pandit Omkarnath Thakur, Veena Sahasrabuddhe and Malini Rajurkar.

Agra Gharana

- The Agra Gharana places great importance on developing forcefulness and depth in the voice, so that the nodes are powerful and resonant.
- Its founders were **Haji Sujan Khan, Ustad Ghagghe Khuda Baksh.**
- Prominent exponents of the gharana are the important singers of this *gharana* are Faiyaz Khan, Latafat Hussain Khan and Dinkar Kaikini.

Kirana Gharana

- It derives its name from the birth place of Abdul Kharim Khan of *Kirana*, near Kurukshetra. In the *Kirana* style of singing, the *swara* is used to create an emotional mood by means of elongation and use of *Kanas*.
- Its founders were **Abdul Karim Khan** and **Abdul Wahid Khan.**
- Prominent exponents of the gharana are Hirabhai Barodekar, Begum Akhtar, Bhimsen Joshi, Gangubai Hangal and Prabha Atre.

Jaipur Gharana

- The most distinctive feature of the Jaipur *Gharana* can be best described through its complex and melodic form, which arises out of the involutedly and undulating phrases that comprise the piece.
- Its founder was **Ustad Alladiya Khan.**

- Prominent exponents of the gharana are Alladiya Khan, Mallikarjun Mansur, Kesarbhai Kerkar, Kishori Amonkar, Shruti Sadolikar, Padma Talwalkar and Ashwini Bhide Deshpande.

Rampur Sahaswan Gharana

- In the Rampur Sahaswan Gharana, there is a stress on the clarity of *swara* and the development and elaboration of the *raga* is done through a stepwise progression.

Mewati Gharana

- The Mewati Gharana gives importance to developing the mood of the *raga* through the notes forming it and its style is *Bhava Pradhan*. It also gives equal importance to the meaning of the text.
- Its founder was **Ghagge Nazir Khan**.
- Prominent exponents of this gharana are Pandit Jasraj, Moti Ram, Mani Ram, Sanjeev Abhyankar and others.

Folk Music

India has a rich legacy of folk music as well, which represents the emotion of the masses. The simple songs are composed to mark every event in life. Folk songs have their special meanings or messages. They often describe historical events and important rituals. Some of the important folk music are as follows :

- **Lavani** Popular folk song from Maharashtra.
- **Maand** Developed in Rajasthan as Veer Rasa.
- **Dandiya Raas** Performed in Gujarat and is associated with Holi and lilas of Krishna and Radha.
- **Bhagwati** Popular folk music in Karnataka and Maharashtra.
- **Baul** It is a type of Bengali music and a religious sect.
- **Wanawan** Folk music from Kashmir which is sung during wedding ceremonies.
- **Alha** Folk song from Madhya Pradesh and is a heroic ballad song.

Dance Forms of India

- Indian dance forms has developed in a rich classical tradition. It has a great power of expression and emotions while telling a story. Dance forms in modern period can be divided into Classical and Folk dance forms.

Classical Dance Forms

Many temples across the country shows the sculptures of the dancers in their different forms. Classical dance forms like Kathakali, Bharatanatyam, Kathak, Manipuri, Kuchipudi and Odissi are an important part of our cultural heritage.

- **Bharatanatyam** (Tamil Nadu) Performed by the women, the dance form is known for its beautiful body movements and gestures, which are called Mudras in the traditional language.
- It focuses on the hand gestures, leg movement and the facial expressions of the dancer.

Bharatanatyam

- **Kathak** (Uttar Pradesh) Kathak comes from the word 'Katha' which means 'story', so the dance is performed in the form of storytelling. It can be performed by both the male and female dancer together. This dance form focuses highly on the ankle.
- **Kathakali** (Kerala) Kathakali is another traditional dance form of India, which relates to the storytelling. It includes the intriguing face movements and the heavy costumes, which include the traditional face masks and body paints (generally green). The music which includes only the vocals is called Soppanam.
- **Mohiniyattam** (Kerala) Mohiniyattam is a classical dance tradition of Kerala, which gained prominence under the rulers of Travancore. It was revived by famous poet Vallathol Narayana Menon along with Kalyani Ammal.

Mohiniyattam

- **Kuchipudi** (Andhra Pradesh) Kuchipudi is probably the toughest form of classical dance in India. Lasya and Tandava elements are important in Kuchipudi dance form.
- **Odissi** (Odisha) This traditional dance form has developed in temples in Odisha. The Odissi dance is considered as the oldest dance forms of India, which includes more than 50 intriguing mudras (body movements).

Odissi

- **Sattriya** (Assam) Mahapurusha Sankaradeva, a Vaishnava saint and reformer of Assam, introduced Sattriya dance in the 15th century AD. Traditionally, this dance was performed by the male monks, but now women mainly perform Sattriya dance.
- **Manipuri** (Manipur) This dance form is performed to narrate the romantic relationship between the Hindu gods Radha and Krishna, which is famously known as Raas-Leela.

Tribal Dances

Some of the prominent tribal dances are :

Muria

- The *Muria* tribals of North **Bastar** area are known for performing the folk dances of *Muria*.
- These dances start with an invocation or prayer to the phallic deity of their tribe and the founder of the *Ghotul* institution.
- One of the popular *Muria* dances comprises of *Har Endanna* dance, performed by boys and girls during marriages.

Saila

- This dance is the dance form of **Chhattisgarh** and is performed by young boys in the post-harvest time. It is basically a stick-dance, in which dancers (each standing on one leg and supporting himself by holding onto the man in front) form a circle.
- Then, all of them jump together, going round and round.

Karma

- Popular among the *Gonds* and *Baigas* of **Chhattisgarh** and the *Oraons* of **Madhya Pradesh**, *Karma* dance is associated with the fertility cult.
- These dance forms represents the coming of green branches on trees, during the spring season. It is related to the *Karma* festival, which falls in the month of August.

Kaksar

- This dance is performed by people in hope of reaping a rich harvest and is popular among the *Abhujmarias* of **Bastar**.
- It is mainly undertaken by young boys and girls, in order to invoke the blessings of the deity.

Folk Dance Forms

Along with classical dance forms, folk dance also flourished.

Practically every region of our country has developed their own rich tradition of folk dances.

Folk Dances

	Folk Dance	Region
1.	Dumhal	Jammu and Kashmir
2.	Chholiya	Uttarakhand referred as 'sword dance'
3.	Bhangra	Punjab
4.	Mayur Nritya	Uttar Pradesh
5.	Giddha	Punjab, Female version of 'Bhangra'
6.	Chhau	Odisha, Jharkhand and West Bengal
7.	Gotipua	Odisha
8.	Bardo Chham	Arunachal Pradesh
9.	Bihu	Assam
10.	Nongkrem Dance	Jaintia Hill, Meghalaya
11.	Jhumur	Assam, Jharkhand, West Bengal and Odisha
12.	Mayil Attam	Temples of Tamil Nadu and Kerala
13.	Theyyam	(Kerala) also known as 'Kaliyattam.'
14.	Lava Dance	Lakshadweep
15.	Garba	Gujarat

Sarhul Dance

It is a traditional dance of the Oraon tribe. It marks the commencement of a new year as per the Hindu calender. It is a worship of the village deity who is considered to be the protector of the tribes.

Sarhul Dance

Theatre Crafts

India has a long, rich and illustrious history of folk theatre. In ancient times, Sanskrit dramas were staged at seasonal festivals or to celebrate special events.

It has also played an important part in the growth of modern theatres in different languages.

Some of the important theatre forms in India are as follows :

- **Koodiyattam** (Kerala) One of the oldest traditional theatre forms of India, Koodiyattam follows the ancient tradition of Sanskrit theatre.

  In 2001, Koodiyattam was officially recognised by UNESCO as a Masterpiece of the Oral and Intangible Heritage of Humanity.
- **Jatra** (Bengal/Bihar/Odisha) The Jatra, originated in Bengal in the 15th century as a result of the Bhakti Movement. It was initially known as Krishna Jatra due to Chaitanya's Mahaprabhu's influence.
- **Yakshagana** (Karnataka) Yakshagana is a popular folk theatre form of Karnataka. It is a unique harmony of musical tradition, eye-catching costumes, improvised gestures and acting.
- **Swang** (Haryana/Rajasthan/Uttar Pradesh) A popular folk theatre form, Swang is characterised by loud rendering of dialogues and songs. It has two important styles –Rohtak (performed in the Bangru language)and Hathras (performed in the Brajbhasha language).
- **Bhand Pather** (Kashmir) Bhand Pather is a unique combination of dance, music and acting. It is the traditional folk theatre of the Kashmir valley. The performances begin in the evening with a ritualistic dance called Chhok.

  The word **Bhand** stands for a jester while pather means a performance.
- **Tamasha** (Maharashtra) A traditional folk Tamasha flourished in the courts of Maratha rulers of the 18th and 19th centuries and attained its artistic peak during the reign of Baji Rao II. Unlike other theatre forms, in tamasha, the female actress is the lead performer.

Puppetry

Puppetry throughout the ages has held an important place in traditional entertainment. Like traditional theatre, themes for puppet theatre are mostly based on epics and legends.

The earliest reference to the art of puppetry is found in Tamil classic. **Silappadikaram** written around the first or second centuries BC.

These are some major types of Puppetry in India:

- **Glove Puppetry** In this particular form, the heads and arms of the puppets are controlled by the fingers of the puppeteer. Found in Odisha, Uttar Pradesh, Kerala and West Bengal. **Pavakoothu**, a glove puppetry form is from Kerala.
- **Rod Puppets** The puppets in this form are manipulated using rods. This form of puppetry expression is found in West Bengal and Odisha.
- **Shadow Puppets** Shadow puppets are flat and operated against a white clothed screen. It is very popular with many styles originating from various states (Odisha, Andhra Pradesh, Kerala, Karnataka, Maharashtra and Tamil Nadu).
- **String Puppets** String puppetry has prospered in Rajasthan, Odisha, Andhra Pradesh and Tamil Nadu. It is the most recognised and spoken form of puppetry around India.

38

Indian Languages, Literature and Philosophy

[SOURCES]

Class-X Old NCERT The Story of Civilisation Volume II, Chap 14 The Heritage of India

- It is one of the Twenty-two languages listed in the Indian Constitutions which are known as **Indian Languages**.
- **Sanskrit**, **Persian**, **Hindawi** and **Urdu** as well as various regional languages were developed over the period of times.

Classical Literature in India

- In Indian sub-continent, there are two main groups of languages. The **Indo-European** or **Indo-Aryan** and the **Dravidian**.
- However, both Indo-Aryan and Dravidian developed simultaneously.

Indian Language Families

- In India, many major languages exist along with other minor languages usually spoken by a small number of people. The Indian languages can be divided into the following four families :
  1. **Indo-Aryan** Speakers of languages from this family account for around 70% of the population of the country.
     Most of the languages in this family are derived from Sanskrit. Hindi, Bengali, Punjabi, Gujarati, Rajasthani, Assamese, etc., are the parts of this family.
  2. **Dravidian** This is the second largest family of languages in India and consists of languages mostly spoken in Southern India like Tamil, Kannada, Malayalam and Telugu.
     The Dravidian languages are older than the Indo-Aryan languages and many of them have classical language status.
  3. **Austric** This is the oldest and most indigenous language in the language family of India. Its speakers are concentrated in the hilly and tribal areas of Central and Eastern India.
     Santhali, Nicobarese, Khond, etc., are the examples of languages from this family.
  4. **Sino-Indian** This includes languages spoken in the North-East and Northern parts of India. It includes Naga, Bodo, Tibetan, Ladakhi, Karbi, etc.
- Apart from this, a fifth family of languages spoken in South Andaman is Ongan, which includes the two languages of Onge and Jarawa. The Great Andamanese is another language family, which is almost extinct.
- The Nihali language spoken by around 2000 people in **Madhya Pradesh** and **Rajasthan** is an isolated language, not a part of any family.
- The **Sidi language**, spoken by Sidi people in Gujarat till the middle of the 20th century, is not extinct and was derived from Swahili and also constituted to be a part of the Niger-Congo language family.
- Classical languages of India are Tamil, Telugu, Sanskrit, Kannada, Malayalam and Odia.

Role of Sanskrit

- Sanskrit was the language of the Indo-Aryans which came to India and belongs to the Indo-European group of languages. Sanskrit was gradually standardised and given a hugely scientific grammar by Panini, in fourth century BC.
- Sanskrit was the language of religion, philosophy and learning and was used by upper castes. The common people spoke a number of dialects, which were called Prakrits. Various spoken languages which developed are called **Apabhramsa**.

The Vedas

The Vedas are the earliest known literature in India. The Vedas were in Sanskrit and were handed down orally from one generation to the other. The four Vedas are Rigveda, Yajurveda, Samaveda and Atharvaveda.

Buddhist Literature

- The Buddhist works can be divided into the canonical and the non-canonical, which were written in Pali language. The canonical literature is known as 'Tripitakas' (three baskets), Vinaya Pitaka, Sutta Pitaka and Abhidhamma Pitaka.
- The non-canonical literature is best represented by the Jatakas. These are the most interesting stories on the previous births of the Buddha. Each birth story is called a Jataka.
- The Jatakas throw invaluable light on the social and economic conditions ranging from the sixth century BC to the second century BC. They also make incidental reference to political events in the age of the Buddha.

Jain Literature

- The Jain texts were written in Prakrit and were finally compiled in the sixth century AD in Vallabhi in Gujarat. The important works are known as Angas, Upangas, Prakirnas, Chhedab Sutras and Malasutras.
- Important Jain scholars were Haribhadra Suri, (eighth century AD) and Hemchandra Suri, (12th century AD).
- Jainism helped in the growth of a rich literature comprising poetry, philosophy and grammar.

Later Sanskrit Literature

- The Milind-Panho is another great Buddhist work consisting of dialogues between the Indo-Greek King Meander and the Buddhist philosopher Nagasena.
- Later, many books were written in Sanskrit, of these, the most famous is the Buddha-Charita or Life of Buddha by Ashvaghosha in Kushana period.
- Another important books were written such as book on medicine by Charak and on surgery by Sushruta. Books written on astronomy by Varahamihira and Aryabhatta.

Dravidian Literature

- About 23 Dravidian languages are spoken mainly in Southern India including Tamil, Kannada, Malyalam and Telugu.
- Tamil the oldest language of these, produced the Sangam literature.

Sangam Literature

- Poets, bards and writers, authors came from various parts of South India to Madurai, were called 'Sangamas' and the literature produced in these assemblies was called Sangama literature.
- The Sangama literature is a collection of long and short poems composed by various poets in praise of numerous heroes and heroines. They are secular in nature.
- There are about 30000 lines of poetry, which are called Ettuttokai. Besides the Sangama texts, Tolkappiyam, deals with grammar and poetry. In addition, we have the twin epics of Silappadikaram and Manimekalai.

Indian Scripts

- **Indus Script** It refers to the script used by the people belonging to the Indus Valley Civilisation. It has not been deciphered yet. Some people have argued that this script was the predecessor of the Brahmi script.
- This script is an example of Boustrophedon style as in one line. It is written from left to right while in other it is written from right to left.
- **Brahmi Script** Brahmi is the originator of most of the present Indian scripts, including *Devanagari*, *Bengali*, *Tamil*, *Malayalam*, etc.

  It developed into two broad types in Northern and Southern India, with the Northern one being more angular and the Southern one being more circular.

  It was deciphered in 1937 by **James Prinsep**. Its best examples are found in the rock-cut edicts of Ashoka.
- **Kharosthi Script** It is the sister script and contemporary of *Brahmi*. It is written from right to left. It was used in the Gandhara culture of North-Western India and is sometimes also called the **Gandhari Script**. Its inscriptions have been found in the form of Buddhist texts from present day Afghanistan and Pakistan.
- **Sharada Script** It was a Western variant of the Gupta script. It evolved into Kashmiri and Gurmukhi (now used for writing Punjabi) scripts. It was also used for writing Sanskrit. It is now rarely used.
- **Nagari Script** It was an Eastern variant of the Gupta script. It is an early form of the Devanagari script.

It branched off into many other scripts such as Devanagari, Bengali, Tibetan, etc. It was used to write both Prakrit and Sanskrit.

- **Tamil Script** It is the script used to write Tamil language in India and Sri Lanka. It evolved from Grantha, the Southern form of Brahmi. It is a syllabic language and not alphabetic. It was written from left to right.

Classical Languages

- There are six languages that enjoy the classical status in India.
- Tamil (Declared in 2004), Sanskrit (2005), Kannada (2008), Telugu (2008), Malayalam (2013) and Odia (2014) are classical language in India.
- The Ministry of culture provides the guidelines regarding classical languages.
- One a language is notified as a classical language, the Human Resource Development (now Education) ministry provides certain benefits to promote it.

Literature in the Medieval Period

- In the early medieval period in Northern India, Sanskrit continued to be the language of literature.
- Many texts were written in this period in Dravidian languages and Apabhramsha (Sanskrit mixed with local dialects) languages as well.

Sanskrit Literature

- **Somadeva's** *Katha Sarit Sagara* is a collection of Indian legends, fairy tales and folk tales with multiple layers of story within a story.
- **Kalhana's** *Rajatarangini* is related to Kashmir, which is a first systemtically written history book.
- Another famous work of this period is the *Gitagovinda* by **Jayadeva**, which is one of the finest poems in Sanskrit literature. **Bilhana's** *Vikramankadeva Charita*, a biography of the **Chalukya king Vikramaditya VI.**
- One of the earliest works in an early form of Hindi was *Prithviraj Raso* by **Chandbardai**. This work marks the beginning of bardic literature.

Kannada Literature

- **Nrupatunga** wrote a first great work of poetry in Kannada called the *Kavirajamarga*, which was deeply influenced by Jainism.
- In Kannada language, **Pampa** wrote the *Adipurana* (life of first Jain Tirthankara) and the *Vikramarjuna Vijaya* based on *Mahabharata*.
- **Ponna** wrote the *Shantipurana*, history of 16th Tirthankara. Another great Kannada writer was **Ranna**, who wrote *Ajita Purana* and *Gadayuddha*.

Note *Pampa, Ponna and Ranna are known as the 'Three Gems of the Kannada Literature'.*

Tamil Literature

- In Tamil, this was the period of composition of the great hymns of the **Alvars** and the **Nayanars**. The hymns of the Alvars are collected into the *Nalayira Divya Prabandham*.
- Some of the Nayanar works are *Thiruvasagam*, *Thiumanairam* and *Thiruttondattagoi*. Another great work was *Kamban's Ramayanam*, which was written during this time.

Telugu Literature

- Under the Vijayanagara kingdom, Telugu literature developed immensely. Krishnadeva Raya wrote the Vishnuchittiya and his court poets Allasani Peddana and Dhurjati wrote the Manucharita and Kalahasti Mahatyam respectively.

Hindi Literature

- The period of Sultanate of Delhi saw a great advance in the growth of various regional forms of Hindi languages. *Braj Bhasa* and *Khari Boli*, forms of Hindi, began to be used in literary compositions.
- The famous ballad *Alha Udal* and *Vishaldeo Raso* belonged to this period. **Mulla Daud** wrote perhaps the oldest poem in Awadhi language called *Chandayana* (commentaries on ancient scriptures).
- Bhakti saints preached in the language of the common people. **Kabir's** *Bijak* written in *Bhojpuri* and Tulsidas's Ramcharitmanas and Malik Muhammad Jayasi's Padmavat were written in *Awadhi* language.
- Hindi language also made significant progress during this period. **Surdas** and **Keshavdas** wrote in this period. **Rahim's** *Doha* or couplets were also written in Hindi language.

Other Regional Literature

- Literature in other languages also developed in this period. In Bengali, the Ramayana by Kritivasa and the hundreds of lyrics by Chandidas were written.
- With **Chaitanya**, the tradition of writing devotional songs began. **Narsi Mehta** wrote devotional songs in Gujarati, **Namdev** and **Ekanath** wrote in Marathi.

Persian and Turkish Literature

- The Turks introduced the Arabian traditions of historical writings in India. **Ziauddin Barani** wrote the *Tarikh-i-Firoz* Shahi which gives a detailed accounts of the Khaljis and Tughlaqs.

- The most outstanding literary figure was Amir Khusrau. He wrote the *Ashiqa*, *Nuh Sipihr*, the *Khazan-ul-Futuh* and other literary works.

Note *Persian was the court language of the Delhi Sultanate. Because of it many Persian words became part of the vocabulary of Indian languages.*

- Babar the first Mughal ruler, was one of the pioneers of Turkish literature in India. His autobiography Babar Nama is written in Turkish language.
- **Gulbadan Begum**, sister of Humayun wrote *Humayun Nama*. **Jahangir** wrote his autobiography, *Tuzuk-i-Jahangiri* in Persian language.

Urdu Literature

- One of the most significant developments during the medieval period as the birth of the Urdu language. It produced great poets like **Wali**, **Mir Dard**, **Mir Taqi Mir** and **Mirza Ghalib** and others.
- This language soon developed one of the richest literature in modern Indian languages. Many states of Northern and Deccan region of India, Urdu language is spoken in large number.

Development of Indian Philosophy

- The six orthodox schools are called as Shaddarshanas and include Nyaya, Sankhya, Yoga, Vaisheshika, Purva Mimamsa and Uttara Mimamsa (Vedanta Philosophy).
- Most of these schools of thought believe in the theory of *Karma* and *Rebirth*.
- *Moksha* (salvation) is believed to be the liberation from the cycle of birth and death and also the ultimate goal of human life.

Nyaya Philosophy

- Nyaya school follows a scientific and a rational approach. **Sage Gautama** is the founder of this school. Nyaya school banks upon various *Pramanas* (mechanism of attaining knowledge).
- It believes that gaining knowledge through the five senses is the sole way of attaining liberation from the cycle of birth and death.

Sankhya Philosophy

- Sankhya is the oldest of all philosophies put forth by the sage Kapila. It is a dualistic philosophy with Purusha (soul) and Prakriti (nature) in it.
- **Advaita Vedanta** derives its base from Sankhya school. Sankhya also devolves philosophical basis for yoga. It emphasises the attainment of knowledge of self through meditation and concentration.

Yoga Philosophy

- The Yoga school, as expounded by **Patanjali** in his second century BC. Yoga Sutras, accepts the Sankhya psychology and metaphysics, but is more theistic, with the addition of a divine entity to *Sankhya's* twenty-five elements of reality.
- The relatively brief Yoga Sutras are divided into eight Ashtanga (limbs), reminiscent of Buddhism's **Noble Eightfold Path**, the goal being to quiet one's mind and achieve *kaivalya* (solitariness or detachment).

Vaisheshika

- The Vaisheshika school was founded by **Kannada** in the sixth century BC and it is atomist and pluralist in nature.
- The basis of the school's philosophy is that all objects in the physical universe are reducible to a finite number of atoms and Brahman is regarded as the fundamental force that causes consciousness in these atoms.
- The Vaisheshika and Nyaya schools eventually merged over the period of time because of their closely related metaphysical theories. However, Vaisheshika only accepted perception and inference as sources of valid knowledge.

Purva Mimamsa

- Purva Mimamsa school believes in the complete authority of Vedas. It is based on sage **Jaimini's Mimamsa Sutras**. It emphasises the power of yajnas and mantras in sustaining the activities of the universe.
- It states that a human being can attain salvation only by acting in conformity with the principles of Vedas.

Uttara Mimamsa (Vedanta)

- Vedanta school is a monistic school of philosophy that believes that the world is unreal and the only reality is Brahman.
- The three sub-branches of Vedanta are **Advaita** of Shankaracharya, **Vishishtadvaita** of Ramanujacharya and **Dvaita** of Madhwacharya. **Uttara Mimamsa** is based on Upanishads (the end portions of Vedas).

Appendix

Historical Events in India

2350-1750 BC	Period of Indus Valley Civilisation
1500-600 BC	Vedic Age
563-483 BC	Buddhist Era
540-468 BC	Mahavira's Era
544-492 BC	Reign of Bimbisara (Haryanka Dynasty)
326 BC	Alexander attacked India through Khyber Pass
322 BC	Chandragupta Maurya became King
305 BC	Battle between Chandragupta Maurya and Seleucus
304-299 BC	Stay of Megasthenes in the court of Chandragupta Maurya
269 BC	Coronation of Ashoka
261 BC	Victory of Ashoka in Kalinga War
185 BC	End of Mauryan Dynasty
183 BC	Attack of Indo-Greeks
57 BC	Vikram Era begins
45 AD	Discovery of Monsoon by Hippalus
78 AD	Beginning of Saka Era Wind
150 AD	Junagadh Inscription (First Sanskrit Inscription)
319 AD	Coronation of Chandragupta I (Gupta Samvat)
350-375 AD	Reign of Samudragupta
375-415 AD	Reign of Chandragupta –II, Fa-Hien (399-414) visited India
415-455 AD	Reign of Kumaragupta, establishment of Nalanda University
455-467 AD	Reign of Skandgupta, Invasion of Huns
510 AD	First signs of Sati-Pratha found in Bhanugupta's Eran Inscription
606-647 AD	Harshavardhana's reign
630 AD	Visit of Hiuen Tsang during Harsha's rule
632 AD	Battle between Harshavardhana and Pulakesin-II
712 AD	Arab attack on Sindh
915-16 AD	Al-Masudi travels in India
1001-1026 AD	17 raids of Mahmud Ghazni on India, Al-Biruni visited India
1015-1044 AD	Reign of Chola ruler, Rajendra -I
1178 AD	Bhima-II emerged, victorious in the battle with Muhammad Ghori
1191 AD	First Battle of Tarain, Prithviraj Chauhan defeated Ghori
1192 AD	Second Battle of Tarain, Ghori defeated Prithviraj Chauhan
1194 AD	Muhammad Ghori defeated Jaichand, ruler of Kannauj in Battle of Chandawar

1199 AD	Bakhtiyar Khilji destroyed Nalanda University
1206 AD	Delhi Sultanate founded by Qutub-ud-din Aibak
1210 AD	Iltutmish ascended the throne of Delhi Sultanate
1236 AD	Razia Sultan ascended the throne
1241 AD	First Mongol invasion during the rule of Bahram Shah
1326-27 AD	Muhammad-bin Tughlaq shifted his capital from Delhi to Daulatabad
1333 AD	Moroccan traveller, Ibn Battuta visited to India
1336 AD	Vijayanagara empire founded
1347 AD	Foundation of Bahmani kingdom
1398 AD	Invasion of Taimur in India
1498 AD	Arrival of Vasco-da-Gama in India
1506 AD	Sikandar Lodhi shifted capital to Agra
1510 AD	Portuguese conquest of Goa
1509-1529 AD	Reign of Krishnadeva Raya
1526 AD	First Battle of Panipat, Babur defeated Ibrahim Lodhi
1527 AD	Battle of Khanwa, Babur defeated Rana Sanga
1533 AD	Dinpanah constructed by Humayun
1540 AD	Battle of Bilgram, Sher Shah defeated Humayun
1555 AD	Battle of Sirhind, Bairam Khan defeated Sikandar Sur. Humayun once again ascended the throne of Delhi
1556 AD	Coronation of Akbar, Second Battle of Panipat fought in which Hemu was defeated
1565 AD	Battle of Talikota between Vijayanagara and Bahmani empire
1567 AD	Akbar introduced Mansabdari system
1575 AD	Establishment of Ibadat-Khana
1576 AD	Battle of Haldighati
1579 AD	Announcement of Mahzar by Akbar
1582 AD	Din-i-Ilahi started by Akbar
1600 AD	East India Company established
1608 AD	William Hawkins visited Jahangir's court
1615 AD	Sir Thomas Roe arrived in India
1627 AD	Birth of Shivaji
1665 AD	Treaty of Purandar signed between Shivaji and Jai Singh
1674 AD	Coronation of Shivaji , establishment of Puducherry by Francis Martin
1699 AD	Khalsa sect established by Guru Gobind Singh
1707 AD	Death of Aurangzeb
1717 AD	Farrukhsiyar gave farman to East India Company for free trade

1724 AD	Establishment of Hyderabad state by Nizam-ul-Mulk
1739 AD	Battle of Karnal, Nadir Shah's invasion on Delhi
1748 AD	Ahmad Shah Abdali invaded India
1757 AD	Battle of Plassey
1764 AD	Battle of Buxar
1772 AD	Warren Hastings appointed as Governor of Bengal
1773 AD	Regulating Act passed
1784 AD	Pitt's India Act passed, Foundation of Asiatic Society of Bengal
1793 AD	Permanent Settlement was introduced
1799 AD	Death of Tipu Sultan
1803 AD	British captured Delhi
1809 AD	Treaty of Amritsar signed by Britishers and Ranjit Singh
1816 AD	Treaty of Sugauli was signed by East India Company and Nepal
1824 AD	Military revolt of Barrackpore
1829 AD	Abolition of Sati
1833 AD	Governor-General of Bengal became Governor- General of India
1839 AD	Construction of GT road from Calcutta to Delhi started
1843 AD	Annexation of Sindh
1853 AD	Introduction of railways in India
1854 AD	Wood's Despatch
1857 AD	Establishment of Universities of Bombay, Madras and Calcutta
1860 AD	Budget system started in India
1865 AD	Telegraph service started between Europe and India
1875 AD	Arya Samaj founded
1876 AD	Indian Association established by Surendranath Banerji
1877 AD	Delhi Darbar held
1878 AD	Vernacular Press Act implemented
1881 AD	Census system started in India
1883 AD	Ilbert Bill Controversy
1885 AD	Indian National Congress established
1888 AD	The United Indian Patriotic Association was established by Sir Syed Ahmed Khan
1893 AD	Swami Vivekananda's speech in Chicago
1896 AD	Vande Mataram was sung first time in INC Session
1902 AD	Lord Curzon appointed a Commission for improvement in University Education System
1905 AD	Partition of Bengal
1906 AD	Muslim League founded
1907 AD	Surat Split of INC
1909 AD	Morley-Minto reforms for separate electorates for Muslims
1911 AD	Annulment of partition of Bengal
1912 AD	Capital was shift to Delhi from Calcutta
1913 AD	Ghadar Party founded, Rabindranath Tagore received Nobel Prize
1914 AD	World War I started
1915 AD	Arrival of Mahatma Gandhi in India
1916 AD	Home Rule League founded, Pact signed between INC and Muslim League
1917 AD	Champaran Satyagraha launched by Mahatma Gandhiji, formation of Saddler Commission
1919 AD	Rowlatt Act passed, Montague- Chelmsford reforms, Jallianwala Bagh Massacre, Khilafat Movement
1920 AD	Non- Cooperation Movement, All India Trade Union Congress established
1922 AD	Chauri-chaura incident, withdrawal of Non-Cooperation Movement
1924 AD	Hindustan Republican Army founded, Mahatma Gandhji appointed President (only once) in Belgaum Congress Session
1925 AD	Kakori Train Case (Kakori Kand)
1927 AD	Simon Commission appointed
1928 AD	Simon Commission came to India, Hindustan Socialist Republican Army established
1929 AD	Bhagat Singh and Batukeshwar Dutt threw bomb in Assembly
1930 AD	Gandhiji's Dandi March, Round Table Conference, Civil Disobedience Movement Launched
1931 AD	Second Round Table Conference, Chandrashekhar Azad shot himself at Alfred Park in Allahabad
1932 AD	Third Round Table Conference, Communal Awards
1933 AD	Gandhiji started a magazine, 'Harijan'
1934 AD	Congress Socialist Party founded
1935 AD	The Government of India Act passed
1937 AD	Provincial elections held, Federal Court of India was established
1938 AD	Subhash Chandra Bose was appointed as a President of Indian National Congress
1939 AD	Forward Bloc founded, World War ll started
1940 AD	Gandhiji launched Individual Satyagraha
1941 AD	Azad Hind Fauj established
1942 AD	Gandhiji gave a slogan 'Do or Die' (Quit India Movement)
1944 AD	Subhash Chandra Bose called Mahatma Gandhiji as the 'Father of Nation'
1945 AD	Wavell Plan
1946 AD	Cabinet Mission, Muslim League's call for direct action day, Royal Indian Navy's Mutiny
1947 AD	Indian Independence and partition of India
1948 AD	Assassination of Mahatma Gandhiji
1950 AD	Implementation of the Constitution of India
1951 AD	First General Elections held
1953 AD	First Linguistic State Andhra Pradesh created
1954 AD	First Bharat Ratna Award was given
1962 AD	India-China War, Integration of Daman –Diu and Goa into India
1964 AD	Death of Pandit Jawaharlal Nehru

Inscriptions of Ancient India

Inscriptions of Ancient India	Ruler	Subject
Piprahwa Buddhist Vase Inscription	Shakya Ruler	• Obtained from Piprahwa situated in Basti district of Uttar Pradesh • Just after the Mahaparinirvana of Buddha • Brahmi Script and Prakrit Language
Sohgaura Copper Plate Inscription	Chandragupta Maurya	• Maurya Record that mentions famine relief efforts
First Ashoka Inscription at Girnar	Ashoka	• Prohibition of animal killing and eating of animals
Second Ashoka Rock Edict of Girnar	Ashoka	• Talks about welfare measure • Order for spread of Dhamma
Ashoka's Triadesh Rock Edict	Ashoka	• Life of Ashoka and discussion of Kalinga War
Seventh Pillar Inscription of Ashoka	Ashoka	• After 27 years of coronation, this incription was made to spread of Dhamma • It is obtained from Topra and established in Firoz Shah Kotla, Delhi
Lumbini Pillar Inscription	Ashoka	• 20 years after the coronation Ashoka came to Lumbini and visited the place of Buddha's birth • Paying Reverence to Buddha, land tax was run away for residents of Lumbini village
Besnagar Garuda Pillar Inscription	Antialcidus (Heliodorus)	• Prakrit language influenced by Sanskrit is used and engraved in Brahmi Script • In Vidisha, Madhya Pradesh and established as symbol of Bhagwat Religion
Hathigumpha Inscription	Kharavela	• Found Udayagiri Hills of Odisha. Written in Sanskrit influenced Prakrit language with Brahmani Script • Life and victory of Kharavela • Description of his campaigns and mention of being a follower of Jainism
Nashik Inscription	Gautami Putra Shatkarni	• Victories of the Satavahana Rulers • Prakrit language and Brahmi Script is used
Junagadh Inscription (Girnar Pillar)	Rudradaman	• Sanskrit Language and Brahmi Script, First Sanskrit Inscription of India • Description of his achievements • Restoration of Sudarshan lake was mentioned

Inscriptions of Ancient India	Ruler	Subject
Allahabad Pillar Inscription	Samudragupta	• Sanskrit language and Brahmi Script is used • Description of War against 12 Kings of Dakshinapatha • Ashoka and Jahangir writings were also engraved
Iron Pillar of Mehrauli	Chandragupta-II	• Qutub Minar complex (formely established in Mihirpuri Village) • Sanskrit language and Brahmi Script is used • Vishnu Flag on Vishnu Padha Mountain installation detail
Mandsaur Inscription	Kumaragupta-I	• Sanskrit language and Brahmi Script engraved • This inscription gives description about Tantuvai class of people from Lat Pradesh to settle in Dispur • Prashasti was written by Vatsabhatti
Junagadh Inscription	Skandagupta	• Inscription in Sanskrit language and it is in Brahmi Script • Vishnu at the beginning of the inscription • Skandagupta's success against the Mlechchhas
Bhitari Pillar Inscription	Skandagupta	• Discovered by Tregear from Ghazipur (Uttar Pradesh) • In this incription, the genealogy of Gupta Dynasty has been engraved • Details of defeat of Pushyamitra by Skandagupta
Harha Rock Inscription	Ishaan Varman	• Sanskrit Language and Brahmi Script is used • Found in Barabanki (Uttar Pradesh), Haraha village of the district Shastri in the year 1915 • Date-611 Vikram Samvat (554 AD) on inscription is inscribed • Description of achievements of Moukhari rulers
Aihole Inscription	Pulakeshin-II	• In Sanskrit and Brahmi Script is used, engraved Ravikirti on the walls of the Temple by Jain • Description of Pulakeshin victory over Harshavardhan
Eran Boar Pillar Inscription	Bhanugupta	• In this the first practice of Sati gets mentioned • Discussion of Huna ruler meets Tooraman

Famous Statements Related to History

Ancient History

- Harappa and Mohenjodaro were the twin capitals of a vast Empire. *Stuart Piggott*
- India is a companion of Greece in the field of astrology. *Gargi Samhita*
- No person could marry irrespective of his caste, change of occupation was also not possible, only Brahmans had the right to change their occupation during an emergency. *Megasthenes*
- Dhammavijay, the favourite of the Gods, enjoys the most important victory. *13th Rock Edict of Ashoka*
- Dhamma is the common property of all religions. In fact, the power prescribed in record was the essence of all religions. *John E. Flint*
- Not a year passed, in which India had not earned ten million sastriyar (Roman currency) from the Roman treasury. *Panini*
- During the period of Harshavardhana, the irrigation of fields was done by 'Ghanti Yantra' and 'Tula Yantra'. *Banabhatta*
- After crossing the Indus river, Seleucus fought Chandragupta and eventually a treaty was made between the two and a matrimonial relation was established. *Appian*
- Mesopotamia is the inspiration of Indus Valley Civilisation. *M. Rafique Mughul*
- Sabha and Samiti are the two daughters of Prajapati. *Atharvanas*
- The way of salvation is not knowledge, but devotion that is love for God. *Ramanuja*
- Hindukush Mountain was the legal boundary of India. *VS Smith*
- Chandragupta with an army of six lakhs defeated all of the India and annexed it. *Plutarch*
- Except the East, i have conquered all other three directions. *Kanishk*
- A king should be respected, even if he is a child, because he is a deity, ruling in the form of a man. *Manu-Smriti*
- During the last days of his life (Ashoka), he was surviving on a half a awala. *Divyavadana*
- Samudragupta was not just fond of war and victory, but poetry and music also has a major part in his life. *Prayag Prashasti*
- Samudragupta was 'Napoleon' of India. *VA Smith (Vincent Arthur Smith)*

Medieval History

- If I am guilty of any wrongdoing, then I can decide against myself also. *Akbar*
- I don't know what is their in the shriyat I do what is good for my kingdom. I am unaware of what will happen to me on the day of judgement. *Alauddin Khilji*
- Daulatabad was a monument of misguided power. *Lane-Poole*
- Firoz Tughlaq was Akbar of the Sultanate Era. *Henry Elliot and Alston*
- The Sultan was freed from his people and the subjects were freed people their Sultan. *Badauni, on death of Mohammad Tughlaq*
- Humayun tumbled through life and he tumbled out of it. *Lane-Poole*
- He is the most brilliant Asiatic prince of his age an worth of a high place among the sovereigns of any age or country. *VS Smith*
- The real soul of the Mughal painter has become infatuated with Jahangir. *Percy Brown*
- Akbar's tomb (at Sikandra) is a complete monument of a great Indian ruler. *Hawell*
- An architectural masterpiece like Fatehpur Sikri was neither in the past nor will happen in future. *VS Smith*
- Fatehpur Sikri is an expression of love in stone and the mind of a great man. *Ferguson*
- Sher Shah's tomb at Sasaram is the best work in the whole of North India. *Percy Brown*
- Had Razia not a woman, she would have been named among the great Muslim rulers of India. *Elphinstone*
- The king is the representative of God on Earth (Niyamat-i-Khudai), so his everything done by him is just. *Balban*
- Aurangzeb's fame and body both got a tomb in the South VA located. *VS Smith*
- I almost lost the kingdom of Delhi for a handful of millets. *Sher Shah (about the Marwar conquest)*
- The Alai Darwaza is the largest diamond in the treasury of Islamic architecture. *John Marshall*
- He (Krishnadeva Raya) was the most learned and complete king. He was among the people who respected foreigners, he was a great and he was a just ruler. *Domingo Paes*

Modern History

- Nehru is a patriot, while Jinnah is a politician. *Iqbal*
- The British rule is a formidable weight and strength, which has its own. There are uses, but is does not help in producing a fertile lump of land. *Rabindranath Tagore*
- I am not a visionary. I claim to be a practical idealist. *Mahatma Gandhi*
- Bengal united is a force, Bengal divided will go in different ways. *Herbert Risley*
- The bones of cotton- Weavers are bleaching the plains of India. *William Bentinck*
- Just as all the currents mix their waters by taking them into the ocean, similarly, all religions lead man towards God. *Swami Vivekananda*
- Gandhiji did the work which 50 thousand armed soldiers could not do. He made peace. *Mountbatten*
- 'Saare Jahaan Se Achcha Hindustaan Hamaraa Hamaraa.' *Iqbal*
- Whole of India is a large prison. *CR Das*
- Remember we will have to make zamindars out friends. *Mahatma Gandhi*
- The Sword of Revolution is sharpened on the whetting-stones of ideas. *Bhagat Singh*
- Better live a day like a lion, than twenty years like a sheep. *Tipu Sultan*
- The peasants will have to free themselves not only from foreign slavery, but also from the slavery of landowners and capitalists. *Bhagat Singh*
- Today our country needs nerves of steel and muscles of iron. *Swami Vivekananda*
- We are all sons of the Earth, we have to live together, believe me, India cannot move forward until the people, Hindus and Muslims do not become one. *Jinnah*
- A theory must be tempered with reality. *Jawaharlal Nehru*
- I will create a bigger movement than the Congress from the sand of the country. *Mahatma Gandhi*
- Give me blood, i will give you freedom. *Subhash Chandra Bose*
- You cannot believe in God until you believe in yourself. *Swami Vivekananda*
- Political freedom is the life-breath of a Nation. *Aurobindo Ghosh*
- 'Swaraj is my birth right and I shall have it.' *Bal Gangadhar Tilak*
- India will be divided on my dead body, as long as I am alive I will not allow partition of India. *Mahatma Gandhi*
- If God is put up with untouchability, I will not call him God. *Bal Gangadhar Tilak*
- India has been won on the strength of the sword and it will be protected only by the strength of the sword. *Elgin-II*
- Go back to the Vedas. *Swami Dayananda Saraswati*
- If we do not accept the demand of Pakistan, then many people in this country Pakistan will be made, there will be a unit of Pakistan in each office. *Sardar Patel*
- Sarfaroshi Ki Tamanna Ab Hamaare Dil Mein Hai. *Ram Prasad Bismil*
- There is nothing more horrifying than stupidity in action. *Jawaharlal Nehru*
- Delhi Chalo *Subhash Chandra Bose*
- Inquilab Zindabad *Moulana Hasrat Mohani*
- Jai Hind *Subhash Chandra Bose*
- The creator of Pakistan was not Jinnah or Mohammad Iqbal but Lord Minto. *Dr. Rajendra Prasad*
- It is a state of looted country, where the robber is continuously robbing and then escapes cleanly. *Dadabhai Naoroji*
- The shots that hit me are the last nails to the coffin of British Rule in India. *Lala Lajpat Rai*
- I think Satyagraha is the only way to stop terrorism. *Mahatma Gandhi*
- The Congress is tottering to its fall and one of my greatest ambitions while in India is to assist it to a peaceful demise. *Lord Curzon*
- By revolution we mean that the existing system based on injustice should end. *Bhagat Singh*
- Home rule is the right of India, India as a nation has its own judicial and authority demands from the British empire. *Annie Besant*
- The main reason behind the establishment of the Indian National Congress was it's the birth fathers were concerned about saving the empire from disintegration. *Lala Lajpat Rai*
- Congress represents the micro minority of the people. *Dufferin (about Congress)*
- Our nation is like a tree, whose root stem is Swaraj and indigenous and boycott its branches. *Tilak*
- My only hope lies in the prayer and its answer. *Mahatma Gandhi*

Ancient Temples of North India and their Patrons (Dravida Style of Temples)

Temples	Places	Time Period	Built By
Kailashnath Temple	Kanchipuram	700 AD	Narasimhavarman (Rajasimha)
Vekund Perumal Temple	Kanchipuram	1720 AD	Narasimhavarman
Mukteshvara Temple	Kanchipuram	8th century AD	Nandivarman
Choleshwar Temple	Kanchipuram	9th century AD	Vijayalaya
Nageshwar Temple	Kumbakonam	9th century AD	Aditya-I
Thiruvalleswarar Temple	Brahmadesam	10th century AD	Raja Raja-I
Rajarajeswara Temple (Brihadeeswarar Temple)	Thanjavur	11th century AD	Raja Raja-I
Vaidyanatha Temple	Tiruchirappalli	11th century AD	Raja Raja-I
Uttar Kailasa Temple	Thanjavur	1106 AD	Logo Mahadevi
Shiv Devalaya Temple	Temple Polonnaruwa	11th century AD	Raja Raja-I
Airavatesvara Temple	Kumbakonam	12th century AD	Raja Raja-II
Kapreshwar Temple	Tribhuvanam	1176 AD	Kulotung-III
Virupaksha Temple	Hampi	14th century AD	Lakkan Dandesha
Varadharaja Perumal Temple	Kumbakonam	3rd century AD	Kulo Hung-I
Meenakshi Temple	Madurai	4th century AD	Pandya ruler

Delhi Sultanate and Mughal Architecture

Sultanate Rulers	Architecture Built
Qutub-ud-Din-Aibak	• Qwati-ul-Islam • Qutub Minar • Adhai-din-ka Jhonpra
Iltutmish	• Tomb of Sultangarhi • Tomb of Iltutmish • Baoli of Gandhak
Balban	• Lal Mahal • Tomb of Balban
Alauddin Khilji	• Alai Darwaja • Shiri Fort • Hazar Satun
Ghiyasuddin Tughlaq	• Tughlaqabad • Tomb of Tughlaq
Muhammad-Bin-Tughlaq	• City of Jahanpanah • Fort of Adilabad • Tomb of Nizamuddin Auliya
Firoz Shah Tughlaq	• Firoz-Shah Kotta • Tomb of Khan-i-Jahan Tilangini
Sikandar Lodhi	• Moth Ki Masjid • Agra Town • Tomb of Bade Khan and Chote Khan
Ibrahim Lodhi	• Tomb of Sikandar Lodhi

Mughal Architecture

Babar	• Kabuli Bagh Mosque • Jama Masjid (Sambhal) • Ram Bagh (Agra)
Humayun	• Din Panah (Delhi)
Akbar	• Agra Fort • Panchmahal • Fatehpur Sikri • Tomb of Salim-Chishti • Buland-Darwaja
Jahangir	• Tomb of Akbar (Sikandra) • Tomb of I'timad--ud-Daulah • Shalimar Bagh (Kashmir)
Shahjahan	• Shanjahanabad City • Chandni Chowk • Taj Mahal • Lal Quila (Delhi)
Aurangzeb	• Badshahi Masjid • Moti Masjid • Tomb of Rabiya-Ud-Dauranni
Sher-Shah-Suri	• Tomb of Sher Shah • Grand Trunk Road • Sher Shah Pavillion

Important Historical Works

Ancient Literatures	Creators
Ashtadhyayi	Panini
Mahabhashya	Patanjali
Kathasaritsagara	Somdev
Katha Manjari	Kshemendra
Arthasastra	Kautilya
Nitisara	Kamandaka
Mrichhakatikam	Sudraka
Harshacharita	Banabhatta
Rajatarangini	Kalhana
Tolkappiyam	Tholkappiyar
Malavikagnimitram	Kalidas
Prithviraj Raso	Chandbardai
Silappadikaram	Ilango Adigal
Manimekalai	Sitalai Sattanar
Civak Chintamani	Tirukkadevar
Ramcharitam	Sandhyakar Nandi
Uttara Ramcarita	Bhavabhuti

Important Works in Delhi Sultanate

Works	Writers
Tahkik-i-Hind	Alberuni
Tajul-Masir	Hasan Nizami
Tarikh-i-Firozshahi	Zia-ud-din-Barani
Fatwa-i-Firozshahi	Firoz Shah
Tabaqat-i-Nasari	Minhaj-us-Siraj
Tarikh-Masudi	Abul-Fazl Muhammad ibn Husayn
Kitab-ul-Rehla	Ibn Battuta
Tarikh-i-Salatin-i-Afghana	Ahmed Yadgar
Kitab-l-Yamini	Utbi
Khazain-ul-Futuh	Amir Khusrau
Fatwa-e-Jahandari	Zia-ud-din Barani

Important Works During the Mughal Period

Works	Writers
Tuzuk-i-Baburi (Baburnama)	Babur
Humayun nama	Gulbadan Begum
Tarikh-i-Shershahi	Abbas Khan Sherwani
Tarikh-e-Rashidi	Mirza Haider Duglat
Tarrikh-e-Farishta	Muhammad Qasim Farishta
Tabakat-e-Akbari	Nizamuddin Ahmed
Akbarnama	Abul Fazl
Tuzuk-i-Jahangiri	Jahangir
Badshah Namah	Abdul Hamid Lahori
Shahjahan Namah	Inayt Khan
Nuskha-i-Dilkusha	Bhimsen
Badshah Namah	Muhammad Amin Kajvini

Important Works of Modern India

Works	Writers
Young India	Lala Lajpat Rai
India Divided	Rajendra Prasad
Pakistan or the Partition of India	BR Ambedkar
Anhilation of Caste	BR Ambedkar
Satyarth Parkash	Dayananda Saraswati
Poverty and un-British Rule of India	Dadabhai Naoroji
India Wins Freedom	Abdul Kalam Azad
Golden Threshold	Sarojini Naidu
Ideas of a Nation	Sarojini Naidu
First War of Independence	VD Savarkar
The Life Divine	Aurobindo Ghosh
Anand Math	Bankim Chandra Chatterjee
Lectures from Colombo to Almora	Swami Vivekananda
Hind Sawaraj	Mahatma Gandhi
Gita Rahasya	Bal Gangadhar Tilak
Discovery of India	Nehru

Important Wars of Indian History

Wars	Periods	Between
Battle of Hydaspes	326 BC	Alexander-Porus
Kalinga War	261 BC	Ashoka-Ruler of Kalinga
Battle of Sindh	712 BC	Mohammad Qasim-Dahir
War of Peshawar	1001 BC	Mahmud of Ghazni-Jayapal
First Battle of Tarain	1191 AD	Muhammad Ghori-Prithviraj
Second Battle of Tarain	1192 AD	Muhammad Ghori-Prithviraj
Third Battle of Tarain	1215 AD	Iltutmish-Yaldoz
Battle of Chandawar	1194 AD	Muhammad Ghori Jaichand
First Battle of Panipat	1526 AD	Babur-Ibrahim Lodhi
Battle of Khanwa	1527 AD	Babur-Rana Sanga
Battle of Chanderi	1528 AD	Babur-Medini Rai
Battle of Ghaghara	1529 AD	Babur- Mahmud Lodhi
Battle of Chausa	1539 AD	Sher Shah-Humayun
Battle of Kannauj (Bilgram)	1540 AD	Sher Shah-Humayun
Second Battle of Panipat	1556	Akbar-Hemu
Battle of Talikota	1565	Vijayanagara-Bahmani
Battle of Haldi Ghati	1576	Akbar-Rana Pratap
Battle of Plassey	1757	Anglo-Bengal Nawab
Battle of Wandiwash	1760	Anglo-French
Third Battle of Panipat	1761	Ahmad Shah Abdali-Maratha
Battle of Buxar	1764	British-United Alliance
First Anglo-Mysore War	1767-69	English-Hyder Ali
Second Anglo-Mysore War	1780-84	English-Hyder Ali
Third Anglo-Mysore War	1790	Tipu Sultan -British
Fourth Anglo-Mysore War	1799	Tipu Sultan -British
First Anglo-Sikh War	1845-46	Anglo-Sikh
Battle of Chillianwala	1848-49	Anglo-Sikh
First Carnatic War	1744-48	Anglo-French
Second Carnatic War	1748-54	Anglo-French
Third Carnatic War	1756-63	Anglo-French
First Anglo-Maratha War	1775-82	Anglo-Maratha
Second Anglo-Maratha War	1803-05	Anglo-Maratha
Third Anglo-Maratha War	1817-18	Anglo-Maratha
First Anglo-Afghan War	1838-42	Anglo-Afghan Ruler
Second Anglo-Afghan War	1878-80	Anglo-Afghan Ruler

Important Personalities of Modern India

Dadabhai Naoroji (1825-1917)

- He was the first Indian to be elected in the house of commons (The Lower House) of the British Parliament.
- He had active participation in the establishment of the Indian National Congress and elected as its President in 1886, 1893 and 1906.
- He is also called 'Grand Old Man of India'.

Mahadev Govind Ranade (1842-1901 AD)

- He was famous social reformer and Nationalist leader of Maharashtra.
- Gopal Krishna Gokhale considered him as his Guru.
- He played an active role in Widow Remarriage Committees, Prathana Samaj, Deccan Education Society, Vidhiva Partha, etc.

Badruddin Tyabji (1844-1906 AD)

- He was liberal Congressman and social reformer.
- He was first Muslim President of Congress (Madras in 1887 AD) the session.

Annie Besant (1847-1933 AD)

- He played key role in the establishment of Central Hindu College (1898 AD).
- In the year 1916, the Home Rule League was formed and the Swadeshi Movement established.
- In the year 1917 (Calcutta Session), she was the first Congress woman to become President.
- In the year 1907, she became the President of the Theosophical Society.
- Important newspapers associated with her are *Commonweal*' and '*New India*'.

Anand Mohan Bose (1847-1906 AD)

- He was leading educationist, social reformer and active of Bengal nationalist.
- He organised Indian National Conference in 1883 AD.
- He was founder and secretary of Indian Association.
- He was President of the Madras Session of Congress in 1898 AD.

Surendranath Banerjee (1848-1925 AD)

- He was nationalist leader, journalist, jurist and educationist.
- Indian Association was founded by him in 1876 AD.
- He established the Indian National Liberal Federation in the year 1918.

Bal Gangadhar Tilak (1856-1920 AD)

- He was supporter of extremist ideology.
- He tried to spread awareness through newspapers like *Kaisari* and *Maratha*.
- He started the Ganpati and Shivaji Mahotsav in Maharashtra in 1897 AD.
- Due to his fearless journalism, he was imprisoned for six years in Mandalay jail, in the year 1908.

Shyamji Krishna Verma (1857-1930 AD)

- He was prominent freedom fighter of revolutionary ideology.
- He represented the Indian Independence Movement in London.
- He established India House in London in the year 1905.
- He established the Home Rule Society in England (1905).

Bipin Chandra Pal (1858-1932 AD)

- He was leader of revolutionary ideas.
- He was the first among all revolutionary thinkers
- He played a prominent role in Swadeshi Movement and Anti-Bengal Partition Campaign.
- He was prominent campaigner of India Swaraj abroad.

Madam Bhikaji Cama (1861-1936 AD)

- She was a freedom fighter from Mumbai.
- She participated in the Socialist Congress at Stuttgart in 1907.
- She founded the free India Society.

Madan Mohan Malviya (1861-1946 AD)

- He was a moderate leader and a lawyer by profession. He served the provincial and Central Legislature for many terms.
- Through his efforts, a memorial was built at the Jallianwala Bagh site.
- He founded the Nationalist Party in 1926.
- He was appointed as the Vice-Chancellor of Banaras Hindu University.
- He served as the editor of *Hindustan*, *Abhyudaya* and the *Indian Union*.

Lala Lajpat Rai (1865-1928 AD)

- He was fearless journalist and Freedom Fighter. He was also known as 'Sher-e-Punjab' or 'Punjab Kesari'.
- He joined the Extremist section along with Tilak and Bipin Chandra Pal.
- He was nominated as the President of the Calcutta special session of the Congress in the year 1920.
- He was one of the founders of Swaraj Dal and also helped in the establishment of DAV College.
- In November 1928, during the demonstration against the Simon Commission, he was injured and martyred.

Gopal Krishna Gokhale (1866-1915 AD)

- Gandhiji regarded him as his Political Guru.
- He was President of the Banaras Session of INC, 1905. He supported the Swadeshi Movement.
- He founded the Servants of Indian Society in 1905 to train people who would work as National Missionaries.

CR Das (1870-1925 AD)

- He was a lawyer by profession. He defended Aurobindo in the Alipur Bomb Conspiracy Case.
- He was the member of the Congress Enquiry Committee set up to look into Jallianwala Bagh Massacre.
- He founded the All India Swaraj Party in 1923.
- He was elected as the First Mayor of the Calcutta Cooperation in 1924.
- He prepared the Das Formula for Hindu-Muslim Cooperation.
- He was nicknamed as Deshbandhu Chittaranjan.
- His works includes Malancha in 1895 (Poems), Mala in 1904, Antaryami in 1915, Kishore-Kishoree and Sagar-Sangit in 1913.
- Newspapers/Journal associated with him are *Narayana* (Bengali Monthly) and *Forward*.

Sohan Singh Bhakna (1870-1968 AD)

- He was a popular revolutionary.
- He founded Hind Sangh in 1913.
- He published letter named *Gaddar*, in context of Komagata Maru incident.
- He was released from jail in 1930 and joined Farmer Movements.

Shri Aurobindo Ghosh (1872-1950 AD)	• He was popular leader during Bengal Partition Movement. • He was leader of Revolutionary Movement in Bengal. • He was editor of *Yugantar*, *Karanuyagi* and *Dharam*. • He was sentenced for one year in Alipur Conspiracy Case.
Tej Bahadur Sapru (1875-1949 AD)	• He was progressive Congress Leader. • He founded National convention. • He was President of Uttar Pradesh Congress Committee. • He was member of Legislative Council of United Province between 1913 and 1916. • He was law member of Viceroy's Council.
Vallabhbhai Patel (1875-1950 AD)	• He was a freedom fighter and social reformer from Gujarat. He is popularly known as Sardar Patel and honoured with the title of 'The Iron Man of India'. • His father, Jhaverbhai Patel, is supposed to have fought in the army of Rani of Jhansi in the Revolt of 1857. • He started the Kheda Satyagraha in 1918 and fought for the rights of the Peasants in Bardoli Satyagraha. Here, he was honoured with the title 'Sardar'. • He was the first national leader to be arrested during the Civil Disobedience Movement. • He participated in Gandhi's Individual Satyagraha and Quit India Movement. • In the Post-Independence Period, he was appointed as the first Deputy Prime Minister of India along with the portfolios of the Information and Broadcasting and Home Ministry. • He played a major role in integrating the 562 Princely States in the Indian Union.
Chakravarti Rajagopalachari (1879-1972 AD)	• He was a politician and lawyer from Tamil Nadu. • He gave up his practice during Non-Cooperation Movement. • He held the post of the General-Secretary of the INC in 1921-1922 and was a member of Congress Working Committee from 1922 to 1924. • He was arrested for leading a Salt March from Trichinopoly to Vedaranyam on the Tanjore Coast. • He was elected as the Chief Minister of Madras in 1937 elections. • He resigned from INC in 1942 for not accepting the Cripp's Proposal. • He prepared the CR Formula for Congress-League Cooperation. • He served as the Governor of Bengal (August-November 1947) and was the first and last Indian Governor-General of India (1948-1950). • He became the Minister of Home Affairs in the country's first cabinet. • He founded the Swatantra Party in 1959. • His rational ideas are reflected in the collection Satyameva Jayate. • He was awarded the 'Bharat Ratna' in 1954.

Sarojini Naidu (1879-1949 AD)	• She was popularly known as the 'Nightingale of India'. She was a nationalist and poetess from Uttar Pradesh. • She was married to Dr. Govindarajulu Naidu in 1893. • Under the guidance of Gopal Krishna Gokhale, she became the first woman to participate in India's struggle for Independence. • She participated in the Dandi March with Gandhiji and presided over the Kanpur Session of Congress in 1925. • She was the first woman to become the Governor of Uttar Pradesh state. • Her famous poetries includes - *The Golden Threshold* (1905), *The Feather of The Dawn*, *The Bird of Time* (1912) and *The Broken Wing* (1917).
Narayan Malhar Joshi (1879-1955 AD)	• He founded of All India Trade Union Congress 1920. • He founded Social Service League in Bombay. • He was President of Bombay Textile Labour Union.
Dr. Pattabhi Sitaramayya (1880-1959 AD)	• He was a doctor by profession and a prominent nationalist. • He was official historian of Indian National Congress. • He was President of Indian National Congress in 1948. • He was first Governor of Madhya Pradesh.
Madan Lal Dhingra (1887-1909 AD)	• He was a revolutionary from Punjab. He was the member of Indian Home Rule Society, the Abhinav Bharat and the India houses. • He was sentenced to death for assassinating Sir William Curzon Wyllie, an advisor to the secretary of State of India during a public function in the Imperial institute, London.
Lala Hardayal (1884-1939 AD)	• He was a revolutionary from Delhi. He took up the cause of India's Freedom to a foreign land in order to win international support for the Freedom Movement. • He was the first President of the Ghadar Party founded in San Francisco in 1913. • He founded the Indian Independence Committee in Germany and an Oriental Bureau to translate the writings in the local language. • His books were *Wealth of Nations* and *Hints for Self Culture*.
Dr. Rajendra Prasad (1884-1963 AD)	• He participated in Swadeshi Movement (established Bihari Students, Conference), Champaran Satyagraha and Quit India Movement • He founded the National College at Patna. • He was Minister Incharge or Food and Agriculture in the Interim Government of 1946. • He was President of the Constituent Assembly. He was first President of the Indian Republic. • He was honoured with 'Bharat Ratna' in 1962. • He published newspaper *Desh* (Hindi Weekly).

Name	Details
Abdul Kalam Azad (1888-1958 AD)	• He joined INC during Swadeshi Movement. • He was President of Khilafat Committee presided over the Congress special session at Delhi in 1923, to become the youngest President. He was also the longest-serving President of INC. • He headed the Jamiat-ul-Ulema, 1924, Nationalist Muslim Conference, Shimla Conference, 1945 and negotiated with Cabinet Mission, 1946. • He was elected as the Member of Constituent Assembly in 1946 and became Minister of Education and Arts in the Interim Government. • He was first Education Minister of independent India. He was also given the portfolios of natural resources and Scientific Research. • He contributed in the foundation of UGC, AICTE and IIT Kharagpur. • His book was '*India Wins Freedom*'.
Sarvepalli Radhakrishnan (1888-1975 AD)	• He was an educationalist from Tamil Nadu. He was associated with many Educational Institutions in India. • He served as the Vice-Chancellor of Andhra University in 1931 and Banaras Hindu University in 1942. • He gave lectures on theology and philosophy in the Universities of Chicago, Manchester, London and Oxford. • He was the leader of the Indian Delegation to UNESCO from (1946-50), its Chairman in 1948 and President of UNESCOS University Education Commission in 1952. • In 1962, he represented the Calcutta University at the Congress of Philosophy at Harvard University. • He was twice elected as the Vice-President of India (1952-1956 and 1957-1962) and served as the President of the Nation from 1962 to 1967. • His birthday (5th September) is celebrated as 'Teachers' Day'. • His works includes — *the Ethics of the Vedanta and Its Material Presupposition* 1908, *the Philosophy of Rabindranath Tagore* 1918, *Idealistic View of Life* 1932, *Eastern Religion and Western Thought, Indian Philosophy* and *Kalki on the Future of Civilisation.*
Acharya Narendra Dev (1889-1956 AD)	• He was a scholar, socialist, nationalist and a lawyer by profession. He gave up his practice and joined Non-Cooperation Movement. • He became the President of Patna's Socialist Conference in 1934 and a member of Uttar Pradesh Legislation Assembly in 1937. • He was appointed as the principal of Kashi Vidyapeeth in 1925 and also became the Vice-Chancellor of Lucknow and Banaras Universities. • He founded the Socialist Party in 1948.
Swami Sahajanand Saraswati (1889-1950 AD)	• He was Dandi Sanyasi of Dasnami Order. • He was a nationalist. • He was a prominent peasant leader of Bihar. • He founded Bihar Kishan Sabha in the year 1929. • He established 'Akhil Bharatiya Kisan Sabha in the year 1936.
Khan Abdul Ghaffar Khan (1890-1988 AD)	• He was given title of Frontier Gandhi, Badshah Khan or Sarhadi Gandhi, Fakhar-e-Afghan. • He founded an organisation of non-violent revolutionaries known as 'Red Shirts' or 'Khudai Khidmatgars'. • He opposed partition of India. He participated in Non-Cooperation Movement and Quit India. • He was newspaper — Pakhtoon (In Pushto), later published as Das Roza. • He was honoured with 'Bharat Ratna' in 1987.
Dr. Bhimrao Ramji Ambedkar (1891-1956 AD)	• He was leader of the Depressed Class and an eminent Jurist. • He founded the Depressed Classes Institute in 1924 and Samaj Samata Sangh in 1927. • He set up a network college in the name of People's Education Society. • He was participated in all the Three Round Table Conferences and signed the Poona Pact with Gandhiji in 1932. • He was in the Governor-General's Executive Council from 1942 to 1946 and organised the Indian Labour Party and Scheduled Caste Federation. • He was Chairman of the Drafting Committee of Indian Constitution. • As the first Law Minister of Independent India. He introduced the Hindu Code Bill. • He started 'The Republican Party' in 1956. • Towards the end of his life, he embraced Buddhism.
Achary Vinoba Bhave (1895-1982 AD)	• He was a prominent participant and leader in Flag Satyagraha, Temple Entry Movement, Salt Satyagraha, Dandi March and Quit India Movement. • He was prominent Satyagrahi of Individual Satyagraha. • He lead Bhoodan Movement and Sarvodya Movement after Independence.
Ram Prasad Bismil (1897-1927 AD)	• He was a revolutionary from Uttar Pradesh. He was a member of the Hindustan Socialist Republican Association. • He was sentenced to death in charge of the Kakori Rail Dacoity Case (9th August, 1925). • His most famous composition is '*Sarforoshi Ki Tamanna Ab Hamare Dil Mein Hai*'.
Subhash Chandra Bose (1897-1945 AD)	• He passed the Indian Civil Services Examination in 1920 in England but left it on Gandhiji's call of Non-Cooperation Movement. • He founded the Independence for India League with Jawaharlal Nehru. • He was elected as the President of INC at its Haripura Session 1938 and Tripuri Session 1939. Resigned from Tripuri due to differences with Gandhiji. • He founded the Forward Bloc 1939 and Kishan Sabha. • He escaped to Berlin in 1941 and met Hitler. He took the charge of Indian Army (Azad Hind Fauz) in 1943 in Singapore and set up Indian Provisional Government there. • He addressed Mahatma Gandhi as the 'Father of the Nation.' • He supposedly died in a plane crash in 1945. • His slogans are '*Delhi Chalo*' and '*Jaihind*' • His autobiography is '*The Indian Struggle*'

Udham Singh (1899-1940 AD)	• He was prominent revolutionary of Punjab and an Associate of Bhagat Singh. • In London, he assassinated General Michel O Dyer, the Governor of Punjab during Jallianwala Bagh Massacre.
NG Ranga (1900-1995 AD)	• He played an important role in Indian Communist Movement. • He founded first Kisan Sangh 1923 in Guntur. • He played important role in formation of Akhil Bhartiya Kishan Sabha in the year 1936.
Jayaprakash Narayana (1902-1979 AD)	• He was a freedom fighter from Bihar. He is popularly known as Loknayak. • He was a follower of Marxist philosophy and advocated for the nationalisation of heavy industries and abolition of Zamindari. • He joined INC on Nehru's offer and was jailed during Civil Disobedience Movement. • He formed the All India Socialist Party in 1934. • He actively participated in Quit India Movement and was imprisoned. • He joined the Bhoodan Movement of Vinoba Bhave. • In 1975, he protested against the National Emergency and founded the Janata Party.

Chandra Shekhar Azad (1906-1931 AD)	• He was a famous revolutionary activist, member of the Hindustan Republican Association and leader of the Hindustan Social Republican Army. • He gained his title 'Azad' during the Non-Cooperation Movement. When he was arrested and the court asked his name, he repeatedly answered 'Azad'. • He was involved in Kakori Conspiracy of 1925, Second Lahore Conspiracy, the Delhi Conspiracy, the Killing of Saunders in Lahore and Central Assembly Bomb Episode. • He shot himself while fighting with the police at Alfred Park in Allahabad (now Prayagraj).
Bhagat Singh (1907-1931 AD)	• He was member of Hindustan Socialist Republican Army. • He started the Militant Naujawan Bharat Sabha in Punjab. • He killed British official Saunders in 1928 and was involved in Lahore Conspiracy. He also bombed the Central Legislative Assembly. • He was executed on 23rd March, 1931.
Ashfaqulla Khan (1900-1927 AD)	• He was a revolutionary. • He was member of Hindustan Republication Association. • He was played an important role in Kakori Conspiracy Case. • He was hanged in Fridabad by the British.